THE REPUBLICAN PARTY
1854–1966

The Republican Party

1854-1966

SECOND EDITION

GEORGE H. MAYER

NEW YORK   OXFORD UNIVERSITY PRESS   1967

Copyright © 1964, 1967 by Oxford University Press, Inc.
Library of Congress Catalogue Card Number: 67–25300
First edition published in 1964 under the title *The Republican Party 1854–1964*

Printed in the United States of America

To my father
a lifelong Republican

Preface to the Second Edition

There is always a temptation in the preface to a second edition to deal with matters that troubled readers in the first edition. A number of readers expressed disappointment in this book over the emphasis on personalities, an apparent reflection of the belief that a definitive explanation of the Republican party could be made in terms of ideological and structural development. Why I did as I did may perhaps be better understood if it is realized that only during the formative years of an American party, when it is developing a reliable base of popular support, is such an approach of any major usefulness. Once this task is accomplished, however, principles tend to be an embarrassment. They cannot be abandoned or ignored except at the risk of offending the faithful. On the other hand, they cannot be implemented in consistent fashion without disrupting the varied pressure groups that constitute the backbone of the successful party. So after the period of *Sturm und Drang,* the spotlight shifts from principles to leaders who keep the party afloat by personal charisma, adroit handling of patronage, and the manipulation of ephemeral issues that attract the voters. The party continues to be identified with traditional principles, but at this stage its credo is subjected to such ambiguous interpretations that the serious historian cannot make political narrative intelligible in ideological terms alone.

Periods of ideological and structural change tend to be much shorter than periods when personalities dominate a party because Americans are tenacious in their political loyalties. Hence, the leaders of a successful party are reluctant to tamper with a winning formula by the injection of new principles. They do so only in times of turmoil, when voter habits have been disrupted. The fact that the Republican party enjoyed long periods of uninterrupted supremacy forces an emphasis on personalities. Even the relegation of the G.O.P. to minority status after 1932 did not provide much justification for a different emphasis. On the contrary, the dominance of personalities persisted precisely because the party was unable to develop distinctive principles.

Perhaps the real source of disappointment with a narrative built around ambitious personalities is the belief that party history ought to be inspiring. It rarely is, and efforts to make it so obscure the truth. Therefore, party history can be justified only on the ground that the party has been an important factor in the development of the United States. This hypothesis provides the rationale for the ensuing effort to chart the vicissitudes of the G.O.P.

In preparing the material on the Goldwater campaign, I received invaluable help from several reflective students of politics. Professor Robert J. Graf of Purdue put his vast collection of newspaper and magazine clippings at my disposal. Mr. Everett Lynch called to my attention contemporary materials that might otherwise have been overlooked. Mr. Lawrence B. Lehman of Sarasota read new portions of manuscript and made perceptive suggestions. Finally, Mrs. Fran Mayers did the indispensable work on the typewriter cheerfully and competently.

Sarasota, Florida   G.H.M.
April 1967

Preface

It is unlikely that a definitive history of the Republican party will ever be written unless the project is undertaken by a team of scholars. The individual historian must concentrate on following the development of the party as a national organization, with side glances at state and local politics whenever they have a decisive effect on its fortunes. Even this modest enterprise is beset with difficulty because of the superabundance of source material. A lifetime could be consumed examining Republican newspapers, to say nothing of periodicals, government documents, private correspondence, and other relevant material. Of necessity, some selectivity must be exercised on a basis that assures coverage of representative sources. For the portion of this study dealing with the nineteenth century, the heaviest reliance has been placed on the letters and telegrams of party leaders, because they reveal most clearly the interplay between impulse and calculation at the root of political decisions. Through such material the researcher can approach the ideal of writing party history as if he had no advance knowledge of the outcome of elections or other decisive events. The increasing use of the telephone for political communication has reduced the amount of information about party strategy in letters, but they still provide a valuable record of public sentiment on controversial issues.

Almost as important as correspondence are the newspaper, the campaign leaflet, the popular periodical, and the many government and party publications. I have tried to supplement the data from these sources by drawing on secondary works, especially the published monographs of specialists and unpublished Ph.D. theses. The dividends from interviews with active political leaders are usually so meager that I avoided this type of research. A series of conversations with Alf M. Landon, who generously offered to answer questions about his letters and private papers and gave his permission for me to quote from them, constitutes the sole exception to the rule. I also wish to acknowledge the following manuscript collections, the custodians of which have given me permission to quote in this book; in each case the specific collection consists of the private papers of the figure involved:

The Library of Congress, Washington, D.C.: Nelson W. Aldrich, Wharton Barker, Jeremiah Black, C. J. Bonaparte, William E. Borah, Ben Butler, Simon Cameron, Thomas H. Carter, W. E. Chandler, Zack Chandler, Salmon P. Chase, W. W. Clapp, James S. Clarkson, Roscoe Conkling, John J. Crittenden, Henry L. Dawes, Hamilton Fish, Moreton Frewen, James A. Garfield, Joshua Giddings–George Julian, William H. Gist–Frank P. Blair, Charles Hamlin, Benjamin Harrison, Joseph Hawley, Thomas Jessup, Andrew Johnson, Philander C. Knox, Abraham Lincoln, Manton Marble, George B. McClellan, William McKinley, John McLean, Charles L. McNary, Edward McPherson, L. T. Michener, Justin Morrill, Harry S. New, John G. Nicolay, George W. Norris, Alton B. Parker, Amos Pinchot, Gifford Pinchot, Whitelaw Reid, Theodore Roosevelt, Elihu Root, John Sherman, John C. Spooner, Edwin M. Stanton, Thaddeus Stevens, William Howard Taft, Roger B. Taney, Lyman Trumbull, Ben L. Wade, Thomas J. Walsh, Elihu Washburne, Henry Watterson, Gideon Welles, William Allen White, John R. Young.

The Yale University Library, New Haven, Connecticut: William C. Beer, Edward M. House, William Kent, James Sheffield.

The Kansas Historical Society, Topeka: Joseph L. Bristow, Arthur Capper, Alf M. Landon, Chester I. Long.

The Indiana State Library, Indianapolis: Will H. Hays.

The Bancroft Library, University of California, Berkeley: Hiram Johnson, Chester Rowell.

The Stanford University Library, Stanford, California: Francis V. Keesling.

The Massachusetts Historical Society, Boston: Henry Cabot Lodge.

The University of Virginia Library, Charlottesville: Miles Poindexter.

The University of Wyoming Library, Laramie: Francis Warren.

A full bibliography on the literature dealing with the Republican party is a major project in itself, while a select bibliography raises as many problems as it solves. So I have taken refuge in extensive footnotes with the full realization that they do not constitute an adequate substitute.

The need for a new history of the Republican party is evident because the available studies are either outdated or highly specialized. Most of them give the misleading impression that the party exists nine months every four years to conduct a campaign for the Presidency. This approach loses the element of continuity in party history and underestimates the enduring influence of sentiment and tradition on party policy. Midway through the twentieth century, Republicans still cherish doctrines arising out of the partisan warfare of an earlier era. This book endorses no theory of political causation save the commonplace one that each successive development has its roots in an earlier event. Allegiance to a venerable institution shapes the attitude of a modern Republican as much as his real or fancied economic interests. The history of his party also points to some broader generalizations about the nature of American politics.

I owe a debt of gratitude to several colleagues who put their insights at my disposal. Professor Robert C. Scott of Williams College broadened my horizons in informal conversations extending over many months while we occupied adjoining desks in the Library of Congress. Professors Charles B. Murphy and Don Paarlberg of Purdue University have drawn on their practical knowledge of twentieth-century politics to help me at critical points. A kindred service was performed by Karl Detzer, a roving editor of the *Reader's Digest*. The curators of manuscript collections all over the United States have done what they could to lighten the burdens of research. Alf M. Landon deserves a special word of thanks for allowing me unrestricted use of his private letters, which contain forthright judgments about his contemporaries. Finally, I want to acknowledge my debt to Marilyn Lehmann, who typed my manuscript and tracked down errant footnotes, as well as to my wife, Merrylees, who did the thankless job of proofreading and indexing.

G. H. M.

Lafayette, Indiana
December 1963

Contents

THE REPUBLICAN PARTY
1854–1966

I

The Golden Age of Politics

Rare are the periods in which the affairs of government become the primary concern of society at large. Usually politics come into national consciousness only during a major election campaign, and for most people interest dies as soon as the campaign ends. Even in political democracies, where mass participation in the political process allows more people to have a direct involvement in the day-to-day operation of parties, most of society remains unaffected by the events in this area. Occasionally, however, political parties have radiated the creative energies of an entire society, expressing its cultural aspirations as faithfully as art or literature. Then the apparatus of party government, the ceremonial rules of political warfare, and the campaign pageantry become more than mere devices for recording the popular will. Under such circumstances, politics become the concern of virtually everyone in the society and involve them in the affairs of government and in the election of officials to serve them. Then it can be truly said that a "golden age" of politics exists. Such an age dawned in the United States with the Presidency of Andrew Jackson, reached its peak in the decade of the '50's when the Republican party was born, and expired with the nineteenth century.

"The cares of politics," noted a herald of the golden age, "engross a prominent place in the occupation of a citizen in the United States, and almost the only pleasure which an American knows is to take part in government and to discuss its measures. . . . If an American were condemned to confine his activity to his own affairs, he would be robbed of

3

one half of his existence . . . and his wretchedness would be unbearable." [1] Speaking in kindred accents in 1860, an Illinois editor observed that politics "seems to be the all-absorbing theme of conversation in the bar-room, and in the drawing room, on the streets, and in the house, morning, noon and night." [2] Political fever persisted until the end of the golden age, as a teen-age daughter of a future Presidential candidate confessed after attending a political rally: "I got so excited," she wrote, "I could hardly stand still and clapped my hands as hard as anybody. I'd love to be a politician and work hard for my candidates." [3] Interest in politics often expressed itself in hero worship and violent partisanship. Political leaders loomed as large to their admiring followers as the legendary warriors of *Beowulf* and the *Cid*. Popular imagination transformed the petty struggles of political jobbers over the spoils of office into an epic encounter of chivalrous knights over lofty ideals. The Lincoln-Douglas debates of 1858 even cast a spell over hardened newspaper editors. One of them lyrically reported that Stephen A. Douglas arrived at Ottawa, Illinois, "like some great deliverer, some mighty champion who had saved a nation from ruin." [4] Out of deference to the democratic credo, political leaders tolerated some familiarity from the rank and file, but they also expected the kind of loyalty that a medieval baron demanded from his vassals. Although voters occasionally rebelled against an individual leader, they rarely left their party. Convinced that it could do no wrong, they applauded each victory at the polls as a vindication of truth and justice. The anti-slavery Whigs felt it "as necessary to be Whigs as Christians." [5] An equally self-righteous Republican proclaimed that "the intelligence and morality of our country is on the Republican side, while nearly every renegade and libertine is upon the side of Democracy." [6] Fully two generations after the Civil War young Theodore Roosevelt was still congratulating himself because his father had been a Republican and had spared him the mortification of living down Democratic ancestors.[7]

No single explanation can account for the tenacity of party attachments during the nineteenth century. Economic interests, family tradition, social environment, political ideals, and accidents of geography all interacted to generate partisan convictions. But the spontaneity and exuberance of nineteenth-century party warfare owed something to a raw energy which a later age either stifled or diverted into new channels. Outside of America the instinct for play had expressed itself in myriad cultural forms, ranging all the way from games of chance to sports contests and tournaments.

Although some types of recreation found their way to the New World, they could not thrive in a Puritan atmosphere. The frontier environment was almost as hostile as Puritanism to sports, for it isolated settlers to such an extent that organized competition was impractical. Yet neither an ethical system nor an inhospitable environment could destroy the zest for competitive games in a lusty frontier society. With the usual outlets partially clogged, the play impulse welled up in the new nation through the party system and spilled out at every level in streams of partisan enthusiasm.

The political contest in nineteenth-century America was simultaneously serious warfare and pure fun. The combatants seldom drew a clear line between serious objectives and the desire for victory. The sheer joy of winning was just as much a goal as the harvesting of concrete political benefits. Lord James Bryce, an acute commentator on post-Civil War American democracy, observed about party warfare: "Men enjoy combat for its own sake, loving to outstrip others and carry their flag to victory. . . . Nothing holds men so close together as the presence of the antagonist strong enough to be worth defeating." [8] A Kansas senator likewise observed that "politics is a battle of supremacy. Parties are the armies. The Decalogue and the golden rule have no place in a political campaign. . . . To defeat the antagonist and expel the party in power is the purpose." [9] Spectators derived as much satisfaction from a political victory as their leaders did. Theodore Roosevelt wryly conceded that "the average American in his party affiliations is largely influenced by a feeling quite as unreasoning as that which makes the average fan depressed or exultant over the victory of a professional baseball team. . . ." [10] By the time Roosevelt made this comment, spectator sports and other recreational activities had begun to compete with the political party as agencies for expressing the play impulse. But when America was half a century younger, the birth of a political party was an event of the first magnitude. To some it marked the beginning of a new contest for power; to others it inaugurated the penultimate stage of the great struggle between good and evil; to the vast majority it heralded both competition and crusade. Irrespective of the terms in which the combatants saw the conflict, they were assured of a simple political choice because America had taken over the two-party system from Great Britain. Like primitive tribes divided into opposing halves or phratriai, Americans conducted their mock warfare on a basis that promoted fierce, uncomplicated partisanship. Since the rules of polit-

ical conflict had been stabilized in the age of Jackson, a brief review of
them is essential to a knowledge of the circumstances surrounding the
birth of the Republican party.

II

As in the city-state of ancient Greece, the village or market town of mid-
nineteenth-century America was the focal point of political activity. Aside
from a few large cities in the East, the typical community was composed
of "a business street pretty compactly built, filled with stores, work shops,
taverns, and a few drinking saloons." [11] Homes clustered around the central
area in random fashion, usually with an adjacent yard for garden plots.
The Southern village was often more untidy than its Northern counterpart,
disfigured by "wooden structures, standing pools of stagnant water, bilious
and listless white people, shiftless and wretched negros [sic]. . . ." [12]
Urbanization, however, acted as a leveling force all over the country, with
the result that filth increased as rapidly as conveniences. A community of
10,000 people seldom provided lighted or paved streets for its citizens, who
were obliged to detour around holes and pigs wallowing in the mud. Despite the hazards of urban life, farmers converged on the nearest community for political discussion. Those who lived in villages or within walking distance met regularly at the country store. In the winter they sat
around the stove, smoking, spitting, and whittling on sticks while they
talked. The first breath of spring brought them out to the front porch. From
both locations they made frequent trips to the whiskey barrel at the back
of the store, which made the discussions more lively and less coherent.
More formal analysis took place under the auspices of the local lyceum,
which usually met once a week in cool weather at the local school. All men
of good character were eligible for membership, and although lyceums
were nonpartisan organizations, speakers could not resist the temptation
to stray from their texts. Even seemingly innocent topics like temperance
and flogging in the navy provided participants with an opportunity for
thrusts at political opponents. People unable to satisfy their appetite for
controversy at the lyceum joined debating societies, which also made half-
hearted efforts to keep discussion to educational subjects. The village
churches fared no better than other organizations in avoiding politics, particularly during the 1850's when America was convulsed by religious re-
vivals. Taking their cue from older evangelists like Lyman Beecher and
Charles Grandison Finney, local preachers exhorted their flocks to fight

slavery, intemperance, and other evils. In the best American tradition, the crusading churchmen represented their opinions as the will of God.

The weekly newspaper provided villagers with ammunition for political warfare. The typical country journal contained only four pages and gave equal space to politics and other matters. Normally the front and back pages featured advertisements, letters from old settlers, and jokes, while the inner pages concentrated on current issues. Inasmuch as most weeklies could not get up-to-the-minute news, they gave full coverage to stale congressional debates. Editorial columns were highly partisan and open to articles by politicians who shared the political faith of the publisher. Limited circulation restricted the number of weeklies, except in election years when unprofitable journals were launched and kept alive by party subsidies. In the 1850's the only journal with a wide circulation outside of its immediate area was a weekly edition of Horace Greeley's *New York Tribune,* which had 200,000 subscribers, mostly in New England and the Midwest.[13] Toward the end of the decade improved service by the Associated Press encouraged the growth of regional dailies and enabled them to provide news as promptly as the New York press.

With so many sources of political information available to the villager, party organizations did not propagandize actively except during the campaign season. Politicians did pay close attention to isolated farm families on the special occasions when they were drawn into town. In New England, town meetings and county musters of militia attracted crowds, while the convening of the circuit court served the same function elsewhere. Farmers combining business with pleasure bought provisions and lingered for social intercourse. Ordinarily the circuit courts did no business the first day except to swear in the local jury. After adjournment the lawyer-politicians who followed the circuit court debated current issues before the assembled farmers. Abraham Lincoln first won widespread attention in this fashion, and Hannibal Hamlin of Maine started his long political career at a county muster in Hampden, where he was proposed for the state legislature.

Militia musters and meetings of the circuit court crowded an already overburdened political calendar. Many state governors were elected on an annual basis, and even the state constitutions which gave them a longer term provided for the selection of a canal commissioner or a judge in the off years. Since few states chose either their own officials or congressmen on the date prescribed for national elections, a campaign was going on somewhere throughout the year. Only January, February, June, and July were free of elections; ceaseless activity during the remaining eight months kept voters in a chronic state of excitement.

Each party built its local campaign around a mammoth political rally, and not even the most insignificant hamlet was overlooked. The rally served the dual purpose of providing entertainment and prompting partisan solidarity. The parades, picnics, and contests accompanying the campaign rally were America's equivalent of the religious celebrations and royal celebrations that existed in the European countries from which its people had come. For a few fleeting hours life took on a magical, operatic quality for spectators and principals alike. Boastful oratory, flamboyant gestures, and emotional battle cries gave the crowd a sense of participation in the great enterprises of the party. Arrangements were invariably made with an eye to outdoing any rally organized by the opposition,[14] and the party press consistently overestimated attendance. Toward the end of the 1850's parties employed semi-military units as means of competition. Composed of young men who purchased their own uniforms, these honor guards provided an escort for speakers, led parades, and kept order at meetings. In impoverished frontier areas where nobody could afford uniforms, the partisans scuffled over party flags and cut down each other's campaign poles. The more imaginative partisans devised a host of campaign tricks to confound the opposition. In an effort to block the re-election of Democratic Congressman S. S. Cox in 1858, Ohio Republicans stole sacks of weevil-resistant wheat seed that the congressman had earmarked for distribution and refilled them with scrapings from barn floors.[15] The Democrats were equally adept. One party orator went to a settlement of newly arrived Germans in Missouri and told them that the Republicans sold wooden nutmegs and broken clocks. He then informed the credulous immigrants that a Republican victory would mean the end of walks, kisses, and cooked meals on Sunday.[16] When a Republican jumped on a wagon to protest this statement, the Democratic owner hitched up the wagon and started to drive away.

The trend toward the all-day rally was first apparent in the "Log Cabin and Hard Cider" campaign of 1840. At dawn people began to converge on Syracuse, New York, for a Whig rally, coming by canal boat, in wagons, and on foot—"singly, in pairs, by dozens, and by hundreds. . . ."[17] A decade later, crowds of 25,000 were not unusual at hamlets like Massillon, Ohio, and Kalamazoo, Michigan. Mornings were devoted to the organization of a parade around the mass of wagons, horse-drawn carriages, and pedestrians arriving from the countryside. While cannon boomed at regular intervals, bands, glee clubs, and floats joined the procession. Marchers carried campaign flags or placards with party slogans. Some parades were seven miles long and took hours to pass a single point.[18] Spectators followed the procession to the fairgrounds or to a spacious grove at the edge of town for a picnic. One held at Greenville, Illinois, in 1860 required 2500 tables and eight sides of beef, hundreds of chickens and hams, as well as innumerable cakes, pies, and loaves of bread. On that occasion a single precinct contributed 1000 pies.[19] Served at noon, the meal was interrupted by oratory, the circulation of political literature, and the raising of a campaign pole. Because it was difficult for a single voice to be heard above the crowd noise, parties usually had several speakers on hand to address the picnic simultaneously. Sometimes the star orator imported for the occasion spoke in the evening following a torchlight parade. There was little change in the basic formula for these mass rallies until the end of the nineteenth century, although after the Civil War, Indians, cowboys, and veterans in uniform enlivened the parades. During the 1880's the parties added balloon ascensions and rodeos to the picnic entertainment.

The individual office-seeker did not rely solely on the mass rally to win support, for he also made a strenuous personal canvas. Whether he was running for county commissioner or congressman, he felt obliged to visit voters and their families. "Mingle with the mudsills," one political boss advised an acquaintance, "for personal contact provides a reliable gauge of sentiment and a way of overcoming mutual suspicions." [20] Still, there was no single formula that guaranteed success. Personal appearance, temperament, and platform manner were variables that no candidate could completely control irrespective of his basic approach to the voters. Some found mileage in cultivating the boisterous, democratic manners of the frontier. One Indiana governor, in an effort to imitate his constituents, spat eighty-two times during his inaugural address.[21] At the other extreme was James A. Garfield, who retained his academic dignity after forsaking the presidency of Hiram College for a political career. A few with aloof and chilly personalities managed to stay in office for extended periods, the most notable being Roscoe Conkling of New York, who dreaded physical contact with the voters and tolerated them only in orderly rows beneath the speakers' platform.

Most campaigners took as much care with their speeches as their personal contacts, especially if they reached higher political office. Seasoned orators were prepared to address groups of ten or ten thousand on a moment's notice. Normally, they had only one speech but constructed it in such a way that sections could be added or deleted as circumstances required. Since the same basic campaign issues often persisted for a decade or more, politicians felt little pressure to revise their arguments. As a result, a speech might be made serviceable indefinitely by the periodic inclusion of new statistics and derogatory references to opposition candidates. A magnetic orator like James G. Blaine could speak for any length of time, and his brief performance from a railroad platform showed the same polish as his two-hour address. Whether good speakers or not, candidates tried to be both informative and entertaining. They knew that a farmer did not travel for hours over a rutted wagon track to hear a dry summary of issues, and so they made every effort to provide an audience with comic relief. Hecklers could be counted upon to brighten a rally, and the more self-assured politicians courted interruptions. For a slow-witted speaker, however, the risk involved in extemporaneous exchanges with an audience outweighed any possible advantages. Ordinarily, speeches combined windy eulogies of party heroes, moral platitudes, ambiguous statements on current issues, and ill-remembered quotations from Scripture. Americans conditioned by years of tedious Puritan sermons regarded length as a criterion of excellence, and politicians made every effort to oblige. The three-hour oration was common. Nature took her revenge on speakers who abused their voices, and the prudent ones had a variety of home remedies to cure hoarseness, the most familiar being the application of cold water bandages to the throat.[22]

On the whole, American audiences treated speakers more courteously than did British audiences, which were known to heave vegetables and dead cats at candidates for Parliament. But after the rise of the abolitionist controversy in the 1840's, a speaker faced considerable danger in a hostile district. Cassius Clay often put a loaded gun on the rostrum before advocating emancipation in the pro-slavery sections of Kentucky. This precaution did not always afford him adequate protection, and on one occasion, after an assailant had hit him with an umbrella, Clay drew a bowie knife and gashed the face of the offender.[23] During the encounter, several shots were fired and both men were lucky to escape with their lives. Violence erupted more frequently in cities than rural areas. The gangs in Baltimore and Philadelphia were especially notorious, and ward bosses regularly employed young thugs to break up the meetings of political opponents.

Before the Civil War, the joint canvass or debate was a customary feature of contests for state offices and for Congress. By prearrangement, each candidate made a formal speech of specified length and a shorter extemporaneous rebuttal. The Whig and Democratic congressional candidates from the Terre Haute district of Indiana not only shared their audience in the 1847 campaign but traveled together.[24] This practice, which reduced expenses, persisted until the end of the century largely because of the fast turnover of elective officials. When incumbents began to enjoy longer periods of unbroken tenure, they refused to advertise an obscure challenger by sharing the platform with him.

Unless a candidate was running for a county office or an elective post in a compact urban district, his efforts to make a thorough canvass were hampered by the inadequacy of transportation. When Orville H. Browning of Quincy, Illinois, became the Whig candidate for Congress in 1852, he started to campaign on August 31 and did not return home until two months later. Browning solved his transportation problem by renting a bay mare named Sallie to pull him around the congressional district in a covered buggy. With considerable ingenuity Browning tied his rental costs to his political fortunes, for he agreed to pay the owner of Sallie $1.50 per day if he won but only $1.00 a day if he lost. Still, Browning was luckier from the standpoint of expenditures as well as comfort than Abraham Lincoln and Stephen A. Douglas, who canvassed all of Illinois in 1858. Altogether Lincoln covered 4300 miles by train, carriage, and riverboat, and made 63 major speeches and many minor ones.[25] Douglas, crisscrossing the state, piled up 900 more miles than Lincoln and delivered 59 set speeches of two to three hours, 17 shorter speeches, and 37 responses to addresses of welcome.[26] The rapid extension of railroad lines made travel easier for candidates in the 1860's. Even so, Garfield confided to his diary in 1866 that he was often routed out of bed to take trains at 3 and 4 in the morning.[27] After one early morning rail journey, he spoke for an hour and a half; then took a nine-mile buggy ride and spoke for two hours.

Unreliable transportation was not the worst hazard of a campaign. Whenever a candidate spoke in a village late at night, he encountered poor accommodations and wretched food. In some cases he was better off at the village inn, however miserable it might be, because he could at least go to bed. If he stayed with a friend he was likely to be faced with further hospitality. Many candidates with convivial instincts shortened their lives by being good guests, and even teetotalers suffered from chronic exhaustion. All candidates risked offending one political supporter by staying with another. Matters did not improve if a local party committee took over the responsibility for housing, because the candidate was then confronted with all the risks of poor accommodations without the compensation of either privacy or good fellowship.

The only office-seekers without travel problems until the end of the nineteenth century were Presidential candidates, who by tradition stayed home. Out of deference to the popular belief that the office ought to seek the man, they displayed outward indifference while engaging in feverish backstage maneuvers to improve their prospects. Any experienced observer knew enough to discount the ceremonial restraint exhibited by Presidential candidates, but the voters lived on the fiction that the party standard-bearer was a modern Cincinnatus who had reluctantly left the plow at the call of his country. The aspirant felt obliged to reside on a modest country estate during both the pre-convention season and the campaign itself, and he was expected to behave like a simple, upright farmer. His time was spent chopping wood, planting crops, and dispensing folk wisdom, a routine which left leisure for writing gloomy letters deploring the current state of the nation and hinting that only virtuous leadership could save it. Lest any of his correspondents miss the obvious conclusion, the candidate usually went on to advertise his position on current issues and to offer his co-operation in rescuing America from her alleged miseries.

No avowed Presidential candidate attended a major party convention during the nineteenth century, but Garfield was on hand when the Republican delegates nominated him in 1880, and William Jennings Bryan became the Democratic standard-bearer in 1896 under similar circumstances. Both escaped open criticism by professing amazement at the outcome, but they were too active and conspicuous during the conventions for their words to be taken at face value.[28] Theodore Roosevelt broke precedent in 1912 by appearing at the Republican convention and working openly for his nomination. The only immediate effect of his behavior was to encourage unavowed candidates and dark horses to pursue the Presidency in bolder fashion from the convention floor.

Campaign tours were taboo for Presidential nominees before the Civil War and for a considerable period thereafter. Stephen A. Douglas defied custom in 1860 and Horace Greeley in 1872, but both were beaten. People expected the candidate to remain in the background. So he remained at home, greeting delegations, conferring with managers, and assisting quietly with the solicitation of contributions. Plenty was said about him but not by him. In fact, the sole official pronouncement of the candidate on issues occurred in a formal response to the committee which notified him of his nomination. If the committee made a personal call, he might accept with a carefully prepared verbal statement; otherwise, he replied by letter. In any case, the response of the candidate became a campaign document. Sometimes he amplified his position by additional letters to supporters intended for publication. This device was a particularly useful one in the days before rapid communication, for it enabled a candidate to take a stand in one section without having it reported in another. If he waited until the closing weeks of the campaign to express these contradictory views, he ran little risk of exposure before election day.

In the pre-platform era of the 1830's and '40's, when the delegates prepared a short statement or none at all, the candidate imitated the silence of the convention. The Whigs regarded platforms with suspicion. They usually gave the voters nothing but the airy assurance that the lofty character of their nominee guaranteed a constructive approach to issues. Lincoln retained enough of his Whig antecedents to maintain silence as the Republican nominee in 1860. He parried all verbal and written queries about his position by referring questioners to the party platform. Grant carried matters further than Lincoln in 1868 by refusing to make statements, answer letters, or even give interviews to his political advisers. As a Presidential candidate, Rutherford B. Hayes was not so much of a recluse as Grant. Nevertheless, Hayes had sufficient regard for precedent to question the propriety of attending Ohio Day at the Philadelphia Fair, although he was governor of the state and the celebration was nonpolitical.

The initial pressure to change the system in 1880 came not from the Presidential candidates but from the voters. An accident of geography placed the Mentor farm of the Republican nominee, James A. Garfield, only eight miles from a station on the main railroad line in northern Ohio. Alive to the commercial opportunities in the situation, the railroad advertised excursion rates from Cleveland and other cities to the home of the candidate. It neglected to say that passengers would still have to take a horse and buggy ride from the railroad stop to the farm. Despite this inconvenience, crowds converged on Mentor in such vast numbers that Garfield found it necessary to appear on his front porch and make innumerable

short speeches. The experience was something of a nightmare for him because he fretted constantly about blundering into an indiscreet statement.
Eight years later, another Republican nominee, Benjamin Harrison, recognized that his Indianapolis home was too accessible to discourage trav-
elers, so he deliberately built his campaign around voter pilgrimages. Bearing the experience of Garfield in mind, Harrison and his managers organized faithful Republicans into delegations and scheduled their appearance
for a particular day and hour. Harrison also insisted on the right of prior
censorship of what was to be said to him. He looked over the salutation to
be delivered by a delegation leader well in advance so that he could plan
his own response. The advent of the "front porch" campaign in the 1880's
doomed the candidate to live in a chaotic atmosphere, but it proved to be
a workable compromise between the established tradition and the newer
demand of voters for personal contact with the candidate. The only nominees to imitate the ill-fated cross-country tours of Douglas and Greeley before the end of the century were James G. Blaine in 1884 and William Jennings Bryan in 1896. Both suffered the fate of their predecessors, but
within two decades exhausting regional or transcontinental tours were common for all candidates, except incumbent Presidents seeking re-election.

The gradual change in the role of the Presidential nominee did nothing
to diminish the responsibilities of party managers who had always borne
the main burden of national campaigns. They continued to raise money,
arrange tours for popular party orators, subsidize the production of campaign biographies, and produce quantities of literature dealing with contemporary issues. The manager's work became even more exacting when
the nominee occupied the White House and hence was exempted from
active participation.

III

Although the discussion of political issues was continuous, it reached a
peak every four years in the months just before a Presidential election.
During the 1850's and '60's the climax came in October when Ohio, Indiana, and Pennsylvania held state elections. Since two of the three were
doubtful states, party strategists made frantic efforts to carry them, on the
theory that a sweep in October would create a bandwagon psychology for
November. Nobody knew whether the voters actually scrambled onto the
winning side for the reasons advanced by the political experts, but in the
case of Indiana and Pennsylvania the theory worked with the regularity of

a scientific law: the party that carried them won the election in November. Understandably, parties spent the bulk of their national campaign funds in these states. Such dishonest practices as bribery, stuffing the ballot boxes, and importation of voters from other states were common in these elections. Pennsylvania ceased to be a doubtful state in the 1870's and Indiana did not hold an October election after 1880, but the corrupt habits of the state machines continued long after the national party organizations had cut off the stream of funds.

Until the general adoption of the Australian ballot in the 1890's, which standardized election procedures and provided private booths for voters, conditions at the polls encouraged lawless behavior. Since each party committee printed its own ballots, it took care to utilize a color and size that would easily distinguish its ballot from those of other parties. Thus, when the voter stood in line at the polls, bystanders knew his preference, even if he had taken the precaution of picking up his ballot in advance. This informal system was an invitation to intimidation and violence. In the cities, employers often voted their employees as a bloc and brought recalcitrants into line by threats of dismissal. Urban bosses employed armies of ward heelers at the polls to use physical force on the defiant. Conditions in rural America were not much better. Elections attracted large numbers to village polling places, and many came full of whiskey. Inevitably, insulting remarks were exchanged that led to biting, scratching, and fist fights.[29] Major brawls occurred with frequency in border towns because party organizations could not resist the temptation to import voters from an adjoining state. Every effort was made to keep the floaters drunk and out of sight until the time they marched to the polls, for their appearance signaled the start of a fight.

Although Southerners were generally considered to be more quarrelsome than Northerners, elections below the Mason-Dixon Line tended to be quiet. Restrictions on the suffrage reduced the voting population, and custom made it still smaller. Most yeomen had given up the habit of participating in elections and acquiesced cheerfully in the domination of politics by the planter class. The few who tried to exercise their rights were discouraged in a variety of ways, with the result that the entire political machinery fell under the domination of courthouse rings. In fact, the only place "to wear a quiet Sunday air" on election day was Washington, D. C., where the residents had no vote.[30]

What often looked like the spontaneous political activity of voters was the co-ordinated effort of massive party organizations which, like icebergs, concealed much of their bulk. By 1840 the national party had come to resemble a huge pyramid with a base composed of county or township committees, and a superstructure of derivative committees. As a rule, in each election district a party committee performed the dual function of calling nominating conventions and naming members to the next higher committee in the hierarchy. At the apex of the pyramid was the state committee which held the state convention and selected delegates to the national convention. Eventually party organizations would take the next logical step and create a powerful national committee, but—in keeping with the states' rights theory prevalent before the Civil War—the national party of the 1850's was a coalition of autonomous state parties. The independent attitude of these units made it virtually impossible for a party to unite on any national enterprise except the election of a President. Even this nominal gesture of co-operation was due to the desire of state parties to control patronage more than policy. Before its collapse in 1854, the Whig party was so badly split on major issues that it settled for a few meaningless statements at national conventions and called them a platform. The Democrats were more successful than the Whigs in agreeing on a statement of national policy, but the platforms of state Democratic parties frequently contradicted the national platform at crucial points. Under the circumstances it was not surprising that party national committees limited themselves to routine correspondence and to raising money for expenditure in doubtful states. When the Republican party emerged in the late 1850's, it started a trend toward centralization of party doctrine and discipline. In the beginning, however, progress was so slow that the Republicans welcomed the affiliation of state organizations in Pennsylvania, New Jersey, and Delaware which maintained their independent status.

While the rise of explosive national issues on the eve of the Civil War promoted the cohesiveness of political parties, other developments were at work undermining the autonomy of state organizations. For one thing, the number of federal jobs grew five times as rapidly as the population between 1792 and 1861, so that the President had some 50,000 at his disposal by mid-century. Even the weak Presidents of the '50's attempted to use this vast degree of patronage control as an instrument for compelling co-operation. State leaders resented the attempt to dictate party policy from Washington, especially if the President applied pressure on behalf of legislation unpopular with their constituents. On the other hand, party bosses recognized that a loyal army of office-holders gave more reliable support to a machine than rank-and-file voters. So when the President and local opinion differed on an issue, the party bosses tended to stick with the President rather than risk the loss of patronage. Although the supply of jobs never caught up with the demand, it increased steadily enough to produce the career office-holder. Living a marginal existence, he became as dependent on a government job as state leaders became dependent on his professional support. Thus the mutual needs of Presidents, state organizations, and career office-holders promoted the consolidation of the party system.

Postmasterships were the backbone of political machines at mid-century, for they provided the party that controlled the Presidency with two-thirds of its patronage. Not only did the postal system extend to the smallest hamlet, but in most communities the postmaster was the sole link between the citizen and the national government. He performed such important functions for the party as testing local sentiment, smoothing over factional quarrels, distributing campaign material, and raising money. His negative power to withhold information was almost as important as his power to issue it, and pamphlets mailed by the opposition party often wound up in wastebaskets instead of postal boxes. The eagerness of local citizens to become postmasters had nothing to do with pay scales. Only eighty-eight postmasters received more than $1000 annually, and many in rural areas received as little as $10. The real attraction of the job was that it was a reward for service to the party and a badge of distinction in the local community. The postmaster enjoyed such fringe benefits as the privilege of franking his mail and exemption from military service and jury duty. The position could also bring indirect advantages to citizens who operated a general store or a newspaper on the side. By locating the post office in his store, a postmaster could count on extra business from people who came to pick up their mail. As the first one in a rural community to receive news, the postmaster controlled a priceless commodity. Quite often, if he was not already an editor at the time of his appointment, he tried to buy a paper soon after. From there it was an easy step to the printing business, which in turn gave him the inside track on contracts for governmental notices and party ballots.

Of the remaining political plums at the disposal of the national Administration the most important was the customs service, which provided many jobs in major ports such as New York, Boston, Philadelphia, and New Orleans. The navy yard at Philadelphia took care of additional party workers, and, unfailingly, every Administration stepped up construction on the eve of an election. Landlocked states got a negligible share of this patronage, but they participated on equal terms in the appointment of federal judges, marshals, and district attorneys.

The distribution of jobs created as many problems for a President as it solved. His constitutional power over appointments was shared with the Senate, which had to ratify them by a majority vote. Presumably the selection of candidates rested with the President, but after the establishment of the spoils system in the Jacksonian era, senators had begun to take a voice in the nomination of judges, customs officials, and postmasters in large cities. Congressmen had tried to whittle away at Presidential power in similar fashion. Long before the Civil War, both senators and members of the House had appropriated the right to name postmasters in their home towns; congressmen had also begun to dictate minor appointments in their respective districts.

Presidents viewed the erosion of their power over appointments with mixed feelings. The need to protect executive prerogatives clashed with their desire to escape the thankless task of parceling out the jobs. No amount of skill and patience could insure a President against the acrimonious claims of rival factions, or the resentment of unsuccessful applicants. The New York customs house jobs, which should have been a source of strength to a party, always were a source of trouble instead. Winning New York was always the prelude to the disintegration of the majority party in the state, a fate which overtook first the Democrats and then the Whigs. Although New York politicians were fighting over the biggest prizes, elsewhere patronage squabbles generated as much discord. The chronic disagreement of local leaders about job recommendations led John Sherman of Ohio to the conclusion that, if a President made all major appointments immediately, he might "hope to recover from the effects" before his term closed.[31]

Security of tenure would have mitigated Presidential patronage problems, but the spoils system assured the chaos of frequent rotation in office. Whenever a new party came to power, the President was expected to clean house. By 1857 the demand for jobs was so explosive that office-holders were rotated, despite the fact that one Democrat had succeeded another in the White House. Besides consuming a disproportionate amount of the

President's time and involving him in idiotic wrangles with Congress, the system tended to lower the tone of public life. The universal acceptance of the idea that jobs ought to be awarded on the basis of party service rather than fitness dulled ethical instincts. The line between a reward and a bribe grew hazy; and party leaders from the President down bartered jobs for legislative support, favorable publicity, and a host of clandestine advantages. Lincoln behaved no better than the rest, although he undoubtedly believed that his goals justified the use of questionable means. The traffic in offices also stimulated the deep-seated instinct of politicians to practice nepotism. The Civil War generation was probably no worse in this respect than others, but powerful senators like John J. Crittenden of Kentucky and Jesse D. Bright of Indiana made no effort whatever to conceal the fact that they had loaded the public payroll with their relatives.[32]

Party leaders made no distinction between relatives and others, however, in levying assessments at election time. A logical result of the spoils system, the assessment program had been in effect since 1840, with payments geared to the salary of the federal office-holder. The minority party always protested piously against the practice, but used it as vigorously to extract campaign funds from employees in the states it controlled. Although there was little outright coercion under the assessment system, those who did not pay usually lost their jobs. Legal attempts to outlaw assessments came to nothing because few of the victims objected to the principle. No President tried to stop levies on federal employees in the '50's, and Lincoln acted only in specific cases called to his attention.[33]

The casual attitude of political leaders toward the abuses stemming from the spoils system was shared by lesser figures in the party hierarchy. The principal trouble did not come from dedicated partisans, who often possessed some scruples, but from professional adventurers drawn to a party by the prospect of financial profit or power. Like soldiers of fortune, the latter led an uncertain existence and used whatever tactics were necessary to capitalize on their opportunities. Reflecting on half a century of experience in managing party workers, Thurlow Weed—who was first a Whig and later a Republican boss—concluded that politics brought out both "the best and the worst aspects of human nature." [34]

On the fringe of the party organization and bearing a varying relation to it was the newspaper editor. Later generations idealized the nineteenth-century editor as an incorruptible tribune of the people who reported facts accurately and voiced opinion fearlessly. The subsequent absorption of independent newspapers by nation-wide chains fed this legend and has evoked a nostalgia for what was imagined to be an era of honesty in journalism. In actuality, editors slanted political news shamelessly. Although a number of editors were colorful, eccentric, and fearless, self-interest undermined their objectivity. Some made a living by editing the personal news-sheets of leading politicians. Still more relied on legal notices, advertising, miscellaneous printing contracts, and other types of party patronage to maintain solvency. Those who did enjoy financial independence were so hopeful of becoming either kingmakers or kings that their newspapers became as much political organs as those of their subsidized brethren.

Party leaders distrusted editors but regarded them as a necessary evil because the political machine subsisted on favorable publicity. Since association was inescapable, the rising politician preferred that the editor be his employee, and either bought a personal organ or induced his followers to do so if possible.[35] Senator Stephen A. Douglas, the leading Western Democrat of the '50's, had a mouthpiece in Chicago; and when Abraham Lincoln began to take his Presidential prospects seriously, he purchased the *Illinois Staats Anzeiger,* a German-language newspaper. It was standard practice for an established leader to multiply the journalistic outlets under his control, and as late as 1908 Senator Thomas H. Carter of Montana managed to take over papers in all but three counties in his state.[36] Until the establishment of the Government Printing Office on the eve of the Civil War, Congress selected the public printer who was expected to edit an Administration organ in Washington.

Lesser politicians who could not afford to own papers were obliged to pay editors for support. Congressman Elihu Washburne of Illinois regarded $50 per editor as the standard fee in the 1850's, although he had to put up $200 to secure satisfactory treatment from the *Chicago Tribune.*[37] An alternate arrangement was to pay an editor in patronage, but this could be done only by incumbents fortunate enough to have printing contracts at their disposal. Party committees helped impecunious candidates in close and important districts. Whatever the arrangements, the subsidy system was so firmly entrenched that it persisted well into the twentieth century.[38]

Subsidies were just as apt to produce discord as co-operation between editors and politicians. Few editors cared to take orders as paid employees or felt adequately compensated by a petty patronage job or local printing contracts. The bulk of them consistently overestimated the power of the pen and hence their value to the party. More often than not they also mistook the natural conviviality of the politician for an invitation to share special confidences. Because they were asked to evaluate local opinion, editors expected to be consulted on over-all party policy and campaign strategy. Worse still, they responded to perfunctory praise from party leaders by dreaming of high office. Yet the very characteristics that made a man an effective editor impaired his chances of becoming an astute politician. A nose for news tempted an editor to betray confidential information and reduced his usefulness as an adviser. Furthermore, the constant pressure of deadlines led the average editor to take hasty and indiscreet positions. Once on the record, his statements provided ammunition for the opposition. If made known frequently enough and on a sufficiently wide variety of subjects, his views might become an insurmountable barrier to his own political advancement.

Each generation produced a few editors who were exceptions to the rule. During the Civil War era, the moderate Henry J. Raymond of the *New York Times* became successively lieutenant governor, chairman of the Republican National Committee, and congressman. The wily Schuyler Colfax of Indiana used his South Bend paper as a stepping stone to the speakership of the House and the Vice Presidency. One or two editors like Thurlow Weed of New York and Alexander McClure of Pennsylvania wielded considerable power by being content to operate behind the scenes. But Horace Greeley, the most conspicuous journalist of the age, doggedly pursued high office and was repeatedly thwarted. The case of Greeley illustrated the problem faced by party leaders in dealing with powerful metropolitan editors who did not need subsidies to survive. Every major Republican politician feared Greeley and tried to placate him. Yet none could predict what would please Greeley, because he changed his mind often and without warning. On the other hand, everyone knew that to oppose his insane desire for office was to make a mortal enemy of the editor and his dedicated readers.

Ministers, educators, and businessmen seldom pursued elective office as vigorously as editors, while the small farmer lacked the leisure during the crop season to be a full-time politician. In the South, the cotton planter played a dominant role, but elsewhere lawyers monopolized the honors at the disposal of parties. The structure of the legal profession helped the lawyer to achieve his commanding position. He was master of his own time and operated in an atmosphere conducive to friendly relations with the voters. Except in the largest cities, the lawyer kept his office door open and turned his reception room into a social center that competed with the courthouse and the general store.[39] People came to discuss legal problems and remained to gossip about politics. Often the small-town lawyer followed the judges on circuit, which gave him additional opportunity to mingle with the voters. Since few county seats had any entertainment facilities, the visiting attorney spent the long evenings after the adjournment of court swapping jokes, drinking, and talking in the local inn. If a lawyer was modest in his charges and agreeable in manner, he could often turn a client into a political supporter. Abraham Lincoln owed his phenomenal grass-roots support to long years on the circuit; he had a great reputation as a storyteller and knew more people in central Illinois by their first name than anyone but the presiding judge.[40]

As the career of the self-educated Lincoln demonstrated, lawyers could be successful in politics even if they were poor. The requirements for admission to the bar were not exacting, and most candidates made the grade after a brief apprenticeship in the office of an established lawyer. Poverty sometimes obliged the would-be lawyer to become temporarily a teacher or manual laborer, but rarely frustrated him altogether. Once he had saved a little money, the embryo politician read law, passed his bar examination, hung out his shingle, and embarked on his twofold career.

Notwithstanding the furious competition of lawyer-politicians for office, the Whig and Democratic parties enjoyed remarkable stability between 1836 and 1848. Shortly thereafter, the aggravation of the slavery issue and other questions shattered the familiar alignments and paved the way for the emergence of the Republican party.

II

A New Party Arises

For a party that was destined to control the Presidency during sixty of its first hundred years, the Republican party had a singularly unimpressive birth. Although numerous party heroes later claimed credit for launching or naming the Republican party, nobody of consequence took any interest in it in 1854. The first Republican President, Abraham Lincoln, protested sharply against attempts to use his name in connection with initial attempts to organize the party in Illinois. Not a single member of his first cabinet was any more willing to accept the Republican label than Lincoln had been in 1854, and the only one who came forward in 1855 thought the word "Democratic" ought to be inserted in front of "Republican." [1] Thereafter the party attracted distinguished recruits at a more rapid rate, but only by partially concealing its name and original character. The national committee omitted the word "Republican" from its call for nominating conventions in both 1856 and 1860,[2] while one of the leading candidates for the Presidency at the second party conclave referred to it as "The National Union Convention." [3]

There is no single explanation to the central paradox that more people approved of the Republican party than were willing to join it. Some hesitated because of the high mortality rates for third parties. This consideration weighed heavily with professional politicians, who preferred a subordinate role in a flourishing organization to leadership in a movement facing an uncertain future. The rank and file were frightened away by the political

23

antecedents of the first Republicans, most of whom boasted long records as militant foes of slavery.

The stigma attached to the anti-slavery cause in an era notorious for its sympathy with reform movements was due to the Abolitionists, a heroic but repellent band of crusaders. Superseding an older and more cautious anti-slavery organization in the early 1830's, the Abolitionists managed to conduct a thirty-year crusade for Negro freedom without picking up any significant support from the public. It was not so much what the Abolitionists proposed as the provocative tone of their arguments that offended people. William Lloyd Garrison, Wendell Phillips, and other New Englanders in the forefront of the movement, always coupled their plea for emancipation with a coarse indictment of the planter class. Phillips described the South "as one vast brothel where half a million women are flogged into slavery," and Garrison talked wildly about the rights of Negroes "to cut the throats of their masters." [4] Apparently the Abolitionists, who had no practical plan for helping the slaves and abused more cautious reformers who did, expected to produce a miracle by unremitting agitation. Abolitionist propaganda backfired in North and South alike. The agitators dared not enter the slave states, and were not entirely safe among their own people. Mobs broke up their meetings, smashed their printing presses, and occasionally an Abolitionist was lynched. The fact that the crusaders persisted was more of a tribute to their courage than to their political acumen. In any case, their behavior increased the danger that anyone who criticized the abuses of the slave system would be branded an Abolitionist.

By 1840 the futility of the Abolitionist crusade had convinced many anti-slavery men that abuses could be remedied only through political action on a piecemeal basis. These more cautious reformers were the men who ultimately organized the Republican party. Many of them were as critical of Southern institutions as the Abolitionists were, and secretly cherished the same ultimate objective. Yet they avoided all connection with the Abolitionists and concentrated their initial efforts on legislation to block the admission of more slave states. The advocates of political action contested the elections of 1840 and 1844 as members of the Liberty party. The public response was so discouraging that the anti-slavery men reorganized as the Free-Soil party in 1848, polling a somewhat larger vote because of the co-operation of the Barnburners. This group was a disgruntled faction of New York Democrats who displayed as much interest in rebuking their own party as advancing the cause of the Negro. Having succeeded in defeating the Democratic Presidential candidate, most of the Barnburners promptly deserted the Free-Soil party, with the result that it suffered the same fate as the Liberty party.

The principal handicap of both third parties was that they could not sell the moral arguments for the containment of slavery. Some imaginative anti-slavery men had tried to connect their program with sectional economic issues, but this formula made no headway until the unexpected breakdown of the Compromise of 1850. Both the Democrats and Whigs thought they had solved the problem of slavery in the Compromise by organizing the territories recently taken from Mexico without any statement about the status of slaves. Their optimism was founded on the belief that no new territories would be organized in the foreseeable future. Since neither the territories created in the aftermath of the Mexican War nor the remaining Louisiana Purchase territory seemed capable of supporting much if any agriculture, the architects of the Compromise imagined that the agitation over the expansion of slavery would subside.

II

In 1854, however, the languishing anti-slavery movement received an unexpected opportunity to revive its crusade when the Democrats reopened the territorial quarrel. Artificial pressures rather than land-hungry settlers were primarily responsible for this blunder.

Innumerable business groups wanted a government-subsidized railroad link with California, and those who favored a northern route thought that the organization of Nebraska territory would improve their prospects. As always, land speculators were interested in new territory and were intrigued by the possibility that a transcontinental railroad would run through it. An epic feud between two Democratic leaders in Missouri also found one outlet in rival plans for the organization of Nebraska. These artificial pressures converged on Stephen A. Douglas of Illinois, chairman of the Senate committee on territories. Whether Douglas acted against his better judgment in reopening the territorial question is debatable, but he was ambitious enough to take the leadership of a dubious project rather than forfeit the spotlight.

Douglas hoped to avoid a squabble by employing the so-called "squatter sovereignty" formula of 1850 and allowing the prospective settlers to fix the status of slavery. The trouble was that Nebraska did not fall into the same category as the areas taken from Mexico. As part of the Louisiana

Purchase territory, Nebraska was governed by the provisions of the Missouri Compromise of 1820, which prohibited slavery north of the line 36° 30′ except in Missouri. Obviously planters could not take slaves to Nebraska territory and compete with free farmers unless Congress repealed the Missouri Compromise. So Douglas reluctantly added a provision for repeal to the bill organizing Nebraska territory, and by so doing caused an explosion throughout the North. Nobody considered the Great Plains suitable for the cultivation of cotton, but the fact that the Douglas bill divided the region into two territories—Kansas and Nebraska—suggested a deal to give the South control of Kansas. Many Northerners indifferent to the plight of the Negro thought the South was trying to swindle them out of territory reserved for the free farmer. They denounced the proposed amendment repealing the Missouri Compromise as a cynical breach of the thirty-year-old contract between the sections. Northern congressmen who could not be reached by anti-slavery arguments found themselves co-operating with Free-Soilers in the fight against the Kansas-Nebraska bill.

The sudden change in the political climate encouraged Free-Soilers everywhere to call anti-Nebraska meetings. Although few people recognized it at the time, the initial round of protest meetings in February and March was the beginning of the Republican party. If the Pierce Administration had heeded these manifestations of popular discontent and shelved the Kansas-Nebraska bill, the opposition would probably have disintegrated. Instead the President mobilized all of the resources at his disposal and pushed the measure through a sullen Congress in late spring. The unexpected size of the defiant House minority revealed that both major parties were honeycombed with Free-Soil sentiment. Acting on this discovery, the Free-Soilers called a second round of meetings to convert the anti-Nebraska forces into a new party. Cognizant of the unpopularity of the Free-Soil label, they held fusion conventions which in most cases took no name. Some Free-Soilers, however, could not stand anonymity and called themselves Republicans. Tactics varied so widely that future historians were left with the perplexing job of deciding which anti-Nebraska convention launched the Republican party.

The principal claimant was Ripon, Wisconsin, where Alvin E. Bovay, a staunch foe of the Kansas-Nebraska bill, had called a protest meeting at the Congregational church on February 28, 1854. This gathering had provided the impulse for a state convention which met at Madison on July 13 and nominated a full ticket for the fall elections. Meanwhile, Bovay had been fretting about what to call the new party, and had written a letter to Horace Greeley proposing the name "Republican." Greeley had commented favorably in his *New York Tribune* on June 16, but remained a Whig and so lost his chance to take credit for the idea. Bovay persisted, however, and the Madison convention, as well as a similar gathering at Jackson, Michigan, a week earlier, raised the Republican banner.

By midsummer 1854, however, it had become apparent that the Republicans would face competition from another new party, which was more upset about immigrants than slaves. For over a decade an unprecedented number of foreigners, mainly Irish and Germans, had been arriving in the United States. An America which was basically Protestant and Anglo-Saxon took alarm at this influx, because many of the newcomers were Catholic and also unfamiliar with democratic institutions. A succession of anti-foreign societies and political parties had grown up in the port towns where arriving immigrants were most conspicuous. Mergers and consolidations eventually resulted in the creation of a single party in time to contest the 1854 elections. Members were called Know-Nothings because they took a vow of secrecy and when quizzed about their activities said that they "knew nothing." Organized in lodges, the initiates learned an elaborate ritual. If deemed trustworthy they could take three degrees, and only those who took the highest degree were eligible to hold office. Whatever the ultimate objective of the Know-Nothings, their immediate goal was to cut off immigration.

The secrecy that shrouded the movement and its leaders alarmed the politicians of the older parties. All that the Whigs and Democrats could learn about the Know-Nothings was their intention to elect "representatives fresh from the people." Presumably "no politician or office seeker" could "have a post . . . with them." [5] Under ordinary circumstances, a clandestine political organization would have lacked mass appeal, but 1854 was not an ordinary year. On paper the Know-Nothings had a perfect formula for people who hated the Democrats or resented the reopening of the slavery question. Immigration restriction could be presented as a way to cut off a major source of Democratic votes or, alternately, as a way to shut down the westward flow of migrants who were making trouble over slavery in the territories.

Temperance agitation also complicated voter resentment and helped to unsettle party alignments on the eve of the off-year elections. Maine had taken the lead by passing successive Prohibition laws in 1846, 1848, and

1851. Thereafter the movement to prohibit the sale and manufacture of alcohol spread westward. Like the Abolitionists, the advocates of Prohibition were single-minded in their devotion to the cause, and nativists joined with them to strike at beer-drinking Germans and whiskey-drinking Irish.

Of the major parties, the Whigs stood to lose the most from the three-fold agitation. They had already been deserted by their followers in the deep South for tepid support of the Compromise of 1850, and they had never been strong in any Midwestern state except Ohio. The Free-Soil Whig element in Michigan, Wisconsin, and New England was tempted to join the new Republican party; whereas the Border-state Whigs, who cherished the Union and abhorred the disruptive influence of the slavery controversy, leaned toward the Know-Nothings. The national Whig leaders did not provide effective guidance for the rank and file. They were too timid to risk the onus of associating with the Republicans, and they were excluded from the inner circle of the Know-Nothings because they refused to take secret vows. Under the circumstances, Senator William H. Seward of New York, Abraham Lincoln of Illinois, and other prominent Whigs decided to remain with the party until the electorate spoke more clearly. Wherever they could promote fusion and give it a Whig flavor, they did so. The success of these efforts was mixed, the outcome depending on the strength of the party and the willingness of Whig leaders to co-operate with groups they distrusted.

The unpopularity of the Kansas-Nebraska Act was bound to hurt the Democrats, but the divided opposition made their position far from hopeless. Many of the Barnburners with anti-slavery tendencies hesitated to repeat their bolt of 1848 and were prepared to act with the Democrats if they refrained from making the Kansas-Nebraska Act a test of loyalty. President Pierce lacked the energy to enforce any policy on a national basis, but the party bore the brunt of popular indignation for sponsoring the Kansas-Nebraska Act. Douglas was hanged in effigy all over the Midwest, and accused of selling out to the South in return for the Democratic Presidential nomination. The fact that Southerners had shown little interest in the fortunes of the Kansas-Nebraska bill made no difference to critics of the Illinois senator. Their sustained attack put Douglas in an ugly mood, and when he returned to Illinois in the summer, he instituted a purge of anti-Nebraska Democrats. Some remained active in the party and defied him; others took no part in the election; but an influential minority defected to the fusionists. In neighboring Indiana, Senator Jesse D. Bright, the state Democratic boss, pursued the same vindictive policy. Elsewhere, mutual recriminations over the Kansas-Nebraska law also knocked splinters off the Democratic party and destroyed the morale of its remaining followers.

During the last months of the 1854 campaign it became obvious that the politicians trying to dominate fusion were determined to avoid using the name Republican. Soundings of popular sentiment convinced them that most voters opposed to the Kansas-Nebraska Act would not accept the proposed Republican ban against the admission of more slave states. Aside from Michigan and Wisconsin, where the Free-Soil Whigs went over in a body to the Republicans, fusionists kept the Republican element in the background. Although the anti-Nebraska forces were the backbone of the coalition in Maine and Vermont, they preferred to call themselves the Opposition. A more nondescript fusionist movement ran without a name both in Ohio and Indiana. The Whigs managed to draw most of the Iowa and New York fusionists under their banner, but they were swallowed up in the Border states by the Know-Nothings.

The situation was so chaotic in some states that three or four parties were contesting the elections. Republicans who tried to defy other elements of the opposition had a discouraging time. The organization in New York attracted so few people that it abandoned plans to nominate a state ticket.[6] Pennsylvania Republicans found their Free-Soil antecedents such a handicap that they did not launch a party until after the 1854 election.[7] In Massachusetts and Illinois the Republicans refused to take a subordinate role in the fusionist movement, nominated separate tickets, and were badly defeated. They would have done still worse in Massachusetts if Garrison and Phillips had not removed the Abolitionist stigma by their attacks on the party.[8]

The most effective fusionist campaigns were made in Connecticut, Pennsylvania, Ohio, and Indiana, where opposition candidates concentrated on nativism, temperance, and anti-Nebraska sentiment. Ohio coalitionists exploited the religious susceptibilities of the voters by holding meetings in churches, conducting them like a worship service.[9] Confronted with a wide Democratic majority, Indiana coalitionists gave the bulk of the nominations for state offices to rebel Democrats and charged the regulars with favoring "the extension of slavery and whiskey." [10] In all four states many lukewarm Republicans tried to insure themselves against a political disaster by becoming Know-Nothings.

When the votes were counted in November 1854, the Democrats knew they had lost, but nobody knew who had won. The Know-Nothings polled two-thirds of the votes in Massachusetts, which was full of Irish immigrants, and made spectacular gains at the expense of the Whigs in the Border. The Republicans carried Wisconsin and Michigan, but had to share victory with the fusionists elsewhere. In the Midwest, as in the East and Border, the Whigs were the principal sufferers, although the Democrats also failed to carry a single Northern state. The dissidents were happy over the rebuke to the major parties; the anti-Nebraska Democrats exulted over the defeat of the regulars; the Free-Soilers in command of the Republicans believed that slavery had been dealt a decisive blow; the Prohibitionists claimed victory for the forces of morality; while the Know-Nothings thought they had routed the immigrants and laid "a soothing bandage on the chafed edge of North and South." [11] There was an element of truth in all these assumptions, but the *Boston Courier* came nearest the mark when it observed that "the foundations of the political deep were broken up—men floated about loosely, and all party ties and ligatures, which had bound them together before, were burst and cast away." [12]

The chaos in party alignments became fully apparent when fusionist legislatures met to elect senators in January 1855. California, Indiana, Missouri, and Pennsylvania could not agree on anyone. Connecticut chose Lafayette Foster, a Whig who had made common cause with the Know-Nothings. The Massachusetts legislature also preferred a political chameleon, Henry Wilson, a Know-Nothing with pronounced Free-Soil tendencies. In Iowa a deadlock was averted only because James Harlan, the compromise choice, had no definite political antecedents. Illinois Whigs tried to put over Abraham Lincoln, and he succeeded in polling the highest vote on the first ballot. Lincoln was too conservative on the slavery question, however, to suit the anti-Nebraska Democrats who held the balance in the legislature and ultimately managed to elect their own candidate, Lyman Trumbull. The Whigs almost lost New York, where the opposition members of the legislature swarmed about like "maggots" on "an old cheese." [13] Eventually, Senator William H. Seward, the Free-Soil Whig, won re-election, but both his party and the rival Democrats were demoralized.

Few of the victorious fusionists had any idea about which issues would ultimately be most important. Fortunately for them, the new Congress did not meet until December 1855, and they took full advantage of the breathing spell to ascertain whether nativist or anti-slavery enthusiasm would become predominant. A hard core of Know-Nothings refused to co-operate with the Free-Soil Republicans, and an equally dedicated anti-slavery group detested the Know-Nothings on principle. In the middle, however, was a large faction willing to move to either side if the occasion warranted.

No one could judge what the anti-Nebraska Democrats would do. Twenty-eight per cent of them had not bothered to vote in Illinois in 1854,[14] and several of their leaders had boycotted the campaign in the apparent hope that they could take command if the Administration was discredited.[15] Hardly any of the anti-Nebraska Democrats favored the abolition of slavery, and only a few advocated containment. The bulk of them would have been satisfied in 1855 with the re-enactment of the Missouri Compromise, and their disgruntled attitude was due as much to grievances over patronage as convictions on the slavery question. Their most articulate spokesmen were ex-Senator Thomas Hart Benton of Missouri, ex-Barnburner Preston King of New York, and Sam Houston of Texas, together with two editors, Frank P. Blair of Maryland and Gideon Welles of Connecticut. As self-appointed heirs of Andrew Jackson, they blamed their own eclipse and the low estate of the Democratic party on the dominant pro-slavery faction. Far more interested in recapturing control of the party than in co-operating with fusionists, they dreamed of a great popular uprising which would by-pass conventions and send either Benton or Houston to the White House.[16] The latter tried to promote a ground swell by touring the country in 1855 and by naming his youngest son for Andrew Jackson.

The Whigs, on the other hand, based their hopes on recapturing deserters from their party. Although some Whigs had left the party for good, a substantial bloc of conservatives disliked the Know-Nothings and considered the Republicans too extreme in their opposition to slavery. Abraham Lincoln was typical of this group, saying nothing publicly but waiting patiently for a revival of the party. As he confided to a boyhood friend in August of 1855: "I think I am a Whig but others say there are no Whigs and that I am an Abolitionist. I now do no more than oppose the extension of slavery." [17] Senator Hamilton Fish of New York and leading Whigs in Boston shared this cautious approach.[18]

III

The voters calmed down in the spring of 1855, but within six months they were upset again over developments in Kansas. New England Free-Soilers raised enough money to dispatch three small companies of settlers to Kansas. But pro-slavery Missourians got there first, elected a legislature responsive to their viewpoint, and returned home. Soon there were two governments in Kansas, a pro-slavery one at Lecompton recognized by Pierce and a Free-Soil one at Lawrence, which the President branded as illegal. A few encounters took place between the Kansas partisans, but both sides went into winter quarters too early to affect the 1855 elections.

Meanwhile, the influential Horace Greeley had decided to join the Republican party, and he was to do a great deal to keep the Kansas issue alive. His zeal for emancipation, slum clearance, milk inspection, and the working man was matched by his hatred of alcohol, tobacco, gambling, and idleness. He combined Puritan morals with the Utopian enthusiasm of the New England Transcendentalists. Visions of a New Jerusalem competed in his brain with Whig doctrines of economic nationalism. Invariably, Greeley's pen worked twice as fast as his mind, but it was a fault shared by a large proportion of *Tribune* readers and lyceum audiences that turned out to hear him lecture.

Most of the time Greeley managed to discipline a crafty streak of self-interest and behaved like a homespun philosopher. The fact that he looked like an urban Thoreau was an enormous help. His bespectacled moon face and pink cheeks radiated benevolence, while his broad-brimmed hat, shapeless duster, shuffling gait, and absent-mindedness added just the proper note of eccentricity. Greeley's numerous and impulsive charities also strengthened his reputation as a humanitarian. Notwithstanding this abundance of good qualities, Greeley could not altogether stifle a demonic passion for public office. In a dormant phase, his political ambition expressed itself in editorial sniping at his party collaborators; but when his appetite got out of control, Greeley was vindictive and destructive. Sooner or later his dislike of slavery would probably have drawn Greeley into the Republican party, but the Kansas issue hastened his conversion. Besides, Greeley had little to lose by deserting the Whigs, inasmuch as the New York Whig organization was controlled by his foes.

A Republican victory in the Ohio gubernatorial election in October 1855 caused several major anti-slavery leaders in the older parties to imitate Greeley. Salmon P. Chase, the winner in Ohio, was a migratory politician who had already changed parties five times. Contemporaries disagreed as to whether the bewildering zig-zags of Chase had been due primarily to his hatred of slavery or his political ambition, but nobody disputed the consistency of his record on the slavery question. Chase was typical of the political Abolitionist who concealed his ultimate aim for tactical reasons. He had belonged successively to the Liberty and Free-Soil parties. Moreover, in 1849 he had persuaded a deadlocked Ohio legislature to elect him to the Senate, where he led the fight against the Kansas-Nebraska Act. His subsequent campaign for the governorship had been a masterpiece of equivocation, for he posed alternately as a Republican, a Know-Nothing, a Whig, and a Democrat. Chase must have found anti-slavery sentiment durable and strong, because soon after the election he decided that he was really a Republican. Chase brought to the party experience, ability, and an impressive physical appearance, but he lacked the warmth that inspires personal loyalty. There was a repellent self-righteousness about his idealism which led a critic to remark that Chase "thinks there is a fourth person in the Trinity." [19] His naked ambition offended people almost as much as his sanctimonious manner.

Nevertheless, Chase's victory convinced his bitter Ohio rival, Senator Ben F. Wade, that it was time for anti-slavery Whigs to become Republicans. Although well educated and canny, Wade, in contrast to Chase, posed as a simple, uncouth frontiersman. His speech was profane and coarse, and his jibes at his political opponents were heavy and sardonic. Wade always overstated his case, a defect aggravated by his bellicosity and scorn for prepared addresses. People found it difficult to reconcile his idealism on the slavery issue with his attitude on other subjects, particularly his sneers at religion. Although Wade was no match for a nimble debater, he stood his ground in the Senate and encouraged other Republicans to do the same. Wade loved to puncture the self-esteem of haughty Southerners, and once squelched a potential duelling partner by suggesting the use of rude squirrel guns as weapons.

The October elections also brought to the Republicans Weed and Seward, who headed the New York Whig machine. Thurlow Weed was a master politician with keen awareness of human nature; he knew instinctively when to use flattery and when to use force. He could bend a merchant prince like Edwin D. Morgan to his purpose as easily as he could an illiterate ward heeler. Born to poverty and apprenticed to a printer at the age of eleven, Weed had worked his way up to the editorship of the *Albany Journal* at the age of thirty-three and had become state boss of the New York Whigs in the early 1840's. Most people believed that Weed was crooked, but he merely encouraged others to do corrupt things which he would not do himself. His basic interest was in pursuing power for its own sake. Yet, on occasion, Weed could be sufficiently distracted by national issues to use his political machine for constructive purposes.

Senator William H. Seward and Thurlow Weed complemented each other ideally, for Seward enjoyed holding public office but cared little about building a personal organization. Seward always charted his political course with great shrewdness, but willingly allowed Weed to take care of the patronage which resulted. Personal friends as well as political allies, they did not have a serious quarrel in over thirty years of close association. Seward was elected governor of New York in 1838, and immediately championed appropriations for parochial schools and other measures in support of the immigrants, who were usually cultivated by the Democrats, and offensive to nativists. During this period, Seward also supported the Free-Soil program, but he did not earn a national reputation as a foe of slavery until he entered the Senate in 1849. Thenceforward he alternately repelled and attracted his anti-slavery colleagues by combining outspoken statements with cautious behavior. His idea of a crusade was to take two steps forward and one step back. He aroused further misgivings by maintaining close personal ties with pro-slavery Senate Democrats and clinging to the Whig party until he had been re-elected in 1855. Even after affiliating with the Republicans, Seward was something of an enigma. The public thought of him as an orator and a statesman, but from the Senate gallery Seward struck one anti-slavery observer as "the most unprepossessing figure in the chamber—thin, pale, eyes-sunken, a retreating forehead hidden by a shock of dishevelled hair, voice high-keyed and almost repulsive." [20] A young admirer thought Seward had a "head like a wise macaw," finding charm in his ugliness, "off-hand manner, free talk, and perpetual cigar." [21] Friend and foe alike found Seward convivial, warm-hearted, and sparkling in conversation. Yet the words that tumbled so freely from his mouth often confused his listeners. For Seward, frankness served as a device to inspire confidence without revealing thoughts. By concealing his own attitude, Seward was able to function as a conciliator on more than one occasion, but he overestimated the capacity of personal friendship to withstand the strain of ideological disputes. Many of his Senate colleagues considered

Seward an opportunist who had joined the Republicans only because the New York Whigs were dead and the Know-Nothings were unwilling to accept him. The close association of Seward with Weed also damaged his standing in the party, but the oratorical ability of the New York senator more than made up for his faults.

Few prominent members of the opposition imitated Seward and Chase. Some would have preferred to join the Know-Nothings, who had made the best showing in the scattered November elections of 1855, but were discouraged by the intensification of factionalism within the movement. The principal trouble came from an anti-Nebraska group headed by Senator Wilson which wanted the party to take a stand on the divisive slavery issue. The Know-Nothing Council made a final effort to prevent a split by abandoning secrecy, going to the voters as the American party, and nominating a Presidential candidate far in advance of the usual time. The obvious choice for a party which wanted to ignore slavery and concentrate on the immigrant was Millard Fillmore of New York, a former Whig who as President had sponsored the Compromise of 1850. So the American party held a convention at Philadelphia on February 22, 1856, nominated Fillmore, and adopted a platform reaffirming the doctrine of 1850 for dealing with slavery in the territories. The moderate anti-slavery Know-Nothings, who called themselves the North Americans, regarded "the nonintervention doctrine" as a pro-slavery position. They had begun dropping hints in January that they would bolt if they could find a suitable group to join and the Republicans obliged them by also calling an "opposition" convention for February 22 at Pittsburgh. By remaining nameless, the Republicans attracted not only the North Americans but restless Jacksonians like Frank P. Blair and ex-Congressman Preston King of New York. The sponsors of the Pittsburgh convention also eased the way for the participation of waverers by promising not to nominate a Presidential candidate and by admitting all interested people as delegates.[22]

IV

With tolerance as their watchword, the Republicans attracted delegates from sixteen free states and eight slave states.[23] The convention opened in Lafayette Hall at 11 a.m., and from the opening prayer until adjournment at the end of the second day, the more militant anti-slavery men held the center of the stage. Old Joshua Giddings, the Free-Soil congressman from Ohio, gave a fighting speech, and Gamaliel Bailey, the Abolitionist editor of the *National Era,* was very active in the hall. Yet the official actions of the convention displayed a spirit of compromise. The moderate Frank P. Blair was chosen to preside, and although the declaration of principles went further than his proposal for the restoration of the Missouri Compromise, it fell far short of the Free-Soil platform of 1848. Some of the bolting North Americans offended the anti-slavery zealots by proposing to "take care of the Dutch and Irish after the nigger question is settled," [24] but on the whole the proceedings were harmonious.

It was easier for the Republicans to imitate the party structure of the Whigs and select a national committee than to agree upon the wording of a call for the nominating convention. The delegates left the problem in the lap of National Chairman Edwin D. Morgan, an anti-slavery New York merchant. Since both North Americans and Jacksonians bitterly opposed the use of the "Republican" label, on the ground that it would offend all but the Free-Soilers, Morgan prudently decided to refer to the national committee as the "Committee appointed by the Pittsburgh Convention." As to who was to be invited to the June 17 convention, Morgan included everybody opposed to the Pierce Administration, the repeal of the Missouri Compromise, and the admission of Kansas as a slave state.[25]

Neither the nameless convention of Republicans nor the American party convention had done much to clarify the murky political situation. The Republicans had gained the support of the anti-slavery Know-Nothings plus some Free-Soil Democrats. The Pittsburgh convention had also absorbed the so-called Republican Association, a radical organization founded in 1855 by Gamaliel Bailey and Louis Clephane to co-ordinate the strategy of anti-Nebraska congressmen. By taking control of the Association the Republicans were able to stop the release of radical statements under their name.

The most disappointing aspect of the Pittsburgh convention was that it failed to attract a significant number of new recruits for the Republican party. The subsequent behavior of some participants proved to be even more disconcerting. Blair confided to ex-President Van Buren that he still favored a mass meeting of Democrats to take from the pro-slavery element "the name they used as impostors." [26] Seward had pointedly boycotted the Pittsburgh meeting as a rebuke to the radicals, and his continued silence checked the drift of anti-Nebraska Whigs toward the Republicans. The aloofness of the anti-Nebraska Whigs was especially disconcerting because they had nowhere else to go. The defection of the nativist Whigs to Fillmore had doomed the party, but the remnant was so conservative that it disapproved of all the current trends in politics.[27]

Although procrastination suited the old Jacksonians and the fossil Whigs who awaited the second coming of Henry Clay, it did not appeal to the younger anti-Nebraska men. Mindful of the adage that every politician needs a party, they recognized the importance of making a decision before state conventions selected candidates and formulated platforms for the fall campaign. The realists concluded that it would be easier to wrest control of the Republican party from the Free-Soilers than to revive the Whigs or devise a workable compromise with the pro-slavery Democrats. The only thing that caused the uncommitted anti-Nebraska men to hesitate was the irresolute tone of public opinion. Fortunately for their peace of mind, fresh trouble developed in Kansas during May of 1856 and with it a wave of sympathy for the Republicans.

The resumption of hostilities coincided with the spring thaw in Kansas, but Eastern newspapers had prepared their readers to expect the worst by reporting nonexistent encounters between the Abolitionists and the pro-slavery forces throughout the winter. Greeley had allowed his imagination free scope, peopling the frozen prairie with the half-crazed widows of murdered Abolitionists. In the process "bleeding Kansas" became a house-hold phrase which evoked an image of innocent, defenseless pioneers suf-fering for their convictions. The situation on the eve of the conflict was not as clear-cut as the North supposed. The people behind the pro-slavery fac-tion had more interest in land speculation than in establishing Negroes on plantations. Moreover, the leadership of the so-called "free state" faction had passed from the original colonists dispatched by Massachusetts to political adventurers as greedy for profits as the pro-slavery crowd. The proposed free state constitution even contained a clause that prohibited Negroes from entering Kansas, but the Abolitionists ignored this embar-rassing fact and spent the winter raising funds to arm Northern settlers.

None of this agitation bore much fruit until the pro-slavery government tried to arrest some of their opponents at Lawrence, the free state strong-hold. A scuffle took place on May 21, and drunken pro-slavery militia fired a few buildings in Lawrence and destroyed the newspaper office. A few men were killed, but Eastern papers reported a full-scale battle. Thereafter they habitually referred to the incident as the "sack of Lawrence." Twenty-four hours later, Northerners were further aroused when Congressman Preston Brooks of South Carolina clubbed Senator Charles Sumner of

Massachusetts, the most outspoken Republican in the Upper House, for an abusive speech. In the ensuing uproar Northerners overlooked the fact that Sumner had been clubbed for a personal attack on Senator Andrew P. Butler, a kinsman of Brooks, rather than for his tirade against the behavior of the pro-slavery forces in Kansas. These two incidents revived the drooping fortunes of the Republican party because they seemed to confirm the Abolitionist thesis that the South was engaged in a conspiracy to spread slavery. Few Northerners accepted the corollary that slavery ought to be abolished, but for the first time they wholeheartedly espoused the Republican principle that the expansion of slavery ought to be stopped. Exploiting popular anger promptly, anti-slavery leaders organized nonpartisan demonstrations in behalf of Sumner, and these were often so successful that the participants reorganized as Republicans on the spot.

These developments had a remarkable effect on the irresolute anti-Nebraska Whigs and Democrats, who realized that it was possible for the Republicans to wage a Presidential campaign on Sumner and Kansas without embracing the cause of the Negro. So in June and July of 1856 the professional politicians from the older parties made a concerted effort to infiltrate Republican state organizations and wrest control of them from the pioneer Free-Soilers. The strategy and timing of the infiltrators depended on local conditions, but they were successful enough to change the character of the Republican party.

The complex realignment in Illinois deserves special attention because it was typical of the pivotal Northern states. The original Illinois Republicans in 1854 had been drawn from the most radical wing of the old Free-Soil movement, their principal spokesmen being Icabod Codding and Owen Lovejoy, the brother of an Abolitionist editor lynched by an Alton mob twenty years earlier. Moreover, the party platform had gone beyond the orthodox Free-Soil position and advocated repeal of the Fugitive Slave Law as well as abolition of slavery in the District of Columbia. Neither the anti-Nebraska Whigs nor Democrats had co-operated with the Republicans in 1854, and at the time of the Pittsburgh convention the rebellious factions within the major parties were still sitting "on the fence like benumbed prairie chickens in winter." [28] Most of the rebels wanted nothing more than the restoration of the Missouri Compromise. This sentiment was especially pronounced among the Illinois Whigs, most of whom disliked anti-slavery agitators more than slavery. Although the Whigs had been the minority party in a normally Democratic state and had already lost their nativist element, a hard core of conservatives preferred impotence to fusion with the Republicans.

It required political leadership of a high order to promote co-operation between the mutually suspicious foes of the dominant pro-slavery Democrats in Illinois. Ex-Congressman Abraham Lincoln undertook the difficult assignment and in so doing set forces in motion that carried him to the White House. At the time Lincoln had little to lose. He had worked his way slowly up the political ladder, reaching top rung in the Illinois organization and a nomination for United States Senator just as the party collapsed in 1855. Already forty-six years old, Lincoln had no alternative but to retire from politics or make a fresh start in a new party. He was well known as a lawyer in central Illinois, but on the other hand he was handicapped, like most Whigs, by an identification with issues that had ceased to be important. For over a decade Lincoln had regarded slavery as a moral evil without knowing what to do about it, and he was reluctant to engage in denunciation unless he could propose a practical solution. The passage of the Kansas-Nebraska Act had convinced him that it was imperative to stop the expansion of slavery, although his moderation made him reluctant to co-operate with Free-Soilers and Abolitionists. A lesser man would have given up in despair, but Lincoln possessed a conviction that he was destined to solve the slavery question. Inner voices nagged him insistently throughout 1855, and by midwinter he felt obliged to act.

Instead of attending the Pittsburgh convention, Lincoln turned up the same day at a meeting of Illinois editors. He persuaded them to adopt a cautious declaration against the extension of slavery and to call a fusion convention at Bloomington for May 24. Then he began the painful task of coaxing anti-Nebraska Whigs and Democrats to attend the convention. The response was decidedly cool until the outbreak of violence in Kansas and the clubbing of Sumner, which took place on the eve of the Bloomington meeting. The sudden change in the political weather caused a number of sullen Whigs to participate. They were even more unhappy when Lincoln unveiled his program. Recognizing that the anti-Nebraska Democrats held the balance of power in Illinois, Lincoln insisted that the convention give them the choice nominations, including the governorship. Not a single member of the original Illinois Republican party was put on the state ticket. Ignored from beginning to end, Lovejoy, Codding, and the Free-

Soilers watched helplessly while Lincoln stole their party. His triumph was complete when the delegates authorized him and others to attend the Republican national convention.

Elsewhere moderates reorganized the anti-slavery movement along the same lines, but were too timid to take the Republican label in New Jersey, Delaware, Pennsylvania, and Indiana. Instead, the fusionists called themselves the People's party in an obvious bid for the large conservative element of the four states. Office-holders followed the lead of their constituents and scrambled onto the Republican bandwagon throughout the North. The most prominent recruits in the Senate were two anti-Nebraska Democrats, Hannibal Hamlin of Maine and Lyman Trumbull of Illinois, and two Vermont Whigs, Jacob Collamer and Solomon Foote. The trend was less clear in the House where many members continued to bid for the support of nativists as well as anti-Nebraska men. In any case, the House had an anti-Administration majority and blocked the efforts of the Democrats to remove Kansas as an election issue. The chief threat was provided by the Toombs bill, which proposed to make a fresh start in Kansas. This Administration measure not only authorized a new census but incorporated reasonable safeguards against dishonest territorial elections. Republicans were desperately afraid that the Toombs bill would solve the problem in Kansas and opposed it on the ground that the Democrats could not be trusted to administer any territorial legislation impartially.[29] Fortunately for the Republicans if not for the country, the Toombs bill perished in the House. Anti-slavery men also managed to get control of a House subcommittee investigating violence in Kansas, and produced a report which was suitable for use as a Republican campaign document.

V

While Congress was skirmishing over the Toombs bill, the national conventions selected their Presidential candidates. The Democrats met first at Cincinnati on June 2. Their traditional strategy had been to nominate a Northern candidate with Southern sympathies, and it was more essential than ever to do so in 1856 because the planters resented the intensification of the anti-slavery campaign. The delegates also recognized the need for a standard-bearer unconnected with the Kansas-Nebraska Act, which doomed both Pierce and Douglas. After considerable balloting, they selected James Buchanan of Pennsylvania, an elderly professional from the Jacksonian era who had never hesitated to reverse his stand on an issue if it would aid his political advancement. As ambassador to Great Britain during the Pierce Administration, Buchanan had missed the acrimonious discussion over territorial policy in Kansas. With his customary pliability, Buchanan agreed to a platform plank reaffirming the principle of "squatter sovereignty." Despite the bitter fruits of "squatter sovereignty" in Kansas, Democratic managers hoped to blunt criticism by promising that Buchanan would appoint territorial officials capable of ending the trouble. In any case "squatter sovereignty" was inevitable because it was the only formula upon which the Northern and Southern wings of the party could agree. Moreover, it embodied the democratic principle of allowing people to decide on their institutions at the local level. Recent events suggested that "squatter sovereignty" would always be difficult to apply, but optimists in the Democratic party expected the territorial problem to disappear once Kansas was admitted to the Union.

The sudden improvement of Republican prospects assured a lively fight for the nomination in the weeks preceding their June 17 convention. The most pressing task was to select a candidate who would draw votes away from Fillmore. The specifications called for a moderate anti-slavery man with some appeal to the nativists. None of the old Free-Soilers like Chase or John P. Hale of New Hampshire would do. Seward looked better to professional politicians, who were onto his trick of concealing cautious views behind radical pronouncements. Yet Seward had carried on an open war against nativism for twenty years, and had been locked in an equally bitter feud with Fillmore for control of New York Whigs. Currently they were continuing the old quarrel under new labels. Seward had also managed to incur the enmity of both Democratic factions in New York, although the anti-Nebraska Barnburners agreed with him in principle. His numerous enemies worried needlessly about Seward in 1856, because he made no real effort to get the nomination. On the advice of Weed he decided to wait four years in the hope that Republican prospects would continue to improve.

Thomas Hart Benton and Sam Houston were more anxious to run than Seward, but neither of the old Jacksonians appealed to the anti-Nebraska Whigs. By a process of elimination the Republicans reached the same conclusion as the Democrats and decided to nominate somebody who had not been involved in the squabble over Kansas. The faction most anxious to conciliate the nativists favored Justice John McLean of the Supreme Court. A rough-hewn man with a large, bald head and Roman nose, McLean had been intriguing for the Presidency since 1836. At one time or another every major politician had received an ambiguous letter from McLean about the slavery question. Couched in an obscure constitutional idiom, these pronouncements only indicated that McLean was a Unionist and would not let convictions stand in the way of political advancement.[30] The wily Justice also retired into the clouds whenever correspondents queried him about the Know-Nothings, expressing guarded sympathy with the nativists, but avoiding criticism of their opponents. His greatest appeal was to the fossil Whigs, who hoped that people would simply stop talking about slavery.[31] His boom alarmed the pioneer Free-Soilers and anti-slavery Whigs. He managed to draw delegates away from Chase in Ohio and developed great strength in Pennsylvania, where opposition to immigrants was stronger than opposition to slavery.

The threat posed by the McLean candidacy caused the Jacksonians and other moderate foes of slavery to rally around John C. Frémont, who had a vague record on current issues. Frémont was attractive because of his identification with national expansion in the 1840's. After an undistinguished youth that included short stints as a librarian, mathematics teacher, and surveyor, he had eloped in 1841 with Jessie Benton, the daughter of Thomas Hart Benton. Frémont immediately began the first of three expeditions to the West which were to bring him the name of "Pathfinder" and enable him to participate in the liberation of California from Mexico. Court-martialed after a quarrel with his superiors in the regular army, Frémont persuaded the California Democrats to elect him senator. A fresh controversy followed with army engineers over the proposed route for a transcontinental railroad, and made Frémont more popular than ever. People close to him found the Pathfinder impulsive, stubborn, and careless about finances, but politicians overlooked these defects because of his boyish charm. At forty-three he looked and acted like an American conquistador, possessing, as Ambrose Bierce remarked, "all of the qualities of genius except ability."

In 1855 both the Democratic and the Jacksonian factions of the Republican party had begun to exhibit interest in Frémont. Up to this point Frémont had not shown much concern over the slavery question, but he was vexed with the Pierce Administration over the railroad survey and discovered that he was an anti-Nebraska man. First, he announced that his anti-slavery views had prevented his re-election as senator from California, and then in two letters he advocated the Republican position on the

Kansas question. The North Americans got behind Frémont as enthusiastically as the Jacksonians, and at their convention on June 12, 1856,
nominated Nathaniel P. Banks, the speaker of the House, with the understanding that he would withdraw in favor of the Pathfinder. This elaborate
maneuver was intended to appease anti-slavery Germans, who would presumably be offended if Frémont received his initial nomination from
nativists.

The McLean and Frémont backers were engaged in a fierce struggle
behind the scenes when the Republicans assembled in Philadelphia on
June 17. Most Free-Soilers had enough political sense to avoid a blanket
denunciation of slavery, but they showed their partisan zeal by blaming
the woes of Kansas on conspiratorial slaveholders, in which they were
joined even by conservative Republicans. In his keynote speech Harry S.
Lane, president of the convention, returned to Greeley's favorite theme
of the Kansas widows whose innocent husbands had been murdered by
pro-slavery ruffians.

The crucial test between the McLean and Frémont men came after the
oratorical fireworks on a platform resolution to maintain the existing
naturalization laws. It was bitterly opposed by Thaddeus Stevens, who
led the McLean forces in Pennsylvania and wanted to inject the nativist
issue in the campaign. The subsequent debate almost broke up the convention, but in the end, the nativist faction accepted the will of the majority.[32]
The passage of the resolution by an overwhelming margin indicated that
Frémont supporters were in control of the convention. Stevens promptly
withdrew the name of McLlean, and Frémont received a first ballot nomination. According to an informal understanding, William F. Johnston, the
Vice Presidential nominee of the North Americans, was supposed to receive second place on the Republican ticket. But the Republican managers
decided that the heavy vote for Frémont relieved them of the necessity for
compromise. So they broke the agreement and selected William L. Dayton
of New Jersey for Vice President.

It was one thing to snub the nativists, but a very different matter to
offend the moderate anti-Nebraska men who were expected to provide the
bulk of the Republican votes in November. So the Republican platform
took a moderate line on slavery. The Free-Soilers had to be satisfied with
the statement that Congress should use its sovereign power to ban "the
twin relics of barbarism," slavery and polygamy, from the territories. The
influence of the conservatives was evident in the omission of reference to

such divisive issues as the Missouri Compromise, the Fugitive Slave Law, and the status of slavery in the District of Columbia. Because of the cleavage between former Democrats and Whigs, the platform also was silent on financial questions. In fact, the only plank that commanded unanimous support was one calling for the construction of a transcontinental railroad with Federal aid. After completing their work, the delegates adjourned to the chant of "Free Soil, Free Labor, Free Speech, Free Men, Frémont," which was to be the Republican rallying cry throughout the campaign.

The Republicans had been correct in supposing that the demoralized North Americans would acquiesce in the decision at Philadelphia. When the anti-slavery nativists reassembled to ratify the substitution of Frémont for Banks on June 19, a few obstructionists charged the Republicans with bad faith on the Vice Presidency, but Frémont made a personal appearance at the convention and persuaded them that Dayton would step aside for Johnston. The North Americans accepted this assurance and adjourned for the final time. Frémont was unable to fulfill this pledge, but the Republican ticket did not lose many votes in the process.

The absorption of the North Americans by the Republican party assured a three-way contest between Buchanan, Fillmore, and Frémont. The only uncommitted voters were old-line Whigs who were waiting hopefully for a reaction in their favor. They failed in their attempt to hold a convention at Louisville on July 4, but a handful did meet September 17 at Baltimore. The delegates blamed the Pierce Administration for chaos in Kansas, condemned the Republicans for preaching disunion, endorsed Fillmore without accepting the principles of his new American party, and disbanded. The death rattles of the Whig party intensified the struggle for the allegiance of its orphaned voters, who, it was thought, held the balance of power in the country.

The Democratic campaign cleverly exploited the apprehensions of conservative Whigs about the future of the Union. Buchanan supporters denounced the Republicans as a sectional party, predicting that the South would secede were Frémont elected. Prominent Southerners did their duty, alternating disunionist threats with assertions that Buchanan was as conservative as Fillmore. They pictured Buchanan as an upright, efficient administrator who would end chaos in Kansas by bringing her into the Union after an honest election.

The Republicans tried to counter this argument with their familiar contention that the squatter sovereignty formula was the cause of all the trouble. Their more canny strategists tried to limit debate to Kansas and the martyred Sumner, but they could not avoid the retaliatory charge that Republicans were Abolitionists. Some of the sting was taken out of this accusation by the decision of the Abolitionists to run Gerrit Smith for President on a platform of "No Union with Slave Holders." Garrison also divorced himself unmistakably from the Republicans with a series of extreme statements that Greeley printed in the *Tribune*. Many Republicans said little about slavery in the territories and a great deal about the desirability of colonizing Negroes abroad. The lack of concern for the Negro disgusted many Free-Soilers, leading George W. Julian to grumble that, if Republicanism won, it would do so "through the conduct of men who were ashamed of it." [33]

Most American party members resented the slavery agitation because it diverted public attention from the immigrant. They also blamed the Republicans for keeping the slavery question alive, and aimed most of their blows at Frémont rather than Buchanan. The Fillmore camp made its greatest headway with the insinuation that Frémont belonged to the Catholic Church. The charge was untrue but difficult to combat, particularly when coupled with the claim that Frémont would speed up the naturalization of his co-religionists. American party literature advertised Fillmore as an apostle of sectional peace and the only one of the three candidates capable of saving the Union.

The brunt of the campaign was borne by party workers rather than the Presidential candidates. The Republicans employed a variety of visual aids to portray the suffering of innocent settlers in Kansas. Parades, floats, and transparencies dwelt on the theme. Lyman Beecher, the great revivalist orator, even exhibited a heavy chain with two large padlocks which he claimed had been placed around the legs of free state men in Kansas.[34] The national committee issued a series of campaign documents on such subjects as "The Border Ruffian Code in Kansas," "The Poor Whites of the South," and "The Vacant Chair of Sumner." The *New York Tribune* printed a stream of reports about innocent settlers being "proscribed and hunted" like wild beasts,[35] while Greeley organized a Kansas relief fund with great fanfare.

As the crucial October elections approached, it was apparent that the Republican campaign had strengthened the party in New England and the upper Midwest but had alienated the fossil Whigs in the doubtful states along the Mason-Dixon Line. These orphaned voters simply did not believe the average Republican orator who denounced slavery in Kansas as a moral crime and then promised to leave the institution untouched in the South. Rufus Choate, the most influential of the old Whigs, wrote a public letter midway through the campaign urging Unionists to vote for Buchanan. His plea was echoed by James B. Clay, the son of Henry Clay, and had a powerful effect on the undecided. Some Whigs, however, who shared the sentiments of Choate could not bring themselves to vote for a Democrat, and preferred to waste their votes on Fillmore. This attitude was especially evident in the crucial October states of Indiana and Pennsylvania, which also contained numerous nativists. Furthermore, the Pennsylvania Germans, unlike their brethren farther west, were indifferent to slavery and irritated by the fact that Frémont had a French father. In raising money to exploit discontent the Pennsylvania Democrats showed great resourcefulness. They assessed every job-holder in the state organization three days' pay and raised enough outside money to provide a fund of $70,000. The Pierce Administration helped by employing additional workers at the Philadelphia navy yard on the eve of the election. The Republicans did what they could, but they had no state patronage and were unable to match the Democratic campaign fund.

And yet, despite all their advantages, the Democrats managed to win the Pennsylvania state election by a plurality of only 3000. They had a somewhat larger margin in Indiana but lost Ohio, the other October state, to the Republicans. The closeness of the results in Pennsylvania encouraged the Republican national chairman to open negotiations with the American party for a fusion ticket on Presidential electors. The mutual antagonism between the followers of Frémont and Fillmore prevented an agreement, but the Democrats experienced some anxious moments during the three weeks between the state and national elections.

As the politicians had expected, the October vote in Pennsylvania and Indiana was an accurate preview of the trend in November. Buchanan won the election by carrying the South plus the five Northern states of New Jersey, Pennsylvania, Indiana, Illinois, and California. Fillmore held Maryland with 8 votes, but the remaining states went to Frémont, which gave the Republicans 114 votes in the electoral college to 174 for the Democrats. The victors had every reason to be sobered by the outcome. They would not have won without the assistance of Whigs who either went to Buchanan with misgivings or helped him indirectly by casting a protest vote for Fillmore. It was impossible to regard this kind of support as an expression of confidence in the Democratic party. Plainly a large number of Whigs had done nothing more than register their fear that a Republican victory would lead to the secession of the South. This dwindling group of conservative Unionists still held the balance of power in the doubtful states of the North, and the future of the Democrats depended upon their ability to terminate the divisive quarrel over Kansas.

For a party that had been in existence barely two years, the Republicans made a spectacular showing, and their leaders were elated. Thaddeus Stevens crowed about the "victorious defeat." [36] Schuyler Colfax, who had begun to cut away from the Indiana nativists, compared the 1856 battle to Bunker Hill, "where those who finally retreated won the victory." [37] Ex-Barnburner Preston King of New York confidently predicted that the Democrats had won their last victory,[38] while Fessenden of Maine was amazed that the Republicans had "accomplished so much in so short a time." [39]

The full magnitude of the Republican victory in the Northern states became apparent when legislatures met at the beginning of 1857 to elect senators. Although it was impossible for them to control the new Senate, the Republicans could take comfort in the defeat of several supposedly invincible Democratic wheel horses. The most conspicuous casualty was Lewis Cass of Michigan, the party Presidential candidate in 1848, who gave way to Zack Chandler. Throughout New England, Democratic dynasties crumbled, and with the assistance of nativists the Republicans gained additional Senate seats. The New York Democrats watched in helpless anger while the legislature elected the renegade Preston King. Nothing gave the Republicans as much joy, however, as their unexpected victory in Pennsylvania, where the Democrats controlled the legislature. The upset sent Simon Cameron, the most artistic wire-puller of the Civil War era, to the Senate. Besides giving the Republicans another seat, the selection of Cameron was a direct rebuke to President-elect Buchanan, who had backed his Pennsylvania campaign manager J. W. Forney for the post. The new President was not to confront the irresolute and disunited opposition of the Pierce era but a militant minority already heartened by a taste of victory.

III

The Secession Crisis

Upon assuming the Presidency, Buchanan knew he must do something about Kansas but was in a quandary about what to do. Squatter sovereignty provided him with little practical guidance. It was a formula for concealing differences of opinion in the Democratic party rather than a plan for action in the territories. Behind the apparent simplicity of the doctrine lurked unresolved problems, the most serious being the question of when settlers fixed the status of slavery in the territories. Southerners contended that slaves could not be excluded until a territory applied for statehood, while most Northern Democrats believed that a territorial legislature was competent to exclude slavery from the outset. The South argued that the institution of slavery existed before the Constitution and had been recognized in it by formal provisions for the protection of property. They also contended that the power to define property rights inhered in states, and hence could be exercised only by people framing a state constitution. Carried to its logical conclusion, this theory entitled Southerners to the protection of slave property until a territory became a state, irrespective of local opinion. There was an irreconcilable difference between the Southern view of squatter sovereignty and Douglas's version of the doctrine, which rested on the principle of local self-government. Ever since the Compromise of 1850 Northern and Southern Democrats had lived with this disagreement only by refusing to discuss it, and in his 1856 campaign Buchanan had endorsed both versions of squatter sovereignty.

Since ambiguity had served the Democrats so well, Buchanan ought to have undertaken state-building in Kansas without reopening the territorial question. Before he reached the White House, however, Buchanan had worked out a dangerous plan to solicit a Supreme Court decision defining the status of slavery in the territories. He had done so on the theory that a judicial opinion would stop the political debate and thereby facilitate the admission of Kansas. It never occurred to Buchanan that a decision might divide the Democrats without silencing the Republicans. For an experienced politician he was incredibly naïve in imagining that people who had affirmed the right of Congress to regulate slavery in the territories since 1840 would subside as soon as a Court with a Democratic majority rendered an opinion.

A constitutional test was easily arranged on a case involving a slave named Dred Scott whose master had transported him to free territory. But Buchanan's project almost foundered on the reluctance of the judges to deal with the territorial question. Their instinct was to pass only on the narrow issue of whether a slave could sue in federal court. So during the weeks before his inauguration, Buchanan worked on two Democratic justices to secure a broader decision. With different motives the Abolitionists pursued the same objective. They did not expect the Supreme Court to free Dred Scott, but believed that any verdict on constitutional issues would intensify the agitation over slavery. Despite the several forces pressuring the Supreme Court, Buchanan received the blame for tampering with the independence of the judiciary because he predicted in his inaugural address that the Court would shortly decide the territorial question. He compounded the indiscretion by asking the nation to accept the anticipated verdict.

On March 6, 1857, the Supreme Court held that Dred Scott was not a citizen, and that neither Congress nor a territorial legislature could exclude slavery from the territories. The Court went out of its way to give the defunct Missouri Compromise a kick by declaring that it had been unconstitutional. Chief Justice Taney wrote the majority opinion and learnedly defended the Southern position. Six of the eight justices concurred in Taney's conclusion but reached it by a different route and wrote separate opinions. Both of the judges in the minority also wrote dissenting opinions, and thus people were left with the impression that the Supreme Court was carrying on a political debate rather than handing down an impartial judicial decision.

It is doubtful whether even a unanimous opinion would have made the

Dred Scott decision a definitive statement on territorial sovereignty. Buchanan learned within twenty-four hours that he had misjudged his countrymen. Horace Greeley rushed into print with the stinging observation that the Dred Scott decision deserved no more respect than the opinion of a majority "congregated in any Washington bar." [1] Many Northern editors agreed with Greeley, and several urged open defiance of the Court. In their sermons the next Sunday, Abolitionist ministers also concentrated on the Dred Scott decision, claiming that it was fresh proof of a vast conspiracy to spread slavery throughout the Western Hemisphere. Explosive as the outburst was, it soon became apparent that the rank and file did not feel as alarmed as the professional agitators. Most Northerners disliked the Dred Scott decision, but their instinct was to suspend judgment until Buchanan acted in Kansas. Accepting the guidance of the voters, Lincoln and other moderate anti-slavery men refrained from public comment on the decision of the Supreme Court.

The Dred Scott decision was as much of an irritant to Northern Democrats as to the Republicans. It made a shambles of their version of the squatter sovereignty doctrine by asserting that slave-holders had an unconditional right to take their slaves to the territories. Southern newspapers expressed unconcealed delight at the outcome, but Southern politicians saw the need for conciliatory gestures. Several of them issued statements to the effect that the legal rights of slave-holders in the territories would mean nothing if the settlers opposed the introduction of slavery. Northern Democrats received the further assurance that squatter sovereignty would survive on a de facto basis despite the Dred Scott decision. Douglas took his Southern colleagues at their word, hailing the Dred Scott decision as a vindication of territorial self-government.[2] Such a display of party solidarity was possible only because the discussion concerned a hypothetical situation. Once the Democrats returned to the problem of Kansas, where sectional interests were at stake, party leaders could be counted upon to speak more candidly.

There was a momentary decline of interest in the Dred Scott decision and Kansas because Congress was not in session. The lack of a national forum hurt the Republicans in the fall elections of 1857, and they lost ground everywhere except in New England. Chase managed to win a second term as governor of Ohio, but his margin was shaved to 1503 votes. The Democrats took the governorship of Pennsylvania, improving on their 1856 plurality by 40,000 votes. For the Republicans the only comforting feature of these scattered elections was an abrupt drop in the nativist vote throughout the East.[3] Although the Republicans were gradually becoming the sole opposition party, they needed an issue badly. Kansas soon came to their rescue, as it had done in the past.

In his effort to prepare Kansas for statehood, Buchanan had persuaded Robert J. Walker, a resourceful Mississippi Democrat, to serve as territorial governor. Walker was realistic enough to realize that Kansas would never become a slave state. He did, however, think it was possible to attract settlers with a Southern viewpoint who would support the Democratic party and the interests of the planter class in Washington. Both Indiana and Illinois were states of the type that Walker had in mind, and he thought a great deal could be accomplished by the judicious use of federal patronage in Kansas. Nevertheless his first job was to promote co-operation between the pro-slavery element and the free state men who wanted to bar Negroes from Kansas. The two groups came closer to sharing a common outlook on the racial question than the Abolitionists and the foes of Negro equality in the free state movement. The trouble was that the free state men demanded honest elections and Walker could not persuade the territorial government to make the necessary reforms. The basic objective of the Lecompton office-holders was to retain their monopoly on political power, and they knew no better way of discouraging free-state immigrants than by establishing slavery in Kansas. This irresponsible project received secret encouragement from Southerners in the Buchanan Administration who had grown weary of abuse in the North.

Walker was unable to cope effectively with the Lecompton-Washington axis. So the free state men boycotted the election held for the constitutional convention, with the inevitable result that it fell under the control of the Lecompton extremists. They proceeded to draft a constitution with an elaborate code protecting the property of all twelve slave-holders. The bolder delegates wanted to defy the popular sovereignty principle and transmit their constitution directly to Congress. This scheme was too raw even for the pro-slavery clique in Washington, which forced its protégés to submit the slavery clause to a popular vote. Fearful that the free state men might not boycott the new election, the pro-slavery men offered the voters a meaningless choice. Even if they voted against slavery, the institution could not be abolished until 1864. This device assured the continuation of the boycott by the free staters. Consequently, the clause establishing slavery without restriction won approval at the referendum of December 21, 1857, on the Lecompton constitution. The territorial government then forwarded the constitution to Congress for action.

Long before the Kansas election, Stephen A. Douglas, who had been the outstanding exponent of popular sovereignty, warned Buchanan publicly and privately that Northern Democrats would oppose the Lecompton constitution. Both Douglas and Walker urged the President to use his influence against it, and make a fresh start in Kansas. The timid Buchanan hesitated until February 1858, but he finally accepted the advice of hotheaded Southern Democrats and announced that the Lecompton constitution was the legal will of Kansas. Then he mobilized all his resources to secure congressional approval of an enabling act.

By endorsing the Lecompton constitution, Buchanan did the one thing certain to revive Republican prospects. Nevertheless, party strategists were in a quandary. One faction wanted the Republicans to stand aside while the Northern and Southern Democrats fought each other, while an equally large group favored an alliance with Douglas.[4] There were hazards in both policies. If the Republicans remained on the sidelines, the Lecompton constitution seemed likely to pass. If they aided Douglas, they were endorsing by inference the popular sovereignty doctrine detested by rank and file Republicans.

Developments in the Senate played into the hands of Republicans who favored co-operation because the Southern Democrats were in complete command. Despite a heroic fight by Douglas, the Lecompton constitution passed on March 23 with only three Northern Democrats voting against it. Although the situation was more favorable for the foes of Lecompton in the House, the Republicans saw they could not block the constitution unless they made an outright coalition with Douglas. The dilemma produced a bitter debate in the Republican caucus and almost split the party.[5] In the end the radical anti-slavery men acquiesced in the caucus decision to support the Montgomery-Crittenden amendment which called for another vote by the people of Kansas. Joshua Giddings of Ohio was so upset at the prospect of House Republicans abandoning their unconditional opposition to the extension of slavery that he was felled by a stroke.[6]

On April 1 the climax came. Dawes reported "a deep, silent excitement, an intensity which forbids noise" as the House prepared for the roll call.[7] The coalition, however, was successful, for the Montgomery-Crittenden amendment passed by the narrow margin of 120 to 112.

The Administration tried to save face and also to disrupt the House coalition with a proposal sponsored by William H. English of Indiana, which, in effect, offered Kansans two alternatives: immediate admission on the basis of the Lecompton constitution, or continued territorial status until the census showed the 90,000 inhabitants required for a congressional district. The English compromise also offered Kansas a large land grant if her voters accepted Lecompton. With Republican opposition certain, the anti-Lecompton Democrats found themselves in a dilemma. Douglas was placed under even greater pressure when Buchanan offered forgiveness and patronage to waverers in the House. For a moment Douglas hesitated, but he, too, preferred defeat to capitulation. Over his protest the compromise cleared the Senate 31 to 22 and the House 112 to 103 on April 30. The Administration's efforts were wasted, nevertheless, because Kansas, with the free staters voting, rejected the Lecompton constitution, 11,812 to 1926.

The bitter quarrel over Lecompton widened the gulf between the North and South as well as between the two sections of the Democratic party. Until that time the only disunionists were Southern fire-eaters and Abolitionists, who denied that Americans shared common values. But during the congressional debates even moderate Southerners like Alexander Stephens and Robert Toombs voiced the views of what was becoming a new national group. They talked about the superior values of their society and glorified the institutions clustered around the plantation system. James H. Hammond of South Carolina expressed this emerging Southern nationalism in eloquent terms during an exchange with Republican senators on February 3, 1858. Asserting that "cotton is king," Hammond warned his tormenters that the South was strong enough and prosperous enough to get along without the North. He went on to extol the aristocratic ideals of Southern society, likening the free Northern worker to a "mudsill." Neither Hammond nor the bulk of his congressional colleagues were advocates of disunion in 1858, but they had lost the incentive to compromise and demanded their own way in Kansas irrespective of public sentiment elsewhere.

II

Instead of trying to heal the breach with the anti-Lecompton Democrats, the Southerners persuaded the feeble Buchanan to continue the intra-party warfare. Despite overwhelming evidence that Northern Democrats approved the stand of the anti-Lecomptonites, Buchanan used the resources of his Administration to purge the rebels in the 1858 elections. No Republican could have prescribed a policy more likely to destroy the Democratic party.

Nevertheless, the political situation confronted the Republicans with problems as well as opportunities. The same faction that had favored coalition in the fight against the Lecompton constitution wanted to fuse with the Northern Democrats in the 1858 campaign. Such prominent Republicans as Horace Greeley, Ex-Speaker Nathaniel P. Banks, and Congressman Schuyler Colfax of Indiana believed that they could entice Stephen A. Douglas and his following into their party by extending the hand of fellowship. They were even willing to help Douglas win re-election as a Democrat on a popular sovereignty platform. This attitude infuriated the militant Free-Soilers, who felt that the Republican party would die if it abandoned its opposition to the extension of slavery. The most outspoken foes of fusion were the Illinois Republicans. Close contact had given them an unflattering view of Douglas, and they concluded that his opposition to Buchanan was based on nothing more than a desire for re-election.

Inasmuch as Douglas was the most famous political leader in the North, his campaign in Illinois became the focal point of factional intrigues in both the Democratic and Republican parties. Facing the simultaneous assault of the Buchanan Administration and the local Republican organization, Douglas refused to rest his fate with an Illinois legislature chosen on the basis of local issues. So he started the campaign early and made a thorough five-month canvass of the state. The Illinois Republicans recognized the difficulty of defeating the famous Douglas with an anonymous candidate who would not normally be named until after the election of the legislature in November, and so they took the unusual step of nominating Abraham Lincoln for senator before the election. The ensuing campaign took on an epic quality when Lincoln challenged Douglas to a series of debates. Douglas knew better than to advertise an opponent by sharing the platform with him, but he was sublimely self-confident. His failure to see beyond the immediate election converted Lincoln from a regional figure into a national one.

A later generation would thrill to the story of Lincoln's obscure birth in a Kentucky log cabin and his uphill fight to overcome the successive handicaps of poverty, inadequate educational opportunities, and his mother's early death. Schoolboys born after the passing of the frontier were to treasure the legends about the youthful Abe who worked as a river boatman, storekeeper, and rail splitter. His painful effort to teach himself would be hailed as proof that any American with grit and determination might reach the Presidency. But the voters in 1858 saw little to distinguish Lincoln from the average lawyer-politician who had built a comfortable practice and had punctuated a relatively undistinguished career with a few years in the state legislature and in Congress. On the platform and in private conversation Lincoln displayed the characteristics of the self-educated frontiersman. He never looked quite comfortable in a suit; his long, awkward frame seemed to rebel against it. He had a tragicomic face which registered moods ranging from playfulness to sadness. He could tell stories with the relish of a country wag. At other times he radiated a melancholy earnestness and conviction which compelled the attention of his listeners.

His chief asset as a speaker was a simplicity and clarity that contrasted sharply with the turgid oratorical style esteemed at the time, a style ornamented by pompous platitudes and quotations from the classics. A slow thinker himself, Lincoln took mercy on his audience and spelled out the logical connection between successive points in his speeches. There was an austere eloquence in his incisive sentences which enabled him to hold his listeners' attention. Those accustomed to losing their way in the luxuriant verbiage of polished orators usually could follow Lincoln from beginning to end. The opening paragraphs of his speeches were marred by a nervousness which introduced a squeaky quality into his high-pitched voice,[8] but, once Lincoln settled down, he talked with a quiet authority. He was neither as quick-witted nor as deft in platform banter as Douglas. Nevertheless, the debaters were well matched.

Altogether, Lincoln and Douglas debated seven times, starting at Ottawa on August 21 and concluding at Alton in late October. The two men agreed to take turns in opening the debate. Their rules provided for the first speaker to talk an hour and to finish with a half-hour rebuttal, after an intervening speech of an hour and a half by his opponent. Five debates were held in the doubtful counties of central Illinois, which contained 37,000 Whigs who had voted for Buchanan in 1856. This strategy reflected the belief of both candidates that Republicans in the North and the Democrats in the South would stick with their respective parties.

Douglas tried to convince the conservative Whig unionists that the Republican formula for excluding slavery from the territories would destroy the Union, and Lincoln countered with assurances that such fears were groundless. On the whole, Douglas managed to retain the initiative by exploiting a passage in Lincoln's June 17 speech to the Republican state convention. Endorsing the conspiracy theory for the first time, Lincoln had gone on to say:

> A house divided against itself cannot stand. I believe this government cannot endure permanently half slave and half free. I do not expect the Union to be dissolved—I do not expect the house to fall—but I do expect it will cease to be divided . . . Either the opponents of slavery will arrest the further spread of it and place it where the public mind shall rest in the belief that it is in the course of ultimate extinction or its advocates will push forward, till it shall become alike lawful in all the states, old as well as new—North as well as South.

Douglas condemned this position as Abolitionist doctrine. He also tried to substantiate his claim by quotations from platforms of Republican county conventions which had been drafted in 1854 before moderate elements wrested control of the party from Free-Soilers. Denouncing Lincoln for promoting war between the sections, Douglas reiterated his belief that the Union could survive only by tolerating a diversity of local institutions. Again and again, he praised popular sovereignty as the one principle upon which North and South could act in harmony.

Lincoln found it easier to convince people that popular sovereignty had failed in Kansas than to persuade them that the Republican formula provided a lasting solution. Starting from the premise that slavery was a moral evil, he reached the common-sense conclusion that the institution should not be allowed to spread. But logic gave way to hope when he predicted that slavery would ultimately die if its expansion was checked. Lincoln tried to overcome the adverse effect of his "house-divided speech" by repeated pledges to respect the constitutional guarantees protecting slave property in the states. He also promised to enforce the unpopular Fugitive Slave Law. When pressed by Douglas in the debates, Lincoln even conceded that he might permit the admission of additional slave states, if the inhabitants of a territory so desired. He felt, however, that such sentiment would not develop, provided the Republicans succeeded in excluding slavery from the territories.

The greatest handicap to Lincoln was the state's attitude toward the Negro, which varied from mild sympathy in northern Illinois to outright hostility in the extreme south. The doubtful middle counties had drawn numerous settlers from Kentucky and Tennessee, who, like most Southern whites, took the inferiority of blacks for granted and enthusiastically supported the policy of excluding the Negro from Illinois. Douglas catered to this racial prejudice with considerable success; he argued that the Republicans favored complete equality between the races. He also forecast unlimited social intercourse and intermarriage in the event of a Republican victory. Lincoln responded with more and more explicit denials of concern for Negro rights. In the debate at Charleston, Illinois, he was finally driven to say:

> . . . I am not, nor ever have been, in favor of bringing about in any way the social and political equality of the white and black races; that I am not, nor ever have been, in favor of making voters or jurors of Negroes, nor of qualifying them to hold office, nor to intermarry with white people; and I will say in addition to this, that there is a physical difference between the white and black races which I believe will forever forbid the two races from living together on terms of social and political equality. . . .

At the end he had nothing left except the contention that the Negro ought not to be a slave. The only hope Lincoln held out to the free Negro was the right to enjoy the fruits of his own labor. Even this proposal was not to be forced on the South or on the five free states that refused to admit Negroes. If Douglas behaved like the modern segregationist politician by raising the bogy of racial mixing, Lincoln exhibited the irresolution of the Northern moderate who did not know what to do about the Negro. The fact that one of the most humane Republican leaders honestly took such an equivocal position illustrated both the depth of racial prejudice in the free states and the political danger of even limited concern for the Negro. Only in New England was there any real sympathy for the rights of Negroes. If the Republicans expected to become the majority party, they would have to check the expansion of the South without upsetting the racial status quo.

Throughout the summer and fall of 1858 the arguments made by the debaters in Illinois were repeated on countless platforms throughout the North. The pro-Douglas Republicans did not actually endorse the senator, but their silence hurt Lincoln. Since centralized direction of the off-year elections was impossible, Republican strategy varied from state to state. Generally speaking, the advocates of fusion carried the day in doubtful states where anti-Lecompton Democrats were strong, but failed to do so in preponderantly Republican areas.

In the November elections the Democrats were swamped in the North, losing every state but Illinois. There the Republican state ticket won by 4000 votes, but Douglas secured re-election by carrying enough legislative seats in the doubtful Whig counties for an edge of 54 to 46 on a joint ballot. Even more humiliating to Buchanan than the victory of his most conspicuous Democratic critic was the loss of Pennsylvania. The depression of 1857 had aggravated the discontent over Lecompton in the Keystone state, causing the angry voters to slaughter every friend of the Administration. The only survivors were anti-Lecompton Democrats. Although a few states were not scheduled to hold congressional elections until 1859, it was a foregone conclusion that the Republicans would control the new House. Apparently mismanagement in Kansas had caused slavery to overshadow the nativist issue because the Republicans also gained at the expense of the American party, which managed to survive only in the Border states.

The results indicated that the North had reached the limit of its patience on the slavery question, and did not intend to be pushed around. Buchanan might have salvaged something by making peace with Douglas and the Northern Democrats, but by the time Congress met it was evident that the President was bent on suicide. Neither he nor the dominant Southern oligarchy in the Senate could forgive Douglas for co-operating with the Republicans to defeat Lecompton. So the Illinois senator was snubbed by his colleagues and displaced from his post as chairman of the committee on territories. They continued to harass him throughout 1859 and 1860 by demanding a federal code to protect slavery in the territories irrespective of the wishes of local inhabitants.

While the Democrats were slowly tearing their party to pieces, the Republicans increased their attacks on the Administration. A quadrumvirate composed of Lyman Trumbull of Illinois, William Pitt Fessenden of Maine, Zachariah Chandler of Michigan, and Henry Wilson of Massachusetts, now shared public attention with more experienced Republicans like Seward and Wade. Trumbull, a descendant of a distinguished New England family, had migrated to Alton, Illinois, practiced law, and identified himself with the Free-Soil wing of the Democratic party. He had defied Douglas on the Kansas-Nebraska Act and snatched a Senate seat away from Lincoln in 1855. Scholarly tastes set off Trumbull from many fellow senators. Cold blue eyes looked out from behind steel-rimmed spectacles, accentuating the solemnity of his face. Normally, Trumbull was shy and withdrawn, but political combat brought him to passionate outbursts, which contained a disconcerting mixture of legal syllogisms and vituperation.

Originally a Whig, Fessenden had taken his seat just in time to oppose the Kansas-Nebraska Act, and had been one of the first senators to join the Republican party. Without a rival as a debater, in an age when most speakers dared not depart from their prepared texts, Fessenden engaged in brilliant extemporaneous exchanges on the floor of the Senate. He possessed a terrible temper, which seemed only to sharpen the clarity and cogency of his remarks. Neither an original nor a profound thinker, Fessenden's firm devotion to principle and sense of justice was rarely clouded by prejudice. Chronic ill-health wasted his body, but he was able to function for extended periods on nervous energy alone.

Chandler was a wealthy dry goods merchant from Michigan who never used his millions to conceal his humble origin and coarse habits. A hard-drinking, two-fisted fighter, Chandler detested the Southern aristocrats and never missed an opportunity to attack them. Although not an especially effective speaker, he relied on persistence to carry his points. A similarity in temperament and outlook drew Chandler into the orbit of Ben Wade, and there was seldom an issue that separated them.

Of the Senate Republicans, none seemed more insignificant than Wilson of Massachusetts. A small, nondescript man, Wilson was an ineffectual speaker but an extraordinary organizer and wire-puller. He had worked tirelessly and with single-minded devotion to convert the Massachusetts Know-Nothings into an anti-slavery party. Wilson had a rare capacity to flatter his fellow citizens by seeking their opinion. Circulating in public places, saloons, and gambling houses, he would search out opinions on current issues with the air of a man who had not made up his mind. He employed the same techniques in the Senate, with a success which his insipid oratory could never have achieved.

The rapid turnover in the House prevented Republican congressmen from achieving the national following of their Senate colleagues, but several enjoyed sufficient security of tenure to command attention. One was young John Sherman of Mansfield, Ohio, who had launched a forty-four-year career of continuous office-holding in 1854. Caution, combined with an uncanny ability to read public opinion, lay at the root of Sherman's success. Dry and humorless, he still managed to stay one step ahead of his constituents on almost every important issue in the last half of the nineteenth century. The anti-Nebraska tidal wave that had washed Sherman into office had also sent Schuyler Colfax of South Bend, Indiana, and Elihu Washburne of Galena, Illinois, to Washington. Colfax made up his mind as slowly as Sherman but was less candid. A manipulator who hid behind more courageous men, Colfax was sufficiently agreeable to rise rapidly in the Republican hierarchy. Washburne, on the other hand, was an open and uncompromising foe of slavery. He had a harsh, disagreeable face which betrayed a thirst for power. Yet hard work, and seniority, gradually brought Washburne to the top. Within a year, the House Republicans would be rejoined by Thaddeus Stevens of Lancaster, Pennsylvania. A former Whig with nativist tendencies, Stevens was soon to emerge as the most effective champion of the Negro in the House.

No divisive issue like Lecompton threatened the solidarity of the Republican minority in 1859–60. The closest thing to a quarrel occurred in the House over the Oregon admission bill, which had passed the Senate before the 1858 elections. Since the Oregon constitution excluded slavery and free Negroes from the state, it annoyed extremists in both parties. Most Southern congressmen were willing to admit Oregon as a free state because it had such an overwhelming Democratic majority. Republicans found the admission bill objectionable for the same reasons.[9] Neither party could pursue its partisan advantage without putting strain on its principles. In the end, enough Republicans were attracted by the prohibition of slavery to vote for admission, and Oregon passed the House by a narrow margin of six votes.

III

Throughout 1859 the politicians were engaged in preparations for the ensuing Presidential election. The likelihood of a split in the Democratic party, and the sectional character of the Republican party, spurred conservative unionists to explore the possibility of organizing a new political movement. What they had in mind was a great center party which would save the Union by persuading the masses to suspend the debate on slavery. The idea caught on in the Border states, and appealed to nativists, Whigs, and other politically displaced Northerners. But the prospects of such a compromise party were blighted in advance of its inception by John Brown's raid on Harper's Ferry, Virginia, in mid-October. Federal troops quickly rounded up Brown and his twenty-two Negro and white followers, but public reaction to the episode strengthened the extremists. Southerners were bound to take a grave view of a raid on a government arsenal for the purpose of arming slaves, but they became more indignant when they learned that Brown had been subsidized by Massachusetts Abolitionists. The fact that several Republican newspapers hailed Brown as a hero only confirmed the Southerners in their belief that Republicans were indistinguishable from Abolitionists. Conversely, many Northerners were irritated because the Virginia authorities insisted on the death penalty for Brown instead of locking him up in an asylum.

The first political repercussions of the Brown episode occurred in the House of Representatives where angry congressmen from the Border blocked the election of John Sherman, the Republican candidate for speaker. The session was paralyzed from December 1859 until after the first of the year while the politicians searched for a compromise candidate. Sherman might have won election eventually if he had not endorsed a plea for funds to circulate *The Impending Crisis of the South,* a book by H. R. Helper which indicted slavery and urged the poor whites to revolt against the Southern planters. As it was, the Republicans had to accept William Pennington, a New Jersey moderate, as speaker to head off the election of a Democrat.

That the handful of moderates who held the balance in the House did not speak for the country was evident from the poor response to the launching of the Constitutional Union party. The new organization was the product of a fusion agreement by the Whig and American national committees on December 29, 1859. The only prominent politician to support the new movement unreservedly was John J. Crittenden of Kentucky, who had succeeded Henry Clay as the chief spokesman of compromise in the Senate. On the strength of Crittenden's endorsement, the fusionists called a national convention for May 1860, but their movement gained little momentum in the intervening months.

The Republicans expected a brisk contest for the Presidential nomination. Ever since 1856 Senator William Seward of New York had been regarded as the leading contender. He had coupled outspoken denunciations of the Buchanan Administration with a cautious approach to the slavery problem. His strategy was designed to convince the voters that he was radical and the professional politicians that he was conservative. This approach worked best at the grass roots, where people knew Seward only through his speeches. Immigrants with Free-Soil proclivities were especially attracted to Seward because of his well-known opposition to nativism. Out of deference to the rank and file, more than half a dozen state conventions in New England and the upper Midwest instructed delegates for Seward, but his strength was not as formidable as it seemed. The old Free-Soil leaders had always disliked Seward because of his equivocal conduct. They would feel obliged to honor instructions for a couple of ballots, but would be looking for an opportunity to switch. The practical politicians did not trust Seward any more than the idealistic anti-slavery leaders. In fact, Preston King of New York was the only senator who supported Seward wholeheartedly.[10] The behavior of Thurlow Weed, his alterego, also hurt Seward. Persistent tales of corruption had circulated about Weed in the past, and he handed the scandalmongers fresh material by pushing some questionable franchise bills through the New York legislature just before the Republican convention.[11]

None of these obstacles seemed likely to stop Seward's campaign as long as the Republican delegates believed that they could elect a candidate with a reputation for radicalism. But in April 1860, W. A. Buckingham, a conservative Republican gubernatorial candidate in Connecticut, won election by only 541 votes. Politicians concluded that a more radical standard bearer than Buckingham would have lost, and their attitude damaged Seward.

Other radical candidates also cut into Seward's strength, among them John P. Hale of New Hampshire, Cassius Clay of Kentucky, and Chase of Ohio. It was wholly characteristic of Chase to imagine that he was the chief competitor of Seward. He had served twice as governor of Ohio and had recently been elected to the Senate for the term starting in 1861. Unfortunately for Chase Ohio politicians were not prepared to support him. Chase had managed to wrench an endorsement for President from the state convention, but his opponents minimized the value of the pledge by arranging for district conventions to select the bulk of the delegation. It was an open secret that Ohio would send many anti-Chase delegates to Chicago and that most of them favored Ben Wade.[12] As always, Chase's personality got in the way of his aspirations. He had used and discarded Whigs, Democrats, and Know-Nothings in his rise to power. Transparent ambition coupled with ostentatious piety was a repellent combination at best, and Chase made it seem still more offensive with a "bland and patronizing smile." [13] One supporter told Chase in plain language that his candidacy was hopeless, but he awaited the convention with foolish optimism.[14]

Long before the Connecticut election killed the radicals, Republican politicians who desired victory above all else had begun to look over the dark-horse candidates. The problem of selection was tied to simple arithmetic. The party needed to carry states with an aggregate of 152 electoral votes for victory. It could count on nine Northern states stretching from New England to Iowa with a total of 54 votes. Most strategists believed that New York with 35 votes and Connecticut with six would wind up in the Republican column. This estimate boosted the total to 95 votes, or 57 short of success, leaving party managers a pair of choices. Either they could select a candidate who would appeal to the 59 votes of the Border states and Delaware or one who would attract the 74 votes of Pennsylvania, Ohio, Indiana, and Illinois. The Border campaign contained the most risks. Although opposition groups under a variety of names dominated all of the Border states except Missouri, none of these organizations accepted the Republican position on slavery or desired to fuse with the organization. Most members of opposition parties were conservative unionists who favored a moratorium on discussion of the slavery question. The two sons of old Frank P. Blair, Montgomery and Frank P., Jr., had been trying to stir up interest in the Republicans with a proposal for colonizing Negroes abroad. Montgomery Blair got nowhere with the dominant nativist leaders in Maryland, but Frank P. Jr. did better in Missouri because of a large anti-slavery German population concentrated around St. Louis.

A miscellaneous assortment of politicians seconded the efforts of the Blairs. This group included the conservative Orville H. Browning of Illinois, a former Whig and close associate of Lincoln; the shifty Schuyler Colfax, who had not completely severed his Know-Nothing connections; and the militant Greeley. Browning thought a cautious program and candidate would appeal to Whig remnants in the North as well as the Border. Colfax was playing several games simultaneously, but believed in bidding for the nativists, who still had considerable strength in Indiana and Pennsylvania. Greeley took a vast and unjustified comfort from the fact that slavery was slowly dying in the Border. He imagined that the process could be accelerated by a protective tariff and other economic projects for the betterment of the poor whites. He also violently opposed Seward, who together with Weed had blocked his New York political aspirations in 1854, and he was determined to back a candidate who could stop Seward's nomination.

The candidate the Blairs and their Northern allies decided to sponsor was Edward M. Bates, a courtly Missouri Whig with a gray beard and a genial air of authority. Bates boasted in private that he had "not changed an opinion on politics for thirty years," and his record bore out the assertion.[15] He regarded the Compromise of 1850 as the ultimate expression of wisdom on the slavery question and had scolded both sides for breaking it. Bates had clung to the Whig organization, presiding over the last national party convention of 1856. Thereafter he had remained inactive until the Blairs and Greeley began to boom him for President in the fall of 1859. Facts meant nothing to Greeley when he threw himself into a course, and he produced a number of editorials describing Bates as an orthodox Republican. After applying considerable pressure, Greeley extracted from his candidate a statement taking Republican ground on the slavery question, but Bates subsequently hedged his commitment. The one thing that became clear was that Bates did not disapprove of slavery on moral grounds. Like an old-fashioned Whig, he wanted to outlaw the institution in areas where the climate precluded a plantation economy.

The Greeley campaign made little headway in the North because the rank and file were more interested in nominating a bona-fide Republican than in thwarting Seward. Even faithful *Tribune* readers distrusted Bates and regarded him as "an old Granny." [16] Aside from the impossibility of selling Bates to their followers, most Republican leaders thought the party had a better chance of winning with a candidate who appealed to Pennsylvania and Indiana rather than to the Border. Several dark horses were available for a campaign based on this conviction. The list included Governor Banks of Massachusetts, Senator Cameron of Pennsylvania, and Lincoln of Illinois. None of the three had aroused much enmity or support. Banks, who had also served as speaker of the House, was a suave adventurer with a reputation for retiring "from something good to something better." [17] He had relied on the support of the Know-Nothings to capture the governorship and had repaid them by securing a constitutional amendment which barred immigrants from voting in Massachusetts for two years. This maneuver strengthened him with the nativists of Pennsylvania and Indiana, but damaged his standing with the numerous German Free-Soilers.

The convention seemed more likely to turn to Simon Cameron than to Banks if it wanted a candidate without a record, because the senator came from the pivotal state of Pennsylvania. Cameron regarded success at the polls as a mandate to reward his retainers with jobs, government contracts, and subsidies. As a man who owned banks, railroads, and a variety of industrial enterprises, he sought personal as well as political advantage from power. Crusaders irritated Cameron because they tried to use government as an instrument for formulating policies and the agitation over slavery struck him as particularly inappropriate. He made a half-hearted effort to substitute the protective tariff for the slavery issue, but his abiding conviction was that he could win elections by doing enough favors for enough people.

Cameron attracted no organized support outside of his own state, for he was neither an orator nor a magnetic personality. Shrewd, restless eyes dominated Cameron's angular face, and although he frequently smiled, he never managed to look relaxed. Despite his limitless capacity for doing favors, Cameron had managed to make some enemies in his own party. Indeed, despite their instructions to support Cameron, nearly half the delegates were disloyal to him and would support him only as long as he had no prospect of being nominated.[18] What kept Cameron's flickering hopes alive was the belief that the convention would take him if it rejected Bates. Like the colorless Missourian, Cameron was not officially a Republican, being a member of a coalition organization, operating in New Jersey and Delaware as well as his state, known as the People's party.

In retrospect, it is easy to see why Abraham Lincoln was the most attractive of the dark horses. He had achieved a national reputation in his dramatic senatorial contest with Douglas, and he was the only favorite-son candidate with solid support from his own delegation. In addition, Lincoln had managed to take a firm Republican position on the slavery question, but he had done so in such temperate and conciliatory fashion that nobody considered him to be radical. Like a good politician, Lincoln had refrained from public comment on such divisive issues as temperance, nativism, and the Fugitive Slave Law. In a quiet and unobtrusive way, he had engaged in a considerable amount of self-advertisement, which included a 4000-mile tour in 1859, and a notable speech at Cooper Union in New York City, February 27, 1860. Lincoln's strategy was to avoid offending the supporters of any other candidate. As one Lincoln backer put it: "The Republican party has a head and a tail to it and a middle. I name William Seward as the head and Bates as the tail—I say that if the convention selects the head, the tail will drop off; and if the tail, the head will drop off. . . ." He went on to add that Lincoln was the middle and "could hold the head and tail on." [19]

Norman B. Judd, the principal Lincoln manager, took full advantage of the fact that the convention was being held in his home territory. Judd worked out seating arrangements which isolated the Seward delegates from the doubtful delegations.[20] He also relied on his contacts as a railroad attorney for free transportation of Lincoln supporters to Chicago on the day of the nominating speeches. Then he printed duplicate tickets of admission to the convention hall, so that they could take the seats of the Seward men while the latter were parading through the city.

Meanwhile, the Democrats had suffered a serious setback in late April. Their Charleston convention broke up without selecting a Presidential candidate, because the South refused Douglas and the Northern Democrats would not accept anyone else. The delegates hesitated on the edge of the precipice and agreed to reassemble for a second try at Baltimore on May 25. This decision was a gesture of desperation rather than the first stage of a new plan to heal the party split.

The good news from Charleston was partially offset on May 9 when the various elements of the opposition who could not stomach the Republicans launched the Constitutional Union party. Holding their convention at Baltimore, the conservative Unionists nominated Senator John Bell of Tennessee for President and Edward Everett of Massachusetts for Vice President. Mindful of the old Whig precept that "platforms are nothing" and the candidate "must be the platform," [21] the new party was content to stand on "the Constitution and the Union" without further explanation. Both Republican and Democratic newspapers greeted the birth of the party with derisive comments. The *Springfield Republican* chided the Constitutional Unionists for failing to nominate "a live ticket," [22] and Greeley said the candidates were unsuitable for "the present geological age." [23]

The tepid response to the convention indicated that the new party would not do much damage to the Republicans. Eight Northern states and two Southern states did not bother to send delegates. Of the twenty-one members on the Whig national committee, only two bothered to attend. Half of the American national committee came, but opposition leaders largely boycotted the convention because they wanted to retain freedom of action.[24] To make matters worse, Crittenden of Kentucky, the moderate with the greatest appeal, flatly refused to be the party standard-bearer. The final blow occurred at Boston, where a ratification meeting of the Constitutional Unionists attracted mostly boys anxious "to hear 100 guns fired on the Common." [25]

With the smell of victory in the air, spokesmen for the various Republican candidates started gathering in Chicago a week before the May 16 convention. Weed had blocked the selection of Greeley but the resourceful editor arrived on May 12 as a delegate from Oregon, and to his delight curious crowds followed him everywhere.[26] The arriving delegates were a cross section of what the party could expect in future years. Some came as crusaders with a single-minded determination to fight for their principles. Others were devoted to the fortunes of a particular candidate, their zeal varying in direct proportion to their expectation of reward for services rendered. A large number intended to combine business with pleasure, and Chicago offered more than ample opportunities for entertainment. Thurlow Weed had democratically given representation to all three types on the huge New York delegation. It contained perennial reformers like George William Curtis, professional organizers like Tom Hyer, and a sprinkling of prize-fighters and gamblers. The coarse behavior and ostentatious spending of the last faction were to hurt Seward during the convention.

Workers had scarcely put the finishing touches on the convention hall when the initial wave of Republican politicians reached Chicago. Known as the Wigwam, the new building had been constructed for the sole purpose of housing the convention. It stood at the corner of Market and Lake Streets and cost $5000, the bulk of which the city had raised by public subscription. The remainder was collected by charging twenty-five cents admission to the dedication ceremonies.[27] The Wigwam was a rectangular structure 180 feet long and 100 feet wide, with a sloping main floor, surrounded on three sides by galleries which seated 10,000. A stage at the open end accommodated an extra 600, but the overflow on the main floor was expected to stand. The decorations conformed to the heavy classical style of the period. A large gilt eagle dominated the center of the stage and was flanked on either side by statues of deceased Americans regarded by the national committee as statesmen. Wreathed in evergreen, the coats of arms of the various states hung from the gallery rails. Although the Republicans had run out of martyrs, they found a conspicuous spot for a portrait of Senator David C. Broderick of California, an anti-Lecompton Democrat who had perished in a duel with a pro-slavery judge named David S. Terry.

National chairman Edwin D. Morgan, the taciturn New York governor with the mutton-chop whiskers, called the convention to order exactly ten minutes after noon on Wednesday, May 16. He then introduced keynote speaker David Wilmot to the 465 delegates. Wilmot was an ideal symbol for the moderate anti-slavery forces. As a Pennsylvania congressman in 1846 he had authored the famous proviso to bar slavery from all territory annexed as a result of the Mexican War. After the keynote address, the convention adopted the slate of the committee on permanent organization and adjourned until the following morning. During the interval the platform committee, under the chairmanship of William Jessup, heard opposing arguments on the slavery plank, with Horace Greeley opposing any criticism of popular sovereignty and the Free-Soilers opposing any dilution of the 1856 platform. After an acrimonious discussion, the committee adopted a plank midway between the extremes. It denounced the territorial policy of the Democrats but backed away from the outspoken anti-slavery doctrines of 1856. The final draft confined itself to the mild assertion that freedom was the normal condition in the territories and advocated legislation to deal with specific violations. Passed over were such explosive questions as enforcement of the Fugitive Slave Law, the admission of additional slave states, and the abolition of slavery in the District of Columbia. The platform indicated that the Republicans wanted to shed their reputation as a party with a single issue. The resolutions of 1856 endorsing internal improvements and a Pacific railroad were emphatically reiterated. Additional planks urged free homesteads and a moderate protective tariff. With their expanded economic program, the Republicans offered something to every section but the South, and in most of its features the platform constituted an endorsement of Alexander Hamilton's economic nationalism.

Ostensibly the convention devoted Wednesday and Thursday to problems of organization and the platform, but behind the scenes the managers of the various candidates had been bidding for delegates from the doubtful states. On Wednesday night there was a festive atmosphere in the Seward headquarters at Richmond House. Champagne flowed freely, and the New York delegates boastfully informed visitors that the nomination of Seward was assured. The New Yorkers would have been less elated if they had recognized the full significance of visits made by Governor John A. Andrew of Massachusetts to doubtful delegations on the eve of the convention. In separate sessions with the delegates from Pennsylvania, Indiana, New Jersey, and Illinois, Andrew had reaffirmed the loyalty of New

England to Seward. But the governor had gone on to say that New Englanders wanted victory above all else and would switch to a compromise candidate if necessary.

Andrew's offer of co-operation provided the doubtful delegations with every incentive to unite. Neither Henry S. Lane of Indiana nor Andrew G. Curtin of Pennsylvania, the gubernatorial candidates in their respective states, believed that they could win with Seward at the head of the ticket. Since the Illinois and New Jersey leaders felt the same way, the four delegations agreed late on Thursday afternoon to appoint a committee composed of three members from each state for negotiations on a compromise candidate. The committee met almost continuously from 6 p.m. until midnight in the rooms of David Wilmot. It adjourned without reaching full agreement, but New Jersey agreed to drop its favorite son, William L. Dayton, after a complimentary vote, and to unite behind Lincoln if Pennsylvania would take similar action. Apprised of this development, Judge David Davis, Lincoln's floor manager, held a hurried conference with the wobbly leaders of the Pennsylvania delegation just after midnight. Like many managers before and after him, Davis took a casual view of instructions from his candidate prohibiting any deal that involved cabinet posts. So Davis promised Pennsylvania a cabinet seat for Cameron if the delegation would back Lincoln. There was some evidence that Pennsylvania intended to take this step without any special inducement.[28] In any case, at the state's caucus on Friday morning at 9 a.m. the delegates decided by a slim margin of six votes to support Lincoln over Bates after an initial ballot for Cameron.

The nominating speeches were mercifully short. William M. Evarts of New York placed the name of Seward before the convention in twenty-six words, and Judd used only twenty-seven to nominate Lincoln. The galleries, packed in advance with Lincoln supporters, cheered mightily.

The balloting started late on Friday morning and was all over by noon. Seward's campaign had been based on an early-ballot victory, while the doubtful delegates were voting for favorite sons. On the first roll call he led with 173½ while Lincoln polled 102. None of the favorite sons had more than 60 votes, while the potentially dangerous Bates received the support of only a few scattered delegates. Seward's plans for a quick victory came to naught on the second ballot when he gained only 11 votes. Many New Englanders felt absolved of any obligation to him and shifted to Lincoln, who picked up 79 votes. More important, the doubtful states were ready to execute their prearranged plan. New Jersey gave the signal midway through the third ballot by switching its entire 8 votes from Dayton to Lincoln. States farther down the alphabet followed suit, giving Lincoln 231½ out of the 234 necessary for the nomination. At this point Judge Cartter of Ohio jumped up on his chair and bellowed that the Buckeye state was shifting four votes from Chase.

Cartter's announcement had touched off a wild demonstration inside the Wigwam and a fresh volley of cheers when it was relayed to the pro-Lincoln crowd waiting restlessly outside. Thousands took part in an impromptu parade through Chicago carrying everything from rail fences to broom sticks.The people of smaller towns fired cannon, rang bells, and sang *Yankee Doodle* and *Hail Columbia*.[29] The next day the delegates nominated Senator Hannibal Hamlin of Maine as Lincoln's running mate.

The exciting month of May closed with the final effort of the Democrats to resolve their differences at Baltimore. Once again Administration Democrats combined with Southern fire-eaters to prevent Douglas from obtaining the two-thirds vote necessary for a nomination. The Douglas backers in turn rejected any compromise candidate, and the party split became irrevocable. The Northern wing nominated Douglas for President and Hershel V. Johnson of Georgia for Vice President, while the Southern wing named John C. Breckenridge of Kentucky and Sen. Joseph Lane of Oregon respectively. After all the discord over the status of slavery in the territories, the two Democratic parties drew up surprisingly mild planks on the subject. Breckenridge also professed to be as good a Unionist as Douglas. Yet nobody could miss the fact that the split destroyed the last national party and with it the only institution capable of adjusting sectional differences under the democratic system. The Democratic party had survived the schism in the Protestant churches and other nation-wide organizations in the 1840's. Its disruption, therefore, foreshadowed the collapse of effective communication between the North and South. With the loyalties of voters oriented toward sectional parties, it was most unlikely that the losers would accept the verdict at the polls.

Although the split had destroyed any chance for the Democrats to carry the North, the Republicans drove the wedge between the sections deeper during the long session of the 36th Congress in 1860. The leaders of the Republican majority in the House knew that it would be impossible to get legislation through the Democratic Senate, but they went through the motions of passing a protective tariff, an internal improvement bill, and a Homestead bill for campaign purposes. The House also established a special committee under John Covede of Pennsylvania to investigate the general topic of executive pressure on Congress. After grilling a number of Buchanan's subordinates, including several who had deserted their chief, the Republican majority on Covede's committee filed a blistering report. Buchanan was accused of using bribes, patronage, and other improper methods to round up votes for the Lecompton constitution. Undoubtedly Buchanan had used all of the dubious practices of his predecessors to promote the Administration's program, but the Covede committee had called unreliable witnesses, ignored judicial procedures, and exceeded its jurisdiction. In so doing, the committee served as a model for later investigating committees which used the inquisitorial power of Congress in arbitrary and reckless fashion to harass Presidents. What started out as a partisan maneuver soon became an article of party faith, with Republicans championing Congress against the Executive. The Covede committee was not concerned about long-term consequences, but about the accumulation of ammunition to use against the Democrats in 1860. It achieved this objective, even though the House tabled both the majority and the minority reports.

The Republican House was far more interested in exposing Democratic misdeeds and in taking a stand on economic questions than in slavery. It passed bills to admit Kansas as a free state, and to organize five new territories as a single unit without any mention of slavery. After all the fuss, the party seemed to stand for nothing more original than the Compromise of 1850. Republican efforts to perpetuate the conservative image established at Chicago were wasted, however, because Charles Sumner resumed his seat after a four-year interval and delivered a long harangue on the barbarism of slavery. If the return of Sumner frightened moderates, it also gave him a unique status in the Republican hierarchy. Few religious leaders achieve martyrdom in their own lifetime, and the odds against politicians doing so are almost prohibitive, but Sumner succeeded. Henceforth, faithful Free-Soilers would hail his frenzied attacks on slavery as prophetic wisdom and blame his vanity, selfishness, instability, and bad taste on the blows administered by Brooks. This worshipful devotion made life easier for Sumner and immeasurably harder for his Republican colleagues, who knew from bitter experience that the disagreeable characteristics of the

Massachusetts senator antedated the beating. As a Harvard student and law clerk of Justice Joseph Story in the 1830's, Sumner had begun to exhibit the smugness and conceit of the proper Bostonian. Subsequent travel abroad had brought him into casual contact with the British nobility and aggravated his snobbishness. Upon his return, Sumner had dabbled in law and thrown himself into the most radical wing of the New England reform movement, where he had espoused everything from abolition to projects for perpetual peace. His handsome figure and commanding platform manner had attracted the attention of Massachusetts politicians, but he was too dogmatic and quarrelsome to succeed in ordinary times. Only a deadlocked legislature in which a handful of Free-Soilers held the balance of power had sent Sumner to the Senate in 1851.

Sumner's resumption of active service during the 1860 session provided Southerners with a perfect target for their charge that the Republicans were a party of Abolitionists in disguise. Like many other Free-Soilers, Sumner combined sweeping indictments of slavery with grudging pledges of loyalty to the cautious Republican platform. Under the circumstances the South could not be blamed for believing that the Republicans would aim fresh blows at slavery once they had succeeded in excluding it from the territories. Lincoln was sincere about his pledge to protect slavery in the states, but many of his followers were not.

IV

After the excitement of the convention season and the party battle in Congress, the fall campaign was bound to be an anticlimax. The near certainty of a Republican victory in the four-party contest also dampened the enthusiasm of all but the most dedicated partisans. Aside from his letter of May 26 subscribing to the Republican platform, Lincoln made no speeches or political statements. He remained at Springfield, Illinois, for the duration of the campaign, spending a few hours daily at a temporary office in the state house, where he received callers and processed correspondence. Bell showed just as much respect for tradition. He left Nashville only once during the canvass, and his trip had nothing to do with politics. Breckenridge intended to behave in similar fashion; but, after the Democrats lost the Kentucky state election in August, he was prevailed upon to speak once at a great barbecue in Ashland. Only Douglas felt his situation was desperate enough to warrant new tactics. Convinced that he alone could save the Union, the "little giant" took the stump in August and campaigned steadily until election day. His speaking tour covered the country except for the Far West.

The other three candidates relied on the best-known orators in their respective parties to debate national issues. As usual, the arrangements for speeches and local expenditures were made by state and county units. For the most part the national committees confined themselves to the twofold task of co-ordinating information from the regional leaders and raising money for the critical October states of Pennsylvania and Indiana. Republican national chairman E. D. Morgan made use of his excellent connections with mercantile and banking interests in New York City to raise a campaign fund. Morgan also organized a foreign department, which worked among immigrant groups, especially the Germans, who were led by Carl Schurz, the most eloquent of the German-American Free-Soilers. Senator Preston King, the secretary of the national committee, presided over the party headquarters in Washington, D. C., handled the bulk of the correspondence, and promoted the organization of local clubs to distribute Republican leaflets.[30] The range of campaign literature was impressive. It included a condensed version of Helper's *Impending Crisis of the South,* the majority report of the Covede committee, speeches of congressional leaders on a variety of issues, and several inexpensive campaign biographies of Lincoln. Greeley distributed a political textbook containing excerpts from Lincoln's speeches, while a youthful journalist named Horace White produced a fresh account of the Lincoln-Douglas debates. Republican workers also brought out medals with inscriptions which dramatized Lincoln's youthful struggle against poverty. The party received far more support from the press than in the Frémont campaign. Particularly valuable were the temperate editorials of Henry J. Raymond in the *New York Times.* A dapper little man with "an open ox-like eye," Raymond reached voters who were immune to the vituperative Greeley.

Semi-military units appeared at Republican torchlight processions, rallies, and barbecues. Known as "Wide-Awakes," these units were modeled after a famous drill team of Zouave cadets. The standard uniform of the "Wide-Awakes" included a black oilskin coat, glazed caps with bands of red, white, and blue, and an imitation Lincoln rail with a swinging tin lamp. An eager young Republican could buy a complete outfit for less than $3, although torches for the lamp cost an additional $1 per dozen. The "Wide-Awakes" maintained order at meetings, guarded ballot boxes against fraud, and sang songs. Some units even learned a special zigzag march which resembled a rail fence. The other parties imitated the Republicans by organizing "Little Giants," "Bell Ringers," and "National Democratic Volunteers."

The campaign was remarkably free of the references to the slavery issue which had split churches, political parties, and other national organizations. Aside from a routine denial that he was an Abolitionist, Henry S. Lane, the Republican candidate for governor in Indiana, made no reference to the subject. Candidates in most other doubtful states followed suit, as orators focused on local economic issues and Democratic corruption. Even such a confirmed Free-Soiler as Chase told an audience at Covington, Kentucky, that the status of slavery ought to be decided by people in the territories.[31]

As might have been expected, the Abolitionists helped the Republicans by denouncing them. An Abolitionist convention in August nominated Gerrit Smith for President and criticized the Republican platform for omitting any reference "to slave hunting, slave holding, slave breeding." [32] Speaker after speaker castigated Lincoln as a hypocrite who stood for the Fugitive Slave Law, the admission of more slave states, and the permanent ostracism of the Negro.

The closing stages of the campaign were devoted to frantic negotiations among Lincoln's opponents. Both wings of the Democratic party and the Constitutional Unionists played with various schemes designed to deprive Lincoln of a majority and throw the election into the House. Bell was the strongest advocate of fusion and had the most to gain by it. Running without a platform, he was out of the main line of fire and a logical compromise candidate. Unfortunately for Bell, the decentralization of party control prevented him from making binding agreements. Negotiations had to be conducted by state party units, and local rivalries often precluded co-operation at the national level. While Bell was willing but unable to work out the practical details of fusion with the two Democratic parties, the latter lacked any real desire to co-operate with each other. As one realist put it: Neither "has any chance of success" and "each is fully resolved if there was such a chance that the other should not enjoy it." [33]

The results of the October elections surprised nobody. The Republicans carried Indiana and Pennsylvania by a narrow margin and Ohio by a wide one. Curtin won the governorship in Pennsylvania by approximately 30,000 out of 500,000 votes cast. Only half as many people went to the polls in Indiana, but the popular Lane was held to a slim plurality of

10,000. Even so, the Republicans on the national ticket seemed likely to receive a bigger percentage of the Indiana vote in November, because the Democrats had been able to fuse only on a state ticket. The October elections made the Democrats press even more urgently for fusion, but the bitter animosity between Douglas and the Buchananites was a barrier to fusion everywhere but in New Jersey.

In the national election the Republicans won as expected by a landslide in the electoral college. Lincoln got an absolute majority with 180 electoral votes; Breckenridge 72 votes, Bell 39, and Douglas 12. What seemed like a great national victory was actually a narrow sectional one, for outside of the North and East the Republicans carried only California and Oregon. None of the other parties attracted support on a broader basis. Breckenridge carried all the cotton states but received few Northern votes outside of areas dependent on trade with the South. Bell's strength was confined to the Border and Unionist enclaves in the upper South. Douglas ran a strong race throughout the North but won only New Jersey and Missouri. The fragmentation of the country along sectional lines was clearly demonstrated in the popular vote, with Lincoln receiving only 1,866,452 votes to 2,813,741 for his three opponents. If the election returns meant anything, they meant that the voters were suffering from indecision. The Republicans had carried too many Northern states by stressing economic issues to claim a mandate for their slavery program. The Breckenridge Democrats were hardly enthusiastic Unionists, but they had no grounds for assuming that their followers favored secession. Nobody knew what the Constitutional Unionists wanted except peace and quiet. Left to their own devices, most party leaders would have waited patiently for a trend to develop. They reckoned without restless elements in the South determined to rule the United States or destroy the Union. Since the election of Lincoln had removed the first alternative, they hastily embraced the second by launching a secession movement.

V

The South Carolina legislature was in session, and so it took the lead and set up a timetable for withdrawal from the Union on December 20. The six Gulf states found it impossible to move so rapidly, but within a week of the November election they had made their intentions clear. The remarkable feature of the secessionist movement was the speed with which it gained momentum. A New Orleans woman noted on November 23 that "the finer men who have been the most conservative . . . are now excited and angry and are urging disunion." [34] Old Frank Blair made a similar discovery, observing that "men who are in full health and sound for the Union on one day—on the next are for dissolving it." [35] Richard Taylor, the son of the deceased planter-President Zachary Taylor, marveled at the joyous and careless temper in which "men, much my superiors in sagacity and experience consummated these acts." [36] A minority in the Gulf states professed to believe that withdrawal would be the prelude to readmission on more favorable terms. Doubtless, some of these people were sincere, but others held out the hope of reunion to secure the co-operation of waverers. In any case, articulate Unionist sentiment virtually disappeared in the lower South, although Bell and Douglas between them had captured 46 per cent of the vote. There was no rational reason for the precipitant action of Southerners. Lincoln had pledged himself to respect the institution of slavery in states where it already existed. Moreover, there was no constitutional way for him to break his promise, because the Democrats would control both Houses of the new Congress. The blind determination of the Gulf states to leave the Union indicated that the nationalist movement had suddenly reached its crest. The attitude of Southerners could be expressed in rational statements, but the impulse behind it was an irrational fear that the values of the group had been endangered. Once this point has been reached, the nationalist always seeks independence because he sees no other way of safeguarding the values which he treasures above all else. The fact that the Southern nationalists were a minority in their own section did not affect the dynamism of the movement. All rebellions are started by minorities who know what they want.

Neither the key figures of the Buchanan Administration nor the bulk of the Republicans were aware of the intensity of Southern nationalism in November. Even if Buchanan had understood the situation, he would have been incapable of action. His objective was to prevent the spread of the secession movement during the remainder of his term by avoiding any coercive measures that might annoy the upper South. Buchanan not only committed himself to inactivity but kept an even balance between Northerners and Southerners in his cabinet to justify the policy. He also underwrote the deadlock with the constitutional doctrine that, although a state could not secede, the federal government could do nothing to stop secession.

Lincoln had no effective way of combating Buchanan's policy until he became President on March 4, 1861. Besides, Lincoln's initial assessment of the secession movement made him less likely to act. Like most Republicans, he had believed that Southern threats during the campaign were sheer bluff. He saw no reason for the South to distrust his intentions, and he assumed that a corresponding degree of common sense would motivate the conduct of Southern leaders.[37] He did not regard the action of South Carolina as a justification for revising his views. On November 9 he told a *Tribune* reporter that hostility to the Union was "limited to a very small number though very intense." [38] The same week Congressman Elihu Washburne found "old Abe in fine spirits . . . and quite undisturbed by the blustering of the disunionists and traitors." [39] At this stage of the crisis, Lincoln was strongly influenced by Senator Trumbull of Illinois, who also expected logic to prevail.[40] Together, they concluded that Lincoln should make no public statement but should incorporate two hundred words in a speech to be delivered by Trumbull at a Springfield victory celebration on November 20. Speaking for Lincoln, the Illinois senator termed secession an "impracticality." He took an equally cheerful view of military preparations in South Carolina, for he felt that they would enable loyal people to identify the troublemakers more readily. Refusing to go beyond the statements in Trumbull's speech, Lincoln politely parried queries about his position by referring questioners to the Republican platform.

Lincoln's attitude was defensible only on the assumption that his constitutional inability to act also prevented him from influencing the course of events. If this assumption had ever made any sense to Lincoln, it ceased to do so once Congress met in December. Before the lame duck session was a week old, the President-elect discovered that the victorious Republicans would melt into a disorganized rabble unless he provided them with some sort of leadership. One faction was prepared to abandon the party platform on slavery and make sweeping concessions to save the Union. The sentiment for compromise predominated on the Eastern seaboard, which faced heavy economic losses if the Gulf states seceded. Dixon of Connecticut on December 8 made a public confession of his willingness to retreat and expressed private doubts that he would act with the party unless it followed his advice.[41] Lafayette Foster, the other Connecticut Senator, was just as wobbly, and his wife sympathized openly with the secessionists.[42] Thurlow Weed advocated compromise on November 24 through the editorial column of the *Albany Journal,* and it was believed in many quarters that he spoke for Seward. The tone of Republicans in the House was not much better. Dawes confided to his wife that the party might break up completely before March 4,[43] and many of his colleagues who blustered on the floor talked about concessions in cloak rooms.[44] Even Congressman Elihu Washburne, who on December 2 had denied that a crisis existed, advised Lincoln a week later that "our friends" in the West "are not fully appraised of the imminent peril." [45]

A second group of Republicans headed by Trumbull, Wade, Chandler, and Fessenden stoutly resisted compromise. Aside from their fear that concessions would destroy the party, they were determined to call what they regarded a gigantic bluff. "We can have no peace," wrote Fessenden, "until the utter folly of this long continued threat of disunion shall have been demonstrated by actual experiment." [46] Councils of firmness were much more popular in the rural Midwest than the metropolitan East, and Republican voters tried to stiffen the backbones of their representatives in Congress.[47] Unfortunately the legislators hostile to concessions disagreed about tactics. Wade wanted to reply to the taunts of Southerners in Congress, while Fessenden feared that such a course would push the irresolute states of the upper South to secede. Additional discord was produced by Sumner, Greeley, and others who opposed secession but preferred it to compromise. Sumner fired off incoherent letters in all directions, and one observer found "something distinctly suggestive of insanity" in his eyes.[48] Greeley bewildered the rank and file with a variety of proposals bound together by nothing but a dread of compromise.

Behind the intra-party dissension over the immediate problem posed by the Gulf states lurked deeper differences. The old Free-Soilers considered the election a mandate for an offensive against slavery. The more moderate Republicans wanted to admit Kansas as a free state and call it a day. As one constituent reminded Trumbull, "the free ones [Negroes] are obnoxious citizens to us." [49] An indeterminate number who had joined the party in expectation of victory preferred to forget about slavery as quickly as possible and divide the spoils. Inevitably, former Democrats distrusted Lincoln because of his Whiggish antecedents. They fretted over the possibility that either Seward or fossil Whigs like Thomas Corwin and Richard W. Thompson would gain control of the new Administration. Conversely, the Whigs feared the influence of Free-Soil Democrats, particularly Chase and the powerful Blair clan. Both groups hated the disguised Abolitionists in their midst, and the latter repaid them with interest.

Although the visible evidence of demoralization caused Lincoln to act, he carefully covered his tracks. His first bid for leadership was through letters to Trumbull, Washburne, and Congressman William Kellogg of Illinois in mid-December.[50] The President-elect made it clear that he had no objections to legislation that would reassure Southerners regarding the safety of slave property in the states. On the other hand, he flatly opposed any modification of the Republican pledge to exclude slavery from the territories. Simultaneously, he bid for party harmony by privately informing callers that the major factions would be represented in the cabinet.

It soon became apparent that Lincoln had not gone far enough. The ink was hardly dry on his letters when a series of remarkable demonstrations took place throughout the urban East for the Crittenden Compromise. Introduced by elderly Senator Crittenden of Kentucky on December 18, the plan called for the extension of the Missouri Compromise line of 36° 30' to the Pacific Coast. There was nothing novel about the central idea of ending the dispute over slavery in the remaining territories of the United States by dividing them between the North and the South. Douglas had proposed the same scheme after the Mexican War, and compromisers revived it repeatedly in the 1850's. The sudden upsurge of popular support for the Crittenden plan was due to bank failures and other signs of business depression in commercial centers triggered by the impending withdrawal of the Gulf states. Confronted with the prospect of economic ruin, many merchants who had voted for Lincoln concluded that another slave state or two south of the 36° 30' line was a small price to pay for the preservation of the Union. The less doctrinaire manufacturers and workingmen felt the same way.

The people clamoring for the Crittenden Compromise overlooked the fact that secessionist leaders in the Gulf states did not regard it as an acceptable settlement. Moreover, most Southern congressmen concealed their opposition because they hoped the Republicans would kill the Crittenden Compromise and thereby drive the wavering Border states to secede. Under the circumstances it was imperative for the Republicans to devise a counter proposal which would not breach the party platform as flagrantly as the Crittenden Compromise. During the last week of December, Lincoln vetoed a number of formulas put forth by party leaders in Washington. By this time Seward had denounced the Crittenden Compromise and been designated as Lincoln's Secretary of State.

The rapprochement of the two men paved the way for Seward to become the chief spokesman of the President-elect in Washington. Collaborating with an old Massachusetts Free-Soiler, Charles Francis Adams, and a former Maryland Know-Nothing, Henry Winter Davis, Seward advanced a plan for the simultaneous admission of New Mexico as a slave state and Kansas as a free state. The party caucus in the House was persuaded to endorse this remarkable repudiation of the Republican platform after hearing testimony from a reputable New Mexico resident that the state would soon become free even if admitted with slavery. Lincoln also reluctantly acquiesced, and so the Kansas-New Mexico plan was introduced in the House on December 28 and was coupled with an amendment protecting slavery. The package cleared the Committee of Thirty-three, which had been organized at the beginning of the session to consider compromise legislation. When Adams brought the measure to the floor in January, matters went according to plan. The Gulf-state congressmen, most of whom were still in their seats, demonstrated their unwillingness to compromise by opposing the measure. Since Adams also regarded his brain child with distaste, he allowed it to die, it having served its purpose of exposing the real attitude of the deep South.

A larger Republican plan began to unfold in January under the skillful direction of Seward. Its over-all objective was to freeze the status quo until Lincoln's inauguration by encouraging every kind of activity that would prolong negotiations. Good intentions lay behind Seward's hypocritical formula of conciliatory talk and no action. He believed that citizens of the Gulf states were victims of a blind, unreasoning panic and would clamor for readmission as soon as the Republican Administration demonstrated its good will toward the South. Seward also thought it was mandatory to conciliate the upper South while waiting for the Union reaction to develop in the Gulf states. From his standpoint, February would be the critical month, because the legislatures of Virginia, North Carolina, Tennessee, Arkansas, and Missouri had authorized plebiscites then on secession.

The Seward policy enjoyed the support of Lincoln but required too much forbearance to suit the average Republican. The advocates of firmness regarded Seward as an incorrigible schemer and resented his efforts to remain on good terms with Southerners. Trumbull was especially indignant at being displaced from his role as Lincoln's chief adviser in Washington. Secessionist senators like Iverson of Georgia and Wigfall of Texas made matters more difficult for Seward by delivering inflammatory speeches. Even so, Republicans might have accepted Seward's policy more readily if it had been restricted to subtle maneuvers for killing the Critten-den Compromise.

Unfortunately, neither Seward nor anybody could prevent the crisis from erupting at new points. Just as the Republicans were sidetracking the Crittenden Compromise in early January, South Carolina provoked a fresh controversy over the disposition of federal property in the Gulf states. A substantial federal garrison held the fortifications around Charleston harbor when South Carolina withdrew from the Union on December 20. The South Carolina government promptly dispatched commissioners to Washington for the purpose of securing the evacuation of the garrison. Simultaneously, state troops surrounded Fort Moultrie on the mainland and made other preparations for military action. Anticipating that the irresolute Buchanan government would abandon the forts, Lincoln approached General Winfield Scott through an intermediary on December 22 and urged him to defend them. The President-elect also informed Trumbull that, if the forts surrendered, he would favor a public pledge to retake them after March 4. While the commissioners were negotiating with Buchanan, Major Robert Anderson, the commanding officer of the federal garrison, decided that his troops would be safer at Fort Sumter in Charleston harbor than on the mainland. Under cover of darkness, Anderson transferred the garrison from Moultrie to Sumter on December 26. Governor Pickens of South Carolina ordered Anderson to return, and upon receiving a peremptory refusal occupied the customs house, the arsenal, the post office, and the abandoned mainland forts of Moultrie and Castle Pinckney. Then Pickens demanded that Buchanan send the garrison back to the mainland. The ultimatum precipitated a cabinet crisis in Washington. Forced to choose between the Southerners who favored capitulation and the Northerners who advocated reinforcements for Anderson, Buchanan took the more heroic course. He reorganized his cabinet on December 30 by dropping the pro-Southern element and dispatching the *Star of the West* with supplies for the beleaguered Anderson.

South Carolina forced the *Star of the West* to turn back, but made no attempt to storm Sumter. The result was an uneasy status quo in Charleston harbor. The President exercised self-restraint in the hope of finishing his term without further trouble. South Carolina showed a similar desire to avoid violence until the Gulf states completed their withdrawal from the Union and organized a government of their own. Besides, most secessionist politicians thought caution was in order until the upper South gave a clearer indication of its intentions. A new crisis was inevitable when the garrison at Fort Sumter ran out of food, but Anderson felt able to hold out for at least six weeks. So tension subsided in mid-January, creating a more suitable atmosphere for the delaying tactics of Seward.

The New Yorker renewed his plea for conciliation in an eloquent speech on January 12 which moved Crittenden to tears and some of Seward's Republican colleagues to cold fury.[51] Seward offered no specific concession but the Kansas-New Mexico plan which the House had already shelved. Extremists on both sides of the Senate chamber killed it, and then the Republicans cast a solid vote against the Crittenden plan, defeating it 25 to 23 on January 15. Undismayed by the rebuff, Seward opened negotiations with Border-state Unionists, who prodded the Virginia legislature into sponsoring a peace conference. All states were invited to send delegates to Washington on February 4 for an exploration of compromise measures. Seward could not have expected much from the peace conference, but it pleased the Border states and seemed likely to keep everybody talking until after the February plebiscites on secession in the upper South. Simultaneously, Seward exploited all of his contacts with Gulf-state politicians and members of the Buchanan Administration for the same purpose. He worked through such improbable go-betweens as foreign diplomats and Southern Supreme Court justices to convince secessionists of the pacific intentions of the Lincoln Administration. Through these channels the South Carolina commissioners received hints that Fort Sumter would eventually be evacuated. Whether Seward exceeded the instructions of his chief in Springfield is a moot point. Unquestionably Seward's charm, conviviality, and persuasiveness created expectations that were unjustified; he had the knack of making profuse expressions of good will sound like commitments. His extraordinary powers of dissimulation deceived as many Republicans as Southerners and laid the foundation for Seward's subsequent unpopularity as Secretary of State. The foes of compromise thought his maneuvers in January and February were treasonable, and they never changed their minds. They also concluded that Seward was operating on orders from Springfield. As a result, they came to distrust the silent, enigmatic Lincoln long before he entered the White House.

It is difficult to evaluate the voluble Seward's contribution during this critical period. Judged from the standpoint of his immediate objective, Seward was completely successful. Each of the February plebiscites in the upper South produced a lukewarm Unionist majority, and thus checked for the moment the epidemic of secession. Yet Seward could hardly claim full credit for the result, because other forces were moving independently in the direction that he wanted to go. One thing was certain: his policy had a demoralizing effect on the Republican party. At the time, many people thought the party would disintegrate, but Seward had no doubt about the verdict of history. "I have brought the ship off the sands," he wrote his wife on the eve of Lincoln's inauguration, "and am ready to resign the helm into the hands of the captain whom the people have chosen." [52]

While Seward was spinning his intricate webs, Congress continued to explore compromise measures in desultory fashion. The withdrawal of most Gulf-state legislators in the third week of January gave the Republicans full control of the House and sharply reduced the Democratic majority in the Senate. Renewed agitation for Congress to support the Crittenden plan subsided when it became apparent that no states besides the original seven were in the control of secessionists. Only a corporal's guard of Douglas Democrats in both Houses really favored the Crittenden Compromise, and the remaining legislators from the upper South combined with the Republicans to keep the plan in committee. The House passed a number of measures designed to guarantee the safety of slave property, but the only one to survive a Senate vote was a constitutional amendment prohibiting further amendments that would modify the status of slavery in the states. Republican Congressmen also joined with Douglas Democrats to clear bills for the admission of Kansas; the organization of Colorado, Dakota, and Nevada territories; and a protective tariff. The effort was wasted on the Democratic Senate, which remained obstructionist until the end of the session. The Washington Peace Conference accomplished as little as Congress. A few states boycotted it altogether, and a number of others under Republican control sent representatives for the express purpose of blocking agreement.

An air of unreality hung over Washington during the last days of the Buchanan Administration. The pronounced pro-Southern sympathies of most Washingtonians convinced many Republicans that the capital was in danger. The impressionable Sumner circulated hair-raising tales about a Southern conspiracy to capture Washington. Other leaders foolishly believed either that the stalemate would continue or that the Gulf states would eventually rejoin the Union. A future President marveled at the spectacle of a country "now three months into a revolution—and yet no militia . . . called out—no troops levied—no streets barricaded—no bloodshed." [53]

VI

In Springfield, meanwhile, Lincoln was constructing his cabinet. By mid-January, he had clearly indicated his determination to include every major faction of the Republican party, although some appointments remained in doubt until the last minute. Lincoln reserved the choice posts for his pre-convention rivals: Seward, Secretary of State; Chase, Secretary of Treasury; and Bates, Attorney General. After innumerable interviews with party leaders, Lincoln settled on Gideon Welles, an old Jacksonian from Connecticut, for Secretary of the Navy, and balanced this selection by offering the Department of Interior to Caleb B. Smith, an Indiana Whig. Montgomery Blair received the Postmaster Generalship in recognition of the significant contribution by the Blair clan. The War Department gave Lincoln the most trouble. It had been promised to Simon Cameron by Lincoln's managers at Chicago, and the first impulse of the President-elect was to honor an obligation contracted in defiance of his instructions. He tendered the post to Cameron at the end of December, but tried to withdraw the offer after it had touched off a storm of protest in Pennsylvania and elsewhere. Of the numerous people who accused Cameron of corruption, none could offer documentary proof. In the end, Lincoln stuck by the Chicago bargain and appointed Cameron Secretary of War. Lincoln unknowingly selected his official biographers when he appointed John Nicolay as his secretary and John Hay as his assistant secretary. The twenty-eight-year-old Bavarian-born Nicolay was "scrupulous, polite, calm, and obliging . . . coming and going about the capital like a shadow. . . ." [54] John Hay had been cut from different cloth. He was a languid, dreamy son of the Illinois prairie—"a girl in boy's clothes," as John Russell Young remembered him thirty years later.[55] Educated at Brown University, Hay had returned home to write poetry and brood when Lincoln, at the urging of Nicolay, started him on a distinguished career. A final hitch developed on the eve of Lincoln's inauguration when Seward withdrew his acceptance in an effort to force the President-elect to part with Chase. Rightly assessing the maneuver as a bluff, Lincoln remained firm, with the result that Seward and Chase were to sit at the cabinet table as bitter rivals.

Like most of his predecessors, Lincoln felt obliged to leave for Washington well in advance of the inauguration. Those who gathered for his farewell speech at the Springfield railroad station on February 11 heard a melancholy plea for divine guidance. After a brief reference to his emotional distress over the prospect of separation from his home and friends, Lincoln confessed:

> I now leave, not knowing when, or whether ever, I may return, with a task before me greater than that which rested upon Washington. Without the assistance of that Divine Being, who ever attended him, I cannot succeed. With that assistance, I cannot fail. Trusting in Him, who can go with me and remain with you and be everywhere for good, let us confidently hope that all will yet be well. To His care commending you, as I hope in your prayers you will commend me, I bid you an affectionate farewell.

Such close Illinois friends as Norman B. Judd, Orville H. Browning, Judge David Davis, and Ebenezer Peck rode with Lincoln as far as Indianapolis. His eldest son Robert and Ward H. Lamon remained at his side throughout the entire trip, while Mrs. Lincoln and his two younger sons joined the President-elect en route. The journey took twelve days, with extended stops at Indianapolis, Columbus, Pittsburgh, Cleveland, Buffalo, Harrisburg, and Philadelphia. Lincoln never gave any precise reason for choosing such a circuitous route, but his unspoken hope was to reassure his fellow countrymen by his demeanor and statements. Everywhere he was received with spontaneous manifestations of enthusiasm and respect. His speeches were much less effective, because he refused to make any explicit pronouncements about policy but for the most part confined himself to platitudes minimizing the current threat to the Union. Some people thought him flippant at Indianapolis when he characterized the Southern idea of the Union as free love and the Northern idea as regular marriage. Others were dismayed by the seemingly casual way in which he dismissed the crisis as "an artificial one" before a large Pittsburgh audience. It is more probable that Lincoln was following Seward's strategy than that he felt the optimism indicated by his remarks.

The weather on March 4 suited the gravity of the occasion. Throngs converged on the Capitol under angry, black clouds occasionally pierced by shafts of sunlight. The Presidential party arrived late, and Lincoln did not take the oath of office until 1:15 p.m. Accounts of the various incidents connected with the ceremony differ, but some observers swore that

Douglas held Lincoln's hat throughout the inaugural address. Even if this symbolic gesture of good will did not actually occur, Douglas had already assured Lincoln informally of support from Northern Democrats in the event of a crisis.

The inaugural address reflected the restraining influence of Seward and Browning. The right of secession was denied in a straightforward statement which termed the Union "perpetual," but Lincoln spoke less clearly about his policy for preserving it. Promising to execute the laws of the Union in all states, he declared that federal power would be used "to hold, occupy, and possess the property and places belonging to the government." Then he proceeded to back away from the implications of this pledge by saying: "Where the hostility to the United States, in any interior locality, shall be so great and universal as to prevent competent local citizens from holding federal offices, there will be no attempt to force obnoxious strangers among the people for that object." Plainly Lincoln was offering residents of the Gulf states federal jobs if they brought their states back into the Union. He also implied that he would avoid provocative action while the secessionists considered his proposition.

Taken at face value, the inaugural message envisioned a continuation of the status quo. The United States would hold Fort Sumter and wait patiently for a pro-Union reaction in the South. In retrospect, it is easy to see that the Gulf states were determined to be independent and would not allow a foreign state to hold property indefinitely within the frontiers of their new Confederacy. Perhaps Lincoln understood the attitude of the Confederacy and wanted to maneuver it into a position where it would be responsible for firing the first shot. But Lincoln's behavior during his first month in office suggests that he really hoped a policy of self-restraint would result in reunion.

The status quo policy ran into snags almost immediately. The day before Lincoln took office, Buchanan received a dispatch from Major Anderson expressing alarm over the rapid depletion of his stores and fuel. He reminded the President that he was entirely dependent on Charleston for food supplies and would need heavy reinforcements to break the siege. Buchanan dumped the problem in Lincoln's lap, and on March 5 the new President ordered General Winfield Scott to study the situation. Simultaneously, the Southern commissioners received fresh instructions from the Confederate government at Montgomery to press for recognition and the evacuation of Sumter. Secretary of State Seward would not engage in direct negotiations, but kept in contact with the commissioners through various intermediaries. He urged patience and predicted that the Administration would eventually withdraw troops from Sumter. Seward gained several weeks in this fashion, because the majority of the cabinet as well as General Scott seemed to favor his policy. Until the end of March there was no evidence that Seward had been working at cross purposes with Lincoln, although the Secretary of State had certainly taken certain steps without the knowledge of his chief. Undoubtedly Lincoln used this three-week breathing spell to get his bearings and explore alternatives. He dispatched two Illinois friends to Charleston for information about Southern sentiment. At the same time he tried to find out whether the Virginia convention, with its slender Unionist majority, would adjourn in return for the abandonment of Fort Sumter.

The Republicans in Congress were becoming increasingly restless as the days passed without any clear lead from the White House. Douglas made matters still more difficult for them by professing to speak for Lincoln. Not only did the Illinois Democrat announce that Sumter would be evacuated, but he introduced resolutions designed to prod the Administration. These tactics were too much for Trumbull, who hated his colleague and had begun to doubt the firmness of Lincoln. After a stormy interview at the White House, Trumbull introduced a resolution designed to force the President into a clear-cut stand on Sumter. Fortunately for Lincoln, congressional Republicans were concentrating single-mindedly on the confirmation of appointments, and they adjourned on March 28 without voting on the Trumbull resolution.

By this time it was apparent that the President could not hesitate much longer. During the special session the morale of the Republicans had steadily deteriorated. Only the desire for patronage had prevented the advocates of firmness from organizing an open rebellion against Lincoln. Scattered elections indicated that the rank and file were as dissatisfied with the irresolute behavior of the Administration as were the Republicans in Congress. In Rhode Island a coalition of Democrats and Constitutional Unionists won the governorship, while Connecticut voters retired two Republican congressmen. The politicians in the cabinet noted the election returns and began to show a firmer tone. At the beginning of March, Montgomery Blair had been the only one to favor reinforcing Sumter, but at a meeting on the 29th the cabinet divided evenly on the issue. Simultaneously, Lincoln was discovering that further equivocation would be useless. Reports from his observers in Charleston convinced the President that Unionist sentiment was non-existent. Moreover, the leaders of the Virginia convention continued to avoid any firm commitment to adjourn it. Plainly they regarded the convention as a lever for prying federal troops out of Sumter; they bargained with the President as if they were representatives of a foreign state. Important as Virginia was to the Union, she seemed pro-Southern enough to leave it on some other issue if not Sumter.

The turning point came after the deadlocked cabinet meeting of March 29, when Lincoln wrote out instructions for Gustavas V. Fox to leave for Fort Sumter with a relief expedition on April 6. Optimistic to the end, Seward vainly attempted to divert the expedition from Sumter to Fort Pickens, which was in no immediate danger. Then he wrote Lincoln a tactless note on April 11, in which he complained that the Administration had no policy and urged a war on France, Spain, and Great Britain to restore national unity. The expedition had already departed when Seward made his final, desperate bid to postpone armed conflict with the Confederacy. Hysterical as he was, Seward understood that an effort to relieve Sumter meant war. Many around Lincoln refused to recognize this fact. His secretary John Nicolay, for example, had no fear of war and assured his fiancée in Illinois that a brush over Fort Sumter would not result in general hostilities.[56] Illusions in Washington and elsewhere were rudely shattered on April 12. Confederate batteries opened a full-scale bombardment of Sumter, and thus left no alternative to Civil War. The ensuing conflict soon unleashed destruction and suffering on a scale that few people anticipated. In the process, it brought about one remarkable side effect: the immediate revitalization of the Republican party, which, on the edge of complete disintegration, was transformed into a patriotic instrument for saving the Union.

IV

Lincoln and the Civil War

With the coming of war, the Republican party became the beneficiary of a wave of patriotic indignation which swept through virtually the entire North. The bellicose reaction of radicals was to be expected, but the display of hostility by conservative Republicans and Democrats alike was surprising. Orville H. Browning promptly denounced the rebels as criminals and traitors,[1] and urged Lincoln to turn the Gulf states into a Negro republic.[2] General John A. Dix, who had worked feverishly with other New York Democrats for compromise until the last minute, called Charleston "a nest in which treason has been hatched" [3] and urged the destruction of the city as a just retribution for its sins. In most cases the bitterness of conservatives was a passing phase and reflected their frustration at being deserted by the Southerners for whom they had sacrificed so much.

Though Stephen A. Douglas did not completely share these feelings, his basic loyalty to the Union was certain. At the request of Lincoln he called at the White House on April 14, the afternoon that the news about the fall of Sumter reached Washington. The onetime political rivals conferred for several hours; the next day Douglas issued a statement reaffirming his opposition to the political principles of the Republican party but promising the President full support in his effort to preserve the Union. Douglas was as good as his word, and at the end of the week started westward to rally the Democrats of southern Illinois to the Administration. En route he spoke at Bellaire, Ohio, and, pointing his finger in the direction of the Ohio River, told his audience that the Almighty intended that this valley "in all time shall remain one and indivisible." On April 25 at Spring-field, Illinois, Douglas delivered an eloquent Union speech before the leg-islature and also dealt indignantly with charges that he had sold out the Democratic party. His exertions during the next month were regarded by friend and foe alike as decisive in swinging "Egypt" (southern Illinois) behind the Union. An iron will sustained Douglas until this crucial task was done, but he had pushed his body to its limit, and on June 3 died at Chi-cago. Memories of his ambition, arrogance, and partisanship receded into the background as citizens of all parties paid tribute to Douglas for his unswerving and heroic devotion to the Union. His death brought the Dem-ocratic party a step closer to disintegration. Already deprived of its South-ern leaders, it now lost the one Northerner with the ability and prestige to keep it intact.

Meanwhile, Lincoln had issued a proclamation on April 14 warning treasonable elements to disperse and calling for 75,000 volunteers to serve three months. Subsequent proclamations in early May provided for further additions to the army and for the suspension of the writ of habeas corpus.

Lincoln felt obliged to announce that Congress would be convened when he first requested troops. But he was reluctant to let the legislators share in the initial planning, and he postponed the special session until July 4. Although the public took little notice of the delay, Republican congress-men fretted privately about alleged encroachments on their prerogatives. Grimes of Iowa complained to Fessenden on May 12 that Lincoln had no right to call up the militia for more than thirty days,[4] while others saw in the Presidential proclamations a serious threat to civil liberties.

For a time Lincoln had more pressing matters to worry about than his relations with Congress. His call for troops reactivated secessionist senti-ment in the upper South; Virginia, North Carolina, and Arkansas with-drew from the Union as quickly as possible. Sentiment was so evenly di-vided in the Border states except Tennessee that a large majority favored the inconsistent policy of remaining in the Union but doing nothing to help it. Neither Washington nor Richmond would have tolerated neutrality in-definitely; but both governments encouraged their local partisans in the Border area to premature seizure of forts and arsenals before their armies were properly organized.

No single pattern emerged out of these initial skirmishes, but Washing-ton managed to establish loyal administrations and retain physical control in Kentucky, Maryland, and Missouri. The eastern third of Tennessee refused to acknowledge the secessionist state government in Nashville, and West Virginia broke away from Virginia in 1862 because of Unionist sentiment. Nevertheless, all five states were battlegrounds from time to time, and guerrilla operations continued even when the rival armies were inactive. The chronic disorder stirred up bitter feelings and hardened political partisanship along lines that have persisted to the present. Aside from a pocket of German Abolitionists in St. Louis, the principal Unionist strongholds were in the Appalachians and the Ozarks, where economic conditions had prevented slavery from taking root. Since the Southern Unionists shared the dominant sectional view that the Negro was inferior to the white, they feared the Abolitionist tendencies within the Republican party, and maintained a separate political organization during the Civil War. After the military victory of the North removed the divisive issue of emancipation, the mountaineers joined the Republican party. They never became numerous enough to dominate the Border states, but the Appalachian counties were to be as consistently Republican as any counties in the North.

Even though there was war, patronage-seekers harassed Lincoln. They thronged the executive offices, buttonholed the President in corridors, or bombarded him with petitions and endorsements. The assault was probably no worse than at the beginning of other administrations, but the magnitude of the crisis made it harder for Lincoln. As usual, there were more applicants than jobs. Besides, Lincoln found himself caught in a cross fire between Seward and Chase, who were continuing their struggle to dominate the party. New York was the focal point of the power struggle because of the numerous political jobs in the customs office. The dominant Seward-Weed organization had been forced to accept Judge Ira Harris, a compromise candidate, for the vacant Senate seat in January 1861. The Chase forces, spearheaded by Horace Greeley and Hiram Barney, tried to exploit this evidence of weakness. Lincoln assumed the role of mediator in New York, with the result that both factions distrusted him. Elsewhere, the President hoped to minimize friction by urging state organizations to present consolidated lists of applicants, but his hope turned out to be illusory.

Notwithstanding the incessant bickering, the displacement of Democrats from minor offices went on at a rapid pace, and by December 1861, Republicans held three-quarters of the 28,000 jobs in the postal service.[5] Many disappointed office-seekers were eventually taken care of by the vast increase in government posts, from 50,000 in 1860 to nearly 150,000 at the end of the war. Military commissions and contracts to supply the armed forces provided an additional safety valve against discontent. Thwarted in his bid for a district attorneyship in Iowa, young William B. Allison, who was destined to serve thirty-six years in the Senate, wasted no time brooding: "Can't we arrange together to make something out of this rebellion or war?" [6] At the War Department, Simon Cameron did what he could to accommodate restless Republicans like Allison, for he awarded contracts with a lavish hand. But often military commissions were more important to unsuccessful competitors than employment in government posts. Although not everybody could make a distinguished service record, those who did virtually assured themselves of a bright political future. Patriotic Republicans converged on Washington or the capitals of their respective states in the hope of becoming generals. The most successful were John C. Frémont, Nathaniel P. Banks, and Frank P. Blair. A few choice commissions went to Democrats, however, because both Lincoln and the Republican governors of Northern states recognized the necessity of fighting the war on the broadest possible basis. Two Democrats who took advantage of their commissions to erase reputations as pro-slavery Northerners were Benjamin F. Butler of Massachusetts and John A. Logan of Illinois.

Both men ultimately became leaders of the Republican party and displayed considerable versatility in making the transition. Butler had graduated from Waterville College and settled in Lowell, Massachusetts, where he quickly developed a following among the local textile workers. As the Democratic candidate for governor in 1858, Butler had gone as far as any Southern fire-eater in condemning the Republicans; and two years later, as a delegate to the Democratic national convention, he had voted repeatedly for Jefferson Davis. Since nothing embarrassed Butler, he coolly reversed himself after Sumter, offered his services to Governor John A. Andrew of Massachusetts, and soon received a commission. Within eighteen months Butler had made himself so obnoxious to Southerners that they dubbed him "the beast." The crafty Massachusetts politician seemed so sincere in his new role that most Republicans welcomed him into their party.

John A. Logan was just as ambitious as Butler but more prone to allow emotions to interfere with political calculations. As a native of southern Illinois and a graduate of the University of Louisville, Logan had identified himself with the pro-slavery wing of the Democratic party. Elected to the

Illinois legislature in 1852 at the age of twenty-six and promoted to Congress in 1858, he had distinguished himself by coarse denunciations of the Abolitionists. When the shooting began, Logan refused to declare himself for three months, and rumors circulated that he favored the cause of the Confederacy.[7] The reaction in his own district was so unfavorable that Logan announced on August 9 his determination to resign from Congress and enter the Union army. Six more months elapsed, however, before he could secure a commission as brigadier general. He was more reluctant than Butler to sever his ties with the Democratic party, but by the end of the war Logan had eased himself into a position where he could join the winners.

Long before the special session of Congress, Republican newspapers had been demanding that Lincoln launch an offensive with untrained troops. In a country where every citizen regarded himself as a military expert, there was considerable support for the impatient clamor of the *New York Times* and the *New York Tribune*. The usually sensible Henry Raymond of the *Times* urged an immediate advance on April 23, and, a week later, he declared Lincoln a failure and proposed that Congress take control of the war. Greeley refused to be outdone by his rival on the *Times* and urged, "On to Richmond." Even a confirmed pacifist like William Lloyd Garrison joined the chorus, for he feared that a prolonged Union military build-up would scare the South into negotiations and so jeopardize the prospects of imposing abolition on it.[8]

II

Congressional critics of the Administration moved into action just as soon as the special session opened. Lincoln wanted the legislators to ratify his emergency proclamations, appropriate the necessary funds to fight the war, and adjourn. He dreaded any tampering with the status of slavery, lest it alienate the wobbly Border states, and he was equally fearful of congressional interference with military operations. In his initial message he confined himself to a constitutional defense of executive action already taken, and he recommended little beyond what was absolutely necessary. Criticism of the South was tempered by the assertion that a Union majority probably existed in all of the Confederate states but South Carolina, while the controversial subject of slavery was ignored altogether.

The legislators found the message disappointing and had no intention of heeding its cautious counsels.[9] Members of both houses promptly introduced a variety of confiscation bills aimed at slaves and other categories of rebel property, but dragged their feet in ratifying emergency measures already undertaken by Lincoln. This display of a legislative *esprit de corps* was an impulsive reaction to alleged executive encroachment on congressional power rather than a premeditated attack on the President. It soon became evident, however, that a small but articulate element of the Republican majority intended to launch a counteroffensive and wrest powers from Lincoln. Known as the Radicals or Jacobins, this faction posed alternately as obstructionists of the President and as overzealous supporters who wanted to save the President from himself. The negative role of the radicals was largely the result of habit. In the 1850's they had opposed the President on partisan grounds and now opposed him as champions of congressional prerogatives. Their positive role was a product of their war aims, which included the conquest of the South and the emancipation of the slaves. Yet the radical policy of pushing Lincoln to energetic military measures involved serious risks. If it succeeded, the North would win the war before public opinion was prepared for emancipation. So the ultimate objective of the radicals really depended on the prolonged war which they tried to shorten. Most of them never saw the conflict between their ends and means, but history was to smile on the radicals and give them the best of both worlds. The war would drag on long enough for them to enjoy the simultaneous pleasure of denouncing the incompetence of the President and forcing him into policies that doomed slavery.

The backbone of radical strength was in the triumvirate of Chandler, Wade, and Trumbull in the Senate. Chandler and Wade were self-made men and determined not to let anybody forget it. They were profane, boisterous, and fluent enough to bully their colleagues, especially when they were stimulated by whiskey. Of the two, Chandler was the more authentic frontiersman, but Wade succeeded in concealing the evidence of a New England background and a good education.

At first glance nothing seemed more improbable than that the quiet, scholarly Lyman Trumbull would collaborate with noisy partisans like Wade and Chandler. But appearances were deceiving, and Trumbull succumbed to periodic fits of irritation that clouded his judgment. The special session found him angry at the Southerners and ready to strike back at them with emancipation, even though he had never before shown any sympathy for the Negro. Trumbull's vindictive attitude was also aimed at Lincoln, whose only offense had been to win the Presidency. Jealousy did not normally influence Trumbull's behavior, but the old rivalry of the two men in Illinois made comparisons inevitable, and Lincoln's good fortune had annoyed him. The ensuing crisis over Sumter and the irresolute response of the President brought all of Trumbull's resentment to the surface. Under the circumstances, it did not require much effort by Chandler and Wade to convert the Illinois senator into a carping critic of Lincoln. Thirty-five years later, Trumbull still remembered the wartime President as a crafty, ambitious trimmer who was deficient in the real qualities of leadership.[10]

The lesser radicals in the Senate were more erratic and doctrinaire than the triumvirate. In bitterness toward the slaveholders and in idealistic enthusiasm for the Negro, Charles Sumner outstripped all of his colleagues, but he brought the radical cause nothing practical but his own vote. Vanity, instability, and egotism made Sumner incapable of teamwork, and his attack at the hands of Brooks had only aggravated these characteristics. The Massachusetts senator knew virtually nothing about actual conditions in the South, and he was unwilling to learn. It was impossible to predict from day to day what Sumner would advocate, but it was certain that he would automatically elevate each proposal into a moral cause. John P. Hale, the old Free-Soiler from New Hampshire, was also a prima donna and something of a trial to the more pragmatic leaders of the triumvirate. Two newcomers, B. Gratz Brown of Missouri and Jacob Howard of Michigan, showed more capacity for sustained work than their more famous colleagues, but they were too busy mastering the procedures of the Senate to be of much use in the special session.

The radical movement in the House was not as well defined. Thaddeus Stevens of Pennsylvania had already begun to exhibit the wit, sarcasm, and capacity for inspiring fear that would enable him to dominate the House from 1864 until his death. But he was a backbencher in 1861 and lacked the seniority to command. George W. Julian operated under a similar handicap. Others like Schuyler Colfax of Indiana and Henry Winter Davis of Maryland had not yet become indiscriminate critics of Lincoln.

Following the lead of the Republican press, the Senate triumvirate insisted on an immediate advance by the Union army. On July 13, Trumbull introduced a resolution in the party caucus asserting that it was the duty of the government to occupy Richmond by July 20. Despite its manifest absurdity, the resolution nearly passed, for the insulting remarks of Wade and Chandler intimidated their critics.[11] Posing as an authority on military tactics, Wade boasted that he could take Richmond immediately with 10,000 men. Only the firmness of Fessenden kept the resolution bottled up in caucus. The Maine senator was not particularly friendly to the President, but he possessed common sense and courage. No amount of blustering could move Fessenden if he thought he was right, and Grimes of Iowa, as well as the two Vermont senators, usually followed his lead.

Although the caucus thwarted the radicals, they made enough noise on the floor of the Senate to achieve their purpose of forcing Lincoln to give battle. On July 21, 30,000 raw recruits marched out of Washington. Numerous congressmen on horseback or in carriages, among them Wade and Chandler, followed closely behind the troops with picnic lunches and whiskey to celebrate the anticipated victory. Unfortunately, the carnival mood vanished almost as soon as the army established contact with the Confederates at Bull Run, for panic set in, and by late afternoon disorderly swarms of Union soldiers reeled back toward Washington. Wade and Chandler tried to take over from the generals, blocking the main road with their carriages in a futile effort to stem the retreat.

Bull Run ought to have discredited the radicals, but they escaped responsibility by blaming the defeat on Union generals, whom they accused of being pro-slavery Democrats. Resuming the offensive immediately, the radicals called on Lincoln and urged abolition on the new ground of military necessity.[12] Nevertheless, they were far ahead of opinion in their own party. The day before their meeting with Lincoln, the House had passed with only two dissenting votes the Crittenden Resolution. Drafted by the elderly Kentucky Unionist, it stated that the war was being fought for the sole purpose of maintaining the Union. The Senate followed suit a few days later, with Trumbull casting the only negative vote, although several other radicals did not answer the roll call.

The legislative setback of the radicals was due to momentary panic and did not constitute an endorsement for the President's policy of ignoring the slavery question. Overnight, the expectation of an easy Northern victory turned into a blind fear that the war was irretrievably lost. Greeley advocated an armistice and a negotiated peace. Even cooler heads feared that an invasion of the North was imminent and hoped the Crittenden Resolution would keep the wobbly Border states in the Union. The sudden change in the political weather doomed all the legislative projects of the radicals except a confiscation bill which fell far short of their demands.

They held out until the last day of the session against resolutions ratifying Lincoln's emergency proclamations and managed to block approval of his suspension of the writ of habeas corpus. On this defiant note, Congress adjourned August 5.

Criticism of Lincoln subsided temporarily with the departure of the legislators and the appointment of General George B. McClellan as Commander of the Army of the Potomac. McClellan arrived in Washington fresh from a series of victories over the Confederates in West Virginia. A thirty-five-year-old West Pointer with a self-confident, aristocratic bearing, McClellan quickly reassured the jittery by a prompt reorganization of the demoralized army. Within a month he had restored discipline and morale and won his soldiers' confidence.

McClellan's rapid success was his undoing, for it revived hope that the Confederacy could be crushed in a single campaign.[13] McClellan, however, was a cautious man, and, when it became apparent in mid-autumn that he planned to postpone military operations until the following year, he lost the good will of the radicals. They remembered that McClellan was a Democrat and attributed his delay to pro-slavery sympathies. They were especially incensed by his policy of treating slaves as property and returning runaways to their owners. General John C. Frémont provided the radicals with fresh ammunition against McClellan by issuing a proclamation on August 30 freeing all the slaves within his Western Department. Lincoln immediately revoked Frémont's proclamation, and on October 24, after further provocations from the general, the President removed him from command. The inefficiency of Frémont and the corruptness of his subordinates probably justified his dismissal, but Lincoln had based his decision on the inability of Frémont to launch an attack. The effect of this reasoning on Wade, Chandler, and Trumbull can well be imagined. They descended on Lincoln and demanded that he apply the same standard to McClellan: McClellan should be dismissed unless he mounted an immediate offensive. Unable to budge the President, the triumvirate vented its fury successively on McClellan and Seward. Chandler found the noncommittal attitude of the Secretary of State so irritating that he lost his temper completely. Choking with rage, he screamed that defeat was preferable to delay.[14] The same evening Chandler penned a solemn note to his wife, announcing that "the end is at hand." [15]

It is difficult to sympathize with the grotesque antics of the triumvirate or accept their assessment of the military situation. Yet Lincoln was not wholly free from suspicion of professional soldiers and impatience for action. Although as commander in chief he necessarily took a more responsible attitude toward the shortcomings of his military staff than did the critics, he changed generals frequently. Experts disagree as to whether Lincoln could have shortened the war by a different strategy, but nobody doubts that Union defeats in the early years multiplied the President's political troubles.

III

Radical prophecies of doom had no visible effect on Administration policy in the fall of 1861, but signs of a sharp cleavage in the Republican party began to multiply. The conservative wing stood on the Crittenden Resolution and insisted that the war be fought for the sole purpose of restoring the Union. The radicals paid lip service to the same objective, but argued that defeat of the Confederacy could not be achieved without abolishing slavery.[16] Playing down the idealistic argument for emancipation, they urged it as a military necessity. The issues raised by the war also had a divisive influence on the Democratic minority, splitting it into three factions. One group accepted Lincoln's policy at face value and offered him full co-operation; a second group gave nominal support to the war while opposing all Administration measures except military appropriations; and a third group took the view that the Abolitionists had already destroyed the Union, and advocated an armistice and a peaceful separation of the states.

The cross currents in both major parties led to a political realignment. Pro-Administration Democrats joined the conservative Republicans, while the other two factions of Democrats formed a new opposition party. The purpose of the conservative coalition was to reduce the influence of the radicals on war policy and make common cause between the Republicans and patriotic elements in the Democratic party. The intentions of the anti-Administration Democrats defy generalization. One faction favored the war in theory but was obstructive in practice because it objected to any measures that threatened the constitutional rights of states. It had little difficulty co-operating with the other faction, which contained both passive Southern sympathizers and outright agents of the Confederacy. Partisan bitterness drove many Democrats into more extreme statements than their real feelings justified, and created the impression that the treasonable element in the party was very large. The electioneering tactics of the Republicans also encouraged this belief. In reality, the bulk of anti-Administration Democrats showed no disposition to aid the Confederacy actively, but displayed a negative attitude toward the war. The conspirators were concentrated in the Democratic counties along the Ohio River,[17] and provided recruits for secret societies like the Knights of the Golden Circle and its successors. Most members of these organizations were illiterate and ineffective.[18]

The political regrouping was first evident in Ohio, which held a state election in the fall of 1861. Since neither of the old parties could be sure of winning on a straight partisan platform, the Republican state executive committee agreed to abandon its party organization and issue a call for a Union convention at Columbus on September 5. Enough War Democrats responded to warrant the nomination of their leader, David Tod, for governor; and the Union ticket won a sweeping victory. The Ohio radicals had the most trouble in accepting the new policy.[19] Chase and Giddings openly complained; but Wade, who was up for re-election, temporarily flirted with the coalitionists.[20] Republican leaders in other evenly divided states such as Delaware, New Jersey, and Pennsylvania imitated the example of their Ohio brethren. It was difficult on the basis of the 1861 elections to tell whether Republican sponsorship of state Union parties was a temporary expedient or the prelude to reorganization on a national basis. In 1864 the Republican national committee made the change official by issuing a call for a Union party convention, but the effect on state organization was variable. In the one-party Republican states of New England and the upper Midwest, party leaders did not need Democratic votes to win elections. So they obligingly took the Union party label but maintained their old Republican organization. Elsewhere the change in name involved a change in the structure and personnel of the party, with War Democrats receiving their share of elective offices and state patronage. On the other hand, Lincoln continued to favor people with a Republican background in the distribution of federal patronage. In general, Republicans and War Democrats co-operated uneasily in the Union party until the end of the war when Reconstruction problems caused another realignment.

When Congress met for the long session in December 1861, it was clear that a majority favored the idea of a Union party dedicated to the one objective of restoring the Union. Nevertheless, the radicals were able to take the initiative on slavery because of widespread dissatisfaction over the management of the war. Chandler led off on December 5 by proposing a special committee to investigate Northern defeats at Ball's Bluff and

Bull Run. Grimes wanted an investigation of all lost battles, while Sherman, who was anything but an Abolitionist, advocated a joint committee to review the general conduct of the war. Overwhelming support developed for Sherman's proposal, and the necessary resolution cleared both houses the next day. In theory the committee was supposed to help Lincoln win the war, but the caucus packed it with radicals bent on blaming pro-slavery generals for all defeats. Ben Wade received the chairmanship and Zack Chandler the other appointment from the Senate. The House also selected three radicals: George W. Julian of Indiana, John Covede of Pennsylvania, and Daniel W. Gooch of Massachusetts. The majority ran the Committee on the Conduct of the War in high-handed fashion; it ignored the Democrats and suppressed information that failed to coincide with the opinions of the radicals. Hearings were often held by Wade or Chandler alone, and they leaked testimony given under pledges of confidence if it suited them. Subordinate officers were encouraged to testify against their superiors, a situation which virtually forced all army commanders to become politicians in order to protect themselves. From time to time, the committee issued reports on atrocities in Southern prisons and the alleged military benefits that would follow from arming the slaves. Greeley obligingly published a number of these reports as *The Tribune War Tracts*. Committee members represented partisanship as patriotism and thought of themselves as incorruptible tribunes of the people who were ferreting out abuses and revitalizing an Administration honeycombed with defeatism.[21] Unquestionably the Committee on the Conduct of the War made Lincoln's position more difficult. It forced him into battles against the advice of his generals and undermined confidence in his leadership. Moreover, the second guessing of the committee was hard to combat because it could criticize without being obliged to suggest practical alternatives. It sniped with deadly effect in the winter of 1861–62 because McClellan refused to invade the South.

While the radicals complained about the inactivity of Northern armies, a special House committee under the chairmanship of Henry L. Dawes of Massachusetts uncovered unmistakable evidence of laxity and mismanagement in the War Department. Secretary Cameron was remarkably efficient by his own standards, but he saw no difference between running the War Department and the state bureaus at Harrisburg. He regarded both primarily as agencies for rewarding old political friends and making new ones. So Cameron had spent money with a lavish hand, purchasing everything from crippled horses to leaky tents at exorbitant prices. He had also shown a predictable partiality to Pennsylvanians in the awarding of government contracts and military commissions. The Dawes committee turned up all of these facts and more. Since the radicals were his principal critics, Cameron tried to pacify them by authorizing the seizure and arming of fugitive slaves without first consulting Lincoln. This gesture exhausted Lincoln's patience, and without prior warning to Cameron, he named him minister to Russia. As a replacement for Cameron in the War Department, Lincoln chose an energetic, ruthless War Democrat, Edwin M. Stanton. The selection proved to be an admirable one so far as administration was concerned, but it did not bring Lincoln any reliable political support. Stanton's previous career had shown him to be deficient in political ethics. As a member of Buchanan's cabinet, he had reported confidential decisions to Seward, and within a matter of months made a rapid transition from a Breckenridge supporter to a militant Republican. Apparently Stanton had embraced Abolitionist doctrine as a youth in Steubenville, Ohio, but concealed his convictions until it was politically advantageous to reveal them. Coupled with his outstanding ability as a lawyer was an appetite for intrigue which often drove Stanton to engage in duplicity when candor would have worked just as well. A Prussian sense of hierarchy made his gropings for power peculiarly distasteful, causing him to curry favor with superiors and browbeat subordinates. Chronic asthma and a series of domestic tragedies accentuated his irritability and gloom. Before he had been in office six months, the wily Stanton was weaving intricate political webs, and at the same time posing as the protégé of Seward and the radicals.

With the encouragement of Stanton and Chase, radicals supplemented the work of the Committee on the Conduct of the War with more direct blows at slavery. In the House they managed to block a reaffirmation of the Crittenden Resolution by a vote of 71 to 65. They also countered Lincoln's cautious request for an appropriation to encourage the voluntary colonization of freed slaves with a demand for general emancipation. This proposal was embodied in a resolution introduced by Thaddeus Stevens which bid for moderate support with a clause for compensation to loyal slaveholders.

The conflicting plans of Lincoln and Stevens were the opening shots in an intra-party war that continued until the eve of the 1864 election, when the President capitulated by endorsing abolition through constitutional amendment. Both practical and legal considerations caused Lincoln to resist an abrupt change in the status of the Negro. It is not altogether clear whether Lincoln believed that the Negro could ever be raised to the level of the white. In any case, he felt that it would require considerable time for the whites to overcome their prejudice against social intercourse between the two races. Lincoln also objected to immediate emancipation because it would offend the Border states. As matters stood, they begrudged their contributions to the war and complained bitterly that the North was repaying their loyalty with abolitionist agitation. The conviction that emancipation by legislation was unconstitutional likewise weighed heavily with Lincoln, and he refused to concede that the war had destroyed any of the legal guarantees respecting slave property. Lincoln's stubborn attitude was reinforced by a mystical devotion to the Union, to which he was prepared to subordinate all other issues.

It soon became apparent that Congress would not settle for voluntary colonization and that it was afraid to proceed with emancipation. In an effort to head off more extreme measures, Lincoln recommended compensated emancipation in a special message on March 6, 1862. This proposal was intended as an olive branch for both the radicals and the Border-state Unionists, but it satisfied neither. The radicals contended that Congress had the power to abolish slavery and denounced the President's plan, which made compensated emancipation contingent on the consent of individual slaveholders. Border-state congressmen blindly resisted concessions. They echoed the aged Crittenden, who asserted: "Let slavery alone. It will go out like a candle." [22]

The stalemate on the legislative front might have lasted until the end of the session if McClellan had succeeded in breaking the stalemate on the military front. But as winter turned into spring without a decisive battle, the clamor of the Abolitionists for further blows against slavery increased. Phillips and Garrison denounced the conciliatory attitude of the Administration toward slaveholders, and Lydia Maria Child prayed nightly to God "to remove from our government that night-mare fear of the Border States." [23] Having banished the specter of Confederate soldiers invading his office, Greeley reversed himself once again and demanded vengeance on slaveholders. Stevens stalked the corridors of the House growling that he was tired of hearing Border-state men talk about their rights, and cowardly Republicans talk about the Constitution.[24] The bolder spirits talked openly about carving Negro freeholds out of plantations and creating a new South "bristling with Africo-American villages." [25]

The cumulative pressure of the assault on slavery undermined the resistance of moderate Republicans, and in the spring the legislative mill began to grind. An amendment to the Articles of War prohibited officers from returning, even to loyal masters, fugitives who came within army lines. Lincoln refused to communicate the amended article to Union commanders, but his defiant attitude only played into the hands of the radicals. In quick succession they rammed through Congress bills for compensated emancipation in the District of Columbia, for the prohibition of slavery in the territories, and for the repeal of the Fugitive Slave Law.

Lincoln signed all three measures, because they did not directly raise constitutional issues regarding the status of slave property. The second Confiscation bill was in a different category. It produced a host of legal questions and reached Lincoln's desk in early July, just as rumors of the collapse of the Peninsular campaign and McClellan's retreat began to circulate. Even earlier, critics of the Confiscation bill had been cowed by cries of treason,[26] and with the country in an ugly mood the President had every incentive to sign the bill. Yet he seriously considered a veto, because it had been formulated on the theory that the Confederate states were out of the Union and that their citizens had forfeited all civil rights. Lincoln objected not only to this constitutional doctrine but to two provisions of the bill: one that ignored the constitutional prohibition against the forfeiture of property in perpetuity, and one that denied a court hearing to those threatened with confiscation.

An outright breach between the President and Congress might have occurred had Fessenden not made a last-minute call at the White House and discovered Lincoln's objections. The radicals resented the meddling of the Maine senator, but sober counsels prevailed, with the result that both Houses attached an explanatory resolution to the Confiscation bill, bringing it in line with the constitutional provision on forfeiture. The peacemakers thought that they had succeeded when Lincoln signed the bill July 17, but the President then took the extraordinary step of sending to Congress the unused veto message. It asserted that the Confiscation Act was really an emancipation measure and flatly denied that the lawmakers possessed any power to modify the status of slavery in the states. This gesture enabled Lincoln to continue his unbroken custom of sending Congress home in a disagreeable humor.

Despite his acquiescence in peripheral assaults on slavery, Lincoln had outmaneuvered the radicals for the time being. The resolutions attached to the Confiscation Act turned it into a hodgepodge of regulations based on the contradictory legal assumptions that Southerners were both domestic rebels and citizens of an enemy state. It suited Lincoln to live with the confusion, because he was not ready to commit himself to any theory regarding the status of rebel states or their inhabitants. Having weakened the Confiscation Act, he turned it into a dead letter by allowing only token proceedings against rebel property within his reach.

Lincoln's victory was a temporary one. It did nothing to arrest the ruinous divisions within his party over slavery, and the pressure for emancipation continued to grow with unfavorable news from the military fronts. The one bright spot was in the West, where Union armies re-established control of the lower Mississippi River and New Orleans. Even this accomplishment became a fresh source of trouble for Lincoln, because General Ben Butler, the commander of the Union occupation army in New Orleans, began to support the Negro cause. On August 22 Butler discontinued the policy of returning runaway slaves to loyal masters. A month later, with the encouragement of Abolitionists in Washington, he began organizing colored regiments,[27] and soon after came out flatly for abolition. Although Butler was not openly defiant, Lincoln would undoubtedly have fired him had he dared. But the winds of abolition which had subsided temporarily with the adjournment of Congress reached gale proportions in mid-August; Lincoln was now confronted with more pressing problems than the dismissal of a scheming general. Throughout the country, the Republican press began to demand emancipation as the one measure that would revive the fortunes of Northern armies. Joseph Medill of the *Chicago Tribune* predicted that thousands of slaves would throw down their tools and enlist in Union armies if Lincoln would issue a proclamation freeing them. On August 19, Greeley struck a kindred note in a combination editorial and open letter to Lincoln entitled: "The Prayer of Twenty Million." Sherman of Ohio was startled by the effectiveness of this propaganda, and found his section ablaze with sentiment for using Negro troops against the South.[28]

Lincoln tried to appease the public by replacing the unpopular McClellan with General John Pope, who promised to seek out the Confederate army and offer battle. Whether the President intended to issue an emancipation proclamation in the event of a Union victory was a matter of conjecture. He concealed his purpose behind tentative preparations for such a proclamation while simultaneously undercutting them by a series of negative statements. The cabinet discussed with him a preliminary draft of an emancipation proclamation on July 22 and gained the impression that it would be released as soon as the Army of the Potomac broke the stalemate. Lincoln said nothing further to his official advisers about the matter for nearly two months. His subsequent letter in response to "The Prayer of Twenty Million" brushed aside the contention that emancipation was a war objective. In language reminiscent of the Crittenden Resolution, he reaffirmed his determination to save the Union, which meant he would use any method necessary to do so whether it involved freeing some slaves, all slaves, or no slaves.

Lincoln also confided to his friend Orville H. Browning, who had replaced the deceased Douglas as senator from Illinois, that he was doubtful whether the President possessed the necessary authority under his war powers to emancipate the slaves. According to Browning, Lincoln also believed that Negroes freed by executive proclamation would revert to their former status as slaves when the war ended.[29] By September 12, Secretary of the Treasury Chase had reached the conclusion that Lincoln's reference to an emancipation proclamation on July 22 was a smoke screen and that the President intended to shelve the project altogether in case the Union won a major victory. If so, military developments culminating in the Battle of Antietam represented a major setback for the President.

In late August, General Pope moved the Army of the Potomac southward to establish contact with the Confederates. As it turned out, General Robert E. Lee was willing to meet Pope more than halfway by invading Maryland with his rebel troops. The two armies collided again at Bull Run on August 30, 1862, this time without picnicking congressmen as spectators, and once more the Union army retreated toward Washington. Lincoln could think of nothing more original than to recall McClellan. The latter again demonstrated his special talent for revitalizing demoralized armies, but public gratitude evaporated as soon as it became clear that Lee intended to retreat and did not plan to attack Washington. With the familiar demand for a battle ringing in his ears, McClellan pursued Lee. Catching the elusive Southern commander at Antietam Creek on September 17, McClellan launched one of the bloodiest battles of the Civil War. He inflicted severe damage on his opponent, but his own army was so badly battered that Lee was able to escape. The indecisive action at Antietam ended McClellan's career as a Union general and removed Lincoln's last chance to avoid issuing an emancipation proclamation.

With the 1862 elections only two months away, Lincoln was reluctant to introduce an emancipation proclamation into the campaign. Apparently Lincoln acted more from fear that Great Britain would recognize the Confederacy than from any desire to placate the radicals. In any case, he issued an emancipation proclamation on September 22, and quickly discovered that he had pleased nobody. The radical Republicans were infuriated because Lincoln made implementation of the proclamation contingent upon a second proclamation set for January 1, 1863, and promised not to emancipate the slaves of any Southerners who resumed their allegiance to the Union in the intervening months. Worse still from their standpoint, the preliminary proclamation restricted emancipation to slaves in rebel states beyond the reach of Union armies. The Abolitionist press also bitterly criticized Lincoln because he refused to touch slavery in the Border states; it charged that the President had perpetrated a hoax on the North.

Conservative Republicans and War Democrats were equally unhappy. John Sherman, who had found Ohio clamoring for the use of Negro troops in Union armies a month earlier, encountered stony silence when he endorsed the proclamation.[30] Orville H. Browning abruptly gave up his campaign for re-election in Illinois. Already marked for political extinction by the radicals for voting against the second Confiscation bill, Browning tersely urged his fellow citizens to vote, but neglected to tell them how they should vote.[31] Many prominent War Democrats also sat on their hands and allowed the rank and file to drift back to the Democratic party. The exodus from the Unionist coalition was particularly large in the free counties along the Ohio River, where citizens harbored the unreasoning fear that the proclamation would discharge a flood of runaway slaves on their doorsteps. The regular Democratic organization in the key Northern states began to make headway with the slogan: "The Union as it was and the Constitution as it is." Party orators denounced the Republicans as Abolitionists and promised to restore peace by applying the Jeffersonian principle of respect for diverse local institutions. The Democratic press fired away at the Administration for alleged suspension of civil liberties, arbitrary arrests, and extravagant expenditures. "A vote for the Republican ticket," the *New Haven Register* informed its readers, "is a vote to mortgage every dollar's worth of property for the Abolitionist Disunionists to carry on this Negro war, and flood the whole North . . . with lazy, thieving Negroes to be supported by charity and the taxes of our people." [32]

With virtually every political faction condemning the Administration, it was apparent that the Unionists would lose ground in the election. The only direct test of Abolitionist sentiment occurred in Illinois, where the electorate turned down by a large majority an amendment to the state constitution which would have permitted colored men to enter the state and vote. The key states of Illinois, Indiana, and Pennsylvania elected Democratic legislatures, which ensured the retirement of three Union party senators. The Democrats also gained 33 seats in the House and elected a governor, Horatio Seymour, in New York. Elsewhere, the Union party retained its majorities. It even managed to gain a little ground in the Border states, because the Democratic leaders in those states openly sympathized with the Confederacy. Unnoticed at the time was the victory of two freshmen congressmen, James G. Blaine of Maine and James A. Garfield of Ohio, both of whom were destined to be key figures in the postwar Republican party.

The radicals derived almost as much comfort from the election as the Democrats, because conservative Unionists were the real losers. Necessity, if not conviction, had required Unionist candidates in closely divided districts to take a moderate stand, and they had been cut down by the withering cross fire of extremists on both sides. Since the Democratic gains were not large enough to jeopardize Unionist control of Congress, the radicals took the line that the voters had rebuked the President and his "incompetent pro-slavery generals." [33]

IV

If the radicals expected Lincoln to accept their interpretation of the 1862 election, they were disappointed. His annual message to the lame duck session in December gave no indication that the President would share his leadership with Congress or modify his attitude toward slavery. On the contrary, he proposed three constitutional amendments to promote gradual emancipation. The first authorized payment in United States bonds to states that voluntarily freed their slaves before January 1, 1900; the second prohibited the re-enslavement of Negroes freed during the war, but made provision for the compensation of loyal owners; and the third empowered Congress to appropriate money for the colonization of freedmen. The President justified his program of spreading out emancipation over a thirty-seven-year period with the familiar argument that it would spare "both races from the evils of sudden derangement."

At first most radicals concealed their negative reaction to the Presidential message, to ensure that Lincoln would have no excuse for with-holding the final Emancipation Proclamation. But they could not resist the temptation to resume open war on the Administration when the Army of the Potomac suffered still another defeat in mid-December. The newest victim of the canny Lee was General Ambrose E. Burnside, whom Lin-coln had appointed to succeed McClellan. Like the radicals, Burnside be-lieved that knowledge of military tactics was not nearly as important as a determination to attack the enemy. When he tested this theory with a wild charge against the Confederate army at Fredericksburg, Virginia, Burn-side was soon forced to retreat toward Washington.

Three days after the battle, Republican senators held a secret caucus to deplore the incompetence of the Administration. Chandler and Wade opened the session by renewing their favorite charge that Secretary of State Seward was responsible for the military misfortunes. They condemned him as an evil genius who dominated the President and infected the cabinet with defeatism.[34] Since the senators were looking for a scapegoat, even cautious members like Fessenden and Collamer joined in the denunciation of Seward. Several hours of indignant oratory produced almost unanimous agreement that, if only Seward were fired, incompetence, disunity, and despair would vanish overnight. The caucus had more trouble in agreeing about positive steps to be taken. Wade wanted a military dictatorship under a Republican general and undoubtedly had himself in mind. Sher-man regarded it as a waste motion to oust Seward unless members were also prepared to lecture Lincoln about his faults. So the Ohio senator urged a mass descent on the White House for a showdown. Displaying more irritability than usual, Fessenden asserted that the Senate ought to dictate the composition of the President's cabinet and eliminate members who did not possess its confidence. Exhaustion set in before the caucus could agree on a policy, but, when it adjourned overnight, the participants were con-fident that they had eliminated Seward.[35] The next day the caucus adopted with minor changes a resolution proposed by Sumner for a committee to call on Lincoln "and urge upon him changes in conduct and in the Cabinet that will give the administration more vigor." The tactful Collamer was chosen to head a committee of nine, and after securing an appointment with Lincoln for the following evening, he prepared a written summary of senatorial complaints.

Since the caucus members were not very good at keeping secrets, both

Seward and Lincoln received advance information about the intentions of the committee. Seward promptly submitted his resignation to the President, who spent the day brooding about the impending meeting with the committee. Lincoln recognized that he, not Seward, was the real target of the critics and wrestled with a dark impulse to give up the Presidency. Yet at the evening meeting on December 18, Lincoln handled the committee adroitly. He parried questions about his intentions toward Seward and wrung from the senators a virtual admission that complaints about the lack of unity in the cabinet and the infrequency of its meetings originated with Chase. Whereupon, Lincoln asked the committee to return the next day for a session with all of the cabinet but Seward. As Lincoln expected, Chase refused to repeat openly the charges that he had made privately. The upshot was that the committee members retired smoldering with resentment against Chase, while the unhappy Secretary of the Treasury, who had walked into Lincoln's trap, submitted his resignation the following morning. Then the President asked both Seward and Chase to remain in the cabinet. After a show of reluctance they agreed, thereby enabling the President to demonstrate that he had repelled the Senate's assault on his executive powers.

Lincoln won a smaller victory in salvaging the compound cabinet. For nearly a year its value as a symbol of unity had been outweighed by its inability to function as an effective arm of executive power. Seward had already ceased to be a source of political strength to the Administration, and Chase lost his influence with the radicals by withdrawing his resignation. The continued presence of two such bitter foes in the cabinet diverted Lincoln's attention from more important matters. Like most politicians, the President must have secretly enjoyed the atmosphere of intrigue in his official family, otherwise he would certainly have ended the situation much sooner than he did.

After their unsuccessful offensive of mid-December, the radicals subsided for the remainder of the session. Their feelings were as bitter as ever,[36] but they made no organized fight on Lincoln's bill authorizing an appropriation of $15,000,000 to compensate loyal slaveholders in Missouri. Coupled with the final Proclamation of January 1, 1863, freeing slaves within the Confederacy, this measure seemed to satisfy the public. But the short-sighted Border-state Democrats played into the hands of the radicals by filibustering the appropriation bill to death in the closing week of the session. It proved to be the last chance for a policy of gradual emancipation, and when Congress met nine months later the sentiment for unconditional abolition was irresistible.

Meanwhile, the President returned to the dreary task of finding a general who could advance on Richmond and end the war. First he tried "Fighting Joe" Hooker, but Lee gave his newest antagonist a good drubbing at Chancellorsville on May 2, 1863; so Lincoln turned to George G. Meade. Before the new Union commander could work out any plans for an offensive, Lee was advancing northward into Pennsylvania. The two armies collided at Gettysburg, and Lee retreated after a grim three-day battle. While the outcome at Gettysburg was still in doubt, Vicksburg— the last Confederate stronghold in the West—surrendered on July 4. Plainly the economy which had supported the Confederate armies was under severe strain, but Meade could not follow up his victory with a knockout blow.

A new round of state elections occurred just as impatient Northerners were discovering that the war would drag through another winter. The Union party had carried New Hampshire in March 1863, but a crucial test of public sentiment took place in Ohio in October. Interest in the election was heightened by the fact that the Democrats had nominated former Congressman Clement L. Vallandigham, an extreme critic of the Civil War, for governor. In many respects Vallandigham was a liability to the Democrats. He had repeatedly defended the states' rights position in language that implied sympathy with the South. He had also offended by advocating an armistice and predicting that it would generate a huge wave of Unionist sentiment in the South.[37] The only reason the Democrats gambled on Vallandigham was because General Burnside had arrested him for seditious utterances in May 1863. The President had subsequently tried to undo the damage of his overzealous subordinate by ordering Vallandigham escorted to the Confederate lines and released. But the Ohio Democrat recognized the political advantages of martyrdom and fled to Canada, where he received the party nomination as a candidate-in-exile.

The Ohio radicals were sufficiently alarmed by Vallandigham's candidacy to accept both a cautious platform and John Brough, a War Democrat, as the Union party candidate for governor. A lively and inconclusive discussion about Vallandigham's loyalty ensued. Union party orators branded him as a traitor but failed to uncover any evidence that he was in contact with Confederate authorities. Most voters cared little about documentary proof, and Vallandigham's earlier statements were sufficiently inflammatory to hurt him. In any case, the loyalty issue enabled the Ohio Unionists to avoid the subject of the Negro, which had backfired a year earlier.

A similar contest developed in neighboring Pennsylvania, where the Democrats chose George Woodward, a bitter critic of Lincoln, to run for governor against the incumbent Unionist, Andrew G. Curtin. Both states erased their Democratic majorities and gave substantial margins to the Union ticket. A noteworthy feature of the 1863 elections was the participation of an organization known as the Union League. Originally a nonpartisan agency which had tried to mobilize public support for the war, the League functioned effectively as an auxiliary arm of the Union party.[38] Eventually its local chapters were to fall under the control of the radicals, but the Union League escaped factionalism until the end of the war.

It is clear in retrospect that the state elections of 1863 in pivotal Ohio and Pennsylvania were a major watershed in political history, for they marked the end of a thirty-year supremacy of the Democratic party. Hitherto voters had refused to believe that the party of Andrew Jackson and Stephen A. Douglas harbored treasonable elements, but the nomination of the notorious Vallandigham caused the suspicion to take firm root in the Northern mind. A crucial number of patriotic Democrats defected to the Union party. The regular Democrats unintentionally contributed to the exodus by blaming their losses on each other, quarreling over strategy, and venting their frustration in ever wilder displays of partisanship. The Ohio and Pennsylvania elections also convinced the moderate Republican element in the Union party that victory in 1864 could be achieved only by strengthening the coalition.

The radicals were less impressed by the change in the political weather, and were in full command of the House, which had been chosen thirteen months before it met in December 1863. The new majority displayed its aggressive temper immediately by electing Schuyler Colfax of Indiana as speaker. Colfax was a soft-spoken intriguer who professed good will toward the President while obstructing his program. The speaker would have made more trouble for Lincoln if he had possessed more ability, but he lacked the robustness and firmness to manage unruly congressmen. Consequently, the real leadership of the House passed to Thaddeus Stevens, whose iron will and acid tongue intimidated most of his colleagues. It delighted him to expose the ulterior motives behind their pious utterances with a few sardonic phrases. Stevens detested hypocrisy so much that he pretended to be more cynical than he really was. Although indifferent to organized religion, he displayed a religious reverence for the ideal of human equality, and he championed the cause of the Negro with zeal and persistence. The most incisive thinker among the radicals as well as the most realistic, he was always willing to accept the full consequences of his beliefs. Stevens saw that any practical improvement in the status of the Negro required the complete destruction of the existing social and economic order in the South. As early as 1863 he had begun to pursue the goal of resettling freedmen on confiscated rebel estates,[39] but he saw the necessity of proceeding a step at a time. The twofold purpose of his piecemeal legislative assaults on slavery was to wreck the Presidential policy of gradual emancipation and to establish the doctrine that Congress alone could fix the postwar status of the rebel states. Not only did Stevens argue that the Southern states had left the Union and forfeited their constitutional rights, but he denied that the President could do anything to restore them.

Despite his uncompromising stand in behalf of the Negro, Stevens was distrusted by most of his fellow radicals as well as their followers. They disapproved of his unconcealed addiction to gambling and his devotion to his Negro housekeeper, Lydia Smith, whom many believed to be the mistress of the lonely old bachelor. Others were tolerant of his personal qualities but appalled by his hatred of the South. Because Stevens so seldom lapsed into the flowery idealism of Sumner and Garrison, the militant Abolitionists suspected that he was motivated more by dislike of rebels than devotion to the Negro.

It would take four years for public opinion to catch up to Stevens, but in 1864 he pushed Congress far enough to kill gradual emancipation. His first move was to secure an amendment to the Enrollment Act, making all able-bodied Negroes subject to the draft. The amendment also provided for the permanent freedom of those called up for service and a paltry compensation of three hundred dollars to loyal owners for each slave liberated in this fashion. Then Stevens, in co-operation with Senate radicals, introduced a constitutional amendment authorizing immediate and unconditional emancipation of slaves. The Senate promptly cleared the measure 38 to 6, but there were enough Democrats in the House to prevent Stevens from mustering the necessary two-thirds vote. Nevertheless, the amendment commanded such overwhelming Republican support that Lincoln capitulated two months before the final House roll call and endorsed it.

In the same session of the 38th Congress, Lincoln and the radicals fired the opening shots in a long battle over the issue of restoring Southern states to full membership in the Union. The more Lincoln yielded on the emancipation question, the more he needed Southerners in Congress to help him thwart radical plans for a drastic alteration of race relations. There was no way that the President could modify congressional control over the admission of members, but he could organize loyal governments in Southern states as rapidly as Union armies liberated them and encourage their elected representatives to reclaim their seats. Lincoln recognized that he was most likely to succeed by avoiding a debate on the constitutional status of the rebel states and by pressing for their admission to Congress on a piecemeal basis. His principal asset was the argument that lenient treatment of the earliest states to be liberated would destroy the fighting spirit of the rest and shorten the war. So Lincoln took the offensive in his annual message of December 1863, by proposing a reorganization plan under the guise of a "Proclamation of Amnesty and Reconstruction." He pledged himself to recognize any state government established by 10 per cent of those eligible to vote in 1860 who would take an oath to support the Constitution, the Acts of Congress, and Executive Proclamations on slavery. All such persons, except a few high Confederate officials, were to be extended a full pardon.

Almost everyone in Congress reacted unfavorably to the plan. The Democrats, who had the most to gain from it, claimed that the President was trying to pack Congress with subservient legislators and promote further assaults on the rights of the states. The radicals denounced the scheme as unconstitutional and insisted that Congress possessed sole jurisdiction over Reconstruction. More disconcerting still was the hostility of moderate Republicans. Fessenden admitted that he could not think of a better plan but believed it nonsensical to tell the rebels "that they may fight as long as they can and take a pardon when they have had enough." [40] Nevertheless, the President proceeded to reorganize the governments of Arkansas, Louisiana, and Tennessee in the spring of 1864. Congressmen-elect from Arkansas appeared in Washington to ask for their seats, and it was understood that if they were successful, applicants from Louisiana and Tennessee would follow. Opponents of the President probably had enough votes to block his plan in any event, but even the moderates deserted him, because none of the three loyal governments were able to exercise any jurisdiction outside of Union lines. The hopelessness of the situation was graphically demonstrated in Tennessee, where an attempt to hold elections in two congressional districts had ended with the Unionist candidates fleeing to escape assassination.[41]

Not content with the negative policy of ridiculing Lincoln's "shadow governments," the radicals launched a counteroffensive by preparing a readmission bill of their own. Known as the Wade-Davis bill, it fell far short of satisfying Stevens and Julian, because its provisions implied that Southerners possessed some constitutional rights. Deserted by key members of their own faction, Wade and Davis were forced to accept amendments which weakened the measure still further. To assure its passage, they even sacrificed a mandatory provision for the participation of Negro voters in the reorganization of Southern governments. In final form, the Wade-Davis bill was a severe version of the Lincoln plan rather than a radical measure. It required the action of a majority instead of 10 per cent of the voters to re-establish state government; it excluded more categories of Confederate officials from the reorganization process; and it stiffened the oath of allegiance to the Constitution. Its most controversial section included requirements that all new state constitutions bar Confederate officers above the rank of major from holding office, abolish slavery, and repudiate debts contracted by Confederate governments.

The bill was an embarrassment to its sponsors, but their hatred of Lincoln and their determination to assert congressional control over Reconstruction blinded them to its defects. By the time the Wade-Davis bill reached the White House, many radicals preferred no legislation at all. Had Lincoln signed it, probably enough Southern congressmen would have been readmitted under its terms to block the more punitive Reconstruction measures of 1866–67. But there was a stubborn streak in the President, which was reinforced by his conviction that Congress had no constitutional power over slavery.

The climax was one of the most dramatic in the long series of feuds between Presidents and legislators. A few hours after adjournment on July 2, when several senators were clustered about Lincoln urging him to sign their pet measures, the forthright Chandler brought up the Wade-Davis bill. "The important point," he asserted, "is the one prohibiting slavery in the reconstructed states." Looking the Michigan senator straight in the eye, Lincoln replied: "That is the point on which I doubt the authority of Congress to act." [42] Convinced that Lincoln intended to kill the bill with a pocket veto, Chandler stormed out of the office. When word of its fate reached Henry Winter Davis, he was still at his desk, although the House had adjourned. Shaking with fury, he rose to his feet and delivered an extemporaneous denunciation of Lincoln to the empty chamber. On the surface the President had won the first round in the struggle over Reconstruction, but it was a costly victory.

V

Lincoln's veto of the Wade-Davis bill also rekindled an intra-party feud over the party Presidential nomination which had been smoldering since the beginning of 1864. At that time the radicals had begun looking for a candidate to replace Lincoln, but none of those anxious to run enjoyed their confidence. To make matters worse, none who met their qualifications possessed any political appeal. The candidate most eager for their endorsement was Salmon P. Chase, who had been running against Lincoln since the polls closed in November 1860. From his strategic position in the cabinet, Chase had employed the patronage of the Treasury Department to build a personal organization. By arranging for his portrait to appear on the one-dollar national bank notes, Chase placed "a campaign picture in every man's pocket." [43] Over a three-year period he wrote more letters about his political availability than about Treasury Department business. At the same time that he was conducting transparent intrigues against Lincoln, Chase was also protesting his loyalty to him. The radicals did not take note of this equivocal conduct until the cabinet crisis in December 1862, but thereafter they were wary of Chase. Their coolness failed to discourage him, and as the official campaign season approached he redoubled his efforts to win their support. Early in February 1864, Chase persuaded John Sherman to send out under his frank a pamphlet called "The Next Presidential Election," a bitter attack on Lincoln's competence. Sherman received so many critical letters about the pamphlet that he lamely pleaded ignorance of its contents. Chase ought to have heeded the warning, but on February 20 he persuaded Senator Samuel C. Pomeroy of Kansas to father a new assault on Lincoln known as "The Pomeroy Circular." This document rehashed all of the radical objections to Lincoln and predicted that the President would be defeated if he ran for re-election. The concluding paragraphs of "The Pomeroy Circular" called for more vigorous prosecution of the war and asserted that Chase was well qualified to provide dynamic leadership.

The immediate response of the radical leaders was decidedly tepid. None of them endorsed Chase, and a few urged a postponement of the Union convention, which could only mean that they wanted time to find another candidate. For a few days it looked as if the clumsy attack on the President would cost Chase nothing more than a damaged ego. Lincoln was not in a position to fight back, and few of his supporters in Washington carried much weight. But Chase had his share of enemies, none of whom were more outspoken than the Blair family. Border-state Abolitionists, they distrusted radical schemes of Reconstruction and considered it a patriotic service to expose Chase, who was vulnerable on several counts. For one thing, the Secretary of the Treasury had received both personal loans and investment opportunities from Jay Cooke, whose financial house enjoyed almost exclusive rights to market government bonds. Chase had also shown favoritism in issuing permits which authorized holders to purchase cotton from "loyal citizens" inside the Confederate lines. Congressman Frank P. Blair did not care much about the debt-servicing arrangements of the Treasury Department, but he was incensed by the fact that all of the trading permits in Missouri had been issued to his enemies in the radical or "Charcoal" faction of the Union party. Blair also hated the permit system because he believed that the cotton trade lined the pockets of Chase's henchmen and provided the South with badly needed resources to continue the war. Blair made all these accusations and more in a hard-hitting speech February 27 on the floor of the House. His words carried unusual weight because he held a general's commission and had recently returned from the front to take his seat in Congress.

The Blair speech dealt a staggering blow to Chase, and his candidacy collapsed altogether a few days later when the Ohio legislature repudiated the Pomeroy Circular by endorsing Lincoln for renomination. Chase announced his formal withdrawal from the Presidential contest and again offered to resign as Secretary of the Treasury. Lincoln listened with a straight face while Chase disclaimed all knowledge of the Pomeroy Circular, and he once again persuaded the Secretary to remain at his post. These developments infuriated the radicals, who thought Lincoln was behind the attack on Chase. With the Secretary of the Treasury out of the race, they were all the more enthusiastic about defending him. They packed with radicals the House committee organized to investigate Blair's charges in order to secure Chase's vindication; in addition, they ultimately deprived Blair of his congressional seat.

Meanwhile, John C. Frémont had come forward to fill the vacuum left by the collapse of the Chase boom. Frémont had been disgruntled ever since his ouster as Department Commander in Missouri, where he enjoyed considerable popularity among the Germans who were the backbone of the Charcoal faction. So when Chase withdrew, this faction quickly transferred its allegiance to Frémont. The foes of the President in Washington saw a certain nuisance value in the Frémont candidacy, but they regarded the Pathfinder as an adventurer. His flirtations with the Democrats only confirmed the radicals' uneasiness about him. Unlike Chase, Frémont showed interest in lost causes and was determined to have a nomination of some kind. In the end, he managed to entice a few dissident Germans and Eastern intellectuals to a convention at Cleveland on May 30. This motley crew called itself "The Radical Democracy" and nominated Frémont on a platform that no bona fide Democrat could accept. Frémont promptly qualified his endorsement of it, and announced that a spirit of vengeance ought not to prevail in dealing with the South. This statement ruined his last chance of securing support from the radical leaders in Congress, who wanted not only a winner but a reliable Abolitionist.

The inability of the opposition to unite on a candidate was a tribute to Lincoln's popularity with the rank and file, as well as a demonstration of his skill in political management. Throughout the winter of 1864 reports reached Washington of his strength "with the unthinking masses." [44] An Ohio editor warned Sherman that five out of six people in the Midwest favored the renomination of the President, and added that "the movement is not managed; it is spontaneous beyond the possibility of doubt." [45] Outwardly the President appeared to be indifferent to his political prospects and preoccupied with the conduct of the war, but appearances were deceptive, for actually he was working furiously through a host of local leaders to secure endorsements from state legislatures. Technically such resolutions were not binding on the delegates, but the vast majority of state conventions honored these instructions. The Lincoln bandwagon also gained momentum because of the popular belief that the President had finally found in Ulysses S. Grant a general who would end the war. Already famous for his capture of Vicksburg, Grant had been elevated to the rank of lieutenant general in March 1864 and vested with control of all Union armies.

In keeping with his strategy of representing the Union party as a truly national organization, Lincoln had arranged for the convention to be held in the Border-state city of Baltimore. No less hospitable site could have been selected for a Unionist gathering outside the rebel states themselves. The notorious Baltimore mobs were belligerently pro-Southern, and Lincoln's arch foe in the city, Congressman Henry Winter Davis, managed to prevent his own party from renting the only suitable hall. So the national committee made arrangements to meet at the Front Street Theater, where heat, poor acoustics, and street noise harassed the delegates.

When the convention opened on June 7, it was apparent that most of the delegates felt less enthusiasm for Lincoln than had the state organizations that selected them. Although Baltimore was only a short distance from the capital, most radical legislators did not bother to attend. Thaddeus Stevens appeared long enough to organize an unsuccessful fight against the seating of delegations from Lincoln's reconstructed state governments. Chase also boycotted the convention, referring to it contemptuously as a "Blair-Lincoln convention."

A spirit of improvisation characterized the sessions. The Reverend Robert Breckenridge set the tone at the outset by touching up the last four lines of the Lord's Prayer so that the Almighty virtually declared himself for a Union party victory.[46] Retiring national chairman Edwin D. Morgan followed with the shortest keynote address on record. Ex-Governor William Dennison of Ohio gave a more typical performance as permanent chairman, but the delegates plodded through their business apathetically. Lincoln got his way in the platform, which was a mild document except for the plank endorsing unconditional emancipation by constitutional amendment. The resolutions advocating the speedy construction of a Pacific railroad and the encouragement of immigration did not have an objectionably partisan ring. Even the animus of the radicals against the Blair family was buried in a veiled request for reconstruction of the cabinet, actually leveled at Postmaster General Montgomery Blair.

As expected, Lincoln received a first-ballot nomination with 506 votes to 22 cast for General Grant by the unhappy Missouri radicals. The maneuvering over the Vice Presidency launched a controversy about the attitude of Lincoln that raged long after the death of the principals.[47] At the time it was commonly supposed that Lincoln favored the renomination of Vice President Hannibal Hamlin of Maine and that the convention defied the wishes of the President in selecting Governor Andrew Johnson of Tennessee. The more probable explanation of the episode is that Lincoln engineered the selection of Johnson through the concealed management at which he excelled. The President could not possibly have wanted Hamlin on either personal or political grounds. Besides being a radical and a quiet, but persistent, critic of Lincoln, Hamlin was from a Republican state and unable to bring any strength to the ticket. Johnson, on the other hand, was a Southern War Democrat, and his nomination seemed most likely to answer the argument that the Union party was only the old Republican organization in disguise. Nevertheless, Lincoln misled a lot of people, including his own secretary, because he wanted to avoid any appearance of dictating to the convention. It is probable that he gave Hamlin backers a noncommittal but sympathetic hearing, which they interpreted as support. Simultaneously, Lincoln must have dropped hints to Simon Cameron, Governor William Stone of Iowa, and others that a War Democrat would be an acceptable running mate.[48] Without intending to help the President, Sumner swung the Massachusetts delegation behind Johnson. His maneuver was part of a devious plot against his enemy Fessenden. Because Hamlin was popular in Maine, Sumner assumed that the Vice President would run for senator if denied renomination and beat Fessenden. The defection of Sumner from the Hamlin camp unsettled the New England radicals; and after an indecisive first ballot in which Daniel S. Dickinson, a War Democrat from New York, drew 108 votes away from the leading contenders, the convention swung behind Andrew Johnson.

There is little doubt that the irresolute behavior of his enemies at Baltimore encouraged Lincoln to take a firmer line. When Chase offered his resignation once again in late June, after a dispute over Treasury patronage, Lincoln amazed him by accepting it promptly. Shortly thereafter, the President also vetoed the Wade-Davis bill. Undoubtedly he did not expect violent criticism, for the leading radicals had been indifferent to the measure, but the reaction was explosive. Horace Greeley led the radical press in a sustained demand that Lincoln withdraw from the contest. The authors of the bill also prepared a broadside against the President known as the Wade-Davis Manifesto. Issued on August 2, it reviewed all the objections to the 10 per cent plan and summarized the alleged advantages of the Wade-Davis bill. In extravagant language, the Manifesto accused the President of making war on Congress. Reaffirming the familiar Whig doctrine that the legislative branch was the only constitutional representative of public sentiment, the Manifesto asserted that the President ought to confine himself to executing the laws. In effect, Republicans were invited to seek a new candidate.

The rebellion of the radicals gained fresh momentum because of discouraging news from the battlefield. With Grant stalled in front of Richmond, many disappointed citizens blamed the stalemate on the President. Pessimism revived and with it the ominous sentiment that the North ought to accept peace at any price.[49] Defeatist sentiment reached a climax during the last week of August. The White House bulged with angry Republicans who clamored for action but had no specific proposals. "Everything is darkness, doubt, and discouragement," wrote Lincoln's secretary, John Nicolay, on August 25. "Our men see giants in the airy and insubstantial shadows of the opposition and are about to surrender without a fight." [50] One of the most panicky was the new chairman of the Union national committee, Henry J. Raymond, whose strategic position as editor of the *New York Times* gave added weight to his words. "The tide is setting strongly against us," he reported to Lincoln, and he added that most Northerners believed negotiations would produce both peace and reunion.[51] Raymond felt sure that the Confederacy would reject an armistice proposal, but he thought Lincoln ought to make one in the hope of blunting the effectiveness of peace talk. The President rejected Raymond's suggestion, but not because he was more optimistic than his advisers. The same week he dictated a memo noting the likelihood that he would be defeated and pledging co-operation to his successor.

The loud clamor for peace sobered and divided the radicals. Zack Chandler recoiled from a third ticket because it would assure the victory of the Democrats whom he hated more than he did Lincoln. The fiery Michigan senator confided to his wife August 27 that he was prepared to accept Lincoln,[52] and his example seemed certain to influence Wade as well as other leading radicals. Henry Winter Davis and the Chase faction in New York were not yet willing to give up their plan for a new nominating convention.[53] They had sent out a circular letter August 18 soliciting the help of prominent politicians, and they planned to meet at the home of Dudley Field Malone on August 30 to discuss the replies. Since the date of their proposed conference fell in the middle of the Democratic convention, the conspirators agreed to delay the final decision a few more days.

Meanwhile, evidence had been accumulating that the Democrats were as badly divided as their opponents. August Belmont, the chairman of the Democratic national committee, had postponed the convention from the beginning of August until the end of the month, on the theory that a decisive battle might take place during the interval and give the delegates a fresh clue about public opinion. None was forthcoming, and the convention opened amidst manifestations of bitter discord. Although the bulk of the War Democrats had gone over to the Union party, a substantial faction led by Belmont opposed a declaration of unconditional opposition to the continuation of the war. Vallandigham headed a group almost as large that wanted to reaffirm the position so fatal to the Democrats in the Ohio and Pennsylvania elections of 1863. The situation called for a compromise, and the delegates made the worst one possible by nominating General George B. McClellan, who favored the war on a peace platform. The one escape hatch for McClellan was the ambiguous armistice plank which did not specify whether the party ought to recognize the Confederacy to obtain a cessation of hostilities. The Vallandigham faction favored an armistice at all costs, and for a time McClellan wavered. In the end Belmont, George T. Curtis, and others persuaded McClellan to write a letter of acceptance requiring from the Confederacy a prior commitment to reunion as a condition for an armistice.[54] Released in this form, the McClellan letter defied the peace faction, but the damage done by the platform was irreparable. It provided Unionist orators with ammunition for their thesis that the Democratic party harbored treasonable elements. Had the military deadlock persisted, this argument might not have been fatal to the Democrats; but no sooner had their convention disbanded than General William Tecumseh Sherman captured Atlanta on September 2.

The spectacular Union victory at Atlanta not only doomed the Democrats but killed the movement for a new Union party convention. Chase supported Lincoln, and Davis even agreed to campaign for the President in his own fashion, telling his Maryland constituents that "the man is neither wise nor honest . . . but if I can vote for him it would be ridiculous for you to be more squeamish." [55] Only the task of securing the withdrawal of Frémont still remained. Chandler undertook the negotiations with the balky general after extracting from Lincoln a promise to oust Montgomery Blair from the cabinet and restore Frémont to an important command post.[56] The Pathfinder kept Chandler on tenterhooks until the end of September, but, when he withdrew, Frémont declined to press for fulfillment of the terms offered by the White House. Nevertheless, so many radicals clamored for Blair's scalp that Lincoln abruptly secured his resignation the same month. The President completed his fence mending by offering the French mission to James Gordon Bennett of the *New York Herald,* who promptly became more enthusiastic about the Union ticket.

After the turbulent summer months, when the schismatics threatened to dissolve the Union party and the voters threatened to support an armistice, the campaign itself was comparatively calm. Victory did not seem as certain as in 1860, but in September the morale of Union party workers improved visibly. Even the gloomy Wilson of Massachusetts gave the President an optimistic report after canvassing in the saloons and gambling dens of Boston.[57]

There were few innovations in party organization or strategy in 1864. The Unionists enjoyed a great advantage because of the wartime increase in federal employees. Wealthy businessmen contributed to the Union party campaign chest more generously than they had in 1860. Lincoln also tried to help his own cause by encouraging Union commanders to furlough as many Union soldiers as they could spare during election week. As usual, the national committees of both parties concentrated expenditures in Ohio, Pennsylvania, and Indiana because of the prevalent belief that a sweep of the three states would generate a bandwagon psychology elsewhere. The major campaign theme of the Union national committee was to represent the Democratic party as the northern arm of the Confederacy. Governor Yates of Illinois insisted that Lincoln was running against Jefferson Davis,[58] while Governor Morton of Indiana used the proof of treasonable activity by a few Democrats to indict the entire party.[59] Lesser figures echoed these charges, which also appeared in editorials and campaign leaflets. This strategy enabled the Union party to harvest the seeds of doubt which Vallandigham had sown in the Ohio campaign of 1863. Voters reminded of his outspoken utterances a year earlier concluded that the Democratic party was the party of treason. Once convinced, many patriotic citizens clung to the belief to their dying day. In fact, the systematic assault on the loyalty of the Democratic party did more than anything else to convert the wobbly Union coalition into a majority party. For every four Democrats whose partisan attachments were intensified by attacks on their patriotism, there was one who went over permanently to the opposition.[60] Illinois and Ohio, which had been doubtful states in the 1850's, did not go Democratic in a Presidential election until 1892, while Pennsylvania held out until 1912. Of the populous states in the lower Middle West, only Indiana possessed so many Democrats that the party was able to weather the defections of the Civil War and compete on equal terms with the opposition.[61]

The wounds of the 1864 election left a legacy of partisan bitterness that was to persist into the 1890's. The great mass of Democrats, who considered themselves anti-Administration rather than anti-war, never forgave their tormentors. Their immediate response was to denounce Lincoln as a "widow maker" whose generals stood for "corruption, conscription, and taxation." Party orators found a parallel between Nero, who had fiddled while Rome burned, and Lincoln, who told stale jokes while the Union fell apart. The *New York World* of September 9 revived an old story that Lincoln had asked Ward Hill Lamon to sing "Picayune Butler," a gay ballad, as they rode over the gory battlefield of Antietam. Neither Presidential candidate took the stump in 1864, but the campaign was lively enough without them.

As the political strategists had anticipated, the October elections proved to be a reliable indicator of popular sentiment. The Union party carried Ohio by a more comfortable margin than Pennsylvania and Indiana. Furloughed soldiers contributed 15,000 of the 20,000 majority in Pennsylvania, while vote buying put over the Union state ticket in Indiana. As Joseph Medill of the *Chicago Tribune* explained to a friend, "I knew the boys were fixing things up pretty steep" (in Indiana), but "it was well to err on the safe side." [62] There was no taint of corruption, however, about the Union party victory in November. Lincoln received 212 electoral votes and 2,206,938 popular votes to McClellan's 21 electoral votes and 1,803,787 popular votes. Historians have pointed out that the redistribution of a few thousand votes in New York, Pennsylvania, Indiana, and Connecticut would have thrown the election to McClellan. Yet, it is difficult to avoid the conclusion that the Lincoln victory was a solid one, for the Union party polled 55 per cent of the popular vote, or approximately 15 per cent more than the Republican party had polled in the same states in 1860.

VI

The election results prodded the House to reverse itself in the lame duck session and pass the Emancipation Amendment by the necessary two-thirds vote. Apparently Lincoln felt bound by the party platform, because he used executive patronage as shamelessly as any of his predecessors to procure affirmative votes from several wobbly Democrats. It is unlikely that Lincoln's enthusiastic support of unconditional emancipation meant he had given up his advocacy of gradual adjustment of race relations. He probably hoped for radical support of bills to admit reconstructed states and believed that enough Southerners could be sneaked into Congress in this fashion to block legislation aimed at immediate racial equality. In any case, the President reached an understanding with Lyman Trumbull, who suddenly deserted the radicals to sponsor the Administration's bill for the admission of Louisiana. Some twenty senators who had supported the Wade-Davis bill reversed themselves and supported the admission of Louisiana, while Sumner led seven radicals in a filibuster against the bill. The filibusterers were supported by a like number of shortsighted Democrats, who did not see that a Lincoln government in Louisiana would be more friendly to the South than one established by Congress. Although Trumbull had a clear majority, he could not bring the Louisiana bill to a vote before the short session expired on March 4, 1865.

Lincoln might have salvaged it by calling a special session of the new Congress, but, with the regular session nine months away, he preferred to let the legislators go home. Time seemed to be working against the radicals, and the President must have hoped that he could complete his own reconstruction program by the time they returned in December. Some of the bolder radicals remained in Washington and clamored for a special session at the end of March, when it became obvious that the Confederacy was about to collapse. The President was conciliatory but vague. Speaker Colfax left for the West Coast in disgust, but Sumner, Wade, and Julian remained to watch the President. They were still there on April 10 when Lee surrendered to Grant at Appomattox Court House. Now they fretted over the magnanimous tone of Lincoln's victory speech.

The radicals had no inkling that death would strike the President, but for months Lincoln had been tortured by monstrous dreams. During one nightmare he imagined that he had walked to an open coffin and seen himself lying in state. Although these forebodings made the President melancholy, he stubbornly resisted the entreaties of his friends to accept a bodyguard. Rumors of impending violence circulated in Washington the night of April 14 when the President went to Ford's Theatre. In the midst of the performance a demented Southern sympathizer, John Wilkes Booth, entered the President's box, fired a bullet into his brain, and fled the theater. Lincoln was mortally wounded and died the next morning.

After his death the Lincoln legend grew to such vast dimensions that it became impossible for either his contemporaries or historians of later generations to put his achievements in perspective. To each successive evaluation of Lincoln's complex personality there was the reply that he really could not have been such a person. Even the more modest effort to judge Lincoln as a party leader is beset with hazards. Although Lincoln had nothing to do with the founding of the Republican party, he was the individual most responsible for its survival. Not only did he make it respectable by moderating its radical tendencies, but he enlarged the base of its support by temporarily converting it into a broad coalition to save the Union. As usually defined, the term "strong President" is not an altogether satisfactory designation for Lincoln. Notwithstanding the fact that he vigorously expanded executive power in all areas related to the war, he showed little interest in other matters. There was nothing that could properly be called a Presidential program. Lincoln invariably signed bills dealing with the tariff, homesteads, and railroads which had been promised in the Republican platform of 1860, but he allowed the initiative in such matters to rest with Congress. He neither attempted to dictate the specific provisions of such legislation nor to shape the strategy for passing it. He likewise avoided special messages, frequent appeals for public support, and other aggressive methods of asserting executive leadership.

Lincoln's conception of Presidential responsibility owed something to his Whiggish antecedents. It was a cardinal doctrine of the Whigs that Congress ought to originate legislation and that the President ought to confine himself for the most part to the execution of the laws. Long before he reached the White House, Lincoln had endorsed this theory, and it is doubtful that he would have taken a different view of executive responsibility except under the pressure of war. Temperamentally he was also predisposed to honor the tradition of Clay and Webster. Despite his simplicity and directness in small matters, Lincoln seldom confided his real intentions fully to others. It suited him to exercise Presidential powers by indirection whenever possible and to stay out of the main line of fire. He was a more vigorous executive than most of his predecessors, and he collided with Congress repeatedly. Nevertheless, most executive-legislative friction arose out of disputes over war powers, and it seems probable that Lincoln would have done little to strengthen the Presidency in the absence of a crisis. As it was, his friction with Congress caused the radical wing of his party to exaggerate the old Whig theory of legislative supremacy. But Lincoln perished before a showdown took place. Both the constitutional relations of the two branches and party doctrine on the subject were now in a state of flux.

V

The Radicals and Reconstruction

If Republican leaders shared in the widespread grief over the sudden death
of Lincoln, they wasted no time in brooding. On the contrary, they began
to maneuver to gain the ear of his successor. When Andrew Johnson was
sworn in as President at 11:00 a.m. on April 15, radical Congressman
George W. Julian noted with dismay that the Blairs, General Halleck, and
old General Scott had been among the handful of witnesses.[1] Although
nobody discussed politics at the simple ceremony in Kirkwood House,
Julian feared the worst, and that afternoon he gathered together Chandler,
Wade, Covede of Pennsylvania, and other trusted radicals. Julian was
troubled by the profanity of his colleagues but saw nothing inappropriate
about their undisguised relief at being rid of Lincoln or their animosity
toward Seward, who lay between life and death as a result of the knife
wound inflicted by one of Booth's collaborators.[2] After their initial discussion, the radicals approached Johnson in the spirit of a fraternity rush
committee trying to keep a prospective pledge from joining a rival organization. They hastily commandeered the services of ex-Senator Preston
King, the only radical on close personal terms with the new President.
King arrived from New York twenty-four hours later and, to the relief of
his sponsors, was soon a member of Johnson's household and a regular
participant in cabinet meetings.[3] Simultaneously, the radicals launched a
drive to isolate the President from conservative influences. A sizable delegation called on him on Sunday morning and, having received a cordial
reception, sought additional interviews singly or in small groups. Chandler

cancelled an appointment to accompany Lincoln's body to Springfield so that he could apply pressure on Johnson, and his cohorts repeatedly postponed departure from Washington for the same reason.

The radicals sought first of all to secure additional representation in the cabinet, since they believed it would dominate the formulation of Reconstruction policy. Among the holdovers, the only one that the radicals could count on was the crafty Stanton, and common sense told them that it would be easier to reinforce the Secretary of War immediately than to undo cabinet decisions when Congress met in December. Presumably, the reorganization of the cabinet would also simplify the task of committing Johnson to Negro suffrage, the subject of greatest interest to the doctrinaire radicals. Sumner, for one, saw it as a cure-all for the ills arising out of the Civil War. Southern whites, he assumed, would respect the right of Negroes to vote, and the latter in their gratitude would support the Republican party for granting them suffrage. Thus, the new Republican organization in the South would become a large bi-racial party which would guarantee the party's ascendancy for a long period to come.

Aside from Chief Justice Chase, few prominent radicals shared Sumner's childlike faith in the capacity of the Negro to perceive his self-interest and to promote it through political action. One radical thought the freedman to be "as ignorant, debased, and totally unfit to exercise the duties of citizenship as any Irishman fresh from Donnybrook." [4] Even the realistic Stevens, who was one of the most outspoken champions of the Negro, feared that at the outset universal suffrage would simply enable Southern planters to vote their former slaves. He considered military occupation of the South an indispensable prerequisite to the establishment of Negro suffrage, and, since Northern opinion opposed army rule, he wanted to postpone the suffrage experiment. Another obstacle for the radicals was the prevalent notion that "nowhere this side of heaven will the Negro count for as much as the white." [5] Many people also feared that the indiscriminate extension of civil rights and the franchise would touch off a northward migration of Negroes. So some radicals felt obliged to conceal their views on the suffrage question until the electorate was in a more receptive frame of mind. Meanwhile, they continued to hope that the South would behave badly enough to generate sentiment for military occupation.

The less cautious radicals sought Negro suffrage through executive action, for then any adverse public reaction would be directed at Johnson instead of at them. It must have cost Wade, Chandler, and Sumner some distress to adopt this tactic, because a year earlier they had loudly claimed for Congress exclusive jurisdiction over Reconstruction. Yet, in supporting this position, less than two weeks after the death of Lincoln, Sumner dismissed as inconsequential any inquiries about the constitutional status of the rebel communities. Showing more elation than discretion, Sumner confided to a friend that the President might have the Southern states reorganized by autumn.[6]

The initial cordiality of the radicals toward Johnson was due to the tone of Presidential statements rather than to their content. At his first conference, Johnson had adroitly parried questions about policy with a plea that his previous record "be regarded as a guarantee for the future." [7] The following week ceremonial calls from various state delegations gave the President an opportunity to amplify his views. "Indulging in bad grammar, bad pronunciation, and much incoherency of thought," [8] he obliged with extravagant threats of retaliation against treasonable elements in the South. A few conservatives thought his observations in bad taste and feared a period of "bloody assizes," but the extremists regarded them as a pledge for a severe program of Reconstruction. Moderate elements, however, took heart when additional weeks elapsed without any specific implementation of these threats.

After a month of inactivity in the White House, the radicals began to insist more vehemently that Ben Butler be included in the cabinet and that Johnson make a clear commitment to Negro suffrage. Johnson showed sympathy for their viewpoint but deplored hasty action. Some radicals were now beginning to wonder about the President's good faith, but at a final caucus on May 12, Sumner and Wade reassured the doubters, whereupon most of them left for home. Seven months later, these same men returned to Washington violently opposed to the President and convinced that he had betrayed them by pardoning thousands of rebels and reorganizing the Southern states without any provision for Negro suffrage.

There will never be a completely satisfactory explanation of the shift in Johnson's attitude, but his subsequent behavior indicates that the President concealed his real beliefs during his first months in office. It was easy for him to do so, because Americans habitually ignore Vice Presidents. The only information readily available was in campaign leaflets which dwelt on Johnson's patriotism and courage as war governor of Tennessee. People with good memories also recalled that Johnson had been born six weeks before Lincoln, had waged an uphill battle against poverty and illiteracy, and had risen from a lowly tailor's bench through a series of state and national offices to the Vice Presidency. Politicians knew that Johnson was a War Democrat who had been chosen as Lincoln's running mate to balance the Union ticket, but the average Northerner either remained ignorant of this fact or dismissed it as a matter of no consequence. Johnson, however, was a Southerner, whose prewar speeches on the status of the Negro betrayed the customary prejudices of his section.[9] As a poor white from the mountainous area of eastern Tennessee, Johnson had nursed a deep and abiding hatred of the planter class. Indeed, he embraced emancipation only as a weapon for striking at this class. The Civil War intensified his bitterness, because eastern Tennessee remained loyal to the Union and the Confederacy retaliated by turning the region into a battleground. When federal troops later occupied Nashville and installed Johnson as war governor, the population of central Tennessee was openly hostile to him. It sabotaged his efforts to hold elections and broke up Union meetings. Johnson had a volatile temperament and was given to extreme statement under ordinary circumstances, and so he responded to the tense atmosphere in Nashville by wildly denouncing the secessionists. The radicals drew misleading conclusions from these inflammatory statements.

Whether or not Johnson consciously deceived the radicals, he was always more interested in giving an oration than implementing a policy. His frank and decisive manner disappeared as soon as he left the speaker's platform. Acutely aware of his educational deficiencies, he refused to expose himself to the direct exchange of the private interview or cabinet meeting. Instead, he would hear advisers or petitioners in silence, waiting patiently for them to lose momentum. A grave, judicial manner and an occasional sympathetic nod of the President's head left the average politician with the notion that Johnson agreed with him. No doubt the President stopped short of deliberate duplicity, but he must have been aware of the impression he created, for he avoided forthright decisions as long as possible. As one contemporary who observed him at close range put it: ". . . he always postponed action and was of an obstinate, suspicious temper. Like a badger, one had to dig him out of his hole; and he was ever in one except when on the hustings." [10]

Although Johnson's calculated silence was the basis for misunderstanding between him and the radicals, the latter had only themselves to blame for not giving proper attention to a comprehensive statement of Johnson's views on March 4, 1865, following his inauguration as Vice President. On that occasion he was outspoken, insisting that states possessed the sovereign power to do virtually anything except leave the Union. It was inconceivable that a man of such views would use federal power to impose Negro suffrage on the Southern states.

II

Even a President with Johnson's exceptional talents for procrastination could not avoid a stand on Reconstruction indefinitely. North Carolina had tried to withdraw from the Confederacy before it collapsed, and Lincoln had discussed the reorganization of the state government at his last cabinet meeting. Stanton pressed for a decision while the radicals were still in Washington. He proposed Negro suffrage for North Carolina on May 9, and the cabinet had a full-dress debate on the issue, with Johnson a silent bystander. Since his official advisers were evenly divided, Johnson bought time by turning the problem over to Preston King.[11]

In all fairness to the President, no solution would have satisfied all elements of the Union party. Some sort of political realignment seemed inevitable, because the party had completed the task for which it was created. The Republicans constituted the backbone of the Union party, a fact to which the Democrats had called attention repeatedly in the campaign of 1864. In the one-party states of New England and the upper Midwest, the Union label was nothing more than a camouflage for the local Republican organization, which continued to control all of the patronage and elective offices. Elsewhere some concessions had been made to Unionist elements outside the party, but the only states in which the Republicans had shared the substance of power were Ohio, Pennsylvania, and New Jersey. Except for Johnson himself, the only major office-holder in the Union party not previously affiliated with the Republicans was Governor John Brough of Ohio. By and large, War Democrats occupied humble positions in the Union organization. Thus, unless Johnson wished to become a President without a party, he had to frame a Reconstruction program broad enough to satisfy the bulk of the Republicans or identify himself with the regular Democrats. Johnson, however, thought he could satisfy both camps through a policy punitive enough to hold the conservative Republicans and mild enough to split the Democrats. He planned to extract from the rebel states a public recantation of their doctrine of secession and a pledge of compliance with the Emancipation Amendment. Once this had been done, he intended to restore them to full membership in the Union. Under the

Johnson plan, the problem of race relations would be left to the states to solve in their own way. Such an approach was bound to appeal to the War Democrats and to former Free-Soil Democrats in the Republican party like Preston King and the Blairs because it revived the theory of states' rights. Many conservative Republicans with Whig antecedents seemed likely to support the policy, if not the theory. Probably even some regular Democrats would back Johnson in order to avoid a more extreme policy, and so, the President thought, only the outspoken supporters of Negro suffrage would remain in opposition.

The initial response to the North Carolina Proclamation, which appeared May 30, 1865, gave Johnson every reason to be optimistic about isolating the radicals. The Proclamation had something for everybody except the proponents of Negro suffrage. The first part of it offered amnesty to the bulk of rebels, if they would take a prescribed oath of loyalty to the national government. High-ranking political and military officials of the Confederacy were excluded from amnesty, as in Lincoln's Louisiana Proclamation. In addition, Johnson excluded rebels with a taxable property of $20,000. The amnesty provisions satisfied most Northerners, who still believed that a wicked minority of aristocratic planters had misled a rank and file of deep-rooted Unionists. Some people were troubled by the fact that Johnson held out the prospect of pardon to those in the excluded categories, but not even the radicals cared to make an issue of the matter in view of the President's fierce hostility to traitors. The second part of the North Carolina Proclamation brought Johnson out into the open on the suffrage question, because it authorized the voters eligible in 1860 to elect delegates for a constitutional convention.

Although the radical high command was stunned by the North Carolina Proclamation, none of the critics rushed to oppose the President. For one thing, Johnson had emphasized that North Carolina was in a special category and he held out the hope that other rebel states would be handled differently.[12] The President also hinted that the constitutional convention in North Carolina would adopt Negro suffrage voluntarily—an inconceivable notion, in reality—but most radicals knew far less about the South than Johnson and felt obliged to wait for the verdict of the convention. Moreover, premature criticism would open them to the charge of splitting the Union party. Some radicals might have been willing to take the risk if Congress had been in session, but they were scattered throughout the country and unable to coalesce behind an alternate program.

Any lingering hopes for co-operation between Johnson and the proponents of Negro suffrage disappeared two weeks after the North Carolina Proclamation when he laid down the same terms for the reorganization of Mississippi. The gloom of the critics turned into open anger as identical proclamations for the remaining states appeared at regular intervals throughout the summer. The most indignant reaction came from Charles Sumner, who had subjected the President to long lectures on Negro rights and had mistaken silence for agreement. By early July the Massachusetts senator was writing everyone he knew, denouncing the President as a foe of Almighty God as well as the Negro.[13] He received a sympathetic response from Stevens who feared that the President would "be crowned king before Congress meets," [14] but the two friends of the Negro could not agree about what to do. Sumner wanted to organize a series of meetings to endorse Negro suffrage, a policy the more realistic Stevens vetoed as "heavy and premature." Recognizing the timidity of the public on the suffrage question, Stevens urged that the rebel states be reduced to a territorial condition where "they can be easily dealt with." [15]

As usual, Stevens was in closer touch with public opinion than Sumner. Few radicals cared to make an issue of Negro suffrage, and those who were to become the bitterest foes of the President professed satisfaction with his initial Reconstruction proclamations. Speaker Colfax urged trust in Johnson, "whose patriotism no one can doubt." [16] Secretary of Interior James Harlan of Iowa assured fellow radical Elihu Washburne that the President "is as firm as a rock and as inflexibly right on all the main points involved in the great struggle as the most ardent could desire." [17] The unpredictable Trumbull amazed Gideon Welles by proclaiming himself to be a Johnsonian.[18] Most significant of all were endorsements from Simon Cameron, John A. Logan, and Ben Butler, a trio of weathercocks who turned with every political breeze.[19] Butler apologized privately to Wade for keeping such strange company, but the astute general could not resist crowded bandwagons.[20]

Johnson's Reconstruction program owed much of its initial popularity to the belief that Southerners had seen the error of their ways and were prepared to co-operate. Since conservatives and radicals alike assumed that military victory had demonstrated the superiority of Northern values, they expected the vanquished to reach the same conclusion and to do justice to the Negro. Except for the Sumner-Julian wing of the Republican radicals, nobody was quite sure what justice involved. Negro suffrage seemed to be ruled out, unless the North insisted on a higher standard for the South than for its own people. Eventually Northern opinion would support the double standard, but in the summer of 1865 the rank and file demanded nothing more than the extension of civil rights to the Negro. What this meant to the North was that the system of white supremacy would be abandoned.

If Southerners had appeared contrite in the months after Appomattox, it was because they were dazed rather than hypocritical. Dissolved in self-pity, they showed little disposition to defend their values or anything else. This defeatist mood slowly disappeared while Johnson was reorganizing the rebel states. As their morale revived, Southerners began to behave like any national group in defeat. They devised rationalizations for military defeat which left intact the supposed superiority of their values. This attitude expressed itself negatively in obstruction of the Johnson program and positively in the formulation of new law codes designed to preserve the superior status of the whites.

By fall, President Johnson found it necessary to put pressure on the balky constitutional conventions of the Southern states. A few had to be prodded to repeal ordinances of secession; more had to be explicitly directed to abolish slavery and to repudiate any obligation for paying off the Confederate debt. Ultimately, Johnson secured compliance with his terms, but in the process Northerners learned that the allegedly loyal Southern masses were as defiant as the Confederate leaders who had been excluded from the constitutional conventions. Then Southern voters drove the point home by turning to their old leaders, irrespective of whether they had received a Presidential pardon. The Georgia legislature chose Alexander Stephens, the former Vice President of the Confederacy, for United States Senator. Not to be outdone, Mississippi and South Carolina selected a pair of rebel military commanders particularly obnoxious to the North. Simultaneously, Southern legislatures were preparing new civil codes, known as "the black codes," which made the Negro a second-class citizen. Admittedly, the former slaves posed a serious problem. They understood emancipation to mean freedom from work and roamed about the countryside in disorderly fashion. Left to their own devices, many Negroes would have died from exposure and starvation. So some regulation of their movements and behavior seemed inevitable. Unfortunately, the average Northerner concluded that the black codes were motivated by the South's desire to make the Negro harvest cotton rather than by any concern for his welfare. Provisions which levied stiff penalties on freedmen for breaking labor contracts drew the most criticism. Even Northerners with no particular interest in the Negro regarded such clauses as an insolent rebel scheme to sabotage the Thirteenth Amendment.

As the date for the opening of Congress approached, there was a growing disposition to blame Johnson for the recalcitrant attitude of Southerners. Some thought his soft policy had caused the trouble,[21] and others were disturbed by his liberal use of the pardoning power. After bristling against high Confederate officials in the spring, the President had gradually taken a more lenient view and had issued some 15,000 pardons to individual petitioners. This abrupt reversal of policy was partly due to the influence of Seward, who returned to active duty in midsummer.[22] Johnson's sympathy was also aroused by reports of suffering and privation in the region. Like many of the aristocratic Southerners, Johnson felt a chivalrous obligation to aid women in distress; and tearful wives exploited this susceptibility with moving pleas in behalf of unpardoned husbands. By autumn Johnson had begun to reflect more and more the attitudes of the typical Southerner.

There was no visible evidence that dissatisfaction over Reconstruction had advanced the cause of Negro suffrage. Voters in Ohio, Connecticut, and Wisconsin rejected Negro suffrage amendments to their respective state constitutions by decisive majorities. The returns were conclusive enough to silence most radicals, but the issue had been postponed rather than shelved. It was bound to revive as soon as the requisite number of state legislatures ratified the Thirteenth Amendment, because the abolition of slavery would change the basis for allotting representatives in Congress. Slaves had been counted as three-fifths of a person, while free Negroes would count as a full person, thereby increasing the representation of the South. With ratification certain by the end of 1865, Republican politicians faced a painful dilemma. As Sherman of Ohio noted, Negroes were not competent to vote, but somebody would benefit from their enlarged representation, whether they voted or not.[23] Like many of the trimmers, Sherman did not know what to do. He opposed both Negro suffrage and increased representation for the South, but, if forced to choose between the two, the irresolute Sherman was almost certain to regard Negro suffrage as the lesser evil. Along with a majority of his colleagues, Sherman hoped that a compromise formula could be devised. Meanwhile, it served Republican interests to postpone the readmission of representatives and senators from the Southern states.

Northern politicians could agree on this strategy, if on nothing else. The radicals were delighted, because they thought time was on their side. The Johnson supporters were unhappy about excluding the Southerners, but they were in a poor position to resist postponement, since the Administration had created widespread suspicion about the loyalty of every congressman elected under its supervision. It was feared that the Southerners, once seated, would block any additional measures of Reconstruction proposed by Congress. Even people ready for amnesty toward the South were reluctant to allow the region to participate in the formulation of terms for its own readmission to the Union. Northern opinion was so emphatic on this point that congressional leaders perfected a plan to exclude representatives from the eleven rebel states a month in advance of the session.[24] Nevertheless, the high command in the House hesitated to collide directly with Johnson and delivered the President a veiled but public warning through Speaker Colfax, who arrived in Washington on November 17. Speaking from his hotel balcony to a noisy crowd gathered by prearrangement, Colfax deplored the election of ex-Confederate generals to Congress as an insult to the President. Warming up to his subject, Colfax indignantly demanded legislation to protect the civil rights of the Negroes, without specifying what he had in mind. He concluded by demanding that Southerners be barred from participation in Reconstruction until a majority of them had demonstrated their loyalty.

The odd combination of bluster and vagueness in Colfax was a confession of weakness. It tacitly acknowledged the popularity of Johnson and the uncertainty of House leaders as to how far they could go in modifying the President's program. Several alternatives were open to Johnson. He could concede that his experiment in Reconstruction had not worked and retain the initiative by imposing additional requirements on the South before Congress assembled. Or he could stand by his basic policy while inviting suggestions from Congress on details. It was even conceivable that he could persuade the lawmakers to seat loyal Southerners immediately and thereby gain practical recognition of his provisional governments. Any of these tactics promised considerable dividends, because the radicals hesitated to split the Union party or drive the President over to the Democrats. Much as they distrusted Johnson, they feared everything would be lost if the congressional majority lost its cohesiveness. The situation invited negotiation, and the President was in a position to drive a hard bargain if he acted in a conciliatory manner.

Unfortunately for Johnson, he lost touch with reality precisely at the time that his critics began to apply pressure. Since midsummer he had nursed a grievance against the most active and outspoken radicals,[25] and, when moderates joined their movement to postpone the admission of Southerners, Johnson felt betrayed. His suspicious attitude was partly the result of physical exhaustion. He had struggled through the hot Washington summer without rest or recreation, piling countless interviews about pardons on top of the routine work of the Presidency. The impossible demands on his time had taken a cumulative toll of Johnson's good humor and flexibility. Members of the White House staff noticed the effect of persistent tension on him, which became so extreme that even the sound of laughter annoyed him.[26] Moreover, circumstances and his own personality deprived him of the partial relief which other Presidents gained by sharing their burdens. Mrs. Johnson was an invalid confined to an upstairs bedroom in the White House and shielded from the anxieties of her husband. Preston King, the only other person the President trusted, cracked under the political pressure and the summer heat of Washington. An autumn appointment as collector of the port of New York unhinged the ex-senator completely. For two months King brooded over his inadequacy and then committed suicide by leaping off a ferry in the middle of New York harbor.

With others Johnson remained distant and aloof. His manner discouraged a candid exchange of views, and he bottled up apprehensions which forthright discussion might have dispelled. The stream of congressmen who called on the President in the week before the opening of the December session were for the most part cordial. Yet, Johnson concluded that their obvious determination to delay the seating of Southern congressmen was the first stage of a gigantic plot to impose Negro suffrage on the South. Some legislators volunteered assurances to the contrary, but the President imagined that they were tools of Sumner and Julian sent to lull him into a false sense of security.

It is altogether possible that Johnson's feeling of isolation was necessary to him. His entire career had been devoted to single-handed combat against overwhelming odds. The youthful quest for an education and security, the lonely crusade for free homesteads, and bitter experience as a Unionist war governor in a strongly Confederate state were all part of the same pattern. For a man who seemed to thrive on fighting the world, Johnson's initial popularity as President must have made him uncomfortable and ill at ease. No single explanation can account for his disastrous course after December 1865, but Johnson behaved as if he found public support irksome and sought martyrdom. Within a year he managed to destroy the Union party, revive the Republican party which he mistrusted, and transfer control over Reconstruction to his worst enemies. Instinct drew him toward a collision which he could not have wanted on the basis of rational calculation.

III

The first phase of the critical struggle commenced with the opening of the 39th Congress in December 1865 and ended four months later with Johnson's veto of the Civil Rights bill. The drama started with exploratory sparring between Johnson and the radicals, but was quickly converted into an open battle between the executive and legislative branches of the government. Even the most astute President would have been forced to yield some of the swollen powers conferred on the chief executive during the Civil War. The stubbornness of Johnson drove Congress beyond its original objective of restoring the balance between the two branches into a drive for supremacy.

At the outset the focal point of opposition to Johnson was in the House, where the Union party had a majority of 107. The radicals enjoyed an influence out of proportion to their numbers because of their seniority and the complexity of House rules, which put newcomers at a disadvantage. Speaker Colfax was a radical at heart, but he was too timid to provide leadership against Johnson. That chore devolved on Thaddeus Stevens, who at seventy-three displayed an unrivaled parliamentary skill, fluency, and alertness. A clubbed foot, a wrinkled face, and an ill-fitting wig gave Stevens the appearance of a medieval court jester; and he possessed unconventional habits to match. The fact that he cut such a grotesque figure made his mastery of the House all the more remarkable. The secret of his success lay in an ironic eloquence. Few dared to tangle with Stevens in debate, and he alternately ridiculed and frightened challengers into submission. Time would show that there were limits to the influence of the iron-willed Lancaster lawyer, but he had an uncanny ability to bully members into positions that they did not really favor.

From almost every standpoint, Henry J. Raymond, who reluctantly acted as Administration spokesman in the House, was a pathetic contrast to Stevens. Although the editor of the *New York Times* doubled as national chairman of the Union party, he was a freshman representative and wholly ignorant of House rules. Raymond faced the added handicap of being a moderate in a period of controversy. He elevated the technique of compromise into a principle and was temperamentally incapable of believing that any differences were irreconcilable. Broad-mindedness drew him into such an erratic voting pattern that on one occasion Stevens scornfully predicted that Raymond would pair against himself. After one term in Congress, Raymond returned with relief to the *New York Times*.

Mindful of Johnson's popularity, Stevens adopted the strategy of subjecting the President to petty slights. He did so in the hope that wavering members of the Unionist majority who would bridle at an open attack on the Administration might be drawn into the radical camp by degrees and that Johnson might be goaded into attacking the needlers and so relieve them of the necessity for self-restraint. The campaign of harassment began at a House caucus on December 2, the day before Congress assembled. Stevens introduced a resolution authorizing the establishment of a joint committee to examine the qualifications of Southern members and to bar their admission to both Houses until the committee reported. This novel proposal was adopted in caucus without a dissenting vote and ratified by the House the next day. The bewildered Raymond watched the entire transaction in silence; it was all over before he grasped its significance. The radicals deliberately provoked Johnson by refusing to exempt the Tennessee members from the terms of the resolution, thus by implication casting doubt on Johnson's record as war governor and on the loyalty of his state. It also barred Horace Maynard, a congressman-elect from Johnson's home district of eastern Tennessee, whose loyalty to the Union was unquestioned. As an added pinprick, the House refrained from appointing a committee to make the customary call on the President.

The immediate response from the White House disappointed the radicals. Johnson passed over his opportunity to retaliate in his annual message. Conscious of his literary deficiencies, the President relied on a ghost writer, who produced a forceful document. In temperate language the President summarized his successive steps to reorganize the Southern states and expressed the belief that they were ready for admission. The conciliatory tone of the message averted the immediate collision which many congressmen had feared.[27]

The Senate promptly postponed action on the Stevens resolution for one week. Shortly thereafter, the Union party caucus removed a source of friction by converting the measure from a joint resolution, which required Johnson's signature, into a concurrent resolution, which did not. The caucus also rebuked Stevens by refusing to bar Southern senators-elect until the joint committee reported, and by naming only one radical, Jacob Howard of Michigan, to the joint committee. Moreover, the chairmanship went to the moderate Fessenden of Maine, who was a personal foe of Sumner. These adjustments, which barely cleared the Senate caucus by the vote of 16 to 14, represented a compromise rather than a wholehearted commitment to the President. Besides, the Senate, like the House, refused any Southerners immediate admission. Plainly, Johnson was being put on his good behavior.

The House continued to harass the President.[28] Congressmen-elect who had been notorious rebels appeared at the Capitol, and Stevens indulgently set aside two weeks for his colleagues to attack them. Indignant speakers inveighed against the admission of traitors "direct from the field of battle, with fresh blood upon their hands, with the odor of Florence and Andersonville prisons upon their garments. . . ." [29] Until this time the only publicized statement Stevens had made on Reconstruction was in September at Lancaster, when he had ignored Negro suffrage but had proposed enough other radical measures to keep Congress busy for several years. On December 18, however, he interrupted the orators long enough to raise the suffrage question again. He pointed out that, if Negroes were counted for purposes of representation, the South would be entitled to 83 members instead of 46. Stevens dryly declined to reward the rebels in this striking fashion or admit their representatives until Negroes were provided with land, civil rights, and the franchise. With logic and bitterness, he pointed out that the vote would not do the Negro much good unless he first received education and property. Few of his colleagues recoiled from the proposition of barring the Southerners until Reconstruction legislation had been completed, but they were still unready to accept the familiar Stevens thesis that the South was conquered territory. Raymond intended to reply for the Administration, but before he could speak, Finck of Ohio —a Vallandigham Democrat—spoke in defense of the President. It was the worst possible misfortune for Johnson to receive praise from a Northern Copperhead. In fact, one Union party member confessed that he felt the way "members of a Christian church do when Sabbath breakers, whore masters, and gamblers praise their preacher." [30]

On January 8 Stevens returned to the attack by mobilizing a big majority behind the Williams Resolution, which put the House on record against any withdrawal of troops from the South. The next day he called up with mock gravity another resolution expressing confidence in the President and had it referred to the committee on Reconstruction by a vote of 107 to 32. Only Raymond and one other member of the Union party voted against the insulting maneuver. Once again, the Democrats damned Johnson by providing the bulk of the votes in his behalf. The very next day Stevens called a caucus to consider Negro suffrage in the District of Columbia. He cared little about the measure, but rightly regarded it as a proposal that would aggravate the paranoid fears of the President. A temporary rebellion of freshman members "against the despotism of committees" reduced the scope of the suffrage bill, but after a fierce tantrum by Stevens the caucus restored the original version.[31] Then the entire bill cleared the House with votes to spare. The President resisted his impulse to make a direct comment on the suffrage bill, but in an interview with Senator Dixon of Connecticut, which appeared in the *New York Herald,* he took exception to the suffrage bill and the craze for constitutional amendments. The same afternoon Stevens read the *Herald* article into the record and accused Johnson of behaving like a British king. Then he rammed through the House by a vote of 120 to 46 his proposed constitutional amendment reducing the representation of Southern states that excluded the Negro from voting.

Although none of these maneuvers produced a direct confrontation between the House and Johnson, Stevens was in no hurry to do so. But the Senate, on the other hand, moved to act promptly on Reconstruction legislation. Since moderate counsels prevailed in the Upper House, the initiative passed to Fessenden of Maine and Trumbull of Illinois. Neither placed much faith in Negro suffrage as a device for helping the freedman or promoting the dominance of the Union party in the South. Trumbull dismissed the idea sarcastically as "the most sovereign remedy . . . since the days of Townsend's Sasparilla." [32] Fessenden clung to the traditional view that the franchise was a privilege rather than a right and that it should be restricted to the literate. He showed far more concern about the establishment of uniform voting regulations than universal suffrage. His attitude infuriated radicals like Howard, who wanted Negro suffrage in the South, irrespective of what "the Northern people may do to their own blacks." [33] In January most Unionist senators agreed with Fessenden and helped him to shelve the House bill for Negro suffrage in the District of Columbia.

Simultaneously, Trumbull was drafting Reconstruction bills with a haste motivated in part by a competitive instinct. As chairman of the Senate judiciary committee, he had been irked by the creation of a joint committee to handle problems normally under his jurisdiction, and he wanted to complete the Reconstruction bills while his rivals were still arguing. The only way Trumbull could do so would be to avoid introducing constitutional amendments. He prepared two companion measures, one extending the life of the Freedmen's Bureau for a year, so that the Negro would be adequately protected during the transition from war to peace, and the second permanently guaranteeing civil rights by the federal government.

Of the two, the Freedmen's Bureau bill was the least controversial. The Bureau had been established in 1865 to help care for Negro refugees who converged on Union army camps in uncontrollable numbers. Unavoidably, its first year's work had been largely concerned with providing food and shelter to helpless blacks. The Bureau had also begun to educate Negroes and had supervised their contractual arrangements with whites. Popular in the North, the Bureau met opposition in the South, where the people resented any outside interference in race relations. The Trumbull extension bill continued the existing functions of the Bureau for a year and also provided for Bureau courts to handle litigation in cases involving the civil rights of Negroes.

The supplementary Civil Rights bill was intended to protect Negro rights after the termination of the military occupation and the Bureau courts. Hence, the first section of the Civil Rights bill defined federal citizenship in terms broad enough to include the Negro and enumerated the same list of rights that appeared in the seventh section of the Bureau bill. The sardonic humor of Trumbull was evident in his provision for enforcing Negro rights with the same machinery that had been used to return fugitive slaves. No Civil Rights bill would have been satisfactory to the South, but the Trumbull bill startled a number of Unionist senators, for it seemed to embody a revolutionary concept of citizenship. Hitherto Americans had derived the bulk of their civil rights from state rather than federal citizenship, and the Illinois senator was proposing that the national

government operate in a vast new area without the formality of a constitutional amendment. People intent on protecting the Negro hesitated over
the Trumbull bill for fear of establishing a precedent which would permit
expansion of national power at other points. As usual, Trumbull made the
most out of a dubious legal position. He silenced critics of the citizenship
clause in the Bureau bill by insisting that it was a temporary measure
authorized under the war power. When they renewed their attack on the
same provision of the Civil Rights bill, he countered with the ingenious
argument that the Thirteenth Amendment not only abolished slavery but
empowered Congress to protect Negro rights. The radicals made more
trouble for Trumbull than senators who doubted the constitutionality of the
Civil Rights bill. They insisted that the citizenship clause covered all rights
including the franchise. Sumner promptly argued that any legislation extending human freedom was constitutional. He may have been wholly sincere in his opinion, but some radicals echoed him in the hope that the
suspicious Johnson would be convinced that civil rights legislation meant
Negro suffrage and so would veto the bill.

While the two Reconstruction bills moved through Congress, Fessenden
was struggling to win the confidence of Johnson. On January 14 the Maine
senator despaired "of keeping peace between the President and those who
wish to quarrel with him." [34] Two weeks later, he still hoped to make
"our friends go to the President's levees so as to have somebody about him
besides Democrats and secessionists." [35] It was difficult for Johnson to see
that if he did not accept the moderate program being offered, Congress
would pass more extreme measures. The discourteous gestures of the
House toward the President had undermined his ability to distinguish between radicals and constructive critics of his policy. On his side, Fessenden
defended his party's policies and also supported congressional prerogatives, thus making an understanding with Johnson next to impossible. The
one wholesome feature of the discussions was that the President found it
impossible to equivocate with the forthright Fessenden. In interviews with
Trumbull and other moderates, Johnson paved the way for subsequent
bitterness by appearing to acquiesce in their program. Trumbull reached
the conclusion that Johnson would sign both bills at about the same time
the President decided that they were really sponsored by the radicals.[36]

Stevens, who had stopped calling at the White House, was better informed as to the President's state of mind than the moderates were. The
astute leader of the House expedited passage of the Trumbull bills, which

he disliked, in order to promote a breach between Johnson and the peacemakers in the Senate. On February 9 the Freedmen's Bureau bill reached
the White House, where it encountered a sharply divided cabinet. The
President was determined to veto the bill, and he received six versions of
a veto message, including a very mild one from Seward.[37] Although rumors
about Johnson's attitude circulated freely on Capitol Hill, Stevens left nothing to chance. With diabolical cleverness, he injected the sensitive Tennessee issue into the controversy. On February 15, a three-man subcommittee
had proposed to the joint committee that Tennessee was entitled to admission, and Stevens sought a postponement by moving that the issue be
referred to a new subcommittee. Ironically, it was Fessenden who held the
deciding vote for postponement in the evenly divided committee. He
made the fateful decision to line up with Stevens and block the admission
of Tennessee. Why Fessenden chose to defy the President is a matter of
conjecture.[38] Although conciliatory in his gestures in this acrimonious
period, Fessenden was still a partisan with all the prejudices of his section.
He had lost a son in the Civil War, and, although he lacked the vindictiveness of Sumner and Stevens, he did believe that the South ought to pay
more for its defiant behavior than did the President. Besides, Fessenden
was an irritable man under the best of circumstances, and it would have
required a superhuman restraint to continue absorbing blows from both
the radicals and Johnson. Probably he had concluded that a sharp rebuke
would clear the air and convince Johnson that it was necessary to co-
operate with Congress.

The effect on Johnson of Fessenden's action can be imagined, for it had
been Fessenden who had repeatedly assured him that the moderates wanted
to co-operate with him. The radicals only made matters worse by hinting
to the President that Tennessee would be admitted promptly if he signed
the Bureau bill.[39] Johnson's answer came on February 19, when he pieced
together an outspoken version of the veto messages. Most of his arguments against the constitutionality of the Bureau bill echoed points raised
earlier in Congress. The last paragraph, however, made it plain that Johnson was smarting over Tennessee. He accused Congress of unconstitutional behavior in excluding the representatives of eleven states from a
voice in legislation affecting their interests and professed ignorance of any
reason for excluding Tennessee. The message also contained veiled expressions of hostility to legislation affecting race relations.

The House promptly overrode the veto and repassed the resolution denying seats to all Southern representatives until the joint committee declared them entitled to admission. Matters took a different turn in the Senate, despite the fact that it had originally passed the Bureau bill by more than a two-thirds margin. Five Unionist senators reversed themselves, and three who had been absent for the initial roll call also supported the President, with the result that the veto was sustained 17–30. The Senate majority was anxious to retaliate by approving the House resolution on Southern representation, but before taking action adjourned for Washington's Birthday. The evening of the holiday, a noisy crowd of Johnson sympathizers gathered on the White House lawn. Senator James R. Doolittle of Wisconsin, foreseeing the impromptu celebration, had warned Johnson against making an extemporaneous speech.[40] Unfortunately, Johnson could not resist the habits of a lifetime, nor could he be convinced that the vituperative stump speech of the Tennessee hills was inappropriate in Washington. So he told the crowd that the joint committee was an "irresponsible central directory" which had assumed nearly all the powers of government, and that it would be necessary for him to fight Northern foes of the Union as vigorously as he had fought Southern traitors. When the crowd shouted for names, Johnson designated Stevens, Sumner, Wendell Phillips, and Forney as Northern traitors. Johnson's words may now seem flat and dry in print, but they were inflammatory to his contemporaries. Some read the speech with "much pain" and thought the President was drunk.[41] Others felt "sadness and humiliation" over the denunciation of patriots.[42] Many more foresaw the end of the Union party and feared that the fruits of victory would be thrown away.[43] Fair-minded Unionists recognized that the fault was not all on one side. Both Dawes of Massachusetts and Henry B. Harrison of Connecticut agreed that the radicals had first goaded the President into behaving badly, and then pointed to his conduct as a justification for their attitude.[44] Nevertheless, the immediate aftermath of the veto was an intensification of hostility to the President.

By emphasizing the unconstitutional behavior of the lawmakers in his message, Johnson enabled the radicals to unite all shades of opinion in defense of congressional prerogatives. Fessenden, Trumbull, and the moderates took up the new issue and threw their weight behind a demonstration of legislative *esprit de corps*. The Unionist caucus in the Senate reversed its stand of December and adopted the House resolution barring the admission of Southern members until the joint committee acted affirmatively on their qualifications. Fessenden justified his new position in a long speech. He asserted that Congress would exercise "the most full and plenary jurisdiction" over Reconstruction, but he also expressed kind feelings for Johnson by saying that disappointment over Tennessee had driven the President further than he intended to go. The House showed no such charity or restraint. Henceforth, Johnson's messages were laid aside unread, and members jeered whenever his name was mentioned. Moderate sentiment had never been very articulate in the House, and it disappeared altogther in the intimidating atmosphere which prevailed. Within a month Dawes, who had blamed the radicals for the split over the Bureau bill, was complaining that the behavior of the President deprived moderates of all excuse for supporting him.[45] The cautious Sherman felt the same way, gloomily reporting that Johnson was "suspicious of everyone." [46]

Nevertheless, when the Civil Rights bill reached the White House at the end of March, it was clear that the country thought more of Johnson than Congress did. Local politicians dreaded a complete break between the President and Congress, lest it disrupt the flow of patronage.[47] A number of national leaders also had second thoughts about pushing Johnson too far, especially after the Senate had failed to pass the Stevens suffrage amendment. The resolutions of scattered state conventions warned the congressional majority to show self-restraint. On March 29, Oregon Unionists took a vague position on Reconstruction, deplored discord, and conceded that loyal men "may honestly differ." [48] A similar straddle was made by the Connecticut Unionist convention in preparation for the crucial gubernatorial election in April. Ohio had elected a Unionist governor in October of 1865 committed to racial segregation, and one prominent party worker reminded a Unionist senator five months later that "we have not gotten full of religion on the subject" of Negro suffrage.[49] Butler and Logan considered the political weather to be too uncertain for the inflammatory stump speeches at which they excelled, and even Greeley spoke well of the President, although he had written an editorial deploring the veto of the Bureau bill.

Although Johnson was known to regard the Civil Rights bill as unconstitutional, many who agreed with him urged him to sign it on the ground of expediency. Governor Jacob D. Cox of Ohio reminded the President that the prevailing mood in the West was "to be pleased with everything which looks like severity." [50] Cox tried to sweeten his recommendation by dwelling on the difficulty of enforcing civil rights. In a dramatic interview, Governor Oliver P. Morton of Indiana told the President that a veto would end their political friendship.[51] Fessenden also called at the White House and pleaded with Johnson to avoid a step that would isolate him from the party.[52] All this pressure, however, was to no avail. Johnson had repeatedly defied party discipline without hindering his political advancement in Tennessee, and he expected to do the same in Washington. He also felt, as Democratic party Presidents both before and after him, that he represented the people more faithfully than Congress.

At the end of March the President vetoed the Civil Rights bill. The House did not even bother to debate the veto but overrode it the same day. The Senate postponed action over the weekend, while Fessenden made a grim effort to muster the necessary two-thirds vote. His partisan instincts were now fully aroused, and he launched a complicated series of maneuvers which unseated one Democratic senator from New Jersey and prevented the other one from voting. Neither act was to Fessenden's credit, and under ordinary circumstances the enthusiastic co-operation of Sumner and Wade would have been enough to make the Maine senator reconsider. The radicals also put pressure on doubtful members like Stewart of Nevada and Morgan of New York.

The ensuing roll call was dramatic, and the outcome remained uncertain until the clerk reached Morgan's name. When the New Yorker voted to override the veto, the galleries burst into wild applause. Another demonstration took place at the end of the roll call "with a terrible rejoicing, waving of handkerchiefs, and clapping of hands. . . ."[53] Only three Unionist senators had stuck with the President, although the ailing Dixon had made arrangements to be carried to the chamber if his vote would change the outcome.

IV

The only real victors in the civil rights controversy were the radicals. Johnson lost most of his remaining support from Union party state organizations and party newspapers, while the moderates lost their opportunity to guide Reconstruction. Fessenden expressed relief because the long weeks of suspense were over, but he felt bitter toward Johnson for splitting the party, and he foresaw only "a long, wearisome struggle."[54] Trumbull reacted with the cold fury of a man who felt he had been deliberately misled by the President,[55] and Stewart of Nevada never spoke to Johnson again. A few moderates tried to believe that the veto would clear the air.

They took comfort from a cordial encounter between Johnson and Stevens at General Grant's reception on April 8,[56] but optimism evaporated as soon as Congress resumed work on Reconstruction.

The severance of relations between Johnson and the Unionist leaders in the Senate reactivated the joint committee, which had not met since the Senate rejected the Stevens amendment. Negro suffrage was still the most divisive question. The radical members of the joint committee would have liked to establish it by constitutional amendment, but the narrow victory of the Unionist gubernatorial candidate in Connecticut indicated that it was not likely to be a suitable issue for the campaign of 1866. Moreover, Northern opinion still resisted the idea of imposing Negro suffrage on the South through military rule. So the joint committee painstakingly devised a package amendment that would include a federal guarantee of citizenship, penalties against conspicuous rebels, and reduced representation for Southern states. Like most compromises, the proposed Fourteenth Amendment aroused no enthusiasm. The joint committee also recommended adoption of an enabling act to authorize the admission of Southern states that ratified the amendment. In justifying the amendment constitutionally, the committee formulated the nebulous theory that the Southern communities were states for the purpose of ratifying the Fourteenth Amendment but not for other purposes. In so doing, the committee gave birth to a new political institution: the state "in suspended animation" which had "forfeited" its rights. As a campaign slogan "the forfeited rights" theory was to do good service for Unionists with different views about the status of the Southern states, but it did not smooth the path of the amendment through Congress.

The House debated the measure first. The principal target of the critics was the third section, which disfranchised supporters of the Confederacy until 1870. Garfield thought it had been designed to make the South "a vast camp for four more years," and Raymond insinuated that its authors wanted to goad the South into rejecting the whole amendment.[57] But Stevens thought the third section to be the only one worth defending, and so he rammed it through the House. The Senate substituted a milder provision disqualifying participants in the rebellion from national office but authorizing the removal of the disqualification by a two-thirds vote of both Houses. The advocates of Negro suffrage in the Senate fought furiously but unsuccessfully to revive the provision from the old Stevens amendment, which reduced the representation of states denying the vote to freedmen. But Howard struck at the heart of the matter when he dryly informed his fellow idealists among the radicals that the real question was "what could be ratified"; Negro suffrage was "impractical for the present." [58] The urgent need for campaign issues produced an unprecedented display of solidarity in the Senate. Even Sumner bowed to the caucus decision, and the amendment secured the necessary two-thirds vote without a Negro suffrage provision.

When the revised Fourteenth Amendment went back to the House, Stevens fumed over the weakening of the third section. In retaliation he introduced a bill to establish military government in the South. There were limits, however, to what the House members would do to please Stevens in defiance of their own constituents, and so the bill was tabled. Then the House accepted Senate modifications of the Fourteenth Amendment in mid-June. The ambiguity of the final version foreshadowed a century of controversy over the meaning of the "due process" clause and other provisions, but most party leaders were thinking of 1866 rather than of posterity. With good reason James Gordon Bennett called the Fourteenth Amendment a campaign document of the anti-Johnson faction in the Union party.[59]

The chief casualty was the enabling act, which would have pledged definite admission to states ratifying the Fourteenth Amendment. Stevens had never liked it in the first place, and the Senate leaders reluctantly sacrificed it to secure the support of Sumner and the Negro suffrage bloc for the Fourteenth Amendment.[60] Tennessee helped the radicals to bury it without political risk by ratifying the Fourteenth Amendment on July 19. When Stevens promptly rushed an admission resolution through Congress admitting Tennessee, the impression was left that other Southern states would receive identical treatment upon ratification.

Countermoves by Johnson kept Congress in session an extra month. In line with his intention of remodeling the Union party, Johnson made plans for a midsummer convention. He also threatened to fire office-holders loyal to Congress. There was little that the legislators could do beyond creating congressional campaign committees to take their case to the country. The radicals answered him, though, by demanding that Congress remain in session all summer to watch the President. At a caucus on July 12 George S. Boutwell of Massachusetts and William D. (Pig Iron) Kelley of Pennsylvania charged that Johnson was planning to turn the government over to the rebels. Dawes of Massachusetts, who retained his sanity, was aghast at the proceedings and compared them to "the wild roaring of the Girondists before the French Revolution." [61] Finally, a second caucus agreed to an adjournment at the end of the month, but the antagonism to the President was still so explosive that the timid Banks of Massachusetts expected the rebels to take over Washington as soon as his colleagues departed.[62]

During the ensuing congressional campaign that fall, the number of Johnson's enemies multiplied with each successive act of his. On June 11 the President had called a conference to determine ways to wrest control of the Union party from the Republicans who opposed him, and he had pledged his entire savings of $20,000 to that end.[63] He would have preferred a simple test between his own Reconstruction plan and the Fourteenth Amendment, but he dropped the idea to win the support of Henry J. Raymond, the chairman of the Union party national committee, who had reluctantly supported Congress's program. In return, Raymond had agreed to issue a call for a Union party convention at Philadelphia on August 13.

Johnson's actions prompted Attorney General Joshua F. Speed, Secretary of Interior James Harlan, and Postmaster General William Dennison not only to resign from the Administration but also to attack the President. Stanton ought to have followed their example, inasmuch as he had lost all sympathy with the Administration. Unfortunately for the President, Stanton's concept of loyalty had not changed greatly since the days when he had peddled secrets to the Republicans as a member of Buchanan's cabinet. So the Secretary of War stayed at his post and used his vast influence in the Freedmen's Bureau and the army to undermine his chief. If Stanton was treacherous, Johnson was foolish, for he had been warned repeatedly about the disloyalty of his Secretary of War. The cabinet replacements chosen by the President brought him little political support, for they were either fossil Whigs or conservative Democrats without any following worthy of the name.

At the lower levels of the Administration, Johnson intended to fire rebellious job-holders who would not resign voluntarily. This policy was easier to announce than to implement. It proved physically impossible for Johnson to oust postmasters and customs officials rapidly enough to affect the fall elections.[64] The selection of suitable replacements turned out to be almost as much of a problem. Neither Democrats nor radicals were eligible, and the President discovered to his dismay that practically all Republicans of standing sided with Congress. It became almost impossible for him to find respectable candidates who would contest incumbent Unionist candidates. The utter futility of Johnson's bid for control of the Union party organization was not apparent until after the Philadelphia convention, but long before it signs of trouble had appeared.

Aside from the difficulty of ousting Republican office-holders who had survived the Union party movement of the Civil War years, Johnson faced a rebellion of Northern voters. The noisy support of the Northern Democrats hurt his cause, particularly when they showed up at the Philadelphia convention in large numbers. Vallandigham and other notorious Peace Democrats were barred, but the participation of Southern Democrats more than cancelled the effect of this gesture. The Johnson managers had invited the Southerners in order to demonstrate the national character of the President's following. A year earlier the tactic might have succeeded. In the summer of 1866 it simply outraged Northern opinion and lent substance to the radical charge that Johnson drew his support from rebels and traitors. The Johnson faction fanned the flames of resentment by then calling an ex-servicemen's convention at Cleveland. Top-heavy with Democratic generals, both Union and Confederate, it also received telegrams of support from several Confederate generals who were known for their mistreatment of Northern prisoners.

The anti-Johnson faction replied by calling a rump session of the national committee, which ousted Raymond and authorized his successor to issue a convention call. Although the backbone of the anti-Johnson faction was Republican, this name continued to be unpopular except in strongly radical communities. So the rump organization called itself the Union-Republican party. It called Northern and Southern "loyalists" together at Philadelphia on September 3 and promoted a soldiers and sailors convention at Pittsburgh on September 24.

Actually, the fate of the Johnson movement was settled at dozens of district conventions rather than at the large ceremonial gatherings. Irrespective of whether they called themselves Unionists, Unionist-Republicans, or Republicans, the delegates to the district conventions renominated the congressmen who had opposed the President. As it became evident that old-line Republicans were in control of the party machinery, the President made frantic, last-minute efforts to effect fusion between his handful of followers and the Democrats. Something might have been salvaged by this policy if Democratic office-seekers had been willing to step aside for War Democrats, fossil Whigs, and the sprinkling of conservative Republicans in the President's camp. The regular Democratic organizations, however, were singularly unco-operative. They had received no patronage for supporting Johnson's policy and saw no reason to run candidates who had abused the Democratic party during the war. On the contrary, they hoped to benefit by the split in the Union party to win the off-year elections. There was no rational basis for the optimism of the Democrats, but in convention after convention they spurned the Johnsonites and nominated candidates with debatable war records. Fusion collapsed completely in mid-September, when the New York Democrats passed over the distinguished Union general and former Barnburner, John A. Dix, and gave the gubernatorial nomination to an obscure Tammany politician from the peace faction of the party. It was the last straw for unhappy moderates like Henry J. Raymond. Confronted with the choice of voting for a radical Republican or a Peace Democrat, Raymond abandoned the crumbling Union party on September 15 and announced that he would vote the straight Republican ticket. Thus, six weeks before the election, Johnson was a man without a party. The President still clutched the Unionist banner tightly, but the rank and file had deserted to either the Democrats or Republicans, thereby restoring a genuine two-party system for the first time since 1854.

Hopeless as his situation was, Johnson refused to accept the popular verdict registered by the political conventions. In early September he converted a nonpolitical trip to Chicago into an extended speaking tour, swinging as far north as Albany and as far west as St. Louis. His handicaps were insurmountable. Nothing he might say could undo the effect of local conventions or produce a new set of congressional candidates. His intention, moreover, was to campaign against Negro suffrage, and he lacked any documentary evidence that his opponents favored it. Congress stood officially on the Fourteenth Amendment, which made no reference to the subject. Under the circumstances, Johnson's best course seemed to be in short prepared speeches, but unfortunately hecklers frequently goaded him into extemporaneous statements and verbal exchanges. His language was not below the customary level of the period and was considerably better than the standard prevailing in his own section of Tennessee. But his slashing attacks on Congress and his promise to remove radical appointees from their jobs produced a violent reaction in the President's critics. Many thought his conduct did not suit the dignity expected of a President. Sherman of Ohio branded his speeches as typical of a grog-house performance,[65] and Secretary of the Treasury Hugh McCulloch conceded that they "were in the worst possible taste." [66] Johnson's tour may not have greatly affected the outcome of the elections, but his extemporaneous tirades provided radicals with material for subsequent attempts to impeach him. At the time, they contented themselves with characterizing him alternately as Judas Iscariot, a filthy demagogue, and a drunken tailor. The radical platform in Kansas struck the dominant note when it accused the President of making treason a virtue and loyalty a crime.[67] Nobody could doubt the effectiveness of these denunciations when three such dedicated students of public opinion as Logan, Butler, and Cameron broke a long silence in late summer to join the chorus of Johnson's detractors.

V

The election in November 1866 returned practically all the old congressmen opponents of Johnson to office, plus Butler of Massachusetts and Logan of Illinois. Radical legislatures were also elected in most Northern states, which in turn forced the retirement of several moderates from the Senate. By campaigning as patriots pledged to preserve the fruits of the victory, the Republicans had swallowed up the War Democrats and other splinter groups from the old Union party coalition. In the process, the center of gravity in the party shifted to the left because the radicals were the element most closely identified with that policy.

The effect of the election became apparent the moment the 39th Congress convened for the lame duck session in December 1866. Dawes reported radicalism "terribly intensified" and extremist measures "the most popular." [68] The House consented to the reading of Johnson's annual message only after a series of close votes, and the Senate repudiated the leadership of Fessenden and the moderates by taking Reconstruction legislation out of the hands of his joint committee, which met only twice during the session. From the outset, both branches operated on the theory that the country had no President and that Congress would have to perform his functions. Recommendations and messages from the White House were ignored, while legislation was shaped with complete indifference to the possibility of a veto. As Sumner put it: "The present incumbent is a nullity and will be treated as such." [69]

For nearly a month Congress waited to see whether Southern legislatures would ratify the Fourteenth Amendment. Nobody expected affirmative action, but the radical leadership wanted to be in a position to say that ratification would have assured readmission.[70] The South did not disappoint the radicals. All ten states rejected the amendment—some unanimously. Their principal objection was to section three, which disqualified rebels from holding office. The attitude of the North Carolina legislature was typical. The members announced that they would entrust the state to the mercy of Congress before they would turn it over to the few Southerners with Northern sympathies who could qualify for office. Meanwhile, the latter descended on Washington with forecasts of violence. They expressed apprehension over their personal safety and a kindred concern for the welfare of the Negro. They also denied that Johnson governments were capable of protecting life and property. These pleas put Congress in the frame of mind to pass a military bill. When Stevens could not get sufficient House support for his scheme to divide Southern plantations among the Negroes, he retaliated by turning back the proposals of Blaine, Raymond, and others for a terminal date on military occupation. The Senate irritated Stevens by converting the military bill into a Reconstruction measure. It imposed upon military commanders the obligation to convene constitutional conventions in the Southern states and supervise the establishment of new governments. In the Senate, after a fierce debate, Sumner persuaded his colleagues to adopt a provision for manhood suffrage. Stevens disliked the enfranchisement of the Negro unless it was coupled with the disfranchisement of Southern whites, because he feared that the planters would control the vote of their former slaves.[71] But he acquiesced temporarily in the Senate amendments, since Congress had at last acted on his theory that Southerners possessed no constitutional rights.

Although public attention was focused on the Reconstruction Act, which cleared Congress just before the end of the short session, the radicals initiated other measures, too. The bill for Negro suffrage in the District of Columbia was pulled out of its pigeonhole by the Senate and passed. The radicals also worked through Congress a Tenure of Office Act, designed to safeguard office-holders against ouster by the President. In an obvious effort to protect Stanton, cabinet members as well as lesser officials were included. This provision introduced the novel doctrine that the President could be deprived of control over the major officials who were supposed to help him execute the laws. Few congressmen had the courage to vote against the coverage of cabinet officials, but they had enough scruples to put the provision in ambiguous form and qualify its usefulness. The Republicans possessed the two-thirds majority necessary to override, and in the party caucus in both houses discipline was enforced with an iron hand.

Those who favored the impeachment of Johnson were busily at work. James M. Ashley of Ohio and Benjamin F. Loan of Missouri pushed a resolution through the House authorizing the joint committee to investigate whether Johnson had been "guilty of acts . . . designed or calculated to overthrow" the government of the United States. This move was based on the hope that some evidence of treasonable intentions could be found by probing Johnson's excessive use of the pardoning power. Ben Wade had the most to gain by impeachment, because he expected to become president pro tem of the Senate, which would put him in line to succeed Johnson. Since Wade also recognized that it would be more difficult to get a two-thirds vote for Johnson's impeachment than for radical legislation, he called up and secured passage of a Nebraska statehood bill, which added two more Republican senators. Wade was not cynical enough to avow publicly the purpose of the bill, but nobody missed the fact that there were now five more Republicans in the Senate than the two-thirds necessary to convict the President.

Some radicals would have been disposed to halt legislation until the new Congress met in December 1867, but their leaders had no intention of allowing the White House to regain the initiative. They pushed through a measure empowering the 40th Congress to convene as soon as the 39th expired on March 4, and interrupted their work only long enough to swear in new members and to fill vacant committee posts. As expected, the radicals selected Wade to replace Lafayette Foster of Connecticut, the retiring president pro tem of the Senate. They also showed their teeth by abolishing the joint committee, which would have been a poor instrument for pushing impeachment with Fessenden as chairman. The aggressive Butler proposed the creation of a special impeachment committee under his chairmanship; and, although Stevens favored the scheme, the House refused to confer such a choice assignment on a new member. The problem passed instead to the judiciary committee, headed by James F. Wilson of Iowa. It proved easier to rebuke Butler, however, than to silence him. The crafty freshman representative from Massachusetts watched while the judiciary committee made an ineffective effort to implicate Johnson in the release of Jefferson Davis. Then Butler renewed his demand for a special committee and succeeded on July 8, 1867; the impeachers searched all summer for evidence against Johnson.

Once the 40th Congress had completed its reorganization, Stevens renewed his drive for a Reconstruction bill that would disfranchise the bulk of the Southern whites. It soon became apparent that he no longer possessed the vitality to push it through single-handedly. Occasional flashes of masterful leadership were interrupted by longer periods of inactivity, brought about by his declining health. With the help of Boutwell and Butler, however, he pushed through a second Reconstruction Act in late spring. It disfranchised most of the former rebels, under the guise of prescribing conditions for the reorganization of the Southern states, but the Senate had softened the measure so that the President was left with some discretionary authority over the military authorities who registered voters. When Johnson attempted to use his power, Congress countered with a third Reconstruction Act on July 12 which disfranchised all but a handful of whites. This act climaxed the long fight of the radicals to establish Republican supremacy in the South. With organizers from the Union League clubs and the Freedmen's Bureau to instruct the Negro about his obligations as a voter, the reconstructed governments passed quickly to the control of Northern Carpetbaggers and their local collaborators.

It is doubtful whether Congress could have devised any program satisfactory to the mass of Southern whites except one of nonintervention in Southern institutional life. The former rebels were more determined than ever to maintain their national values, including white supremacy. They had acquiesced in a new legal status for the Negro but had no intention whatever of tolerating a change in his social or economic position. They were prepared to let him vote if he accepted their dictation. This concession represented the absolute limit of their flexibility, and the Southern whites intended to obstruct clandestinely any other aspect of Reconstruction. It was expecting too much of the Northern mind to imagine that it would understand the outlook of another national group. In 1867 the average Northerner believed that the Negro might be used as an instrument for imposing a new value system on the South. The outcome of such a program would have been a dubious one, even if Congress had conferred land and educational opportunities on the Negro, as Stevens had urged. The enterprise was doomed from the start by the refusal of Congress to go beyond Negro suffrage. The policy represented by the third Reconstruction Act was too severe to attract any Southern support but not severe enough to prepare the Negro for competition with the whites on even vaguely equal terms. Radical Reconstruction brought the Republican party to the South under the worst possible auspices and was bound to produce an extreme reaction to it as soon as federal troops were removed. Few

Republicans experienced misgivings at the time. The third Reconstruction Act promised the party immediate benefits in the South and did not expose it to the political danger that might have resulted from the establishment of Negro suffrage on a nation-wide basis.

Sumner and other leading Radicals wanted to remain in Washington all summer, but Fessenden ridiculed their exaggerated fears of Johnson and successfully carried a motion for a recess, with the result that Zack Chandler read his Maine colleague out of the party. "The path of the conservative Republicans," he thundered, "is clearly marked by tombstones as is the great highway to California by the carcasses and bones of dead mules. . . ." [72]

Instead of bearing out Chandler's predictions, the scattered elections of 1867 resulted in a sharp rebuke to the radicals. In the Border states of Kentucky and Maryland the voters rebelled against Negro suffrage by sweeping the Unionists out of power and turning to the discredited Democratic organization which had opposed the war.[73] Connecticut also elected a Democratic governor in April by a narrow margin. But the biggest surprise came in Ohio, where the October election produced a 38,000 majority against Negro suffrage and a Democratic legislature which would assure the retirement of Ben Wade on March 4, 1869. The Republican gubernatorial candidate squeaked through by only 3000 votes. A month later, Kansas voters rejected a Negro suffrage amendment to the state constitution.[74]

VI

Meanwhile, the complicated triangular relationship between Johnson, Secretary of War Stanton, and General U. S. Grant was producing a new impeachment crisis and a new Presidential candidate. As early as 1864, politicians had thought about running the squat, silent general for President, but on that occasion Grant proved unco-operative. He seemed just as allergic to politicians during the first part of Johnson's term; but as the popularity of the President declined, prominent Republicans took the precaution of exploring the antecedents and opinions of Grant. What they found would have discouraged most king-makers. In fact, until the middle of the Civil War, he had seemed determined to fail. Born in Georgetown, Ohio, on April 27, 1822, Grant had spent an unhappy childhood under the tutelage of a father who made a practice of comparing him with more energetic brothers. Eventually he had received an appointment to West

Point, and had plodded through his courses and graduated near the bottom of the class of 1843. Grant had performed creditably in the Mexican War, but the peacetime army was not likely to stimulate a young man with a lethargic disposition. Matters had gone from bad to worse after Grant married Julia Dent in 1848. Separated from her by a succession of assignments on the West Coast, he had begun to drink heavily and resigned in 1854 to avert a possible court-martial. During the next six years Grant tried a number of jobs without success. Then he was so preoccupied with making a living that he had seldom bothered to vote, and, if he possessed any opinions about the explosive issues of the '50's, he kept them to himself. Apparently Grant committed himself to the preservation of the Union by re-entering the army at the beginning of the Civil War, but his dominant motive was to terminate an unbroken series of failures. He was cool under fire and quickly won the confidence of his troops. Victories and promotions followed one another until, by the end of the war, Grant was Supreme Commander of the Union Armies and a military hero. After a lifetime of failure, Grant had suddenly become a success, and to his amazement remained one. Admiring citizens showered him with swords, horses, libraries, and testimonial dinners. Universities awarded him honorary degrees, and the press reported his activities with worshipful enthusiasm. Grant was grateful but inarticulate. Yet silence did not dim his success. If he stammered a few platitudes at a testimonial dinner, they were hailed as imperishable wisdom. Even his indifference to politics was taken for the aloofness of a statesman rather than the calculated evasiveness of an office-seeker.

At the outset, Johnson and Grant seemed to be made for each other. Both were shy, insecure, and unembarrassed by long periods of silence in social intercourse. Besides, Grant's lack of interest in a political career was so genuine that even the suspicious Johnson found it impossible to mistrust him. They had co-operated during the first phase of Reconstruction, because Grant felt sympathetic toward the South and was instinctively repelled by the vindictiveness of the radicals. Friction had begun to develop between them in the fall of 1865, however, when Grant discovered that his army of occupation was being used to shield civil authorities who harassed it. His distress deepened as state courts in the South began to hand down verdicts against Union officers in damage suits. A polite undercover war had broken out in the spring of 1866, with Johnson trying to restore full civil government in the South and Grant secretly countermanding the instructions of the President.[75] In these maneuvers Grant had enjoyed the full support of Stanton, but he disliked the overbearing Secretary of War and was reluctant to break with Johnson.

The situation did not remain static very long, because the President made the general an unwilling participant in the ill-fated campaign tour during the fall. Grant was annoyed at being exploited for political purposes and had displayed distress when the Peace Democrats turned out in overwhelming numbers to greet Johnson.[76] After the election of 1866, Grant concluded that the President ought to acquiesce in the will of the voters rather than oppose Congress. By March 1867 the general had reached the point where he was willing to co-operate in drafting the provisions of the second Reconstruction Act, which made the army more independent of the President. Grant, nevertheless, kept his opinions to himself and administered the Reconstruction laws as impartially as possible, which made many people regard him as a Johnson supporter. Not as much could be said for Stanton, who worked at cross purposes with the President and gradually became more open in his insubordination. In August 1867 Johnson finally ousted Stanton and offered the War Department to Grant.

By this time the general had discovered that he could not stay out of politics. He was not yet an active Presidential candidate but had become receptive to a nomination and charted his course with more calculation than usual. He agreed to accept the War Department portfolio only if Johnson would comply with the Tenure of Office Act by suspending Stanton and making an ad interim appointment. The President met Grant's conditions in the letter of appointment on August 12, but he cleverly avoided referring to the Tenure of Office Act as his authority for ousting Stanton. Trouble with Grant developed almost immediately, because the President removed two radical generals, Sheridan and Sickles, from their commands in the South. Grant made a formal protest against the ouster of Sheridan on August 17, but the President stood his ground and quieted Grant with lectures on the Constitution.

At this point politicians were assessing the effect of Grant's appointment on his Presidential prospects. Various factions in both parties had been trying to promote his candidacy since the winter of 1866, and his continued silence in the midst of controversy had only enhanced his attractiveness as a compromise choice. Even the radicals who distrusted Grant were afraid to oppose him for fear that his popularity would be used against them. The general's chief backer, Congressman Elihu Washburne, tried

to still the critics by reassuring them that Grant was not a Johnson supporter, despite his presence in the cabinet.[77] Nobody knew, however,
whether Grant was encouraging Washburne's activities. As Wade snorted
in disgust after an interview with Grant: "As quick as I'd talk politics, he'd
talk horses." [78]

Grant's silence caused a serious division among the radicals who favored
impeachment. One group led by Ashley and Boutwell wanted impeachment immediately. They considered Johnson to be a black-hearted traitor
and did not regard the lack of evidence as detrimental to their case. Butler
headed a second faction which cared as little about evidence as Boutwell
and Ashley but was concerned about proper timing. Despite his denunciation of Johnson, Butler dragged his feet. He wanted to be President and
saw that Wade might receive the nomination if he replaced Johnson in
the White House so far in advance of the convention season.[79] The boom
for Grant in the fall of 1867 caused Butler to change his mind and press
for immediate impeachment. He hated Grant in a bitter personal way and
preferred to take Wade immediately, if such a maneuver would stop the
convention from nominating Grant. Two obstacles upset his timetable:
one was the Grant supporters headed by Washburne, who saw that the
abrupt removal of Johnson would give Wade the inside track for the nomination; the second was the flimsy character of the evidence on which to
base impeachment charges. The latter consideration would have made little
difference before the fall elections, but the Democratic revival caused the
wobblers to hesitate. Without the active help of Stevens, little could be
done with the irresolute, and the master of the House was unable "to hurl
the discus or bend the bow of Ulysses." [80] Sheer will power kept Stevens
alive, but he was too feeble for the exacting burden of floor leadership.
Butler attempted to take his place, and although he applied the lash vigorously, he lacked the prestige to do so successfully. Even Greeley became
apprehensive over the antics of the impeachers.[81] The inexperienced Butler
misread the signs and, after forcing an impeachment resolution to the floor
of the House on December 7, was defeated by a vote of 108 to 57.

Matters were far from settled, however, for, five days later, Johnson sent
a letter to the Senate in which he set forth his reasons for suspending Stanton. In so doing, he complied with the procedure outlined in the Tenure
of Office Act, but he omitted any reference to the statute. Instead, Johnson
referred cryptically to the Constitution, as if his action was based on an
implied executive power to remove subordinates. His critics had no inten-

tion of letting the President escape in this fashion. On Saturday, January 10, 1868, the Senate Judiciary Committee officially refused to concur in the suspension of Stanton. Since it seemed probable that the full Senate would ratify the committee action on Monday or Tuesday, Johnson tried to force a court test on the constitutionality of the Tenure of Office Act. This strategy required the co-operation of Grant, and Johnson thought he had secured it on the same Saturday that the committee rebuked the President. Presumably, Grant would either retain physical possession of the War Department in defiance of the Senate or resign in time for the President to appoint another Secretary of War. It is possible that Grant deceived Johnson, but more likely that the President had at last met his peer in the art of making silence seem like consent. In any case, Grant acted as if he had agreed to nothing and yielded his office to Stanton on Tuesday morning following a Senate vote which sustained the judiciary committee. Grant was now shaping his conduct with the Presidency in mind, and he knew better than to offend the Senate. What seemed like a misunderstanding to Grant seemed like betrayal in the White House. An angry encounter between Grant and the President took place in front of the cabinet. A still more heated exchange of letters followed, and both parties released their version of the quarrel to the press. Within a week relations were severed, and Grant joined the ranks of the impeachers. It was the most popular step he had taken since receiving Lee's surrender, and it turned Grant into the radical candidate for President.[82]

If Senate action helped Grant, it created an impossible situation for the President by depriving him of control over a key subordinate without relieving him of responsibility to execute the laws. Full implementation of the Tenure of Office Act would destroy the separation of powers and turn the executive into a creature of the majority party in Congress. Some Republicans were troubled by the prospect and others by the current behavior of Stanton, who clung to the War Department after denying the constitutionality of the Tenure of Office Act.[83] Under the circumstances, Johnson would have done well to advertise his helplessness and wait for a popular reaction against the excesses of Congress. He was determined, however, to test the Tenure of Office Act. It took the President nearly a month to find a high-ranking military officer who would take the War Department portfolio for this purpose. Eventually Adjutant General Lorenzo Thomas agreed to force the constitutional issue. He appeared at the War Department on February 21, armed with his certificate of appointment from the

President. Stanton declined to give up possession of the office, and shortly thereafter Thomas was arrested for violating the Tenure of Office Act.

Nobody worried very much about the hapless Thomas, who was released almost immediately by a radical judge, to avoid a court test. But the attempt of Johnson to oust Stanton produced mass hysteria in the House. Logan of Illinois, who had just been elected commander in chief of the new organization for Union veterans known as the Grand Army of the Republic, made preparations to march a detachment to Washington and protect Congress.[84] Other members succumbed to the unreasoning fear that Johnson would install himself as a dictator. After scaring each other for two days, Republican congressmen cast an almost unanimous vote for impeachment. Just before the roll call, senators who were supposed to serve as judges had appeared on the House floor and urged wavering brethren to do their duty. Having inverted the normal procedure by voting impeachment first, the House began to prepare charges that would justify it. Speaker Colfax tried to keep the public as hysterical as the legislators by reporting on February 29 that 300 pounds of nitroglycerin had been stolen from New York and would probably be used to start a revolution. Taking their lead from Colfax, the press speculated about the possibility that some American Guy Fawkes would blow up Congress. The excitable Logan moved down to the War Department and slept in a room adjoining Stanton's quarters, so that he could summon the G.A.R. to Washington at a moment's notice.[85]

For a time, hysteria was self-sustaining. Repeated tugs on the alarm bell also intensified the opposition to Johnson, but eventually the House was obliged to devise some sort of legal case for impeachment. It had been hoped that Stevens would rally sufficiently to take a hand in impeachment proceedings, and the House selected him as one of the seven managers. By some miracle Stevens managed to stay alive throughout the trial, but, although his mind was clear, his body was unable to do its bidding. He had to be carried to his seat in the House and propped up on pillows where he sat motionless. His voice seldom rose above a whisper, while his face bore "the crooked autograph of pain." [86]

Leadership passed from Stevens to Butler because he alone possessed the necessary cunning to make a legal case out of the fanciful charges against Johnson. His appearance was a decided handicap to Butler. A bald head crowned a massive brow and beneath it were a pair of eyes which pointed disconcertingly in opposite directions. Heavy lids gave a sinister cast to his face, reminiscent of the villain in an old-fashioned melodrama. On occasion, Butler puffed out his cheeks with the comical exuberance of a clown, but when he was earnest or angry he had the sullen look of a bully. Some of his contemporaries could not stand the sight of him. An aristocratic Rhode Island hostess confessed that she had the impulse to trample him under foot.[87] James Garfield thought him "devoid of sensibility" and "of conscience." [88] Butler repaid his critics with epithets worthy of Stevens and once confessed to a friend his way of dealing with enemies: "make them fear me as badly as they hate me." [89] His honesty was repeatedly under attack, and many believed that he had used his opportunities as a military commander at New Orleans and elsewhere to improve his financial condition. Others who professed indifference to his financial ethics were appalled by Butler's opportunistic political maneuvers, which had transformed him in six years from a hard-money, pro-slavery Democrat into a paper-money, Negro-suffrage Republican. Nevertheless, he had his defenders. He knew how to talk the language of the working man and dispensed loans to his poorer retainers in Massachusetts with the liberality of Simon Cameron. The most durable source of his popularity was a remarkable facility for fanning sectional hatred.

Because it had impeached Johnson for violating the Tenure of Office Act, the House majority imagined that the Senate would convict him for the same reason. Accordingly, articles of impeachment dealing with other matters were initially rejected. This optimistic mood survived less than two weeks. The more realistic radicals in the House had always known that the Tenure of Office Act did not cover Stanton or other cabinet members appointed by Lincoln. They also recognized that the Tenure of Office Act might be declared unconstitutional if Johnson succeeded in getting the statute before the Supreme Court. It was just as evident that Johnson had not committed "a high crime or misdemeanor" in the accepted sense of the phrase. So the radicals shifted the emphasis by redefining "misdemeanor" to include misdeeds that were political rather than criminal. Then they added an eleventh impeachment article which covered all aspects of Johnson's alleged misconduct. Butler had favored this strategy from the first and demonstrated his leadership by forcing the House to reverse itself. The adoption of his catch-all article was a bid for the votes of conservative senators who wanted to convict Johnson but needed some pretext besides violation of the Tenure of Office Act. In a long speech for the prosecution, Butler contended that any "abuse of discretionary powers from improper motives, or for any improper purpose" was an impeachable crime. He blandly assured senators that impeachment was a political inquest rather than a trial, and hence did not need to be conducted as a judicial proceeding. According to Butler's interpretation of the Constitution, senators would not be violating their oaths if they convicted Andrew Johnson for political policies obnoxious to the Republican party. His speech was a persuasive misinterpretation of the Constitution, which enjoined the Senate to act as a court in impeachment cases and specified that a President should be tried for criminal offenses. Butler's logic prompted James G. Blaine to observe some years later that "the President was impeached for one series of misdemeanors and tried for another." [90]

Radical senators immediately endorsed Butler's theory that the Senate was not a court. Howard, Chandler, Sumner, Cameron, and Roscoe Conkling of New York declared Johnson guilty three weeks before the trial opened. Once the proceedings got under way, Conkling pushed through a resolution declaring that the Senate was sitting as "a constitutional tribunal" rather than as a court. Whatever it was, the Senate treated the country to an extraordinary display of partisanship throughout the six-week trial. It stripped Chief Justice Chase, the presiding officer, of the power to make final rulings on the introduction of evidence, and admitted or excluded witnesses by a straight party vote. Defense attorneys were not allowed to call on cabinet members or others likely to say a good word for Johnson. Midway through the trial, the dying Stevens made an Arkansas statehood bill a special order of business in the House—a hint that more tractable senators would be added if the existing membership did not reach a proper verdict.

At the outset, the impeachment managers had been confident that the Senate would convict, but toward the end they began to display signs of uneasiness. Colfax, who had expected "deliverance from the shameless apostate" on March 7,[91] noted with apprehension on April 28 that spokesmen for Wade "are making Cabinets and proffering patronage openly and undisguisedly." [92] Others were more indignant than Colfax. They objected to the elevation of Wade to the Presidency on the ground that he was a vulgar partisan who had never thought seriously about any subject but slavery and who had surrounded himself with the most disreputable elements in the party.[93]

Fessenden, Grimes, and Trumbull had never favored impeachment in the first place, and the activity in behalf of Wade gave them another reason for opposing it.[94] The three senators took the view that impeachment was a criminal proceeding and that Johnson was not guilty of any crime. They also felt that a conviction on political grounds would establish a precedent for future impeachments and thereby destroy the separation of powers. As displaced leaders of the Senate, they resented both the policies and bullying tactics of the radicals. The only thing that made the triumvirate hesitate was the attitude of Johnson himself. They feared an acquittal would cause the President to "act like a mad elephant" who had escaped from his keepers.[95] So on April 25 Grimes sought and received a pledge of good behavior from Johnson.[96] This interview convinced the triumvirate, that it ought to fight for acquittal. The defection of the courageous Fessenden seemed likely to influence others, and so he was subjected to unremitting pressure. On May 3 he warned a cousin that he expected to be "denounced as a traitor and perhaps hanged in effigy." [97] Shortly thereafter, John Russell Young, the managing editor of the *New York Tribune,* called on Fessenden and showed him the draft of an article "to prepare the minds" of citizens "for the sentence we must pronounce upon every Senator that proves recreant to his country in the hour of its agony." [98] Young had threatened the wrong man. Fessenden preferred "tar and feathers to life-long regret" and announced that he would honor his oath as senator to do justice, even though "villains and fools set him down as a friend of the President." [99] Four days after the Senate had gone into secret session on May 7, Grimes, Trumbull, and Henderson joined with Fessenden in a declaration that they would vote for acquittal. Since nobody supposed that they would defy the party without reserve strength, this announcement touched off a campaign of intimidation toward waverers. Two Republican senators from Tennessee, two from West Virginia, Sprague of Rhode Island, and Ross of Kansas bore the brunt of the radical onslaught. Robert Schenck, the chairman of the congressional campaign committee, telegraphed Republican organizations in states with doubtful senators to bombard the culprits with resolutions and petitions. The Methodists, who were holding a convention in Chicago, passed a resolution beseeching God "to save our Senators from error." [100] Spies and lobbyists stalked their prey in the cloakrooms, at social gatherings, and in homes. Stevens tried to make resistance useless by proposing the immediate admission of five reconstructed states with ten more votes for impeachment.

Neither side was completely certain of the outcome when the Senate convened to vote on May 16. Some doubt existed as to whether Grimes would be present, for he had suffered a massive stroke on May 13, immediately after reading a Greeley editorial comparing him to Benedict Arnold and Jefferson Davis. The impeachers felt similar anxiety over Howard, who had been desperately ill for several days. Both were carried in for the vote on stretchers, to the relief of their respective supporters. The majority decided to take the initial ballot on Butler's catch-all eleventh article, rather than the first article, which charged Johnson with violating the Tenure of Office Act. This strategy was designed to save the face of Sherman and one or two other senators whose earlier statements prevented them from supporting the first article. The tension mounted as the roll call proceeded, and by the time Van Winkle's name was reached in the alphabetical order it was evident that the impeachment would fall one vote short of the necessary two-thirds. The final count was 35 to 19, with 12 Democrats and 7 Republicans voting "not guilty." Chief Justice Chase, who detested Wade and resented the behavior of the other impeachers,[101] promptly sought a roll call on the first article, but the radicals forced a ten-day adjournment in the hope of reversing the verdict. During the interval, they concentrated their efforts on Ross of Kansas, because he had cast a reluctant vote against article eleven and hinted that he might support articles one and two.[102] When the Senate reassembled on May 26, it voted on article two and article three. Neither roll call changed a single vote, whereupon the Senate adjourned as an impeachment court.

The opponents of Johnson expressed their displeasure in frenzied fashion. Butler, who had predicted that Wade and prosperity would "come with the apple blossoms," [103] charged bribery and launched an investigation. Boutwell repeated his famous demand that Johnson be hurled into the empty hole in the sky near the Southern Cross, while the practical Stevens drafted new impeachment articles from his death bed. The seven Republican senators who had voted for acquittal were denounced by the party press and by their own state organizations. None were re-elected, but only Henderson of Missouri lost his seat because of his vote against impeachment. The invalid Grimes resigned in 1869, and Fessenden died the same year. Two Border senators were replaced by Democrats, while Trumbull disqualified himself for re-election in 1872 by deserting the Republicans on other issues. Far from being hounded out of the party for their vote on impeachment, the seven rebels were soon restored to good standing. Even Ross, who was beaten up by an irate friend of impeachment soon after his return to Kansas, considered the issue dead in 1870.[104]

VII

The truth was that the Republican party needed all of its supporters for the impending 1868 election, and the wiser heads did what they could to stifle the agitation. Once congressmen escaped from the menacing atmosphere which the radicals had created in Washington, they discovered that impeachment was popular only with the firebrands. Most Republicans still despised Johnson but wanted to forget about impeachment. There was some danger that monetary issues would overshadow Reconstruction in the impending campaign. The controversy revolved about the problem of servicing the national debt, part of which was in the form of short-term bonds known as 5–20's. Since many people had bought these bonds with depreciated greenbacks, considerable sentiment existed for paying off the 5–20's in the same currency. An equally large and articulate group took the contrary position that the terms of the 5–20's called for payment in lawful money, which meant gold. The division of opinion cut across party lines. Former Democratic Congressman George Pendleton of Ohio had first proposed to pay off the bonds in greenbacks in 1867, and the idea was so favorably received in the Middle West that Ben Butler endorsed it. As usual, he made the most of the issue by arguing that, if greenbacks were good enough for the poor, they were good enough for the bondholder. Butler's agitation alarmed the Eastern financial interests in the Republican party and created considerable bitterness on the eve of the national convention.

Nobody knew where Grant stood on the money issue, but his identification with the radicals had given his candidacy irresistible momentum. The congressional leaders were not really comfortable with Grant but concluded that they would have to accept him. Butler was the most miserable. He had never forgiven Grant for removing him from command after the failure of an attack on Fort Fisher in the closing months of the war. Butler's favorite remark in Washington drawing rooms was to the effect that there was no more difference between Grant and Johnson than between a drunken tanner and a drunken tailor. Unfortunately for Butler, he stood to lose more than Grant by continuing the feud, and so the slippery congressman made a formal gesture of reconciliation.

The Republican national committee had picked Chicago as a convention site, but unfortunately the convention opened on May 20, in the midst of the impeachment fight. Efforts were made to recognize the military achievements of the party without jeopardizing its image as the guardian of peace. White doves were released in the convention hall when Grant was nominated. Since the candidate refused to interfere in the Vice Presidential contest, it took five ballots to nominate Speaker Colfax over Ben Wade, Henry Wilson, and Governor Reuben Fenton of New York.

The most troublesome responsibility of the convention was the drafting of a platform. Nobody objected to the endorsement of congressional Reconstruction, but Negro suffrage was unpopular outside of New England. In the end the delegates settled for a compromise formula which endorsed Negro suffrage in the South and left the matter to the discretion of the loyal states. The monetary plank was even more ambiguous. It denounced all forms of repudiation and called for payment of the national debt in accordance with the spirit and letter of the law. Since the controversy resulted from different interpretations of the funding laws, no one was the wiser. The platform committee found it impossible to bridge the gulf between low-tariff Westerners and high-tariff Easterners. The problem was further complicated by disagreement between importers and manufacturers.[105] Pennsylvania industrialists added to the confusion by denouncing everybody who disagreed with them as "free traders." [106] So the convention prudently passed over the tariff in silence.

The Democrats tried to revive their reputation for patriotism by meeting on July 4 in New York City. The convention was held in newly completed Tammany Hall, which featured such mechanical wonders as a 24-foot chandelier with 320 gas jets. The delegates entered from 14th Street, where triumphal arches of evergreen, flags, streamers, and portraits of Democratic Presidents reminded them that they were part of a great tradition. Unfortunately, the level of the proceedings did not match the setting. The Democrats were demoralized and continued to make the mistakes typical of a frustrated minority, justifying Kate Chase's sneer "that when the South seceded the brains of the party went with it." [107] In 1864 the Democrats had nominated suitable candidates on an impossible platform; in 1868 they nominated impossible candidates on a suitable platform. The party might have taken Pendleton and emphasized the money issue, or Chase—who had suddenly discovered he was a Democrat again—and emphasized their acquiescence in the results of the war. In the end, "the implied censure upon the great body of their party" kept the Democrats from nominating Chase or any other strong Union man.[108] Instead, they selected former Governor Horatio Seymour of New York, who had strongly protested against the arrest of Vallandigham in 1863. He had also expressed sympathy for rioters resisting conscription,[109] and presided over the convention of 1864, which drafted the peace resolutions. None of these incidents proved that Seymour was a traitor. Yet the emotions of many Northerners were still too inflamed to accept a Civil War governor who had been a bitter and outspoken critic of Lincoln.[110]

The choice of Frank P. Blair, Jr. as Seymour's running mate proved to be still more unfortunate,[111] because he had written a much-publicized letter on June 23 denouncing in extravagant terms the Reconstruction Acts. The most dangerous passage was one in which Blair asserted that the victorious Presidential candidate ought to "declare these Acts null and void, compel the army to undo its usurpations in the South, disperse the Carpet Bag state governments, and allow the white people to reorganize their own governments. . . ." The Blair letter was a priceless boon for the Republicans. It enabled them to campaign on the issue of disloyalty and to keep the dangerous financial issues in the background.[112] Sectional antagonism also could be revived to good effect, as Blaine discovered when he read an official account of the Fort Pillow Massacre to his audiences.[113] This tactic subsequently came to be known as "waving the bloody shirt," and it was a standard feature of Republican campaigns for over a generation. Southern Democrats only hurt their own cause by replying in kind, for such exchanges invariably redounded to the benefit of the Republicans.

In the 1868 campaign, the Republican high command began to cultivate systematically the pressure groups which became the basis of the postwar party. These included the Grand Army of the Republic, Eastern manufacturers, and the larger Protestant denominations in the North.[114] Already the Republicans had concluded that the largest pressure group of all—the Midwestern farmers—would remain loyal without any special recognition of their interests.

The campaign organizational structure that had been developed in the '50's persisted after the Civil War with little modification. The function of the national committee continued to be advisory, and the canvass in most states was run by local leaders. Whatever funds the national committee collected were spent in traditional fashion on the doubtful October states of Pennsylvania and Indiana. The only innovation in 1868 seems to have been that the national committee shared the responsibility of assessing federal office-holders with the newly created Congressional Campaign

Committee. This step freed the national committee to concentrate its attention on corporations enriched by Republican policies during the war and hopeful of future favors. Even so, the national committee appears to have collected only about $200,000.[115] Headquarters in New York City consisted of three rooms in the Fifth Avenue Hotel, where Secretary W. E. Chandler supervised a small clerical force. Although just over thirty years old, Chandler already had a decade of political experience behind him and an organizational ability second to none. He had been the secretary of the first Republican club in New Hampshire before he was old enough to vote and had served as speaker of the lower house at twenty-seven. Aside from his responsibility for coaxing a few speakers with national reputations into campaign tours, Chandler's most disagreeable task was to settle disputes about money. Complaints occurred frequently both from the hapless office-holder who was victimized by multiple assessments and from the local campaign manager who claimed that the national committee had dried up his source of funds.[116]

While campaign orators were ranging over the country, Grant lived in virtual seclusion with his family at Galena, Illinois. Having won the nomination without contracting any obligation to the politicians, he intended to win the election in the same way. He made no speeches, gave no interviews, and answered no letters about political matters. His only activity during the campaign consisted of brief trips to the scenes of his early life and participation in a military reunion in Denver. His self-imposed isolation was so complete that he confessed he would not know a campaign was going on but "for the accounts we read in the papers of great gatherings all over the country." [117] The only politicians with direct access to Grant were Congressman Elihu Washburne, his long-time political mentor, and John A. Rawlins, an old comrade-in-arms. Chandler managed to establish indirect contact with the candidate through Grant's secretary, Adam Badeau, who received $300 a month to relay information from the national committee to the general.[118] Badeau's activities were secret and subtle. Often he did no more than place campaign pamphlets in places where Grant might see them. The only matter which really seemed to interest the Republican Presidential candidate was the defeat of Butler. The national committee made arrangements for Richard H. Dana to run against the congressman. It also subsidized Dana so that he could remain in the contest as an Independent after Butler had won the Republican primary. In the ensuing campaign, Dana discoursed on the evils of greenbacks, while Butler ridiculed his cultured foe for wearing gloves. The national committee might as well have saved its money, because Butler won an overwhelming victory.

Although individual radicals like Butler won re-election, it is doubtful if a radical could have won the Presidency. With all his handicaps, Seymour polled 46.3 per cent of the popular vote, or about 1.3 per cent more than McClellan four years earlier. Apparently many people voted for Grant because they believed that he meant it when he wrote in his letter of acceptance: "Let us have peace." [119] What they looked forward to was the end of turmoil over Reconstruction rather than an extension of the radical program. The electoral college divided 214 for Grant and 54 for Seymour. In the Solid South, where a secret organization known as the Ku Klux Klan tried to frighten Negroes away from the polls, the Democrats managed to carry Georgia and Louisiana. Even so, the Southern Republicans were despondent about their future because of "the disloyalty, the obstinacy and blind folly of the Southern whites; [and] the ignorance, inexperience and changeableness of the negroes." [120] They were not much more hopeful about the Border states of Missouri, West Virginia, and Tennessee, where the disfranchisement of many Democrats gave Grant a narrow victory.

Outside the South, the distribution of party strength in 1868 was to persist with only minor changes until 1896. New England and most of the Mississippi Valley could be counted upon as Republican territory. Indiana remained the only Midwestern two-party state after the Civil War. Outside the big Eastern cities, Republicanism was synonymous with patriotism.[121] One Northern woman ruefully recalled that she had been a Democrat "when they hunted them with dogs." [122] It would require more than a generation to shatter the political prejudices developed by the Civil War.

VI

The Age of the Condottiere

The election of Grant closed a chapter in the history of the Republican party. The heroic days of its youth were gone, the burning issues settled, and the goals óf the founders fulfilled. Leaders who had been willing to risk denunciation, ridicule, and social ostracism for their principles settled down to enjoy what they hoped would be a long twilight of respectability. Relying on the gratitude of the voters for past services rendered, Republican Presidential candidates time after time ran against Jefferson Davis and the secessionists. The Democrats were as biased, and so a fierce partisan warfare continued to rage over the issue until the agrarian crusade of the 1890's. At first the Republicans succeeded in holding the initiative by dwelling on the iniquitous behavior of the South, but after 1876 they were on the defensive because of public discontent over the spoils system and party monetary policy. Unable to resume the offensive on the basis of the Southern question, the Republicans relied increasingly on the protective tariff as their bread-and-butter issue.

The shift of voter interest in 1876 coincided with a major political upheaval. Until that time, the Republicans had enjoyed a comfortable majority, confirming the normal American pattern of extended periods of one-party supremacy. The sudden disruption of the pattern, however, opened an exceptional period of five Presidential elections in which the major parties competed on virtually equal terms. Between 1876 and 1892 the election map showed a remarkable stability, despite a rapid increase in the population. During this era the Democrats maintained a firm grip on the Solid South and the Border, while the Republicans enjoyed a similar position in New England and the Upper Mississippi valley. Partisan loyalty was so strong in both Democrat and Republican strongholds that angry voters organized third parties rather than co-operate with the opposition. Occasionally, Prohibition and the issue of state support for parochial schools contributed to discontent, but most third parties were a response to acute distress in rural areas and disappeared as soon as economic conditions improved. Disgruntled farmers might possibly have forced a redress of grievances by switching from one major party to the other, but they dissipated their bargaining power in ephemeral splinter movements. Although a third party occasionally gained control of a state government, it seldom showed vitality on a national scale until the 1890's. Before that time third parties went through a predictable cycle, flourishing in off-year elections and losing ground in Presidential years. Since major party leaders could count on the traditional partisanship to reassert itself eventually, they either did nothing or gave the rebels meaningless concessions.

The fact that most states basically supported either one party or the other left the settlement of Presidential elections to the three states that possessed a genuine two-party structure: New York, New Jersey, and Indiana. The two latter states had been so overwhelmingly Democratic before the Civil War that the party was able to withstand the defections of the '60's and still compete on equal terms with the Republicans. The political complexion of the Empire State resembled the rest of the North, but it became a doubtful state in the 1870's when the Democrats absorbed the bulk of the immigrants who congregated in New York City. All in all, these states decided four of the five Presidential elections during this period.

After 1876 the Republicans tried to escape dependence on the capricious voters of the doubtful states by regaining their foothold in the Solid South. At first party leaders tried to woo the upper-class whites by turning protection of Negro rights back to the states. After a negative response, Republicans bid for the poor whites by promoting coalitions with debtor and agrarian splinter parties. This arrangement worked no better, so by the end of the 1880's the Republicans had reverted to the Reconstruction policy of cultivating the Negroes. The collapse of this effort reduced the party in the South to a skeletal organization which existed for the sole purpose of enjoying patronage whenever the Republicans controlled the national government. These successive Republican improvisations foundered on the antipathy of the whites and the apathy of the blacks. Without the Carpetbag regimes to prod them, some Negroes stopped voting. The rest slowly became discouraged by the equivocal attitude of the planter class and the smouldering antagonism of the poor whites.

I

The existence of so many one-party states in the post Civil War era reduced the need for issues and stimulated factionalism. As a result, leadership of the Republican party passed into the hands of political condottieri, whose mentality and behavior resembled that of professional soldiers of fortune during the Italian Renaissance. Neither the sixteenth-century soldier of fortune nor his later counterpart cared about principles. Both were engaged in an amoral quest for spoils, and fought a noisy but highly stylized warfare. These modern-day spoilsmen were more numerous and quarrelsome in the Senate than in the House. A quadrumvirate composed of John A. Logan of Illinois, Simon Cameron of Pennsylvania, Oliver P. Morton of Indiana, and Roscoe Conkling of New York managed the business of the Upper House during most of the Grant era.

Time had not mellowed John A. Logan. He espoused radicalism after the war as violently as he had defended slavery in the 1850's. An ugly temper and an exaggerated notion of his own importance prevented Logan from exerting much influence on legislation, but, like a true condottiere, he was more interested in patronage than policy. In 1872 he almost bolted the party as a result of trivial disputes with Grant over appointments.[1]

Simon Cameron did not have to make any adjustments to the post-Civil War era. He had lived through a decade of turmoil without becoming emotionally involved in public issues. Until the late 1860's his talents as a manipulator had not been appreciated outside of Pennsylvania; but during the Grant Administration he attracted a host of imitators. In 1877 his durable organization passed intact to his son, J. Donald Cameron, who ran it for an additional eighteen years.

Oliver P. Morton of Indiana, a newcomer to the Senate in 1867, had been war governor of a badly divided state, where he had displayed unscrupulous partisanship to keep the Republicans in control. After the collapse of the Confederacy he became undisputed party boss in Indiana, and remained so until his death in 1877. Under different circumstances, Morton might have been a constructive force in the party. Like many Hoosiers, he disliked Negro suffrage and had initially tried to co-operate with Johnson.

When the President stubbornly rejected compromise, Morton went over to the radicals and became one of the bitterest foes of the South. Throughout the Grant Administration he devoted his keen intellect to the negative task of preserving Republican supremacy in the Gulf states. In appearance, Morton resembled Napoleon, with a huge head anchored to a short body. His face showed strength and determination, an impression reinforced by his deep, resonant voice. Far from discouraging him, a severe stroke in 1865 had stimulated his vitality and will to power. Rutherford B. Hayes had watched the crippled Morton batter an opponent in the Senate and thought him the greatest statesman of the day.[2] On the other hand, Whitelaw Reid of the *New York Tribune* regarded the Indiana senator as "an unprincipled demagogue of large ability," [3] while another journalist called him "the devil on two sticks." [4] Despite the conflicting estimates of Morton's character and motives, nobody doubted his energy or skill as a parliamentarian.

Roscoe Conkling, like Morton, possessed many talents that ought to have been used in a better cause than controlling the swollen patronage machine of New York state. He had served three terms in the House before being promoted to the Senate in 1867. A musical voice heightened the attractiveness of a face with finely chiseled features and glittering steel-blue eyes, while wavy yellow hair made Conkling seem even taller than his six feet three inches. A careless elegance in dress and a fondness for exotic colors vaguely suggested a Byronic temperament, but his ruthless pursuit of power dispelled any illusion that Conkling was a dreamy nineteenth-century Romantic. Behind an arrogant manner lurked a gnawing sense of inadequacy. Not only was Conkling abnormally sensitive to slights, but he brooded over unimportant remarks that most men would have ignored.[5] While boasting that no one could outwit him, Conkling lived in constant fear that others might think they could. His defense mechanism was a haughtiness unprecedented in American politics. He ordered subordinates around like lackeys, and, although he treated a favored few as colleagues, he repelled all gestures of intimacy. Occasionally when in pursuit of a favor, he stooped to flatter an individual,[6] and then denounced him behind his back. The only person for whom Conkling showed a genuine admiration was the plodding, reticent Grant.[7] It was an open secret that Conkling rehearsed his speeches as carefully as Sumner; he labored for weeks to perfect a sneer or a devastating characterization of an opponent.

He even carried notes and pretended to consult them so that his oration would appear extemporaneous. Few people knew where Conkling the actor ended and Conkling the human being began, but the unwary who tried to find out risked a fearful retaliation.

The condottieri had few effective opponents in Congress. The Democrats showed little interest in any issue but the restoration of home rule in the South. Among the House Republicans, veterans like Dawes of Massachusetts and Garfield of Ohio consistently pursued more important questions than patronage and subsidies for business. But even they temporarily lost their perspective in the atmosphere of jobbery and corruption and became involved in financial transactions that were dubious if not downright dishonest. Devotion to the principle of party regularity also silenced them at critical moments. Matters were not much different in the Senate, where the custody of party morality fell into the hands of Sumner and Schurz. Egotism and a lack of discretion had always hampered Sumner's leadership, and by the late '60's old age was beginning to aggravate both characteristics. As interest in the Negro receded, he groped about for other causes but destroyed everything he touched. Carl Schurz showed more ability, but was handicapped by an insecure political base in Missouri and by a heavy Teutonic style of oratory which many people equated with bossiness.

At the outset of the Grant Administration, no one believed that the new President would fall under the influence of the condottieri. He neither consulted the politicians about his cabinet nor replied to their unsolicited letters of advice. His intentions were to provide a nonparty administration for the country and to heal the wounds of the Civil War by impartial enforcement of existing laws. Since he intended to do nothing more, he imagined that he could avoid both dependence on the party organization in Congress and quarrels of the type that hurt his predecessor. Grant's oversimplified view of executive-legislative relations owed much to his experience in the army, where areas of responsibility were clearly defined and orders from the proper authorities were promptly obeyed. Just as he anticipated that Southerners would accept Reconstruction laws without dispute, so he believed that politicians would accept orders from the President, irrespective of political attachments. Grant did not propose to destroy the party system but to ignore it.

In this spirit, the President made cabinet selections without regard to geographical considerations or the political standing of proposed candidates. Supposedly, fitness was the sole test that he applied, but Grant's idea of fitness was the possession of great wealth, coupled with the unwillingness to solicit a cabinet post. Both Adolph Borie, the Secretary of the Navy, and Alexander T. Stewart, the Secretary of the Treasury, fit this description. Stewart had taken no part in politics, but he was a sufficiently prominent merchant to be known outside of New York. Borie, on the other hand, was a wealthy Philadelphian financier unknown outside his city. The appointment of E. Rockwood Hoar of Massachusetts as Attorney General was more orthodox, but Grant startled Republican leaders once again by selecting Hamilton Fish, a fossil Whig who had retired from politics in the mid-'50's, to be Secretary of State. For a time the President had considered including an intellectual in the cabinet. His tentative choice was John Lothrop Motley, the distinguished historian, but he finally settled on an Ohio reformer, ex-Governor Jacob D. Cox, as Secretary of the Interior. Some of the appointees were as surprised as the politicians by Grant's selection. In fact, Borie did not know about his selection until he read about it in the newspaper.

The initial reaction of Congress to the cabinet nominees was remarkably restrained, but the lawmakers quickly took their revenge. They objected to Stewart on the basis of an old law prohibiting the Secretary of Treasury from engaging in the mercantile business. Senators would not have regarded this difficulty as insuperable had Stewart been nominated after they had been consulted; but, since the President had ignored them, they refused to repeal the offending law. The chamber rang with pious expressions of concern over a possible conflict of interest, and the bewildered Grant was forced to withdraw the nomination. A few days later, senators showed their teeth again by refusing to approve a House bill repealing the Tenure of Office Act. In retaliation, Grant threatened to make no appointments until the Senate reversed itself. This tactic did not work any better for Grant than for his predecessor. After some bargaining, he settled for a senseless and confusing law which deprived the Senate of practical power over removals but reaffirmed its theoretical right to review suspensions made by the President.

Increasing disorder and violence had characterized the 1869 elections in the Reconstructed states. Organizations like the Ku Klux Klan and the Knights of the White Camellia kept Negroes away from the polls, with the result that Democrats regained control of North Carolina, Georgia, Virginia, Tennessee, and West Virginia. At first Grant was disposed to be lenient with the South, but after the loss of Virginia he gave full support to the Carpetbag governments. Congress in turn provided him with additional authority. In May 1870 it passed the first of three Force Acts to establish federal supervision of Southern elections. Periodic use of federal troops, plus more energetic manipulation of executive patronage, prevented the Democrats from capturing any more Reconstructed states in 1872. Yet the cost of Grant's holding operation in the South was very high. Northern Carpetbaggers and their Negro allies pursued graft with a candor that some people found distasteful, but the real reason for Southern resentment was the participation of Negroes in Carpetbag regimes.

The gradual drift of the President toward a repressive policy in the South reflected his increasing dependence on radical Republicans for support and advice. There was little difference between the radicals and other Republicans on Reconstruction issues, but factionalism began to develop in the fall of 1869 over appointments. Some party leaders objected to Grant's patronage policy because he was filling minor offices with mediocrities. Others had no objection to mediocrities, but resented individual appointments. In any case the critics began to snipe at the bewildered and inexperienced President and their attacks drove him over completely to the radicals. By March 1870 Morton, Conkling, and Butler were regular callers at the White House and had become Grant's main advisers on party policy. Their responsibilities expanded steadily because Grant followed the military practice of delegating broad discretionary power to subordinates. This system also suited Grant's temperament, for, since he worked by fits and starts, he had to rely on assistants who would keep the administrative machinery going during his recurrent periods of torpor. Contemporaries were struck by the abrupt changes in the tempo of Presidential activity; one of his intimates characterized Grant "as intermittent energy, immensely powerful when awake, but passive and plastic in repose." [8] Grant found so many aspects of the Presidency irksome and confining that he rarely inquired into the day-to-day operations of the Administration. His indifference proved to be Grant's greatest weakness in a system where the President is held constitutionally responsible for the blunders of his subordinates. Grant had never been a good judge of character, and although some of the radicals were, they did not put their insight at the disposal of the President. They recommended and he appointed men who had performed service for the radical faction, irrespective of their competence. Many were naïve and careless, but the conduct of others bordered on the criminal.

The first result of Grant's casual approach to public administration occurred in the fall of 1869 when Jim Fisk and Jay Gould, two unscrupulous speculators, attempted to corner the supply of gold available on the New York stock exchange. Aside from a few merchants who had to purchase gold at astronomical prices until the government broke the monopoly through its purchases, nobody but the speculators suffered. What attracted public attention was the fact that Grant's brother-in-law had been connected with the shady operations of Fisk and Gould. A congressional investigation, however, failed to establish any evidence of collusion between speculators and either Grant or his Secretary of the Treasury.

Grant's attempt to annex Santo Domingo, by contrast, produced an open split in his party. In his off-hand fashion the President had initially bypassed the Secretary of State and negotiated an amateurish treaty of annexation through one of his personal secretaries. Eventually Hamilton Fish persuaded him to put matters on a more formal basis; however, the real problem was not the Secretary of State but Charles Sumner. By the beginning of 1870 Grant had learned enough about constitutional procedure to solicit the support of the volatile chairman of the Senate foreign relations committee. The President thought that he had received a definite commitment from the Massachusetts senator at a private interview, but, instead, Sumner emerged as the most violent opponent of the project. It would have been easy to object to annexation on the ground that Santo Domingo was in a state of chaos and that the Baez government did not speak for the country. But Sumner could never state a case temperately. He characterized the Presidential secretaries and their collaborators who favored the treaty as corrupt adventurers and implied that Grant was a pliant tool of this group. The Massachusetts senator also fretted about the proposed addition of 300,000 Negroes to the American population, although he had spent the previous decade predicting that Negroes would make more useful citizens than the Southern whites. Grant was furious at Sumner and increased his efforts to force the treaty through the Senate. In the end, Sumner's control over the foreign relations committee enabled him to block ratification, but it was a costly victory. Several months and three speeches later, the Senate caucus at Grant's request removed Sumner from his committee chairmanship and put Simon Cameron in his place.

II

As the 1870 election approached, Grant's enemies multiplied. Secretary of Interior Cox and Attorney General Hoar were ousted from the cabinet and joined the opposition to Grant. The Fenton-Greeley wing of the party in New York openly fought the President, while Schurz tried to wrest control of the Missouri party organization from Grant's friends. The dissidents were by no means united, but they complained about everything from Reconstruction policy to the Santo Domingan treaty. Champions of civil-service reform and reduced tariffs added their voices to the clamor against the Administration. As a result, the Republicans received a sharp setback in November 1870; they lost 41 seats in the House and 6 seats in the Senate.

The most ominous development for Grant occurred in Missouri, where a Republican split led to the election of B. Gratz Brown, the anti-Administration candidate for governor. What worried the President was the behavior of the Democrats, who had made no nominations of their own but had thrown their support to Brown. There was danger that in 1872 the anti-Grant Republicans might be encouraged to follow the same strategy on a national scale. The victorious Brown faction was alive to this possibility, but it saw the danger of an open coalition with the Democrats, whom many Republicans still regarded as disloyal to the Union. A safer alternative was to exploit fears of a Republican split in the hope of blocking the renomination of Grant. The architect of this policy was Senator Carl Schurz, who seized leadership of the Missouri rebels. Immediately after the 1870 elections he began promoting a fusion of civil-service reformers, low-tariff advocates, and critics of the Administration's harsh Reconstruction policy. In a bid for the support of moderate elements, Schurz proposed a universal amnesty for all disfranchised rebels and a withdrawal of troops from the South. Concentrating on the Border states, he organized Reunion and Reform Associations. Ex-Secretary of Interior Cox launched a similar organization in Ohio, and dissident Republicans on the Atlantic seaboard followed suit. Within a year the fusion movement had gained so much momentum that the Missouri rebels, who took the name Liberal Republicans, to distinguish themselves from the radicals, proposed a mass convention at Cincinnati on May 2, 1872. The call disclaimed any intention of making a nomination and seemed to be aimed at purifying the party from the inside. Six weeks later, the Reunion and Reform Associations announced that they would meet in Cincinnati the same day. Other splinter groups, including a Labor Reform party, decided to join in the deliberations of the fusionists.

Simultaneously, dissident Republicans renewed their attacks on Grant. Trumbull, who had joined the movement, criticized patronage abuses in the New York customs house. With an eye to the German vote, Schurz launched an investigation of armament sales to France during the Franco-Prussian War. In the manner of a modern Cicero, Sumner bewailed the decadence of the Republic and called upon his fellow citizens to defeat Grant. By early spring the Liberal Republican tide was so strong that it threatened to engulf regulars like Garfield, Dawes, Sherman, Logan, and Hawley of Connecticut, who were up for re-election. All of them disliked Grant and grumbled in private about the arbitrary behavior of "his majesty." [9] Garfield confided to Cox on February 29 that he was ready to join the reformers if the movement continued to gain ground in the next six weeks.[10]

Grant and the radicals were so alarmed that they tried to head off the Liberal Republican movement by stealing its program. The President cut the ground out from under his civil-service critics by establishing competitive exams for federal jobs on a trial basis in Washington and New York City. The experiment came to nothing, because Grant broke his own rules and Congress withheld the necessary appropriations, but the inadequacy of the program was not apparent until after the 1872 elections. The President experienced more difficulty in working an amnesty bill through Congress, because Sumner attached a civil-rights measure to it that offended Southern Democrats. After several false starts, Butler managed to draw up an omnibus measure that met Southern objections. He rushed it through Congress on May 22 over violent protests of Sumner, who left his sick bed to denounce the compromise. Having stolen the civil service and amnesty issues from the Liberal Republicans, the regulars made a token gesture to tariff reformers by cutting all industrial rates a flat 10 per cent.

The belated action of Grant and the 42nd Congress deprived the Liberal Republicans of their argument that the party was doomed unless it nominated a reformer. Many fence sitters decided to avoid Cincinnati, rather than invite retaliation by participating in a futile demonstration against Grant. Simultaneously, the reformers saw that they would be obliged to nominate a candidate or disband the movement. This discovery did not bother Schurz, who took party obligations lightly, but it depressed Trumbull and others who had hoped to liberalize the Republican organization from the inside. Matters were complicated still further by the refusal of the Democrats to dissolve their party and as individuals support the Liberal Republicans. Trumbull justifiably dreaded the prospect of a campaign in which the reformers would be saddled with the organized support of former secessionists, yet he was too deeply involved to withdraw.

A highly discordant group met at Cincinnati. In addition to the proponents of specific reforms, there were Southern Democrats, spoilsmen who had broken with Grant, and old-fashioned, anti-slavery Republicans, including four members of Lincoln's cabinet. The situation invited management by the more disreputable element, as the original reformers either could not or would not assume leadership. Schurz had been born in Germany and was ineligible for the Presidency. Trumbull thought defeat inevitable and put forth only a half-hearted effort for the nomination, while Charles Francis Adams, a pioneer Massachusetts Free-Soiler and former ambassador to Great Britain, refused to do anything that would promote his own candidacy.

The disorganized reformers thwarted the effort of the spoilsmen to nominate Supreme Court Justice David Davis, who was already the choice of the Labor Reform party. Yet the reformers continued to behave in irresolute fashion, with the result that the convention moved completely out of control. To their amazement on the sixth ballot the delegates nominated Horace Greeley for President and Governor B. Gratz Brown of Missouri for Vice President. What seemed to be a sudden stampede was actually the product of a carefully planned deal between the two nominees. It was also a direct rebuke to Schurz, who had quarreled with Brown over the control of the Liberal Republican movement in Missouri. Greeley accepted every item of the Missouri platform of 1870 except tariff reform, for which he substituted a noncommittal plank.

The reformers were depressed and the Republican regulars elated by the outcome. At a small dinner the night after the nomination, Schurz expressed his feelings by playing Chopin's Funeral March on the piano.[11] Grant himself confided to a friend that "no one is satisfied but Greeley himself and a few Tammany Republicans who expect office under him if he is elected." [12] In general, Greeley had an unfavorable reputation, mainly because of his eccentricity and his notorious thirst for public office. His nomination was especially troublesome for the reform movement, since one element regarded tariff reduction as the most critical issue of the campaign and Greeley was a militant protectionist. His zeal for Prohibition also offended the Germans, with whom Schurz had great strength.

The critics found their voices immediately. The venerable, reformer and editor of the *New York Evening Post,* William Cullen Bryant, announced that he would not support Greeley under any circumstances. E. L. Godkin of the *Nation* was even more waspish and grumbled that to avoid betraying the reformers "Greeley would have to change his nature at the age of sixty-two." Midwesterners found themselves in agreement with the Eastern intellectuals. Schurz spent two weeks in a futile effort to secure Greeley's withdrawal before reluctantly deciding to support him. A splinter group of revenue reformers, however, nominated a fourth-party ticket. The gesture was a futile one because neither of the intended candidates would agree to run. In the end most revenue reformers supported Grant because he had lowered the tariff 10 per cent, which was more than they could expect from Greeley.

The aging Sumner, who had boycotted the Cincinnati convention in the hope that the Republicans would drop Grant, continued his assault on the President. While the Republican delegates were arriving in Philadelphia for their own convention in early June, he delivered a diatribe marked "by great ability, greater bitterness, and indiscretions in quoting the conversations of dead men." [13] Unfortunately for the Massachusetts senator, the age of martyrs was over, and it is doubtful that Grant could have restored it even if he had appeared on the floor of the Senate and caned Sumner.

The atmosphere of the Philadelphia convention was dull and the delegates languid. W. E. Chandler, in charge of seating arrangements, scattered the handful of anti-Grant delegates throughout the hall so that they would have difficulty communicating with each other. His fears were groundless, for Grant easily secured a first-ballot nomination. The President wanted to substitute Senator Henry Wilson of Massachusetts for Vice President Colfax, and the delegates obediently complied. They were just as obliging about the platform, which paraphrased the planks of 1868, and answered the reformers by declaring that the Republican party had solved all the problems troubling them.

The Democrats met at Baltimore a week later amid indications that Greeley was more unpopular with them than with the Liberal Republicans. Greeley's life-long motto had been "anything to beat a Democrat," and the Northern wing of the party, which had suffered his abuse at close range, opposed him. Since most Southerners rarely read Northern papers, they found it easier to support Greeley. In their current mood they would have nominated the devil on a platform calling for the withdrawal of federal troops from the South. So they provided the votes to nominate a candidate who had been their consistent critic for thirty years. A handful of bitter-enders spurned the counsels of expediency. Calling themselves the Straight Out Democrats, they held a convention at Louisville, September 3, and nominated Charles O'Conor of New York for President and J. Q. Adams of Massachusetts for Vice President. Neither accepted the dubious honor, but the Straight Out Democrats did succeed in putting themselves on the ballot in twenty-three states. Few Democrats bothered to support the splinter ticket. Instead, many of them announced they did not intend to vote at all. A number of reformers felt the same way.

Grant spent most of the campaigning season by the sea at Long Branch, New Jersey. Greeley started out with the same intentions. After retiring from active management of the *Tribune,* he took up residence on his estate at Chappaqua, New York. For a time he was content to chop wood, pitch hay, and entertain visiting delegations with quaint aphorisms. But, finally, he could not resist the opportunity to see and be seen by the voters. In September, Greeley toured Pennsylvania, New Jersey, Ohio, and Indiana. In his effort to give a new speech each day, Greeley talked on too many subjects and confirmed his reputation for being garrulous, foolish, and erratic.[14]

For the first and only time North Carolina held the first of the state elections, on August 1st. The Republicans under the direction of E. D. Morgan, who was once again chairman of the national committee, tried out their arguments against Greeley there. Republican orators spent more time joking about Greeley's personal appearance and eccentric beliefs than in discussing issues. They ridiculed his devotion to vegetarianism, Prohibition, and communal living projects. Simultaneously, the Republican press produced caricatures of the bewhiskered, moon-faced philosopher, with his crumpled white hat and untidy clothes. More damaging were Republican pamphlets which charted Greeley's bewildering zig-zags on the major issues of the Civil War era. The files of the *New York Tribune* provided his tormentors with an endless supply of source material, and the Republican congressional campaign committee spent $30,000 putting it in convenient form for the voters.

These tactics enabled the regular Republicans to carry North Carolina by a narrow margin, and seemed likely to produce larger majorities in the North. Nevertheless, national secretary W. E. Chandler was pessimistic and Greeley was overly optimistic. As a result the final stage of the campaign saw mud-slinging on such a determined scale that Bayard Taylor claimed he could smell the stench in Switzerland.[15] Greeley was called "renegade," "rebel," and "apostate," while Grant was branded as a "drunkard," a "crook," and "a low demagogue."

There is little evidence that character assassination affected the outcome. Nothing Greeley said could convince many Democrats that they could vote for him and still maintain their self-respect. On the other hand, nothing Grant had done could dissipate his great reservoir of popularity. When the vote was counted, the country learned that it had administered a worse rebuke to Greeley than to Seymour. The Republicans piled up 3,596,745 popular votes and 286 electoral votes, while the Democrats got only 2,843,496 popular votes and 63 electoral votes. New York returned to the Republican column, and New Jersey went Republican for the first time in its history. The Republicans regained their two-thirds majority in both houses of Congress.

Greeley promptly turned a political defeat into a personal tragedy. Although he had vilified political opponents and misrepresented their motives for over a generation, he could not survive under the same pressure. After brooding over his mistreatment for three weeks, Greeley died of a broken ego. If his career offered any object lesson, it was that good intentions were no substitute for common sense and consistency of purpose.

III

Republican congressional leaders wasted little time on self-congratulation. Some of them had an uneasy feeling that most of their followers had voted against Greeley rather than for Grant. Speaker Blaine noted with prophetic insight that "parties are never in a more dangerous attitude than when loaded down with their own strength," [16] while Garfield confided to his diary that the Republicans had probably won their last victory.[17]

Apprehension about the future did not prevent the Republicans from dealing harshly with bolters when the lame duck session convened in December 1872. House rules made retaliation difficult, because committee assignments were made at the beginning of a Congress and could be changed only by a suspension of rules. Some regulars wanted to try, but the leadership equivocated, because all Liberal Republicans in the House had been defeated in the election and would soon be out of office. So the House rebuked the bolters by showing hostility to their legislative projects. The Senate carried retribution further than the House, owing partly to the fact that the terms of Schurz, Sumner, and Fenton did not expire until 1875. The three renegades, along with Trumbull, who was a lame duck, lost their committee assignments and were excluded from the party caucus. Sumner died before his political future was settled; Trumbull rejoined the Democratic party, which he had left in 1854; and Schurz became a genuine Independent. The bulk of the Liberal Republicans in the House imitated Trumbull, closing their careers as Democrats.

Inaugural day, March 4, 1873, was a cold and clear day, which grew rawer as the afternoon progressed. That evening the Inaugural Ball was an icy ordeal. The committee on arrangements had spent $60,000 decorating the vast, barnlike structure on Judiciary Square where the ball was held. Despite provisions for 2500 gas-burning chandeliers, tons of paper streamers, and innumerable cages of canaries, the committee had made no arrangements for heat, so the guests wore their fur wraps and overcoats at the banquet table, ate in haste, and departed. By 10 p.m. the hall was empty and the canaries frozen. The speed with which the merrymakers deserted the Inaugural Ball was symbolic. It foreshadowed Grant's desertion by most of his supporters during his second term.

Few Presidents profited as little as Grant from the mistakes of their first years in the White House. Much of his embarrassment had stemmed from boredom with the details of administration and indifference to the qualifications of his subordinates, yet after 1872, Grant continued to rely on the professional spoilsmen for advice about appointments and policy. In addition, he developed a morbid sensitivity to criticism. Grant imagined that all charges of corruption against his subordinates were really aimed at him and thus felt he must defend them. He even reached the point where he refused to believe documentary evidence of his subordinates' wrong-doing. This stubbornness ultimately destroyed his great reputation and exposed him to understandable but inaccurate reflections on his personal honesty.

Grant's carelessness and indifference to the dubious financial practices of public officials was not an isolated phenomenon of the postwar era. This spirit had infected many of the critics in his own party. Few congressmen or senators consciously promoted corruption, but the practice of showering special favors on industry had dulled their sense of propriety and sapped their resistance to reciprocal favors from grateful businessmen. Until 1872 the White House had been the principal target of reformers; but shortly after the election, criticism shifted to Congress, where an investigation of relations between prominent Republicans and railroad builders over the granting of government subsidies to a construction firm known as Crédit Mobilier produced a national scandal. Congress was reluctant to expose itself, but eventually a House committee uncovered evidence that retiring Vice President Schuyler Colfax and his successor, Henry Wilson, and a host of lesser figures had accepted Crédit Mobilier stock at nominal prices. Even foes of corruption like Garfield and Dawes had put themselves into an equivocal position.[18] Some of the accused felt indignant because they had not been asked to do anything specific for Crédit Mobilier, but their attitude merely showed how casually Congress viewed the distribution of railroad subsidies.

Public indignation over Crédit Mobilier had hardly subsided before the House voted its members a retroactive pay raise of $2500, and the Senate followed suit with a more generous boost of $4000. The fact that Butler had sponsored the proposal was enough to prejudice most people against it, but the outcry against the so-called "salary grab" was explosive and universal. Even congressmen who had opposed it were denounced for not blocking the pay raise.

Matters went from bad to worse when a severe business panic occurred in the late summer of 1873. The rapid rate of industrial expansion since the war had been accompanied by the usual symptoms of speculation, price inflation, and overextension of bank credit. A readjustment at some point was inevitable; the immediate cause occurred in Europe, where leading financial houses went bankrupt in May and June. The repercussions of the panic in the United States put more than 5000 concerns out of business. There were heavy casualties among railroads and banks, which were already objects of popular suspicion. Especially damaging to the Administration was the failure of Jay Cooke, whose banking firm had contributed heavily to Republican campaigns since 1864. Before he went bankrupt, Cooke had already been under fire because Congress awarded his Northern Pacific Railroad Company a land subsidy twice as large as that granted to any other builder of transcontinental railroads. The party in power would have been blamed for the panic in any case, but the close identification of Cooke with the Republicans convinced many people that the party had jeopardized national prosperity to help greedy entrepreneurs and railroad builders. The critics of the Administration might have had shorter memories if the effect of the panic of 1873 had ended as quickly as the "black Friday panic" of 1869. The abrupt collapse, instead, was the prelude to a general depression which lasted for six years. As many as three million were unemployed at one time or another. Farmers suffered still more, as agriculture prices fell drastically and remained near their 1873 floors for much of the next two decades.

The scarcity of money and credit resulted in a renewed clamor for the government to increase the supply of greenbacks in circulation. Since an election was imminent, enough Republicans became converted to the doctrine of currency inflation to pass a bill enlarging the supply of greenbacks from $382,000,000 to $400,000,000. Grant showed considerable courage, if not political wisdom, by vetoing the measure. It is doubtful that the 18 million which separated Grant from the inflationists would have made any real difference to the duration of the depression, but the President was repeatedly condemned as a foe of the farmer.

As grievances against the Administration accumulated, opposition groups came alive. The Liberal Republican organization had disappeared without leaving a trace, but in the staunchly Republican areas of the Midwest a series of soft-money and anti-monopoly parties filled the vacuum. These new organizations, which drew their strength from the farmers, seldom grew beyond the state level. They owed much of their momentum to the Patrons of Husbandry, more often called the Grange, a nonpartisan movement founded by Oliver Kelley in 1867 to promote the social and economic betterment of farmers. Although the Grange steered clear of politics, it stimulated the political impulses of members by sponsoring discussion of farm-relief measures.

The dissident farmers were unwilling to become Democrats, but they were sufficiently irritated at the Grant Administration to form coalitions with the Democrats. In the East the discontented went over to the Democrats directly. Their dissatisfaction appeared in the election of 1874, which produced one of the most violent upheavals in party history. Eighty-five seats changed hands in the House, giving the Democrats 169, the Republicans 109, and the Independents 14. The fusionists also gained control of several legislatures in the Midwest, and replaced pro-Administration senators with Independents or Democrats. The most conspicuous casualty was Zachariah Chandler of Michigan, who was retired from the Senate after eighteen years. The Senate still remained Republican by a margin of 45 to 29, but several members of the majority were unreliable.

Fusion did not survive the election in most states of the Midwest. It had been a marriage of convenience, and most farmers could not bring themselves to long-term co-operation with the Democrats. Not only did the stigma of treason cling to the party, but it catered to Catholics and foes of Prohibition in a heavily Protestant area where temperance sentiment was strong. The fusionists held together in Illinois long enough to pass legislation imposing state regulation on rates charged by railroads and grain elevators. Such reforms did not work well enough to sustain the coalition, and after 1874 farmers turned increasingly to Congress for legislative relief. The Democrats made more durable gains in the East than in the Midwest, and they recaptured control of all but three states in the Solid South, despite the exertions of the Carpetbaggers and their Negro allies.

The Republicans used the lame duck session of Congress to answer their rebuke from the voters by passing controversial legislation. Senator Sherman of Ohio pushed through a bill for the resumption of specie payments in 1879. He tried to placate the inflationists by holding out the hope that greenbacks retired under the law might be reissued later, but few critics were impressed. The Republicans also passed a sweeping Civil Rights law which called for racial mixing in all public places except churches, cemeteries, and schools. This measure was designed to stop the erosion of Republican strength in the South and hearten the Negro allies of the party. So far as they were concerned, the law came too late. The Grant Administration made little effort to enforce it, and the Supreme Court saved lukewarm friends of civil rights embarrassment by declaring the measure unconstitutional in 1883.

With the adjournment of the lame duck session on March 4, 1875, the focus of popular dissatisfaction shifted from Congress to the White House. Secretary of War William Belknap was forced to resign for taking bribes from operators of Indian trading posts under his jurisdiction. A few months later, Secretary of the Treasury Joseph H. Bristow uncovered the operations of a whiskey ring involving Orville E. Babcock, who was both private secretary and military aide to the President. The investigation indicated that Babcock had shared in the profits from the forgery of revenue stamps, but Grant ignored the evidence and fired Bristow rather than Babcock. Eventually Babcock was acquitted on a technicality by a military court, and Grant rejoiced over the vindication of his secretary. Grant's behavior led many citizens to the false conclusion that Grant was as corrupt as Babcock.

At the same time the Administration's Reconstruction program was collapsing. To his dying day the President never understood why the South defied the law. He was just as bewildered by the attitude of Northern voters, who had endorsed his program in 1872 and then criticized it with increasing vigor in 1875. Nevertheless, Grant responded to the pressure of a new generation which was weary of the Negro problem and gradually withdrew support from the beleaguered Republican organizations in the Gulf states. He kept token forces in South Carolina, Florida, and Louisiana to protect the surviving Carpetbag regimes, but it was plain that Reconstruction would end as soon as the Democrats reclaimed the three states.

IV

Preparations for the 1876 election took place amidst increasing evidence of Republican demoralization. One party renegade gleefully likened his erstwhile associates to "an army whose terms of enlistment had expired." [19] Speaking in kindred tones, a Democratic journalist compared the Republican party to an "old tree" which was dead at the top and accessible only to "birds of prey." [20] Discouraged as they were, most Republicans felt relieved when Grant declared himself out of the race. The aspirants who sought to fill the vacuum were numerous but not especially distinguished. Two of the condottieri leaders, Roscoe Conkling and Oliver P. Morton, sought to acquire delegates in January 1876; but neither had any real following outside his own state. They were further handicapped by being identified with the spoils system. It is likely that the real reason for the activity of Conkling and Morton was to block candidates of whom they disapproved. Persistent rumors circulated that these soldiers of fortune intended to scatter the vote on the initial ballots and then stampede the convention to "Old Mahogany" for a third term.[21] Whatever their ultimate goal, the immediate purpose of the spoilsmen was to stop Speaker Blaine, the leading candidate for the nomination. Blaine enjoyed widespread support throughout the North, and his wife had been discussing furniture in the White House with the confidence of a future occupant since the spring of 1875.[22] It was impossible to distinguish between Blaine and his senatorial foes on the basis of principle. Personal antagonism and disputes over patronage accounted for their mutual hostility. Conkling had hated Blaine since the '60's when the ex-speaker had made his oft-quoted reference to the New Yorker's "turkey-gobbler strut." It was a trivial reason to pursue a feud for over a generation, but Conkling sought vengeance with persistence and single-mindedness.

Blaine was the leading candidate, but his stock fluctuated wildly during the pre-convention period. In January 1876 he taunted the House Democrats by moving to exempt Jefferson Davis from the provisions of their general amnesty bill. Raking up old controversies with a brilliant extemporaneous outburst, Blaine accused Davis of starving Union soldiers at Andersonville prison and of other Civil War atrocities. This transparent attempt to divert public attention from the depression, the Negro question, and corruption by waving "the bloody shirt" struck a responsive chord in Blaine's fellow Republicans. But in February, Blaine began to be tormented by rumors that personal letters dealing with his questionable financial transactions had fallen into the hands of the Democrats.[23] The House thereupon established a special committee to investigate the relations between Blaine and various railroads. In late May a bookkeeper named Mulligan confessed to the committee that he had some letters written to his employer, Warren Fisher, Jr., by Blaine about the Little Rock and Fort Smith Railroad. Blaine promptly conducted a private interview with Mulligan, during which he secured possession of the letters on the pretext of wanting to examine them; afterwards he refused to return the letters. Exposure of the theft, plus the publication of another Blaine letter about railroad bonds by the hostile *New York Sun* on May 27, strongly damaged his candidacy. Nevertheless, he fought back at his tormentors in daring fashion. On June 5 he took the floor and, after denying the right of the committee to examine the Mulligan letters, he proceeded to read excerpts from them. Even his edited comments revealed a suspiciously close association with railroads seeking financial favors from the government, but the adroitness of Blaine's performance brought cheers from the Republicans. Despite his mixed feelings about Blaine, Garfield conceded that "the effect was dramatic and electric." [24] Before the net effect of the Mulligan letters could be assessed, Blaine was overtaken by a fresh blow. On the Sunday before the opening of the convention, he collapsed on the steps of his church and was carried home more dead than alive. For twenty-four hours he remained in a partial coma, but he recovered rapidly enough to reassure his supporters.

While Blaine partisans held the spotlight, realistic politicians were discovering that splinter groups held the balance of power between the Democrats and Republicans. Some of the discontented founded a Greenback party at Indianapolis on May 15 and nominated Peter Cooper, a New York philanthropist, for President. The rest preferred to put pressure on the major parties for a compromise candidate. The tireless Carl Schurz tried to rally the remnants of the Liberal Republican movement behind Bristow of Kentucky, who had been fired for his zealous pursuit of the Whiskey Ring. Bristow's chief asset was his honesty, but he lacked personal magnetism. More to the taste of the professionals was another dark horse, Governor Rutherford B. Hayes of Ohio, who had carried the state as a hard-money candidate at the height of the greenback agitation in 1875. The Hayes record on national issues consisted of nothing more than cautious endorsements of clean government, balanced by partisan outbursts worthy of Blaine. The spoilsmen mistrusted Hayes, but not enough to wage an all-out fight on him. Thus, Hayes occupied a good strategic position, although he came to the convention with few actual delegates.

The Republicans met at Exposition Hall in Cincinnati, where the ill-fated reform movement had nominated Greeley four years earlier. Completed in 1869, Exposition Hall was a tasteless Victorian structure topped by two lofty towers which made it vaguely resemble a cathedral. Apparently the architecture affected the oratory, for the nominating speeches were flowery and endless. The simple statement of 1860, which did little more than name the candidate, had now been replaced by the extended eulogy. In piling up the tributes, orators carefully withheld the name of their candidate until the last possible moment. It was on this occasion that Colonel Robert G. Ingersoll stirred the delegates by describing Blaine as the "plumed knight." Some observers felt that Ingersoll's eloquence would have carried Blaine to victory, if the gas lights had not gone out, thus forcing an adjournment before any ballots were taken.

The outcome of the convention in 1876, however, was not determined by speeches but by the cohesiveness of the stop-Blaine movement. On the first ballot Blaine led Senator Morton, his nearest competitor, 285 votes to 125. Several favorite sons had less than 100 votes, and Hayes polled only 61. Blaine made small gains on the next three ballots, while Morton, Conkling, and Cameron tried to concentrate their strength behind a member of the Grant faction. By the fifth ballot Morton was convinced that the convention would have to take Hayes, if it were to stop Blaine, and he presented the Indiana delegation to the Ohio governor. The big break came on the next ballot when Hayes received the bulk of the New York and Pennsylvania delegations, which gave him the nomination with six votes to spare. The fierce backstage struggle added fire to the feud between Blaine and Conkling, and kept it alive for a full decade to come, Blaine men being known as "Half Breeds" and the Grant-Conkling faction as "Stalwarts."

The convention next quickly agreed on Congressman William Wheeler of New York for Vice President. The platform featured the standard denunciation of the Democrats as the party of treason and the customary pledge to enforce the Fourteenth and Fifteenth Amendments, but it took notice of Northern restlessness over Reconstruction policy by promising to pacify the South. The controversial subject of civil-service reform was passed over in silence, save for a congratulatory reference to "the quickened conscience of the people concerning political affairs." Hayes clarified some points in his letter of acceptance on July 8, in which he flatly supported sound money and civil-service reform. The most significant section of the speech was a paragraph which blamed the aggravation of the spoils system on Congress. Hayes accused the lawmakers of usurping executive control over appointments and distributing jobs on the basis of loyalty to individual leaders. Then he came close to a declaration of war with a pledge to end corruption by recapturing Presidential powers over patronage. Hayes was far less explicit in his statements about Southern policy, for he confined himself to an endorsement of local self-government and a promise to defend Negro rights. Since most people thought the two policies were mutually exclusive, they had no idea what to expect if Hayes reached the White House.

Voters outside Ohio knew little about the Republican candidate and had to rely on campaign biographies for the routine facts of his life. They learned that Hayes had been born at Delaware, Ohio, in 1822; was graduated from Kenyon College twenty years later; attended Harvard Law School briefly; and began practicing law in Fremont, Ohio, in 1845. Hayes served in the Civil War and had risen to the rank of major general; had served two terms in Congress; and was currently in the middle of his third term as governor of Ohio. Campaign photographs revealed a large, rawboned man in oversized clothes with a straggly beard. The face gave little inkling that Hayes possessed a shrewd mind. Like Lincoln he enjoyed being underestimated, and he encouraged this by listening more than he talked. Only his restless, twinkling eyes provided a clue that Hayes was both astute and mischievous.

The Democrats also nominated a candidate with an equivocal record, Samuel J. Tilden of New York. Although Tilden had been an active politician since the 1850's, he took pride in his ability to conceal his opinions. Tilden's craftiness and subtlety were overcompensations for chronic ill-health, but neither quality damaged him in the campaign. Southerners assumed that Tilden's long association with the Democratic party was the equivalent of a pledge to end Reconstruction; civil-service reformers imagined that his ouster of Republican office-holders in New York was a commitment to clean government; and hard-money men supposed that no New Yorker could favor greenbacks. Tilden held his peace on these questions, and let his running mate, ex-Senator Thomas A. Hendricks of Indiana, encourage each group in its beliefs.

Familiar faces again presided over the Republican campaign, with Zack Chandler head of the national committee and W. E. Chandler its secretary. It was evident, in his reliance on these regular Republicans, that Hayes would not sacrifice his chance of victory to please the independents. For once, Ohio received as much attention as Indiana, for the Greenback party was strong in the state. Aside from the money issue, there was no campaign topic that had not been discussed in 1872. Voters showed little disposition to change their basic views, but they were weary of Grant and blamed the Republicans for the depression.

The October state elections were too close for either side to take comfort. Ohio went to the Republicans and Indiana to the Democrats by narrow margins. The indecisiveness of the outcome made both sides intensify their campaigns in the month remaining. Indiana politicians, who already had a reputation for bribing, colonizing, and intimidating voters, demanded heavy contributions from New York financiers. One Republican manager requested $10,000 from Jay Gould; he assured him that the money would be used only where the party controlled "the election boards and a large floating population." [25] Nobody knows how handsomely Wall Street responded to the wails of Indiana Republicans and Democrats, but the state had its usual close and corrupt election.

None of these eleventh-hour exertions helped the Republicans in the large doubtful states. Not only Indiana but New York, New Jersey, and Connecticut went Democratic. A large and enthusiastic crowd braved disagreeable weather to watch the returns on the *New York Herald* bulletin board, and dispersed about midnight when it appeared that Tilden had captured 184 of the 185 necessary electoral votes. Like the crowd, Zack

Chandler and his associates at Republican headquarters stopped following the election about the same time.

The only Republican who continued to watch the returns was John C. Reid, editor of the *New York Times*. Concluding that the Democrats would carry no more Northern states, he examined the results in Florida, Louisiana, and South Carolina, where the Republicans still maintained troops and controlled the all-important election boards. To his delight, Reid noticed that the Democratic pluralities were small, except in Louisiana. A quick calculation indicated that, if the electoral vote of the three Southern states were added to the Republican total, Hayes would win 185 to 184. Reid rushed off to the deserted lobby of the Fifth Avenue Hotel, Republican election headquarters. There he found a solitary figure hunched up in an overcoat reading the *New York Tribune*. It was W. E. Chandler, who had just returned from voting in New Hampshire. Chandler immediately saw the significance of Reid's analysis and roused Zack Chandler, who, while not comprehending, did agree to dispatch telegrams to members of the election boards and special agents of the post office in the three states. At the same time, other statements were prepared claiming the electoral votes of the three Southern states and the Presidency for Hayes. W. E. Chandler left the next day for Florida "with full power to act and make terms," while Grant invited John Sherman, Garfield, and Stanley Matthews, a close personal friend and political associate of Hayes, to observe the canvass in New Orleans. Abram S. Hewitt, chairman of the Democratic national committee, promptly retaliated by dispatching a similar group from his own party to watch the Republicans. The press euphemistically referred to these rival groups of observers as "visiting statesmen."

In the ensuing contest, the Republicans possessed every advantage except the support of the white Southerners. The Reconstruction laws had given the local returning boards virtually unlimited power to change election returns. Federal troops and postal authorities were available to uncover Democratic chicanery where it existed and to fabricate it where it did not. The only problem for the Republicans was the unreliability of their party officials who staffed the returning boards and other federal posts in the disputed states. In most cases their partisanship was only skin deep and their services were for sale to the Democrats at the proper price. Thus, the Republican national committee had to make their loyalty worthwhile by offering money, jobs, and other inducements. Chandler conducted some matters through New York by means of coded telegrams, but he made a number of other deals on the spot in Florida. He was aided by W. S. Dodge, the assistant postmaster of the Senate, who fulfilled his assignment so efficiently that the national committee sent him to Nebraska, beyond the reach of investigating committees.[26] Trusted postal officials volunteered for special outdoor jobs, which required them to wade through swamps in pursuit of "evidence." [27]

Not to be outdone, Tilden's nephew, Colonel W. S. Pelton, and Manton Marble, the editor of the *New York World,* dispatched coded telegrams of their own in an effort to buy an election which Democratic orators were insisting that the party had already won. The Presidential nominees showed no curiosity about the methods employed to manipulate the democratic process in their behalf. Whether their ignorance was due to choice or the deliberate misrepresentation of subordinates, both naïvely expected that justice would prevail.[28] Neither candidate took an open position on the merits of his case, but Hayes worked far more aggressively behind the scenes to devise a winning strategy than Tilden. The Ohio governor was in constant touch with party leaders, whereas Tilden became a virtual recluse.

To this day nobody knows which candidate was entitled to a majority of the electoral college in 1876. The Republicans needed all three of the disputed Southern states to win, but they could only make out a good case for their claims to South Carolina and Florida. In both states, the Democratic plurality was small and the evidence of Negro intimidation plentiful. On the other hand, the Democrats carried Louisiana by 6000 votes, and this margin could not be overturned without broadening the definition of intimidation which had been used in Florida and South Carolina. The Republicans would have been more consistent and persuasive if they had proposed to throw out the returns in all Southern counties with Negro voters, but they used the issue of intimidation on a narrowly partisan basis.

By the end of November the Republicans had completed their recount and induced the pliant governors of South Carolina, Florida, and Louisiana to certify the electors designated by the party. The Hayes strategists were enormously pleased with themselves, because they did not think the Democrats would repudiate the sacred doctrine of states' rights by arguing that Congress could review the election returns of individual states. The Democrats, however, were no more disposed to let ideology interfere with their interests than the Republicans were. They demanded that the dispute be settled by the House, which they controlled. The Republicans countered with the same claim for the Senate, which happened to be Republican.

Several other constitutional positions were possible, and partisans developed them as the need arose. In December extremists in both Houses talked wildly of civil war to vindicate their claims.

Behind the bluster each party was divided by internal dissension which eventually worked for compromise. For all their bellicose talk, few Southerners were willing to fight. A New Orleans resident said, "If there is conflict, let the North engage in it"; [29] while Ben Hill of Georgia dryly observed that the Northern Democrats "were invincible in peace and invisible in war." [30] Southern congressmen who wanted compromise visited Garfield in mid-December to explore the possibilities of a deal with Hayes.[31] Simultaneously, the Republicans in the Senate were discovering that not all of the party favored the plan to have their presiding officer count Hayes into office.[32] Conkling and Blaine, who disagreed about everything else, preferred a Democrat in the White House to a civil-service reformer from their own party. To take the election away from the Senate they supported a proposal of George F. Edmunds, chairman of the Senate judiciary committee, for the establishment of an electoral commission to hear the evidence from the contested states and to render a verdict. Unlike his colleagues, Edmunds favored Hayes, but he took delight in pursuing partisan objectives by judicial methods. Grant also threw his weight behind a peaceful solution, and eventually both houses passed a bill calling for a commission composed of five senators, five representatives, and five Supreme Court justices. Since the terms of the legislation guaranteed the selection of seven Democrats and seven Republicans, a complicated compromise was devised for choosing the fifteenth member. It put the crucial decision in the hands of the four justices already designated on the understanding that they would name David Davis, a colleague who was classed politically as an independent. Justice Davis did not relish the responsibility of choosing a President, and managed to escape when the Illinois legislature elected him to the Senate.[33] This development worked out better than Edmunds had hoped, because the four justices then chose Republican Justice Joseph P. Bradley as the fifteenth member. As expected, Bradley supported Hayes, with the result that the three disputed states were awarded the Republican candidate by a straight party vote of 8 to 7. The more combative Democrats in the House retaliated by launching a filibuster to prevent the counting of the electoral votes. It collapsed on March 3 after spokesmen for Hayes promised that the President-elect would withdraw troops from the

South and sponsor federal subsidies to stimulate construction of a transcontinental railroad through the South.

V

No President had a shorter honeymoon with Congress than Hayes. He stunned the condottieri by appointing David M. Key, an ex-Confederate officer from Tennessee, Postmaster General. Immediately after, Hayes withdrew troops from South Carolina, Florida, and Louisiana. Just as these gestures foreshadowed a new Southern policy, so the appointment of Evarts as Secretary of State and Schurz as Secretary of Interior foreshadowed a new patronage policy. Both were Independents, and with the approval of the President drafted a new code governing the selection and removal of subordinate office-holders. Designed to prevent the ouster of efficient federal employees, the code achieved limited success. Half the incumbent postmasters were reappointed, and Hayes made fewer removals in the opening months of his Administration than in any comparable period since the days of John Quincy Adams.[34] Despite the emphasis on merit, the reforms were not quite as impressive as policy pronouncements suggested. Each cabinet member retained jurisdiction over his own employees, and enjoyed considerable leeway in applying the Schurz-Evarts rules. Moreover, merit was not defined broadly enough to include Democrats, and none bothered to apply for jobs.

As might have been expected, Hayes pleased neither the militant civil-service reformers nor the spoilsmen. The former objected to the intrusion of partisan considerations, and the latter denounced the President for ignoring the recommendations of senators and representatives. Hayes faced open warfare with the spoilsmen in October 1877 when he fired Chester A. Arthur, Collector of Customs in New York and a political colleague of Conkling. Senators retaliated by blocking confirmation of Presidential appointments. Altogether, they rejected 51 out of 92 nominees to major positions before Hayes retired.[35] Defeats did not disturb the serenity of the President. He expected permanent reform only when the public demanded legislation to relieve congressmen from the undignified task of hunting jobs for constituents.[36] On the other hand, Hayes believed he was advancing the cause of civil service by contesting congressional control over appointments. The struggle ended on an inconclusive note, and was resumed by his successors.

His Southern policy made almost as many enemies for Hayes as his approach to patronage. Old radicals like Ben Wade grumbled that Hayes was worse than Andrew Johnson, and said he surrounded himself "with political eunuchs." W. E. Chandler attacked the President in a public letter. Written in December 1877, it accused Hayes of betraying his platform pledge to protect the Negro, and it condemned him for a shameful bargain with the Democrats. The first opportunity to test the policy of conciliation in the South occurred in the off-year elections of 1878. Six of the nine Republican congressmen in the Gulf states lost their seats, and the party vote decreased in both the white and black belts. Elsewhere Hayes took as bad a beating, for the Democrats won both houses of Congress for the first time since 1856. Confronted with the failure of his effort to divide the Southern whites and build a bi-racial Republican party, Hayes contended that he had at least improved race relations.[37] His assumption was a dubious one, as the steady decline of the Negro vote would demonstrate in the years ahead.

The Democrats in Congress behaved as if Hayes were as bad as they thought Grant had been. Many Southern senators had voted with the spoilsmen to block the confirmation of Presidential appointees, while a Democratic committee in the House had tried to force the resignation of Hayes by reviving the stale controversy over the disputed election. Apparently the Democrats regarded their victory in 1878 as a mandate for further harassment of the President, for they paralyzed Congress during the last two years of his term. Internal dissension prevented the Democrats from taking action on the tariff or monetary questions, but they made persistent efforts to dismantle federal election machinery in the South. Although Hayes checked them with a series of vetoes, he had little to show for his efforts. The election laws were a dead letter after the withdrawal of troops from the South, and neither Hayes nor his Republican successors could reinstate them.

The Republicans demonstrated some solidarity in the fight over the election laws, but they resumed their ferocious infighting on the eve of the 1880 election. Hayes had pledged himself to retire after one term, and thus there promised to be a scramble for the party nomination. The leading candidate of the Stalwarts was ex-President Grant. After leaving the White House, he had embarked on an extended world tour, and the longer he stayed away from the United States the better he looked to the demoralized Republicans. Party members found it easy to forget his faults, and

Grant was anxious to run, provided his nomination could be managed so that it looked unmanaged. Except for Ben Butler, who had defected to the Democrats, and Blaine, all of the condottieri supported Grant, on the theory that he would restore the old dispensation. Conkling and Logan swung their big delegations behind the general, while J. Donald Cameron, who had replaced his father Simon as senator and state boss, did the same in Pennsylvania. The Grant managers also acquired a sprinkling of delegates in the South and the mountain states, thus assuring Grant of 310 first ballot votes. He might have accumulated the remaining 68 votes necessary for a majority if he had followed the advice of his backers and deferred his return to the United States until the eve of the convention. As it was, he returned in the autumn of 1879, which gave his opponents time to organize. The Half Breeds, Blaine's faction, backed him as loyally as in 1876, and he entered the convention with nearly 250 delegates from the smaller states.

The dark horses were more numerous and enthusiastic than ever because of Hayes's success four years earlier. Senator Edmunds of Vermont commanded the support of civil-service reformers, who were strategically placed in the Massachusetts and Vermont delegations. Every active Ohio politician thought he was Presidential timber, but the official favorite son was John Sherman, who had served successively as congressman, senator, and secretary of the treasury under Hayes. Despite his experience and long record of service to the party, Sherman carried the political cross of dullness. "People will be knocked down for calling Blaine a thief," noted one observer, "but who ever heard of anyone knocked down for calling Sherman a thief." [38] His greatest virtue was a knack for framing a hard-money policy in such a way that it looked like a soft-money policy. With the Greenbackers active in pivotal Midwestern states, Sherman found support among Eastern financiers, who contributed generously to his campaign fund. By adroitly manipulating Treasury Department patronage, Sherman also gained the support of Southern delegates which would otherwise have gone to Grant.[39]

The worst problem for Sherman was his own Ohio delegation, which contained Blaine and Garfield supporters. Sherman could do nothing about the Blaine men, but he tried to make disloyalty difficult for Garfield. His first step was to promote Garfield's election to the Senate, and he followed this gesture by making him his floor manager. Neither of these favors stopped Garfield from pursuing the nomination. The truth was that Garfield had become restless and impatient after eighteen years in the House. A decade earlier, he had become known as an authority on financial questions and as a cautious civil-service reformer. Until the mid-'70's Garfield had discussed these and other questions with urbanity and restraint, but then he decided that the highest political honors went to noisy partisans. He began imitating Blaine in 1876, starting with a fiery denunciation of Jefferson Davis and gaining momentum by opposing all efforts to compromise the disputed election. His behavior was so out of character that old friends remonstrated with him, but Garfield persisted with his new tactics.

Although Garfield was too intelligent to overlook the hazards of undermining Sherman, his conception of an effective pre-convention campaign drew him down this dangerous path. "Few men," he told his diary, "have gained the Presidency by trying to obtain it. In most cases, it is got as the result partly of accident and partly of popular sentiment seizing hold of a man who has not done much about it himself." [40] Using this kind of logic, Garfield concluded that he would make himself "available." Late in 1879 he permitted Governor T. L. Pound of Wisconsin and Wharton Barker, a Pennsylvania industrialist, to approach delegates to support him in case of deadlock.[41]

When the Republican delegates convened on June 3, 1880, at Chicago's Exposition, the anti-Grant forces concentrated their initial effort on blocking the imposition of the unit rule, which would have bound each delegation to support the wishes of the majority of its members. Their strategy was sound, because some sixty-three foes of Grant scattered through the Illinois, New York, and Pennsylvania delegations would have to vote for Grant if the rule applied. The skirmishing in the rules committee and on the convention floor occupied nearly two days, but under the leadership of Garfield the delegates rejected the unit rule. Garfield was so conspicuous in this fight that after the victory of the coalition Conkling sent him a message of congratulation "on being a dark horse." During this period Garfield also made several well-timed entrances into the convention hall to loud applause.[42] Struggling with his conscience, Garfield confided to his wife that despite a trend in his favor he would faithfully support Sherman. His equivocal feelings expressed themselves in his nominating speech for Sherman, a flowery, elaborate piece of oratory which barely mentioned the candidate or his virtues.[43]

Soon after the balloting started, it became evident that neither Grant nor his leading rivals could be nominated. Between the second and the twenty-eighth ballots, their strength remained almost stationary, with Grant drawing 302 to 309, Blaine 280 to 285, and Sherman 93 to 97. The most obvious way out of the deadlock was for Blaine and Sherman to join forces, but the "plumed knight" had mortally offended the Ohioan by making a contest for delegates in his own state.[44] Conkling might have salvaged something for the Stalwarts by switching from Grant to Edmunds, but he gave orders to stand firm. Three hundred and six delegates obeyed him until the end. Chauncey Filley, one of the loyal Grant men, later sent each of them a medal bearing the phrase "Old Guard," a designation which was to enjoy a long life in Republican politics.

When Conkling snuffed out the hopes of the Edmunds delegates, most of them drifted over to Sherman, and his total rose above 100 for a few ballots. This development actually hurt Sherman, because, when he failed to gain additional momentum, Governor Charles Foster and other Ohioans had an excuse for deserting him. From the second to the thirty-fourth ballot, one or two Pennsylvania delegates had regularly voted for Garfield, and at the end of the thirty-fourth ballot, Governor Pound threw him the 16 votes from Wisconsin. On the next ballot Indiana switched to Garfield, and invited the Sherman and Blaine managers to unite behind him. A telegram from the Ohio delegation asking Sherman to release them crossed one from Sherman suggesting that they go to Garfield. Blaine was just as acquiescent as Sherman, with the result that Garfield received the nomination on the thirty-sixth ballot. In the confusion surrounding the vote on the last ballot, Garfield vainly attempted to secure the floor to protest the use of his name. There was some difference of opinion as to whether he spoke as loudly as a determined man ought to have done. In any case, a protest would have been more effective if Garfield had made it the first time he received a vote. The fact remains that he had won the nomination by not doing "much about it himself." As if to register divine approval of the convention verdict, an eagle lit on Garfield's house in Washington at the hour he was chosen in Chicago.[45] In a clumsy attempt to placate the disgruntled Grant supporters, the convention gave second place on the ticket to Chester A. Arthur, the collector of the Port of New York, whom Hayes had ousted for inefficiency. The platform did not break new ground on any important issue and was understandably vague about the controversial policies of the Hayes Administration.

Many Democrats would have preferred to renominate Tilden in order to inject the disputed election into the campaign. This dubious strategy was thwarted by Tilden himself. Just before the convention began to ballot, he took himself out of the race, whereupon the Democrats tried to shelve the "bloody shirt" issue by nominating a distinguished Union general, Winfield S. Hancock of Pennsylvania. The convention gave second place on the ticket to W. H. English, a former Indiana congressman who had been an active politician since the 1850's.

With prosperity reviving and the scandals of the Grant Administration all but forgotten, the Republicans entered the campaign of 1880 in better standing with the voters than at any time since 1872. It soon became evident, however, that the condottieri were unhappy, although only Ben Butler openly went over to the Democrats. On June 15 Dawes found Conkling, Logan, and Cameron to be in such an ugly mood that he was fearful over the outcome of the election.[46] Garfield's cryptic statement about civil service in his letter of acceptance did not improve matters. It was not emphatic enough to satisfy Schurz and the civil-service reformers, but too positive for the condottieri. The displeasure of Cameron and Logan could be ignored, inasmuch as Pennsylvania and Illinois were almost certain to go Republican in any event. New York, on the other hand, was closely divided, and Conkling's hostility represented trouble for Garfield. Through intermediaries Garfield learned that Conkling wanted an explicit repudiation of civil-service reformers. As Stephen W. Dorsey, retired Carpetbag senator from Arkansas and Stalwart representative on the national committee, put it: ". . . They (i.e. Conkling) want to know whether the Republicans of the state of New York are to be recognized or whether the 'Scratchers' and Independents and 'Featherheads' are to ride over the Republican party of this state. . . ." [47] Garfield eventually agreed to visit New York for a conference on campaign finances, but Conkling boycotted the meeting. His lieutenants were on hand, however, and conferred secretly with Garfield after the general meeting. Although Garfield confessed that he passed a sleepless night as a result of the discussions, he told his diary that he wore "no shackles." [48] The New Yorkers, however, believed that Garfield had pledged himself to "consult" and "be guarded" by the regular Republican organization in the Empire State.[49] For the moment both sides were satisfied, and the Stalwarts rallied behind Garfield.

When the Republican candidate returned from New York in early August, he remained at his farm near Mentor, Ohio, for the duration of the campaign. Previous candidates had courted intrusions upon their privacy by the press, key politicians, and campaign managers, but 1880 was the first year that a Presidential candidate was overwhelmed by visits from voters. Swarms of school children, businessmen, party workers, and Union veterans converged on the Garfield farm. Some visitors like the Fiske Jubilee Singers and the Lincoln Club of Indianapolis were well organized and considerate enough to give the candidate advance notice of their intentions. Others simply jumped off the train at Painesville, seven miles away, and arranged with the nearest farmer for a buggy or wagon ride to Mentor. Nearly all of them had the impulse to bring Garfield some kind of gift and to present it with a song, a poem, or a speech. The hardier souls refused to get in line at the gate but instead scrambled over fences and trampled flowers. Petitioners posed even more of a problem than admirers, for they marched about with banners and distributed leaflets. Garfield was annoyed by the experience and apprehensive of the political implications. "I could not play dummy on my own doorsteps," he later told a friend, "when my yard was filled with voters from all parts of the country hurling speeches at me on all subjects." [50] He recognized that to say nothing implied agreement with the speakers and that to reply extemporaneously might result in a blunder. His way of handling the problem was to make short statements about subjects unrelated to campaign issues. After such a performance, he often confided to his diary, with an air of relief: "I think no harm has been done." [51] The era of the front-porch campaign had begun almost by accident.

Republican campaign strategy settled into the familiar grooves. Like his predecessors, Garfield believed that the outcome of the election would depend on the ability of the Republicans to carry Indiana in October.[52] National chairman Marshall Jewell contributed generously to the state's party organization,[53] on the assurance of local politicians that the vote of a Hoosier was "worth a crisp two-dollar bill." [54] One of Garfield's close friends was shocked by conditions in Indiana. He reported to the candidate that 30,000 votes were for sale, and that the Republican state organization would make an energetic effort to outbid the Democrats.[55] Under the circumstances, it was probably fortunate for the country that 1880 marked the end of October elections in Indiana.

Elsewhere, Republican politicians relied more on issues than on bribery. They unveiled a brand new "Conspirators' Song" which recounted the history of Democratic treason from 1860 to 1880.[56] They also warned veterans that pensions would be cut if the Democrats won. An abrupt change of strategy took place in mid-September when a coalition of Prohibitionists, Greenbackers, and Democrats carried the state election in Maine. Since both the Prohibitionists and Greenbackers had nominated Presidential candidates, Republican orators made a concerted effort to stop defections in other states. Even more important was the decision to emphasize the protective tariff, a switch in strategy advocated by Blaine, who thought the money question dangerous and the Southern question stale. Party placards appearing in the shop windows of Eastern industrial cities contrasted the high wages of America with the low wages of Europe and predicted that the low-tariff policy of the Democrats would reduce the worker to abject poverty.[57] Hancock tried to counter Republican propaganda by asserting that the tariff was a local issue.

Republican headquarters felt more confident when the party carried Indiana in October, but neither side was certain of the outcome until New York went Republican in November. Although Garfield had a comfortable edge of 214 to 155 over Hancock in the electoral college, his popular vote margin was only 30,000 out of approximately 10,000,000 cast. The minor party vote of 325,000 prevented either of the major parties from winning an over-all popular majority. The Republicans won the House, but control of the Senate depended on two Independents, who were receptive to bids from both parties.

VI

Since the election of Jefferson, no victorious Presidential candidate had developed such a widespread reputation for erudition as Garfield. Before entering Congress in 1862 at the age of thirty-three, Garfield had been graduated from Williams College and served successively as professor and president of the Eclectic Institute, the denominational college maintained by the Campbellite sect, to which he belonged. Not only did Garfield have a broader perspective than his co-religionists, but he managed to pursue his interest in literature, philosophy, and science amid the distractions of Washington. Along with the detachment of the academician, Garfield had a conciliatory manner, which his contemporaries interpreted as a sign of weakness. Under other circumstances his flexibility might have been an asset, but it was a definite handicap in the winter of 1880–81 when the spoilsmen resumed their struggle for power. Garfield's position was further complicated by the fact that he owed his nomination to Blaine and his election to Conkling, the principal antagonists in the protracted war between the Half Breeds and the Stalwarts. Although Garfield might have developed his own organization in time or taken over leadership of the reform movement, he was forced to take sides prematurely by the factionalists, who wanted a showdown.

Garfield intended to be fair to both sides, but Blaine knew how to manage him and slowly drew the President-elect into a frontal encounter with the Stalwarts. Garfield ought to have been placed on his guard by a letter of December 10, in which Blaine announced that the Stalwarts "must have their throats cut with a feather." [58] Yet, he continued to solicit the advice of Blaine and kept Conkling at arm's length. The suspicions of the New York boss were aroused when the press in late December leaked the news that Blaine had been appointed Secretary of State. A month later, Blaine through his supporters intervened in the New York senatorial election and held up the selection of Tom Platt, Conkling's henchman, until Platt promised to vote for the confirmation of Half Breed appointees in the state. This maneuver threatened Conkling's grip on the New York Custom House, the source of his political power. In retaliation, Conkling attempted to place a Stalwart in the Treasury Department because it had jurisdiction over the Custom House. His bulldozing tactics offended Garfield, who chose a compromise candidate. Tension was high on inauguration day, and Garfield declared open war on Conkling two weeks later by appointing Judge William H. Robertson, the leading New York Half Breed, as Collector of Customs.

Undoubtedly the slippery Blaine had pushed Garfield further than he intended to go. Nevertheless, a collision was inevitable sooner or later, because Conkling wanted dictatorial control over New York patronage. Garfield unwisely turned the Robertson appointment into a constitutional issue by asserting that it would test whether the President is "head of the government or the registering clerk of the Senate." [59] Conkling promptly exploited his opportunity with an extravagant defense of senatorial prerogatives, which brought him support from legislators who had no interest in his vendetta with the Half Breeds. It was a commentary on the sterile character of this era's party politics that the struggle over the Robertson appointment continued until mid-May.

Eventually Conkling proposed that the Senate act on all nominations but the Robertson appointment and so adjourn the special session. Garfield countered by withdrawing every New York nomination except Robertson's. When Conkling discovered that the Democrats would provide Garfield with enough votes to confirm Robertson, the New Yorker lost contact with reality. On May 16 he resigned from the Senate and forced his unhappy colleague Platt to do the same.

A wave of misfortunes successively engulfing Conkling, Garfield, and Blaine, followed this impulsive act. First, at Albany Conkling mobilized all his retainers, including Vice President Arthur, in a vain attempt to secure re-election. As a result, Conkling smashed the Republican organization in New York, and Platt, who succeeded him as party boss, could not put it back together until 1896.

Time ran out almost as quickly for Garfield. Far from settling the squabbles over patronage, the resignation of Conkling intensified them. The President found it impossible to concentrate his attention on any other subject. At the end of June he sought relief from job-seekers by fleeing Washington for a class reunion at Williams College. While he was leaving the station, a half-crazed Stalwart named Charles J. Guiteau stepped out from behind a pillar and pumped two bullets into the President's back. Garfield lingered between life and death for 79 painful days. Efforts to remove a bullet lodged near the base of his spine only succeeded in producing an infection, and he finally died September 19 at Elberon, New Jersey.

The death of the President was also fatal to Blaine, because it left him at the mercy of Chester A. Arthur, the new Stalwart President. Overnight, Blaine lost the fruits of his nine-month intrigue; he resigned from the State Department before Arthur could fire him. The senseless chain of events that killed Garfield and wrecked the Republican party did more for the cause of civil service than the decade of agitation by reformers. Public demand for curtailing the ruinous patronage wars was so overwhelming that Congress finally passed the Pendleton Law on January 16, 1883. It fell far short of converting the government bureaucracy into a genuine civil service, but it did establish the principle of basing appointments on competitive examination. Subsequent legislation eventually extended the policy to all of the major federal departments.

Arthur soon demonstrated afresh that responsibility sobers a mediocre politician. In reorganizing his cabinet, Arthur drew appointees from every element of the party, including members of the Blaine faction, who were willing to forgive and forget. Even the reformers received recognition through the appointment of Benjamin H. Brewster as Attorney General. The selection of Brewster was all the more remarkable, since he had prosecuted Arthur's personal friend, Stephen W. Dorsey, for defrauding the government on mail contracts. The President also promoted the passage of the Pendleton Law and made worthy appointees to the new civil service commission. Arthur showed just as much sense of responsibility in 1883 when he vetoed a large rivers and harbors appropriation. This courageous act prevented Congress from dissipating a large Treasury surplus, and forced it to reduce taxes. Even protective tariff rates were cut by the unhappy Republicans. Although Senator Justin Morrill of Vermont, the high priest of protection, apologized to manufacturers for the "shameful treatment of tin plates, wire rods, cotton ties, nickel, and quinine," it was the last time that Morrill felt ashamed of his colleagues.[60] A quarter-century would pass before the Republicans reduced tariffs again, and by that time high protection was the most sacred principle of the party.

Although the conscientious leadership of Arthur surprised his fellow countrymen, the President was simply displaying talents that he had previously taken great pains to conceal. He had graduated Phi Beta Kappa from Union College in 1848; passed his bar examination shortly thereafter; and developed a successful law practice before the Civil War. Yet for a bright man, Arthur was unbelievably indolent until he reached the White House. During the '70's he had been content with a subordinate role in the Conkling organization, and he seemed to prefer the company of ward heelers to that of his intellectual equals. Arthur's list of callers changed in Washington, at least during the day. After hours, however, he continued to see his old friends. The White House billiard room, which "Lemonade Lucy"—the Prohibitionist wife of President Hayes—had turned into a conservatory, was restored to its original function and fitted out with a bar. There the handsome widower-President with the mutton chop whiskers presided over lively supper parties in fawn-colored trousers. The combination of hard work and hard play shortened Arthur's life, but no President overcame a dubious reputation so rapidly.

VII

The appointment of William E. Chandler as Secretary of the Navy was Arthur's way of notifying the country that he intended to seek the nomination in 1884. Chandler did his work well, as he secured 163 out of the 240 Southern delegates and 100 delegates elsewhere. Unfortunately for Arthur, by spurning a narrow factional party he had served his country better than himself. In the process the Stalwarts had lost their cohesiveness, but the Half Breeds had clung to Blaine, who made a remarkable comeback. He bid for the support of civil-service reformers by advocating an elaborate plan to give government employees a seven-year term. Office-holders would have greater security of tenure, but not so much that they would forget their benefactors. Blaine hinted to critics of Southern policy that, if he were elected, he would establish Negro suffrage in the rebellious states. None of these promises disarmed Blaine's old enemies, but he was still the favorite of the party at large.

Other familiar figures tried for the Republican nomination. Ohio again offered John Sherman, who had little chance of victory but was determined to stop Blaine. Logan was the favorite son of Illinois and enjoyed scattered support in the smaller delegations. His bad grammar and devotion to pensions made him a favorite of the veterans, while his tirades against the South endeared him to the shrinking faction of die-hards. As usual, Edmunds, in his dual aspect of civil-service reformer and spoils-man, had picked up some New England delegates, but he aroused no interest whatever west of the Appalachians. It required faith in miracles to believe that Blaine could be stopped by such a motley crew, but all of the candidates hoped that 1880 would happen again.

The convention met on June 3 in the same Chicago auditorium where Garfield had been nominated four years earlier. The party had reached a transitional stage, with several old leaders appearing for the last time and a host of potential new leaders on the scene. From Ohio came Joseph B. Foraker, Marcus A. Hanna, and Congressman William McKinley, a trio whose paths were soon to cross in a complicated pattern on the national stage. The older Ohio leaders regarded Hanna, the level-headed Cleveland industrialist, as especially valuable because of his knowledge of "men and measures." [61] New York sent young Theodore Roosevelt to Chicago. Twenty-six years old, he had a pugnacious manner that was belied by a squeaky voice and a pince-nez. Adopting the pose of the Eastern intellectual, Roosevelt told his sister that the Edmunds group included "all the men of the broadest culture and highest character. . . ." [62] Roosevelt made friends with Henry Cabot Lodge, a kindred spirit from the Massachusetts delegation, who was representing his state for the second time at the national convention. One other youthful leader named Stephen Benton Elkins made an impact on the convention as a Blaine manager. Like Mark Hanna, the shrewd Elkins was one of the new style industrialist-politicians soon to be a familiar figure in the upper levels of the party. Elkins, after brief service in the Civil War, had made a fortune in land speculation and mining in New Mexico. A decade later he married the daughter of Henry Gassaway Davis, a multimillionaire and senator from West Virginia; and with the help of his father-in-law he had entered into banking, railroads, timber, and coal. By 1884, he was a leading Republican in New York, New Mexico, and West Virginia.

Remembering the adverse effect of untimely adjournments on Blaine's fortunes in the past, his managers forced the convention into continuous balloting the morning of June 7. This strategy was sound, because many delegates instructed for favorite-son candidates actually wanted Blaine and could not be held to their original commitment for more than a few ballots. The initial roll call showed 334½ for Blaine, 278 for Arthur, 93 for Edmunds, 63½ for Logan, 30 for Sherman, and a scattering for other candidates. Blaine gained 14½ more votes on the second ballot and slightly more still on the third. For several weeks rumors had circulated that Logan would throw his delegates to Blaine in return for the Vice Presidential nomination; and so at this juncture, the scheming Ohio politicians, who wanted the office for one of their number, tried to upset the anticipated deal. They announced that their delegation would switch from Sherman to Blaine.[63] The action of Ohio started the stampede to Blaine, who won overwhelmingly on the fourth ballot. The Ohioans received nothing for their support, for Blaine backed Logan as anticipated. The reaction of many party leaders to Blaine's nomination was distinctly cool. Sherman, Morrill, and others believed that he could not carry New York and hence would lose the election.[64] The reform wing of the party had expected the outcome without being reconciled to it: "James G. Blaine's audacity, good humor, horror of rebel brigadiers, and contempt for reformers," snorted E. L. Godkin, "made his nomination sooner or later inevitable." [65]

The Republican platform featured new planks in 1884, but none likely to revolutionize voting behavior. A plank calling for the exclusion of Chinese labor repaired an omission in 1880, which many people felt had cost the party California and Nevada. Another plank promised the suppression of polygamy in Utah, and a third endorsed the eight-hour day and the regulation of corporations. Neither of these last two proposals committed the party to do anything specific, but they reflected an awareness of public interest in new problems. Much space was devoted to more familiar matters: civil rights in the South, civil-service reform, and the protective tariff.

The Democrats served notice that they regarded New York and Indiana as pivotal states by nominating Governor Grover Cleveland of New York for President and Thomas A. Hendricks for Vice President. Cleveland was an unknown quantity, but he had quarreled with Tammany, which made him attractive to reformers. The selection of Hendricks reassured old-fashioned Democrats, since he had been an outstanding champion of the party in the Senate during the Reconstruction era. Except for partisan jabs at the Republicans, the Democratic platform contained nothing very distinctive. Some Southerners would have liked to fight the campaign on the tariff, but the Eastern wing of the party, led by ex-Speaker Randall, was strongly protectionist, and it blocked a clear-cut statement on the subject.

The lack of strong issues turned the campaign into a contest between personalities. One observer predicted that victory would go to the party "that can cast the most stink pots." [66] Apparently the party managers agreed, because the campaign of 1884 was certainly the dirtiest since 1872 and perhaps the dirtiest in American history. A Buffalo newspaper set the pattern for the Republicans on July 21 by revealing that Cleveland was supporting the illegitimate son of a widow of doubtful morals named Maria Halpin. Further investigation indicated that Cleveland was uncertain of the child's paternity but desirous of behaving honorably. Whatever the truth in the matter, it received an indecent amount of attention, and gave rise to a Republican campaign chant: "Ma, Ma, where's my Pa? Going to the White House! Ha, Ha, Ha!" [67] The Democrats replied in kind with whispers that Blaine's first child was born only six months after his marriage.[68] The charge was untrue and easily dealt with. The Democrats, meanwhile, turned their attention to Blaine's private finances, and in September they produced some new Mulligan letters. They also dredged up old material about Blaine's dealings with railroads in the early '70's when he had been Speaker of the House. As the principal journalistic spokesman for the anti-Blaine reformers, Godkin revived the tactic which the Republicans had used on Greeley. He printed contradictory Blaine statements in parallel newspaper columns. Since Blaine had been saying different things to different people for years, there was an inexhaustible supply of material. The *New York World* also put their new reproductive process for cartoons at the service of the Democrats. Hitherto confined to magazines, cartoons suddenly achieved mass circulation, and throughout the campaign the *World* featured merciless front-page caricatures of Blaine.

Nobody knows how many voters were swayed by the mud-slinging of the two parties in 1884, but their efforts probably cancelled out each other. A number of other factors converged to deprive Blaine of New York and the Presidency. For one thing, a large number of reformers who had supported Edmunds at the convention decided to bolt the party and vote for Cleveland. Derisively called Mugwumps, they waged a furious campaign under the leadership of Carl Schurz, who refused to "look upon Mr. Blaine as a mere jolly, prince Hal who has lived through his years of indiscretion and would make a good President." [69] After much indecision, Roosevelt and Lodge decided to remain regular, but they had little influence on others. In mid-October, Reid ruefully reported to Blaine that he had lost both the Civil Service Reform Clubs and the normally Republican Knickerbocker and Union Clubs in New York City.[70] Edmunds might have been able to help Blaine with these groups, but he blamed the latter for a *Tribune* article attacking his financial integrity, and so he flatly refused to participate in the campaign.[71] Other splinter groups hurt Blaine. The Prohibitionists had been rebuffed at the Republican convention. Their Presidential candidate, John F. St. John, gave forty speeches in New York, and ultimately polled 25,000 votes, mostly at the expense of Blaine.[72] Roscoe Conkling also worked to settle an old score with Blaine.[73] Conkling's home county of Oneida had given Garfield a majority of 2053 in 1880 and was to give Cleveland a majority of 19 in 1884.[74] A further erosion of Republican strength took place because Whitelaw Reid persistently refused to settle a strike of the typographical union against his *New York Tribune,* despite Blaine's pleas.[75] The union magazine, *The Boycotter,* came out against the Republican ticket, and union sources later claimed that most of the 3500 members voted for Cleveland.[76]

To reduce the influence of these defections, the Republicans frantically tried to draw the Irish away from the Democrats in New York. Blaine made discreet references to his Catholic relatives and visited a large number of seminaries. W. E. Chandler and Elkins arranged for Ben Butler, who had been nominated by the Anti-Monopoly party, to be paid $5000 per week to concentrate his campaign on the Irish in New York City.[77]

Near the end of the campaign, the Republican managers feared that they had overdone the appeal to the Irish Catholics, and so they brought Blaine back to New York for a meeting with 400 Protestant clergymen at the Fifth Avenue Hotel. To avoid interdenominational frictions, it was agreed that the oldest clergyman in point of service would read a resolution endorsing Blaine. This responsibility fell to the Reverend Samuel D. Burchard, who also appended some extemporaneous remarks. One of these described the Democrats as the party of "Rum, Romanism, and Rebellion." Since Blaine was thinking about his own response,[78] he missed these inflammatory words, and they floated through the parlor uncontradicted. They might not have escaped the four walls but for the fact that the Democratic manager, Senator Arthur P. Gorman of Maryland, had assigned a stenographer to trail Blaine, on the chance that he might make a slip.[79] Gorman worked fast, and "Rum, Romanism, and Rebellion" leaflets were spread over the whole state within forty-eight hours. Later the same day, Blaine's managers had arranged a dinner with a cluster of millionaires at Delmonico's, a gathering which the Democrats effectively depicted as a Belshazzar's feast.

The electorate had only a few days to digest these dramatic last-minute developments before it went to the polls. Few voters behaved differently than in 1880, and the 900,000 new voters divided their allegiance almost equally between Republicans and Democrats. A mere five states changed from one column to the other; and two of these, California and Nevada, actually returned to their normal Republican allegiance. As expected, however, the election was decided in New York, and its 36 electoral votes went to Cleveland by the slim plurality of 1000. Any one of the dissident groups, from Conkling's Oneida County organization to the typographical union, might have dealt the deciding blow to the Republicans. Blaine himself blamed bad weather and the Reverend Samuel D. Burchard for the outcome.[80] In any event, Cleveland received 219 electoral votes to 182 for Blaine. The Democrats carried the House by a comfortable margin, but the Republicans increased their Senate majority from one to nine, which meant there would be at least two more years of divided government.

For most of the Republicans in Congress, the acceptance of minority status did not require much adjustment in outlook. They had been obstructing Presidents off and on since the inception of the party and felt more comfortable about their tactics with a Democrat in the White House. The new situation invited the party to reaffirm its traditional role as the defender of congressional powers against encroachment by Presidents. It did so with relish.

During his first months in office, Cleveland was engaged in a fierce wrangle with his own party over patronage. Friction developed so quickly because the ravenous appetite of rank-and-file Democrats for spoils collided with the President's evident intention of honoring his pledge to civil-service reformers. In the end, most of the 110,000 jobs not covered by the Pendleton Act went to Democrats, although Cleveland let some competent Republicans serve out their four-year terms. His policy displeased both the impatient Democrats, who wanted a general housecleaning, and the Mugwumps, who wanted no removals on political grounds. When Congress assembled in 1885, the Republicans added their voices to the chorus. Edmunds led off by trying to revive the Tenure of Office Act. He assured his colleagues that they lived under the baleful shadow of executive tyranny. The Vermonter sounded as if he was rereading his old speeches, and some of the more excitable Democrats expected him to propose the impeachment of Grover Cleveland. Republican senators enjoyed twitting the President for inconsistencies in appointment policy, but they knew better than to launch a counter-offensive. Despite the outbursts of florid oratory, both sides were willing to settle for the status quo. Henceforth, Presidents would control appointments and removals in the cabinet, but would have to share an ill-defined jurisdiction over other patronage with Congress as in the past. Thanks to the stubborn fight by Hayes and Garfield, the executive branch had regained the position which it occupied before the Civil War. Since Cleveland was not disposed to fight for more, the powers of the President did not expand markedly until the twentieth century. The voters seemed satisfied with the terms of the truce, because the off-year elections of 1886 left the composition of Congress virtually unchanged.

With a Presidential election only two years away, both Cleveland and the Republicans began to search harder for issues. The rumbling in the West against railroads finally scared enough congressmen into passing an interstate commerce law in January 1887. It outlawed railroad pools, drawbacks, and rebates, and prohibited the carriers from charging a higher rate for a short haul than for a long one. The railroad question was a little too volatile for the senators, and some twenty-five of them declined to be recorded for or against the interstate commerce law. Even the sponsors were decidedly cool toward it. To protect themselves, they refrained from giving the interstate commerce commission established by the law adequate power to enforce its provisions.

Pensions were a safer issue and evoked more spirited partisanship. Reflecting the views of Southerners ineligible for benefits, Cleveland vetoed a dependent pensions bill in the short session and gave the same treatment to a spate of private bills which reached his desk. This tactic showed more courage than political intelligence, because nearly 750,000 Union veterans drew some kind of pension. Cleveland increased their indignation by ordering the return of Confederate battle flags to Southern states. He also pointedly went fishing over Memorial Day to avoid participation in G.A.R. celebrations. Republican Governor Joseph Foraker of Ohio, who had recently won election by waving the bloody shirt, responded defiantly to the Presidential order about rebel flags, and said that none would be surrendered while he was governor.[81] The Democrats derisively dubbed Foraker "Fire Alarm Joe," but he stirred up such a storm of protest that Cleveland had to rescind the order.

Cleveland now turned hopefully to the protective tariff—an issue on which his party had prudently avoided a clear-cut stand for a quarter of a century. First, the President used patronage to destroy the political influence of ex-Speaker Samuel J. Randall, the high-tariff Philadelphia Democrat who had helped the Republicans to block drastic rate reductions in the '70's and '80's. Then Cleveland devoted his entire annual message of December 1887 to a plea for tariff reduction. He characterized the protective tariff and "its illegitimate child" the trust, as unjust, unwise, and wicked. Mindful of growing economic discontent, he added that the protective system made the masses poorer and the wealthy richer. Finally, Cleveland pleaded for tariff reduction as the proper way to reduce an embarrassingly large Treasury surplus. Democratic congressmen were willing to sponsor the issue, as long as they did not have to defend any specific law. They pushed a modest tariff cut known as the Mills bill through the House in the summer of 1888; they knew it would be defeated by the Republican Senate. Most Republicans welcomed the challenge on the theory that the Democrats were running the greatest risk by adopting a new position. Nevertheless, the Mills bill put Republican senators in a quandary. Some wanted a new high-tariff bill, while others thought that any tampering with rates would offend some pressure group or other. John Sherman, who once more represented the Republicans in the Senate on financial measures, urged his colleagues to do nothing except assail the Mills bill as a free-trade measure.[82] But by this time the Presidential campaign was on, and the national committee thought industrialists would contribute more money to the party if the Senate revised key rates upward. A Republican caucus in the Upper House supported his plan, and it appointed a committee of eleven to draft a bill. William B. Allison of Iowa did not report the bill out of committee until October 3, and it was immediately tabled. Thus, most of the electorate saw that the Republicans favored protection, but no one knew to what extent.

Meanwhile, the search for a Republican Presidential candidate was on. The 1884 election was the last to be waged under the influence of old issues and concepts of leadership. Retirement and death had continued to thin the ranks of the condottieri after 1884. Grant, Arthur, and Logan died within a year of the election, and soon after Butler retired from politics. William E. Chandler baffled his old Stalwart associates by turning into a foe of corporations and heavy campaign expenditures, which left Blaine as the sole remaining representative of the old era.

Between 1885 and the nominating convention more industrialists like Elkins and Hanna had become active in Republican politics. The condottieri had never been indifferent to pressure from business, but they had regarded political power as an end in itself. The new leaders, on the other hand, built machines as a means for controlling the economic policy of government, and assumed that the prosperity of business was equivalent to the prosperity of the country. Without apology or equivocation, they tried to identify the party with the emerging entrepreneurial class.

Probably the most adroit of the new bosses was Matthew Stanley Quay, who, after a long apprenticeship in the amoral politics of Pennsylvania, became a senator in 1887 and undertook active management of the Cameron machine. A scholarly face and considerable personal charm made the shrewd Quay an ideal fund-raiser among the wealthy Philadelphia manufacturers. Platt of New York was a holdover from the old days, but he shared the newer concepts of political management. As the principal figure in the United States Express Company, he saw the desirability of a marriage between business and politics. By 1888, Platt was Republican state boss, but for a time he had difficulty controlling such energetic Blaine adherents as Whitelaw Reid, Warner Miller, and Chauncey Depew.

With some nineteen candidates in 1888, there was no prospect of a first-ballot nomination at the Republican convention. During the pre-convention maneuvers, the ever hopeful John Sherman accumulated the largest number of delegates. As usual, his principal handicap was the Ohio delegation, which contained all the ambitious politicians who had made their debut in 1884, plus several more. As early as February 5, one would-be President-maker predicted that Sherman would be destroyed in his own state by the dashing, versatile Governor Foraker.[83] Hanna imagined that he could be loyal simultaneously to Sherman and Congressman McKinley. All these inveterate schemers pledged their support to Sherman, but this ritual demonstration of solidarity did not impress leaders outside the state.[84] Others wrote off Sherman because of his animosity to Blaine and Platt.[85]

The Midwest also had as candidates Senator Allison of Iowa, former Governor Russell A. Alger of Michigan, Walter Q. Gresham of Indiana, and ex-Senator Benjamin Harrison, also of Indiana. Allison attracted interest primarily because of his ability to represent the policy of Eastern Republicans as if it were designed to help the Midwest. As a prominent Civil War general, Alger benefited from the upsurge of indignation against Cleveland's pension policy. Gresham was not nearly as prominent as Allison or Alger, but he had served briefly in Arthur's cabinet and for a longer period as a judge. He was popular with the farmers because of his bias against railroads. Like Alger, ex-Senator Harrison of Indiana had a strong Civil War record and a formidable reputation as a debater. Harrison was further strengthened by the fact that he was a grandson of President William Henry Harrison and a resident of a doubtful state. But his failure to secure re-election to the Senate in 1886 and his life-long antagonism to his fellow Indianian Gresham militated against his chances.[86] The only noteworthy Eastern candidate was Chauncey Depew, president of the New York Central Railroad, and nobody took his aspirations seriously. It was commonly believed that Platt intended to use Depew as a stalking horse and then throw the New York delegation to some candidate who would agree to appoint him Secretary of the Treasury.[87] In any case, a life-long career with an unpopular railroad constituted an insurmountable barrier to Depew.

The chief obstacle to the Eastern bosses like Platt and Quay was Blaine. Since the middle of 1887 the aging warhorse had consistently denied that he was a candidate.[88] He pleaded ill health and inadequate financial resources, but his real reason for retiring was his belief that he had been disqualified by defeat in 1884. Repeatedly, Blaine insisted that a beaten candidate needed unanimous party support, and he expressed doubt that he could command it.[89] To make his position clearer, Blaine ostentatiously went to Europe before delegates were chosen and indicated that he would remain abroad until after the convention. He dispatched letters reaffirming his position. These gestures had no effect on his chief supporters, who tried to organize a draft.[90] The principal figures in this movement were Reid and Elkins. They promoted the selection of uninstructed or favorite-son delegations sympathetic to Blaine and predicted that Blaine would accept a unanimous call from the party.[91] This strategy was predicated on the belief that a protracted deadlock would develop and leave the delegates with no alternative but Blaine. The wily Elkins, though, was taking no chances of being caught without a candidate. He had taken the precaution of opening negotiations with Harrison in February and continued to keep lines of communication intact throughout the spring. Elkins tried to avoid charges of duplicity by telling Harrison's manager, Louis T. Michener, that Blaine's nomination was a remote possibility and that Harrison was the logical heir of the "plumed knight."

Against this background of high-level intrigue, the Republican delegates assembled in Chicago on June 21. Contrary to precedent, the Democrats had met first, renominated Cleveland by acclamation, and adopted a platform emphasizing tariff reduction. The Republicans countered with a plank vowing to uphold the protective system, but, while the platform committee was drafting the party manifesto, the foes of Blaine were laying plans to avert a stampede. Their program called for no more than two ballots per session,[92] and they succeeded in imposing this pattern on the convention both Friday and Saturday. On the initial ballot, Sherman led with 229, followed by Gresham with 111, Depew with 99, Alger with 84, Harrison 80, Allison 72, and Blaine 55. No substantial changes occurred until the fourth ballot, when 58 of New York's 72 votes shifted from Depew to Harrison. Just before the switch, Hanna advised Sherman to step aside for McKinley.[93] Foraker moved in a different direction, and, after telling the Ohio delegates that Sherman could not be nominated, the Governor hinted he might support Blaine.

At this point the convention was adjourned until Monday morning. During the weekend Blaine cabled two Maine supporters, S. A. Boutelle and J. H. Manley, reiterating his earlier stand and requesting that his decision be made public.[94] Simultaneously, Elkins received a coded cablegram from Blaine's host, in Scotland, the iron magnate Andrew Carnegie, which read: "Too late Victor [i.e. Blaine] immoveable; take trump [Harrison]. . . ."[95] With this message in his pocket, Elkins took a carriage ride with Platt and promised him the Treasury portfolio if the rest of the New York delegation swung to Harrison. It is doubtful that Elkins was authorized to make an explicit pledge to Platt, although Harrison had granted Michener wide discretionary powers in a letter of June 12.[96] In addition, on Sunday Sherman and Harrison agreed to unite their strength if either made a substantial gain after the initial ballot on Monday.[97]

Rumors of the Sunday deals produced belated co-operation between Allison and Gresham on Monday morning. Harrison made the anticipated gains on the fifth and sixth ballots. By this time the trend was evident, but Manley read Blaine's telegram before the seventh to increase its effect. It took one more roll call to convince Quay of Pennsylvania that Harrison was inevitable, and he delivered 50 votes on the eighth ballot. The convention then named Levi P. Morton, a prominent New York banker, for Vice President and adjourned.

From the standpoint of organizational cohesiveness and morale, the Republican party emerged from the convention in better shape than in any election year since 1868. There were no disgruntled factions to conciliate. In the end, every element of the party had co-operated in the nomination of Harrison. This advantage was consolidated by the selection of Quay and James S. Clarkson of Iowa as chairman and vice chairman of the national committee. The two men possessed complementary talents. Quay was an excellent money-raiser and Clarkson an excellent organizer. Aided by generous contributions from businessmen apprehensive about the tariff, Quay accumulated a record campaign fund of $3,000,000. He was helped by John Wanamaker, the Philadelphia department-store executive, who headed a special sub-committee and raised an additional $300,000.[98] Wanamaker spent half of the total, bet the other half on Harrison, and after the party's victory returned the original investment to the contributors, plus 30 per cent profit.[99]

Clarkson capitalized on a revival of local Republican clubs that had begun in the late '70's, and had gained momentum in 1887 through the formation of a National League of Republican Voters. With Clarkson co-ordinating the organizational drive, some 10,000 individual clubs were functioning by the end of the campaign. Charters prohibited members from using their clubs to promote either nominations or appointments. This wise restriction forced officers to focus their attention on the enrollment and transportation of new voters to the polls. The clubs also held rallies, distributed literature, and promoted enthusiasm. The efficient Quay-Clarkson organization worked carefully to win back the splinter groups that had cost the party so heavily in 1884. Quay managed to secure mailing lists of *The Voice,* the official journal of the Prohibitionist party, with the result that subscribers received literature telling them that the best way to promote their cause was to vote Republican.[100] Considerable attention was also devoted to the Irish, although friction developed between Quay and Wharton Barker, a fellow Pennsylvanian, over the expenditure of funds.[101] Behind their disagreement was a difference of opinion as to which of the numerous Irish organizations could deliver the vote.[102] Barker ended the campaign on bad terms with Quay, but between them the two men managed to convince a number of Irish to vote Republican. Other factors helped the party divide this strongly Democratic group. Cleveland's tariff policy was described as pro-British. Party leaders also made the most of the famous Murchison letter. Written by British Minister Sackville-West to a California Republican, who was posing as a former British subject and soliciting advice on the election, the letter urged a vote for Cleveland. The letter was published in the *Los Angeles Times* on October 21 [103] and convinced some Irishmen that Cleveland had become a tool of the British.

Harrison surprised observers by his effective front porch campaigning. He delivered ninety-four extemporaneous speeches without making a single blunder.[104] He mainly discussed the tariff, pensions, and Negro rights at the polls. Quay had wanted the candidate to confine himself to platitudes, but the Pennsylvanian was so elated by the treatment of thorny issues that he jokingly said, "We could safely close these headquarters and he [Harrison] would elect himself." [105] Harrison drew all the attention, because Cleveland neither campaigned nor went beyond the position outlined in his letter of acceptance. The President had staked his future on the tariff, and as far as he was concerned no other issue really mattered.

During the campaign Harrison had made the statement that he would rather carry Indiana than the whole country,[106] and his state's Republicans took him at his word. As a result, the state campaign was waged with a corruptness remarkable even for Indiana. Both sides imported voters and tried to stuff the ballot boxes. "Divide the floaters into blocks of five," wrote a Republican organizer to his lieutenants, "and put a trusted man with necessary funds in charge of these five and make him responsible that none get away and that all vote our ticket." [107]

Harrison displayed a sound instinct in wanting to carry Indiana. Along with New York, it switched from the Democratic to the Republican column, and gave him the electoral college by a margin of 233 to 168. The closeness of the election was emphasized by the fact that Cleveland actually received 80,000 more popular votes than Harrison. For the first time since 1880, the Republicans won both houses of Congress. The Senate ratio of 39 Republicans and 37 Democrats remained unchanged, while the Republicans held a slim majority of 7 in the House, which included 18 Southerners.

It was evident that Harrison intended to devote his attention to such familiar problems as pensions, the protective tariff, and the South. But his plans were shaken by the emergence of a new issue. A serene ex-President in Fremont, Ohio, told his diary that the new issue was the question of wealth and asked: "Shall it be held, controlled, owned by a few?" [108] Harrison did not see the issue in the same way, nor was he prepared to deal with it, but before he retired from office many voters were demanding an answer.

VII

Tariffs, Silver, and Expansion

No President was more effective as a campaigner and less effective as a party leader than Benjamin Harrison. The conflicting impulses that contended for mastery in his enigmatic personality proved to be his undoing. He loved politics but disliked politicians; he possessed a fine sense of humor but kept it a carefully guarded secret; [1] and he displayed a superb ability in the analysis of problems but none in the management of men. Piled on top of the other contradictions was a streak of blind partisanship which Harrison seldom exhibited outside the arena of politics. Not only did he defend party policies that had been out of fashion for a decade, but he did so with a conviction and logic that amazed his contemporaries. If Harrison had shown half the deference to Republican leaders in Congress that he showed to Republican principles, he would have avoided much trouble. As it was, the President often greeted congressmen and senators with the coolness of a man who expects to be asked for a personal loan. His demeanor became more ungracious when he was drawn into discussions of patronage; and since the topic overshadowed all others for several months after the election, Harrison had unlimited opportunities to make enemies.

At the outset, he damaged himself by his peculiar approach to cabinet-making. His only realistic alternatives were to balance off the claims of party bosses and reformers or to reward indiscriminately younger politicians with a promising future. Harrison acted on neither principle but selected a disproportionate number of cabinet members with no political following. In New York the claims of both Platt and his factional foes were ignored; the obscure Benjamin Tracy represented the state in the Navy Department. A similar pattern developed in Pennsylvania, where the choice of John Wanamaker as Postmaster General did not strengthen Harrison with either Boss Quay or the reform element headed by Wharton Barker.[2] His worst problem, however, was Blaine, whom he distrusted but to whom he had promised the State Department portfolio in return for support at the convention.[3] A prompt and cheerful offer of the post might have brought Harrison as much loyalty as the calculating Blaine was constitutionally capable of giving anyone. Unfortunately, the President-elect postponed the inevitable until mid-January. Then he sent Blaine a terse, official offer of the position, accompanied by a longer private letter informing him of the rules for chivalrous conduct in the Administration.[4] Blaine was too hungry for office to take public notice of this reflection on his character. But he had a good memory, and more incentive than ever to use his talent for intrigue. Harrison failed to improve his position in the distribution of patronage. Some were offended by the substance of his policy. Others received what they wanted but took exception to the President's manner.[5] Cullom of Illinois reacted badly because he was never offered a seat during patronage interviews.[6] Another disgruntled suppliant reported that the President "was a purely intellectual being and had no bowels." [7]

Civil-service reformers quickly became as dissatisfied with Harrison as the regulars. His appointment of J. S. Clarkson as supervisor of personnel in the postal department heralded an abrupt return to the spoils system. Clarkson regarded civil service as "the toy of a child," [8] and began firing Democratic postmasters at the rate of one every three minutes.[9] While this efficient work was going on, Harrison tried to conciliate Mugwumps by appointing young Theodore Roosevelt to the civil service commission. In the end, this gesture came to nothing, because the President ignored Roosevelt's recommendations.

With virtually all Republicans in an irritable mood, the prospects for the party legislative program looked bleak. Slim majorities of seven in the House and two in the Senate left the dissidents in a commanding position. They were not likely to block measures that promised such obvious political dividends as increased appropriations for pensions or internal improvements. But they might wreck tariff revision, to say nothing of an Administration-sponsored bill for federal supervision of Southern elections. Old wire-pullers such as Sherman of Ohio, Allison of Iowa, and Cullom of Illinois were back in the Senate and ready to disarm opponents of the party program with meaningless concessions. The House, however, was under new management and hence a more doubtful quantity. The speakership fell to Thomas B. Reed, a shrewd and sarcastic congressman from Maine, who was starting his second decade of service. His understudy, Joseph G. Cannon of Danville, Illinois, had entered the House in 1872 and specialized in concealing his astuteness behind a smoke screen of rustic platitudes. Two junior congressmen came forward to share the leadership burdens of the session: William McKinley and Henry Cabot Lodge. The former had already become a power in Ohio politics, and as chairman of the ways and means committee he was entrusted with the all-important task of framing the tariff bill. This trio seemed better fitted than Lodge to subordinate their judgment to the demands of party discipline. At the age of thirty-eight, Lodge could look back on a career which had successively featured graduation from Harvard, editorship of the *North American Review,* a professorship in colonial history at his alma mater, and a ten-year flirtation with reform politics. Lodge lacked Cannon's inclination to cover up his attainments. Not only was he a Boston aristocrat, he behaved like one. Lodge might have finished his life as a frustrated Beacon Street Mugwump if his fellow intellectuals had not ostracized him brutally for supporting Blaine in 1884. In retaliation he embraced the doctrine of party regularity with the fervor of a dervish and was rewarded in 1886 with a seat in Congress.

The leaders of both Houses saw an opportunity to increase their majority by admitting territories with Republican voting habits. Moreover, a substantial backlog of appropriate candidates existed, since the Democrats had blocked all statehood bills during the decade they controlled the House. The Republicans barred Democratic Arizona and New Mexico for obvious reasons, but inducted North Dakota, South Dakota, Montana, Wyoming, Idaho, and Washington as a bloc. Although this maneuver gave the Republicans six more seats in the House and twelve in the Senate, the new members were so unreliable that they did the party more harm than good. All of them represented frontier communities which at the moment were feeling the effects of such familiar pioneer diseases as over-expansion and land speculation. Drought, low agriculture prices, and depressed conditions in the silver-mining industry added to the misery of the settlers and made them more bellicose. Besides, the western two-thirds of Kansas and Nebraska were suffering the same difficulties and sending the same kind of representatives to Washington.

The radical views of the new members did not produce much of a problem in the House. They soon learned that good committee assignments were contingent upon an orthodox voting record and came to prefer the wrath of their constituents to the wrath of Reed. In addition, the speaker succeeded in reducing his dependence on maverick Westerners by a revolutionary interpretation of House rules. To establish a quorum, he started counting as present Democrats who were in their seats but refused to answer roll calls, and after a brief struggle the House sustained the Reed rules. The outraged Democrats dubbed the Speaker "Czar Reed," and he lived up to the title by enforcing discipline with the thoroughness of Thaddeus Stevens. Under his leadership, the tiny Republican House majority thwarted the obstructive tactics of the opposition and passed every major Administration bill.

Matters did not go so well in the Senate, where the twelve newcomers made common cause with their colleagues from Nebraska, Kansas, Colorado, and Nevada. Altogether, they amounted to more than 20 per cent of the total membership. In addition to holding a casual view of their party obligations, the newcomers took full advantage of the Senate rules, which encouraged independent action. Seniority meant nothing to them, and lectures on deportment by glacial New Englanders like Edmunds and Hale only made the Westerners more defiant.[10] As a group they had little interest in the tariff and still less in federal supervision of Southern elections. But they wanted to do something for distressed farmers and silver miners. In fact, they were so insistent on both points that they were prepared to act with the Democrats if necessary.

The session was hardly a month old before it became apparent that the newcomers were a third force in the Senate and held the balance of power between the party regulars and the Democrats. Hitherto the pointless quarrels of the condottieri had constituted the sole threat to Republican stability, and sectional economic disputes had been compromised with a minimum of disturbances. Henceforth, however, the party would have to deal with a chronically disgruntled minority of Westerners which it was unable either to assimilate or to exclude permanently from its counsels. Because they came from sparsely settled states, the dissidents would seldom be able to influence the outcome of national elections, but their twenty-odd senators would often succeed in wrecking the party's legislative program.

As anticipated, all Republican factions co-operated in passing a huge pork-barrel appropriation and extending pension coverage to virtually all Civil War veterans and their dependents. Trouble started for the Administration when the McKinley tariff bill reached the Senate. Like the extravagant appropriations for pensions and internal improvements, it was intended to reduce a large Treasury surplus as well as to provide generous protection for industry. Raw sugar, which had offended the protectionists by contributing over $50,000,000 annually to the budget, was placed on the free list. The bill also featured selective rate cuts on other high-revenue producers that were not central to the protective system. Consumers seemed unlikely to benefit from the proposed sugar schedule, because the bill retained the duty on refined sugar and offered a bounty to cane-sugar producers. The most ingenious feature of the McKinley tariff was a blanket increase of industrial rates to levels that would exclude imports altogether. This arrangement would serve the dual purpose of rewarding industrialists for their campaign contributions and shutting off an embarrassing source of revenue.

It was hoped that the extension of the protective principle to eggs, butter, wheat, barley, and potatoes would reduce the opposition in the farm states, even if it did not help the farmer. But Plumb of Kansas, Pettigrew of South Dakota, and Teller of Colorado attacked the high industrial rates in the McKinley bill. Even the hesitant Cullom grumbled that hundreds of protected articles "are carried abroad and sold in foreign markets at from 25% to 60% less than is charged to the American consumer." [11] Not all the critics intended to vote against the McKinley bill, but it became clear that they would continue to talk until something was done about silver and the trusts. Since it was mid-summer of 1890 before the McKinley bill cleared the Senate finance committee, the prospect of a protracted deadlock during the campaigning season frightened the protectionists into concessions.

Silver was the more perplexing of the two issues. During the halfcentury before 1873, one ounce of gold had been worth approximately 15½ ounces of silver on the world market. The stability of this relationship had encouraged many countries, including America, to establish a bimetallic monetary system and to provide for coinage at the commercial ratio. The bimetallic system had never fulfilled the expectations of its creators, because a statutory ratio seldom coincided with the commercial ratio for more than a few weeks. Even a slight change in the latter encouraged enterprising citizens to melt down and sell coins made of the dearer metal, with the practical result that only the cheaper metal remained in circulation. The American government had established an official ratio of 16 to 1 in 1837, which slightly undervalued silver. Under the circumstances, it had proved impossible to keep silver in circulation, and Congress had dropped the silver dollar from the coinage list in 1873. Shortly thereafter, Western mines began to produce silver in tremendous quantities. Simultaneously, several European countries abandoned bimetallism for the single gold standard. The commercial ratio quickly reflected both the increase in silver production and the reduction in demand by increasing to 18 to 1. This development quickly revived interest in re-establishing the statutory ratio of 16 to 1.

Senators from silver-producing states, who had made no protest at the time the silver dollar was dropped, began denouncing "the Crime of '73." [12] Enlisting the support of the miners, they clamored for bimetallism in the hope of increasing both the use and the price of silver. Inflationists of every description added their voices to the chorus. They had been indifferent to bimetallism as long as the official ratio reflected market conditions, but they hoped to discharge with cheap silver dollars debts contracted in gold dollars with a higher purchasing power. Congress had temporarily stifled their agitation by passing the Bland-Allison Act in 1878, which obliged the government to purchase and coin a minimum of $2,000,000 worth of silver per month. Provision was also made to issue silver certificates for silver dollars deposited at the Treasury. In effect, the Bland-Allison Act provided a modest subsidy to the silver producers and an annual increase in the money supply, while avoiding unlimited coinage at the ratio of 16 to 1. This compromise policy maintained the gold standard and permitted restricted use of silver. Many conservative Republicans went a step further by declaring for the restoration of full bimetallism through international agreement. Neither Harrison nor the Senate leaders, however, showed any interest in going beyond the terms of the Bland-Allison Act until the silver faction forced their hand.

As usual, the task of providing the rebels with illusory concessions fell to John Sherman, who was now sixty-seven years old but still unrivaled as a legislative operator. He cannily proposed to replace the Bland-Allison policy of silver purchases in terms of dollars with one of silver purchases in terms of ounces. If silver prices continued downward as he anticipated, the new arrangement might cost the government less than the old one.[13] The silver group warily swallowed the bait, because the Sherman bill provided for the monthly purchase of 4,500,000 ounces, which was roughly equivalent to the national output. Senate managers also hinted that a free-coinage bill would follow as a reward for party regularity, although they were purposely vague about the date. The agrarian allies of the silver senators took mild pleasure in the inflationary provision for the issuance of silver certificates in amounts equal to the silver purchased by the government. The soft-money men were encouraged to believe that the Secretary of the Treasury would exercise the option granted him by the bill to redeem the silver certificates in silver as well as gold. Nobody who had bothered to check Harrison's record on monetary legislation could have possibly entertained such a hope, but a few naïve Westerners confidently expected the establishment of bimetallism by administrative action. So the Sherman Silver Purchase bill floated through the Senate at the end of June 1890 on a wave of misconceptions and delusions.

Simultaneously, the judiciary committee was completing action on an anti-trust bill which bore the name of Sherman although drafted mainly by Edmunds.[14] After a rough debate, Edmunds persuaded the Senate to delete amendments designed to apply anti-trust procedures selectively. In the end, the Sherman Anti-Trust Law was stripped down to a simple statutory reaffirmation of the old common-law prohibition against illegal combinations in restraint of trade. The bolder spirits felt tricked by the outcome, but they would have felt still worse had they foreseen the unwillingness of the government to prosecute the trusts and of the courts to convict them.

The ardent Senate protectionists who had co-operated with the Westerners to clear the tracks for the McKinley bill found another obstacle awaiting them. It was the Force bill, which passed the House on July 2 and reached the Senate a few days later. The pressure for the Force bill had originated in the White House, where Harrison was energetically reversing the Hayes policy of friendliness toward the Southern whites. Except in the Border, the policy had brought few recruits to the party, and Harrison regarded federal protection of the Negro vote as the sole way to promote a Republican revival. The President also expected important side effects from a vigorous enforcement policy. He believed it would create a permanent majority for the protective tariff in Dixie and prevent Southern tactics of intimidation at the polls from spreading northward.[15] Harrison would have preferred the original Lodge bill authorizing the government to control federal elections, but was prevailed upon to accept a weaker measure which left the elections in the hands of state officials. The Force bill sought to control the behavior of state officials by increasing the powers of federal supervisors and empowering circuit courts to review and reverse returns upon a petition from 100 citizens in a congressional district. With these adjustments, the Force bill had passed the House on a straight party vote, after Speaker Reed had explained that it was just as fair for the Republicans to poll ignorant Negroes in the South as for Democrats to poll ignorant immigrants in the North.[16]

Reed's logic was never tested in the Senate, because Southern Democrats filibustered with great resourcefulness. On August 7, Quay and Cameron, the Pennsylvania protectionists, convinced the Republican caucus to postpone consideration of the Force bill until the short session so that the Senate could act on the tariff. More weeks of debate followed, and the McKinley bill became law just in time for its shortcomings to have a maximum effect on the congressional elections of 1890.

II

In the House, the party suffered its most severe reversal since 1874. The party lost over eighty seats to the Democrats, who emerged with an overwhelming majority of 235 to 88. Both McKinley and Cannon lost their seats, while other Republican leaders had to be content with sharply reduced pluralities. Popular dissatisfaction with the tariff and the extravagant appropriations of the 51st Congress were primarily responsible for the upheaval in the industrial East, whereas drought and the intensification of agricultural depression produced the same result in the Mississippi valley. The Republicans lost senators only in Kansas and South Dakota, but the unreliability of their Western bloc deprived them of effective control in the Upper House. More ominous than the gains of the Democrats was the victory of nine Independent representatives and two senators in the Great Plains and Rocky Mountains. The storm center of third-party activity was in Kansas, Nebraska, and the Dakotas, but it swept over neighboring Minnesota and Iowa as well. Legislatures in four of the five states fell either partly or wholly under the control of the new movement, which just missed electing several governors as well.

Precinct workers who had been in touch with recent political developments in the West knew that the third-party movement was the fruit of agitation conducted for nearly a decade by the Northern Alliance. This organization had inherited most of the discontented agrarian groups previously active in the Grant era. During the early '80's, it had tried to improve the position of the farmers by encouraging them to organize a variety of business enterprises and compete directly with corporations. None of these efforts had been very successful; and in the late '80's, the Alliance had decided to engage in direct political activity and bid for the co-operation of various labor groups. Simultaneously, an alliance movement with similar economic objectives had emerged in the South. Since it was logical for the two groups to unify and launch a nation-wide political party, a joint alliance convention met at St. Louis in December 1889 to explore the possibilities. The conference accomplished little, because the Southern Alliance wanted to work with the Democratic party rather than to challenge it and thus jeopardize white supremacy. Behind this attitude was the fear that the Republicans would be the beneficiaries of a third-party movement and would then restore the Carpetbag era. So the two Alliances went their separate ways in 1890, with the result that the Southerners elected several insurgent Democratic congressmen to co-operate with the Northern Independents. This development strengthened the third force in the 52nd Congress and produced virtual deadlock.

With time running out on the Republicans, they made a desperate effort to complete the Administration program in the lame duck session of the 51st Congress which met in December 1890. Senator Hoar of Massachusetts, the floor manager of the Force bill, had extracted written pledges from the members of the Republican caucus to give it priority in the short session. This precaution ought to have assured its passage, but several factors caused a critical number of senators to violate their pledges. Some of the silver senators interpreted the recent election as a mandate for a free-coinage bill and were infuriated upon receiving word that Harrison would veto it.[17] They believed the President had violated the party platform and felt absolved from their own commitments. The elderly Stewart of Nevada, who was allergic to Presidents generally and disliked Harrison as much as he had Andrew Johnson,[18] worked tirelessly on his fellow silverites.[19] Senators responsive to the views of Eastern industrial protectionists were equally cool to the Force bill, because they feared it would create an unfavorable climate for the investment of capital in the

South. A few waverers also blamed the loss of the recent election on the Force bill and wanted to shelve it as quickly as possible. First, the dissidents combined to displace it from the top of the calendar on January 5 in order to take up the free-coinage bill. The Eastern Republicans had no intention of abandoning the gold standard, however, and they promptly dropped free coinage on January 16. Debate was then resumed on the Force bill, and the Democrats began to repeat their familiar complaints about the unconstitutionality of legislation for honest elections. Inasmuch as the session would end on Monday, Aldrich of Rhode Island unsuccessfully tried to choke off discussion with a closure motion on January 20, and two days later the Senate ended the long struggle by voting 35 to 34 to take up a reapportionment measure.

The death of the Force bill marked the end of the twenty-five-year effort of the Republicans to establish a flourishing party in the South. By this time it was evident that the whites would not join the Republican party and that the Negroes would not vote for Republican candidates unless protected at the polls. Only Harrison and several senatorial holdovers from the Civil War generation like Edmunds of Vermont and Chandler of New Hampshire really cared about the plight of the party in the South or the fate of the Negro. Most Republicans had a bad conscience about abandoning the Negro and did not want to be reminded of it. Their unmistakable display of apathy toward the Force bill was not lost on Southerners. It coincided with the agrarian upheaval, which brought the most ignorant and prejudiced members of the white community to power in the South. Fearful of the Negro as an economic competitor, these poor whites rewrote their state constitutions between 1890 and 1901 in a fashion that disfranchised former slaves entirely. Constitutional revision enabled Louisiana to reduce the number of registered Negro voters from 130,334 in 1896 to 1,342 in 1904. Other Southern states were achieving similar results while Northern Republicans looked the other way. It is doubtful that passage of the Force bill would have arrested the slow erosion of Negro voting power that had begun in 1876, but it might have prevented the mass disfranchisement program of the '90's. In any case, the Republican party ceased to be a factor in the South. For the next half-century it consisted of nothing but a few federal office-holders, who were only active before national conventions, when they held the key to the vote of the Southern delegations.

Elsewhere, no clear political trend could be detected in the aftermath of the election of 1890. Within a year after he had been retired from Congress, the resourceful McKinley won the governorship of Ohio. Scattered elections in other Midwestern states in 1891 indicated a modest Republican revival. This trend coincided with a perceptible loss of momentum in the third-party movement. Enthusiasm was dampened by the meager achievements of the Alliance in states where it had gained control of the legislature. More plentiful rain on the Great Plains also cooled the tempers of farmers who had survived the break in land and crop prices during the late 1880's. Simultaneously, their less fortunate brethren were completing their retreat eastward and were finding it difficult to infect the older agricultural communities with the bitterness of frontier agrarianism. Even silver prices enjoyed a modest recovery in 1891, as government purchases under the Sherman Act took substantial quantities of the metal off the market.

To the immense relief of the major party politicians, who were perplexed by the irresolution of the voters, the 52nd Congress accomplished nothing. On the theory that popular discontent against the McKinley bill could be further exploited, the Democratic House passed a tariff-reduction bill in April 1892. It proposed to put tin plate, binding twine, and other consumer items on the free list, but the measure perished in the unfriendly Republican Senate. The latter passed a free-coinage bill, which failed in the House by a tie vote. The heavy support for silver was not so much a vote of confidence in bimetallism as a desire to force Harrison into a veto and thereby reduce his prospects for renomination. Through this cagey maneuver, many congressmen in both parties were able to record themselves as friends of silver without taking any real risk.

III

Long before the Republican national convention of 1892, Harrison had driven into uncompromising opposition the party bosses responsible for his nomination in 1888. The President seemed almost as anxious to vacate the White House as his party foes were to have him leave it. Mrs. Harrison suffered from chronic illness, and the President was weary with the wrangling over patronage. In the summer of 1891 he informed the disgruntled Clarkson through an intermediary that he would withdraw from the Presidential race at the proper time.[20] If the bosses had taken Harrison at his word, they might have saved themselves and the party much trouble later. But they refused to believe the President and began a feverish search for a candidate. So many Presidential hopefuls had been eliminated in the election of 1890 that the field was decidedly limited. Only Blaine possessed a nation-wide reputation, and ill health made him a poor risk. Platt and Quay had never cared for him; but on the theory that anyone was better than Harrison, Platt indulgently approached the Blaine faction in New York, which he had been fighting since 1880, and together they launched a boom for the "plumed knight." [21] By late fall of 1891, reports from Blaine backers indicated that he was growing stronger every day.[22] Callers found him interested but irresolute. Because he was Secretary of State, Blaine's receptive attitude toward the nomination worsened his relations with Harrison. No cabinet member since Chase had taken a similar position while his chief was a potential candidate for renomination. Blaine, however, saw no impropriety in his conduct. In fact, he confessed in private his intention of withdrawing, once it was conceded that he hadn't violated "good taste or morals." [23] On February 6, Blaine wrote a letter to Clarkson which was designed to take him out of the Presidential race, but the practical value of this gesture was destroyed by his refusal either to endorse Harrison or to disown Clarkson, who continued to collect Blaine delegates, just as though he had never seen the letter. The net effect of the episode was to make Harrison more distrustful than ever of Blaine. During the spring of 1892 the friction got worse because Blaine was frequently too ill to work but not too ill to encourage his political supporters. The President had to take on the burdens of the State Department while his ailing Secretary was plotting behind his back. By May, Harrison had had enough. He called his political advisers together, told them that "no Harrison ever ran from a fight," [24] and announced his decision to seek renomination. With only two weeks remaining until the convention, he faced a steep uphill fight. Blaine countered by resigning on June 4, but gave his bewildered supporters no clue as to his political intentions. Although his resignation was timed to do the maximum damage to Harrison, Blaine apparently acted on impulse rather than calculation—old age, illness, and a venomous hatred of Harrison had clouded his political judgment and increased his capacity for self-pity. Only his most deluded followers believed that Blaine could survive another canvass, and the leaders of the "stop Harrison" movement quietly made preparations to abandon the "plumed knight."

The difficulty of transferring Blaine's strength to another candidate handicapped the Eastern bosses almost as severely as Harrison had handicapped himself by his belated entry in the contest. Senator Cullom of Illinois had been advertising his availability for the Presidency since February,[25] but nobody took him seriously. Aside from a slight physical resemblance to Lincoln, Cullom's only asset was his reputation as a compromiser. Despite repeated disappointments, old John Sherman awaited the call to duty,[26] but he was hampered by the customary factionalism in Ohio. At the beginning of the year, Sherman had incurred the enmity of the ambitious Foraker by slipping past him to win an unprecedented sixth term as United States Senator. Foraker's power to do damage was weakened, however, by differences with Mark Hanna dating back to the 1888 convention. Hanna found it expedient to encourage Sherman, although the Cleveland industrialist had already transferred his loyalty to McKinley and formed a partnership with the Ohio governor. On the eve of the convention, Hanna was torn between his desire to secure the nomination for McKinley and his fear that any Republican candidate would lose in November. The temptation to gamble increased when it became evident that Platt and Quay wanted to concentrate Blaine's strength behind McKinley. The chief stumbling block was the Ohio governor himself. He had maneuvered himself into a position as awkward as Garfield's in 1880 by repeatedly urging Harrison to run.[27] McKinley's subsequent conduct at the convention suggested that he had encouraged Harrison on the assumption that the latter would not only retire but show his gratitude by designating the Ohioan as his successor. In any case, McKinley had backed the President too openly to become an avowed candidate. So he took refuge in evasion, refusing to acknowledge repeated invitations to give a nominating speech for Harrison or to commit himself in any other way.[28] Simultaneously, McKinley prepared a fiery defense of the tariff to be delivered when he took over the gavel as permanent chairman. On the chance that the speech would start a stampede, Hanna arrived at the convention with several boxes containing McKinley portraits and badges.

The convention opened June 7 at the Industrial Exposition Building in Minneapolis. The national committee had chosen Minneapolis because of its proximity to the rebellious farm belt and to the cooling breezes of Lake Minnetonka. Although the delegates would probably have been equally dispirited in another city, the selection of Minneapolis proved unfortunate. For one thing, Minneapolis was in the grip of a heat wave, and the surrounding lakes only added to the misery of the politicians by increasing the humidity. Resin dripped sporadically from the unseasoned pine roof of the convention hall, forcing delegates either to sit on gummy benches or stand in the aisles and receive direct hits on their bare heads.

Listlessness characterized the opening sessions of the convention, although the delegates spiritedly applauded a pro-tariff speech by eighty-three-year-old Colonel Richard W. Thompson, a perpetual Whig who had lived long enough to become a perpetual Republican. The platform gave a thumping endorsement to the McKinley tariff and a more restrained approval of Blaine's reciprocity agreements. The explosive monetary question was disposed of with the cryptic assertion that the party demanded the use "of both gold and silver as standard money" and believed that "every dollar, paper, or coin" should be equally good. The Sherman Anti-Trust Act, civil-service reform, and "purity of elections" also received favorable attention. To be on the safe side of the growing agitation for women's rights, the convention took the revolutionary step of allowing a woman to make a speech.

While the routine business of the convention continued for three days, the uninstructed delegates were wooed by supporters of the major candidates. Some who had received patronage drifted toward the President; others had the familiar instinct to back a winner and little faith that the anti-Harrison forces could concentrate on a single candidate. Harrison's manager, the ingenious Louis T. Michener, sought to capitalize on this situation by drawing the waverers into a demonstration for the President. His gambit was to call a meeting for the afternoon of June 10 at Market Hall, without specifying its purpose. Many responded out of curiosity, and reliable Harrison men coaxed some of the suspicious to attend.[29] More delegates than the 453 necessary to nominate attended; and when they found that they were on a Harrison bandwagon, the bulk of them stayed put.

Later the same day, Harrison won a first-ballot nomination with 535 votes to 183 for Blaine and 182 for McKinley. In a desperate effort to stem the tide the Ohio delegation cast 44 votes for McKinley, who, in imitation of Garfield tactics in 1880, challenged the vote, insisted on a poll of the delegation, and vacated the chair to overrule his proxy and cast a ballot for Harrison. The stampede failed to materialize. After the session Hanna consoled McKinley with the observation that he had escaped by "a damned close squeak." [30] Hanna subsequently informed Sherman that he had been abandoned only to block a first-ballot nomination for Harrison.[31]

Second place went to Whitelaw Reid, who replaced his fellow New York, Vice President Levi P. Morton, on the national ticket. Reid had been active in party councils since his ill-fated bolt in 1872, and his *New York Tribune* had done yeoman service for successive Republican candidates. He had just completed four years as Harrison's minister to France, and possessed both ability and energy. For an Ohio farm boy, he was remarkably aristocratic and aloof. His bearing seemed unlikely to be as much of a handicap to the ticket as his ownership of the *New York Tribune,* which had a bad record from the standpoint of organized labor. At the time of Reid's nomination, his paper was in the midst of a long controversy with the typographical union. Reid never yielded ground gracefully, and the strike dragged on, to the detriment of the Republican party in New York.

The Democratic convention selected Cleveland to run for a third time. The party professionals disliked him almost as much as their Republican counterparts disliked Harrison, but Cleveland's name was synonymous with "low tariff," and the issue looked like a winner in 1892. For the preceding decade, both Cleveland and his party had been cool to free silver. Nothing in the Democratic platform indicated a change of heart. Nevertheless, it was thought best to appease the inflationist element in the South by giving the Vice Presidential nomination to Adlai E. Stevenson, an Illinois bimetallist.

Although the protest movement on the Great Plains had lost ground since 1890, the members of the Northern Alliance finally persuaded their reluctant Southern brethren to join in launching a nation-wide third party. Known as the Populist party, the new organization extended the hand of fellowship to single taxers, Knights of Labor, Utopian Socialists of the Bellamite school, and agrarian reformers of every stripe. A nominating convention was held at Omaha on July 4, and chose James B. Weaver of Iowa as its standard bearer. The Populist candidate had been identified with various third-party movements since the middle 1870's and had run for President on the Greenback-Labor ticket in 1880. Despite his devotion to lost causes, Weaver was far more conservative than most of the other visionaries at Omaha. The Populist platform contained several planks that the major parties denounced in 1892 and adopted a generation later. Emphasis was laid on various devices to make the election system more responsive to popular control. The Populist platform also endorsed the graduated income tax. The aspirations of organized labor evoked their sympathy, but the Populists remained vague about their legislative plans in this area. The sections of the platform dealing with railroads and money were more forthright. One plank condemned the railroads for exploiting the farmer and advocated public ownership of transportation and communication. Another plank proposed free and unlimited coinage of silver at a ratio of 16 to 1, but placed primary emphasis on the need for a flexible currency and an increase in the circulating medium to $50 per capita. The Socialist Labor party concluded that the Populists were not radical enough and entered their own ticket. The Prohibitionists likewise sought to capitalize on public unrest by nominating a Presidential candidate and addressing themselves to a variety of social and economic questions in addition to alcohol.

From the beginning of the campaign, it was evident that the Democrats rather than the splinter parties would benefit from the unpopularity of the Harrison Administration. The untimely emergence of several large trusts, coupled with a rising price level, seemed to confirm Democratic prophecies about the evil effects of the McKinley tariff. Dissatisfaction was growing among laborers in protected industries that had not shared the wealth but had reduced wages instead. Carnegie locked out protesting workers at his Homestead plant in Pittsburgh, and violent industrial warfare erupted at such widely scattered points as Coeur d'Alene, Idaho, and Buffalo, New York. Under the circumstances, the Republicans should have promised adjustments to make the protective system more equitable, but instead they made a blanket defense of the existing law. The delighted Democrats countered by peddling 25¢ tin dippers for $1.00 in the rural areas and blaming the high prices on the McKinley tariff.[32] This trick had helped the Democrats defeat McKinley in his own district in 1890, and it was employed with equal effectiveness in the Presidential campaign. While the opposition attacked the Republican tariff, it had the good sense to retreat from the virtual free-trade declaration in its own platform. Cleveland gave the cue in his letter of acceptance by paying lip service to the protective principle, and other orators took up the theme. For once, honesty and political self-interest coincided. Neither the American people nor the Democrats were free-traders, but a majority of voters thought the McKinley tariff was too high.

The Populists unintentionally gave aid and comfort to the Democrats by their inability to expand beyond their original geographical base. Once the campaign got under way, the Southern farmer quickly demonstrated that, when he had to make a choice, he was a Democrat first and an Alliance man second. A Georgia Populist, Tom Watson, said the argument against independent political action could "be boiled down to one word— nigger." [33] Whether it could be or not, local Democratic leaders took no chances with wavering farmers. They stole popular planks from the Populists and incorporated them into Democratic state platforms. A Southern tour by Weaver and Mary Ellen Lease, a militant Kansas Populist, turned out to be a disaster. Weaver was distrusted because he had been one of the Union officers quartered in the South during Reconstruction, while Mrs. Lease aroused the antagonism of people unaccustomed to female politicians. Their speeches were interrupted by catcalls, flying rocks, and eggs; and Mrs. Lease wryly observed later that Georgians made General Weaver "a regular walking omelet." [34] Populist efforts to work out local fusion tickets with Republicans also backfired, because the Force bill had made the latter more unpopular than ever below the Mason-Dixon Line.

The Democrats, on the other hand, threw their support to the Populist party and withdrew Presidential electors in six Western states where they had no chance to win.[35] They also persuaded half their electors in Minnesota to retire in favor of the Populists.[36] Negotiations for fusion tickets at the state and local level were less successful because Populists and Democrats quarreled over the allocation of offices. Fusion worked best in Kansas, where Democrats-Populists displayed genuine solidarity, and worst in Nevada, where four anti-Republican parties, including a silver party, squabbled over local offices.

Although the third-party movement hurt the Republicans, the election of 1892 was decided in the doubtful Eastern states where the Populists ran a poor fourth. Disgruntled workers and consumers blamed their troubles on the tariff, and the campaign only strengthened their conviction on this point. The faction-ridden Irish deserted Harrison because of friction over patronage.[37] Neither of the Presidential candidates was very active. Harrison had intended to tour New York state after a summer vacation in the Adirondacks, but the illness of Mrs. Harrison, followed by her death in the middle of the campaign, caused the President to cancel his plans. Except for a long letter to the voters on September 5, he remained on the sidelines. Cleveland had never shown any taste for the stump and behaved with the restraint of an incumbent seeking re-election.

Signs multiplied in 1892 that the highly stylized campaign techniques of half a century would soon be abandoned. Parades, picnics, and torchlight processions were becoming less popular in the urban East, although they still persisted in the frontier states.[38] Reductions in the cost of printing brought about a vast increase in the distribution of campaign literature, while the increasing sophistication of the electorate caused an improvement in the intellectual level of these pamphlets.[39] Americans would never succeed in stifling the exuberant political spirit that had characterized the golden age, but the manifestations of it that survived the nineteenth century gradually became more stylized. Transition pains were eased by the passing of leaders identified with the old order. Blaine survived the election of 1892 by only a few months. A few of his contemporaries like Sherman of Ohio and Morrill of Vermont lingered on in the Senate, but their careers were destined to end with the nineteenth century.

On election day the Democrats overwhelmed the Republicans by sweeping all of the doubtful states in the East and carrying Illinois for the first time since the days of Stephen A. Douglas. Not since 1856 had the Democrats won the Presidency and both houses of Congress. The Populist party drew electoral votes away from the Republicans in several Western states where the Democrats had withdrawn, with the result that Cleveland received 277 electoral votes, Harrison 145, and Weaver 22. Although the Democrats gained a nation-wide plurality of approximately 380,000 over the Republicans, they fell far short of an absolute majority.

IV

No sooner did the Democrats take office in 1893 than they discovered that the risks of holding political power and responsibility outweighed the advantages. Not only was the country in a ferment, but the Democrats were as badly divided on the tariff and monetary policy as the Republicans. Furthermore, President Cleveland lacked the necessary tact and patience to lead a party of states' rights obstructionists. He shared the combative instincts of his fellow Democrats, and felt more at home thwarting the policies of others than promoting his own. His idea of a successful administration was one that lowered the tariff, dammed up the flow of pensions, and preserved the status quo at all other points. This limited concept of Presidential responsibility had worked well enough in the middle '80's, when people still thought largely in terms of the old Civil War issues, but by 1893 the focus of interest was shifting to a host of new social and economic questions. Cleveland would have experienced difficulty conducting his Administration along traditional lines under the best of circumstances. The task became impossible when the country was overtaken by a severe financial crisis a month after he moved into the White House.

Some sort of readjustment was probably inevitable after twenty-five years of uneven economic development. Industry had grown more rapidly than agriculture, and farmers who had tried to push wheat cultivation westward suffered chronically depressed conditions after the collapse of the land boom in 1887. The outcry in the Populist states against railroads, grain elevators, banks, and trusts helped to conceal the role of overproduction in the troubles of agriculture. Bad harvests in Europe from 1889 to 1892 had postponed the day of reckoning for the American farmer by enabling him to dispose of mounting surpluses abroad at stable prices. The European demand for staple crops abroad began to weaken during the American election, foreshadowing distress for farmers in the older areas as well as on the frontier.

Although danger signals in agriculture could be detected when Harrison vacated the White House, the first evidence of panic occurred in the great financial circles when the gold reserve in the Treasury dropped below $150,000,000. There was no reason why $150,000,000 should be a magical figure, except that it was the amount John Sherman had in reserve when he successfully undertook the resumption of specie payments in 1879. Thereafter, it had been an article of faith in orthodox financial circles that a reserve of $150,000,000 was necessary to maintain the gold standard. Despite the steady rate of government silver purchases under the Bland and Sherman acts, and the large expenditures of the Harrison Administration, the gold reserve had remained well above the minimum figure until 1892. Then the reduction of revenue under the McKinley tariff, plus the repercussions of depression in Europe, caused a drain on the gold. Fearful that the government would suspend specie payments, investors began exchanging currency issued under the Silver Purchase Acts into gold. Their behavior further depleted the gold reserve, which in turn fed the panic. Credit vanished; hard-pressed debtors were forced to liquidate; and numerous businesses went into bankruptcy.

The process of contraction was well under way when Cleveland took office. A Republican chorus promptly began to chant that the Democrats had started all the trouble by unsettling businessmen with their threats to lower the tariff. Since it is axiomatic that the voters blame the party in power for a depression, Cleveland seemed certain to face stormy weather whatever he did. From a political standpoint, it would probably have been wisest for the President to implement the party pledge on the tariff first and postpone a decisive stand on the explosive monetary question until later.[40] But Cleveland displayed a remarkable indifference to political considerations by calling Congress into special session and demanding the repeal of the Sherman Silver Purchase Act. He did so on the defensible ground that prompt action might stop the panic. This decision need not have offended the silver men in the Democratic party since they had neither sponsored the law nor considered it as an adequate solution to the monetary problem. Unfortunately, the President made a vice out of courage with uncompromising assertions of hostility toward bimetallism. In the process, he picked up loud support from all the wrong people—the financiers, monopolists, and high-tariff men whom the country had repudiated in the 1892 election. The clamor frightened the trimmers among the silver men, but it enraged the representatives of depressed farmers in the South and West. The latter had voted Democratic on the basis of state platforms which endorsed an inflationary monetary policy, but such pronouncements were not binding on Cleveland or the national party. Nevertheless, Western Democrats felt betrayed and rebelled against White House leadership. The canny David B. Hill of New York was a better politician than the President and tried to repair the damage. When the repeal bill reached the Senate, the New Yorker devised an artful amendment denying that bimetallism was being abandoned, but it perished after a long filibuster.[41]

The Republicans in Congress cheerfully assisted the Democratic majority in destroying itself. While they took little part in the debate, they engaged in every conceivable parliamentary maneuver to prolong the civil war in the enemy camp. When their opportunity for making mischief had been exhausted, the Republicans furnished the necessary votes to carry the repeal of the Sherman Silver Purchase Act. This tactic permitted the Republicans to get rid of a controversial piece of legislation without committing themselves to an alternate policy. Nobody was any wiser as a result of the three-year experiment. The Sherman Act had failed to arrest the fall in the value of silver, but it had also failed to produce price inflation, even though it added approximately $1,500,000 to the volume of money in circulation.[42] Such inconclusive results ought to have thinned the ranks of the self-appointed experts on monetary policy. But they were as loud and dogmatic as ever, and many people agreed with the confused Senator

W. P. Frye of Maine when he said it made his "brain buzz to read their opinions."[43]

Whatever therapeutic effect the repeal of the Sherman Act might have had on the business panic was lost through delay. Filibustering senators blocked action until October 1893, and by that time the country was in the grip of a crippling depression. Congress reassembled for the regular session in December amid mounting evidence of demoralization in the Democratic party. Thanks to the adoption of the Reed rules, which the Democrats had denounced four years earlier, their House leadership pushed through a tariff bill in harmony with the party platform. Known as the Wilson bill, it put iron ore, sugar, coal, and some three hundred other items on the free list and made modest reductions in the rates on manufactured products. It was anything but a free-trade bill. Nevertheless, Senate Democrats were unable to pass it without drastic modifications. The Louisiana senators wanted to protect sugar, and their colleagues from Alabama wanted to protect iron ore. Faulkner of West Virginia insisted on a duty on coal as the price of his support. Other senators demanded support for their products, too. In the face of this opposition, Gorman of Maryland called a party caucus and redrafted the measure so that it could pass.

In final form, the Wilson-Gorman bill more nearly resembled a Republican tariff of the pre-McKinley era. Even so, Senate Republicans vied with one another in extravagant denunciations of the measure. Platt of Connecticut said he preferred the original version, because it would kill American industry quickly instead of subjecting it to slow death.[44] Lodge of Massachusetts, who had been promoted to the Upper House in 1893, proposed an amendment to double the duty on goods from the British Empire until England acquiesced in an international silver agreement. Other Republicans simply contented themselves with denouncing free trade, and one member of the House gave an irrelevant speech against the tariff of 1842.[45] In view of the performance on the Senate floor, it was difficult to take the professed principles of either side seriously. A decade earlier, Lodge had conceded privately that the tariff was "a question of expediency,"[46] but neither he nor anyone else cared to make the admission publicly. During the next half-century both parties were to focus public attention on the tariff, and individual congressmen were to load successive bills with amendments pleasing to their constituents. From 1894 on, high-tariff arguments of the Republicans tended to make a better impression on the voters than the low-tariff arguments of the Democrats, because the latter were unlucky enough to undertake downward revision during a depression. In any case, everybody thought the Wilson-Gorman tariff was an abortion. Cleveland let it become a law without his signature but denounced Gorman and his colleages for "party perfidy and party dishonor." By the end of the session, Eastern Democrats hated Western Democrats and both groups hated the President.

Meanwhile, the relentless advance of depression in 1894 angered the voters and provided the Cleveland Administration with opportunities for additional blunders. The prices of such staple crops as wheat, corn, and cotton dropped to new lows, with resulting distress in all farming areas. After relaxing its grip for two years, drought returned to the Western plains. Country merchants suffered as much as their customers, and thousands of small businesses failed. In the silver states, most of the mines shut down, as declining prices made operations unprofitable. Miners were not the only workers to feel the squeeze. Industrial stagnation in urban centers idled thousands of workers, and brought protests in the form of strikes from other workers protesting against wage cuts. In Chicago, in a strike against the Pullman Company, the Cleveland Administration secured an injunction against the strikers, and then called out the national guard when they ignored the court order. The intervention of the federal government was decisive and broke the strike. Besides dealing a devastating blow to organized labor, it provided workers with an additional reason for voting against the Democrats.

The nation-wide unrest in the summer and fall of 1894 revived third-party activity. With low prices forcing farmers to grow more crops to pay their debts, free silver looked more attractive than ever. By this time, the market ratio of silver to gold had dropped to 32 to 1, which seemed to mean that free coinage at the old rate of 16 to 1 would reduce debt burdens 50 per cent. Farmers saw nothing immoral in this prospect. They felt that Wall Street had been engaged in a conspiracy to preserve the gold standard and make the dollar more valuable, so they were unmoved by cries that a cheaper dollar would mean repudiation. As an angry Iowan put it: "If somebody must lose . . . let the creditor stand it; he is best able and can recover more quickly." [47] Most Eastern Republicans listened to such assertions with dismay but handled the silver issue shrewdly in the 1894 campaign. A number of them became active in the American Bimetallic Society, and the rest either remained silent or endorsed bimetallism without committing themselves to free coinage. Their enthusiasm for silver seemed all the more genuine because it was combined with a murderous assault on the monetary policies of the Democrats. Republican campaigners argued that the repeal of the Sherman Silver Purchase Act would have been unnecessary if Cleveland had not touched off a panic by expressing lack of faith in bimetallism.[48] They also denounced the President for floating costly bonds to maintain the gold standard. Voters immune to Republican arguments about monetary policy were told that the depression had been aggravated by the Wilson-Gorman tariff.

V

When the voters showed their discontent at the polls in November 1894, the Democrats suffered their most disastrous defeat since the early Reconstruction era. Their seats in the House dropped from 218 to 105 and in the Senate from 44 to 39. Since the Populists lost four representatives and gained only one senator, the results left the Republicans firmly in control of both houses. They had recaptured all of the rebellious states in the Great Plains and the Rocky Mountains except Nevada. Even the Populist stronghold of Kansas returned to the fold. Throughout this area the Populists actually increased their vote 42 per cent over the 1892 total, but the breakdown of fusion with the Democrats accounted for their poor showing. Far more significant for the future was the Republican comeback in the industrial East, which had been doubtful territory since 1876. The party's representation in the House jumped from 2 to 8 in New Jersey, 13 to 28 in New York, 17 to 25 in Pennsylvania, and 10 to 19 in Ohio. The Republicans made still more spectacular gains in the normally Democratic Border state delegations, with 8 seats in Missouri, 4 in Kentucky, and 3 in Maryland. Even North Carolina produced four Republican congressmen. The rapid reversals in the political fortunes of major parties between 1890 and 1894 reflected the irresolution of the voters, indicating that a major realignment impended.

Neither party could accomplish anything in the new Congress. The Republican majority possessed enough partisan spirit to harass Cleveland but not enough to pass a program of its own. Silver Republicans held the balance of power in the Senate and blocked tariff revision, since their Eastern colleagues would not support a free-coinage bill.[49] In the absence of a clear mandate from the voters, the Republican high command was grateful for the deadlock. It enabled the party to postpone a stand on the explosive issues before the country until the national convention. The tactical advantages of an uncommitted position became more marked in 1895, as both the economy and fortunes of the Democratic party went from bad to worse. Cleveland could not maintain the gold standard without resorting to a fresh bond issue. Bimetallists were infuriated because his policy succeeded, and farmers because the operation put a handsome profit in the pockets of Wall Street bankers. Others illogically blamed the Administration for the well-publicized misdeeds of the trusts, as well as for a Supreme Court decision invalidating the income-tax provision of the Wilson-Gorman tariff. The hapless Democrats also caught the backlash of a fresh wave of anti-foreign, anti-Catholic sentiment spearheaded by a nativist organization known as the American Protective Association.

The declining popularity of the Democrats increased the attractiveness of the Republican Presidential nomination and aroused absurd hopes on the part of several Senators. Sherman of Ohio had finally given up after four tries, but Cameron of Pennsylvania, Cullom of Illinois, Allison of Iowa, and Elkins of West Virginia were available.[50] Only Cullom planned an active campaign. The other three intended to do what they could to promote a deadlock. The 300-pound, acid-tongued Speaker Reed also entered the contest. Time had soured the Speaker. In fact, he revolted "against hypocrisy to the point of always seeming" more cynical than he was.[51] The poor prospects of Reed encouraged another Easterner, Governor Levi P. Morton of New York, to put his hat in the ring. None of these candidates attracted much popular interest, and by January 1896 it was apparent that their only hope lay in combining against the front runner, Governor William McKinley of Ohio.

McKinley possessed several advantages. Everyone had heard of him through the McKinley tariff; he had won re-election as governor in 1893 by a sizable majority; and he possessed in Mark Hanna a very able campaign manager. Contemporaries were baffled by the close relationship of two men so different in temperament and behavior. Hanna had a well-deserved reputation for bluntness. He was an aggressive, hard-driving industrialist who had first amassed a fortune by thoroughness and shrewdness and then turned these talents to politics with equally satisfactory results. Hanna was a perfect subject for Populist cartoonists. He had the look of a well-fed, predatory Wall Street financier, and they enjoyed portraying him as one—complete with cigar and vest covered by dollar signs.

But Hanna's appearance was deceiving. Material success had not stifled an inbred egalitarian instinct or an impulsive warmth and generosity. Unlike the bulk of his contemporaries in the business world, Hanna displayed a sympathetic attitude toward the problems and aspirations of organized labor. He had never embraced the Social Darwinism of the '70's, which counseled indifference to exploitation of workers on the ground that they were unfit to survive unless they could do so unaided. Nor did Hanna show any sympathy for the current view of businessmen like Carnegie and Pullman, who regarded striking workers as anarchists and Socialists. On the contrary, Hanna had raged against Pullman for refusing to "meet his men halfway" and branded him as "a God-damn fool." [52]

It would be claiming too much for Hanna to picture him as an exponent of trade unionism or collective bargaining.[53] His approach to labor relations was practical rather than doctrinaire. He believed that capitalists and workers alike were born stupid or bright, and he displayed genuine concern for the welfare of alert, industrious workers. He did not want the government to interfere in labor-management relations but relied instead on the joint stake of employer and employee in prosperity to draw them together. Yet, Hanna was more like his fellow employers than a reformer in believing that the welfare of business was the welfare of the country. His distinctive contribution to the politics of the '90's stemmed from this conviction. It consisted of coaxing huge campaign funds out of businessmen and promising them sympathetic government policies in return. Hanna's greatest defect was a certain moral obtuseness to the dangers in such a relationship. He did not feel that his obligation to generous campaign contributors was discharged by the promotion of pro-business policy in Washington. On the contrary, he considered it his personal duty to secure special favors for them. In the heyday of his power at the turn of the century, Hanna was to become a part-time errand boy for business groups seeking special subsidies. Neither in 1896 nor later would Hanna conceal these activities or profit personally from them.[54] Unfortunately, his example attracted a host of corrupt imitators who ultimately damaged the reputation of the Republican party. But on the eve of the Presidential election, the danger and the impropriety of soliciting large campaign expenditures were apparent only to disgruntled Western farmers.

The fact that Hanna was to draw more fire than his Presidential candidate tells us as much about McKinley as about his campaign manager. The Ohio governor cultivated with unusual success the difficult art of seeking the limelight without appearing to do so. Except with his intimates, Mc-Kinley limited himself to small talk. This habit convinced some that he was unintelligent and others that he was weak. His kindly manner also suggested a certain softness, which prompted Roosevelt on one occasion to snort that he had the backbone of a chocolate éclair. Other critics doubted McKinley's sincerity. Not only did he accept trivial acts of kindness with a gratitude out of proportion to the service rendered, but he was sometimes moved to tears. The hardboiled politicians of his own generation and the historians of the next found something distasteful about a man given to extravagant expressions of friendship. They could not make up their minds whether McKinley was hypocritical or hopelessly naïve. In either case, they derided him as the exponent of a sickly Victorian sentimentality. They mistook dignity for stuffiness and never forgave him for refusing to be photographed with a cigar in his mouth.

Contemporaries who took McKinley's warmth and kindliness at face value were probably closer to the truth. Domestic misfortune left him with a deep craving for affection. An initially happy marriage to Ida Saxton became a burden to McKinley when his wife fell victim to melancholia and nervous disorders. The initial symptoms had appeared following the death of Ida Saxton McKinley's mother in the mid-'70's and were aggravated by the loss of her two small daughters in rapid succession. Mrs. McKinley never recovered from these blows, and she gradually sank into an endless round of fainting spells, headaches, and nausea. As Mrs. McKinley became more pathetic, her husband became more protective; but as the years went by, he turned increasingly to politics for the intimate companionship that he could not find at home. What seemed like casual contacts to others took on more importance for the lonely McKinley.

Much as McKinley treasured the conventional tokens of friendship, he possessed the judgment to prevent the unworthy from exploiting him and the tact to say "no" without giving offense. One devoted follower thought that McKinley's exquisite courtesy merely softened the impact of "his irresistible will." [55] At times his countenance could harden into a mask if he wanted to protect himself from unwanted confidences or requests for favors. John Hay saw the mask in the 1896 campaign and pronounced it "a genuine Italian ecclesiastical face of the xvth Century." [56] Whether McKinley's demeanor invited intimacy or repelled it, there was a tireless and alert quality in his make-up. Rivals in the snake pit of Ohio politics thought McKinley tricky and unreliable, but his standards were far above average in a state where every office-holder considered himself a potential Presidential candidate.

For all his astuteness, McKinley did not have a very original mind or active imagination. He embraced the main articles of Republicanism with a veneration that disconcerted some of his colleagues. He regarded the protective tariff as a sort of Aladdin's lamp which, if rubbed vigorously, would produce permanent prosperity. His practical approach to political and economic problems appealed to Hanna, whose mind worked the same way. Yet the underlying bond between them was mutual admiration. The blustery Hanna looked up to the Canton attorney who handled men with such quiet confidence, while McKinley was drawn to the genial, open-handed Cleveland industrialist.

In the spring of 1894, Hanna had withdrawn from active management of his varied enterprises to promote McKinley's candidacy. A series of speaking tours had taken the Ohio governor through some three hundred towns in sixteen states. Early the following year, McKinley turned up at Hanna's estate in Thomasville, Georgia, ostensibly to improve his health but actually to round up Republican delegates in the South. Hanna's organizational work and fund-raising activities were so effective that McKinley was practically assured of the nomination by the end of 1895. For the first time in two decades, the Ohio delegates were united behind their own favorite son. The prospect of a Senate seat induced even the temperamental Foraker to co-operate with his arch-foe Hanna. Platt and Quay would have been willing to jump on the bandwagon if McKinley had met their price. But it was too high, especially in view of the probability that McKinley could win without them. Belatedly the two bosses tried to encourage the entry of additional favorite sons to deadlock the convention. Old Senator W. E. Chandler of New Hampshire joined the dissidents with an indignant letter to the *Washington Post* on March 26. It accused the McKinley managers of trying to raise $250,000 from the protected industries and contended that nobody could spend such a vast sum of money for legitimate purposes. Hanna's denial was unconvincing,[57] but the McKinley bandwagon continued to roll. The opposition virtually caved in at the end of March when the McKinley forces under the leadership of youthful Charles G. Dawes snatched a sizable bloc of Illinois delegates from Senator Cullom. This development, coupled with a revival of confidence in Republican prospects, brought the hitherto reluctant Wall Street financiers into the McKinley camp.[58] Once they reached the conclusion that the

Republicans could ignore the silver wing and win the election, big businessmen were bound to favor the leading high-tariff candidate.

The national committee had made a mistake in choosing St. Louis as a site for the Republican convention. The city was overwhelmingly Democratic, and, in addition, had been devastated by a tornado two weeks earlier; hotelkeepers refused accommodations to Negro delegates; and angry party leaders from Massachusetts threatened legal action for breach of contract.

It was just as well that the nomination of McKinley was virtually settled, because the Republican delegates exhausted their energy fighting over the platform. The era of compromise on the currency question had passed, and the silverites were no longer to be pacified by a vague endorsement of bimetallism. The Colorado state convention had instructed its delegates to the national convention to demand free and unlimited coinage of silver at a ratio of 16 to 1 in language that resembled an ultimatum. Moreover, Senator Henry M. Teller, head of the delegation and acknowledged leader of the silver forces, arrived at St. Louis early to co-ordinate strategy with the representatives from other mining states. The sound-money men were as well organized and as unyielding as the silverites. Most of the Reed delegates from New England and a substantial bloc from the Middle Atlantic states favored an explicit endorsement of the gold standard. Platt of New York had spent the winter mobilizing the business world behind a gold plank.[59] McKinley, on the other hand, displayed little sympathy with the extremists and favored some kind of straddle on the monetary question which would enable him to concentrate his campaign on the tariff. Hanna later professed to have been a gold-standard man from the start,[60] but at a strategy session in his hotel room the Saturday before the convention the Ohio industrialist wobbled on the issue.[61] Prolonged discussion with Henry C. Payne of Wisconsin, H. H. Kohlsaat, an Illinois editor, Foraker, Lodge, and others indicated to Hanna that the gold-standard men had the votes. The same evening Hanna reported his findings over the long-distance phone to McKinley in Canton and received the reluctant consent of his candidate to a gold-standard plank. Until the end of the campaign, a large number of hard-money Republicans doubted the wisdom of an explicit reference to the gold standard.[62] But, once the pre-convention decision had been made, they closed ranks for a showdown with the silverites.

The crisis came midway through the convention when the majority report of the resolutions committee reached the floor. The cleverly worded monetary plank held out the hope of bimetallism through international agreement but flatly declared that until that time "the existing gold standard must be preserved." Immediately, Teller of Colorado was on his feet urging the convention to substitute a free-silver plank. Teller was not an inspiring orator, but on this occasion he labored under an obvious emotional strain that gave new authority to his words. A life-long Republican whose political career had begun before Colorado became a state, the silver-haired senator was wrestling with his soul while he talked about the money plank. Teller said nothing about a bolt, but every delegate in the hall knew that he was pleading for a reprieve. Hanna sensed that Teller had won the sympathy of the convention, and his mouth "twitched irritably" [63] as the senator sat down weeping. Immediately, Cannon of Utah was on his feet threatening a bolt. Fearful of the effect that the silver advocates might have on the more timid delegates, Hanna bellowed, "Go, go." In retaliation, Cannon shouted for a "parting of the ways," and again the aggressive Ohioan tried to drown him out by screaming "Goodbye." Others took up the chant and to this gloomy accompaniment Senator Teller marched out of the hall followed by 34 delegates. Whereupon the convention adopted the gold plank and the rest of the platform, which reaffirmed familiar Republican doctrines.

When the convention turned to nominations, Joe Foraker presented McKinley. Still grateful for the deal with Hanna which was sending him to the U. S. Senate, Foraker spoke in the dual role of politician and prophet: "My countrymen, let not your hearts be troubled; the darkest hour is just before the day. The twentieth century will dawn bright and clear; God lives, the Republican party is coming back to power and William McKinley is to be President of the United States." [64] The delegates paved the way for fulfilling at least part of the prophecy by giving McKinley a first ballot nomination. The combined vote for all of his opponents was only 268½ out of 930. Then the convention balanced the ticket by selecting Garret A. Hobart of New Jersey for Vice President.

The bolt of the Republican silverites at St. Louis only stimulated the silver fever that raged among the Democrats. When the party convention opened in Chicago three weeks later, the radical Democrats promptly wrested control from forces representing the Administration. Heartened by visions of fusion with the Silver Republicans and Populists, the radicals rammed through a platform that repudiated Cleveland's policies. It called for free silver, condemned the bond-selling policy of the Administration and the use of the injunction in labor disputes, urged a constitutional amendment authorizing an income tax, and proposed stricter control of the railroads. The convention had more trouble agreeing on a candidate. The famous radical and the champion of the underdog, Governor John P. Altgeld of Illinois, was ineligible because he had been born outside the United States. Some Democrats in their zeal for a standard bearer with a national reputation urged the nomination of Senator Teller, but the wiser silverites recognized that it was unrealistic to expect the Eastern Democrats to support a Republican as well as a radical platform. The elimination of Altgeld and Teller narrowed the choice to a number of dark horses. Congressman Richard P. ("Silver Dick") Bland of Missouri was the most conspicuous of these, but aroused little enthusiasm. Meanwhile, a youthful ex-congressman from Nebraska, William Jennings Bryan, had been testing fragments of a speech about silver on successive prairie audiences. He had done so in the hope of putting together an oration that would stampede the convention. His opportunity came in the debate on the platform, and Bryan delivered the famous "cross-of-gold speech" which rekindled the enthusiasm of the delegates. In print the speech was commonplace enough, but the alchemy of Bryan's rich baritone voice transformed it into a revolutionary manifesto. The prolonged applause was the prelude to the nomination of the thirty-seven-year-old champion of silver. The radicals made a belated gesture to the Eastern wing of the party by selecting Arthur M. Sewell of Maine as Bryan's running mate. With these formalities completed, the Democrats made preparations to campaign against the record of their own party. It was a novel policy, but none of the radical leaders thought they were doing anything remarkable at the time.

Bryan's nomination was ratified by the Populist convention in late July over the bitter protest of Southern delegates. To most of the dissidents, fusion meant being swallowed up by their mortal enemies, the Democrats. It also meant the subordination of Populist issues to free silver. The Democrats managed to fuse with the Populists on Presidential electors in twenty-eight states but no consistent pattern developed at the state level. The Populists held the lion's share of the congressional and gubernatorial nominations in Western states where the party was strong. They also benefitted from the tactics of the Silver Republicans, who presented their own ticket in the mountain states and drew votes away from the regular Republicans. Elsewhere, the Populists did not fare so well. Below the Mason-

Dixon Line their antipathy toward the Democrats resulted either in separate Populist state tickets or fusion with the Republicans. The ultimate in confusion was achieved in North Carolina, where the Populists fused with the Democrats on Presidential electors and with the Republicans on the state ticket. On the Eastern seaboard the Populists had a negligible following and were completely ignored by their Democratic allies.

Most of the prominent Eastern Democrats accepted their convention defeat quietly and either gave weak support to the Bryan ticket or remained inactive. In late summer, however, a splinter group called a national convention of Gold Democrats at Indianapolis and nominated Senator John M. Palmer of Illinois for President. The real purpose of the convention was to help the Republicans by bidding for the votes of conservative Democrats who would not support McKinley directly.[65] The Republicans financed the campaign of the Gold Democrats, and Hanna later confessed to "a soft feeling for them," since they consulted his wishes "at every step." [66] He had every reason to be pleased, because Palmer concentrated his efforts in four doubtful Midwestern states and Kentucky.[67]

The campaign of 1896 started earlier and was contested more fiercely than any campaign in recent American history. Political leaders of both major parties had misgivings about being committed so unconditionally on the money question. The subsequent bolts of splinter groups made the outcome even more uncertain. Nobody was quite sure what to do, but everybody thought something should be done quickly.[68] This sense of urgency was increased by the widespread belief that class war was imminent and that the fate of future generations rested on the outcome of the election. Congressman Jonathan P. Dolliver of Iowa feared the country was on the eve of changes which might upset "the very foundations of the social fabric." [69] A fellow Republican, Senator O. H. Platt of Connecticut, thought that Altgeld, Bryan, and Tillman resembled the bloodthirsty leaders of the French Revolution, Robespierre, Danton, and Marat,[70] while young Theodore Roosevelt refused to meet Altgeld for fear that some day he would have to fire on the Illinois governor at the head of a regiment.[71] The Democrats were just as convinced that a crucial stage had been reached in the age-old struggle between exploiters and exploited. Bryan repeatedly told his audiences that their votes would determine the outcome. One of his followers insisted that the tendency of the times was toward "crushing out the yeomanry and building up an oligarchy" and that only a Democratic victory would reverse the trend.[72]

The Republicans have always been at their best when saving the country from a real or fancied threat to its value system, and in 1896 they had their best opportunity since the Civil War. Nevertheless, the alarmists had some difficulty convincing McKinley and Hanna that they stood in the shadow of the guillotine, and for a time the Republican candidate stubbornly clung to the idea that the campaign could be waged on the tariff issue. Like John Hay, McKinley regarded the monetary question as "a matter utterly unfit for public discussion," [73] but it was a poor year for anybody to try to restrict the campaign agenda. Free coinage interested the voters, and they were not to be diverted by other issues. Even before the opening of the Democratic convention, Hanna noticed with dismay that silver feeling "is developing more strongly than expected." [74] Two weeks later, McKinley was reported to be "very upset" by the persistence of the silver craze.[75] On August 1 he was still clinging to the conviction "that the proper settlement of the tariff question will relegate the financial question to the rear." [76] While the candidate sat at Canton brooding over the obstinacy of his fellow Americans, Republican headquarters was bombarded with reports of mass defections on the silver issue and pleas for literature. Correspondents also made it clear that the old-style campaign document was useless and that the party would have to produce material nonpartisan in tone.[77]

In the face of such overwhelming evidence, Hanna capitulated and agreed to defend the gold standard and American civilization. Once the decision was made, Republican prospects began to improve. Iowa, which had appeared to be lost in July, was reported safe in early September.[78] By this time the organizational genius of Hanna had begun to pay dividends. Two headquarters had been opened, one in Chicago and the other in New York. Money was being raised from every businessman who feared inflation, and tons of literature on the silver question were being distributed to the voters. In the end, the Republican national committee admitted that it had collected $3,500,000. The total expenditures were still larger, although they probably fell far short of the sixteen million estimate made by the Democrats. Even the official figures indicate that the party spent more than twice what it had spent in 1892 and more than in any subsequent campaign until 1920.[79] But by any standards money was plentiful for the Republicans in 1896 and scarce for the opposition. Dawes, who shared control of the Chicago headquarters with Payne of Wisconsin, reported on September 11 that Hanna had turned over to him an envelope from a railroad "containing 50 one-thousand-dollar bills." [80] Apparently, contributions of that size were by no means an uncommon occurrence. Opinion differed as to whether Hanna used the money for improper purposes. One observer predicted that Indiana would have to be bought as usual,[81] and it is likely that some campaign funds flowed into notoriously corrupt areas on the traditional basis.

The bulk of Republican expenditures, however, was for educational purposes. Repeated warnings had led Hanna to insist that pamphlets dealing with the monetary question be analytical in tone. One of the most effective was *Coin at School in Finance* by G. S. Roberts, a rebuttal of W. H. Harvey's famous pro-silver classic, *Coin's Financial School*. The production of campaign literature that read like textbooks in economics had an important side effect. Editors of independent agricultural journals were persuaded to incorporate Republican material in their articles and pass it on to unsuspecting readers.[82] Nobody knows how much campaign literature was reproduced in this fashion, but it has been estimated that the Republican national committee prepared 275 different pamphlets and distributed some 250,000,000 copies of them.[83] Although some Republican campaigners doubted the wisdom of such vast expenditures for education, they were happy about Republican affluence in the face of Democratic poverty. As one Ohioan put the matter: "They [the Democrats] depend, as they say, on the good people and the justice of their cause, all of which is pure sentiment and does not get votes." [84]

While Hanna struggled to win control of America's mind, McKinley sat on his front porch at Canton, Ohio, and tried to capture its heart. Like Garfield and Harrison before him, McKinley met delegations of the faithful, listened to short speeches that his advisers had edited in advance, and responded with cautiously worded policy pronouncements. McKinley possessed all of the characteristics popularly associated with the statesman and took full advantage of them. He had regular features, a handsome profile, and penetrating eyes. A slight touch of heaviness about the jowls enabled McKinley to appear wise when he frowned and dignified when he smiled. His public-speaking style was sermonic, and sanctified even commonplace utterances. McKinley's formal attire and manner just missed being funereal, but he was no more serious about the campaign than were his fellow countrymen.

The coincidence of public curiosity with low railroad rates to Canton turned McKinley's front-porch campaign into a real ordeal for the candidate. One Saturday in early October, the candidate was obliged to make fourteen speeches to delegations totaling 15,000.[85] The casual pilgrims constituted an even worse problem. Although most of them were complete strangers to McKinley, they showered him with a flood of useless gifts. By the end of October the house was "a veritable museum . . . overstocked with campaign curios. . . ."[86] A disorderly array of bath tubs, ink stands, embroidered suspenders, and bicycles filled the halls and overflowed into the living rooms. One admirer even gave the defenseless McKinley a pair of live American eagles.[87]

McKinley could not avoid the assaults on his privacy at Canton, but Bryan courted exhaustion and frustration by stumping the country from one end to the other. Despite the fact that the Presidency had hitherto eluded active campaigners, Bryan ignored precedent and broke all travel records. He embarked on three major tours, traveled 18,000 miles, and made about 600 speeches.[88] Tirelessly reiterating his major theme, he argued that depression and the gold standard were inseparable, and that economic revival could not take place until the country adopted free silver. Rural audiences usually responded more enthusiastically to Bryan than urban ones, but his vibrant voice carried conviction wherever he went.

The analytical tone employed by the Presidential candidates was frequently praised but seldom imitated. Old-fashioned mudslinging and pageantry characterized the campaign at the grass roots; orators alternately irritated the voters and provided them with comic relief. One zealous Republican tried to woo the Italians in New Jersey by praising Columbus and telling them that if Bryan won it would cost more to send money back to Italy.[89] "Sockless Jerry" Simpson, a Kansas Populist seeking re-election to Congress, promised his constituents as much circulating medium as they wanted. According to Simpson, a committee would be appointed to "figger an estimate" on the gold and silver in the mountains "not found" as a basis for the issue of paper money.[90]

Until mid-September the great debate between the Democrats and Republicans on the monetary issue appeared to be a stand-off. Thereafter, economic developments worked to the detriment of the Democrats. Despite Bryan's dogmatic assertion that commodity prices could not rise under the gold standard, market quotations on wheat edged slowly upward. Though few commodities imitated wheat, Bryan's error about a major commodity was enough to shake confidence in his entire economic analysis. Republican orators and newspapers were quick to exploit their opportunity. On October 3, the *Chicago Tribune* gloated over the repeal of the law which had bound wheat and silver prices together: "What agency," sneered the editor, "has dared to separate those whom Altgeld and Bryan have joined together in the unholy bonds of rotten money." [91] The same day McKinley repeated for a delegation of farmers at Canton his well-worn argument: "You don't get customers through the mint, you get them through the factory." [92] Avoiding any hint that farmers bore responsibility for overproduction, he assured the delegation that a protective tariff would reduce the surplus by increasing wages.[93] Few farmers shared McKinley's childlike faith in the tariff, but east of the Missouri River they were increasingly receptive to Republican predictions that free silver would cut the value of the dollar in half.[94]

The September swing toward McKinley in the rural areas was duplicated in labor centers, where some entrepreneurs frightened their employees. From the steel mills of Pennsylvania to the forests of Minnesota, seasonal operations were shut down earlier than usual.[95] A large number of factories remained open but told their workers not to return to work if Bryan won the election. On October 19, the Democrats took public notice of these tactics and charged their opponents with a conspiracy to coerce labor. Hanna promptly termed the charges "absurd." His attitude may have been true in a technical sense. Nonetheless, the pressure on the workers was so well timed that it must have been planned with the knowledge and approval of Republican leaders. On the other hand, Republicans in Bryan country experienced something akin to social ostracism. Senator Edward A. Wolcott of Colorado, who had refused to imitate the example of his colleague Teller by bolting the Republican party, found audiences sullen if not openly hostile.[96] Elsewhere in the great plains and mountain states, businessmen found it prudent to support free silver. Ministers were as active and bitter as politicians. On November 2, the Sunday before the election, wealthier congregations heard anti-Bryan sermons all over New York City. Some were told that nobody could be a Christian and vote for the Democratic "anarchists." [97]

By Wednesday morning it was obvious that the Republican strategy had been successful, for the party had piled up decisive majorities in the populous Eastern states. For the first time since 1872, the Republicans had won a decisive victory. In the final tally, McKinley won the electoral college from Bryan 271 to 176, and a popular vote of 7,035,638 to 6,467,946. At the time few people realized that the election of 1896 was one of the great watersheds in American party history and foreshadowed a long period of Republican supremacy. Cleveland's victory four years earlier had seemed almost as decisive, and many Democrats believed that their party would stage a great comeback in 1900. Statisticians fanned optimism by noting that Bryan would have won if he had been able to capture the 135,000 votes of the Gold Democrats and distribute them as he chose. The crucial factor that enabled the Republicans to consolidate their gains of 1896 was America's rapid recovery from the depression. Grateful Americans dubbed the Republicans the Grand Old Party; the nickname G.O.P became a symbol of prosperity for the faithful. Until 1932 the party could count on a reliable backlog of voters who regarded it as the custodian of good times, irrespective of its blunders in dealing with other questions. Conversely, the Democrats picked up a reputation as the party of depression, which hampered their efforts to win waverers in close elections.

Hindsight indicates that the party realignment of 1896 had begun two years earlier in the congressional elections which reduced the Democrats to impotence in the populous East. Their strategy in the Bryan-McKinley election accelerated the trend. By adopting a radical monetary policy they offended the Atlantic seaboard states, which had been doubtful territory since 1872. Before the election of McKinley, Republican pluralities in Pennsylvania had never exceeded 85,000, but in 1896 the party piled up a margin of 304,000.[98] The switch was just as dramatic in New York, New Jersey, and Connecticut, and was much more important, because hitherto all three states had been evenly divided.

Free silver and Populism did additional damage to the Democratic party in the Border, which had already been weakened by the factional infighting of the Cleveland era.[99] Maryland, West Virginia, and Kentucky went over to the Republicans in 1896, and Missouri followed in 1900. They stayed there most of the time until 1912. The only compensation that the Democrats received for sacrificing their support in the Atlantic seaboard and the Border was the doubtful loyalty of sparsely settled Western states. From the standpoint of electoral votes, the trade proved to be disastrous. It ended the era of close elections, and re-established the more typical American pattern of extended periods of one-party supremacy. Nobody knows precisely why voters behave as they do, but the prevalence of one-party domination suggests that they stay with their party except in times of unusual stress. It is tempting to conclude that the bulk of the 2,000,000 who voted for the first time in 1896 not only supported McKinley but took on the habit of voting Republican.

VI

As usual, the incoming Republican Administration did not have enough jobs to reward the army of workers which had been mobilized in 1896. Yet few Presidents have been as adroit as McKinley in the art of sending disappointed petitioners away happy. When he could not accommodate requests for a particular post, McKinley often promised to find the job-seeker something just as good. If he had to defy senators in making a selection, the President employed a variety of diversionary tactics. A protest from Cullom about a particular appointment in Illinois launched McKinley into a series of reminiscences about the Civil War service of the individual in question. Eventually the narration of hardships under fire reduced McKinley to tears, although the proposed appointee was currently in splendid health. Cullom recorded giving up in despair.[100]

In the distribution of cabinet and lesser posts, McKinley discriminated only against the old Harrison faction, which had denounced his political conduct at the Minneapolis convention in 1892. A personal friend, John Davis Long of Massachusetts, went into the cabinet as Secretary of the Navy; but young Theodore Roosevelt, an outspoken Reed supporter before the St. Louis convention, was made Undersecretary there. Other appointments were distributed with due regard for geography, seniority, and standing in the party. Despite his experience and skill, McKinley came to grief when he tried to satisfy rival claims in his native Ohio. The principal problem was presented by Mark Hanna. None of his factional foes could have objected to his inclusion in the cabinet, but unfortunately Hanna wanted to be senator.[101] To make matters worse for McKinley, there was no senatorial vacancy, and he had to create one by offering John Sherman the State Department. The offer was open to objections on several grounds besides its obviousness. John Sherman had never shown any particular interest in foreign affairs. His skill lay in the area of parliamentary management, and there was no reason to believe that he would be useful to the State Department. Few people found this an insuperable objection, since foreign affairs were not thought to be very important. More serious, however, was Sherman's failing health. He experienced difficulty in remembering names and concentrating on business for any prolonged period. The fact that McKinley knew Sherman's situation and still persisted in the appointment did not help the President. The Democratic press promptly accused him of being a petty politician who was more interested in Ohio politics than the welfare of the country. After a considerable delay, Governor Bushnell of Ohio, a member of the Foraker faction, finally appointed Hanna, but not until he had made the damaging point that he was capitulating to pressure from the White House.

Meanwhile, matters had gone well for McKinley in Congress, largely because he asked it to do so little. He called a special session on March 15, 1897, primarily to raise the tariff, but he quickly discovered that the Republican Senate majority was honeycombed with silverites who set a price on their co-operation. Nothing could be done with the free-coinage element, but it was possible to work with the silverites like Wolcott of Colorado and Chandler of New Hampshire who advocated bimetallism through international agreement.[102] Accordingly, McKinley appointed a three-man commission headed by Wolcott to negotiate with the major European states. This gesture, plus judicious rate concessions to Western senators, enabled the Dingley bill to clear both houses of Congress by late summer. Reincorporating the principle of the ill-fated McKinley tariff, it raised rates to prohibitive levels and authorized reciprocity agreements to modify specific schedules on a bilateral basis. Despite McKinley's reputation as the high priest of protectionism, Congress took special precautions against executive generosity by requiring legislative ratification of reciprocity agreements.

It was always easier to establish a connection between the protective tariff and prosperity in a political speech than in an analysis of production and foreign trade. But in 1897, economic revival followed so closely on the heels of the Dingley Act that the voters were more responsive than usual to Republican claims about the magical properties of the protective tariff. A gradual increase in the supply of gold also reduced the demand for free silver or bimetallism at home. McKinley had to wait until after the election of a new Congress in 1898 for legislation establishing a gold standard. Until then McKinley—like his predecessor, Cleveland—maintained the gold standard through careful control of Treasury policy. Otherwise, the Administration interfered little with economic activity. No effort was made to enforce the anti-trust laws or to interfere with business consolidation. Popular discontent evaporated in the unfamiliar warmth of prosperity, and voters temporarily forgot their animus toward the trusts. McKinley's concept of executive responsibility was about as narrow as Grant's. He avoided collisions with Congress about appointments and minimized the friction over legislation.

The resulting "Pax McKinlica" might have lasted until the Presidential election of 1900 but for the rapid deterioration of American relations with Spain in the spring of 1898 over Cuba. Although the United States had coveted Cuba repeatedly in the past, she did not tackle the problem with much energy before the middle 1890's. But it was an axiom of American foreign policy in the nineteenth century that whenever the country really wanted something she took it. Florida, Texas, and California, to say nothing of Indian territory, were testimonials to her large, if erratic, appetite. Before the Civil War the Democrats had owed their popularity in part to the fact that they were the party of expansion. After Appomattox the Republicans stole the issue from the Democrats with mixed results. A faction of the party had revolted against Grant and blocked his effort to annex Santo Domingo in 1870. For the next two decades, Americans were too busy opening up the western half of the continent to welcome the distraction of overseas projects. In the early '90's, however, signs began to multiply that the country was once more ready for expansion. Government circles had begun to discuss *The Influence of Sea Power on History,* in which Admiral Alfred Thayer Mahan contended that a strong navy would assure national greatness. Mahan's concept of naval power implied more than a dirty string of overseas coaling stations. He wanted "all that tends to make a people great upon the sea or by sea." His emphasis on a strong navy dovetailed with the designs of business groups who had long favored the acquisition of Pacific bases to expand "the China trade." Many Christian denominations were impelled in the same direction by the desire to convert and civilize the heathen. Underlying all of these impulses was a revival of the traditional American appetite for expansion: "The American people . . . simply liked the smell of empire and felt an urge to range themselves among the colonial powers of the time. . . ." [103]

Simultaneously, Cuban revolutionaries increased their operations against the Spanish regime in Havana. The Republican platform had taken note of this situation in 1896 and pledged the party to use its good offices to promote peace and the independence of Cuba. During the subsequent campaign, the plight of Cuba had been temporarily forgotten, but, once the election was over, Senator Cameron of Pennsylvania introduced a resolution calling on the President to recognize the independence of the Spanish colony. Cleveland refused to be intimidated by Republican harassment about Cuba, and the resolution never came to a vote. He likewise resisted Republican efforts to force the annexation of Hawaii. Both issues were passed on to McKinley.

For a time, the situation in Cuba continued to deteriorate as guerrillas intensified their attacks on life and property. Spanish and American sugar plantations were burned with a fine spirit of impartiality. In retaliation, the Spanish authorities herded captured revolutionaries and their families into prison camps. It is doubtful that the government intended to kill the prisoners, but Spanish inefficiency, coupled with the inadequate sanitary facilities in the hastily erected camps, resulted in thousands of deaths. Bad as the situation was, newspaper reports managed to exaggerate it. The so-called yellow press, directed by Joseph Pulitzer and William Randolph Hearst, saw in the Cuban crisis an opportunity to increase newspaper circulation. They kept the issue before the American public with screaming headlines about Cuban atrocities.

The cautious McKinley did not have any strong feelings on the problem of Cuba. His interest in foreign affairs had always been negligible, and he lacked sufficient conviction to be either an expansionist or a noninterventionist. Genuine humanitarian impulses predisposed the President to a peaceful policy and reinforced his instinct to avoid a showdown on any question as long as the American public was irresolute. Accordingly, he sent off U.S. Minister Woodford to Madrid in the summer of 1897 with a warning that hostilities in Cuba must stop. Spain responded by reshuffling her cabinet and recalling General Weyler, founder of the concentration camps. For a time the atmosphere improved; and in his annual message of December 1897 McKinley, with evident relief, praised Madrid's constructive attitude and asked Congress to avoid provocative action.

Two developments in February 1898 destroyed whatever disposition the lawmakers might have had to follow the President's recommendation. One was the publication of a letter stolen from the Spanish diplomatic pouch which reflected unfavorably on the character and intelligence of McKinley. Shortly thereafter, the American battleship *Maine* blew up in the harbor of Havana, killing 258 members of the crew and two officers. Spain tried to blunt the effect of the first incident by recalling the offending diplomat. She could do little about the destruction of the *Maine* but proclaim her innocence. No evidence was uncovered which shook her story or placed the guilt on other parties. McKinley went through the motions of appointing a board of inquiry and asking the American public to await its report patiently. But the explosion of the *Maine* touched off a loud clamor for war with Spain which the yellow press did everything it could to encourage and sustain. The small but influential coterie of Mahan disciples was delighted by the prospect. Senator Cushman K. Davis, the chairman of the Senate Foreign Relations Committee, hoped that the crisis was the prelude to America's emergence on the world stage,[104] while Lodge and Roosevelt wanted war with Spain on the chance that it would provide an excuse for America to grab the Philippines. They remained outwardly silent about their objective while working furiously behind the scenes to precipitate a break with Spain.

On February 25, when Secretary Long was absent, Roosevelt redeployed ships, ordered ammunition, and drafted a message to Congress asking for authorization to strengthen the navy. He also cabled Dewey a warning that war might be near and urged preparations for an attack on the Spanish fleet in the Philippines. The Assistant Secretary did not act in defiance of his superiors, but he pushed them further and faster than they would have gone if left to their own devices. Badgering McKinley was a tactic that Roosevelt pursued with relish. Senator Lodge behaved in a more conciliatory fashion, because he had already begun to see the need for united party action. Yet Lodge schemed as tirelessly as Roosevelt and thought time was on the side of the interventionists.[105]

Other warmongers in the party had simpler reactions to the events of February. A sense of outrage over the insult to American honor was mingled with sympathy for the Cubans, which produced the comforting conclusion that American expansion into the Caribbean would be the same thing as the liberation of Cuba. This attitude was based on the older and quainter delusion that all people wanted democracy and would welcome incorporation into the United States to get it. Even realistic senators like Teller of Colorado and Platt of Connecticut talked airily of annexation without conquest.[106] If expansion was going to start, it would be in a fit of anti-imperialism.

During the month of March, McKinley stoutly resisted the unrelenting pressure from the warhawks. During the first two weeks, he waited for the report of the board of inquiry. When it failed to implicate Spain clearly in the blowing up of the *Maine,* McKinley consumed the rest of the month in negotiations with Madrid about autonomy for Cuba. Senator Charles W. Fairbanks of Indiana, who saw the President on the 6th, reported that McKinley had "no intention of being swept off his feet." [107] On the 27th, Dawes found him still determined to secure Cuban rights by peaceful methods if possible.[108] A noisy bloc of New England Republicans sustained the President. Senator Hoar of Massachusetts annoyed his colleague Lodge by opposing war, and many Boston businessmen shared Hoar's view.[109] Platt of Connecticut had no real objection to expansion; but it occurred to him that America might lose a war, and he lacked the appetite for gambling.[110] Speaker Reed simply thought the war party was silly. When Senator Procter of Vermont, who owned large marble quarries, spoke on the iniquities of Spanish misrule in Cuba, Reed snorted that a war would "make a large market for grave stones." [111]

As the war fever spread at the end of March, McKinley looked increasingly harassed and unhappy. Euchre games with his wife and Dawes failed to relax him, and the President's powerful self-control showed signs of snapping when Mrs. McKinley made her customary intrusions on conferences to solicit his opinion of a dress. Lodge and others tried to sap McKinley's resistance with the attractive but unrealistic suggestion that responsibility for the war could be transferred to Spain by recognizing Cuban independence.[112] The importunities of his callers failed to ruffle McKinley outwardly. He listened silently until they lost momentum and then ushered them out of his office. As late as April 2, Platt of Connecticut, who was on close terms with the President, professed ignorance of McKinley's intentions.[113]

Despite the persistent silence in the White House, decisions were being made. McKinley dreaded the possibility that Congress might take the bit in the teeth and draft a war resolution if he did not. Having stalled throughout March in the vain hope that the war fever would subside, he knew that little time remained for the assertion of executive leadership. Accordingly, on March 28, he issued a secret ultimatum to Madrid demanding the release of all Cuban rebels in prison camps.[114] At this stage, the acquiescence of Spain could only have been an embarrassment to McKinley. Yet he had told Dawes the preceding day with evident sincerity that his only objective was to stop suffering.[115] Spain closed the trap on the miserable President April 1 by agreeing to dissolve the prison camps, appropriate $600,000 for relief, grant an armistice to the Cuban rebels, and convene a legislative assembly at Havana in May to inaugurate autonomous government on the island.

Since the President had anticipated that Spain would reject the ultimatum and had written a war message on the basis of his expectation, the conciliatory reply from Madrid forced him into hasty revisions. A fresh delay became necessary on April 5 to evacuate Americans from Cuba.[116] By this time the warhawks were so pleased with news from the White House that they allowed the President to move at his own pace. Simultaneously, they applied pressure on wavering congressmen by talking calmly about the liberation of Cuba. Roosevelt even assured a New York friend that he would "most emphatically oppose the annexation of Cuba unless the Cubans wished it." [117]

The warhawks had overplayed their hand with all of the talk about Cuban independence. So when McKinley's war message reached Congress on April 11, a coalition of New England Republicans and Democrats tried to amend it with a provision recognizing the Cuban revolutionaries as the lawful government on the island. The House spurned the proposal of coalition and displayed an exemplary vagueness in its war resolution. But the mischief-makers were in control of the Senate, where they tacked on the Teller amendment pledging the United States to grant Cuban independence and the Turpie amendment pledging the United States to recognize the rebel government. The expansionists were vexed by this display of bad manners, especially since they dared not state the real grounds for their objections. The Teller amendment was allowed to stand, but it was not particularly dangerous, because most Americans thought liberation and annexation were the same thing. The Turpie amendment, however, committed the United States to a group of revolutionaries who might have ideas of their own about the destiny of Cuba. McKinley saw the inconvenience of tying his own hands, so he threatened to veto the war resolution unless the offending amendment was deleted, and, as a result, it perished in the conference committee. After these time-consuming delays, hostilities officially began the next day.

The Republicans had unmistakably seized the custodianship of the expansionist movement and American patriotism amidst mounting evidence that the issue would be as profitable for them as it had been for the Democrats in 1844. The rank and file had forced the policy on McKinley, and he had suffered the acute embarrassment of having to concede in his war message that Spain was willing to back down on every point at issue.

He did so in two short paragraphs and salved his conscience with the rationalization of the expansionists that "forceable annexation cannot be thought of. . . ." No doubt he believed his statement at the time. He did not foresee that a victorious war would release pressures for the establishment of a protectorate in Cuba and for outright annexation elsewhere. In his shortsightedness, McKinley was not unlike most Americans, who had never felt obliged to ask themselves whether the foreign policies they adopted were likely to achieve the goals they professed.

The Spanish-American War quickly justified John Hay's description of it as "a splendid little war." Within three months, Spain was completely defeated. Not only did America overrun Cuba and Puerto Rico with almost effortless ease, but her Pacific squadron under Admiral Dewey smashed the Spanish fleet in Manila Bay and occupied the capital of the Philippines. As might have been expected, the appetite of the expansionists increased as American prospects improved. Roosevelt resigned his post in the Navy Department and organized a regiment of "rough riders" to fight in Cuba. In Washington, by May 5, Lodge was advocating the annexation of Cuba, and when the war was all but over, he began urging McKinley to retain Manila and Luzon Island. Similar advice came from Lincoln's former secretary, John Hay, whom McKinley had appointed Ambassador to Great Britain. Hay reported that London was delighted with American action in the Far East. Lodge later returned to the White House to urge McKinley to claim the entire Philippine chain. The President had misgivings about going beyond the stated aims of the war, but when Spain sued for an armistice on August 12, he forced her to give up Cuba, Puerto Rico, and the Philippines. Presumably Cuba was to be independent, and the wording of the clause on the Philippines left the same impression, although it transferred authority over the archipelago to the United States pending a final settlement. The only unequivocal language of the protocol occurred in relation to Puerto Rico, which was plainly earmarked for annexation by Uncle Sam. Considering the fact that the expansionists had already managed to push through the annexation of Hawaii as a "strategic necessity," they could look back on the sixteen-week war with genuine satisfaction.

VII

While an American peace commission dominated by two avowed expansionists—Cushman K. Davis and Whitelaw Reid—worked in Paris on a final treaty, the politicians prepared for the 1898 congressional elections. To the degree that he could control matters, McKinley kept the discussion away from the terms of the impending treaty. Voters were invited to show their gratitude for victory, but the Republican campaign textbook for 1898 emphasized the domestic achievements of the McKinley Administration. Meanwhile, a number of party orators talked lyrically about the alluring markets of the Orient, the white man's burden, and the magnificent destiny of the Anglo-Saxon race. The most exuberant apostle of empire building was young Albert J. Beveridge of Indiana, who would soon replace the troublesome Turpie, a Democrat, in the Senate. Lodge spoke cautiously, because he was up for re-election and wanted to avoid a factional squabble with his colleague Hoar, who had opposed the war. Even Roosevelt found it expedient to avoid the subject. He had returned from Cuba a conquering hero because of a much-publicized charge up San Juan Hill and had been awarded the gubernatorial nomination of New York by Boss Tom Platt, who was also a senator. Platt cared little about foreign affairs and less about the exploits of Roosevelt in Cuba. But he needed a hero and a clean-government man to rescue the graft-riddled party machine from the wrath of the voters. So Roosevelt stumped the state talking about the need to vindicate national honor and civic virtue. The Democrats found it hard to criticize either victory or prosperity. They suspected the Republicans of misrepresentation on the peace treaty but were uncertain as to the proper strategy and left the anti-expansionist argument to intellectuals like Carl Schurz, William James, and President David Starr Jordan of Stanford University.

By off-year standards, the Republican campaign of 1898 was a success. The party won the governorship in New York, held its own in the House, and actually picked up a few Senate seats. The gains were not substantial enough, however, to justify delaying the treaty until the new Congress took office on March 4. So the lame duck Senate received the handiwork of the Paris Conference on January 4, 1899. The American delegation had exploited the opportunities for annexation of Spanish possessions made possible by the armistice terms of the preceding August. The most controversial provision of the treaty was the one calling for the retention of the Philippines. The Administration and most Republican senators hoped to avoid a fight on the question by insisting that no decision had been made on the final disposition of the Philippines. As Senator Chandler put it: "The wisest and most conservative Senators" do not want a premature solution.[118] But wise senators had never succeeded in silencing their colleagues before, and the debate on the Spanish treaty was no exception. A steady drumfire of hostile questions goaded expansionists into the statement that America ought to retain the Philippine archipelago for a time. Platt of Connecticut even tried to establish a connection between Plymouth Rock and Manila Bay, assuring senators "that each ship in Manila Bay was a new *Mayflower* boldly steering through the winter sea." [119]

No opposition senator was quite as graphic as the philosopher William James, who claimed that America "would puke her ancient soul" if she ratified the treaty. But all senatorial foes of the Philippine annexation denounced the proposal as a repudiation of traditional principles and branded the expansionists as "imperialists." At the time, the label was considered to be such a reprehensible one that it ought to have damaged the expansionists more effectively than it did. But foes of the treaty could not attack expansion per se without attacking American history. They had to argue that expansion somehow became evil only if it took place overseas. Although the distinction was subtle, the Democrats might have blocked ratification of the treaty in the short session if they had voted solidly against it. All segments of the party recognized that a crusade against imperialism would be more promising in 1900 than a crusade against the gold standard. Unfortunately for the Democrats, Bryan thought the issue would be more clear-cut if the party furnished the votes to ratify the treaty and then denounced it later. Few Democratic senators accepted this curious line of reasoning, but enough did to make a difference. Nearly all of the Republicans stayed with the President, who had helped his cause by appointing several senators to the peace commission. As it was, when the treaty came up on February 6, 1899, ratification carried by only one vote more than the necessary two-thirds. Two days before the Senate vote, however, word reached Washington that fighting had broken out between the American army and a band of Philippine revolutionaries under Aguinaldo. Having secured liberation from Spain, the Filipinos now sought liberation from the United States as well. Their defiant behavior was a perplexing epilogue to the "splendid little war."

Bryan might have lost his election issue if violence in the Philippines had ended quickly. Aguinaldo, however, proved to be a resourceful guerrilla fighter, and military operations against him continued for two years. Not only did the Philippines cause more trouble than the empire builders had bargained for, but the Islands were also a disappointment as a springboard to the China trade. Meanwhile, the United States had begun to define the status of the areas annexed as a result of the Spanish-American War. None of them received full self-government immediately, nor did the United States feel obliged to impose uniform governmental institutions on Cuba, Puerto Rico, and Hawaii. Nobody could agree on a vocabulary to describe them or the Philippines, but everyone thought it would be bad form to refer to America's dependencies as colonies.

If there had been such a discrepancy between expectation and results in domestic policy, Americans would have rebuked the offending Administration at the polls. But for several reasons the voters measured performance in foreign affairs by a different standard. They were poorly informed about actual conditions in the new dependencies and not concerned enough to worry whether or not America's new subjects received democratic government. In fact, many supporters of expansion actually opposed the extension of full civil rights to the colored men who constituted the bulk of the new empire. The wiser Democrats and Populists realized that to advocate the withdrawal of American forces was an offense to national pride. Not having any alternative to suggest, they condemned the Administration for taking the Philippines in the first place. McKinley answered this criticism effectively: "It is no longer a question of expansion with us; we have expanded. If there is any question at all, it is a question of contracting; and who is going to contract?" [120] For better or worse, the tariff expert from Canton, Ohio, had broadened his horizons considerably since the winter of 1898. He had honestly come to the conclusion that it was America's mission to "educate the Filipinos and uplift and civilize and Christianize them and by God's grace do the very best we could by them."

VIII

The election of 1900 was as dull as that of 1896 had been exciting. The monetary question no longer interested the average American, who now took the existence of the gold standard for granted. A number of Republican leaders unwilling to father the gold plank in June 1896 suddenly discovered that they had been for it all along. By 1900 more authors claimed responsibility for the gold plank than any party doctrine since the Emancipation plank of 1864. The issue of imperialism had been discussed so thoroughly that it was almost as stale as the monetary issue.

The certainty of a rematch between McKinley and Bryan deprived the voter of the last excuse for becoming excited. Despite the absence of a pre-convention fight about the nomination, there was a residue of bitterness in the Republican party over imperialism in addition to the usual factional antagonisms. Speaker Reed had resigned in 1899 in protest against the expansionist policy of the Administration. He was more vitriolic privately than publicly, confiding to an acquaintance that he supposed "we had niggers enough in this country without buying any more of 'em." [121] Reed and several of his New England colleagues remained regular, but their disapproval of party policy was no secret.

The only public outburst of factionalism occurred in the contest over the Vice Presidential nomination, and Quay and Platt took full advantage of the opportunity to settle some old scores with Hanna. Quay had been part of the "stop McKinley" bloc in 1896 and had suffered in the distribution of patronage. But his special grievance against Hanna was that the latter had voted to deny Quay a Senate seat in 1899. Platt's grudge was more subtle and complicated. He, too, had joined the "stop McKinley" movement and suffered for his behavior like Quay. But by 1900, the New York boss was more concerned about removing Governor Roosevelt from New York than about annoying Hanna. Roosevelt had not exactly defied Platt in New York, but the Governor was too unpredictable and independent to suit the state boss. Furthermore, it seemed easier for Platt to promote Roosevelt to the Vice Presidency than to deny him a renomination as governor. Since Hanna detested Roosevelt, the scheme was doubly appealing to the two bosses, and they co-operated enthusiastically.

At the outset, the principal obstacle proved to be Roosevelt himself. Notwithstanding his youthfulness, the Rough Rider was impatient and expected rapid promotion. He wanted to be Secretary of War or Governor General of the Philippines and had begun to intrigue for those posts almost before he was comfortably settled in the governor's chair at Albany. After several hints from Roosevelt, McKinley had invited the governor down for consultation in the summer of 1899 [122] but had ignored Roosevelt's poorly concealed offers to serve in the cabinet. When Hobart's death left the Vice Presidency open, Lodge began to urge his friend for the post. Roosevelt knew that the Vice Presidency was a graveyard and flatly rejected the idea [123] about the same time Platt got interested in it. Roosevelt was mystified for nearly two months as to why Platt should want to promote him, and when the Governor finally found out, he became more negative about the Vice Presidency than ever.[124] In fact, Roosevelt demanded a place on the New York delegation for the specific purpose of blocking his nomination, and he extracted a promise from Platt not to push him against his will. As an added measure of safety, Roosevelt went to Washington and told McKinley that he would not run. He received in return the disconcerting reply that the President did not want him on the ticket.[125]

These precautions would have killed the chances of most candidates. The difficulty was that, despite his violent disclaimers, Roosevelt had not really made up his mind, and the negative attitude of McKinley made the job more attractive to him. Furthermore, Roosevelt had such an insatiable thirst for the limelight that he could not turn down anything if people cheered enough. This streak of exhibitionism drew Roosevelt to the Philadelphia convention on Saturday, June 16, three days before the convention opened. It was a strange gesture for a man who claimed he did not want the nomination, but Roosevelt compounded the error by wearing a broad-brimmed, rough-rider-style hat and mingling freely with the delegates. The following Monday on the eve of the convention, Hanna wrenched a new statement out of Roosevelt that he was not a candidate and that no man should be nominated against his will.

Meanwhile, Platt and Quay had concluded that Roosevelt would accept if it could be made to appear that he commanded enthusiastic support outside of New York. Quay artfully rounded up Roosevelt delegates, recruiting the bulk of Southerners with a threat to reduce the representation of their section at future conventions if they did not co-operate. Westerners fell into line when Quay and Platt told them that New York was against Roosevelt.[126] By Tuesday evening, the Roosevelt boom had gained so much momentum that Hanna phoned McKinley in alarm. The latter declined to interfere, and by Wednesday evening the result was settled. Roosevelt reacted just as the bosses had anticipated. After the convention he wrote a friend that he had accepted only because of the "absolutely unanimous" sentiment for his candidacy outside of New York.[127]

The unwillingness of McKinley to stop the Roosevelt movement indicated a growing coolness in the relations between the President and Senator Hanna. Already McKinley had hurt his friend by delaying until the last possible moment the request that Hanna direct the Republican campaign. Further signs of friction developed in August when the President made public a letter rebuking the Cleveland industrialist for certain campaign practices.[128] Still later, the White House attempted through an intermediary to discourage Hanna from a Midwestern speaking tour. Part of the difficulty was due to Hanna's relaxed view of the ethical standards governing public servants. Still more disconcerting was his outspoken defense of big business. By imperceptible degrees, he had reached the point where he believed that the enemies of big business were the enemies of prosperity. At a Chicago campaign rally, Hanna actually denied that trusts existed, and was induced to modify the statement only after considerable pressure. His business friends could do no wrong as long as they treated labor fairly, and Hanna stormed about the country defending them with the slogan: "Let well enough alone." [129] Few Presidents had a more complacent attitude toward the trusts than McKinley, but he was alarmed at the defiant manner in which Hanna defended them. As it turned out, Hanna had unerringly chosen the one campaign in a quarter-century in which it was safe to ignore the public prejudice against trusts. McKinley's instinct told him that the voters had been pushed far enough on the trust question, but he died before his judgment was confirmed.

What the candidates said and did in the campaign seemed to make little difference in the outcome. McKinley stayed home, and Roosevelt barnstormed the country, defending national honor. Bryan tried to talk about the monetary issues, which were dead, and imperialism, which was dangerous. Chandler of New Hampshire attacked the excessive use of money by business but few listened.[130] As one perceptive Kansas editor put it: "The issue is prosperity." [131] Nobody spoke against it, and the Republicans took credit for it. The only unhappy people were those who wanted to vote for the gold standard and against imperialism. Some of them must have followed Cleveland's example and gone duck-hunting on election day, because the total vote decreased. Nevertheless, McKinley won by a bigger margin than in 1896. He captured 292 electoral votes and 7,218,491 popular votes against 155 electoral votes and 6,356,734 popular votes for Bryan. A few of the sparsely settled Western states like Kansas and Nebraska, for which the Democrats had paid such an excessive price in 1896, slipped back into the Republican column. The most spectacular reversal occurred in Utah, where Hanna enticed the Mormon leaders and hence the state into the Republican camp.

The opening months of McKinley's second term were uneventful. Obviously he intended to continue the hitherto reliable formula of nurturing prosperity and accommodating himself to Congress. There was not a cloud on the horizon when the President and Mrs. McKinley entrained for Buffalo in early September 1901 to visit the Pan American Exposition.

But McKinley sensed the need of his party for a new issue and tried to introduce one in a major speech at the fair grounds on September 5. Although nothing very controversial could be expected from so cautious a politician, the crowd of 50,000 was surprised by the eloquence with which McKinley endorsed reciprocal trade agreements as the key to American prosperity. The next afternoon, the President appeared for a public reception at the Temple of Music. Despite a recent wave of assassination attempts by anarchists against heads of states, no special precautions were taken for McKinley's safety. Secret Service men had not yet perfected the technique of flanking a President to shield him from would-be killers. Thus, nobody was in a position to interfere when Leon F. Czolgosz joined the reception line and approached McKinley with a revolver concealed in a handkerchief. The demented young anarchist pumped two bullets into the President at close range. In the shadow of death McKinley behaved with his characteristic restraint. Instinctively, he straightened up to his full height before shock caused him to collapse in the arms of stunned bystanders. Still conscious, he tried to stop soldiers from beating Czolgosz.

During the anxious week that followed, cabinet members and leading Republican politicians gathered at Buffalo to be near their chief. For a time McKinley seemed to improve; and on September 10, Vice President Roosevelt was persuaded to leave Buffalo and resume his vacation. But the President's condition deteriorated rapidly on September 13, and he died the following morning. A few hours later, Roosevelt was sworn in as President at a private home only a short distance from where the mourners clustered around the body of McKinley.

The death of McKinley marked the end of an era. Not only was he the last President who had served in the Civil War, but the last one to believe that America's problems were simple and easily solved. Like most of his generation, he had no real comprehension of the squalor and misery that lurked beneath the surface of national prosperity. It was not so much that McKinley had deliberately avoided reality as that the conventions of Victorian society had insulated him from it. If McKinley had lived a few years longer, muckraking magazines would have shocked him with their revelations about the ugly political and economic foundations upon which his own power rested. As it was, he completed his career serenely confident of the power of Christian impulses to erode away the injustices which he had only occasionally glimpsed.

VIII
Theodore Roosevelt and the Progressive Movement

Of all the unhappy politicians who accompanied McKinley's body from Buffalo to Canton, Hanna was the most bitter and despondent. Unable to contain himself, Hanna exploded before a friend: "I told William McKinley it was a mistake to nominate that wild man at Philadelphia. . . . Now look, that damned cowboy is President of the United States." [1] Hanna lived long enough to learn that his characterization did Roosevelt an injustice. Yet, the hard-headed party boss was undoubtedly right in believing that no Republican convention in the nineteenth century would have given a man like Roosevelt a Vice Presidential nomination had it thought the President would die in office. From the time of Lincoln to McKinley, the Republicans had selected candidates with a remarkable gift for self-restraint in public. As Presidents, some had been fiercely partisan, but for the most part their prejudices had spoken through deeds rather than words.

McKinley's successor was a more controversial candidate than the Republicans customarily selected for President. He welcomed noisy combat and excelled at it. He also embraced the Jacksonian doctrine that the President ought to provide vigorous national leadership and thwart the divisive influence of Congress. Roosevelt had made his national debut at the Republican convention in 1884 as a militant civil-service reformer and an outspoken foe of Blaine. Moreover, the habit of controversy had grown on him with the passing of the years. As civil-service commissioner under Benjamin Harrison, he had waged a loud but futile war with the spoilsmen. A brief tenure as police commissioner in New York City had followed, during which Roosevelt had carried on a two-pronged conflict with the organized forces of vice and with his own apathetic law-enforcement officers. In 1897 he had returned to Washington as Assistant Secretary of the Navy and promptly campaigned for a big navy. His superiors had been relieved when Roosevelt joined the cavalry, but he had returned in four months with his appetite for combat undiminished. His next target was Secretary of War Russell A. Alger, who had carelessly allowed "embalmed" beef to be supplied to American troops in Cuba. Election to the governorship of New York had distracted him from his vendetta with Alger, but he made so much trouble for Platt that the latter wished that Roosevelt would "take the veil." [2] Under normal circumstances, the Vice President remains as obscure as a novice in a convent, and McKinley scrupulously refrained from giving Roosevelt any responsibility that would broaden his activity in the Administration.[3]

The new President actually was a much more complex person than the politicians had supposed. When they knew him better, they discovered that his inflammatory language was a vehicle for expressing orthodox American ideals. Born in a brownstone mansion in New York City two years before the Civil War, Roosevelt had grown up with an aristocratic sense of obligation toward the poor. A Harvard education had strengthened his sense of duty, and he might have hardened into a typical Boston Puritan but for his contact with the American frontier. As it was, Roosevelt had purchased a ranch in North Dakota and become an advocate of the strenuous outdoor life. The personality that emerged from his immersion in high society and the primitive Western community eludes description. It contained elements of tension, but it was remarkably harmonious, for in many ways the New York squire and the North Dakota rancher reinforced each other. Roosevelt's concern for the weak and unfortunate ceased to have an air of aristocratic condescension about it after he mingled with simple farmers and stockmen. Even his upper-class taste for hunting strengthened his egalitarian tendencies, for it put him on informal terms with trappers, explorers, and Texas rangers. Roosevelt felt as comfortable with people who had no formal education as with the Harvard graduates, and he had a natural flair for putting them at ease.[4]

To a degree, Roosevelt's empathy with the common man was an inverted form of snobbery. Like all men born into a family which had enjoyed a secure status for several generations, Roosevelt disliked the new class of capitalists coming to power at the end of the nineteenth century.

He thought them irresponsible, uncultured, and without character. He especially disliked their efforts to win recognition by flaunting their wealth. "To spend the day with them at Newport," Roosevelt confided to a friend, "or even to dine with them save under exceptional circumstances fills me with frank horror." [5] Roosevelt's dislike of the *nouveaux riches* did not drive him into doctrinaire radicalism. Despite his interest in providing practical help for the underprivileged, he distrusted labor unions and agrarian protest movements as much as he did the new class of industrial entrepreneurs. In fact, he often baffled his contemporaries by denouncing all three groups in the same breath. Behind Roosevelt's impartial antipathy to political organization on an economic basis was a coherent philosophy. He cherished the democratic ideal of a classless society, and opposed any policy that promoted the hardening of class lines. "It would be a dreadful calamity," he wrote in 1904, if the country were divided into two parties, "one containing the bulk of the propertied people . . . the other the bulk of the wage workers." [6] Since big business possessed greater cohesiveness and power than other groups at the beginning of the twentieth century, Roosevelt directed most of his energy as a reformer to restraining it. Inevitably, Wall Street regarded him as an enemy and a traitor to his own class. The financial magnates who had recently risen from rags to riches were especially antagonistic. Unaccustomed to the possession of vast wealth, they viewed even the most innocent reforms as attempts to take it away from them, and could not understand the mentality of this aristocrat. They distrusted the restlessness of the masses, whereas Roosevelt wanted to guide it into constructive channels. Though he was as dedicated to property rights as his critics, Roosevelt believed that he could preserve them only by a prompt redress of grievances.

Paradoxically, Roosevelt also combined an ability to analyze an issue dispassionately with a blind partisanship in promoting solutions. He saw that the emphasis on the tariff as a cause of economic developments was overdone [7] and informed one reformer that "no given set of measures will work a perfect cure for any serious evil." [8] On another occasion he observed: "I believe in men who take the next step; not those who theorize about the two hundredth step." [9] He was Roosevelt the pragmatist one minute and a moralizing Republican the next. In a campaign speech in 1900, he said that the "triumph of the Democrats would mean misery so widespread that it is almost unthinkable. . . ." [10] Not only did Roosevelt regard the Republican party as the custodian of respectability but as the only reliable instrument for correcting evils in American society. He was a conservative and reformer, a crusader and a practical politician. Each of these characteristics dominated in turn, because Roosevelt never succeeded in concealing an opinion very long. As President, he exploded like some capricious volcano, showering advice on the nation and epitaphs like "mollycoddle," "malefactor," and "skunk" on his foes. His policy of indiscriminate opposition to pressure groups came to be known as the Square Deal, a designation that was popular both with Roosevelt and the voters.

Lack of verbal self-restraint had been the undoing of Andrew Johnson, but it failed to damage Roosevelt, perhaps because his feuds were carried on with a certain boyish exuberance and charm. "You must always remember," the British ambassador confided to a friend, "that the President is about six." [11] Like all six-year-olds, Roosevelt had a superabundance of enthusiasm and animal spirits. It was easy to get irritated with him but difficult to stay so for very long. His insatiable curiosity about the world around him disarmed all but the most confirmed critics. Roosevelt could become equally excited about a Tolstoy novel [12] and the protective coloring of birds.[13] Yet despite a wide acquaintance with history, the classics, and modern literature, Roosevelt shared his fellow countrymen's instinctive distrust of overindulgence in culture. After a brief visit in Italy during the late 1880's, he had written: "Being a healthy man with a brain and the tastes that any manly man should have, I of course would not wish to stay in Europe too long." [14] Both his preferences and aversions were so orthodox that Roosevelt became a symbol of the older America slowly vanishing in the wake of the new industrial society. He believed in large families, praised the farm as the nursery of statesmen, and urged youth to cultivate physical fitness. Above all, he bristled with pride in America and defended what he conceived to be national honor with the pugnacity of a Jacksonian. Roosevelt's every act seemed to say: We can preserve our national character irrespective of the challenges delivered by the twentieth century.

II

Not all these traits were apparent to the public when Roosevelt entered the White House in September 1901. Indeed, his initial moves reassured nervous Republican politicians. He promptly announced his intention of carrying out McKinley's policies and invited all members of his predecessor's cabinet to remain. He even asked Aldrich of Rhode Island and other senior senators to look over his first annual message in advance. It was just as well that Roosevelt did so, because on Capitol Hill suspicion of the President was poorly concealed. At the moment, the seniority system was placing the levers of congressional power firmly in the hands of the generation that had displaced the condottieri of the 1890's. Advancing age would have strengthened the conservative instincts of the new leaders in any case, but the rapid turnover in Congress during the turbulent Populist era also promoted men who came from the older and less radical sections of the country. The frontier had moved so far beyond states like Illinois, Iowa, Wisconsin, and Ohio that their representatives in Washington often displayed the cautious tastes of New Englanders. These leaders saw no reason to develop new issues as long as prosperity prevailed and the voters remained reasonably quiet.

Except for the first year and a half of Roosevelt's tenure, the House was ruled with an iron hand by "Uncle Joe" Cannon. He had been the principal lieutenant of the autocratic Reed; but at the outset of his eight-year tenure as Speaker, Cannon aroused far less antagonism than his sardonic predecessor.[15] He stifled legislation which displeased him by sidetracking it in committee. Cannon also declined to recognize members unless they consulted him in advance. Occasionally, he ignored the rules of seniority and bumped recalcitrant congressmen off key committees. For the most part, however, Cannon secured co-operation by an artful mixture of compliments, threats, and buffoonery, dispensing a salty brand of folk wisdom through great clouds of cigar smoke. He was so negative in his approach to all but routine legislation that it was said that, if Cannon had attended the caucus on creation, he would have remained loyal to chaos. His reverence for the status quo was instinctive, although the fact that the Speaker owned a variety of industrial enterprises in Danville, Illinois, strengthened his feelings.

Senate leadership was just as conservative as the leadership in the House but more dispersed because committee chairmen held enormous power. Since voters were mainly interested in tariff, monetary, and pork-barrel legislation, the chairmen of the finance and the appropriations committees were the most powerful leaders in the Senate. Usually one of them also held the dual post of chairman of the Republican conference and floor leader, and so he also filled vacancies on important committees. Throughout most of the '90's, Sherman of Ohio and Morrill of Vermont had divided the leadership; but near the end of the decade, Aldrich of Rhode

Island replaced Morrill as chairman of the finance committee and Allison of Iowa became chairman of the appropriations committee. Both men were exceedingly clever and habitually used their power behind the scenes. Of the two, Allison came the closer to filling Sherman's old role as mediator between the Eastern and Western wings of the party. Allison had served in the Senate continuously since 1873 and was a shy, uncommunicative statesman. Few people knew what he really thought, although his invariable policy was to modify legislation pleasing to Wall Street so that it would be palatable to the rural areas. Like Sherman, he gave business the substance of what it wanted without seeming to do so. He took particular pride in framing innocent-looking amendments which drew the fangs from legislation obnoxious to him. Throughout Roosevelt's Presidency he was a dominant force in the Senate. His colleague Nelson Aldrich of Rhode Island had entered the Senate eight years after Allison and, like most New Englanders, displayed a touch of haughtiness which often infuriated Westerners. Unlike Allison, Aldrich lacked the incentive to compromise, because his Rhode Island constituency was so completely dominated by industrial interests. His own extensive commercial interests and family ties with the Rockefellers reinforced Aldrich's predisposition to believe that the welfare of big business and that of America were identical. His outlook was narrow but honest, and he never understood why others regarded him as a representative of special interests.

Among others in the Senate hierarchy, Orville H. Platt of Connecticut was an unimaginative, hard-working logician who avoided public attention, while John C. Spooner of Wisconsin was an unusually able lawyer who awed his colleagues with bursts of eloquence on dull subjects. Despite his brilliance, Spooner never operated as effectively as he might have because of his carelessness and distaste for practical politics. Few leaders went so far with so little effort on their part, and after 1900 Spooner was increasingly distracted by rebellion in Wisconsin, with which he either could not or would not deal.

On the periphery of the inner circle were Lodge, Cullom, Elkins, Francis C. Warren of Wyoming, Eugene Hale of Maine, and the feuding Ohio senators. The glacial and erudite Lodge could not make up his mind whether his future would be brighter if he co-operated with his long-time friend Roosevelt or with the Senate oligarchy, whom he seldom crossed. It was relatively easy for Lodge to have the best of both worlds because his interest in foreign affairs kept him out of the line of fire. The oligarchy seldom bothered itself about this area unless the President encroached upon the treaty-making power of the Senate. Whenever he did so, Lodge had some anxious moments; but his principal problem was Senator Cullom rather than the President or the oligarchy, for Cullom stood between Lodge and the chairmanship of the foreign relations committee throughout the decade.

Seated near Lodge in the Upper House was the affable, unreliable Elkins, now near the end of a long political career. His great wealth and seniority ought to have made Elkins a powerful force among the conservatives, but Elkins had learned his politics under Blaine and was an incurable schemer. As late as 1904, he was shaping his conduct with an eye to the Presidency,[16] and making zigzags from his strategic post as chairman of the interstate commerce committee to suit the taste of West Virginia constituents. After a short term in the early 1890's, Warren of Wyoming returned to the Senate in 1895 along with Elkins and rose rapidly in the hierarchy. Warren displayed as much diligence in pursuing appropriations for the arid West as Aldrich did in pursuing subsidies for the industrial East. Like his Rhode Island colleague, he had a personal interest in much of the legislation before Congress. Besides accumulating a substantial mercantile empire, Warren became the largest wool producer in Wyoming. Warren behaved like a simple sheep rancher, at home, but, once he crossed the Mississippi River, he became the urbane socialite with Eastern principles. For years rumors circulated that Warren illegally grazed his sheep on public lands, and although he admitted his guilt privately, he succeeded in evading prosecution.[17]

If the Senate had not adhered strictly to the rules of seniority, nobody would have ever noticed Eugene Hale. Although he belonged to the second generation of what was to become a famous political dynasty in Maine, Hale was "a morose and selfish man." [18] Unpopular from the start, he managed to overcome this handicap by sheer longevity, and eventually succeeded Allison as chairman of the appropriations committee and as Republican floor leader. The two Ohio senators had ability without seniority, which restricted their influence in the Senate. Hanna's access to the White House during McKinley's tenure kept him from being as badly neglected as most freshmen senators. Foraker waited his turn for power more patiently than Hanna, but he was a lone wolf and never worked his way into the oligarchy.

Under the circumstances, it would have required a political revolution to shake the grip of the oligarchy on the Senate. In 1901 only the brilliant but egotistical Albert Beveridge of Indiana showed any disposition to challenge the powerful committee chairmen who presided over their miniature legislatures in the Senate. Beveridge was soon to receive help from the President in his challenge to the Senate leadership. After allowing his wary critics on Capitol Hill a six-month breathing spell, Roosevelt launched the first phase of a twofold campaign to consolidate his own power in the spring of 1902. He was wise enough to avoid a frontal attack on Congress, and instead relied upon executive implementation of old laws to turn the flank of the oligarchy.

The focal point of his assault was big business, which had been growing bigger since the Spanish-American War. J. P. Morgan, the investment banker who served as midwife of the trusts, had presided at the birth of the United States Steel Corporation in 1901, a consolidation that revived public suspicion of business power. The only weapon that Roosevelt could use against such consolidations was the Sherman Anti-Trust Act. Since successive Supreme Court decisions had narrowed the application of the law to the point where the statute was virtually useless, the entire business world was startled on February 18, 1902, when the President instituted a suit to dissolve the Northern Securities Company, a newly created railroad trust. Roosevelt had chosen his target well. Railroads were the most unpopular symbols of monopoly, and the events preceding the formation of the Northern Securities had demonstrated afresh the indifference of big business to the interests of the public. Initially, two Western railroad kings, James J. Hill and Edward H. Harriman, had fought for domination of other railway systems controlling access to Chicago. After their financial struggle had produced, among other results, a panic in Wall Street, they calmly pooled their resources in the Northern Securities Company. So Roosevelt's suit to dissolve it received strong public support.

Litigation dragged on for more than a year, and, surprisingly, the Supreme Court sustained the government. The decision came on the eve of the 1904 campaign, and conferred on Roosevelt the politically appealing title of "trust buster." Many newspapers had ridiculed the suit, and the *Minneapolis Journal* had predicted that the two railroads would continue to be "managed in the same general way . . . for the same general ends." [19] Subsequent trust-busting indicated that the critics of the President were good prophets. Physical separation of large business units did not prevent them from co-operating, nor did fresh government suits against offenders stop the formation of new trusts. In fact, the number of trusts increased from 149 in 1900 to 10,020 in 1908. Nevertheless, Roosevelt had made the toothless Sherman Act work for the first time since the days of Grover Cleveland. The agitation that he started prodded Congress into establishing the Department of Commerce in 1903, with a subsidiary fact-finding Bureau of Corporations. Even the reluctant Elkins was pressured into sponsoring the same year a companion piece of legislation which outlawed railroad rebates.

Simultaneously, Roosevelt proceeded with a conservation program which increased his personal strength and gave the Republicans a popular issue for the 1904 campaign. He later recalled in his *Autobiography* that conservation was his first love. Fortunately for the President, two articulate groups were also ready for a new policy to govern the disposal of the remaining public lands in the West. Many Easterners wanted to stop the wasteful exploitation of natural resources by businessmen, while settlers in the arid regions of the Rocky Mountains wanted an irrigation program to sustain agriculture. The Western campaign for reclamation and the Eastern campaign for conservation were separate and conflicting ventures, but Roosevelt forced a shotgun wedding of irrigation and forestry. In his annual message of December 1901 he announced that water for the arid West depended upon the preservation of forests. Under a law of 1891 he began withdrawing forest lands from settlement. He also worked through Congress in 1902 the Newlands Act, the first in a long series of laws earmarking federal funds for irrigation. Like most shotgun weddings, the one between irrigation and forestry was a mismatch. In keeping with American tradition, the Westerners grabbed with both hands for funds to develop their own area. But they showed a predictable resentment against the government policy of withholding forest lands from settlement—a resentment that grew as rapidly as Roosevelt enlarged the forest reserves. Easterners exhibited the same sectional reflexes and obstructed appropriations for irrigation. But at the outset the quarreling was subdued, and few critics openly challenged Roosevelt.

The anthracite coal strike of 1902 and the controversy over the Panama Canal provided two more popular issues for Roosevelt. In its early stages, the anthracite coal strike, which started on May 12, 1902, appeared likely to end in another defeat for the 140,000 miners who had walked off the job. The railroads owned most of the large mines and had perfected certain techniques for ending strikes. They forced the marginal mine operators into a united front by threatening to raise freight rates and prodded local police units into systematic harassment of strikers. If these tactics failed, the operators hauled in private detectives and carloads of strike-breakers; they relied on public disapproval of violence to sustain their position in case labor resisted.

On this occasion, however, the miners' desperate economic condition made them show unexpected determination and discipline. The strike attracted little attention in the summer of 1902; but by September coal prices had jumped from the normal price of $5 a ton to $30 a ton, and many people faced a heatless winter. An increasing clamor arose for federal intervention. Hitherto, government action had been taken in response to state requests, usually for breaking the strike with federal troops, but Roosevelt instead offered his services as a mediator. It was a remarkable reversal of attitude for a man who had advocated shooting the Pullman strikers eight years earlier. Yet Roosevelt found considerable public support for mediation, partly because magazines with a national circulation had created sympathy for the plight of the miners and partly because George F. Baer, the principal spokesman of the operators, had made unfortunate public statements. In a widely quoted letter, Baer had contended that the welfare of the miners would be secured not by "labor agitators, but by 'Christian men to whom God in His infinite wisdom has given control of the property interests of the country.' " When people found out that the self-righteous Baer opposed mediation, the solution became more popular. Hanna conferred with his fellow industrialists, and Roosevelt hinted that it might become necessary for federal troops to mine coal with bayonets. Under these pressures the operators agreed to accept the award of an arbitration commission appointed by the President. In the end, the miners gained far less than they had demanded, but Roosevelt emerged from the crisis with a new reputation as a friend of labor.

While the arbitration commission was working out the terms of settlement in the coal fields, Roosevelt turned his attention to the project for an Isthmian canal. After long negotiations, Secretary of State Hay had persuaded the British to waive the restrictions in the Clayton-Bulwer Treaty of 1850 against exclusive operation and fortification of a canal by the United States. And in January 1903, he signed an agreement with Colombia whereby the United States received a 100-year lease of the proposed canal zone in return for a down payment of $10,000,000 plus an annual rental fee. The American Senate ratified the treaty on March

17, but the Colombian Senate rejected it in June. Bogota hinted that there was no objection to the treaty that could not be overcome by a larger down payment.

At this point the United States might either have raised the ante or resumed negotiations for a canal through Nicaragua, which many senators had favored in the first place. Roosevelt, however, was furious with Colombia, and tried to organize an independence movement in Panama, with a view to negotiating a new treaty. By May 1903 Roosevelt was in touch with dissident groups in Panama, and a month later the New York papers were predicting a revolution. United States naval units took up strategic positions in the Caribbean to prevent Colombia from sending troops to Panama, and the revolution began on November 3, 1903. Three days later, Roosevelt extended recognition to the Panamanian government, pushed a new treaty through the United States Senate on February 23, 1904, and received the concurrence of Panama a month later. American construction engineers could not imitate the breathtaking timetable of the diplomats in Washington, but digging began immediately and the canal was completed in 1913.

Outside the United States, the Panamanian revolution and its aftermath were regarded as a typical imperialist adventure. At home the episode only increased the popularity of Roosevelt. Americans overlooked the fact that Colombia was a sovereign state and had a perfect right to reject the treaty. Instead, they accepted Roosevelt's airy assurance that the venal Bogota politicians had insulted American honor by demanding a higher price.

III

Although Roosevelt repeatedly insisted that the initiative for his renomination in 1904 ought to come from the people, his bid for control of the Republican party was anything but a spontaneous affair. He had begun to think of the Presidency even before he succeeded McKinley,[20] and the night of his predecessor's death Roosevelt put his brother-in-law to sleep discussing tactics for 1904.[21] Precedent offered Roosevelt no encouragement. Not a single Vice President who had been promoted to the White House in mid-term subsequently secured a renomination from his party. To make matters worse for Roosevelt, the powerful figure of Mark Hanna was planted squarely between him and the nomination. Roosevelt obviously needed professional help, and he called upon James S. Clarkson, an ancient foe of civil service who had good contacts with Southern Republicans. Clarkson was brought out of retirement to serve as surveyor of the port of New York. As Civil Service Commissioner under Harrison, Clarkson's efficiency as a spoilsman had been distasteful to Roosevelt; but under the circumstances, the President saw no reason to harbor a grudge. Adversity had driven Clarkson into an equally charitable frame of mind. Toward the close of the nineteenth century he had sold his interest in the powerful *Des Moines Register* and abandoned his political base in Iowa. His dreams of national service had then been shattered by successive quarrels with Harrison and McKinley, which had reduced him to the status of a politician without a following. His sole asset was the National Republican League, a network of local clubs he had founded for the 1888 election. Hanna had viewed the clubs as a threat to his own power and had allowed them to decay.[22] Roosevelt recognized their usefulness as a nucleus for his own organization and restored Clarkson to favor. The partnership worked well. In addition to routine organizational work, Clarkson wrote innumerable letters to local Republican leaders. Those out of favor with Hanna were told that "the money God" had left Washington. Others heard the reassuring news that Roosevelt is "the safest and surest" defender of property "in all of its real rights." Clarkson conceded that Roosevelt seemed to act quickly but insisted that he "never passes on any subject until he has fully investigated it." [23] Roosevelt had equally good luck with Henry C. Payne, his other major appointee from the ranks of the professional politicians. As Postmaster General, the methodical Wisconsin spoilsman weeded Hanna men out of key spots in the postal service.

For nearly eighteen months Hanna watched the erosion of his power without visible protest. He had never overcome his initial dislike of Roosevelt; but deteriorating health and the prospect of a hard re-election campaign in Ohio kept Hanna quiet, until Foraker, who had no particular love for Roosevelt, forced his hand. Foraker could not resist the opportunity to embarrass Hanna, whose political future depended upon the election of a Republican legislature in November 1903. In May, Foraker proposed that the G.O.P. state convention endorse Roosevelt for re-election. This maneuver forced the angry Hanna into the open, and he wrote the President that the local political situation would require him to oppose Roosevelt's endorsement. The latter responded with an adroit telegram. After disclaiming any responsibility for raising the issue, he went on to say, "Those who favor my Administration and my nomination will endorse both, and those who do not will oppose." This ultimatum extracted a terse promise from Hanna not to oppose the Roosevelt resolution in Ohio. Thereafter an uneasy truce prevailed between Roosevelt and the senator while Hanna waded "in gore up to his neck" to secure re-election in 1903.[24]

The Wall Street millionaires were neither as quiet nor as inactive as Hanna. In October 1903 Clarkson found them "blind and implacable" in their opposition to Roosevelt.[25] But they could not find a suitable candidate. Only Hanna possessed the necessary prestige to contest the nomination with any chance of success, and he steadfastly resisted the pressure of his unrealistic supporters. The most he would agree to do was withhold an endorsement of Roosevelt while they looked for a substitute. For a time the financiers put their support behind Arthur P. Gorman of Maryland, who was, embarrassingly enough, a Democrat.[26] Gorman could arouse no enthusiasm beyond Wall Street, though. By the beginning of 1904 the moneyed interests had turned back to Hanna. Although he became increasingly bitter in his private remarks about the President,[27] Hanna avoided a public break. Moreover, his health was failing rapidly. By mid-February he was dead, less than six weeks after his re-election to the Senate. Like McKinley before him, Hanna belonged to the nineteenth century. Although he did not know it, his beloved party was soon to repudiate his advice "to stand pat." Hanna would not have liked the era of reform that lay ahead, but he would have adjusted to it better than many of his fellow businessmen.

The passing of Hanna removed the last barrier to the renomination of Roosevelt, and most of the disgruntled Wall Street figures reluctantly backed him. Once the task of rounding up Roosevelt delegates had been completed, Clarkson and Payne faded into the background, and other associates of the President came into prominence. During the convention and the ensuing campaign George B. Cortelyou and Elihu Root were especially noticeable. Both had served McKinley—Cortelyou as his private secretary and Root as his Secretary of War—but both easily transferred their allegiance to Roosevelt. Cortelyou's contacts in the business world were as extensive as Hanna's, and the younger man had widened them further after becoming Secretary of the newly created Department of Commerce in 1903. Cortelyou likewise showed a pronounced gift for organization and money-raising, but he seemed smooth, cold, and slippery by comparison with the generous, straightforward Hanna. Nonetheless, he was to serve Roosevelt well as chairman and secretary of the Republican national committee and as financial manager of the campaign. In his own day Cortelyou was an unfamiliar type of politician—a forerunner of the talented public relations man who would be held in great esteem by candidates two generations later. Elihu Root was also an unfamiliar type for very different reasons. Root belonged to the nearly extinct species of gifted lawyer-politicians who had flourished before the Civil War. During the intervening years, the ablest legal minds had forsaken politics for corporation law. Root made his fortune, too, but, having made it, he became an active reformer in the New York Republican party. In 1904, he served as a link between Roosevelt and the Wall Street bankers who were fuming over the bear market and blaming the President.[28] Few excelled Root in good looks, charm, and persuasiveness as a speaker, yet he was too aristocratic in his tastes to develop the popularity that he deserved.

Root's most important single assignment in 1904 was to serve as keynote speaker and Administration spokesman at the convention. Roosevelt wisely allowed the older generation to share honors by acquiescing in the selection of "Uncle Joe" Cannon as permanent chairman. When the delegates assembled at Chicago on June 26, it quickly became apparent that they were less than enthusiastic about Roosevelt. Although the convention of 1904 acted more graciously than the Baltimore convention that had renominated Lincoln forty years earlier, nobody could miss the undercurrent of resentment against Roosevelt. In the interests of solidarity, both the convention speech-makers and platform-drafters either ignored the President's controversial domestic program or praised it in tepid, noncommittal fashion. Root's keynote address did not discuss the issues nor did it laud Roosevelt "at McKinley's expense." [29] Instead it dealt with safe topics like the gold standard and achievements in foreign affairs. The platform gave no hint that the party was in transition. It endorsed lawful combinations of capital and labor and denounced unlawful ones. It also tried to satisfy Western advocates of tariff revision by hinting that the Dingley tariff was not as sacred as the Ten Commandments. The older generation received another concession to its viewpoint in the selection of the rich and cautious Senator Charles W. Fairbanks of Indiana as Vice Presidential candidate.

Two weeks later, the Democrats met in an atmosphere of despondency reminiscent of their post-Civil War conventions.[30] Successive defeats had reduced William Jennings Bryan's appeal, and the party was eager to avoid nominating him for the third time running. Most Democrats also thought it desirable to bid for their erstwhile supporters in the populous Eastern states, a strategy which required both a conservative candidate and a conservative platform. Gorman of Maryland had been training for the nomination ever since his return to the Senate in 1903, but his stock dropped abruptly in the spring of 1904 when he failed to mobilize a solid party vote against the Panama treaty. The only candidate upon whom the dispirited delegates could agree was Judge Alton B. Parker of New York. Nobody knew Parker well enough to dislike him, until he made his acceptance contingent on the adoption of a gold plank in the platform. Thereafter, Parker enjoyed the enmity of Bryan's numerous followers. In case any voters had missed Parker's dramatic endorsement of financial orthodoxy, the convention drove the point home by awarding the Vice Presidential nomination to ex-Senator Henry Gassaway Davis of West Virginia, a wealthy octogenarian and father-in-law of Stephen B. Elkins.

The Democrats turned sharply to the right at the exact time the public was moving in the opposite direction. The cumulative effect of Roosevelt's leadership and the switch in Democratic tactics was to revitalize the Republican party at a critical time. Under the direction of McKinley and Hanna, it had threatened to stagnate in the role of defender of the status quo. Four years later, it was on the verge of becoming both the party of prosperity and the party of reform.

The campaign of 1904 was dull, although not as dull as 1900. The trend away from brass bands and pageantry continued. For the Republicans the important activity went on beneath the surface, with Cortelyou systematically wooing various pressure groups.[31] At the insistence of his advisers, the restless Roosevelt remained on his "front porch" either at his family home on Oyster Bay or at the White House. Parker adopted the same tactics from choice. Only Bryan took the stump, but his activity had the effect of diverting the spotlight from the Democratic standard bearer, who was not very well known to start with. The sole excitement occurred in the closing days of October when Parker made a short speaking tour and a sensational charge against the opposition. Accusing the Republicans of extorting large contributions from Eastern corporations in return for pledges of immunity from anti-trust suits, Parker received great attention from the newspapers. Roosevelt angrily denied the charge and was technically correct in insisting that the party had not contracted improper obligations to big business. Nevertheless, the corporations had made far larger contributions to the Republicans than to the Democrats, and Roosevelt was hardly candid in trying to produce the opposite impression. Subsequent developments indicated that Cortelyou did not inform the President accurately about either the size or source of contributions. There was some evidence that Roosevelt remained ignorant from choice, as well as some evidence that the national chairman ignored Presidential orders about contributions.

At the time, Parker's charges made more impression on the newspapers than on the voters. The election on November 8 was a personal triumph for Roosevelt, who ran ahead of his party in several states. The Republicans swept the East and the Midwest, held their own in the Border, and recaptured silver states like Colorado, Nevada, and Idaho which had voted Democratic since 1896. The Roosevelt margin in the electoral college was 336 to 140, and he won the popular vote by an unprecedented majority of 2,544,343. The Republicans also strengthened their grip on Congress, with an edge in the House of 250 to 136 and in the Senate of 57 to 33.

IV

Roosevelt regarded the election of 1904 as a mandate to proceed with his reform program. He had found the role as custodian of McKinley's policies an irksome one, and now that he was President in his own right, Roosevelt quickly displayed more self-confidence and aggressiveness. He bombarded Congress with special messages on a great variety of subjects and pursued them with energetic campaigns. His two-year fight for legislation to enlarge the jurisdiction of the Interstate Commerce Commission over freight rates displayed Roosevelt's remarkable power as a party leader. As matters stood, the commission could, upon application of shippers, make investigations and recommendations regarding discriminatory railroad rates, but this power had not been very effective in practice. Enforcement of Commission recommendations was vested in the federal courts, which suspended contested rates during litigation. As a result, railroads could and did obstruct an I.C.C. order indefinitely by instituting costly suits. Roosevelt wanted to correct this grievance by empowering the I.C.C. to investigate a rate that had been challenged and to authorize a substitute rate. There was nothing very radical about this solution. The President did not propose to free the Commission from court review nor to allow it to establish rates on its own initiative. Nevertheless, the issue touched off the most heated and extensive debate about the constitutional powers of Congress since Reconstruction.

A small but articulate group of Westerners voiced the traditional sectional antipathy toward the railroads, although few were willing to go as far as Bryan, who advocated public ownership. At the same time, many congressmen from former Populist territory considered Roosevelt's remedy to be superficial because it did not touch such important sources of discrimination as freight classification and the rate differential for short and long hauls. The more militant Westerners preferred no bill at all to one that provided for the elimination of rate discrimination without rate reduction, especially since such a measure would provide little relief to farmers. In fact, the critics of the bill prophesied that its sole effect would be to stabilize for the convenience of manufacturers the charges that they passed on to consumers.

At the opposite extreme was a larger group of conservatives who criticized the Roosevelt proposal on constitutional grounds. Some invoked the Constitution to conceal their objection to any further regulation of business. Others were wholly sincere in believing that the authority to pass on the validity of rates and the responsibility for enforcing them could not be combined in a single body. Hence, they opposed any curtailment whatever of court power to suspend contested rate decisions. Fully cognizant of the fact that congressional leaders were cool to rate legislation, Roosevelt began applying pressure on them immediately after his re-election. He cared nothing about tariff revision but knew that Cannon and the Senate oligarchs dreaded it. He began dropping hints that his annual message to the lame duck Congress would contain a recommendation for tariff revision. Cannon understood this kind of executive blackmail and promptly shoved a railroad bill through the House, knowing it would not clear the Senate before the short session ended on March 4, 1905.

Temporarily thwarted, Roosevelt continued the war of nerves throughout the summer until the congressional leaders capitulated in return for a pledge to shelve tariff legislation. Cannon promptly honored his part of the agreement by repassing the Hepburn bill in a form satisfactory to the President. The Senate oligarchs, however, moved at a leisurely pace and loaded the bill with crippling amendments. When it finally reached the floor at the end of March 1906, Aldrich passed over Republican proponents of the bill and designated "Pitchfork Ben" Tillman of South Carolina as its floor manager. This gesture was particularly diabolical since Roosevelt was not on speaking terms with Tillman. The President, nevertheless, promptly opened negotiations with the South Carolina Democrat through ex-Senator Chandler of New Hampshire, who was spending his retirement in a furious crusade against the railroads.

While Tillman tried to line up the Democrats for the unamended version of the Hepburn bill, Aldrich worked as furiously to prevent any enlargement of the powers of the Interstate Commerce Commission. As a result the parliamentary skirmishing took place over amendments defining the scope of court review. So many Republicans were under pressure from their constituents to support the President that they searched frantically for a compromise. Callers at the White House found Roosevelt prepared to meet them halfway and desert his Democratic allies. On April 11, he sounded out Knute Nelson of Minnesota about a new amendment leaving the courts to define the extent of their review powers.[32] This compromise proposal circulated inconclusively in the cloakrooms for several weeks. In the process the name of the venerable Allison was attached to it, although the latter was ill and unfit for business.[33] The White House cleverly avoided evincing much interest in the so-called Allison amendment until the oligarchy began to do so. Then Roosevelt called a press conference on May 4 and publicly accepted the Allison amendment. This compromise restored solidarity in the Republican party and ensured the passage of the Hepburn bill. Nobody could be sure who had won until the courts spoke, but Roosevelt emerged from the encounter with greater prestige than the Senate oligarchy. Once the myth of its invincibility had been destroyed, other Administration measures cleared Congress, the most important of which were the meat inspection and pure food and drugs acts. The passage of both laws climaxed a long agitation against the dangers of misbranded and adulterated foods. Upton Sinclair had focused attention on the need for sanitary packaging with *The Jungle,* his novel describing the revolting conditions in the Chicago stockyards. Stubborn to the last, Aldrich fought progress in the name of freedom: "Are we going to take up," he asked, "the question as to what a man shall eat and what a man shall drink and put him under severe penalties if he is eating or drinking something different from what the chemists of the Department of Agriculture think desirable. . . ."[34]

While Roosevelt was vigorously applying the lash to Congress, he also pursued with his customary energy the policies he had launched during his first term. He had already withdrawn 25 million acres of forest from entry by 1904; and between July and November 1906, he withdrew an additional 66 million acres. Western foes of conservation also discovered to their dismay that Roosevelt intended to enforce government regulations regarding tree cutting, grazing, and fire prevention. He appointed Gifford Pinchot, a trained silvaculturalist, as chief forester and provided him with a sufficient staff to chastise violators. Pinchot was such a zealous conservationist that he soon made the Forest Service an object of hatred in every Western state. Angry lumbermen and ranchers complained bitterly against the Administration. Only the timely adjournment of Congress in the summer of 1906 postponed a showdown on conservation.

The President continued to harass big business, although he became increasingly vague about his objectives. He gave less prominence to antitrust suits but insistently demanded legislation to require the federal licensing of corporations. Nobody knew what Roosevelt intended to accomplish with this weapon. At times he talked as if the licensing of corporations would be made contingent upon their compliance with lawful business practices. At other times he implied that a licensing system might be used to promote positive government direction of corporation policies for public welfare. Businessmen were almost as disturbed by the prospect of more rigid enforcement of existing legislation as by the threat of domination from government commissions. In either case it was evident that there would be greater executive discretion in defining evil business practices and in imposing penalties. Roosevelt confirmed this apprehension in his annual message of 1906, for he termed the Sherman Act "a calamity" because it failed to distinguish between good and bad combinations.

Few corporation executives cared for Roosevelt in the role of judge of their economic behavior. But what the President said alarmed them even more than what he did. He compounded lectures on the responsibilities of wealth with threats of government action to encourage a responsible attitude among the wealthy. On one occasion in 1906, he told the businessmen that they were "singularly callous to the needs, sufferings, and feelings of the great mass of the people." He spoke ominously about the need for federal income and inheritance taxes. The President also urged restrictions on the use of the injunction in labor disputes, the removal of legal barriers against labor unions, and the reduction of working hours. Wall Street regarded these proposals as the prelude to a general assault on property rights. It was bad enough from the standpoint of the big industrialists and financiers for Bryan to talk in this fashion, but it was treasonable for a Republican President to do so. The fact that they had contributed to the campaign fund of their tormentor only aggravated their fury.

The Republican leadership in Congress shared Wall Street's misgivings. A Roosevelt faction had already begun to form as a result of grass-roots support for his program. In a dozen states political mavericks were proclaiming their allegiance to Roosevelt and contesting at every level the renomination of Republican incumbents.

This development was part of a larger political upheaval known as the Progressive movement. First noticeable around the turn of the century, Progressivism had gained momentum ever since. Although the movement was originally nonpartisan, the Progressives gravitated toward Roosevelt because he came the closest to representing their political aspirations. Like the President, the Progressives worried about the multiple threats to traditional American institutions posed by monopolists, radical labor organizers, and corrupt political bosses. They also shared with Roosevelt the refreshingly simple belief that existing wrongs were the result of special privileges rather than impersonal economic forces. Therefore, the Progressives had a predictable enthusiasm for the Square Deal and the Presidential crusade against "the evils of human nature." [35] They thought that trust-busting, conservation, and the overthrow of political bosses would rejuvenate American democracy.

Indignation against special privilege was kept at fever pitch by a group of "muckraking" magazines that built up circulation on the exposure of dark corners in American life. *McClure's* showed the greatest accuracy and objectivity of the "muckrakers." Shortly after 1900, it published in serial form a damaging exposure of the Standard Oil trust written by Ida F. Tarbell. Another series by Lincoln Steffens traced the intimate relationship between corrupt political and business leaders in municipal politics. From its source in the great municipalities, Steffens followed the broadening stream of corruption as it flowed through state governments toward Washington. Ray Stannard Baker did a similar analysis of corrupt labor unions for *McClure's*. Irrespective of their journalistic standards, the muckrakers accustomed many Americans to believe that neither political nor business leaders could be trusted.

By 1906 the Progressives were riding a wave of reform sentiment that lapped at the foundations of durable municipal and state machines which in some cases antedated the McKinley era. In the South, Progressivism tended to equate the elimination of special privilege with improvement in the economic position of the farmer. It expressed itself both in the transfer of political power to the poor whites and in a renewal of the agrarian crusade against railroads and other corporations. By contrast, Northern Progressivism started out as an urban reform movement. Even in predominantly rural states like California and South Dakota,[36] the backbone of Progressivism was formed by middle-class citizens who had no economic axe to grind but who reacted to abuses in American society with the same indignation as Theodore Roosevelt. Since the Civil War, moreover, political discontent had usually expressed itself as factionalism within the Republican party rather than as third party movements. There was no evidence that voting habits had changed at the beginning of the twentieth century. The average rural Protestant was as stubborn as ever in his refusal to co-operate with the predominantly urban and Catholic Democratic machines when the Republican party displeased him. Thus, the Progressives' first impulse was to capture control of the Republican party from within.

Once it became clear that the Progressive movement possessed political vitality, state Republican leaders at odds with the dominant party organization joined the reformers and often elbowed them out of key positions. In fact, the local professionals could easily enter the new movement by raising the age-old cry of the disgruntled factionalist against the inefficient, corrupt incumbents. As so often happens in politics, some men who began by using Progressive slogans to further their own ends eventually became confirmed reformers. The careers of such Progressives as Albert B. Cummins of Iowa, Jonathan Bourne of Oregon, William E. Borah of Idaho, Coe Crawford of South Dakota, Joseph Bristow of Kansas, and Robert M. La Follette of Wisconsin illustrate that to a degree reform leadership was an unconscious rationalization of political interests. Some showed considerably more sincerity and courage than others in advocating Progressive principles, but they were established politicians whose efforts for advancement had been thwarted by the regular Republican organizations in their states.[37] Of the major Republican figures in the Progressive movement, only Charles Evans Hughes of New York and Hiram Johnson of California could be classed as political amateurs.

Cummins of Iowa, who attracted national attention in 1906 as a railroad reformer, had co-operated with the Rock Island Railroad in the 1890's.[38] His conversion was slow and he became a full-fledged Progressive only after the Allison machine had repeatedly blocked his efforts to enter the Senate.[39] Bristow of Kansas reversed himself more abruptly. As late as 1906 he was bidding for the political help of the dominant Long organization by disclaiming any intention of campaigning against railroads and corporations.[40] Like a good conservative, Bristow came out publicly as an opponent of the direct primary the same year.[41] Yet within eighteen months Bristow was running for senator on a direct-primary, anti-railroad platform. Borah of Idaho reached the Senate through a trade with factional foes whom he alleged to be corrupt.[42]

The case of Robert M. La Follette, the most outspoken and fearless of the Progressives, was more complicated. He had always been a passionately honest man with a deep-seated sympathy for the underdog. Yet he somehow managed to overlook the close tieup between the lumbering and railroad interests of Wisconsin and his own party until the early 1890's. According to La Follette's version of the story, his eyes were opened at that period by an attempt of Senator Philetus Sawyer to bribe him. Sawyer flatly denied the charge, but thereafter La Follette waged war on the state Republican organization with the single-mindedness of a fanatic. Two unsuccessful tries for governor of Wisconsin chastened La Follette sufficiently to moderate his assaults on the railroads. With their benevolent neutrality, he won the governorship,[43] and then he launched a six-year fight against them and other privileged groups in the state. La Follette lacked many of the personal characteristics that make politicians successful. He was cold, stubborn, humorless, and wholly devoid of the instinct for teamwork. He sought the Presidency as persistently as any candidate in American history and honestly believed that the sole motive for his action was selfless devotion to a cause. In pursuit of the White House, La Follette imposed on his Wisconsin supporters a discipline that nobody would have dared to impose on him. Any fellow Progressives in Wisconsin who showed an independent spirit were treated as traitors and broken politically if La Follette could reach them.[44]

Nevertheless, La Follette's very weaknesses were a source of strength. The cynical Lincoln Steffens conceded that La Follette had built an autocratic machine but argued that he had done so for the good of the people.[45] Almost as many people applauded La Follette for his independence of party obligations as criticized him for his disruptive tactics. Others saw in his scorn of compromise a courageous love of principle rather than an egotistical aversion to co-operation with colleagues. Even La Follette's coldness on the hustings had a fierce indignant quality like "the passionate expression of a man declaring the truth to his God." [46] Moreover, he belonged to a generation that was still receptive to two-hour speeches crammed full of statistics. With the possible exception of Roosevelt himself, La Follette was the most powerful and controversial figure to emerge from the Progressive movement.

Between 1900 and 1906, Progressive candidates won several governorships in the Midwest as well as in New York. Progressive victories produced a fairly standard pattern of state laws. Direct primaries were substituted for nominating conventions, on the theory that voters would control the selection of candidates and thereby eliminate corrupt political machines. Corporations in general, and railroads in particular, fell under stricter regulation. Often they were also required to pay heavier taxes. Despite the threat that the courts would undo their efforts, most Progressive legislatures passed laws shortening hours and improving working conditions in factories. By 1906 the infection of Progressivism was spreading to other states. Simultaneously, Progressive Republican governors who had completed their work at home sought to continue their activities in Washington by dislodging members of the oligarchy from the Senate.

It is doubtful that the controversy over Progressive legislation alone would have precipitated a struggle for the control of the Republican party. The older G.O.P. leaders who composed the oligarchy had grudgingly given ground in the 1906 session of Congress and demonstrated that they were responsive to public pressure. Their dispute with the reformers often involved a judgment about facts rather than ideology, an admission which Roosevelt made obliquely a few years later when he insisted Lodge was a Progressive "without knowing it." [47] The oligarchy simply denied the Progressive assertion that corrupt interests dominated business or politics. A few of its members opposed direct primaries and other devices for more direct participation of voters as contrary to the principles of representative government. A larger number denied that the federal government possessed the constitutional power to implement some of Roosevelt's proposals. But not even Aldrich advocated special privilege, unlawful business activity, or discrimination against working men. In short, the oligarchy thought reform had gone far enough for the time being. Its position was summed up in Hanna's famous injunction to "stand pat," which Cannon reiterated in the 1906 campaign despite a scolding from Roosevelt. In the best Republican tradition, the oligarchy imagined that abnormal activity in the White House was a pretext for reducing "the coordinate branches of the government . . . from three to two." [48]

Eventually the ideological gulf between the two wings of the Republican party would widen and tear it apart, but in 1906 the members of the oligarchy were principally concerned about retaining control of their local party machines. They had every reason to be worried, because a new note of bitterness characterized the infighting between the Progressives and the stand-patters. Muckraking magazines responsive to reform sentiment taught the voter to believe the worst about Republican incumbents and branded factional opponents of Progressives as conservatives or reactionaries, irrespective of their political principles. The success of reform journals attracted ever more irresponsible ventures in the literature of exposure. The worst offender was William Randolph Hearst, who launched *Cosmopolitan Magazine* in February 1906 with a series of articles by the novelist David Graham Phillips called "The Treason of the Senate." Phillips produced a vicious smear of several members of the Senate oligarchy which angered Roosevelt, although he was the principal beneficiary of the agitation. He applied the epithet "muckrakers" to the reform journals, but their circulation continued to rise. As a blanket designation, the term was unfair. On the other hand Roosevelt had a right to be alarmed over the gullibility of the public and its growing appetite for sensationalism.

Just as disturbing to the oligarchy as the indiscriminate attacks on the integrity of its members were the party-wrecking tactics of La Follette. In 1904 he had tried to purge Republican legislators in Wisconsin who had opposed his program, and after Congress adjourned on June 30, 1906, he applied the technique on a national scale from the Chautauqua platform. In each state which he visited, La Follette discussed national issues, analyzed the voting record of its congressmen and senators, and urged the voters to retire fellow Republicans who disagreed with him. While La Follette was undoubtedly correct in believing that some of his colleagues had outlived their usefulness, they considered him a traitor for attacking his own party. They resented even more his tacit assumption that he was the conscience of the Republican party and the custodian of its morality.

V

The 1906 elections neither reduced the Republican majorities in Congress nor seriously damaged the oligarchy. Only Borah of Idaho and

Bourne of Oregon came to the Senate as avowed Progressives. But the irritable mood of the voters showed no signs of abating. Shortly after the election the oligarchy received its first blow when Spooner of Wisconsin voluntarily resigned his Senate seat two years before the expiration of his term. Undoubtedly Spooner had been responsive to the powerful economic interests in his state, but no more so than any Wisconsin senator for the previous quarter-century. His lack of curiosity had shielded him from contact with the corrupt tactics of the Wisconsin machine and drawn him into the defense of some unworthy associates. In other cases, he had backed men whose only sin was to disagree with La Follette. Whatever his sins of omission, Spooner was personally honest and preferred to quit rather than absorb the systematic assaults on his character for another two years.[49]

The retirement of Spooner coincided with preparations elsewhere for attacks on the oligarchy. Kansas Progressives were so encouraged by the effect of the anti-railroad agitation on the state that they marked Senator Chester I. Long for extinction. Long possessed a colorless personality, but he exhibited abundant courage and common sense. He had fought energetically for the Hepburn bill and had quietly worked for other Administration measures in 1906. His only sins were an unwillingness to make intemperate denunciations of the railroads or to promote the political ambitions of Joseph L. Bristow.[50] Although the senatorial election was two years away, the Progressives began to train their heavy guns on Long early in 1907. Besides Bristow, who hoped to replace Long as senator, the principal skirmisher in the Progressive ranks was William Allen White, the editor of the *Emporia Gazette*. White had attracted national attention in 1896 by writing a famous anti-Populist editorial entitled, "What's the Matter with Kansas"; he would remain active in journalism and politics for half a century. Because White had the acumen to continue as an independent country editor in an era of large urban newspaper chains, he became something of a national institution. Americans identified White as a representative of a vanishing society and hailed his erratic statements on politics with uncritical sentimentality. A homespun manner and a face "as featureless and innocent as a baby's bottom." [51] helped White to reinforce the popular impression of his character. This image of White was extremely deceptive. Like Horace Greeley, he coined devastating phrases and flung them about without regard for the consequences. White also resembled the famous *Tribune* editor in his belief that good intentions excused him from responsibility for the consequences of frivolous behavior. White never made up his mind whether he wanted to be a king-maker or a king, but he sensed that the time was ripe for the *Cosmopolitan* style of muckraking in Kansas. On January 15, 1907, he urged a friend to "join the hell raisers" [52] and sent out scores of letters urging the founding of an organization to "clean up the mess in Kansas." [53] Then he promoted an article about Long in the *Collier's* series on "Senate Undesirables," [54] and followed it with a widely circulated article of his own linking Long with "Wall Street." White did not bother to document his charge. He simply assured his readers that Long had the Wall Street "temperament." Wearing his readers out by repetition, White used the term "Wall Street" seventy times in 3000 words.[55]

The Progressives were also active in Iowa. Cummins had barely managed to win a third term as governor in 1906 and then only after promising not to run against Senator Allison in 1908.[56] Once Cummins succeeded in ramming a direct primary law through the legislature, however, he reversed himself and became a candidate for senator. The clarity of the Progressive crusade in Iowa was thus blurred by fierce factionalism and bitterness over a broken pledge. The Progressives confused battle lines still further by pushing the "Iowa idea," a plan for selective tariff reduction which would aid farmers and penalize business. Allison was slowly dying and seemed unlikely to survive the campaign. Yet echoes of the conflict drifted back to Washington, where the oligarchs feared tariff revision even more than the loss of Allison.

The cumulative effect of the incessant political warfare in the states was to worsen relations between the President and Congress. The oligarchy blamed Roosevelt for the Progressive agitation and brought his legislative program to a virtual standstill in 1907 and 1908. It was encouraged in its defiance by the comforting assurance that Roosevelt would not be a candidate for re-election. He had taken this position immediately after his 1904 victory out of deference to the third-term tradition, and those who chafed under Presidential leadership became increasingly vocal as their day of liberation approached. Far from being intimidated by the critics, Roosevelt stepped up the volume of his legislative recommendations and unleashed his picturesque vocabulary on the obstructionists.

The ugly temper of Congress first became apparent when Westerners tried to hobble Roosevelt's conservation program by passing a bill which prohibited the creation of additional forest reserves in six Rocky Mountain states. While the bill was lying on Roosevelt's desk, he withdrew from entry all remaining land that could possibly be used for forestry purposes. Then he signed the bill amid great protestations about executive tyranny.

A short but severe financial panic in the summer of 1907 produced further controversy. Roosevelt promptly blamed the Wall Street financiers and denounced them as "malefactors of great wealth." Fearful that the panic might spread, however, the President responded favorably to feelers from George W. Perkins of the House of Morgan for constructive action. He was told that the purchase of the Tennessee Iron and Coal Company by the United States Steel Corporation would have a stabilizing effect on the market. Perkins also informed Roosevelt that the U.S. Steel Corporation would make the necessary sacrifice, provided the government agreed not to regard the transaction as a violation of the Sherman Act. The President gave his blessing to the arrangement, and U.S. Steel enlarged its vertical monopoly by adding a valuable property at negligible cost.

The panic was over before Congress met in December, but many members who had been indifferent to mergers sponsored by businessmen professed alarm over the action of the President. Several committees investigated U.S. Steel, and eventually the Senate produced a resolution censuring Roosevelt for his approval of the enlargement of a trust. His retaliatory messages demanding additional trust and labor legislation were treated as contemptuously as Andrew Johnson's communications to Congress. The poisonous atmosphere in Washington precluded constructive legislation; and as a result, the only noteworthy measure to clear the 60th Congress was a law establishing the liability of interstate carriers for injuries sustained by their employees.

Notwithstanding Roosevelt's belligerent defense of his policies, the President left a confused legacy to his followers. He had established an undisputed reputation as champion of the common man without leaving any clear principles for the guidance of his followers. Although he seemed to be the perfect embodiment of Progressivism, he ignored complaints about tariff favoritism and distrusted leading Progressives like La Follette and Hughes.[57] His position on the trusts was erratic and perplexing. Even though he vigorously attacked big business, he had misgivings about substituting big government for it. During his last months in office, Roosevelt seemed to be groping his way toward a policy which would enable the government to enforce certain standards of behavior for big corporations without positively directing their affairs. This same ambivalence showed up in the President's attitude toward the workers. He wanted them well enough organized to defend themselves against business, but he was furious in 1906 when the American Federation of Labor had diverted union power into politics and worked for the defeat of anti-labor congressmen.

It is unfair to criticize Roosevelt for being unable to make up his mind about problems that would elude the best efforts of his successors. One conclusion seems clear: his principal contribution to Progressivism was as an educator rather than a legislator. For nearly eight years he appealed tirelessly to the conscience of the nation for honesty in government and self-restraint in the conduct of business. Although frequently ridiculed for his "original discovery of the Ten Commandments," Roosevelt, by his forthright demands for moral behavior, improved the tone of public life. The government bureaucracy functioned more efficiently, and the civil service was extended into new areas. More important still, national, state, and local machines were made accountable to the voters. Before 1906 the Progressive crusade harassed the corrupt with nonpartisan zeal; thereafter shrewd politicians increasingly exploited the popularity of Progressivism for their own purposes. Nonetheless, many citizens received a wholesome political education and became aware for the first time of the forces operating below the surface of government. Nobody knew where the crusade would end in 1908, but everybody knew that Roosevelt had been the key figure in promoting it. He had dominated the opening years of the new century so completely that one contemporary observed after an interview with the President: "You go home and wring his personality out of your clothes."

IX

The Bull Moose Movement

The masterful Roosevelt did not allow his vendetta with the 60th Congress to distract him from selecting his successor. In the brief interlude of party harmony following his re-election in 1904, a number of candidates had discreetly advertised their interest in the post. The hopefuls included Vice President Fairbanks and Senator Beveridge of Indiana, Speaker Cannon, Secretary of State Elihu Root, and Senator Foraker of Ohio. For a variety of reasons, Roosevelt came to regard all of them as unsuitable. Fairbanks and Cannon disqualified themselves by giving covert aid to the foes of the Square Deal in Congress, and Foraker by doing so openly. Beveridge was a militant Progressive and more to the taste of the President, but a towering ego and a protracted feud with the dominant Indiana organization ruined his prospects. The astute and energetic Elihu Root had all of the qualities necessary for a Presidential candidate, except the proper political antecedents. His long career as a corporation lawyer made him suspect in the eyes of many Westerners. After the 1906 elections, the spotlight fell momentarily on Governor Hughes of New York and Senator La Follette of Wisconsin, but the President did not care for either of them.

Rather than allow matters to drift, the President selected his successor from the second rank of Republican leaders. His choice fell on Secretary of War William Howard Taft. Born of a distinguished Ohio family in 1857, Taft had been educated at Yale and had earned a law degree at Cincinnati College in 1880. He was admitted to the bar the same year and soon became assistant prosecuting attorney of Hamilton County, Ohio.

During the ensuing decade, Taft held various judicial posts and then came to Washington in 1890 as solicitor general. As a member of the Harrison Administration, he struck up a friendship with Civil Service Commissioner Theodore Roosevelt, who lived in the same section of Washington. Their paths momentarily separated when the Democrats returned to power in 1893 but converged again eight years later. By that time, Roosevelt had become President, and Taft was on his roster of employees as head of the Philippine commission. Roosevelt was so pleased with Taft's performance in easing the transition from military to civil government in the archipelago that he brought him back to Washington in 1904 as Secretary of War.

Just when Roosevelt began to think of Taft as his successor is not clear, but an informal understanding must have been reached by 1906 when Taft rejected a Supreme Court appointment. It would have been desirable for the Taft build-up to exhibit a spontaneous, unmanaged air, but Taft was too obscure politically to proceed very far under his own momentum. Furthermore, his mentor in the White House was not very good at covering his tracks. By March 1907 everybody knew that Roosevelt had mobilized Administration patronage behind Taft, and three months later the President graciously offered to break the necks of any federal officeholders his heir-apparent considered obstructive.[1] Roosevelt also persuaded Frank H. Hitchcock, first Assistant Postmaster General and a specialist in the management of Southern delegates, to resign and devote full-time service to the Taft candidacy. These maneuvers were accompanied by repeated hints from Roosevelt that the convention would have to take him or Taft.

Although the threat of a third term for Roosevelt would probably have been sufficient to swing most of the anti-Administration forces behind Taft, the President had chosen the man best suited to disarm the opposition. Not only had Taft never held an elective office, but from his sheltered post in the War Department had managed to remain aloof from the party's factional quarrels. Taft appeared to be a singularly tactful spokesman for the Square Deal. Weighing over 350 pounds, he displayed the Falstaffian geniality expected of fat men without losing the dignity expected of judges. Properly exploited, great bulk can be an important political asset, and Taft made the most out of it. Good-natured jokes about his obesity redounded to Taft's advantage, including the one about his inability to make "a complete revolution" on the dance floor.[2] In any case, all but the professional Roosevelt-haters realized that the campaign would have to be waged on the record of the Administration, and the judicial Taft seemed best qualified for the job. Several stubborn holdouts, including Fairbanks, Foraker, Hughes, and La Follette, were determined to have their names go before the convention. But by the convention, the nomination of Taft seemed certain, and the only remaining threat was a subterranean effort to stampede the delegates for Roosevelt.

The collapse of organized resistance to Taft did not end the intra-party warfare but simply drove it underground. National chairman Harry S. New of Indiana ignored Roosevelt's recommendation of Beveridge for temporary chairman and substituted Senator Julius Caesar Burrows of Michigan, a colorless follower of the oligarchy. A large number of states sent contesting delegations to the convention, and spokesmen for a variety of causes arrived. Farm groups wanted downward revision of the tariff, while organized labor clamored for a restriction on the use of injunctions. The Wisconsin delegation served notice that it would seek platform planks for the direct primary and physical valuation of the railroads. The Progressive credo attracted some and repelled others. Sectional interests which had been more or less dormant since the mid-'90's also threatened to revive.

The warring groups converged on the Chicago Coliseum June 16, 1908. The exterior must have heartened the skirmishers, because it resembled a Norman castle. Roosevelt enthusiasts constituted a problem at the outset. When the President's name was first mentioned by permanent chairman Henry Cabot Lodge, they started a wild demonstration. Lodge had strict instructions from Washington to block a stampede, but he allowed the shouters to wear themselves out, on the theory that their activity would be harmless until nominations were made. After 47 minutes of demonstrations, Lodge threw a cold blanket on the convention by asserting that Roosevelt's decision to retire was "final and irrevocable." The bolder spirits tried again after the nominating speeches by hoisting an old lithograph of Roosevelt in the galleries. The ensuing roar revived the suspicion that the President was managing matters to ensure his renomination. Even the Taft household shared this ungenerous attitude and received news of the ovation with "a silence of death." [3] Eventually the convention quieted down and nominated Taft in listless fashion. It then chose Congressman James S. (Sunny Jim) Sherman of New York for Vice President. Together, the two men made the heaviest ticket in the history of the party—over 500 pounds.

Tempers flared over the platform. President Samuel Gompers of the A.F. of L. denounced the injunction plank because it did not meet the wishes of labor; on the other hand, J. W. Van Cleave of the National Association of Manufacturers complained because the subject of injunctions was even mentioned. More friction developed over the tariff. The Westerners finally accepted a pledge for revision without the proviso that it be downward. Taft had advocated reduced rates since 1906, however, and Eastern delegates were too well mannered to dispute this interpretation before the election. In a final display of irritability, the convention shouted down the Progressive planks proposed by the Wisconsin delegation with cries of "socialistic" and "take it to Denver."

No Republicans were angry enough to go to Denver, but Gompers appeared there at the Democratic convention two weeks later and secured an injunction plank satisfactory to labor. In general, however, the Democratic party's prospects were not bright. Since 1896 the party had slowly contracted until only the municipal machines in the East and the Solid South remained bases of strength. The urban bosses disliked Progressivism for obvious reasons, and the South grafted onto it both Populism and white supremacy. Under the circumstances, there was little for the Democrats to do but nominate the chief Populist, William Jennings Bryan, once again. Roosevelt had stolen most of his planks and incorporated them into the Progressive credo by purging them of their obvious agrarian bias. The ghost of free silver no longer dogged the footsteps of Bryan, but in his frantic search for an issue he had conjured up an even more frightening demon—public ownership of the railroads. The Democratic convention was sensible enough to avoid any reference to the proposal, which Bryan had unveiled on August 30, 1907. Even "the boy orator of the Platte" blithely dismissed his own brain child as "a suggestion," but Republicans ignored the retreat and campaigned against socialism. It was about the only issue upon which their quarrelsome followers could unite enthusiastically.

The ensuing campaign was lively but without much suspense. Bryan traveled as extensively as in previous campaigns, starting with a nonstop sixty-day tour on August 20.[4] Showing a fine disregard for genealogy, he claimed to be both the father and the heir of the Roosevelt reform movement. He created some interest in a plan for federal insurance of bank deposits and tried to exploit the fears of Midwesterners that the Republicans were too closely connected with big business to make an equitable revision of the tariff.

The strategy at Taft headquarters was to keep the candidate on his front porch and to invest heavily in precinct polls. This approach suited national chairman Frank H. Hitchcock, who thought a campaign ought to be a series of secret picnics for professionals, but it did not suit Theodore Roosevelt. Although the President had promised not to intervene, he was as incapable of staying away from a campaign as a small boy from a circus parade. Upon his return from a summer vacation at Oyster Bay, Roosevelt told newsmen, "We must put more ginger in the campaign," and he proceeded to do so. He bluntly ordered Taft to give the impression that he was working hard and to stifle stories about golf and fishing.[5] Roosevelt then launched a controversy with Bryan about campaign expenditures. In September it threatened to backfire when William Randolph Hearst released a stolen letter which revealed that Senator Foraker had received huge retaining fees from Standard Oil. But Roosevelt regained the initiative by driving Foraker out of the campaign and forcing the Democrats to ask for the resignation of their treasurer, Charles N. Haskell, who was also smeared by the Hearst revelations.

Fearful that the voters might believe Roosevelt was running against Bryan, Taft started a series of short speaking tours in late September. He was on the road thirty-nine days and covered every section of the country but the Rocky Mountains and the Far West. Toward the end of the campaign, both Taft and Roosevelt became almost as concerned about the activity of Speaker Cannon as the opposition.[6] Cannon's speeches displayed a cynical attitude toward tariff revision, and he dismissed "the Iowa idea" with gross inaccuracy as free trade. The Speaker managed to annoy other pressure groups besides Western farmers. He had feuded openly with Samuel Gompers for two years and had added the suffragettes and Prohibitionists to his list of enemies in 1908. Progressives also disliked the speaker because of his dictatorial rule and his ill-concealed hostility to their program.

Cannon was only a minor irritant in a year when pressure groups and Progressives between them managed to exploit the restlessness of the voter. The day after the election, it was apparent what a good job they had done. Although Taft received 321 electoral votes to 162 for Bryan and came within 15 votes of Roosevelt's total in 1904, the popular vote told a different story. The Republican margin had dropped in four years from 2,544,343 to 1,269,606. Bryan attracted some of the dissidents, but five minor candidates polled an aggregate 8 per cent of the popular vote. The bitter fruits of Republican factionalism were apparent in the state results. Ohio, Indiana, Minnesota, North Dakota, and Montana elected Democratic governors, despite the fact that Taft carried all five states. Although the regular Iowa organization had saved Allison in the primary, the aged senator had died before the November election. As a result, his mortal enemy Cummins went to the Senate to reinforce the Progressive bloc. The election of Coe Crawford in South Dakota was equally unfortunate for the Senate oligarchy. A still larger number of Progressive congressmen entered the House in 1908 to join older Progressives like George W. Norris of Nebraska, Victor Murdock of Kansas, and Charles A. Lindbergh of Minnesota. The returns made it obvious that the Republican party was on trial.

II

The interval of relaxation and rejoicing which usually follows an election victory failed to materialize in 1908. Not since the grim November of 1864, when the country waited uneasily to see how Lincoln would deal with the collapsing Confederacy, had the atmosphere been so tense. On the day after the election, the politicians began to maneuver for position in preparation for tariff revision. Their preoccupation with this issue was so intense that they paid little attention to cabinet-making and allowed Taft the unprecedented luxury of selecting his official family in peace.

Never had popular interest in the tariff been so high. The sentiment for revision was most pronounced in the Republican states of the Mississippi valley, where farmers clamored for lower rates. What the farmers wanted was wholesale reductions in industrial schedules but none in agricultural schedules. Ordinarily the Republicans frankly recognized sectional interests in their tariff policy, and their bills represented a compromise between the various sections. The prolonged agitation of the Progressives, however, had fostered the delusion among Midwestern Republican farmers that their tariff position rested on principle. For the most part, their moral hypocrisy was unconscious and fed on an older belief by which the welfare of agriculture was identified with the public welfare. Couched in the jargon of Progressivism, this belief seemed to mean that tariff protection was special privilege only if conferred on any group other than the farmers.

It also encouraged the hope that lower rates would expose dishonest trusts to competition, reduce prices, and send the "special interests" reeling in retreat. By 1908 hope had been converted into faith because of the failure of trust busting and railroad legislation to halt the rise in prices. Thus the stage was set for an attempt to make a sectional economic issue a test of Progressivism.

Progressive congressmen opened the fight by trying to unseat Speaker Cannon. In this maneuver they could count on the support of several regulars like Hepburn of Iowa and Charles N. Fowler of New Jersey, who cared little about the tariff but hated the arbitrary Cannon. President-elect Taft promptly showed interest in the rebels but decided not to support them after a hurried poll indicated that Cannon would be re-elected. Nevertheless, the activity of the mutinous congressmen had a remarkable effect on Cannon. Although in mid-November he angrily denied that any man was big enough to dictate to the House about its organization, the speaker gave Taft explicit assurances of co-operation. This timely gesture kept the President-elect out of an abortive fight waged by twenty-five Republican congressmen to strip Cannon of his swollen powers under the old Reed rules. The fact that this struggle lasted until the end of the lame duck session on March 4, 1909, also made Cannon more anxious than ever to return the President's good will. So the speaker reiterated his pledge to support downward revision of the tariff when the special session opened eleven days later.

Unfortunately for the inexperienced Taft, nothing that the House agreed to do would be binding on the Senate. If either Taft or the Midwesterners had bothered to listen to the campaign speeches made by members of the Senate oligarchy, they would have been very uneasy. For obvious reasons, the Senate leaders had not challenged Taft's pledges of downward revision. Instead, they merely praised the protective system and conceded that some rates ought to be revised. Their self-restraint in the interests of party harmony had alarmed businessmen so much that Warren of Wyoming found it necessary to reassure a wool firm in September 1908 that, after the election, senators "will speak more plainly." [7] Elkins and others grumbled privately about the folly of downward revision,[8] but little was said in public before the special session. The joint ravages of death and Progressivism had thinned the ranks of the oligarchy and conferred the leadership on a taciturn pair of New Englanders whose silence was imitated by the junior members. Of the new leaders, Hale had the greater initial influence, because as head of the Republican conference he would fill the all-important committee vacancies. But Aldrich as chairman of the finance committee would have the decisive influence in framing the tariff bill. Both were high protectionists and displayed an air of condescension in dealing with their disputatious colleagues from the Midwest. Aldrich possessed a more genial manner than Hale, but over the years he had accumulated a number of enemies who were waiting hopefully for him to blunder. The able and opinionated Beveridge fell into this category, as did Dolliver of Iowa, whose very existence Aldrich had virtually ignored.

Although Aldrich and Hale were arrogant, they were certainly not stupid, and so they perfected their arrangements during the lame duck session. Lodge of Massachusetts and Reed Smoot of Utah, both high-tariff supporters, received vacancies on the finance committee. Other choice assignments were made with a view to isolating Progressives and minimizing their opportunities to make trouble. Once the organizational problems were out of the way, Aldrich quietly tested sentiment for a tariff that offered generous and indiscriminate protection. He soon discovered that the erstwhile Populist states and the Atlantic seaboard could be mobilized behind such a bill. Without the money question to distract them, all these senators apparently were ready for log-rolling on the tariff. Progressives like Borah of Idaho and Dixon of Montana were just as concerned about adequate protection for hides, wool, lumber, and metals as the regulars were about products from their areas.

Meanwhile, Cannon was having trouble with his charges in the House. The principal mischief came from the Democrats, who had hitherto remained aloof from the controversy over rules. Their change in strategy was due to their new leadership under Champ Clark of Missouri. His predecessor, John Sharp Williams of Mississippi, had co-operated with Cannon in return for the privilege of naming minority members to House committees. Clark defied Cannon and struck up an alliance with the Republican insurgents. Although there was no possibility that the coalition could block the re-election of Cannon as speaker, an informal poll of the members indicated that it might overthrow the Reed rules and take control of tariff revision. Cannon temporarily enlisted Taft's support by lecturing the President on the virtues of party regularity and disclaiming any responsibility for tariff legislation if the rules were amended. Under ordinary circumstances, the intervention of a new President with abundant patronage to distribute would have been decisive, but insurgents like

Norris of Nebraska and Murdock of Kansas had fought the autocratic speaker too long to heed Taft. Lucius N. Littauer, a wealthy New York glove manufacturer, came to Cannon's rescue, providing him with enough votes of Tammany Democrats to counterbalance defections.[9]

Even with his powers intact, Cannon had some anxious moments over the tariff. Although he took the precaution of reporting the bill prepared by Sereno Payne of New York under a rule which virtually choked off both debate and amendments from the floor, Norris almost managed to attach an income-tax rider to the bill. Then Minority Leader Clark was nearly successful in having the House recommit the measure. In final form the Payne bill gave generous concessions to embryo Southern industries and rewarded New York Democrats who had helped sustain the Reed rules with higher duties on gloves and hosiery. Otherwise, the Payne bill lowered rates about as much as any Republican majority would be likely to tolerate. Hides, coal, and iron went on the free list, and the duty on oil was drastically reduced. For a man whose heart was not in his work, Cannon had done very well.

The arrival of the Payne bill in the Senate scarcely ruffled the calm of the finance committee, which continued to hold leisurely secret hearings. Excluded from these deliberations, the Midwestern Progressives could do little but devise strategy to combat the rumored increases. Bristow of Kansas thought there were probably 18 to 20 Progressives who could combine on all issues,[10] but his estimate proved to be too optimistic. For one thing, the Progressive senators lacked an acknowledged leader. The new members like Bristow and Cummins were willing but lacked experience and knowledge of the Senate rules. La Follette possessed more ability but was too much of an introvert. Aside from acting as host at an occasional stag dinner, La Follette remained aloof and buried himself in research.[11] His quiet preparations seemed to foreshadow another lonely and frustrating La Follette crusade. A more basic problem for the Progressives than the vacuum in leadership was their inability to hold together. The only way to prevent any tariff from reflecting special privilege was to abolish the protective system. This position could not be taken by the Progressives because they believed in protection and were divided by sectional interests. In one breath, Bourne of Oregon confessed that tariff legislation disgusted him and in the next asserted his determination to seek "what may be termed special privileges for the people of my state." [12] Bristow promised to do what "is best for Kansas"; [13] and when Crawford was criticized for supporting the wool tariff, he pointed out that even La Follette had defended a $4 duty on print paper to aid the Wisconsin mills.[14]

Such a divided coalition of critics would probably have collapsed within a few weeks if Aldrich had made even superficial concessions. Several factors, however, caused his attitude to harden. For one thing, he possessed the necessary votes to push through a high tariff and saw no need either to oblige his critics or to work up a defense of his handiwork. He had always been indifferent to public opinion, and his intention of retiring in 1910 made him less willing to hide his dislike of his opponents in the Senate.

When the Aldrich version of tariff revision was reported in mid-April, it contained 847 amendments to the Payne bill. No effort had been made to pay even lip service to the downward revision. Most cuts made in the Payne bill were rescinded, and some of the existing rates were actually raised. When Joseph W. Bailey of Texas twitted Aldrich for ignoring the Republican platform, the latter replied that it had not specified downward revision. Still, indignation might have subsided into isolated protests about broken pledges and discrimination against the farmers but for the high-handedness of Aldrich.

Trouble started when his old foes Dolliver and Beveridge began to ask searching questions about the duties on cotton and wool which affected their rural constituents. Hitherto, Dolliver had not shown any unorthodox views on the tariff or any sympathy with Progressivism. In fact, until Allison died Dolliver had lived in the shadow of his more famous colleague. His wit and erudition had sparkled at Iowa county fairs, but neither Dolliver's Senate colleagues nor the country were prepared for his sudden display of leadership in 1909.

Dolliver had listened to the final debates on the tariff in the House, and when Aldrich sneeringly threatened to silence him with facts and figures, the Iowa senator met the challenge. For two weeks, he buried himself in research and paid an assistant out of his own pocket. Then on May 4 he began a two-day analysis of the textile business with the assurance of a manufacturer and the animus of a consumer. Americans received instruction on the difference between light-shrinking wool and shoddy wool, with factual illustrations of how the proposed duties on both would profit the industry. Warren of Wyoming, the wealthy sheep-raiser, tried to ridicule Dolliver's statistics, but was silenced with the observation "that the chief practical use of statistics is to keep the other fellow from lying to you."

In a later exchange, Dolliver described Warren as "the greatest shepherd since Abraham." Warren foolishly denied owning sheep, only to be challenged by Dolliver's statement "that when the Senator took me over that territory, he had all the airs of ownership." [15]

Dolliver's speech was an innovation in tariff debate and did far more to establish the popularity of careful research on legislation than had earlier efforts by La Follette. A handful of insurgent senators then began accumulating information on other schedules, and in mid-May they too launched attacks on the Aldrich bill. Since the muckraking magazines had already conditioned the public to regard businessmen as conspirators, there was a morbid curiosity about the details of tariff-making in 1909. Collier's actually increased its circulation with weekly articles on tariff debates that would have bored earlier generations. It even mailed free of charge to interested subscribers a simplified digest of the votes by individual senators on 117 separate tariff schedules. At the end of May, it had become obvious that the critics of the Aldrich bill were making an impression on the country.

The oligarchy could dismiss the sniping of the Democrats as wicked partisanship, but it had no real answer to a clear exposure of tariff benefits by fellow Republicans. The Midwestern insurgents had broken an unwritten party rule. Individual senators were expected to fight rates that discriminated against their section but not to expose details of the process by which sectional interests benefitted. The embittered regulars could think of nothing to do except insult the insurgents and hold night sessions to cut down their research time.[16] This behavior did not improve relations. The insurgents continued to expose tariff favors through the heat of June and July, and the country listened. Most Republican senators, however, had promised to vote with Aldrich and so ignored the endless speeches. Aldrich took a long vacation at the end of June and ostentatiously napped in his seat while waiting for the insurgents to run down.

No one really knew what President Taft's position would be. He took a more restricted view of executive responsibility than Roosevelt and tried to avoid interfering in the preparation of the tariff bills. At the outset, the insurgents believed that Taft was on their side, but they fretted about the frequency of his business and social contacts with the regulars.[17] In June, Taft sent a special message to Congress recommending a 1 per cent corporation tax without consulting them. This gesture seemed especially hostile to the insurgents, because it blocked their effort to attach an income-tax rider to the tariff.[18] The real truth was that Taft had become disgusted with both sides. But he wanted to fulfill his pledge of tariff revision, and an income-tax rider would have killed it altogether.

The President had to show his hand more decisively when the Aldrich bill passed in mid-July and went before a House-Senate conference committee for seventeen days of grim bargaining. He was successively battered by three groups: Cannon, out of gratitude for the New York Democrats' help in the rules fight, threatened to adjourn the House without a vote unless the President raised the duty on gloves; the regular Republican senators from the range country threatened to oppose the conference report unless hides were taken off the free list; [19] and the insurgents threatened to split the party unless Taft killed tariff revision with a veto. The President stood up manfully to his tormentors, and pleased none of them. He secured reduced rates on glass, lumber, coal, and iron. He also managed to keep petroleum and hides on the free list. His worst reversals occurred on cotton and wool, which greatly interested consumers. The rate on cotton went up to buy some Southern votes and the wool rate remained stationary. The unhappy Taft concluded that he had forced enough reductions on key consumer items to justify signing the Payne-Aldrich bill, even though more rates were raised than lowered in other categories. After all the controversy the only Republican senators who defied party discipline and voted against the bill were Dolliver, Cummins, Beveridge, Bristow, La Follette, and Moses Clapp of Minnesota. So it seemed possible that the issue would subside.

The special session was followed by an uneasy period of political calm, while insurgents and regulars alike returned home to test grass-roots sentiment. From the Great Plains westward, insurgents found much opposition to the tariff in general, and to Cannon and Aldrich in particular.[20] The President did not seem to be so directly in the line of fire, and in late August, Cummins of Iowa declared that Taft still stood for the right things.[21] Further east, opinion was more evenly divided, and Beveridge of Indiana had reason to feel uneasy about his vote against the tariff.

Instead of capitalizing on his ambiguous position, Taft embarked on a 13,000-mile tour in September 1909 to explain his views to the people. As a former judge, he imagined that he could discuss the tariff issue in abstract terms without offending the recent combatants. The atmosphere in Washington, however, had not prepared him for the intensity of popular feeling about the Payne-Aldrich Act. In any case, Taft ought to have taken the precaution of preparing his speeches on controversial topics. But without Mrs. Taft to nag him about his diet and his appointments, the President passed the time on the train convivially with politicians. Speeches remained unwritten, and he delivered short, extemporaneous remarks to rear-platform crowds en route. The President managed to avoid any serious indiscretions until he reached Winona, Minnesota, where he praised the Payne-Aldrich tariff as the best ever passed by the Republican party.

The insurgents could not believe their ears. Both Beveridge and Cummins thought the President had been misquoted.[22] Once the statement was confirmed, the insurgents prepared for total war on the Administration. Matters did not improve when Cannon began to make speeches in October denouncing the insurgents as traitors. The timing suggested that Taft and the unpopular speaker were political allies. On the contrary, Taft wanted Cannon to announce his retirement for the good of the party, but the public had no inkling of the President's attitude.[23] The muckraking magazines lumped Taft and the regulars together as "stand-patters" and designated their foes as Progressives. Thus, by the fall of 1909, an issue that had never been anything but a matter of sectional economics was becoming the acid test of Progressivism. Through the subtle alchemy of muckraking, Western protectionists qualified as heroes and Eastern ones as villains.

III

Simultaneously, a controversy over conservation policy developed within the Administration which ultimately forced Taft to choose between his Secretary of Interior, Richard A. Ballinger, and the gifted but erratic Gifford Pinchot. Pinchot wanted to continue the Roosevelt policy of mass withdrawals of public land from settlement on a scale beyond the intent of congressional law. Ballinger, with the backing of Taft, refused to act on such a dubious legal basis; throughout the spring and summer of 1909, the Secretary of the Interior reopened to public entry power sites withdrawn by the Roosevelt Administration pending reclassification. Some 3,450,460 acres were involved, and after a geological survey report, 421,-129 acres were again withdrawn by Ballinger. The long-range effect of Ballinger's policy was to coax Congress into enlarging executive powers over conservation, but the immediate result was disastrous for the Administration. Throughout the fall of 1909, Pinchot sniped at his superior. He revived an old charge that Ballinger, as Commissioner of the General

Land Office under Roosevelt, had handled an Alaskan coal lease in corrupt fashion. Then he induced one of his subordinates, Louis R. Glavis, to carry the evidence to Taft, who promptly fired Glavis. The well-oiled publicity machine of the Forest Service leaked parts of the Glavis testimony to newspaper correspondents and muckraking magazines. This development followed Taft's blunder at Winona and gave the insurgents a fresh opportunity to embarrass the President. Most of them had either been indifferent or hostile to conservation. Bristow regarded Pinchot "as a good deal of a fake," but he energetically promoted an investigation of Administration conservation policies and confided to a friend in December that the "muckrakers will pave the way for us." [24] *McClure's, Collier's,* and *Hampton's* did their duty as Bristow had predicted, and their articles produced a demand for a congressional investigation. In early January Pinchot rejected Taft's conciliatory gestures and wrote Dolliver a letter full of intemperate accusations, which the latter obligingly made public on January 7, 1910. The President was left with no alternative but to fire the insubordinate Pinchot. The same week, Congress authorized an investigation.

Up to this point the bewildered President had struggled to avert a break with the insurgents.[25] He had assured them that his Winona speech was not intended as a criticism of their position,[26] and had invited suggestions from Cummins about pending railroad legislation.[27] He had also resisted repeated demands from the regulars that patronage be used against the insurgents. But the systematic campaign against his sincerity as a conservationist was the last straw. On January 5 a veiled warning appeared in the *Washington Post* that the Administration would use its power to crush insurgents, and within a month the axe began to fall on their appointees.

Matters went from bad to worse. The insurgents pushed the investigation of Ballinger with indecent zeal. The evidence turned up by the congressional committee was inconclusive, and after four months it exonerated Ballinger. But muckrakers had already convicted him, and the Secretary of Interior resigned as soon as he could do so without appearing to quit under fire. Despite the fact that many of his accusers had acted in good faith, Ballinger's only authenticated crime was to cross the high-strung, arbitrary Pinchot.

The insurgents were carrying on a parallel campaign against Speaker Cannon. Like the agitation against Ballinger, it had begun in the fall of 1909 with a series of attacks on the speaker which solicited intemperate and vindictive responses from him. *Success Magazine* and *Collier's* assisted with articles tying Cannon to the special interests and emphasizing the obvious fact that he did not run the House democratically. When the session opened, Norris of Nebraska waited patiently for an opportunity to offer a privileged motion overthrowing the Reed rules. On March 17 the vigilant Norris found a way of forcing the issue onto the floor. Cannon stalled for twenty-six hours while trying to rally the regulars. A brief adjournment followed while the more conciliatory members sought a compromise. Imminent defeat, however, only made Cannon more belligerent, with the result that he sabotaged the effort of friends to salvage a part of his powers. The final blow came on March 19 when the House transferred the bulk of the speaker's authority to a twelve-man rules committee. Taft felt that Cannon had outlived his usefulness, but his real feelings were misconstrued because at this very time the President revived the custom of the Speaker's Dinner and so paid public respect to Cannon.

Taken at face value, however, Taft's annual message of December 1909 placed the President squarely within the Progressive tradition. Besides seeking additional power to classify public lands, he recommended enlargement of I.C.C. authority over the railroads; mandatory federal charters for corporations engaged in interstate commerce; establishment of postal savings banks; exemption of labor unions from suits under the Sherman Act; and redefinition of judicial procedure to allow a labor hearing before the issuance of an injunction. Roosevelt had never asked for more.

The experiences of the special session had made the Senate oligarchy a little grimmer, and it scuttled most of these recommendations. Conservation legislation slipped through, as well as bills multiplying the restrictions on railroads and establishing postal-savings banks. Nowhere was the animosity of the insurgents toward Taft more evident and more unjustified than in their attitude toward the railroad bill. Known as the Mann-Elkins Act, it plugged up many of the loopholes in the Hepburn Act and even incorporated a La Follette provision for a physical valuation of the railroads. Progressives of every stripe would have been delighted with such a blow at special privilege in 1907, but four years later the insurgents saw tricks lurking in every provision. They complained bitterly against the plan of vesting the discretionary power to institute suits with the executive branch, and they were equally incensed at the effort to legalize the establishment of uniform railroad rates by exempting the common carriers from the

Sherman Act. When the President instituted a suit against the railroads for raising rates, they dismissed it as a cheap political maneuver whereby he hoped to gain credit for something that he really opposed.[28] The insurgents were equally cool toward the trust-busting activities of the Administration, although Taft instituted far more suits under the Sherman Act than Roosevelt. It is difficult to resist the conclusion that their judgment had been affected by annoyance over the patronage warfare conducted against them. Toward the end of the session, Dolliver's humor deserted him, and he complained bitterly about an organized defamation of the Progressives. The muckraking magazines continued to publicize Dolliver's side of the story and inflicted fresh damage on the President. At this point, too, many voters detested congressional leaders so much that they believed the blanket indictment of the muckraking magazines.

Signs that irrational attitudes prevailed were numerous in the spring of 1910 and pointed to a party disaster in November. Massachusetts held a congressional bi-election on March 22, and the Democratic candidate, Eugene N. Foss, carried a normally Republican district by opposing Speaker Cannon and the Payne-Aldrich tariff. Henry Cabot Lodge felt endangered by the outcome and complained to a friend about "a vague discontent abroad which it is almost impossible to meet with argument." [29] Simultaneously, alarming reports from Montana reached Senator Thomas H. Carter, a consistent Taft supporter who was up for re-election. Carter had supported most of Roosevelt's Square Deal as well as subsequent Progressive legislation, but he had voted for the Payne-Aldrich tariff. He had never concealed his responsiveness to the interests of the Anaconda Copper Company and the Great Northern Railroad, and his constituents had not seemed to object. But in 1910 voters became convinced that Carter was corrupt, although nobody ever proved that he had profited personally from his connection with local corporations. If Carter's letters provide an accurate index of his state of mind, he was frankly bewildered by broadsides from erstwhile supporters accusing him of selling out to reactionaries. Pleas from Carter for concrete objections to his conduct produced only vague charges of guilt by association with Cannon and Aldrich.[30] Perhaps by Progressive standards Carter deserved political extinction, but his actual voting record was not so different from that of the insurgents lauded by *Collier's*. Unfortunately for Carter the voters were not in a mood to make distinctions. They were tired of the old faces and wanted a new generation of leaders to take command.

Developments in Massachusetts and Montana were duplicated else-where. Employing the technique of guilt by association, insurgents kept the regulars on the defensive.[31] Many Taft supporters were badly defeated in summer primaries and nominating conventions, while those who sur-vived faced a rejuvenated Democratic party in November.[32] Only in Cali-fornia and New Hampshire did the insurgent campaign retain the unselfish crusading fervor that had originally characterized Progressivism. Hiram Johnson, an important lawyer, led the fight of the California insurgents against the dominant Republican organization, which had been an obse-quious servant of the Southern Pacific Railroad. Johnson was too honest to make a regional position on the tariff a test of Progressivism. He focused his entire attention on rescuing California from a government hostile to the spirit of democracy.[33] In New Hampshire, Robert P. Bass conducted a similar campaign to rescue his state from the grip of powerful economic interests.

Fresh discord developed in Republican ranks when Theodore Roosevelt landed in New York on June 16 after a fifteen-month absence from the United States. He had gone hunting in Africa immediately after his re-tirement from office so that Taft could launch his Administration without interference or embarrassment. At the time of Roosevelt's departure, few people suspected that relations with his hand-picked successor were al-ready strained. Mrs. Taft had always disliked and distrusted Roosevelt, however, and once in the White House she pointedly reversed all of Mrs. Roosevelt's arrangements for White House receptions.[34] Such matters were trivial, but for the Roosevelts the cumulative effect was disagreeable. Moreover, the fact that Roosevelt's daughter, Alice, had married Con-gressman Nicholas Longworth of Cincinnati, whose family was on close terms with the Tafts, assured that the Roosevelts would be informed of petty gossip in the White House about themselves. Taft himself made a serious blunder shortly after the election by telling Roosevelt, "I owe my victory to you and my brother, Charlie." Roosevelt never forgave Taft for equating the President's contribution with that of a Cincinnati publisher.[35] Taft lost most ground with his mentor in his cabinet choices. Apparently the President-elect volunteered to retain some of the members close to Roosevelt and then ended by retaining only the two in whom his predeces-sor had little interest.[36] Doubtless Roosevelt's irritation about the cabinet was aggravated by feelings of depression over his forthcoming retirement.

Lodge did what he could to make trouble, partly out of jealousy toward Taft as heir-apparent.[37]

When Roosevelt emerged from the jungle, Gifford Pinchot was waiting to help convert the ex-President's personal misgivings about Taft into political misgivings. Roosevelt had additional weeks to brood while he toured the capitals of Europe. Frantic letters from erstwhile political associates urged him to avoid comment on the party's factional squabbles, and Roosevelt tried to follow their advice. Lamentably, protracted silence required a greater capacity for self-restraint than Roosevelt possessed. Although he rejected an invitation to the White House and also managed to avoid contact with Taft's foes for seventy-two hours, Roosevelt soon turned Oyster Bay into a place of pilgrimage for restless politicians. Regulars and insurgents alike came for lunch and political discussion. The guest lists indicated that the host had a marked preference for insurgents. In fact, Roosevelt began inviting those who had not appeared voluntarily.[38] The suspicious La Follette came by request on June 27 and in an uncharacteristic fit of generosity told reporters that Roosevelt was "the greatest living American." Congressman Miles Poindexter, who headed the insurgent organization in the state of Washington, conferred with Roosevelt on July 5, after publicly endorsing him for President a day earlier. With the approval of Roosevelt, Poindexter issued a statement at the conclusion of the conference that "we . . . found ourselves in entire agreement." The effect of this announcement on the White House can well be imagined in view of Roosevelt's repeated pledges that he would not take sides. Subsequent developments indicated that his version of neutrality was public silence and private encouragement of insurgents.[39] Roosevelt even suggested material for speeches that he himself was unwilling to father.[40]

Despite his clumsy effort to hide his sentiments, Roosevelt's impulsive intervention in New York politics almost led to a direct collision with Taft. Swallowing his dislike for Governor Hughes, Roosevelt responded to Hughes's request for help in pushing a direct primary bill through the state legislature. When the legislature rebuffed the ex-President, Hughes convinced him to take the issue to the Republican state convention. Shortly after Roosevelt had committed himself to do so, Taft appointed Hughes to the Supreme Court, which made Roosevelt angry at Taft for removing Hughes during the primary fight, and angry at Hughes for accepting the appointment.

The ensuing state convention at Saratoga was a Pyrrhic victory for Roosevelt and carried the Republican party one step closer to defeat and schism. First Roosevelt got himself elected temporary chairman. Then he forced the convention to accept a direct primary plank as well as his choice for governor, Henry L. Stimson, a tweedy squire and lawyer from Cold Harbor, Long Island, who reminded the Rough Rider of himself. The spectacle of a former President participating in a factional brawl offended the voters and caused numerous Republicans to desert their party ticket in November.[41] The regulars got their revenge on Roosevelt at the convention coupling his direct-primary plank with a flat endorsement of the Payne-Aldrich tariff. Roosevelt could never take tariff agitation seriously, but he was embarrassed at being identified with the one measure detested by all his insurgent friends. Roosevelt's solution was to travel about the country adjusting his tariff pronouncements to the taste of his audience. Any other year this performance might have been hailed as a selfless gesture to keep the party together. In 1910 it did little damage in insurgent areas but hurt the Republicans east of the Mississippi, where foes of the Payne-Aldrich tariff voted Democratic.

Election day confirmed the worst fears of the Administration. The Democrats won governorships in New York and New Jersey for the first time since 1892, and unseated Senator Beveridge in Indiana. They gained control of the House by the comfortable margin of 228 to 161, and cut the Republican Senate majority from 20 to 10. Still worse, the Eastern regulars suffered heavy casualties, while only three of 98 insurgent congressmen failed to secure re-election. Such a striking vindication was certain to make the rebels more defiant than ever.

IV

The 1912 Presidential contest started immediately after the 1910 election. The insurgents organized the National Progressive Republican League on January 21, 1911, as the first step in a drive to block the renomination of Taft. Most Midwestern senators became members, along with an assortment of conservationists, intellectuals, and political adventurers. Theodore Roosevelt was invited to join the League but confined himself to private expressions of sympathy with its objectives. His own political intentions were difficult to estimate. At times he adopted the tragic pose of the repudiated leader and spoke of retirement with an air of finality. As it turned out, Oyster Bay was too close to New York and

Washington for Roosevelt to be a melancholy squire full time. Within two weeks of the November debacle, he appeared at the Washington Press Club and engaged reporters in spirited banter, parrying questions about his political future like an avowed Presidential candidate.[42] Depression soon set in again, however, and by early 1911 visitors found Roosevelt apparently reconciled to the renomination of Taft.

Meanwhile, Taft was engaged in the suicidal policy of convening a special session of the new Congress in April 1911 to ratify a reciprocity agreement with Canada. He expected the measure to appeal to all sections of the country and imagined that the proposed reduction in rates would cut the ground out from under the insurgents. Instead it reopened the ruinous factional controversy within the party. The Midwest objected to the admission of the Canadian goods duty free, since the bulk of them were agricultural products and raw materials. Accordingly, the insurgents denounced reciprocity as a device to provide Eastern trusts with cheap raw materials, and predicted that Canadian grain would flood the United States and depress the income of farmers.

Eastern Republicans thought well of reciprocity, and for once Taft had the muckrakers on his side, for reciprocity would result in the admission of Canadian paper for newsprint duty free. The Democrats were delighted by the opportunity to make trouble and were now numerous enough to do so. They combined with the Eastern Republicans to support the reciprocity agreement and with the insurgents to confront Taft with a series of flat rate reductions on individual items. The only working principle behind Democratic tariff votes was to aggravate the divisive forces within the G.O.P.

The Senate oligarchy was seriously weakened by the retirement of Aldrich and Hale, as well as by the election of more insurgents. Nevertheless, Lodge, Smoot, Jacob Gallinger of New Hampshire, and W. Murray Crane of Massachusetts retained control of the Senate organization and rammed through the reciprocity bill by a vote of 53 to 27 on June 21, 1911. The House had already acted affirmatively, but the Democratic arguments for reciprocity were couched in inflammatory language that made the program unpalatable in Ottawa. Speaker Clark, for example, advocated reciprocity to hasten the day "when the American flag will float over every square foot of British North American possessions." As might have been expected, Canada rejected reciprocity, leaving the President with nothing to show for the acrimonious three-month session.

By the time Congress adjourned in the summer, it had become apparent that the word "Progressive" possessed political magic and that both factions of the Republicans as well as the Democrats were eager to appropriate the label for 1912. In the process, the meaning of the term continued to lose clarity. Despite the denunciation of Taft as a reactionary, he adhered to the definition of Progressivism employed at the inception of the movement. In his clumsy way, the President had pursued conservation, trust busting, railroad regulation, and other policies designed to root special privilege out of government. He had also found a provisional answer to the perplexing question of how to outlaw monopolistic business practices without centralizing power in Washington by proposing federal regulation of economic giants affected with a public interest and dissolution of all the others. This solution reflected Taft's judicial training and applied an old common-law rule to twentieth-century economic problems. The distinction between the types of business was becoming blurred precisely at the time that Taft applied it, but no subsequent President discovered a completely objective formula for dealing with monopoly. In any case, Taft believed that the possibilities of disciplining special privilege through legislation had been exhausted by 1910, and that the future of Progressivism lay in the honest administration of existing laws. His position reflected the conservative bias of the early Progressives, who wanted to purify American institutions rather than change them. Aside from unfavorable publicity on the tariff, Taft's reputation as a Progressive was most hurt by his determination to work through the regular Republican state organizations. Except in Illinois, California, and Wyoming, they were neither corrupt nor obligated to special interests in the direct fashion that early Progressives had found outrageous. In fact, the bulk of the dishonest municipal and state leaders had been eliminated by the time Taft became President. Yet many insurgents demanded such additional devices as the initiative, referendum, and recall to promote political purity. Since Taft opposed the substitution of direct government for representative government, he widened the gulf between himself and the insurgents. By the same token he regained the support of the Mark Hanna style of regular who had always regarded all Progressives as self-seeking demagogues.

A full *rapprochement* with the stand-patters was impossible for Taft because of his persistent devotion to trust busting. Nevertheless, a new factional alignment was beginning to replace the old cleavage between Progressives and stand-patters, with the insurgents on one side and the

Taft Progressives and the stand-patters on the other. No clear-cut ideological distinctions accompanied the factional realignment. In general, the insurgents wanted to proceed beyond the purification of institutional life to social and economic reforms. On the other hand, the Taft Progressives thought that the main goals of the reform movement had been achieved, and they sought nothing more than the preservation of existing gains. Most stand-patters thought the whole Progressive crusade had been unnecessary, but they were prepared to settle for Taft's new status quo.

Although the insurgents felt they were the true Progressives, they suffered from internal dissension. La Follette headed a faction that pushed for elimination of the convention system and other impediments to more direct popular control, presumably with the idea that special interests would lose their power once this had taken place. Borah and Bourne shared this general viewpoint, although they did not believe that tariffs for their constituents or the opening up of forest reserves to local lumber companies constituted special privilege. Bristow and the Iowa senators were cooler to the agitation for direct election than their colleagues. The insurgents were even more vague about the proper role of the national government in regulating economic life. Borah and Bourne hoped to keep power decentralized, while the rest tended to favor some enlargement of government authority over business. La Follette was especially optimistic about supervisory commissions and thought that they could be staffed by disinterested experts who would make "the special interests" behave. Unquestionably, there was considerable appeal in this position. Farmers, organized labor, and other groups had expected the Progressive crusade against corrupt machines to produce tangible improvement in their economic position. Since the reform movement had thus far failed to do so, the discontented were responsive to the idea that the national government ought to take positive steps for promoting the prosperity of underprivileged groups. In short, the insurgents and their followers seemed to be on the verge of a redefinition of Progressivism that pointed toward the New Deal.

As the opposition party, the Democrats were in an enviable position, for they did not have to take a positive stand on national issues dividing the Republicans. They loudly claimed that they were Progressives without specifying what kind. The states' rights tradition of the Democratic party encouraged the inference that its version of Progressivism was closer to Taft's than to the insurgents. Yet the record of the Democratic state administrations did not clarify matters.

In the summer of 1911, a small but energetic group of insurgents began looking for a Presidential candidate. The guiding spirits behind this enterprise were intellectuals like Amos Pinchot, Charles Crane, Harold Ickes, and Gardner Gilson; muckraking journalists like E. W. Scripps, E. A. Van Valkenberg, and William Allen White; and disciples of Roosevelt like Gifford Pinchot and ex-Secretary of the Interior James R. Garfield. From the outset, the stop-Taft movement was handicapped by the failure of insurgent senators to co-operate and by the difficulty in deciding on a candidate. Only Roosevelt possessed the requisite political stature to challenge Taft with any chance of success, but the ex-President firmly rejected the initial feelers from the group. Although the sole alternative to Roosevelt was Senator La Follette, nobody felt very optimistic about his chances for wresting the nomination from Taft. Nevertheless, La Follette's love for lost causes and the pledge of $100,000 was sufficient to coax him into a formal declaration of his candidacy on June 17, 1911. From the outset, coolness marred the relations between the Wisconsin senator and his backers, most of whom secretly favored Theodore Roosevelt. At the back of their minds was the unspoken hope that La Follette would stumble and give way to the ex-President at the proper moment. Until then, they imagined that they could support the candidacy of the Wisconsin senator in good faith.

Besides being too transparent, this scheme made no allowance for La Follette's character. He had no intention of being a stalking horse for anybody, least of all Theodore Roosevelt, whom he regarded as a noisemaker rather than a reformer. So La Follette spent the summer and fall of 1911 campaigning on the theory that, if several hundred speeches had made him governor of Wisconsin, several thousand would make him President. Persuasive as he was on certain topics, La Follette could have campaigned forever without changing the mind of a single foe. Most Easterners regarded him as a twentieth-century Cromwell who would march on Washington some day with a fanatical army of wheat and dairy farmers. The Rocky Mountains and the Far West appreciated La Follette more, but with the same mixture of admiration and distrust accorded a preacher in a lawless mining camp. By mid-October it had become apparent that La Follette was not making much headway in his quest for delegates.[43]

Simultaneously, signs multiplied that the squire at Oyster Bay was finding retirement irksome. The unwillingness of insurgents to support La Follette undoubtedly increased his restlessness. At some point in early fall a dangerous idea began to take form in the back of Roosevelt's mind. It was the product of a half-formed hope that the American people would set up an irresistible clamor for him to return to public life. Back in 1908 he had brooded about his decision to spurn a third term, and expressed the fear that he was evading responsibility, like Pietro Morone, a medieval churchman who had refused to accept the papacy.[44] He never forgot the parallel nor overcame his indignation at the cowardly Morone for spurning the call to duty.[45] The episode was in his mind at the time he struggled for rationalizations to justify another term. He found a fresh incentive to run in October when the Taft Administration launched an anti-trust suit against U.S. Steel and tacitly criticized Roosevelt for having allowed the mammoth trust to absorb the Tennessee Coal and Iron Company in 1907. Roosevelt retaliated in an article in *Outlook Magazine* but did not mention Taft by name. Taft's renewed harassment of business reduced his political stock still further, and encouraged even the financial community to think of Roosevelt. Daniel Willard, president of the Baltimore & Ohio Railroad, went so far as to predict the election of a Progressive and to declare Roosevelt the safest Progressive.

At this point the La Follette forces pressed Roosevelt to clarify his position. He met a query from the La Follette camp on December 12 by saying that he did not want the nomination but would neither declare himself out nor support anyone else.[46] Two weeks later, La Follette's manager, Walter Houser, and the Pinchot brothers took note of the senator's disintegrating campaign by flatly requesting him to turn over his following to Roosevelt. Not only did La Follette refuse to withdraw, but he spent January checkmating their attempts to organize joint Roosevelt-La Follette delegations.[47]

Roosevelt did not lose much sleep over the efforts of the amateurish king-makers to wriggle out of their moral commitment to La Follette. Once he had made up his mind about accepting a draft, they were an embarrassment to him and were bound to get in the way of practical politicians rounding up delegates. Some professionals became active for Roosevelt about the time La Follette's campaign collapsed. A triumvirate composed of Borah, Dixon, and Frank Knox of Michigan quietly began "sounding out sentiment."[48] A month later, Roosevelt, still imagining that he was waiting passively for a great ground swell, cautioned a zealous supporter that he did not want the nomination by "artificial stimulation" or the "slightest manipulation."[49] The pretense of spontaneity was harder to maintain after the establishment of a formal Roosevelt organization in Chicago on January 16. Within two days, Roosevelt was ready to advertise his passivity more forcefully. He had already received letters from three Republican governors asking him to run for President, and he decided to use the reply as a discreet hint of his availability. The news, however, was leaked to the press, and so Roosevelt put off replying to the letters for the moment. Still Roosevelt persisted in the misconception that he was a spectator. Root warned him that there was "no resting place" between his present position and an active contest with Taft.[50] But for a time, the Colonel managed to infect Root with his own delusion by describing the current activity of his henchmen as spadework for a great crusade that looked far beyond 1912.[51]

On February 2, La Follette was virtually removed from the race by his collapse during a speech at the banquet of the Periodic Publishers Association. Already mentally distraught over the impending desertion of his managers and the serious illness of a daughter, La Follette had fired several devastating volleys into an audience full of his worst critics in the newspaper world. In the process, the senator had lost the place in his manuscript, and when a few of his tormentors walked out, La Follette had lost his temper completely and delivered a rambling two-hour tirade. The incident gave the Pinchot brothers and others a plausible reason for abandoning La Follette and made it all the more vital for Roosevelt to make a forthright statement, if he expected to inherit La Follette's followers intact.

The strenuous efforts of Roosevelt to ignore the implications of his conduct was nothing new in the world of politics. At fifty-four he was too active for retirement and too ambitious to settle for any lesser post than the Presidency. Personal irritation against Taft played more of a role in Roosevelt's determination to make a comeback than he would admit to himself. But there were other grounds for his attitude. During 1907 and 1908 Roosevelt had become increasingly dissatisfied with the fruits of the Progressive crusade that he had done so much to promote. In fact, Roosevelt had begun to fear that the industrial forces could not be properly disciplined within the existing framework. A book by Herbert Croly called *The Promise of American Life* had helped to convince him that the national government ought to regulate but not destroy trusts, and should promote the welfare of underprivileged groups. Calling this policy "the new nationalism," Roosevelt had first advocated it at Osawatomie, Kansas, in the 1910 campaign. At the time, Lodge had found nothing alarming in it, and the aging Root had scornfully made the private remark that professors taught "the new nationalism" in law school when he was a student; [52] but most other Republicans had missed it. Thereafter the doctrine had appeared regularly in Roosevelt's correspondence. By February 1912 he was ready to put himself at the head of the discontented insurgents in the name of his new movement. Roosevelt connected the New Nationalism to the Progressive movement by blaming Taft—first privately and later publicly—for betraying the Progressive movement. This contention put a serious strain on the facts, but it was an essential part of the complex motives that prompted Roosevelt to run.

Meanwhile, Roosevelt's managers had solicited letters of support from four more Republican governors, bringing the total to seven. They even interrupted the honeymoon of Robert P. Bass of New Hampshire to secure his signature. Roosevelt professed to regard these manifestations of support as "perfectly spontaneous," and announced his candidacy by answering the letters on February 25.[53] The same night he confided to a friend: "I feel as fine as silk." [54] There was nothing like the prospect of a bruising political battle to raise his spirits.

Roosevelt had seldom entered a fight against such formidable odds. By virtue of his patronage power, Taft already held a large bloc of delegates and seemed certain to enter the convention with a majority. The core of his strength was the rotten-borough delegates from the Solid South, plus those from several populous Eastern states where the regular organization had survived the reversal of 1910. Roosevelt's sole chance of undermining the Administration's strength depended upon his showing in thirteen states which had adopted Presidential primaries. Even if he won all of the 388 delegates at stake, he would be far short of a majority. Nevertheless, Roosevelt expected a decisive number of Taft delegates to switch to him if he received noteworthy margins in the primaries. The ex-President also hoped to put pressure on his opponents elsewhere by accusing them of fraudulent practices in the selection of delegates. Wherever possible, contesting Roosevelt delegations were to be organized and sent to the convention. It is unlikely that the Roosevelt managers expected either the national committee or the convention credentials committee to seat these delegates, because the Taft forces would control both bodies. The cries of dishonesty were intended for an excitable public already conditioned to believe the worst about the regular Republican organization.

If popular indignation reached a suitable pitch, some of the more unreliable Taft delegates might bolt. Then the Roosevelt forces could overturn the preliminary rulings and gain control of the convention.

Whatever the outcome of this strategy, it was bound to complete the demoralization of the Republican party. No party could expect to win an election after a pre-convention campaign in which one faction insistently questioned the integrity and good faith of another. Undoubtedly the convention rules governing the selection and apportionment of Southern delegates encouraged abuses, but until 1912 these abuses had not provoked a word of complaint from Roosevelt, as long as they worked to his advantage. Conventions under his management had seated regular delegations selected by machine methods, and had thwarted insistent demands for a reduction in the number of Southern delegates. As might have been expected, Roosevelt was blind to the element of self-interest in his conduct, and imagined that he was complaining about dishonesty in the interest of purifying the party.

Roosevelt's campaign began with a serious blunder. In a speech at Columbus, Ohio, he advocated the recall of judicial decisions. As President he had alienated several conservative Republicans by criticizing the courts and ought to have known that he was playing with dynamite. Most influential Republican politicians were lawyers and had an abiding faith in the institutions of their profession. An attack on the judicial system offended them far more than Roosevelt's murky pronouncements about the need for a new social and economic order. Nobody knows how much he damaged himself by the Columbus speech, but friend and foe alike agreed that it drove influential waverers to Taft.[55]

Roosevelt's decision to campaign actively in the states with direct primaries forced the unhappy Taft into a frontal encounter that he had struggled to avoid. The President was no match for his predecessor as a mudslinger, and under pressure Taft chose a number of unfortunate metaphors. The worst of his self-inflicted wounds was the observation that "even a rat in a corner will fight." [56] Indeed, the primaries turned out to be a series of nightmares for Taft. In North Dakota, the first primary, the President polled 1659 votes, or exactly 16 more than the number of federal office-holders in the state. The White House derived some comfort from the fact that the enraged La Follette had also filed in North Dakota and snatched victory away from Roosevelt. It was clear that La Follette would do anything within his power to defeat Roosevelt, and at this point his activity seemed likely to be decisive. But the Progressive following of the Wisconsin senator was limited to a few North Central states, and so the North Dakota primary represented the high-water mark of his campaign. Roosevelt swept the pivotal states of Illinois, Ohio, and Pennsylvania with heavy pluralities. Only in Massachusetts did Taft hold his own; there he split the convention delegates with Roosevelt.

Roosevelt's primary victories showed him to be the choice of rank-and-file Republicans but failed to generate the bandwagon sentiment which he was counting on. As the convention approached, the Roosevelt managers redoubled the clamor about fraud and corruption, and organized contesting delegations in most states they had failed to control. Yet, although Roosevelt's supporters were willing to argue before both the national committee and the convention itself that several Taft delegations had been selected in irregular fashion, they were hopelessly divided about the proper course of action if this strategy failed. While some favored a bolt, most of them intended to stay in the party. The more candid Roosevelt supporters also recognized that they did not have a very good case for changing the rules in the middle of the game. As one of them privately admitted: "In the Southern states, the Republican primaries and conventions are always farcical whether gotten up for or against the administration." [57]

Yet Taft's margin over Roosevelt was so slim when the national committee met a week before the convention that its hearings on contested delegates attracted as much attention as the convention itself. The Roosevelt managers challenged the credentials of 252 Taft delegates and dumped a mass of affidavits on the national committee. It would have taken several weeks to examine these documents alone, to say nothing of verifying the facts on which they were based. But since neither side wanted to settle the cases on their merits, the customary allotment of one hour per contest was adequate for propaganda purposes. No one really thought the Taft-controlled national committee would unseat Taft delegates. Hence, much of the argument by the Roosevelt managers was aimed at the arriving delegates in the hope that the convention would reverse the national committee. Meanwhile cleavage developed between the bolters and non-bolters in the Roosevelt camp, and rumors that Roosevelt might bolt spread through the convention.

Roosevelt took a long step toward confirming these rumors by arriving in Chicago forty-eight hours before the convention and aggressively pressing the charges of fraud. He had already staked his prestige on a direct bid for the Presidency, and his decision to lead his followers in person shut the last exit to a dignified retreat. Hitherto, no avowed candidate had ever appeared at a national convention, but Roosevelt's defiance of precedent seemed a logical outcome of the Presidential primaries. After telling reporters that he felt "as strong as a bull moose," Roosevelt established his headquarters at the Congress Hotel. The evening of his arrival he held a mass meeting at the auditorium. He condemned Taft for trying to steal the nomination, and concluded on an ominous note by promising to fight for right, whatever the cost. "We stand at Armageddon," he told his cheering supporters, "and battle for the Lord." Taft forces took up Roosevelt's challenge by distributing thousands of handbills announcing that their adversary would walk on the waters of Lake Michigan at 7:30 the next evening.

Meanwhile the national committee had been making careful preparations to prevent physical violence in the convention hall. Decorators erected a barbed-wire fence around the speaker's platform and artfully concealed the fortifications with red, white, and blue bunting. A large police force was also recruited and placed under the direction of W. W. "Pudge" Heffelfinger, a former All-American football guard at Yale and fellow alumnus of Taft.[58] Rumors from the Roosevelt camp seemed to justify these precautions. The professionals expected a Taft man to be elected temporary chairman and anticipated a crisis when he ruled negatively on the inevitable proposal to unseat contested delegates. Some of the hotbloods from Roosevelt's California delegation wanted to demonstrate so violently against the decision that they would be ejected from the hall and provided with an excuse to organize a competing Republican convention.[59] This plan was not put into operation, but the major test came as predicted on the election of a temporary chairman. The Roosevelt forces put up Governor Francis McGovern of Wisconsin in the hope of picking up the votes of the favorite-son delegations pledged to La Follette and Cummins. But Senator Root of New York, the Taft candidate, won over McGovern, 558 to 501. Immediately thereafter, Root ruled that delegates whose titles were contested could vote in every case except their own. This decision enabled Taft to poll his full vote. Despite the adverse effect of his ruling on Roosevelt's prospects, Root had logic on his side. If he had taken the opposite position, Root would have established a precedent for disqualifying all contested delegates irrespective of the merits of individual cases.

At all events, the Root ruling foreshadowed a Taft nomination. The convention had opened on June 18, and it was to continue for four more days. Everybody expected Roosevelt to bolt, and he confirmed this suspicion by ordering his delegates not to vote on any proposition before the convention because of "robbery and fraud." Two factors caused him to delay his decision until the eleventh hour. He hoped to carry his own followers who opposed a party split by allowing them to discover that compromise was impossible. And he needed time to line up the necessary journalistic and financial support before organizing a third party. The prospect of a split stimulated regulars and Roosevelt men alike to find a compromise candidate. Ever fearful of what a Democratic victory would do to the price of sheep, Senator Warren of Wyoming tirelessly promoted compromise.[60] To his dismay, Warren found that the lukewarm delegates preferred Taft or Roosevelt to a third candidate. In the end, compromise failed because Roosevelt would not admit defeat and because the bulk of the regulars intended to keep their grip on the party machinery, regardless of what happened in November.[61]

While the conciliators were engaged in futile negotiations, Frank A. Munsey promised to back a third party with his newspaper chain, and George W. Perkins of the International Harvester trust agreed to provide financial support. Roosevelt then called upon his followers to bolt the evening of June 22, just as the convention was renominating the Taft-Sherman ticket. The bolters reconvened at Orchestra Hall and heard Roosevelt call for the formation of a Progressive party that would enforce the commandment: "Thou Shalt Not Steal." In conclusion, Roosevelt urged them to return home for a sounding of local opinion, and to reconvene August 5 to launch a new party.

These dramatic events temporarily distracted attention from the Republican platform, which made a strong bid for the support of restless Progressives. It advocated maximum-hour laws for women and children in industry, workmen's compensation legislation, the broadening of anti-trust laws, extension of conservation, and complete publicity on campaign contributions. The only part of the document that bore the stamp of the standpatters was a high-tariff plank.

The future of the embryo Progressive organization depended less on what the Republicans said in their platform than what the Democrats did at their Baltimore convention. The old party of Jefferson and Jackson met on June 25 amid indications that it would allow Roosevelt to inherit all of the discontented voters by nominating Speaker Champ Clark, an un-imaginative professional politician. It took a week of wrangling and 46 ballots for the delegates to choose instead Governor Woodrow Wilson of New Jersey. Of all the Democratic Presidential hopefuls, Wilson was the best suited to contest Roosevelt's claim to the custodianship of public morality. As governor of New Jersey, Wilson had smashed a corrupt polit-ical machine and given the state a model Progressive administration. Moreover, he had developed a remarkable talent for coining inspirational generalizations, first as a professor and later as president of Princeton Uni-versity. The Democratic party had also simplified Wilson's problems as a campaigner by adopting a platform in harmony with his record. The vari-ous planks were Progressive but coated with a vague "states' rights" patina. For the first time since 1892, the traditional Democratic commitment to a low tariff was a distinct asset to the party.

The damage done at Baltimore to the prospects of the Progressive party was immediately apparent. Chase S. Osborn of Michigan, one of the Re-publican governors who had asked Roosevelt to run in February, issued a statement that the nomination of Wilson made a third party unnecessary. Amos Pinchot confided to a fellow Roosevelt supporter that both the fraud and the tariff issues were lost. With irrefutable logic he concluded that people could not be asked to vote against Wilson because Taft stole Roose-velt's delegates.[62] Both Osborn and Pinchot finally supported Roosevelt, but many Democratic Progressives stayed with Wilson. Most Republican office-holders who had been in the Roosevelt camp at Chicago also de-clined to desert their party. Except for Dixon of Montana, no governor or senator who was up for re-election in 1912 followed Roosevelt. A few prominent hold-overs like Bristow of Kansas, Poindexter of Washington, and Hiram Johnson of California enlisted in the third party. Against his better judgment, ex-Senator Beveridge joined up, too, and thereby signed his political death warrant in Indiana. But for the most part the upper levels of the Progressive party were staffed by lame duck factionalists at odds with Taft.

The aloofness of the office-holders contrasted sharply with the enthu-siasm of the rank and file. Large numbers of Republicans flocked to the August 5 convention which launched the Progressive or Bull Moose party. There was a religious air to the proceedings. Delegates sang the "Battle Hymn of the Republic" and "Onward Christian Soldiers." Imaginative newspapermen compared them to Cromwell's Covenanters or the crusading army of Peter the Great. "There was room on that platform," one Progressive reported, "for anyone who had seen Peter Pan and believed in fairies." [63] The atmosphere resembled too closely the Populist conventions of the 1890's for Roosevelt to feel comfortable. He had always been a cautious, practical reformer, and now he was attracting the support of the fanatics and dreamers. Fortunately, Roosevelt could be a good actor when he tried and on this occasion he let himself go. As one observer saw it: "People poured up from the floor to have him wring their hands and the Colonel would whirl about from waving a bandanna at the gallery directly behind him and pounce upon whoever happened to be in line with the air of suddenly, at the crisis of his life, meeting the one person who could solve it." [64]

Roosevelt's nomination was a foregone conclusion, and the platform clearly reflected his belligerent mood. It endorsed the protective principle but denounced the Payne-Aldrich tariff. It also advocated most of the Progressive measures already approved by the Republican and Democratic platforms. The novel doctrines of the Bull Moose party were confined to three planks. One proposed to suspend trust busting and to substitute regulation of business by federal commission; the second contained a blanket endorsement of the various devices for direct government; and the third demanded a variety of laws for "social and industrial justice." The last was by far the most popular plank with Progressive campaigners, because it held out the hope of national action to improve health standards, to prohibit child labor, and to promote economic welfare. Before adjourning, the Progressive convention chose Hiram Johnson, the grim-faced governor of California, for Vice President.

When the cheering delegates had departed for home, Roosevelt was left with the insoluble problem of organizing the Progressive party. In six states his Progressive followers controlled the Republican party, and some would rebel if he ordered them to form a new party. On the other hand, Roosevelt could not hope to build a durable national party without promoting local organizations and local tickets. Undoubtedly his personal preference was to tolerate a variety of arrangements. Such a solution seemed to promise the most votes in November, and Roosevelt was not interested in thinking beyond November. Unfortunately, he had coaxed Hiram Johnson, Beveridge, and others into the third party movement by promising that it would be permanent. Thus Roosevelt went through the motions of ordering his followers to organize the Progressive party at every level. He must have been happy to discover that state laws and local political considerations prevented full compliance. In California and South Dakota, the Progressives not only remained in the Republican party but controlled it so completely that they instructed Republican Presidential electors for Roosevelt. As a result, frustrated Republican regulars could vote for Taft only as a write-in candidate.[65] A similar situation developed in Oklahoma, with all but two electors being committed to Roosevelt.[66] Elsewhere, both Progressive and Republican electors appeared on the ballot, but four more states managed to avoid a suicidal contest for local offices. In general, Republican candidates sought to arrest the disintegration of the party by some sort of fusion arrangement on state tickets.[67] This tactic failed in most instances because of the bitter partisanship at the grass roots.

After the vituperative Roosevelt-Taft contest in the spring, the main campaign of 1912 was anticlimactic. The voters were suffering from an overdose of elections. Most of them were determined to vote once more in November, but they had built up an immunity to campaign pageantry. Part of the listlessness was due to the general belief that nothing could avert a Wilson victory, and thus the customary sources of Republican campaign funds were missing, and the morale of local organizations was low.

Personalities outweighed issues in the minds of most voters. Roosevelt and Taft had already spent so much time attacking each other that they welcomed the opportunity to shift their fire to Wilson. Still, the fact that all three candidates claimed the Progressive label kept the discussion at a fairly high level. Roosevelt's endorsement of direct government drove the conservative Republican businessmen into the arms of the Taft Progressives. Although Taft had sponsored the constitutional amendment for direct election of senators, he campaigned against the indiscriminate enlargement of popular participation in public affairs.[68] Elihu Root did the same, but complained that nobody was interested in "the threatened change in our system of government." [69]

Since discontented farmers and workers were supposed to be the backbone of the Progressive party, Roosevelt bid for their support with a promise of bold economic reforms. By this time he had cut away completely from his original belief that traditional American institutions could be preserved in their original form. As amended, his Progressive credo accepted the existence of big business and called for big government to make it behave. Roosevelt had advanced cautiously in this direction since 1907, but his personal rivalry with Taft made him move faster and further in 1912 than he intended.[70]

Wilson defined his position on the role of government in a series of campaign speeches. But nobody was the wiser after listening to them or reading them. In one breath, the Democratic candidate would endorse a return to the states' rights philosophy of Jefferson, and in the next announce the advent of a new era which made the enlargement of government responsibility mandatory. If Wilson's philosophy was perplexing, it was couched in the language of the crusader, which enjoyed great popularity in 1912. Few noteworthy incidents occurred during the campaign. Vice President Sherman died in the middle of it, and the Republican national committee replaced him with President Nicholas Murray Butler of Columbia University. A would-be assassin also put a bullet into Roosevelt's chest at Milwaukee. But the wound was superficial, and the Colonel finished his speech, all the while waving a bloody handkerchief to emphasize his points.

On election day the Republicans suffered the worst reversal in their history in the electoral college. Wilson received 435 electoral votes to 88 for Roosevelt and 8 for Taft. Many normally Republican states went to Wilson because of the Taft-Roosevelt split. The popular vote offered a more reliable index of party strength with Wilson polling 6,286,000 to 4,126,000 for Roosevelt and 3,486,000 for Taft. Not only was Wilson to be a minority President, but his 42 per cent of the popular vote was the lowest for any winner since Lincoln in 1860. Vermont and Utah remained Republican, while Minnesota, Michigan, Pennsylvania, South Dakota, California, and Washington went to the new Progressive party. No third party since the Civil War had done as well as the Progressives, but Roosevelt was distinctly disappointed. He had hoped to attract the bulk of the labor vote in the populous East and to make substantial inroads on Democratic strength in the Solid South. Neither expectation materialized, and the bulk of his support was restricted to a widely scattered string of states near the Canadian border who feared Taft's reciprocity program.

The Republicans took an even worse drubbing in the congressional elections, as they lost districts that the party had controlled since its inception. Even Joe Cannon was defeated, cursing the college professors and the uplift magazines to the end. As a result, the party division in the new House was to be 291 Democrats, 127 Republicans, and 17 Progressives.

The new Senate would contain 51 Democrats, 44 Republicans, and a single Progressive, Miles Poindexter of Washington. The shift also completed the destruction of the old Republican Senate oligarchy. Only Lodge of Massachusetts, Smoot of Utah, and Warren of Wyoming survived to carry on the old traditions.

In retrospect it is clear that Progressivism first revitalized the Republican party and then disrupted it. In 1904, the reform movement gave the party a fresh set of issues when it was sorely tempted to "stand pat" as Mark Hanna and Joe Cannon had advocated. Roosevelt deserves the principal credit for channeling the moral energy of Progressivism into the Republican party and translating the reform impulse into a constructive political program. But moral energy is a divisive as well as a cohesive force, and in the end neither Roosevelt nor Taft could control it.

In a sense the political disorders accompanying Progressivism were birth pains which released durable humanitarian impulses. All subsequent reform movements drew on some portion of the diffuse Progressive credo. Whatever inspiration it provided for social and economic legislation, Progressivism unquestionably helped to destroy the autonomous character of political parties. The first blows had been delivered by civil-service reformers in the 1880's, who curtailed the power of the party organizations over spoils. Next they had fostered adoption of the Australian ballot at elections, thus depriving parties of the right to print their own ballots and guaranteeing a secret ballot. The Progressives took the third step when they stripped parties of control over the nomination of their candidates. As part of the Progressive agitation for direct government, the states passed primary laws which placed parties in legal strait jackets. Not only were the time and place of primaries prescribed, but conditions of party membership were defined in detail. In short, parties lost their private, voluntary status and became public institutions. Four years after the 1912 election, the helplessness of the party under the new conditions was dramatically illustrated in North Dakota. There an agrarian socialist movement entered the Republican primary, gained control of the party, and enacted its radical program under the Republican label. Doubtless, the direct primary laws curtailed fraud and corruption at the polls, but it would be difficult to contend that the revolutionary change in the status of parties was an unmixed blessing. Democrats and Republicans alike faced a new era when it would become virtually impossible to control or discipline their membership.

X

The League of Nations Debate

Most Republicans expected their party to make a rapid recovery from the disastrous 1912 elections. Virtually all the opposition group elected to Congress was Republican, and the party organization remained intact. Optimism sprang from the belief that the Progressive party was a one-man party; it could not live without Roosevelt nor could it be successful with him as a candidate.[1] Sooner or later, the Progressives would have to return to the Republican party.

The Progressives were outwardly sanguine but inwardly depressed. Even crusaders like Hiram Johnson and Harold Ickes recognized that their party had no future if Wilson stole its program.[2] They hoped to persuade Roosevelt to continue his educational campaign for the electorate, but the ex-President was in no mood to do so after successive rebukes in 1910 and 1912. Indeed, within a week of the election, Roosevelt had privately expressed doubt that the Progressive party would survive.[3] Two months later, he wrote Hiram Johnson that "attachment to the Republican name" would ultimately draw disgruntled Progressives back to the Republican party.[4] Roosevelt's pessimism was a reflection of his weariness with reformers and reform. He had welcomed the support of the intellectuals and idealists in his haste to settle scores with Taft. Now he resented their sustained clamor for vigorous leadership. Feeling that he could not abandon the movement altogether, since too many career politicians like Beveridge and Johnson had responded to his impulsive promise of a permanent crusade, Roosevelt decided to ignore the problem in late 1913 by departing for the Brazilian jungle.

Meanwhile, President Wilson took advantage of his large congressional majority by formulating an ambitious legislative program and calling a special session in April 1913. The first item on his agenda was downward revision of the tariff; and after six months of wrangling, Congress passed the Underwood-Simmons bill. It reduced the industrial schedules of the Payne-Aldrich Act a modest 10 per cent and put a hundred items of raw materials and food on the free list. The delaying tactics of the opposition upset Wilson's timetable, but he retaliated by keeping Congress in continuous session until the fall of 1914. Once Wilson had demonstrated the futility of obstructive tactics, the opposition allowed the Democrats to pass three other major pieces of legislation: the Federal Reserve Act, which centralized the banking system; the Federal Trade Commission Act, which established a quasi-judicial agency to supervise business; and the Clayton Anti-Trust Act, which attempted to plug up loopholes in the venerable Sherman Act.

The legislative skirmish in the 63rd Congress did more to establish Wilson's reputation as a skillful parliamentary leader than to clarify his goals. It was impossible to identify Wilson's program explicitly with either version of Progressive doctrine presented to the voters in 1912. Tariff reduction was too modest to expose trusts to foreign competition. Moreover, defenders of the Underwood-Simmons Act sounded like Republicans when they argued that it limited protection to the difference in the cost of production at home and abroad. The formula had been used to justify the sectional appetites of Republicans, and in 1913 it performed a similar service for Democrats. During the tariff debate, Republicans had made the usual denunciation of their opponents as "free traders," but nobody wanted to eliminate special privilege badly enough to breach the protective system.

Wilson's anti-trust legislation incorporated the conflicting principles of Roosevelt's "new nationalism" and Taft's older version of Progressivism. The Federal Trade Commission Act was a tacit acknowledgment that big business ought to be regulated rather than destroyed, while the Clayton Act strengthened the machinery for trust-busting. On the other hand, the Federal Reserve Act conformed to the centralizing tendencies of the Bull Moose philosophy.

If the Democratic party faced in both directions simultaneously, the two opposition parties were not much clearer about their principles. The Pinchot brothers, George L. Record of New Jersey, and other intellectuals tried to formulate a policy for the tiny group of Progressives in Congress, on the theory that the party could not survive by following counsels of expediency. Their ambitious effort failed partly because the Constitution made no provision for minority leadership outside of Congress and partly because they lacked the confidence of the practical politicians. Roosevelt might have been more successful than the intellectuals, but since he had no desire to lead, the Progressive legislators behaved as individuals rather than as members of a party group. The need for a policy was not so urgent in the case of the Republicans. Identified with a patriotic tradition and important economic interests for over half a century, the Republicans needed to do nothing more than oppose the Wilson Administration. Moreover, a negative attitude was the only basis for co-operation between stand-patters and Progressive Republicans who had remained regular in 1912. The withdrawal of Roosevelt from the party and the retirement of Taft to a professorship at the Yale Law School also removed an important source of intraparty friction. In fact the ideological quarrel abated once the principal antagonists had departed from the scene.

Other forces, too, were promoting the reunion. At the outset of the special session in 1913, Wilson had offended potential collaborators in both opposition parties by his determination to pin a Democratic label on all legislation. Insurgent senators who were up for re-election in 1914 had a special incentive to compose factional quarrels so that they could poll the full Republican vote. In mid-May 1913, Cummins of Iowa called a conciliation conference for the purpose of persuading the party to change the basis of Southern representation at conventions. The conciliators would have preferred a national convention for rule revisions, but the Taft-dominated national committee was unwilling to make such an open recantation. Nevertheless it conceded the substance of insurgent demands at a meeting in December 1913 by quietly authorizing a convention rule which deprived the South of 78 delegates. The national committee also made it mandatory for the national convention to seat delegates chosen by direct primary in states with compulsory primary laws. These rule changes were to go into effect when ratified by G.O.P. state conventions representing a majority of the electoral votes. By the summer of 1914, the necessary number of state conventions had done so. Pointing to this achievement, Cummins repeatedly told wavering Bull Moosers that they could accomplish more by reforming the Republican party from the inside.[5] He was seconded by Borah, who was an enthusiastic advocate of regularity as long as it did not oblige him to vote with the party on legislation.

II

Probably none of these gestures would have helped the Republicans in the 1914 elections had it not been for the disagreeable effect of Wilson's foreign policy on Progressives, including Roosevelt himself. Most Roosevelt admirers were nationalists, with a genuine commitment to the aggressive assertion of American rights in the Western Hemisphere and the Far East. They listened with consternation to Wilson's lofty avowals of anti-imperialist sentiments, coupled with proposals to reverse the policy of his predecessors. The implication that men of superior morality were now directing policy infuriated Rooseveltians, and the concrete measures of the Administration drained their last reserves of charity. Wilson's clumsy effort in 1913 to oust the undemocratic Huerta from power in Mexico launched a disorderly seven-year counter-attack on American lives and property below the border. Wilson not only refused to start a war for national rights but the lesser measures he employed only made the situation worse. The President's attempt to repeal the American exemption from canal tolls added fuel to the fire, while his proposal to award Colombia $25,000,000 in damages was an unmistakable condemnation of Roosevelt for fomenting the Panamanian revolution of 1903. By the spring of 1914, Progressives and Republicans of every stripe were attacking Wilson's foreign policy. Borah snorted at an "attenuated and overcapitalized cosmopolitanism" which made Wilson apologize for everything American,[6] while Bristow candidly conceded that his dislike of the President's foreign policy blinded him to other virtues of the Administration.[7]

Taft had predicted that Roosevelt would explode over the Colombian treaty when he got "through running his river up hill," [8] and upon his return from Brazil Roosevelt responded as expected. Besides being personally irritated at Wilson, Roosevelt welcomed the foreign policy issue because he thought it would bridge the gulf between the Republicans and Bull Moosers. For a time he was kept inactive by the diseases he had contracted in the Brazilian jungle, but by mid-summer he was trying to promote fusion between Progressives and insurgents in New York.

All over the country Progressives reacted so violently against fusion that Roosevelt put down his disappointment and made a speaking tour for third-party candidates in the off-year elections. The fusion talk, never-theless, weakened the resolve of many Progressives. Republican billboards in Indiana encouraged them with the slogan: "Eventually, why not now?" In most states the Progressives did not run a full ticket. The party contested only half the House seats outside the Midwest, and did worse still at the local level, where the rivalry over petty offices is an indispensable stimulus to party organization. Even in a state containing as much reform sentiment as Oregon, the Progressives filed for only 14 of 252 local offices.[9]

In the 1914 election the Republicans scored important gains by concentrating their fire on the Wilson Administration. The party won 69 more seats in the House and in the process cut the Democratic majority to 34 and the tiny Progressive delegation from 17 to 9. Although the Progressives ran a poor third in most contests, they drew enough votes away from the Republicans to defeat them in 39 congressional districts. Besides depriving the Republicans of control over the House, the Progressives caused the party to lose Senate seats in four normally Republican states. This achievement was cold comfort to the Progressives, whose total vote dropped from more than 4 million in 1912 to less than 2 million in 1914.

Since the Progressive party still had enough supporters to hold the balance between the Republicans and Democrats in 1916, Republican leaders responded by simultaneously cultivating Bull Moosers and discouraging the Presidential ambitions of their leader. Roosevelt was uncertain about his political future. Whenever he thought about election statistics, he wanted to retire from politics; whenever he thought about his irreconcilable enemies in the Republican party, he wanted to fight for the Republican nomination; and whenever he thought about Wilson, he had an unreasoning desire to sacrifice himself and the Progressive party if necessary to defeat the President. Oyster Bay was as gloomy as Elsinore until the sinking of the British oceanliner *Lusitania* in May 1915. But when it became apparent that Wilson would not declare war on Germany in retaliation for the loss of American lives on board the ship, Roosevelt began to dream of leading a great crusade to rescue national honor. He prodded the dispirited Progressive national committee into outspoken pronouncements for preparedness and made militant statements of his own.

Although Roosevelt continued to avoid an authoritative announcement about his personal plans, it was evident by the spring of 1916 what he would not do. He refused to enter his name in any Presidential primaries, and he made it clear that he would spurn a Progressive nomination unless he also received the Republican nomination. To emphasize the latter point, Roosevelt arranged for the Progressive convention to be held simultaneously with the Republican convention. His prospects for a joint nomination deteriorated steadily as the convention time approached. For one thing, the Republican minority in Congress was unresponsive to Roosevelt's plea for protecting American lives on the high seas. In February 1916 more than half the Republicans in the House supported the Gore-McLemore resolution, which was an unsuccessful attempt to ban Americans from traveling on belligerent ships. Republican party members in Western primaries indirectly endorsed the party stand by choosing convention delegates who ran on a peace platform. Wilson, meanwhile, stole the preparedness issue from Roosevelt. The President succeeded in gaining support for preparedness by assuring the nation it was not directed against anyone in particular, whereas Roosevelt had frightened many people by demanding rearmament against Germany.

Nevertheless, the Republicans needed a Presidential candidate acceptable to Roosevelt and the Progressives. Former Vice President Charles W. Fairbanks, Senator John W. Weeks of Massachusetts, and two ex-senators, Elihu Root and Theodore E. Burton of Ohio, were receptive, but they were all too conservative to attract the Progressives. Conversely, Borah of Idaho and Cummins of Iowa appealed to the Progressives and repelled the regulars. The only Republican who could be represented as all things to all men was Charles Evans Hughes. As associate justice of the Supreme Court, Hughes had taken no part in the disastrous quarrel of 1912. Moreover, both factions mistrusted Hughes enough to believe that his selection would be a heroic sacrifice for party unity. The regulars remembered Hughes as a reform governor of New York who had flouted the state organization, while the Progressives regarded all judges as tools of the corporations. Hughes ignored inquiries as to his availability and refused to help his nomination. Even so, Taft favored him as did ex-Senator W. Murray Crane, a sly politician from Massachusetts. With their encouragement, Frank H. Hitchock came out of retirement to approach Southern delegates for Hughes in the spring of 1916. The New York state boss, William Barnes, whose principal objective was to select anti-Roosevelt delegates, made no effort to block Hughes.

When the Republican convention opened in Chicago on June 7, it was evident that the organization had done its work effectively. Never were delegates so completely bossed with so little complaint from the press or public. In fact the party faithful at the Coliseum were so well disciplined and solemn that observers rechristened it the Mausoleum. Proceedings moved slowly, so that party leaders would have time for negotiations with the Progressives, who were meeting concurrently at the Chicago Auditorium.

The regulars demonstrated their control of the G.O.P. convention by selecting Warren G. Harding, a handsome freshman senator from Ohio, as temporary chairman. Harding had given the nominating speech for Taft in 1912, but his keynote address was an obvious attempt to conciliate the absent Bull Moosers. He assured them that the party had been divided over personalities and procedures rather than issues, and he pleaded for their co-operation in the forthcoming canvass. Other speeches in the same vein followed on the 8th and 9th.

At the same time, five Republicans, headed by Nicholas Murray Butler, and five Progressives, headed by George W. Perkins, conducted negotiations about the terms of the merger. The Progressives would name nobody but Roosevelt, while the Republicans seemed willing to take anybody else. The latter tried to break the deadlock on Friday night by balloting twice, with Hughes in a commanding lead, but the Progressives ignored the hint.

By this time Roosevelt knew that the Republicans would not nominate him, and he was reconciled to a compromise candidate. The stubborn loyalty of the Progressives had begun to be a real inconvenience, and so at 4 a.m. on Saturday the 10th he urged them through Perkins to take either General Leonard Wood or Henry Cabot Lodge. It was obvious to the Progressives that Roosevelt did not want the unpleasant responsibility of turning down a third-party nomination. Some of them would have been more disposed to save his face if he had suggested an authentic Bull Mooser as an alternate candidate. But they were infuriated by his recommendation of Lodge, which was a tacit invitation to disband the party. So the Progressives nominated Roosevelt just before noon on Saturday; selected ex-Governor John J. Parker of Louisiana as his running mate; and adjourned to await a reply from Oyster Bay.

The same morning on their third ballot, the Republicans gave Hughes 949½ votes and the nomination. The delegates selected former Vice President Fairbanks as his running mate and adjourned shortly after twelve noon. The Republicans' platform was broad enough to satisfy every Progressive untainted by low-tariff heresy. Criticism of Wilson's progressive legislation was carefully muted, while his conduct of foreign affairs received a blanket commendation.

The Progressives reconvened after lunch the same day. Roosevelt's message came late in the afternoon and was a conditional rejection of the nomination. His equivocation did not mean that Roosevelt might change his mind, but that he was trying to prevent the party from running a candidate. This cynical attempt to deliver the Progressives to their Republican tormentors doomed fusion. Some Bull Moosers became Wilson men on the spot, and others, who had cheered wildly for Roosevelt eight hours earlier, tore off their badges, stamped on them, and howled with rage. A handful subsequently called a Progressive convention at Indianapolis, but the response was so poor that the participants disbanded without making a nomination. Most leaders went home, dissolved their Progressive state organizations, and told the rank and file to go their own way.

It is clear in retrospect that both Roosevelt and the Republicans were right in believing that the Progressive tide had ebbed. The statutory remedies for corruption, misuse of the public domain, and unfair business practices had been carried far enough to satisfy most voters. A restless minority wanted to proceed further under Roosevelt's banner, but it was far in advance of public opinion. In his old age, William Allen White recalled a feeling of despair over the breakup of the Progressive party, but his memory was poor. At the time, White, along with many others, wanted the reformers to join the G.O.P. in a "stiff preparedness program" and an aggressive foreign policy.[10]

If Roosevelt correctly sensed that people were weary of reform, he bungled his effort to guide the zealots back to the Republican party. Some felt so bitter over his tactics that they took out their frustration on Hughes.[11] This was particularly true of the intellectuals, who refused to "blindly follow the Mahdi." [12] Others resented Roosevelt's social and economic reform. Like the Duke of Wellington, who for thirty-seven unrewarding years survived his great victory at Waterloo, Roosevelt had reached the climax of his career too early. Repeated frustration had warped his political judgment and weakened his capacity for self-restraint, making Roosevelt a liability to the cause he wanted to help. It was ironic that the voters preferred Wilson to Roosevelt because both men possessed many of the same qualities. Both periodically succumbed to fierce partisanship and mistook it for statesmanship. Both lacked any objectivity regarding their own conduct, but saw through each other. Neither could wholly conceal his dogmatism and self-righteousness, although Wilson showed the greater restraint in 1916 because the political breaks were going his way. While Roosevelt scolded the country, Wilson radiated the serenity of the statesman. For the moment Wilson even managed to listen to advice without construing it as criticism, and since the advice was good, he waged an astute campaign for re-election.

III

The basic strategy of the Democrats in the election was to bid for the support of the Bull Moosers and the advocates of peace by representing the President as a Progressive who opposed war. The "peace" theme was unmistakably emphasized at the Democratic national convention, which renominated the Wilson-Marshall ticket by acclamation. Both keynoter Martin H. Glynn and permanent chairman Ollie James enumerated the successive crises that Wilson had confronted, climaxing each with the assertion that the President had kept America out of war. As befitted an incumbent President, Wilson did little campaigning, but the Democratic national chairman, Vance McCormick, plastered the country with colored posters of a happy home in peace bearing the caption: "He kept us out of war." Wilson took a more realistic view of his achievement than the Democratic national committee, for he observed privately that "any little German lieutenant can put us into war at any time by some calculated outrage." But German submarines showed great restraint during the campaign, and the President did nothing to correct the impression that he treasured peace above American rights on the high seas.

Hughes had more reason to be evasive than Wilson, because he was trying to coax teamwork from leaders morbidly suspicious of each other. Yet his reputation as a trimmer was due primarily to the differing impressions he made on the platform and in private. At a public meeting people were so fascinated by his imposing appearance that they tended to forget what he said. Hughes resembled an Old Testament prophet—austere, upright, and preoccupied with cosmic issues. His audience was no more likely to analyze his speeches or cheer them enthusiastically than an earlier one would have been to applaud Moses on his return from Mount Sinai. Voters felt respectful and a little uncomfortable in the presence of Hughes. Accustomed to humor and a warm, if slightly partisan, personal touch, they regarded Hughes's scholarly treatment of issues as an attempt to minimize their importance. Party workers were also a trifle irritated when Hughes omitted reference to local candidates, an oversight that he did not remedy until the closing stages of the campaign.

Off the platform there was another Hughes. His aloofness and dignity did not evaporate altogether, but he became agreeable, persuasive, and approachable. The hypercritical Bristow was prepared to dislike the candidate, but he changed his mind completely after riding 150 miles across Kansas with him. Bristow described Hughes as a man who was willing to discuss everything frankly and to stand up for his convictions.[13] Hughes was clearly not a good candidate but he gave promise of making a good President.

Hughes began his campaign with the wise maneuver of ignoring the national committee and vesting control in a seventeen-member group divided between stand-patters, Progressive Republicans, and Bull Moosers. The effect of this gesture was largely wasted by placing the inexperienced William R. Willcox in charge of his campaign. Willcox did the routine things well; for instance, he raised $2,441,565, or about a million dollars more than the Democrats. But Willcox was insensitive to the problems created by the party split in 1912. He could not believe that grown men really cared who introduced Hughes at a whistle stop.

The situation in California was typical of the factional problems that confronted Willcox, and his response demonstrated his ineptitude. Upon his return from Chicago, Hiram Johnson had dissolved the state's Progressive party, and had announced that he would file for senator in the Republican primary. The regular Republican organization was understandably vexed at Johnson's effort to regain control of the party after abandoning it two years earlier. Both factions bid for the support of Hughes, and the only safe thing for him to do was postpone his tour of California until after the August primary. Unfortunately, Willcox underestimated the depth of factional bitterness and sent Hughes to the state on schedule. Even though Hughes was monopolized by the regulars, he stumbled through his schedule with a minimum of blunders until Sunday morning, August 20. At that point, the local committee on arrangements persuaded him to visit Long Beach. As an added inducement it proposed a side trip to Exposition Park so that Hughes could view the fossil remains at the La Brea pool. The candidate did not anticipate political repercussions from either part of his itinerary, but he was only half right. The regulars had arranged for a reception on the veranda of the Virginia Hotel at Long Beach without telling Hughes that Governor Johnson was inside. Later in the day, Hughes wrote a note of apology for the unintended snub, but when he left the state Johnson was in an ugly mood. At the time nobody imagined that California would decide the election. Nevertheless, Willcox had exposed Hughes to needless risk, and he continued to take a cavalier attitude to factional problems elsewhere.

If the outcome of the election had depended on hard work alone, Hughes would have won by an overwhelming margin. He took a transcontinental tour in August, returned East to campaign in Maine for the September election, and concentrated his remaining time in the pivotal Midwestern states. In general, he avoided discussion of Wilson's domestic policies, which were popular, and centered his fire on foreign affairs. Hughes handled the thorny question of American rights on the high seas with discretion but left the impression that he would uphold national honor more emphatically than his opponent. Mexico seemed to be a safer topic, because there was evidence of widespread dissatisfaction over developments south of the border. Not only had Mexicans stepped up their assaults on American lives and property, but Yankee troops under General John J. Pershing had been engaged in a bloody and ineffectual war along the border with a bandit army led by Pancho Villa. With all the rhetoric at his command, Hughes castigated the Administration for its inability to end disorder in Mexico.

The negative tone of the Hughes campaign struck some Republicans as inappropriate, but the regulars agreed wholeheartedly with his tactics. Lodge commended Hughes for his assaults on Wilson's foreign policy, and declared that it was not the business of the Republicans to propose constructive alternatives.[14] Hughes might have succeeded if he had adhered to his original strategy until the end of the campaign. In early September, however, he got caught in the middle of a labor controversy involving the Railroad Brotherhoods and the carriers. Before Hughes intervened, the Railroad Brotherhoods had spurned arbitration and threatened a nationwide strike, which Wilson headed off by persuading Congress to grant their demands for the eight-hour day. Known as the Adamson Act, this law had been passed September 3. Although Hughes had championed a number of laws to improve working conditions in New York state, he thought the behavior of the Railroad Brotherhoods was hardly distinguishable from blackmail. In a forthright statement, he predicted that free institutions would be endangered if the government allowed labor or any other group to pressure it into passing laws. The Democrats promptly misrepresented the Hughes position to make him seem opposed to the eight-hour principle. Nobody knows how many votes the G.O.P. lost by making an issue of the Adamson Act, but in the Maine election the following week the normal Republican majority of 18,000 was cut to 14,000. Senator Warren reported from Wyoming that Union Pacific workers had the "eight-hour bug" and would vote for Wilson.[15] Similar warnings came from Montana, which had 2100 miles of railroad.[16]

The luckless Hughes, however, did not have the stage to himself. Roosevelt stormed about the country bellicosely affirming solidarity with the Allies and making frenzied tirades against Wilson. Dropping all self-restraint, he pictured a cowardly, cringing President surrounded by ghosts: "The shadows of men, women, and children who have risen from the ooze of the ocean bottom and from graves in foreign lands; the shadow of the helpless whom Mr. Wilson did not protect lest he might have to face danger." This kind of campaign oratory made the Republicans the war party, and the mild-mannered Hughes could neither silence Roosevelt nor undo the damage. Hughes talked about Wilson; Roosevelt talked about Roosevelt and Wilson; the Democrats talked about Roosevelt; but nobody talked about Hughes. The Democrats knew how to make the most out of this situation. Throughout the West, where peace sentiment was strong and women were voting in the Presidential election for the first time, the Wilson managers "hammered into all of the simple ones" the message that the election of Hughes meant war.[17] In Washington state the local Democratic candidates frightened mothers by exaggerating the casualty lists at Verdun and promising that a vote for Wilson would spare them this horror.[18] William Jennings Bryan confided to a fellow campaigner that " 'He kept us out of war' is our strongest slogan." [19]

Since most of the Western states affected by Democratic propaganda had a small electoral vote, the Republicans could still win by making a clean sweep of the Midwest, New England, and the Middle Atlantic states. Matters were well in hand throughout these normally Republican sections except in Ohio. Three weeks before the election, the secretary of the G.O.P. national committee found to his dismay that the Ohio Republicans had "infantile paralysis," [20] by which he meant that local candidates were working for themselves and not for Hughes. In addition, Governor Frank B. Willis was an exceptionally weak candidate whose campaign consisted of extolling the virtues of the flag, buttermilk, and horseshoes.[21] The election of 1916 was not one in which to run on a platform of nostalgia and rural bliss.

With the outcome so uncertain in Ohio, the Western states took on added importance to the Republicans in the closing days of the campaign. Yet neither Hughes nor his managers saw any reason to worry about the area when election night came, for the populous Eastern states voted overwhelmingly Republican. To be sure, little New Hampshire went to Wilson, as well as Ohio, the latter by the decisive margin of 89,000 votes. But the Republican trend east of the Missouri River was so strong that many newspapers announced the election of Hughes in their early-morning editions. Later in the day, no one felt so sure. Minnesota gave Hughes a scant 300-vote margin, but it was to be his last victory in the West. Even Kansas voted for Wilson. As time passed, state after state in the Rocky Mountain area and the Far West went to the Democrats by small but decisive margins.

At the end of election day, the country had thought it would have a Republican President. Twenty-four hours later nobody was certain who had won, but it appeared that California would decide the outcome. With returns from 47 states in, Wilson had 264 electoral votes and Hughes 254. Another night passed while election officials tabulated the votes from the widely scattered precincts in California. Finally, the results showed that Wilson had carried the state by a few thousand votes. The same trend showed up in the popular vote with 9,127,695 for Wilson to 8,533,507 for Hughes. The congressional elections demonstrated that Wilson was more popular than his party. The Democrats lost three seats in the Senate, to reduce their margin to 10, and they lost 14 House seats, which left them two short of an absolute majority and forced them to negotiate with a handful of Independents to re-elect Champ Clark as speaker. Hughes ran behind Republican state tickets in 26 of the 36 states contested by the party, although cries of treachery were confined to California, where Johnson won a Senate seat by a large majority.

IV

After election it became apparent that Wilson intended to assume world leadership with the approval of the country. He had already appropriated the G.O.P. issue of preparedness and had moved into the League To Enforce the Peace in May 1916, a movement for international organization sponsored by prominent Republicans. Next, he offered to act as peacemaker in the war, and when his offer was rejected, he then formulated his war aims. On January 22, 1917, he declared to the Senate that the participation of the United States in postwar arrangements was inevitable. Urging "peace without victory," the President endorsed a League of Nations to guarantee a peace based on freedom of the seas, equality of rights for all nations, and universal acceptance of self-government. Borah and Cummins promptly denounced the League proposal as "immoral and full of madness," but most Republicans felt the program was too vague to warrant a public attack. Their confusion mounted when on February 1 the Germans announced the renewal of unrestricted submarine warfare. Earlier policy statements by Wilson had indicated that such a violation of neutral rights would be a cause for war, but, mindful of the peace vote in the recent election, he proposed a policy of armed neutrality. Although it is unlikely that the President had any faith in armed neutrality, he wanted to mark time until the Germans made a direct attack on American lives or property. By waiting for the enemy to make the first move, he expected the voters to acquiesce in the abandonment of a peace policy.

The Republicans in Congress intended to filibuster the appropriation bills to death to force the President to call a special session of the new Congress. Luckily they were spared the responsibility for this maneuver by a bipartisan group of twelve senators who talked to death Wilson's request for authority to arm merchant ships. Wilson went ahead without Congress and armed the ships under an eighteenth-century law, but the controversy was overshadowed in March by incidents on the high seas. An intercepted dispatch from German Foreign Secretary Alfred Zimmerman to Germany's ambassador in Mexico also helped to stir up sentiment for a war declaration. The offending document offered Mexico a military alliance. Activation of the proposal was made contingent on the outbreak of war between the United States and Germany; but Wilson, without much effort, convinced people that a treacherous plot had been uncovered. Finally, the intensified German submarine campaign brought Wilson to a decision for war. On April 2 he asked Congress for a declaration of war.

Only a handful in Congress contended that the United States was unjustified in going to war. For the most part they complained about Wilson's previous policy of enforcing neutral rights against Germany but not against Great Britain; a partial neutrality in their view was no neutrality at all. Most of the dissidents also argued that the international bankers posed a greater threat to democracy than the German militarists. The opposition cut across party lines, coming mainly from the left wing of the Progressive movement, which thought war would interrupt social reform at home. Although La Follette and Norris of Nebraska, who moved to the Senate in 1913, were most active in opposition, they talked themselves out in four days, whereupon Congress ratified the war resolution by a large bipartisan majority.

There was far more agreement about the desirability of going to war than about the cloudy goals enunciated by the President, but few took issue with him at the time. Most members of Congress undoubtedly concurred with the part of Wilson's message which held out the hope that the United States could resume her traditional aloofness once the German militarists had been destroyed. A smaller group subscribed to the notion that America would have to assume long-term responsibilities for stabilizing the postwar world. The size of the second group was a matter of conjecture and would ultimately depend on the character and extent of the responsibilities that Wilson wanted America to take. His vagueness about war aims postponed trouble for the Republicans as well, for they were badly divided. Borah spoke for the Republican isolationists when he tartly warned that he was not voting for war to support a crusade, but to defend American soil. Republicans with a broader outlook did not bother to dispute Borah in April 1917. The statements of Roosevelt and Lodge during the previous decade nevertheless indicated that their wing of the party took a more comprehensive view of America's role in the postwar world. What they had in mind was a new international order ruled by the English-speaking people, with help from the French. They were fully prepared for America to redraw the map of Europe in pursuit of this objective. They also favored a postwar international organization to uphold the settlement. Yet the sort of League they envisioned was not an organization including all states, but a permanent alliance of the "good" powers to keep the "bad" ones in their place.[22] Lodge had been thinking along the lines of a league of victor powers when he had joined the League To Enforce Peace in 1916.[23] At that time he had expressed apprehension that Taft and other Republicans would try to mobilize the organization behind a plan for a universal league.

It is well to bear this distinction in mind in view of subsequent charges that Lodge and Roosevelt opposed a universal League out of sheer animus to Wilson. As early as 1916, both men knew in a general way what they favored, while Wilson did not. In July 1918 the President still was uncertain about the type of League he preferred. Indeed, his alter ego, Colonel House, confided to his diary in distress that the President's ideas on other aspects of the peace settlement had not taken concrete form on the eve of victory.[24] Few Republicans would have been likely to consider in objective fashion any peace program presented by Wilson. Throughout the war, though, the President dealt in moral platitudes to which no patriotic Republican could take exception. The opposition could only find its voice when Wilson reduced his platitudes to a program.

Although the President was vague about war aims in 1917, he prosecuted the war from the outset like a man who knew what he was fighting for. Wilson's firmness meant little to leading Democrats in Congress, who opposed much of his legislation mobilizing manpower and material resources. Ranking Republicans on the military affairs and agricultural committees repeatedly came to his rescue by steering critical measures through bottlenecks, but they received little gratitude or recognition for their services.[25] The bulk of the G.O.P. also supported passage of the Espionage and Sedition Acts, which concentrated tremendous power in the hands of the President. Most Republicans in Congress were so strongly nationalistic that they applauded executive harassment of anti-war groups. They had second thoughts, however, when it became apparent that the Administration regarded as unpatriotic all critics including members of the opposition who demanded more energetic prosecution of the war. Whatever the intentions of the President, his subordinates used the Committee on Public Information and other government agencies to spread the doctrine that opposition to the Administration was opposition to the war. Fearful of being tagged as obstructionists, the bulk of the Republicans fell into a dismal routine: they complained that legislation enlarging Presidential powers was unconstitutional and then voted for it. Midway through the war they mounted a counteroffensive by trying to force the creation of a supercabinet along the lines of the Committee on the Conduct of the War which had harassed Lincoln. The maneuver backfired, and Wilson used the agitation to extract from Congress the Overman Act, conferring on him virtually dictatorial powers over mobilization. The undercover warfare intensified bitterness on both sides. The Republicans were furious over the fact that the President used their votes, cast aspersions on their patriotism, and managed the war on a narrow partisan basis. Wilson got just as angry at criticism from the Republicans, and assumed that all of it was politically motivated. There was some truth in his complaints as well as in those of the Republican opposition.

The accumulated frustration of both sides boiled over in a Wisconsin by-election held in April 1918 to replace Democratic Senator Paul O. Husted. The President was in a vindictive mood and wrote a letter casting unjustified doubt on the loyalty of the Republican candidate, Congressman Irvine Lenroot. He then sent Vice President Thomas R. Marshall to Wisconsin for a series of campaign speeches built around the theme that the voters ought to spurn partisanship by electing a Democratic senator. Few dared to criticize the tactics of the Administration openly, but the private statements of Wisconsin Republicans were unprintable. Apparently the voters also thought the Administration had been unfair, because they gave Lenroot a plurality of 15,000 over Joseph K. Davis, his Democratic opponent. The real surprise was provided by Victor Berger, an anti-war Socialist candidate who got nearly 25 per cent of the total vote. The Wisconsin election was a twofold rebuke to the Administration for questioning the loyalty of Republicans and for attempting to suppress the free speech of minority groups. The lesson was not lost on Wilson, who called for a moratorium on politics until the end of the war.

This remarkable announcement in mid-May only served to drive the preparations for the 1918 elections underground. From an organizational standpoint the Republicans were in better shape than at any time since 1908. The tactics of the Democrats had driven the Progressive Republicans and the stand-patters to make common cause, despite their differing attitudes toward taxes on war profits and other issues.[26] The rapprochement in Congress was accompanied early in 1918 by the selection of Will H. Hays, an able conciliator, as national chairman. In 1916, Hays as Indiana state chairman had presided over the successful reunion of the Bull Moosers and the regulars. He quickly gained the confidence of all Republican factions,[27] and his platform for the Indiana state convention in May 1918 served as a model in the impending campaign. The platform stressed the loyal support of the Republicans for the war and deplored the partisan politics of the Administration. Not to be outdone, the Indiana Democrats allowed Wilson to write the section of their platform dealing with national issues some three weeks later.[28] Neither Indiana platform took a stand on specific issues arising out of the conduct of the war, but subsequent G.O.P. state platforms, particularly in the Midwest, charged the Democrats with administering prices for the benefit of the South. Congressional candidates from wheat- and wool-growing areas hammered away at Wilson for putting price ceilings on both commodities while allowing cotton prices to soar. The Republicans got considerable mileage out of this charge, exploiting sectional discontent over the alleged inequality in war burdens and aroused latent Yankee resentment over the conspicuous role of Southerners in the management of the war.[29]

The Democrats retaliated with a muted version of the formula which they had used in the Wisconsin election. A pamphlet issued by the national committee proclaimed that the election of a Republican Congress "would be a source of comfort to the Kaiser and his cohorts," while the slogan of the Democratic senatorial candidate in Maine was "Beat the Huns and the Governor." [30] Hays regarded such tactics as a breach in the truce. Both he and Lodge hoped that Wilson would come out in the open and start talking politics, but they were afraid to make a counterattack as long as the chief Democrat remained quiet.[31] The ominous silence of the voters encouraged hesitancy. Nobody knew whether they were apathetic or fearful of expressing their real views; a flu epidemic added to the problem of testing opinion by keeping political rallies to a minimum.[32]

The cautious sparring of Democrats and Republicans might have continued until election day but for the sudden collapse of the Germans. When they sued for an armistice at the end of September, the issue of war aims was injected into the campaign. This development was unfortunate for Wilson because he had not yet clarified his war aims. The closest he had come to an authoritative statement was in the Fourteen Points of January 8, 1918. This document displayed a benevolent spirit toward victors and vanquished alike; proposed a revision of boundaries that would recognize the aspirations of national minorities for self-government; and again endorsed the League of Nations. Neither the Republican isolationists nor the Rooseveltians had liked the Fourteen Points when they were issued. The isolationists viewed with horror the prospect of America redrawing European boundaries, while the Lodge-Roosevelt wing of the party regarded the Fourteen Points as nothing more than Administration propaganda.[33] Convinced that Wilson was "a dexterous juggler with words" who says "something and means anything," the Rooseveltians did not want to be trapped into a premature statement. They also recognized that the Fourteen Points was a unilateral assertion and did not bind any of the warring powers. The Germans changed the situation, however, when they sought an armistice on the basis of the Fourteen Points. Even so, most Republican candidates were as unhappy about the injection of war aims into the campaign as the President and kept quiet. But Roosevelt was not a candidate and nothing could keep him quiet. He telegraphed Republican senators to oppose a soft peace based on the Fourteen Points and to insist on unconditional surrender. Behaving more cautiously than usual, Roosevelt took the patriotic line that he was helping Wilson resist the temptation to be easy on the Germans. Privately he bristled about the President, characterizing him as a "silly doctrinaire at times, and a cold-blooded politician always." [34]

Wilson had every incentive to ignore Roosevelt and to accept Republican professions of patriotic support at face value. If the Republicans won control of Congress on this modest platform they would not be in a position to claim that the voters had repudiated the President. But Wilson took the momentous step of appealing for a Democratic Congress on October 24. Besides breaking his own promise to adjourn politics for the duration, the President invited Republican obstruction by asserting that Europe would regard a G.O.P. victory as a rejection of his leadership.

The Republicans were elated by Wilson's appeal and contrasted the partisan behavior of the President with their own patriotic self-restraint. Citing the congressional votes on war measures as evidence that they had supported Wilson better than the Democrats, they charged the President wanted to be a dictator. The voters did not react very decisively in November. Although both houses went Republican, the Senate did so by the bare margin of 49 to 47. There would have been little justification for the Republicans to claim a mandate if Wilson had not made his ill-advised election appeal. But they were now in a position to harass the Administration with a clear conscience. The armistice which occurred a week after the election destroyed the last reason for self-restraint on the part of Republicans, for they could no longer be considered disloyal if they opposed Wilson. Quite apart from the personal antagonism many Republicans felt toward the President, they considered themselves bound by party tradition to champion Congress against the executive. They were also certain of some Democratic support for this policy because after every war Congress seeks to cut down the swollen powers of the President.

The confusion about war aims provided Republicans with further opportunity to make trouble. Wilson had repeatedly told Americans that the defeat of Germany would end the threat to world peace, an assertion at variance with his insistence on a League of Nations to preserve world peace. Thus, the signing of the Armistice convinced many Americans that the nation's obligations to Europe had ended and that it could resume its normal activities without additional sacrifice. Not all of these people opposed a League, but they saw no need for establishing one quickly. When Congress reassembled in December, Republicans responded to this sentiment by demanding the immediate return of American soldiers, the prompt negotiation of a peace treaty, and the postponement of conversations about a League until the peace treaty had been completed. This policy was supported not only by isolationists who opposed having "An American army policing the world and quelling riots in all peoples' backyards," [35] but by Rooseveltians who favored a larger role for the United States in the postwar world.

Wilson chose to ignore completely the attitude of the opposition in Congress. He promptly announced that he would head the American delegation to the peace conference, and at the same time he refused to put prominent Republicans on the delegation. There was no constitutional reason to preclude the President from attending a peace conference; his decision merely meant that executive prerogative would be exercised in novel fashion since no previous President had gone abroad. This breach with precedent would not have attracted as much unfavorable comment if the President had included representative spokesmen of the opposition in the negotiations. Nobody expected him to take to Paris such bitter personal enemies as Lodge or Roosevelt nor such avowed isolationists as Borah or Johnson, but he might have worked with Taft, Root, or Hughes, all of whom had expressed approval of a League of Nations. Instead, he chose as Republican representatives two obscure officials—Henry White, a retired diplomat of the Roosevelt era, and General Tasker Bliss, who had been as politically inactive as most Republican army officers.

Having served notice that he intended to manage the peace as arbitrarily as he had managed the war, Wilson threw a fresh challenge to the Republicans by proclaiming that the creation of a League would be of prime importance at the peace conference. The best explanation for this extraordinary conduct is that Wilson expected to produce a peace treaty in a few weeks and submit it to the lame duck Senate, which would be under Democratic control until March 4, 1919. Once the President arrived in France, however, he discovered that European diplomats could not be hurried. They diverted him with the grand tour of western Europe, where he was enthusiastically received. As a result, the Paris conference did not begin until the end of January.

In the wake of Wilson's departure for Europe, Republican senators launched a counteroffensive. The excitable Lawrence Y. Sherman of Illinois introduced a resolution declaring the Presidency vacant; Johnson of California thundered at the President for withholding information about American troops in Russia; and the cagey Borah tested his isolationist sentiments on bar associations. The most ominous feature of the eruption was that some Democratic senators joined in. Gilbert M. Hitchcock of Nebraska, who was destined to be Wilson's floor leader, even introduced a resolution directing that eight senators be empowered to attend the conference at Paris. It seemed as if the high-handed tactics of Wilson were producing the kind of esprit de corps in Congress that had been fatal to Andrew Johnson half a century earlier.

The senators subsided on the eve of the Christmas holidays, and waited uneasily for results from the peace conference. Wilson made a number of speeches about the League in Europe but none of them were very enlightening. At Dover on Christmas he talked as if he favored a League of victor powers and four days later as if any League should be a universal one.[36] A further amplification proposing that the League have a tribunal for making and enforcing international decrees prompted wishful thinking on the part of some senators. Poindexter anticipated some sort of useless conciliation board; [37] and Lodge, with his customary contempt for Wilson, privately predicted on January 29 that the President would return "with a lot of general propositions resting on moral suasion" which he would call a great triumph.[38] Taft who had espoused a universal League from the beginning expressed fear that Wilson would not fight for one.[39]

Since the transactions of the peace conference were closely guarded, uncertainty about the arrangements for an international organization persisted until mid-February.[40] Then, for the final time, Wilson confounded his detractors by announcing that the Great Powers had accepted the principle of a League open to all states and that he was returning with a draft of its constitution. Anticipating some trouble with Congress, the President on the eve of his departure cabled dinner invitations to members of the foreign relations committees of both houses, and requested that his guests defer discussion of the League until he reached the United States. Wilson then added insult to injury by announcing that he would land at Boston, the home town of Lodge, to give a speech for the League. The reaction in the Senate was immediate and violent. Poindexter read off a list of organizations propagandizing for the League and announced that senators would not stifle their opinions until Wilson had yielded the floor. Borah made an eloquent denunciation of internationalism and called the proposed League a great triumph for British diplomacy. James A. Reed, a Democratic senator from Missouri, described the League as a sort of world octopus whose tentacles would reach into the local affairs of all states. Along with most members of the foreign relations committee, Lodge honored the President's request for silence until after the Thursday dinner. But he expressed his frustration to Governor Calvin Coolidge of Massachusetts, who had congratulated him for keeping still, with the vow "to speak Friday if I live that long." Confiding to a friend that he would speak about Wilson "with entire civility," Lodge grimly added: "Others . . . are of course free to say what they really think. It will have to come to that sooner or later." [41]

The atmosphere at the White House dinner on February 26 was strained. Although the President appeared to be exceedingly nervous, he tried to be patient and answered questions for more than three hours. His performance was wasted on his critics. Lodge observed privately that he "came away as wise about the League of Nations" as he had been before.[42] Frank B. Brandegee of Connecticut evaluated the session with the President for reporters by saying, "I feel as if I had been wandering with Alice in Wonderland and had tea with the Mad Hatter."

When the senators left the White House that night, they shed the last vestige of self-restraint. Republicans consumed the last week of the short session denouncing the League with a passion reminiscent of the Reconstruction era. Tangled in his own rhetoric, the eccentric Sherman called it "a nameless thing to sit in star chamber judgment" and "embargo our commerce, close our exchanges, leave our merchandise rotting at the piers, shut the Isthmian canal . . . and dispatch our men to every quarter of the globe. . . ." Lodge dryly reminded the Senate that the universal desire for peace transcended party lines, and launched into a scorching analysis of the League's shortcomings. Then, just before midnight on March 3, he interrupted debate to ask unanimous consent for a resolution rejecting the current version of the League of Nations. When the Democrats objected, Lodge read into the record the names of 39 senators and senators-elect who would have voted against the existing version of the Covenant if given a chance. After demonstrating by the so-called Round

Robin Resolution that he commanded more votes than the necessary one-third to defeat the League, Lodge joined Sherman in filibustering the appropriations bills to death.

In the frenzy of the moment, many senators had gone further than they intended, but there was some evidence that the country had been swept by a gust of anti-Wilson feeling. Borah's brother wanted the League rejected so that Wilson would not "have the satisfaction of putting it over as he does everything else." [43] Taft heard from Pennsylvania that conscientious citizens were opposing the League "because of their hatred of Wilson," and from Rhode Island that the state would not support anything "if it is remotely connected" with the President.[44] Others frankly admitted that their attitude was partly a product of political fears. The isolationist Beveridge feared that establishment of a League would be hailed as the greatest achievement in history,[45] while Warren of Wyoming suspected that the President was pushing it to obtain a third term.[46] Warren's suspicion was uncharitable, but members of Wilson's inner circle shared it.[47]

These manifestations of political antagonism did not cause Wilson to moderate his tone. Within twenty-four hours of the Round Robin Resolution he defiantly lashed out at his tormentors. Speaking from the same platform as Taft, he challenged them to do their worst; "when the treaty comes back," he asserted, "gentlemen on this side will find the Covenant not only in it, but so many threads of the Treaty tied to the Covenant that you cannot dissect the Covenant from the Treaty without destroying the vital structure." Behind this boast was Wilson's assumption that the Republicans would not dare reject the entire settlement for the sake of eliminating objectionable clauses from the Covenant. Three months of adulation by the masses of Europe had clouded the President's judgment of political reality at home.

Once Congress adjourned, Republican politicians experienced misgivings, because the League seemed to be more popular than Wilson. Borah heard from an Idaho supporter that he ought to find some way to make the League acceptable rather than "do the unpopular thing" and vote against it.[48] Johnson of California had been temporarily frightened into silence by pro-League letters from civic clubs, labor unions, and councils of defense in February,[49] and when he finally came out against the League he received letters from religious people calling him "every name on the calendar." [50] A poll of newspaper opinion in early April indicated that editors favored the League by a margin of nearly 4 to 1, although many were uncommitted.[51] In addition, thirty-two state legislatures endorsed an international organization of some kind. The principal source of the League's popularity was a general feeling that it would provide added insurance against war.[52] Businessmen thought it would promote international trade, while taxpayers thought it would reduce costly armament burdens.

A deceptive calm settled over Washington after the close of the lame duck session. At a press conference in mid-April Lodge left the impression that the League would ultimately be accepted. Some observers predicted only five negative votes against a Treaty with the League, and few expected more than fifteen.[53] Meanwhile, Wilson was forced to call Congress back into session on May 17 in order to pass appropriation measures which would give him money to run the government. Just a few days before, on April 29, the Paris conference had completed and approved the final draft of the League Covenant. Lodge reacted immediately by urging all Republican senators to refrain from comment on the amended Covenant until after a party conference.

It was evident that Lodge, in his dual role of chairman of the Republican conference and chairman of the Senate foreign relations committee was seizing control of the Republican Senate oligarchy. His ensuing struggle with Wilson invites comparison with the earlier conflict between Thaddeus Stevens and Andrew Johnson. In both cases, the political stakes were high, and in both cases stubborn Presidents invited disaster by appealing to the people over the head of Congress. Their kindred responses were motivated by egotism and by the curious Jacksonian creed that the President knows the real aspirations of the voters better than the voters themselves. On both occasions, Congress answered by championing the legislature over the executive. The smallness of the G.O.P. majority in 1919 promoted self-discipline, which Lodge also fostered through his enormous power as chairman of the Republican conference in the Senate. For a time it appeared Roosevelt would attempt to seize leadership in the struggle against Wilson, but he died suddenly on January 2, 1919.

Although Lodge never found occasion to call Wilson a traitor, he stalked his opponent as relentlessly as Stevens had pursued Johnson. There is no single explanation of the antagonism between the two men. Both were extremely self-confident and violently partisan, and in addition had a common background as scholars in politics.[54]

Friction had first developed in 1914 when Wilson intruded on Lodge's special preserve of foreign relations. The Massachusetts senator reacted all the more negatively because he had waited over a decade to become the ranking Republican on the Senate foreign relations committee and reached his goal just as the Democrats returned to power. Then for nearly six years, Lodge had watched helplessly while Wilson held the stage. In the process, the President had transformed himself from an apostle of peace into a military crusader; he had denounced imperialism in Latin America and sent troops to Haiti; and he had self-righteously insisted that American capital be withdrawn from the international railroad consortium in Manchuria, only to revive the same policy in 1917. Never a charitable observer of his rival, Lodge came to live for the day when Wilson would "be found out" [55] and when the Republicans could promote exposure with safety. The pursuit of this objective was simplified for Lodge by the belief that his own vindication, his party's triumph, and the welfare of the country were identical.

Towering egos prevented both men from attracting either affection or personal loyalty. Both were cold, calculating, and contemptuous of most of their followers. Of the two, Lodge was the better politician. He understood the importance of organization, whereas Wilson nursed the absurd belief that a program could be carried by oratory alone.[56] Adversity had also taught Lodge a patience that was conspicuously lacking in his opponent. He likewise possessed a reverence for the Senate which contrasted sharply with Wilson's low and poorly concealed opinion of the Upper House. The most important factor working in Lodge's favor was the willingness of senior members in the new G.O.P. oligarchy to accept his lead in the formulation of foreign policy. Warren cared little about anything but sheep, reclamation projects, and the maintenance of army posts in his native Wyoming. As successor to Cameron and Quay, Penrose showed a flair for political manipulation and interest in securing protective tariffs for Pennsylvania manufacturers. A huge, shapeless man who could rest a glass upright on the folds of his stomach, Penrose had all of the requisite qualities for party leadership except curiosity about national affairs. Like Penrose, Reed Smoot of Utah displayed the same indifference as his colleague to issues that did not affect his native state. The pro-League attitude of the Mormon hierarchy in Utah made Smoot uncomfortable from time to time, but he solved the problem by saying little on the subject and voting with Lodge.

James Eli Watson and Harry S. New of Indiana, Frank B. Brandegee of Connecticut, and Charles Curtis of Kansas, the junior members of the oligarchy, had a religious devotion to the Republican party and would have followed any leadership that seemed likely to promote victory in 1920. New and Brandegee came the closest to having an articulate conservative philosophy. They had neither flirted with Progressivism nor allowed the exposures of the muckrakers to destroy their reverence for businessmen. Moreover, their militant economic nationalism made them suspicious of any entanglements abroad. Watson and Curtis had cultivated the folksy manner of the Midwest so successfully that it was almost second nature to them. Where the glacial Lodge tended to affront waverers with his air of superiority, Watson and Curtis overpowered them with good fellowship.

Despite the cohesiveness of the Senate oligarchy, Lodge was dependent on the co-operation of the party's mavericks to organize the Senate. Ordinarily La Follette would have given him trouble, but the Wisconsin Progressive had lived under the threat of expulsion from the Senate for over a year because of an allegedly disloyal speech at St. Paul, and so Lodge secured his co-operation by restoring him to good party standing. Borah was more of a problem. From the day he took his seat in 1907, Borah had imagined that defiance of party leaders was Progressivism. Since Borah opposed all entanglements abroad, Lodge expected the Idaho senator to accept party discipline. Indeed, Lodge thought he had worked out an agreement whereby Borah would fight the Covenant in his own way, but would vote for changes in it sponsored by the party's leadership.[57] When the session began, however, the erratic Borah threatened to vote with the Democrats and allow them to organize the Senate unless Warren and Penrose were barred from committee chairmanships.[58] Eventually Borah was persuaded to call off his war on the two stand-patters after issuing a futile declaration that he would never return to "old principles and systems of taxation." [59] Nevertheless, he continued to embarrass Lodge throughout the session.

Even after Republican organization of the Senate was assured, Lodge had to struggle for control of his own foreign relations committee, because the ranking Republican, Porter J. McCumber of North Dakota, favored Wilson's League. With such a small majority, the Republicans were only entitled to a 9 to 8 ratio on the foreign relations committee, in which case McCumber would have held the deciding vote. Lodge neutralized McCumber, however, by persuading the Senate to authorize a 10 to 7 ratio and filling the four Republican vacancies with outspoken foes of the League.

Outspoken as he was in opposition to Wilson's League, Lodge did not express open hostility to American participation in an international organization at any time during the long parliamentary battle. On the contrary, he twice voted for the League with reservations which he had helped to devise. His conduct seems all the more perplexing in view of the fact that he displayed a consistently critical attitude toward the League. He secretly encouraged others to attack the Covenant in an indiscriminate way that he would not employ himself, and then he disowned their position.[60] The most plausible explanation of Lodge's conduct is that Lodge believed outright opposition to the League would hurt the Republican party and subordinated his personal feelings to the welfare of the party. Although he apparently operated on this assumption, Lodge nevertheless hoped that a savage exposure of the flaws in Wilson's League would bring the public to the point where it would tolerate Republican opposition to any League. Lodge gave a guarded account of his strategy:

> The situation . . . must be treated with great care. I have no doubt that a large majority of people are naturally fascinated by the idea of the eternal preservation of the world's peace . . . They are told that is what this League means. They have not examined it; they have not begun to think about it. . . . I think the second thought is going to be with us, but the first thought is probably against us. Therefore we must proceed with caution. . . . I shall not oppose a blank negative to any League. I shall discuss the one before us.[61]

Lodge marked time between the beginning of the session and July 10, when Wilson returned from Paris with the completed treaty. The President had made changes in Paris to meet some of the most violent objections to the League. A section had been added authorizing members to withdraw after two years, while new sections exempted tariffs, immigration, and regional agreements like the Monroe Doctrine from League jurisdiction. Wilson had stood firm, however, on the most controversial provision of all, Article X, which he called "the heart of the Covenant." Article X pledged members to preserve the territorial integrity of fellow members and authorized the League Council to specify how members should meet their responsibilities in case of aggression. Other articles indicated that the League Council might order economic sanctions against aggressors and in extreme cases even military action, but the details were vague. At all events, Article X seemed to qualify the sovereignty of member states by obliging them to honor a League command specifying retaliatory measures against aggression. Alarmists raised the spectre of

American troops being ordered all over the world to quell petty boundary disputes. This interpretation of Article X was fanciful, because all great powers, including the United States, had seats on the Council and any one of them, if it so desired, could block League action on a particular dispute. Such a safeguard meant little to senators who distrusted Wilson and anybody that he would have been likely to appoint as American representative on the Council. Indeed, past experience indicated that the American Senate would not approve Article X or any substitute provision reducing its control over foreign policy.

The initial reaction of Republican senators to the revised Covenant was compounded of indignation and panic. If they had dared they would have torn "the Covenant to pieces," but "the jelly legs" were too uncertain of public opinion to take a public stand.[62] Only a dozen Republican isolationists plus Reed of Missouri took an uncompromising position against the League from beginning to end. Under the leadership of the able but indolent Knox of Pennsylvania, they made an abortive effort to separate the League Covenant from the peace treaty while the Paris conference was in session. Thereafter they supported all amendments and reservations for the purpose of making the League as unworkable as possible. The most effective of the irreconcilables were Borah and Johnson, whose talents were complementary. Borah excelled as an orator and Johnson as a fighter. In fact, one observer who watched Johnson perform during the League controversy concluded that "guts" was the only quality he valued "unconditionally." [63] The irreconcilables would have been more influential if their hysterical members had remained silent. Nevertheless, their persistent attacks made some impression, because public enthusiasm for the League waned in the summer of 1919.

News from Paris about the territorial settlement also had an adverse effect on many Americans because it appeared as if the League would be asked to enforce cynical bargains rather than idealistic terms. Citizens of German ancestry objected to the harsh terms of the treaty, especially since they seemed to be a flagrant betrayal of the Fourteen Points. Italian-Americans were annoyed at Wilson's role in thwarting the territorial ambitions of Rome in the Adriatic. Latent anti-Japanese feeling revived because the conference had awarded Shantung to Japan. The volatile Irish-Americans were stirred up because the peacemakers had ignored Ireland's claim for independence. Returning soldiers brought stories that the Europeans did not like Americans, which made the nation feel that the League would only entangle the United States in insoluble quarrels of ungrateful people.[64]

A simultaneous outbreak of strikes, unemployment, and other reconversion problems were also blamed on the League. Republicans indignantly insisted that Wilson had wrecked the economy by concentrating his attention on international organization.[65] The combined efforts of all of these groups generated a vigorous assault on the League. Hearst contributed his extensive newspaper chain to the cause. Two millionaire Pittsburgh industrialists, Henry Frick and Andrew W. Mellon, financed a League for the Preservation of American Independence, while Wilson's numerous personal enemies swelled the chorus of denunciation.

Lodge felt that further delay would only increase dissatisfaction with the treaty. When Wilson delivered the peace treaties to the Senate on July 11, the day after his return from Paris, Lodge held leisurely hearings before the foreign relations committee. Two weeks were spent in reading the entire treaty out loud, and an additional month and a half in public hearings. Critics were encouraged to state their objections in detail. Nevertheless, Lodge professed to regard the pace of the proceedings as rapid. He rejected with a shade of indignation a suggestion from Beveridge that the committee ought to stall and he complained to a friend that the "miserable League" was delaying peace.[66] From time to time, Lodge interrupted the hearings to harass Wilson for withholding information. The President had foolishly pocketed both a defensive treaty of alliance with France and the Polish minorities treaty on the theory that both would complicate his political position. Lodge had read the draft of both agreements in the Paris newspapers, however, and forced the President to submit them to the Senate on July 29. Isolationists insisted that the President release the records of the Paris conference and Wilson countered by inviting the foreign relations committee to meet with him on August 19. The three-hour session hardened the mutual mistrust of the participants, for Borah and Johnson caught the President in a transparent lie when he pleaded ignorance of the existence of the secret treaties before the armistice. They then confided to the press that their worst fears about immoral territorial bargains had been realized.

V

The public harassment of Wilson by the opposition in August and September concealed a much more important struggle going on behind the scenes. Lodge was trying to frame changes in the Covenant that would be acceptable to 49 Republican senators. He controlled 40 votes for purposes of weakening the Covenant, although 12 irreconcilables intended to vote against the final draft in any case. His real trouble came from nine or ten other Republicans who favored changes in the League Covenant by reservations rather than amendments. Behind this preference for reservations was a sympathetic attitude toward the League, since amendments required the concurrence of signatory powers and reservations did not. According to most legal experts, a state adopting reservations announced how it would interpret a specific provision of the League Covenant and presumably that interpretation stood if it was not challenged. Dubbed "mild reservationists" because they wanted modest changes in the Covenant, this group of Republicans held the balance of power in the Senate. The only way Lodge could bypass them was to use his 40 votes to kill the League altogether, and he did not want the responsibility for such a policy. What followed was a wily battle over the phraseology of reservations between Lodge and Taft, who now assumed the leadership of the pro-League Republicans. Taft knew that some reservations were necessary, if only to save the faces of senators who had signed the Round Robin, but he sought to keep the changes to a minimum. Lodge, with the assistance of Root, worked just as hard to draft restrictions that would pull the ten mild reservationists further than they intended to go.

Although Taft attempted to weld the mild reservationists into a cohesive unit for bargaining purposes, he found the job a discouraging one. Only McCumber, the two Minnesota senators, and Le Baron Colt of Rhode Island were enthusiastic about the League, and Taft discovered that Frank B. Kellogg of Minnesota would not submit to any kind of discipline. Nervous and testy under the best of circumstances, Kellogg lost his temper repeatedly in the strategy sessions of the mild reservationists. Long before the voting began, he had become so resentful of pressure that he was unwilling to discuss the League. The other six presented Taft with a different kind of problem. Selden Spencer of Missouri was interested in nothing but a straddle acceptable to his constituents. He changed his mind every time he read his mail, and by the admission of his own colleagues did not know a mild reservation from a piece of cheese.[67] Arthur Capper of Kansas had already begun to replace William Allen White as the confused but authentic voice of Midwestern agrarians and despite his good intentions was unreliable. Getting agreement from such a group of chameleons became harder and harder for Taft as Lodge intensified the pressure on them.

Taft's job might have been easier if he had received wholehearted co-operation from the White House. Any assistance from mild reservationists was to Wilson's advantage because, with the help of the Democrats, they could strike out amendments and severe reservations when Lodge reported the Treaty to the floor. The President, however, was out of touch with reality. He imagined that pressure from their constituents would force the mild reservationists to remove restrictions from the Covenant without any encouragement on his part. He also supposed that once a majority had taken this step, enough wobblers would desert Lodge to ratify the Treaty in its original form. So the most Wilson agreed to do was hold personal interviews in August with some of the mild reservationists. These negotiations did not have much practical effect. The President talked well about generalities but could not explain satisfactorily the intricate details of the Covenant that caused misgivings. He had a particularly bad experience with Le Baron Colt who disliked abstractions and could not understand what the President meant by a "moral obligation" under Article X.[68]

Even so, the President might have gotten the Covenant with superficial changes if he had continued negotiations and avoided inflammatory statements. This line of conduct required more self-restraint than Wilson possessed. He misconstrued the irresolution of doubtful senators and suspected them of bad faith, an attitude which Lodge encouraged by convincing a couple of duller ones that his own reservations were "mild." [69] Moreover, Wilson had begun to tire of the constant sniping by the irreconcilables and was determined to talk back. On September 3 he embarked on a transcontinental tour in which he planned to take his case to the country. His decision had the worst possible effect on the waverers, who thought he was more interested in promoting his third-term aspirations than seeking a constructive solution to the deadlock.[70] Wilson compounded his error with a careless statement in Salt Lake City, lumping the mild reservationists with the rest of the Republicans and questioning their good faith. He really seemed bent on destroying himself because he insisted that there was no difference between amendments and reservations.[71] Since the position of the mild reservationists was predicated on this distinction, they lost heart and ceased to act as a group.[72]

In seeking to appeal to the people, over the heads of senators, Wilson clearly lost ground in the Senate. Whether the tour improved his standing at the grass roots is uncertain. His speeches were rambling, repetitious, and extravagant in their claims for the League, but they drew large crowds and carried tremendous emotional appeal.[73] Political observers disagreed about the significance of the crowds, especially after a Republican "truth squad" had attracted crowds of comparable size as it trailed the President across the country. Obviously some people who favored the League were beginning to suffer from overexposure to Wilson; but others were affronted by the dour, bellicose Johnson who led the truth squad.

Midway through Wilson's trip, Lodge reported the Treaty to the floor with forty-five amendments and four reservations. The tone of his document was ugly, sarcastic, and partisan, and both the Treaty and the Covenant were loaded down with every conceivable change that Lodge thought public opinion would tolerate. His frame of mind was just as disagreeable as his report. Not only Wilson, but the irreconcilables and the trimmers in his own party as well, felt his wrath. He was furious with Johnson and Borah for barnstorming about the country and making wild statements that Wilson might be able to turn against them. He felt just as bitter toward the "jelly legs" who would not follow his directions and send the Treaty back to Paris.[74] Lodge had even managed to work himself into a condition where he believed that Wilson wanted a deadlock to justify a third term.[75]

The atmosphere, which was murky and menacing for both parties, cleared suddenly on September 25 when Wilson collapsed following a speech at Pueblo, Colorado. He had already overtaxed his physical powers at the Paris peace conference, and the long speaking tour in behalf of the League brought him to the breaking point. He was rushed back to Washington and the fourth day after his return suffered a stroke which paralyzed the left side of his body and incapacitated him for six months.

Leadership of the Democratic forces devolved on Gilbert M. Hitchcock of Nebraska, the ranking minority member of the foreign relations committee. No choice could have been more unfortunate. Hitchcock both shared and had helped to promote Wilson's delusion that the Covenant could be passed without reservations. How Hitchcock could continue to hold this view after circulating in the corridors and cloakrooms of the Senate is something of a mystery. Nevertheless, Hitchcock had certain factors working in his favor if he was willing to be realistic. Many of the mild reservationists were fearful that the voters would regard Wilson as a martyr to a great cause, and so they decided to oppose amendments which would force the resubmission of the Covenant to the Paris Conference. What the mild reservationists would not do was accept the League without change. Specifically, they wanted reservations attached to Article X and other articles of the Covenant which removed any restrictions on national sovereignty or the prerogatives of the Senate. Some of their proposed reservations were reasonable and others were designed to needle the President. The reasonable ones proceeded from the premise that the United States ought not to assume obligations she had no intention of fulfilling. Clearly America would never accept a League order to impose economic sanctions against another power or make war on it without first securing an affirmative vote from Congress. Even Taft felt that clarifying reservations on these points were justified, particularly if they facilitated ratification of the Treaty.

It is unlikely that Hitchcock pressed the White House to accept changes or that such advice would have been welcome. Wilson was too ill to transact business, but nobody knows whether he would have subsequently repudiated Hitchcock if the latter had gone ahead on his own. In any case, Hitchcock passed up his opportunity to bargain with the mild reservationists in a meaningful way. Lodge, meanwhile, was having difficulties of his own because in October a Democratic-Republican coalition voted down every one of his forty-five amendments that would have sent the Treaty back to Paris. All he could do was rewrite some of his amendments as reservations and consolidate his handiwork into a list of fourteen. Clearly Lodge had failed in his effort to delay American entrance into the League. On the other hand, some of his reservations had been formulated in the hope that Wilson would do the job for him and this expectation proved to be justified.

Shortly before the critical roll calls on November 17, Democratic senators received instructions from the sick room that the League with reservations was to be opposed. The first vote was taken on the League with the fourteen Lodge reservations, which the Democrats and the irreconcilables defeated by 55 to 39, and 51 to 41. Next the Senate voted on the Treaty without reservations, and, after both the Democrats and irreconcilables changed sides, the Treaty was defeated, 53 to 38. Hitchcock would have liked another roll call on the procedural reservations drafted by Wilson months earlier, but Lodge blocked the maneuver and adjourned the Senate.

When the long session began in December 1919, there was every evidence that Lodge wanted to keep the League in mothballs. He promptly brought forward the Knox Resolution, which proposed to drop the League from the Treaty and to establish peace with Germany by a simple majority of both Houses. He also confided to a friend that the passage of the Knox Resolution would "win the fight in . . . the best possible way." [76] But trouble developed almost immediately. The Republican House majority was balky and resentful because it had hitherto been excluded from discussion of the treaty.[77] Moreover, the evening of December 21, Lodge received the unwelcome news from Charles McNary of Oregon that six mild reservationists were against the Knox Resolution and wanted the resumption of negotiations with the Democrats on the League.[78] This development killed all prospects of the Knox Resolution's clearing the closely divided Senate.

It quickly became apparent that the handful of mild reservationists represented public opinion better than either Lodge or Wilson. A minority of the electorate had grown weary of the controversy and did not care what happened.[79] Most Americans, however, saw little difference between the Lodge and Wilson positions and thought each side should give enough ground to ratify the Covenant.[80] National chairman Will Hays received emphatic warnings from Republican national committeemen in Rhode Island and West Virginia that many people resented the negative record of the party and thought the League had been used as a political football.[81] Such prominent figures as Hoover, Taft, Bryan, House, and Cardinal Gibbons urged compromise on Wilson. The drive for compromise gained additional momentum as the result of semi-official assurances from the British and French that they were willing to accept American membership on the basis of the reservations.

Lodge could not afford to resist the pressure for the Lodge reservations, but Wilson was harder to reach because his wife and physician kept him in almost complete isolation. The President had a tendency to ignore advice even when it was available, and his current dreams of a third term on the League issue bore little relation to reality. Just how much of his mind had been affected by the stroke was uncertain, but he became abnormally suspicious of his associates and broke successively with those who smuggled compromise suggestions into the sick room.[82] Despite the hostile attitude of the President, negotiations between Hitchcock and Lodge were renewed in mid-January after spokesmen for twenty-six organizations representing twenty to thirty million people clamored for action.[83]

Lodge gave some ground, but the old dispute over Article X, plus Borah's threat to bolt the party, prevented a meeting of minds. Even so, the Lodge reservations claimed few prerogatives for America that other League members did not intend to exercise as a matter of course. A final vote was set for March 17, 1920; and despite pleas to the President to let the Senate vote its own way, he wrote a second letter to Hitchcock demanding that the Democrats stand firm. Only four had deserted Wilson in November, but with an election in the offing nearly all the Northern Democrats broke ranks. Thus, the final count for ratification with the Lodge reservations was 49 to 35, or seven less than the necessary two-thirds. Enough Southern Democrats had voted with the irreconcilables to thwart the will of the majority. Many Democrats believed that the entire effort was a waste of time and that the President would have exercised his constitutional prerogative to pocket the Treaty, even if the Senate had ratified it.[84] The outcome left America's relation to the League unsettled, but it convinced many wavering voters that Wilson rather than Lodge was responsible for the result. After a year of parliamentary maneuvers, the Massachusetts senator had achieved his goal of wrecking the League without placing himself or his party on record against international organization. In one of his rare moments of elation, Lodge confided to a friend that he felt "like a boy out of school for weeks and Sundays." Lodge would not have been himself had he not gone on to gloat over the "unenlightened and stupid" behavior of Wilson for twice killing his own creation.[85] Not everybody was as sure that the League was dead, but by the summer of 1920 popular fears of a Bolshevist conspiracy and nation-wide protests over high food prices had begun to compete with the League for public attention.

VI

The national conventions followed so closely on the heels of the long, exhausting struggle over the League that the politicians were unable to take the usual care in choosing delegates. National chairman Will Hays also encouraged an open convention by refusing to intervene in local contests. Asserting that his business was to elect the candidate and not select him,[86] Hays followed this policy so scrupulously that he cancelled trips when they would have landed him in a community on a day delegates were to be chosen.[87] Because he acted as an honest broker, Hays achieved remarkable success in mediating factional disputes. The impartial zeal of Hays improved morale within the party, but also encouraged a diffusion of leadership. Republican Presidential candidates with national appeal would have been scarce in any case. Neither Taft nor Hughes could shake their reputations as losers. Lodge was too old and further handicapped by a tradition of long standing against the selection of senators, while Root was older than Lodge. Republican governors lacked their usual lustre because they had been overshadowed by developments in Washington.

With 529 out of 984 G.O.P. delegates uninstructed and a vacuum at the top, the opportunities for the connivers were almost unlimited, and they approached the convention in the spirit of a lottery. Huge pre-convention expenditures added zest to the scramble for the nominations. Big business, which had not backed the party heavily in 1912 and 1916, was now weary of wartime regulations on profits and alarmed by the postwar aggressiveness of organized labor. A group of new war millionaires was interested in the success of the Republicans, for they recognized in the swollen powers of the federal government an opportunity to secure valuable favors from a President with a proper sense of gratitude. Some looked forward to the disposal of surplus government property on advantageous terms, while others sought a reversal of conservation policy that would reopen oil and mineral reserves to private exploitation. A few of these men backed a single candidate, but many spent money indiscriminately in the hope that they would be remembered by the successful candidate. Among these business leaders were Harry F. Sinclair, Edward L. Doheny, Jake Hamon, and Ambrose Monell, who were interested in natural resources; Samuel Vauclain and Dan Hanna, who were spokesmen for heavy industry; H. M. Byllesby, the utilities magnate; and a number of bankers, including Herbert L. Satterlee, J. P. Morgan's son-in-law.

The vacuum at the top of the G.O.P. was dramatically illustrated by the obscurity of the front runner, General Leonard Wood, who had taken little part in party politics. Wood was a Rooseveltian rather than a Republican, and he had suffered the same abrupt reversals in influence as his sponsor. The re-election of Wilson in 1916 had doomed Wood to a minor role in World War I, and so he made his bid for the Presidency as the successor to Roosevelt rather than as a military hero. Wood suffered from bad management, due largely to the fact that he forced the professionals to share leadership with Colonel W. Cooper Procter of the Cincinnati soap company. The latter ruined morale by trying to make Wood organizers account for their expenditures and by trying to merchandise the candidate like a bar of soap.[88] Procter also lost potential second choice votes by his foolish policy of pushing Wood into contests against favorite sons.[89]

Wood's major rival, Governor Frank O. Lowden of Illinois, was unembarrassed by a voting record on national issues. His campaign was devoted largely to the need for economy in government. Far behind him came Hiram Johnson of California, the old Progressive warhorse and foe of the League. There was probably room for one Rooseveltian in the contest, but not for two. Wood held the Roosevelt men who were bristling nationalists, and Johnson the rest. Imitating his mentor, the senator entered most Presidential primaries and denounced war profiteers, the persecution of radicals, and the League. As Johnson himself recognized, Progressivism was going out of style, but he made such a good showing that everyone wanted him for Vice President.

Other candidates included Herbert Hoover, the War Food Administrator, Nicholas Murray Butler, Governor Calvin Coolidge of Massachusetts, and virtually all the Republican senators. Besides Johnson, only Warren G. Harding of Ohio and Miles Poindexter of Washington bothered to announce their candidacy and make a formal campaign for delegates. The rest of the senators tried to withhold as many delegates as possible from the front runners. Altogether the senators controlled about 300 delegates, which was nearly one-third of the total. Nobody took the senators as seriously as they took themselves. Five months before the convention Harry M. Daugherty, Harding's campaign manager, had come close to the truth, however, by predicting that his candidate would be nominated "about eleven minutes after two, Friday morning of the convention, when fifteen or twenty men are sitting around a table. . . ."[90] Few people paid any attention to Daugherty at the time, and Harding suffered so many setbacks in pre-convention maneuvers that he had little hope of winning.

The one development that helped all of the dark horses was an investigation of expenditures by a Senate subcommittee under the chairmanship of William S. Kenyon of Iowa. Shortly before the convention it produced a report that the Wood forces had spent $1,773,303 and the Lowden backers $414,000. This exposé was designed to help Johnson, but it actually hurt him, because many delegates resented his willingness to smear the party for his own benefit.

The Republican convention opened at Chicago on June 8, 1920; heard Lodge as temporary chairman denounce Wilson's League; and then witnessed an encore performance when he took the gavel as permanent chairman. The delegates gave the recently deceased Roosevelt a standing tribute and then turned to the platform. Debate on it took longer than usual, partly because Will Hays had appointed a preliminary advisory committee which wanted to state its conclusions at the convention. Once the orators talked themselves out, the domestic planks were formulated with little friction. The party pledged itself to serve as guardian of prosperity by raising the tariff, restricting immigration, and aiding the farmers. The League plank caused more trouble. The internationalist faction wanted a straight endorsement of a League with reservations, while the irreconcilables opposed any kind of commitment to world organization. The cagey Lodge identified himself with both sides.[91] But threats of a bolt by the irreconcilables gave him an excuse to retreat further from identification with the League. He turned his back on the Lodge reservations and consented to an ambiguous statement that the party stood for "agreement among nations to preserve the peace of the world." This plank resembled the Wilsonian platitudes to which Lodge objected but it had the virtue of pacifying both sides and clearing the way for nominating speeches.

Balloting started Friday afternoon, and none of the front runners could gain any momentum. On the first four ballots Wood picked up only 27 votes; Lowden did three times as well, but only drew even with Wood; Johnson remained a poor third; and Governor Sproul of Pennsylvania occupied fourth place as a favorite son. Delighted at the disorder, the senatorial oligarchy urged Lodge to adjourn the convention from 4 p.m. until the following morning so that it could take matters in hand. When Lodge put the motion to adjourn, the chorus of nays was deafening, but Lodge proved sufficiently hard of hearing to bang the gavel furiously and tell the delegates to disperse.

After supper, members of the oligarchy and their retainers began to drift in and out of a suite of rooms at the Blackstone Hotel. Composed of two bedrooms and a parlor on the thirteenth floor, the suite had been rented by Will Hays. Although Hays never appeared to entertain visitors, his roommate George Harvey, a financier-journalist and rabid foe of Woodrow Wilson, dispensed both hospitality and advice to the scheming senators. The sequence of events is not very clear, but apparently Harvey, Brandegee, and Lodge reached the decision that they ought to name the nominee and began soliciting suggestions from reliable colleagues. Watson, Smoot, Curtis, New, Crane, Calder of New York, and McCormick of

Illinois came by invitation, and others arrived later unannounced. Some members of the oligarchy attended competing conferences and discussed additional names, including that of Will Hays. The oligarchy finally decided to throw its 300 votes to Warren G. Harding, mainly because the more prominent figures refused to step aside for each other. The absent Penrose, with a fine dramatic instinct, came out of a coma just in time to bless Harding by private wire from his hospital bed. Even so, some members of the oligarchy had misgivings about Harding, because of separate rumors that he had an illegitimate child and that his family had Negro blood. Harvey and Brandegee asked Harding directly about these rumors, and when he answered in the negative they went away satisfied.

When balloting began again Saturday morning, Smoot predicted the nomination of Harding, and Curtis urged the Kansas delegation to switch from Wood to Harding. During the next four ballots the Ohio senator jumped from 78 to 133½, but the situation was still fluid, and Lodge recessed the convention until 4 p.m. Some senators now urged a weekend adjournment, presumably to reconsider the choice of Harding,[92] but delegates were running out of money, and the oligarchy had no alternate plan. Therefore, Lodge reopened the convention and asked the clerk to call the roll for the ninth ballot. Kentucky started a movement to Harding, and his total increased to 374½. The tenth ballot brought him more than two-thirds of the delegates and the nomination.

The convention was weary of supervision by senators and rebelled against their choice for Vice President, Irvine Lenroot of Wisconsin. An obscure delegate named Wallace McCamant nominated Governor Calvin Coolidge of Massachusetts from the floor. All that was known about Coolidge was that he had broken the Boston police strike, but the convention proceeded to select him over Lenroot by the margin of 674½ to 146.

The choice of such an inconspicuous partisan as Harding was a setback for Woodrow Wilson, who had hoped to run for a third term against an uncompromising foe of the League. His illness gave the Democratic convention a graceful excuse for passing over the President, when it met at San Francisco, but its real reason for doing so was a rising hostility to all things Wilsonian. The delegates turned instead to James M. Cox of Ohio, one of the two Democratic governors in the Northeast to survive the election of 1918. The convention selected Assistant Secretary of the Navy, Franklin D. Roosevelt, as his running mate, partly in the hope that some Republicans would think he was Teddy. The party's platform, which called for immediate ratification of the Treaty without the Lodge reservations to the League Covenant, also advocated independence for the Philippines and expressed sympathy for Ireland. Other planks endorsed the domestic legislation of the "New Freedom" and promised to preserve its benefits.

Although the issues of the war era had divided Progressives, a corporal's guard known as the Committee of 48 tried to launch a third party with a fusion convention at Chicago on July 12. The Bull Moose intellectuals were there in full force, as well as single taxers, Nonpartisan Leaguers, right-wing Socialists, and others, but there was no common agreement. The Nonpartisan Leaguers, who controlled the Republican party in North Dakota, stood for agrarian socialism, while the labor groups demanded nationalization of the basic industries. Such a program was too radical for the Bull Moosers, who walked out, whereupon the extremists took the name of Farmer-Laborites and nominated Parley P. Christensen of Utah for President. The Progressives then tried to run La Follette, but he rejected the bid. The anti-war Socialists ignored the Farmer-Labor party and nominated Eugene V. Debs, who was still confined in federal prison for opposition to the war.

The activity of the splinter groups reflected widespread discontent with the major parties. Had the dissidents been able to co-operate, they would have polled several million votes. But the controversy over the Russian Revolution and the League introduced so many cross currents that most reformers wound up voting for Harding or Cox.

The most important asset of the major parties in the 1920 campaign was their decision to present new faces at a time when many voters were tired of the old ones. Despite six years in the Senate, Harding had enjoyed a phenomenal obscurity. He had been born in 1865 at a little crossroads Ohio community called Blooming Grove; passed an unexceptional youth and graduated from Ohio Central College; and had later become editor of the *Marion Star*. Thereafter, Harding had moved up the political ladder in routine fashion, serving as state senator and lieutenant governor before Ohio sent him to the Senate in 1914. In a state notorious for the bitterness of its factional warfare, Harding made few personal or political enemies. As senator during the turbulent years of the war and the League fight, Harding had neither attached his name to an important piece of legislation nor said anything that the papers bothered to report. Although he had missed 43 per cent of the roll calls, Harding seldom ducked votes on important issues. He was just a little less energetic and less hypocritical about feigning interest in trivia than his colleagues. When his convictions were involved, Harding asserted himself. He had opposed the League without bitterness and had spoken against Prohibition at a time when the political advantage lay on the other side. He also possessed the courage to denounce the New York assembly for expelling five Socialist members in 1919. There was nothing very startling about his voting record, but Harding could hardly be termed a stooge of the oligarchy.

The impression that emerged from Harding's campaign biographies and from his contacts with the voters was of a warm-hearted man who displayed the habits, the tastes, and the outlook of small-town America. Like many of his fellow countrymen, Harding had difficulty in expressing his convictions except in vague, pompous phrases. His bearing was far more reassuring than anything he said. His quiet confidence assured people that not many problems existed and those that did had simple solutions. After nearly a decade of cold-blooded leaders like Lodge and Wilson, who had converted every question into a complicated, intellectual issue, voters responded to the disarming simplicity of Harding. Some Republicans fretted about the Ohio politicians in Harding's entourage and about a certain softness and lack of moral fibre in the candidate.[93] But for the moment Harding's virtues overshadowed his weaknesses.

By late summer the Republicans were as certain of victory as experienced politicians can ever be in advance of an election. Reports of an irresistible anti-Wilson tide was recognized by leaders in both parties.[94] The Republicans did nothing to interfere with the trend. Harding, who conducted a front-porch campaign, stayed home except for five short speaking tours in the Middle West and the upper South.

Much more was said about Harding than by him. Party publicity glorified the candidate as a straightforward homespun son of the pioneers. Nostalgic dispatches from Marion described the town as having "the comfortable look of an old shoe" and its chief citizen as a rural Benjamin Franklin who worked at an ancient flat-top oak desk. The idea that the Republican party would end "one-man government" and restore the simple virtues of an earlier era also found expression in campaign literature about Coolidge.

Harding did little to clarify the League issue. At one time or another he denounced the League, endorsed the League idea, and expressed the belief that some sort of world court would be preferable to an international political organization. Since his private statements were just as bewildering, individual Republicans picked out the position that suited them and declared it to be the official party doctrine. Thirty-one top Republican educators, elder statesmen, and jurists signed a manifesto proclaiming that the election of Harding would assure American entrance into the League, while Borah and Johnson took the opposite view. One G.O.P. congressional candidate in Oklahoma even ran on a platform of opposition to any League "which includes nations that worship idols." [95] Cox, on the other hand, flatly endorsed the League and exposed the inconsistencies of the Republican position. In any other year, the voters would have resented the frivolous way in which the G.O.P. handled the League issue, but by the fall of 1920, many people were indifferent or hostile to international organization. In September farm prices broke sharply, adding to the woes of the Democrats. The same month Maine went Republican by four times as large a majority as in 1916.

In the election Harding received 61.02 per cent of the popular vote. He carried 37 states and decisively beat Cox everywhere except in the Solid South. Rightly or wrongly, the Republicans interpreted the election as a defeat for Wilson rather than Cox. They were so positive on this point that they interred the League with hardly a complaint from the internationalist wing of the party. Several legends developed in the aftermath of the League fight and flourished in the 1940's when America again found itself at war. One was that, had America joined the League of Nations, she would have been able to prevent World War II. A second was that a Republican conspiracy promoted by the diabolical Lodge prevented United States participation in defiance of the majority will. The disheartening experience of America after World War II with the United Nations, which was organized along the same lines as the League, has done much to kill the first legend. By the same token, it has led many historians to reconsider "the conspiracy theory" and to concede that many Republicans sincerely favored a League but objected to some features of Wilson's version.

The underlying purpose of Lodge will always be an enigma. He never concealed his dislike of the League nor his sense of relief when it was buried.[96] Unquestionably he did more than any senator to kill it. Yet, during the entire struggle Lodge had never expressed opposition to the principle of international organization. Some of his objections to Wilson's League could have been anticipated from statements made before the controversy began. Others were a response to the tactics of the President and his bitter personal antipathy to Wilson. Being first and foremost a strong party man, Lodge was prepared to swallow his convictions and take a type of League he didn't like as long as public opinion favored it. He twice voted for the League, and until March of 1920 Wilson could have secured it with minor concessions. Few contemporaries felt affection for Lodge, but he managed things well for his party. Whether he managed things well for the United States is another question. Although he clearly opposed isolationism, one unintended by-product of his fight against the League was to reinforce national antipathy to foreign entanglements. Wilson also shared responsibility for this development by stubbornly resisting compromise. The revival of isolationism was probably more unfortunate in the long run than America's decision to stay out of the League, because the country refused to meet its foreign obligations in the 1930's on any basis. The previous behavior of Americans, however, suggests that they would probably have returned to their old foreign policy of aloofness irrespective of Wilson and Lodge. It is easier to make a firm judgment about the immediate impact of the League fight on politics: it restored the Republicans to their customary role as the majority party.

XI

From Normalcy to Depression

If good luck and good intentions were important qualifications for the Presidency, Harding would have gone down in history as one of the greatest Presidents. Nature had equipped Harding with the face of a statesman. In repose, it radiated dignity, serenity, and wisdom. Unfortunately, the image faded whenever Harding's face registered emotion. His laugh was pleasant enough, but it gave a certain slackness to his chin, hinting at self-indulgence and inviting familiarity. His frown more often betrayed perplexity and petulance than determination. Since photographers seldom caught Harding in moments of relaxation or tension, the public missed the weakness lurking behind the mask. Even political associates who were in a better position to observe the President than the voters stifled misgivings because of his kindliness and good will.

With the bulk of the press and public indulgent, Harding escaped criticism for an approach to cabinet-making and patronage that would ordinarily have outraged all Democrats and the reform wing of the G.O.P. First, the President appointed his campaign manager, Harry M. Daugherty, Attorney General. The announcement came so soon after the election that Harding must have intended to forestall complaints. Outside of Harding's immediate entourage, nobody spoke well of Daugherty, who aspired to the same role in the new Administration that Hanna had enjoyed under McKinley. For over a decade, unflattering reports had persistently followed Daugherty as politician, lobbyist, and lawyer. The consensus was that Daugherty used a shrewd mind to accomplish by dubious methods what might have been done straightforwardly. There was considerable difference of opinion as to whether Daugherty was dishonest. The fact that he had hitherto managed to escape prosecution was a point in his favor, but not even the broad-minded lawyer-politicians of Ohio cared to give Daugherty the benefit of the doubt. Although Harding might have been expected to do something for his campaign manager, his expression of gratitude was overgenerous and betrayed a defective sense of propriety.

It was bad enough for Harding to put a lawyer of dubious reputation in charge of law enforcement, but he carried bad judgment to extremes by turning over the administration of conservation laws to a foe of conservation. He chose for the Interior Department, which was empowered to prosecute violators of the land laws, an old Senate colleague and poker-playing friend, Albert B. Fall of New Mexico. A land speculator, miner, and rancher, Fall habitually wore a broad-brimmed Stetson hat and a flowing black cape. Fall not only had the bluff manner to match his appearance, but the violent regional prejudice against Indians, Mexicans, and conservationists.

It was characteristic of Harding's casual approach to public administration that he first offered Fall the State Department. The New Mexico senator had the good sense to refuse, although it is doubtful if recognition of his unfitness for the post played much part in Fall's decision. He told Harding that it would be politically unwise to pass over the claims of Hughes and Root to the State Department. In this case, good advice for Harding coincided with self-interest for Fall, because he saw vast opportunities in the Interior Department. What made it especially attractive was a law of 1920 authorizing the Secretary to lease mineral lands hitherto withdrawn from entry, and Fall looked forward to inauguration of a more liberal leasing policy. There was nothing inherently wrong about Fall's being opposed to conservation, but for a President who ostensibly favored conservation, the Fall appointment was an odd one to make.

Since Harding was not nearly so impervious to the orthodox considerations governing cabinet-making as Grant, the President completed his official family in approved fashion. Hughes as Secretary of State and Andrew W. Mellon as Secretary of Treasury provided recognition to New York and Pennsylvania respectively. Hughes was destined to give distinguished service in foreign affairs, although his internationalist orientation vexed the simon-pure isolationists. Mellon's background as head of the Aluminum Company of America provoked misgivings in some quarters, but he also became an able if somewhat biased public servant. Hoover received the Commerce portfolio, and in his job he managed to show as much sympathy for business interests as Mellon. Other selections were not up to the level of Hughes, Mellon, and Hoover, but the public accepted the cabinet cheerfully, and one of Lodge's followers called it the best in Republican history.[1]

Below the level of the cabinet, few of Harding's appointees attracted attention, and so the President was free to indulge his penchant for rewarding friends irrespective of their qualifications. He quickly revived the spoils system on a franker basis than any of his Republican predecessors with the exception of Grant. Less than three weeks after Inauguration Day, the Comptroller of the Currency received a personal phone call from Harding asking that the insurance contracts on currency shipments be turned over to his brother-in-law.[2] Systematic attempts were made to force the Federal Reserve Board and other independent commissions to provide jobs for friends of the President.[3] Civil-service rules were stretched to the limit or ignored. In fact, Harding tolerated—if he did not sponsor— the illegal practice of assessing Republican appointees to pay off election debts of the party.[4] A small group of Harding's comrades from Ohio established themselves in a house on K Street and developed a profitable business based on their influence with the President. Daugherty undoubtedly was the guiding force, but much of the actual peddling of influence was done by Jesse Smith, a small-town politician from Washington Court House, Ohio, who wore flamboyant sports coats and neckties. Although Harding could have guessed why his friends repeatedly solicited favors, he salved his conscience by remaining ignorant.

II

Left to his own devices Harding would have given the country the same kind of administration as McKinley. From his Republican predecessor, Harding had inherited the belief that the welfare of business, and that of labor and agriculture were identical. Like McKinley, he also assumed that the twin policy of high tariffs and lax administration of the Sherman Act would bring prosperity. Unfortunately, Harding was faced with a host of postwar problems which did not fit the McKinley program. The backlog was unusually large because since the Armistice Wilson and his Republican Congress had been unable to agree about anything but returning the railroads to private ownership. Harding proposed to give high priority to the reduction of wartime taxes and the disposal of surplus government property, but he soon discovered that the solution of these problems was contingent upon the establishment of peace. Neither Congress nor the country was prepared to settle the basis for tax reduction until something had been done about disarmament and the repayment of war debts. To make matters more difficult for the Administration, the economy was suffering from reconversion pains.

The downward trend in business quickly reversed itself, and boom conditions prevailed in the industrial sector of the economy through the decade. Investment was stimulated by the pent-up demand for consumer goods which had been in short supply during the war and by the emergence of new industries. Factories turned out an increasing stream of automobiles, radios, and household appliances, while utility companies generated ever greater quantities of power to produce and operate the new equipment. As in earlier periods of industrial growth, business consolidation proceeded at a rapid rate, evolving new forms of monopolistic structure like the holding company. Although the fruits of prosperity were distributed unevenly, most urban groups enjoyed some increase in purchasing power.

According to the traditional rules of politics, the boom should have assured the party in power a series of harmonious administrations. The voters did behave predictably enough to elect Republican Presidents throughout the decade. Their administrations, however, were anything but harmonious. The basic reason for the trouble was that farmers did not participate in the general prosperity. They had greatly expanded production in response to high wartime prices, pushing their luck hardest in the arid section of the Great Plains. Worse still, many farmers had mortgaged their property to purchase additional acres and were vulnerable to any sudden change in market conditions. Drought had hit the Great Plains in 1919, and a year later an abrupt drop in the abnormal European demand for farm products touched off a general agricultural depression. Conditions reminiscent of the Populist era returned in the same areas where the Populists had been strong. Heavy mortgage burdens aggravated rural distress, and a rash of foreclosures and bank failures followed the break in prices.

The most obvious cause of the crisis was overproduction, and although farmers could not ignore the visible evidence of the surplus they felt no responsibility for it. Insisting that overproduction was temporary, they blamed foreign governments for flooding the American market and domestic speculators for depressing prices. Congress cheerfully accepted this diagnosis and in 1921 passed an emergency tariff to stop dumping from abroad, as well as a series of laws regulating the grain trade. These measures made no perceptible dent in the surplus and except for brief rallies agricultural prices were depressed throughout the decade. Within a year farmers began to demand additional relief, shifting their emphasis from punitive legislation against hostile pressure groups to proposals for subsidies at the expense of the taxpayer. Business interests stoutly opposed this kind of solution, with the result that the old cleavage between the Eastern and Western wings of the Republican party reappeared. Caught in the middle, successive Republican Presidents tried to do something for agriculture despite their pro-business orientation. Unfortunately, the compromises formulated at the White House always fell short of expectations in the distressed areas, so that by 1922 farm leaders were drifting into the role of chronic obstructionists.

Consequently, political history repeated itself in the Great Plains and the Rocky Mountains, with Western Republicans reverting to the tactics of the 1890's. Instead of becoming Democrats, they harassed the G.O.P. from the inside and encouraged third party movements without joining them. The only innovation of the rebels in the 1920's was the organization of a bipartisan farm bloc in Congress to formulate legislative strategy. Most members maintained their formal party ties, but co-operated more frankly on sectional economic legislation than before. National elections and the subsequent relations between the White House and Congress went through a repetitive pattern. Republican Presidents invariably rode into office with substantial party majorities in both houses which just as invariably proved to be unreliable. Throughout the decade the farm bloc dominated by Western Republicans held the balance of power in Congress. It was able to block passage of legislative recommendations from the White House but could not muster the necessary two-thirds vote to repass its version of agricultural relief over a Presidential veto. The persistent deadlock on major issues reduced the antagonists to inconclusive sparring over a host of petty questions, which the farm bloc represented as the age-old battle between the masses and the special interests. The farm bloc made a spirited effort to retain the high wartime taxes on income and inheritance, which fell primarily on the wealthy. It also harassed electric utility holding companies in a variety of ways. The most popular proposal was one by George W. Norris of Nebraska to force the completion of government dams started during the war at Muscle Shoals, a thirty-five-mile strip on the Tennessee River. The purpose of the agitation was to force the government into the generation and sale of electric power. Norris finally worked his proposal through Congress in 1928, but it was killed by a pocket veto. Investigations of prodigal expenditures in Republican primaries were also sponsored by the farm bloc in 1927, partly on the theory that the funds had been furnished by the holding companies.

The farm bloc got little satisfaction out of sabotaging Administration proposals because there were so few of them. The three Republican Presidents of the 1920's concentrated on creating a favorable atmosphere for business, and their policy required little in the way of legislation except tariff revision and tax reduction.

Harding received a taste of the troubles that lay ahead when he called a special session of the 67th Congress soon after his inauguration. Although the express purpose of the session was to repass an emergency agricultural tariff which Wilson had recently vetoed, representatives from the farm states wrested control from the regular Republican leaders. Under the chairmanship of William S. Kenyon of Iowa, the bipartisan farm bloc operated with an efficiency hitherto confined to business groups.

Having received generous rate boosts for their constituents in 1921, the members of the farm bloc were in a poor position to resist similar demands from other groups. So they co-operated with the Republican leaders to produce the Fordney-McCumber tariff bill which passed Congress after a long debate in September 1922. The Democrats injected a new problem into an old issue with a warning that high tariffs would prevent European states from paying war debts. Senator Thomas J. Walsh of Montana even forced arch-protectionist Smoot to concede that Europe could meet its obligations only by exports. Nevertheless, the Fordney-McCumber Act established the highest wall against imports in American history. No sooner was the tariff law passed than farmers repented their co-operation with business and organized labor. As one grumbler put it:

> The farmer's day begins when he is aroused by an alarm clock, and the new tariff bill raises the duty on this article 67%. His first act is to throw off the bed covering on which the duty has been increased 60%. He jumps from his bed, on which the duty is advanced 133%, and dons a summer bathrobe with the duty up 60% and slippers with the duty increased 33%.

Meanwhile, Harding made a move toward international stability which would disarm objections to tax reduction. At his invitation, the principal naval powers had met in Washington on November 11, 1921, to discuss disarmament and the related problem of peace in the Orient. Remarkable progress had been made, because the United States was willing to scrap battleships under construction in return for abrogation of the Anglo-Japanese Alliance and a multilateral guarantee of the Open Door in China. Some of the isolationists bridled at a supplementary four-power pact to maintain the status quo on fortifications in the Pacific, but the Washington Treaties produced general satisfaction and relieved the United States of a costly armament burden. Harding also ended the technical state of war with Germany by ratifying the Treaty of Versailles without the League. Finally, he extracted from Congress an authorization to negotiate debt settlements with the various European powers.

Despite these efforts to cut down both the commitments and costs of foreign policy, the farm bloc turned a deaf ear to Harding's request for the reduction of wartime taxes which fell principally on business groups. In fact, Congress tried to make tax cuts more difficult by passing a Soldiers' Bonus bill, which Harding killed with a veto. As a result, the long session ended in deadlock, casting doubt on the theory that the promotion of a senator to the White House would assure better executive-legislative co-operation.

Harding was far more successful in pursuing pro-business policies that did not require the consent of Congress. He curtailed executive supervision of economic activity whenever possible, and on the independent regulatory commissions replaced prewar reformers with businessmen. The process of restaffing commissions was a slow one, because statutory regulations prescribed fixed tenure and staggered terms. Harding began the process, though, and his Republican successors expanded it further. By the end of the 1920's officials sympathetic to business dominated every level of the federal government.

III

From the political standpoint, 1922 was a year of unrelieved misery for the President. Factionalism erupted in states with large Republican majorities, and west of the Mississippi the farmers were in opposition. Trouble started first in Pennsylvania, where the successive deaths of Penrose and Knox in 1921 left the party organization without a recognized leader. Careless to the end, Penrose refused to train a successor, and in the subsequent confusion the old maverick, Gifford Pinchot, snatched the gubernatorial nomination away from the regulars. A worse surprise occurred in May when Beveridge swept the Indiana primary, unseating Senator Harry S. New. Local politicians considered the result merely the latest incident in a twenty-year feud between the two men, but Harding felt that he had been personally rebuked. Besides being a close friend of the President, New had run as a supporter of the cautious internationalism represented by the Washington Treaties, whereas Beveridge had remained a militant isolationist.

Primaries in the Great Plains were just as unfavorable for the regulars. In North Dakota, Porter J. McCumber lost to the radical Nonpartisan Leaguer Lynn Frazier, after twenty-four years in the Senate. Harding had tried to deprive the farm bloc of effective leadership by appointing William S. Kenyon to a federal judgeship, but the strategy backfired in the Iowa primary when the voters selected Smith W. Brookhart to replace Kenyon. For nearly a decade Brookhart, whose middle name, appropriately enough, was Wildman, had espoused a variety of extreme measures for agricultural relief, and he continued to harass the regulars throughout the 1920's. Physically, Brookhart resembled Hiram Johnson, with a short, stocky body and a belligerent face to match, but unlike the California senator, who overpowered an audience with logic, the volatile Iowan stirred farmers into millennial ecstasy by impassioned denunciations of Wall Street.

The general election in November 1922 completed the rout of Republican regulars who had not been liquidated in the primaries. The congressional majorities of 1920 shrank from 22 to 6 in the Senate and from 167 to 15 in the House. The outcome was an even worse setback for the Administration than the figures suggest. The rebellious Republicans in the farm belt won easily, while Democratic gains occurred for the most part in populous Eastern states like New York, New Jersey, and Massachusetts. Lodge was re-elected by a scant 8000 votes. There was some evidence that the G.O.P. stand for Prohibition hurt the party among the foreign-born of the big cities almost as much as agricultural depression hurt it in the Midwest. Minor-party representatives also reappeared in Congress from traditionally Republican areas that refused to register discontent by voting for the Democrats. The most noteworthy realignment took place in Minnesota, where the Nonpartisan League organizers launched a Farmer-Labor party instead of taking over the G.O.P. from within as they had done in North Dakota. As a result, the Farmer-Laborites won three Minnesota congressional districts, and elected Henrik Shipstead to replace Frank B. Kellogg in the Senate. The next year, a second Farmer-Laborite senator, Magnus Johnson, was sent to Washington when old Knute Nelson died.

The victory of the farm bloc in the 1922 elections has often been hailed as a revival of the prewar Progressive movement. In actuality, the relation was a tenuous one, because the original Progressive impulse came from middle-class urban reformers who objected to special privileges or subsidies for any group, including farmers. Even after Roosevelt and Wilson had converted a disinterested crusade for the purification of American institutions into a program of subsidizing underprivileged groups, Progressivism embraced many elements besides agriculture. By contrast, most farm bloc politicians of the 1920's were interested exclusively in government aid for agriculture.

Several factors had caused the disintegration of Progressivism into discordant pressure groups. For one thing, the original crusading element, which before the war had regarded big business as a menace, began to fear organized labor after the war. Moreover, the propaganda campaign against Germany had generated an intolerant, nationalistic spirit at odds with the older Progressive faith that informed citizens would be practitioners of democracy irrespective of racial or national background. Many people who still paid lip service to the prewar reform doctrines now proposed to preserve democracy and equality of opportunity by warring on radicals, immigrants, Catholics, and other minority groups. The alleged menace of foreign ideas attracted the most attention in rural areas where traditional behavior patterns persisted. Farmers tended to blame everything they disliked, from jazz to communism, on alien influences operating in the urban East. Here the farm bloc parted company with its middle-class allies of the Progressive era. In the process, it restored the old cleavage between the city and country and drew the lines as sharply as in the Populist decade. As farmers distrusted Catholics, foreigners, radical labor leaders, liquor drinkers, and other city dwellers, they had more reasons than the Populists for antagonism toward the urban East.

The surviving warriors of the reform era were as unsuited to become leaders as the farmers were unsuited to become followers in a new Progressive crusade. Only La Follette of Wisconsin and George W. Norris of

Nebraska had emerged from the war with all their old convictions intact. Although La Follette tried to lead, he was as theatrical and autocratic as ever, while Norris was too quiet and scholarly for the farm bloc. Seniority and choice committee assignments conferred on Borah an excellent opportunity to provide leadership either as a spokesman of the discontented or as a mediator between the Eastern and Western wings of the party. Unfortunately, the Idaho senator was incapable of using power for any purpose except to promote confusion. He had the temperament of a prima donna and regarded the Senate as a stage for the display of his oratorical powers. Borah's concept of hard work was to give an occasional set speech on a general topic.[5] These performances entertained the gallery but seldom influenced Congress, for Borah rarely was informed about the details of legislation. His devotion to abstractions revealed a certain craftiness, for it freed him from facing the inconsistencies which would have been exposed by a specific application of his muddled philosophy. To Borah, Progressivism meant limited campaign expenditures, direct primaries, high taxes on business, isolationism, and anything that his Idaho constituents wanted at the particular moment. Such flexibility made it difficult to predict what Borah would favor, and he compounded the uncertainty by sporadic denunciations of big government. He professed alarm over the centralization of power that would follow an amendment outlawing child labor, but favored the enlargement of federal authority to enforce Prohibition.

His old comrade-in-arms, Hiram Johnson, became just as obstructionist as Borah, but for different reasons. Unlike his Idaho colleague, Johnson took Progressivism seriously and felt troubled by the difficulty of applying the prewar credo to the problems of the 1920's. Although Johnson sympathized strongly with organized labor, he recognized that neither the subversive elements nor the more militant trade unionists could be satisfied within the old Progressive framework.[6] Johnson also saw that the demands of the farm bloc and the tariff reformers did not provide the basis for a new crusade. A more favorable atmosphere for reform or the presence of more genuine reformers in Congress might have encouraged Johnson to use his prestige for constructive purposes. As it was, his latent cynicism reasserted itself, reinforced by his bitterness over the way self-styled Progressives and regulars alike had knifed his candidacy at Chicago in 1920. He spent the ensuing decade exposing foolish proposals and searching for sinister internationalist implications in every aspect of foreign policy.

None of the newer farm bloc senators trusted the old Progressive leaders or were capable of providing leadership themselves. Arthur Capper of Kansas had the meditative eye of a Buddhist monk and was both diligent and well-intentioned. He introduced a vast number of bills every session for thirty years, but was addicted to simple solutions. Naïvely confident of the curative power of legislation, he was something of a problem as a party leader. E. F. Ladd of North Dakota had been associated for many years with the agricultural college of his state and was less visionary than Capper. But Ladd's effort to please his political sponsors in the Nonpartisan League warped his approach to farm problems. Despite the fact that much was expected of Shipstead of Minnesota, it soon became apparent that his heavy Scandinavian dignity concealed a mediocre mind. He quickly turned his principal attention to satisfying the wants of his constituents, while Magnus Johnson, the other Farmer-Labor senator, busied himself with such trivia as cow-milking contests and bills to prevent airplane passengers from flushing toilets over farms.

When Congress reconvened for the lame duck session in December 1922, it believed that only the President had been rebuked at the polls and so brushed aside all his recommendations. The farm bloc could not rally its forces for effective action. Robert M. La Follette, who was still nursing dreams of the Presidency, called a strategy session of farm bloc members at the beginning of the session. Johnson, McNary of Oregon, Norbeck of South Dakota, and other key Republicans boycotted the meeting. The ingenious Borah attended for ten minutes so that he could be regarded as "both a part of the gathering and not a part of it." [7] The inability of either the President or La Follette to provide leadership doomed all legislation but a new Farm Credit Act.

The adjournment of Congress on March 4 must have been a relief to Harding, but the incessant wrangling with the lawmakers left its mark on the President. His health deteriorated in the spring of 1923, and he sought relief through longer periods of recreation with his boon companions. Instead of restoring his vitality, these diversions only left him more exhausted, irritable, and perplexed. Undoubtedly Harding would have preferred to retire at the end of his term, but the rising tide of criticism drove him to seek renomination. In an effort to strengthen his position against the extremists who would dominate the new Congress, the President launched a transcontinental speaking tour on June 20, 1923. Although few people suspected it at the time, Harding was also seeking temporary respite from problems of a grave character. Rumors had begun to reach him about the misuse of funds in the Veterans' Bureau and of improper activities in the Alien Property Office and the Justice Department. A senatorial subcommittee headed by Thomas J. Walsh of Montana was also investigating a series of oil leases made by the Interior Department. How much Harding knew about the details of wrong-doing is uncertain, but he did know that charges would soon be made against members of the Administration who were his close personal friends. The available evidence suggests that the President left Washington brooding over his misfortunes.

Harding did not live long enough to suffer the full consequences of his cavalier approach to public administration. His conduct on the tour was that of a man trying to forget his troubles in campaign acrobatics. From St. Louis to Seattle, he fondled chickens, pitched hay, kissed babies, donned cowboy hats, joined Indian tribes, and consumed quantities of fried food. Coupled with major speeches in defense of his policies, this effort reduced the President to the verge of breakdown by the time he reached Seattle. It was hoped that a view of the midnight sun would revive him, but the cruise to Alaska merely added ptomaine poisoning to his existing woes. When the Presidential train reached San Francisco, Harding was confined to bed with what was diagnosed as pneumonia on July 31. Two days later, when it appeared that he was recovering, Harding suddenly died of an embolism.

Subsequent exposure of scandals in the Harding Administration generated a spate of rumors in the yellow press and elsewhere that the President had been murdered. Eventually, there appeared a full-length book by Gaston B. Means titled *The Strange Death of President Harding*. No evidence for this view has ever been found, and certainly no one at the time had reason to doubt that the President had died of natural causes. Crowds gathered respectfully along the route of the funeral train from San Francisco to Washington, and then to Marion, Ohio. The consensus was that Harding had been the victim of an overexacting job and that America had lost a warm, lovable President. His moderation had done much to soften the animosities engendered by the League fight and to pave the way for the solution of diplomatic problems left over from the war. He had also shown great restraint in dealing with the farm bloc and accepted its relief program despite grave reservations. Even his hasty withdrawal of government controls over business was commended at the time. The subsequent exposure of corruption in his Administration did severe damage to the reputation of the President. Nevertheless, Harding might have been rated as an average President rather than a poor one but for the animus of historians who took the scandals far more seriously than the public. Nobody has ever devised an objective standard for measuring the effect of corruption on the achievements of an Administration. It is a fact, however, that several Presidents who placed unworthy friends in high office and tolerated their corrupt activities have been treated more kindly by posterity than Harding.

IV

Few men relished the obscurity of the Vice Presidency as Calvin Coolidge did. For two years he had borne the neglect of Harding, the Washington hostesses, and the press with the air of a man who craved privacy. To discourage the curious, Coolidge had developed the disconcerting habit of refusing to talk, a characteristic which provided the initial impulse for a Coolidge legend. The circumstances surrounding his elevation to the Presidency gave it additional momentum. On the evening of August 2, Coolidge was at the remote Vermont farm of his father, Colonel John Coolidge, and had retired early as usual and was sleeping quietly when a Western Union messenger arrived shortly after midnight to inform him of Harding's death. Two hours later under the flickering light of a kerosene lamp, Calvin Coolidge took the oath as President from his father, a notary public and local magistrate. After this brief ceremony the new President went back to bed.

For the first time since the founding of the Republic an incoming President had literally fulfilled the American dream by coming to Washington straight from a small farm. It made no difference that Coolidge lived in Northampton, Massachusetts, and was on vacation at the time. The nation intended to cling to its myth of the simple, upright farmer reluctantly leaving the green hills of Vermont at the call of his fellow countrymen. What made the myth so irresistible was the fact that city dwellers still regarded the farm as a nursery of statesmen. Devoted to money-making, indoor plumbing, and urban amusements that would have shocked their grandfathers, Americans vigorously applauded when a man with the old Yankee virtues entered the White House. From the outset, the shy, parsimonious Coolidge was lionized by his free-spending, pleasure-loving contemporaries in the way that the homespun Ben Franklin had been lionized by the jaded aristocrats of eighteenth-century France.

Because America was so willing to accept Coolidge on his own terms, the new President felt less obligation than most Presidents to modify his normal habits of behavior. He continued to be silent almost to the point of rudeness and seldom made an effort to put people at ease. He detested outdoor life and most types of recreation, even though Presidents were expected to make gestures establishing their identity with the hardy pioneer tradition. His concept of executive duties was considerably narrower than Harding's, and, although he was graduated from Amherst, Coolidge kept his intellectual attainments secret. He lacked a political philosophy, but he had inherited all the traditional prejudices against a strong central government. He believed that a President should do little except promote a favorable climate for business and placate the farmer by expressing concern over agricultural problems. Like a good New Englander, Coolidge doubted that there was any legislative remedy for the woes of the farmer. Since he disapproved of people who contracted debts, Coolidge wasted little sympathy on the mortgage-ridden Midwestern farmer. His puritanical devotion to frugality expressed itself in household finance as well as in public policy. He practiced rigid economy over such matters as food, drink, and entertainment, approaching overindulgence only in the consumption of peanuts.

Coolidge soon discovered that his provincial habits could be turned to political advantage. With an unexpected flair, Coolidge carefully nurtured the public image of "Silent Cal." Before he had been in office a year, "Silent Cal" had inspired a host of amusing stories. When Henry Ford set up a colonial restoration at his birthplace, Greenfield Village, Coolidge lived up to his reputation by contributing an antique sap bucket with the terse explanation: "My father had it. I used it; now you've got it." [8] His most famous statement was the six-word declaration of his Presidential intentions in 1927: "I do not choose to run." In a country accustomed to garrulous politicians, people were inclined to equate taciturnity with wisdom. Nobody could have become successively mayor of Northampton, state senator, and governor of Massachusetts by being as inarticulate as Coolidge seemed in the White House. Around friends he could become quite talkative, and he also could be playful on occasions. He took special delight in eluding the Secret Service agents assigned to guard him.

Coolidge's habitual silence was a definite political asset at the beginning of his Administration, as the accumulated scandals of the Harding Administration were being exposed. Almost as soon as Coolidge moved into the White House, Attorney General Daugherty was charged with the diversion of confiscated alcohol into the hands of bootleggers. A probe of the Alien Property Office and the Justice Department led to the little house on K Street, where Jesse Smith dispensed favors and advice for a fee. Colonel Charles R. Forbes, head of the Veterans' Bureau, was not a frequent visitor on K Street, but he was soon linked with the group there when it was discovered that he had embezzled $250,000 from the Bureau. Jesse Smith thwarted his pursuers by committing suicide.

The disclosures about K Street and the Veterans' Bureau were a mild sensation compared to the Teapot Dome scandal, which implicated everyone from an ex-cabinet officer to a playboy millionaire publisher. The storm center was Secretary of Interior Albert B. Fall, who had retired from the cabinet on March 4, 1923, taken a leisurely trip to Europe, improved his Three Rivers Ranch in New Mexico, and given other evidence of sudden revival in his financial affairs, which had been at the point of bankruptcy two years earlier.[9] Over the years Fall had made many enemies in New Mexico and elsewhere. His personal enemies joined forces with his perennial foes, the conservationists, and by the late summer of 1923 they had traced Fall's wealth to oil leases. It was well known that Fall had persuaded Harding to transfer jurisdiction over the naval oil reserves from the Navy Department to his Interior Department, and had then dropped a curtain of secrecy over his leasing arrangements. As early as April 1922, Senator Kendrick of Wyoming had introduced a resolution requesting information on oil leases at Teapot Dome in his own state, but Fall had not obliged him, and the investigation languished for over a year, as no one could find any evidence of irregularities. Only La Follette really wanted action, and his interest was enough to destroy Republican support for the investigation. The Democrats responded half-heartedly to further prodding by Fall's opponents in the summer of 1923. Kendrick of Wyoming lacked sufficient concern with the matter to interrupt his vacation and return to Washington, but Walsh of Montana reluctantly agreed to resume the investigation. Walsh was not a very promising choice, since he had been a zealous supporter of the leasing bill which offended the conservationists in the first place.

Hearings started on October 22, 1923, with the examination of a number of witnesses, including Fall and the larger oil operators with whom he had negotiated leases as Secretary of the Interior. Nobody was startled to learn that Fall had enjoyed close personal relations with a pair of multi-millionaire leasees, Harry F. Sinclair and Edward L. Doheny, or that he had leased the naval reserves at Elks Hill to Doheny and at Teapot Dome to Sinclair without competitive bidding. The law did not clearly forbid such arrangements, and, moreover, Fall declared that prompt action had been required to prevent drillers on adjacent land from draining government oil reserves. Geologists confirmed Fall's statement, and so Walsh temporarily adjourned the hearings on November 2.[10]

Fall's position would have been seriously impaired if he had admitted at this point that he had received substantial loans from both Sinclair and Doheny. Yet, the three had demonstrated with apparent conclusiveness that the leases protected government interests. Thus, a voluntary disclosure of their private financial arrangements in October might have meant nothing more than a scolding by reform journals. Instead, Fall and the two oilmen concealed the existence of the loans. In so doing, they were putting themselves in an untenable position, should the investigators subsequently discover the truth. In that case the loans were certain to be regarded as bribes.

In November, Walsh received enough tips to warrant resumption of the investigation, and within a month Fall was desperately searching for someone outside the oil business who could pose as the source of his $100,000 loan from Doheny.[11] Ned McLean, the erratic playboy editor of the Washington Post, agreed to help Fall. By this time, the methodical Walsh had uncovered the true source of the $100,000, and had followed McLean to Palm Beach, where the latter was golfing with Fall. Coolidge became so alarmed by the direction of the investigation that he sent his secretary south to join them. But matters had gone beyond the point where White House intervention could affect the outcome. McLean broke down under questioning and admitted that he had not lent Fall the $100,000. Then, late in January 1924, Fall was recalled to the stand. Three months earlier he had responded insolently to the questions of Walsh and the subcommittee, but in the interval he had lost his nerve and vitality. The spectators saw a broken old man with stooped shoulders admit that he had borrowed $100,000 from Doheny and $200,000 from Sinclair.

The testimony produced a violent reaction among Republicans in Washington. Borah found the scandal too terrible "to think about," [12] and Lodge groaned that it was a manifestation of the "shattering effect of the war on morals, manners, society, business . . . and civilization." [13] McNary gloomily expected the evidence of corruption to grow "from day to day." [14]

Despite his previous efforts to hamper the investigators,[15] Coolidge posed as an innocent bystander once Fall confessed. In a terse public statement, he promised that the guilty would be punished, and he appointed a distinguished lawyer from each party to serve as special prosecutors. Next he dropped Daugherty from the cabinet. Beyond these gestures, Coolidge took no public notice of the scandal and hoped that the voters would forget the matter.

Indeed, there was surprisingly little reaction against the Administration. For one thing, the suits against Fall, Doheny, and Sinclair dragged through the courts for several years, with the three men using every available resource to avert conviction. Eventually all three escaped conviction for conspiracy, and by the time Fall was convicted of bribery in 1929 the country had more pressing concerns. Secondly, subsequent disclosures of the Walsh committee involved enough Democrats in questionable oil leases to limit the usefulness of corruption as a Democratic campaign issue. Besides, murder cases and divorce scandals of the tabloid press seem to interest the average citizen more than the exposure of political corruption.

Meanwhile, in 1924 the farm bloc continued its war on the Administration. The House contingent under the leadership of Cooper of Wisconsin held up the election of a speaker for several weeks to force a liberalization of the rules, but the revolt collapsed after some meaningless concessions from the regulars. The chief target of farm bloc senators was old Cummins of Iowa, who had joined the oligarchy. Although they succeeded in depriving Cummins of the chairmanship of the interstate commerce committee, they were outmaneuvered in the end. Rather than accept La Follette, who was next in line for the chairmanship, the regulars backed the Democrats' choice of Ellison D. Smith of South Carolina.

The ugly factionalism displayed at the opening of the 68th Congress persisted throughout the session, during which the farm bloc rewrote the Administration plan for tax reduction. The only important subject upon which Republicans could agree was a reduction of income tax rates and the elimination of the levy on excess profits. Immigration restriction was put on a permanent basis by the Johnson Act. Designed to discriminate against ethnic groups from southeastern Europe, it provided for the limitation of immigration to 150,000 annually after July 1, 1927.

V

Congress adjourned amid signs that the public was paying little attention to it or the impending Presidential election. On the surface Coolidge appeared to be as apathetic to politics as the country, but appearances were deceptive. Professionals had recognized that his appointment of Representative C. Bascom Slemp of Virginia as his secretary in the fall of 1923 was a sign that Coolidge wanted renomination. Slemp divided his life into compartments. In his capacity as businessman, church member, or social companion, he observed all the conventional rules of morality, but as a politician he acted always with expediency. His native environment had a great deal to do with his attitude. Born and raised in the mountainous triangle where Virginia, Tennessee, and North Carolina join, Slemp had accepted the local custom of vote-buying as a normal feature of politics. Later, he learned to accumulate party funds by taking kickbacks from appointees for whom he managed to secure civil-service jobs.[16] He systematically weakened party organization outside of his area so that he could control all of the patronage. At the conclusion of fifteen years as congressman, Slemp had achieved complete domination of the Republican organization in Virginia and an influential role in party affairs throughout the South.

Coolidge could not have been ignorant of Slemp's political tactics, but he remained more concerned with gaining the support of Southern delegates at the forthcoming convention. He must have felt his own conscience was salved when, at the time of Slemp's appointment, he asked him with a straight face "not to have anything to do with politics." [17] Slemp took this injunction in the spirit in which it was meant and started to work immediately. His first problem was to secure the repeal of the rule for allotting delegates which had been provisionally adopted at the 1920 Republican convention. Under this plan the delegates from Mississippi, South Carolina, and Georgia were to be reduced from 41 to 17.[18] With a discreet assist from Coolidge, Slemp persuaded the national committee to shelve the plan. Then he rounded up Southern delegates so efficiently and quickly that he began to interfere elsewhere, much to the annoyance of Coolidge's Northern managers. Since neither William M. Butler, the chairman of the national committee, nor Frank W. Stearns, the dry goods merchant and financial backer of the President, possessed the political acumen of Slemp, chronic friction in the Coolidge organization was inevitable. Nevertheless, the President built up a commanding lead in delegates before his potential rivals got their campaigns started.

Pinchot and Lowden recognized that 1924 was not their year, and declined to contest Coolidge. It took longer to convince Hiram Johnson that the voters were no longer interested in him nor in Presidential primaries, but he, too, withdrew from the race in May. By convention time only La Follette remained as a serious contender, and he was much more concerned with organizing a third party than with contesting the Republican nomination.

Despite the prospect of a three-party race, public interest in the election was at a low ebb. The issues arising out of the war had subsided, and the dramatic impact of nativist sentiment on national politics was still four years off. Part of the apathy in 1924 was a result of reviving prosperity. Except for coal, textiles, and railroads, industrial activity pushed steadily higher. Agricultural prices showed only a modest improvement, but it was sufficient to take the edge off rural discontent. If prosperity blunted interest in the election, so did the old-fashioned campaign techniques, which since 1896 had been slowly losing their appeal. Particularly in urban areas, politics was being divorced from recreation, and, as public taste in entertainment changed, there was a simultaneous decline in the popularity of barbecues, parades, and rallies featuring prolonged oratory. Within a decade the large-scale transmission of speeches by radio would revolutionize campaigning, but Coolidge was seeking re-election in a colorless transitional period between the old and the new.

The Republican convention which met at Cleveland in mid-June demonstrated the need for new electioneering practices. The auditorium was never more than half full, and the delegates drifted about listlessly. Slemp and Butler had done their job well, for Coolidge received a first-ballot nomination, with 1065 out of a possible 1109 votes. The President would have preferred Borah as Vice President, but the latter declined. Over the objections of Slemp, Butler tried to push several other candidates through the convention. With the Coolidge managers divided, the convention rebelled and selected Frank O. Lowden, who also turned down the Vice Presidency. After an open quarrel between Butler and Slemp on the platform, the nomination finally went to Charles G. Dawes, a blunt-spoken Chicago banker who was Director of the Budget. The platform generously credited the Administration with reviving prosperity and promised continued good times for the next four years. Mindful of the Teapot Dome scandal, the delegates included planks denouncing corruption and praising conservation. Child labor was deplored, and a constitutional amendment was recommended to prohibit it. Farmers and veterans received a courteous reminder that the party had befriended them, as well as a hint of more blessings to come. Foreign affairs received little treatment beyond an endorsement of the World Court and a denunciation of the League of Nations. Anti-foreign sentiment was recognized by a pledge to preserve the policy of immigration restriction. But nothing was said about the coercive tactics of anti-foreign, anti-Catholic groups like the Ku Klux Klan which dominated several Republican state organizations.

The Democrats met at Madison Square Garden, New York City, two weeks later in such a state of disorganization that they hardly deserved to be called party. The Northern wing was reduced to a series of urban machines supported by immigrant Catholics and foes of Prohibition, which the Southern wing detested even more than it detested the Republicans. Under the circumstances it was not surprising that the Democrats had difficulty agreeing on a nominee. The urban delegates pushed Governor Alfred E. Smith of New York, while those from the South and West backed Wilson's Secretary of the Treasury, William G. MacAdoo. Neither could muster the necessary two-thirds vote nor transfer his supporters to a compromise candidate until the convention was thoroughly exhausted. After 102 fruitless ballots the delegates finally nominated John W. Davis of West Virginia, largely because nobody knew him well enough to dislike him. Aside from two prewar terms as congressman and brief service as ambassador to Great Britain, Davis had been inactive politically. Since he was both an Easterner and a corporation lawyer, the Democrats made a bid for the discontented farmers by giving second place on the ticket to Governor Charles Bryan of Nebraska, the younger brother of William Jennings Bryan. The Democrats had as much difficulty drafting a platform as selecting a candidate. They tried to take a stand against the Ku Klux Klan, but so many Southerners approved of the organization that the anti-Klan plank was beaten by five votes. Although identification with the League of Nations had obviously become a liability to the party, Wilsonians forced adoption of a resolution advocating American membership in guarded language. All other issues were either ignored or treated ambiguously.

La Follette tried to meet the need for a party with a distinctive stand on current issues by initiating a call for a convention of Progressives for

July 4. The backbone of his support was the Conference for Progressive Political Action. Organized in 1922, the Conference was composed of unrelated groups, including the sixteen Railroad Brotherhoods, a few other unions, the remnants of the old Committee of 48, and various committees of Eastern intellectuals. Although the Socialist convention at Milwaukee had authorized its delegates to attend the Cleveland meeting, it also instructed them to bolt unless a labor party was organized. La Follette finally prevailed upon the Socialists to settle for fusion under his leadership, but he repudiated the support of the Communists. Because of its traditional policy of non-alignment with political parties, the A.F. of L. was not represented at Cleveland, and the most that La Follette could extract from Gompers was a weak personal endorsement. After the convention nominated the seventy-year-old Wisconsin senator, it chose as his running mate Senator Burton K. Wheeler of Montana, a Democrat who had been dubbed "Bolshevist Burt" because of his flirtation with the Nonpartisan League.

The platform adopted by the Progressive party was dictated by La Follette and contained fourteen points. It was almost indistinguishable from the Populist platforms of the 1890's, featuring their standard denunciation of monopoly and such familiar remedies as government ownership of the railroads and popular control of the judiciary. Its credo seemed more dangerous and un-American to conservatives than earlier third-party documents, because the Russian Revolution had engendered an unreasoning fear of radicalism. In addition to their pronouncements on domestic problems, the Progressives of 1924 denounced the Versailles settlement as imperialistic and advocated total disarmament. This militant call to action produced a sluggish response. Sympathy for agriculture had never been strong in the East, and organized labor had lost ground steadily since the end of the war. Inasmuch as the Socialists frightened more people away from La Follette than they attracted, the crusading army found few recruits except disgruntled farmers on the high plains. La Follette at least knew who his supporters were, because he campaigned principally on the issue of how Wall Street had siphoned off income from the rural areas. Since his traditional three-hour speech crammed with statistics proved to be too heavy for a postwar audience, Wheeler provided comic relief by addressing questions to empty chairs on the pretext that they were occupied by Coolidge and Davis, whom he denounced as the "Gold Dust twins."

Whatever the shortcomings of the La Follette-Wheeler campaign, it was considerably more lively than the efforts of the major party candidates. Davis bored his listeners talking about Teapot Dome and morality, while Coolidge lived up to his reputation by remaining silent. He undoubtedly would have found a way to avoid campaigning, but the tragic death of his younger son in midsummer provided ample justification for him. His sole contribution to the debate was an occasional statement urging economy in government. Republican orators concentrated on La Follette, representing him as a kind of American Kerensky whose advent to power would be the prelude to a Communist revolution.

The most effective opponent of the third party was prosperity. The *New York Herald* put the matter cynically but accurately near the close of the campaign: "With wheat at $1.23 a bushel, keeping the 'discontented' farmer discontented becomes more of a problem." Still other problems dogged the grim, conscientious La Follette. Election laws kept him off the ballot in some states and forced him to run under misleading labels in others. Like previous reform movements, the Progressives suffered from lack of funds and quarrelled incessantly over their distribution. Finally, La Follette was hurt by the defections of farm bloc colleagues, who as usual remained regular in a Presidential year. Only Norris of Nebraska and the two North Dakota senators came out for La Follette. Borah played his customary double game in Idaho and won re-election as a Republican by praising everybody and supporting nobody but himself.

When the ballots were counted, it became clear that Coolidge had duplicated Harding's landslide in the electoral college four years earlier, with 382 votes, to 136 for Davis, and 13 for La Follette. The South furnished all of the electoral votes for Davis, and La Follette ran ahead of him in 17 farm-belt states. Nevertheless, La Follette was unable to carry any state except his native Wisconsin. Out of nearly 29,000,000 popular votes, Coolidge polled 15,726,016, to 8,386,503 for Davis and 4,822,856 for La Follette. The apathetic atmosphere in which the campaign was conducted was reflected in the fact that less than half the eligible voters bothered to go to the polls on election day.

Coolidge interpreted the election as a mandate for four more years of the kind of executive inertia which he had displayed since becoming President. "Our most important problem," he observed with customary brevity in his inaugural address the following March, "is not to secure new advantages but to maintain those we already possess." It was just as well that Coolidge planned no legislative program, for the new Congress was as balky as the old one. On paper the G.O.P. majorities were impressive. The Senate contained 50 Republicans, 40 Democrats, and 6 irregulars who had supported La Follette. A similar ratio existed in the House, where 233 Republicans faced 183 Democrats and some 20 Progressives. The G.O.P. Senate leaders first moved against the traitors in their ranks. Ladd and La Follette thwarted them by dying before retaliating action could be taken, but when Congress met in December 1924 the other two La Follette Republicans were deprived of their committee assignments and excluded from the party conference. It was impossible to do anything immediately about the rebellious Brookhart of Iowa, because he did not take office until March. But the regulars expelled him in the spring of 1926 and awarded his seat to Daniel Steck, an Iowa Democrat who had contested the legality of Brookhart's election. Although the oligarchy was able to muster the full party vote in dealing with traitors, it was too weak and unimaginative to enforce discipline on other matters. Death had claimed the masterful Lodge in 1924, and none of his lieutenants possessed the capacity or the incentive to replace him. Warren was too old to be majority leader, and Smoot declined the post because he preferred the chairmanship of the finance committee. The job then went by default to plodding Charles Curtis of Kansas. With his limited horizons, Curtis was an ideal collaborator for Coolidge, but his approach helped to revive the political delusion of the Grant era that the retention of power was an adequate substitute for policy. The high command in the House displayed more energy and imagination than did the Senate oligarchy. The new speaker, Nicholas Longworth, a resident of Cincinnati and a son-in-law of Roosevelt, did not show the resourcefulness of Reed or Cannon, but he was much stronger than his immediate predecessors. Longworth made a resolute effort to halt the erosion of the speaker's power which had begun in 1910, and with a little prodding from the White House he might have formulated a constructive legislative program.

The sluggishness of the President and Congress was partly a response to public indifference. The persistence of economic boom promoted complacency, while the drift toward stability in Europe without a direct contribution by the United States caused even the isolationists to relax their vigilance. For the moment the European states found it possible to pay installments on their war debts. They also made enough gestures toward disarmament that even Borah supported the multilateral Kellogg-Briand

Pact of 1928, outlawing war as an instrument of national policy. Negotiated by Frank B. Kellogg, who had replaced Hughes as Secretary of State, and French Foreign Minister Aristide Briand, the pact encouraged Americans to believe that problems abroad would settle themselves.

As usual the farmers attracted the most attention in Congress and persistently demanded passage of the McNary-Haugen bill, which was designed to stabilize farm prices without any curtailment of production. The bill authorized a government corporation to deal in basic commodities for the express purpose of assuring the producer a return on his crop equal to the world price plus the increment from the protective tariff. Presumably this goal could be reached if the government corporation purchased at the same total price the portion of a crop that was not sold on the domestic market and dumped it abroad for whatever price it would bring. The McNary-Haugen bill also provided a mechanism for recouping losses on exports in the form of a fee assessed against each farmer on the percentage of his crop marketed abroad.

No bill so difficult for its intended beneficiaries to understand ever enjoyed such persistent support in Congress. Four versions of it reached the floor of at least one branch of Congress between 1924 and 1928.

The initial pair of attempts to pass it failed because the commodities singled out for special treatment were grown primarily in the Midwest. When cotton and tobacco were added to the list of key commodities, the bill cleared both houses in February 1927. Coolidge promptly vetoed it, with a message that criticized it on every conceivable ground. He assailed it as special-interest legislation for the growers of a few staples, and denounced the price-fixing features as a departure from American principles. He also predicted that the plan would lead to further overproduction and retaliatory dumping by foreign powers. Much of the analysis of the veto was sound, but it would have been more to Coolidge's credit if he had been a consistent opponent of all pressure groups. The proponents of the bill could not muster the two-thirds vote needed to override the veto. History repeated itself in May 1928 when Congress passed a fourth version but again sustained a Coolidge veto. The issue was now certain to be injected into the ensuing Presidential campaign.

Because of the President's negative attitude toward the few measures that Congress passed on its own initiative, executive-legislative relations deteriorated in the last years of the Coolidge Administration. The Republicans suffered the normal off-year losses in the 1926 election, reducing their majority in the House and leaving the Senate evenly divided. The oligarchy managed to organize the Senate by restoring the 1924 rebels to their old committee posts and inviting Shipstead, the Farmer-Laborite, to participate in the party conference. Organization of the Senate did not really put the Republicans in control. Not only did Brookhart return with a fresh mandate from Iowa to disrupt the party from within, but a freshman North Dakota senator, Gerald P. Nye, carried on his state's tradition of irregularity with greater eloquence than his predecessors.

VI

The dissidents were not as strong in the country at large, for a considerable number of state and local party leaders wanted to renominate Coolidge. In August 1927 the President gave a setback to his own candidacy with a cryptic statement of withdrawal. His backers ignored it, and nobody was the wiser when Coolidge amplified his position in December by asking that his wishes be respected. The "draft Coolidge" movement continued throughout the spring, led by William M. Butler, who had replaced Lodge as senator from Massachusetts, and by C. D. Hilles, a prominent New Yorker and former secretary of Taft. Coolidge gave every evidence of enjoying the situation, as he ignored all requests that he amplify his position.[19] Even his closest friends did not know his intentions, and it is altogether possible that the President hoped to be drafted. In any case, he did not say a single word to discourage the movement in his behalf until the Sunday before the convention. Even then, Butler, Mellon, and Hilles refused to believe that Coolidge would not run, until he so informed them in writing.[20]

Meanwhile, several candidates had been approaching delegates while at the same time trying not to offend the President. By far the most active was Secretary of Commerce Herbert Hoover. He would have liked to be the Administration candidate and made unsuccessful efforts to wrest a conclusive statement of intentions from Coolidge.[21] Baffled by persistent silence in the White House, Hoover formally launched his campaign in September 1927, although in one way or another he had been a candidate ever since he first came to Washington in 1917 as War Food Administrator. During the intervening decade he had showed a remarkable knack for securing favorable publicity on a nonpartisan basis. Hoover trained the employees of the War Food Administration, and later those of the Commerce Department, to dramatize their activities and in the process they inevitably reflected credit on him. Hoover also held frequent press interviews, where he explained his policies with cautious pride. He benefitted greatly from the fact that Americans had begun to idolize men of his type. In this time of prosperity, the average citizen had developed an almost worshipful admiration for efficiency experts, and Hoover was not only a dynamic administrator but an architect of business co-operation. In addition, Hoover had a previous reputation as a humanitarian, based on his organization of Belgian relief during the First World War. By the time he was forty, Hoover had already become a millionaire as a mining engineer in the Orient and England. His political credentials also included birth in a weathered Iowa farmhouse on August 10, 1874, a heroic fight to overcome childhood poverty, and a bachelor's degree in the first graduating class at Stanford University.

Hoover's assets were counterbalanced by liabilities that his critics persistently exploited. Long years of residence abroad made him vulnerable on two counts. Some questioned the sincerity of his patriotism, and others drew unflattering conclusions about the source of his great wealth. Hoover's endorsement of the League of Nations in 1919 provided the basis for further insinuations that he was really a man without a country, while his prewar financial operations in China and Great Britain drew considerable fire. There was little factual evidence to justify rumors linking Hoover's name with unsavory manipulations in international money markets, but the Secretary of Commerce persistently refused to dignify these attacks on his prewar business activities with a response. Even under oath, his answers were vague, and as late as 1917 he could not remember whether he had ever voted or lived in the United States at election time.[22]

Midwestern farmers disliked Hoover almost as much as the isolationists and the professional baiters of international financiers. Their grudge went back to the war years, when Hoover, as War Food Administrator, had tried to limit the rise in food prices. The postwar depression in agriculture kept their memories fresh, and by 1927 farm bloc politicians were saying, "Anyone but Hoover."

Although the Hoover opposition was vocal enough, it was badly divided. The strategists who wanted to nominate Coolidge could not find any basis for co-operation with the McNary-Haugenites in the Midwest. Even the latter were badly split and unable to agree on strategy. In October 1927 a conference of farm bloc legislators met in Borah's office and agreed to enter Senator Norris in fourteen Presidential primaries. His candidacy never gained momentum, partly because Norris made no secret of his determination to support the Democrats if the convention nominated a regular Republican. This attitude was too uncompromising for most of the farm bloc. Rival ambitions within the group hurt Norris, and trimmers like Borah were soon exploring possibilities elsewhere. Frank O. Lowden of Illinois seemed to others to be a better choice, but he was too wealthy and conservative for the taste of the more radical agrarians. Lowden weakened his position still further by announcing that he would not accept the nomination unless the party platform explicitly endorsed the McNary-Haugen plan. Coolidge then let it be known that he would interpret such a plank as a repudiation of his Administration. Lowden immediately retreated, but the damage had been done.

The "stop Hoover" movement was now reduced to running favorite-son candidates. Senator Guy D. Goff bid for his native West Virginia with blasts at "Sir Erbert Hoover of Downing Street"; [23] Senator James Eli Watson tried to hold Indiana by similar tactics; Senator Raymond Willis of Ohio ran through the stale platitudes that had driven his state to Wilson in 1916; and the majority leader, Charles Curtis, bid for Kansas with a stirring appeal to the veterans of all wars.

Considering the intellectual level of these campaigns, their early success indicated the existence of deep-seated opposition to Hoover long before the outbreak of the Depression. Not only did he lose four primaries to nonentities, but in Ohio Hoover suffered a further indignity when the voters selected twenty delegates pledged to Willis, despite the fact that the latter had died some weeks before the May election. Although such reversals would ordinarily have been fatal, Hoover went to the convention with overwhelming strength. Part of his good fortune was due to the fact that Slemp gave up hope of nominating Coolidge in February and swung a huge bloc of Southern delegates behind Hoover. In his native California, too, Hoover's old foe Hiram Johnson was disinclined to jeopardize his own chances for re-election by fighting him.

When the convention met at Kansas City in mid-June, the nomination of Hoover was inevitable. The dissidents, however, spared no opportunity to register their displeasure. Three hundred demonstrators converged on the convention armed with hoes and pitchforks. Although the police prevented their admission, the demonstrators established headquarters across the street and shouted anti-Hoover slogans. Nominating speeches in behalf of other candidates made pointed references to their Americanism; the inferences were unmistakable that Hoover was lacking in patriotism. Curtis of Kansas specifically denounced the Secretary of Commerce and stated that under no circumstances would he accept second place on a Hoover ticket. These outbursts had no effect on the delegates. After giving Hoover a first ballot nomination, they named Curtis for Vice President. The Senate majority leader immediately expressed delight in running with his "old friend." Apparently the Hoover managers thought they were extending an olive branch to the farm bloc by selecting Curtis. But the latter had made a religion of regularity in his voting record and had no strength with the dissidents. His only contributions to the campaign were a spread-eagle style of oratory and his Indian ancestry, which led the sardonic journalist, H. L. Mencken, to refer to him as "half Choctaw and half windmill."

Like other Republican platforms of the decade, the platform of 1928 was largely self-congratulatory. The party again took credit for prosperity and promised to safeguard it. Hoover was as opposed to the McNary-Haugen program as Coolidge had been, but he tried to prevent a repetition of the 1924 revolt in the farm belt by pledging government support for a co-operative agricultural marketing system. Another plank placated irritable "drys" with the promise that the 18th Amendment would be vigorously enforced. The section dealing with foreign affairs contained a denunciation of the League of Nations, but proposed further limitations of armaments and the outlawing of war.

When the Democrats met at Houston, Texas, two weeks later, they were more demoralized than they had been in 1924. Strictly speaking, the Southern wing was not really a party but a series of state organizations exclusively preoccupied with local enforcement of Prohibition and white supremacy. The average Southern politician cared so little about national affairs that he lacked the incentive to work for a national victory. The convention reduced his incentive still further by nominating Governor Alfred E. Smith of New York, who symbolized all of the forces obnoxious to the South. Not only was Smith a representative of the new immigration, but a Catholic and a "wet" as well. In addition, New York represented for rural America the most decadent, corrupt aspects of modern civilization.

In retrospect, it is easy to see that the Democrats blundered in selecting Smith for President, but at the time they had no realistic alternative. Smith was literally the only major Democratic office-holder in the North to win re-election with regularity, and in 1928 was serving his fourth term as governor. The Southerners had precipitated the long deadlock in 1924 to block the nomination of Smith, but four years later they sullenly bowed to the inevitable. Close associates did not regard Smith as a radical in any sense of the word. His record revealed a consistent interest in good administration of existing laws rather than a reformer's preoccupation with further experimentation. Aside from a bias for urban consumers, which aligned him with the foes of privately owned utilities, Smith's views were as conservative as those of most successful politicians in the East. What aroused the ire of the South was his objection to the law discriminating against immigrants from southern Europe and his poorly concealed animus toward Prohibition. Smith did not advocate repeal of the 18th Amendment, but he wanted to legalize the manufacture of beer and light wines. Like many urban leaders in both parties, he argued that this concession to the "wets" would assure more effective enforcement of Prohibition.

In an effort to make Smith acceptable to rank-and-file Democrats, the convention wrote a platform which straddled practically every question, including Prohibition, farm relief, and the public utility issue. For the first time since the war, there was no plank dealing with the League of Nations. As a final gesture to disgruntled Southerners, the convention nominated Senator Joseph T. Robinson of Arkansas for Vice President.

None of these concessions made the slightest difference to the hard core of anti-Smith Democrats. They disliked him for what he was, and Smith could not have won their support even if he had advocated the re-enslavement of Negroes. He also lost many waverers by renewing his advocacy of beer and light wines in his acceptance speech, despite the party platform's silence on the subject.

Since it was risky for a Southern politician to take the lead in any movement that would aid the Republicans, Democratic office-holders allowed Baptist and Methodist religious officials to raise the flag of revolt at Asheville, North Carolina, on July 19, 1928. Among the conspicuous Southern churchmen attending the Asheville meeting were Methodist Bishop James Cannon, Jr., a key official of the Anti-Saloon League, and Arthur J. Barton, who enjoyed a similar status on the Baptist Temperance Board. The presence of C. Bascom Slemp spoiled the effort of the participants to pass the meeting off as a spontaneous religious gathering. They left no doubt, however, about their determination to launch a crusade. Keynoter Barton denounced Smith as a menace to civilization, and the Resident Methodist Bishop of North Carolina, E. D. Mouzon, amplified the warning: "This is no mere threat to Prohibition" but "the uprising of the lawless elements in the great cities." The bishop added, "We may be at the beginning of the downfall of American Democracy." [24] Nobody was surprised when the Asheville convention endorsed Hoover, and Slemp showed his gratitude by raising $65,000 to finance the Southern churchmen.[25] Timid Southern politicians were so delighted by the popular response that they judged it safe to come out in the open. Two Democratic senators, Furnifold Simmons of North Carolina and Thomas J. Heflin of Alabama, led the bolt to Hoover, and a host of lesser figures followed their example. Disclaiming any connection with the Republicans, the rebels organized Hoover committees as independent Democrats.

At the beginning of the campaign Smith hoped to make compensating inroads on Republican strength in the farm belts. He persuaded George N. Peek and other leading McNary-Haugenites to support him. In return they received a large sum from the Democratic national committee for propaganda purposes. Peek worked hard for Smith, but his efforts were hampered by the equivocal stand of the Democratic candidate on the equalization fee. Farmers also sensed that Smith did not have very much interest in agriculture and made a lukewarm response to his appeals for support. They were just as apathetic to Republican claims that Hoover was the friend of agriculture, with the result that most of them based their votes on other issues.[26]

The Republicans pictured Hoover as the ideal custodian of prosperity. Campaign literature represented him as an omniscient administrator who would run the United States the way Henry Ford ran an automobile factory. One leaflet called Hoover "Ten Candidates in One," an authority on public administration, engineering, business, agriculture, aviation, conservation, commerce, domestic politics, and international affairs.[27] Hoover fostered these illusions in a speech at Palo Alto, California, accepting the nomination. He cheerfully predicted that "we in the United States are nearer to the final triumph over poverty than ever before in the history of any land." Even Borah sounded as if he believed the election of Hoover would solve all remaining problems. With a zeal worthy of Curtis, Borah said that the election of Hoover would mean four more years of the full dinner pail.

The safe but stale issue of prosperity seemed likely to keep voter interest as low as in 1924. Smith's candidacy, however, generated an unwholesome excitement that drew an additional eight million citizens to the polls in 1928. Most of them were attracted by the nativist crusade for home, mother, morality, and Anglo-Saxon institutions. Underlying the diverse manifestations of prejudice was a legitimate fear about how the election of a Catholic might affect the traditional separation of state and church in America. Over the centuries the Catholic Church had supervised the secular authorities wherever it gained full control. Moreover, Catholic theologians left no doubt as to their preference for a church-dominated society. On the other hand, the Catholic Church was a flexible organization and had learned to operate for extended periods under other institutional arrangements. Thus, the situation in America was perplexing enough to warrant restraint and frankness on both sides, but the campaigners aggravated religious prejudices. The most articulate offenders were rural Protestants, particularly in the South, who vented their anti-Catholic bias in hysterical fashion. Numerous pamphlets allegedly written by ex-Catholics gave lurid accounts of the inner workings of the Church and represented priests as immoral, grasping, and corrupt tipplers. The Ku Klux Klan amplified its familiar charge that a Catholic take-over of the United States impended and that a rifle was placed in a cathedral vault at the birth of each Catholic child. A faked version of the Knights of Columbus oath was circulated to substantiate the charge that Smith could not conscientiously discharge the duties of the Presidency.

The Republican high command officially deplored the injection of the religious issue into the campaign. With a brevity worthy of Coolidge, Hoover went on record "for religious toleration both in act and in spirit." For a candidate billed as an efficient administrator, Hoover displayed a curious indifference to the implementation of his principle. There was little that he could have done about the activity of religious groups, but he might at least have cut off funds for the more extravagant partisan broadsides on Smith. As it was, he let local Republican leaders use their discretion, and most of them showed none. Oliver D. Street, Republican national committeeman in Alabama, admitted responsibility for distributing 200,000 copies of an inflammatory leaflet on the religious issue.[28] Others were as active if not as candid. Frequently churches served as outlets for campaign material,[29] and many Hoover rallies, particularly in the South, featured hymns, prayers, and other religious trappings.

The reaction to Smith as a campaigner only reinforced opinion against him. Dressed in a pin-striped suit and derby, and employing the raspy nasal accent of New York City's lower East Side, Smith seemed to resemble exactly the caricatures drawn by hostile cartoonists. Rural audiences thought that Smith behaved more like a traveling salesman than a Presidential candidate. As one Kentucky editor put it: "But his speeches turned away many who were at first inclined to swallow everything else. His raucous voice, his intemperate language and that strange menacing voice which was audible over the radio as the milling crowds applauded him in the half foreign and wet centers of population" provoked unreasoning fear.[30]

When the votes were counted, Smith suffered a staggering defeat in the electoral college, 444 to 87. In the popular vote, however, Smith received approximately half of the new votes. Even more dramatic, the Republicans had breached the Solid South for the first time since Reconstruction by carrying Florida, North Carolina, Texas, and Virginia. Although G.O.P. headquarters hailed this development as a political revolution, a closer look at the returns suggested that Southerners had deserted Smith rather than the Democratic party. Nowhere in the region had Hoover polled a significant number of votes under the Republican label or improved the popularity of the party's organizations. As usual, the latter had not bothered to run tickets in most areas of the South.

In their elation over the outcome, Republicans overlooked certain disquieting trends. For one thing, Catholics had displayed as much solidarity as Protestants, and had pushed Massachusetts and Rhode Island into the Democratic column. A heavy Smith vote in the urban centers of the East indicated that the nativist crusade had speeded the erosion of Republican strength among the foreign-born. The conspicuous fraternization of Hoover with white politicians in the South had also cost the Republicans 10 to 15 per cent of their huge Negro majority in Northern cities like Chicago.[31] In the farm belt, Smith polled 1,977,921 more than Cox had done in 1920, while Hoover picked up only 1,249,319 more than Harding.[32] Without the religious issue to help him, Hoover probably would have lost several states west of the Mississippi. Montana, Wyoming, Utah, Washington, Nevada, and Arizona gave him majorities, but also elected Democratic senators by substantial margins. Minnesota was unwilling to elect a Catholic President, but it rebuked the Republicans by piling up a landslide victory for Henrik Shipstead, the unimaginative Farmer-Labor senator. Ticket-splitting on this scale was unprecedented in a Presidential year.

Hoover's supporters continued to publicize his virtues in glowing terms. Early in December 1928, Governor Owen Brewster of Maine revealed the existence of a Hoover program for public works that would be activated if the economy showed any sign of faltering. According to Brewster, fact-finding agencies would recognize preliminary warnings of depression far in advance. Business analysts also helped the politicians promote faith in the President's infallibility. The public was assured that economics had achieved the dignity of a science and would usher in greater prosperity. Although Coolidge believed in good times as much as anybody, the repeated predictions about what a genuine engineer would accomplish in the White House began to irritate him. With increasing frequency, his office staff heard Coolidge dismiss last-minute problems by snarling: "We'll leave that to the wonder boy."

VII

Both his popularity and the production indexes were still rising on March 4, 1929, when Hoover took office. Industry was operating at full steam; skyscrapers were being dedicated and opened for occupancy; consumers were feverishly buying a variety of new electrical appliances on the installment plan; and investors were expressing faith in the future by pushing the stock market steadily higher. Under the circumstances neither Coolidge nor Harding would have found any need for energetic activity in the White House. But the new President took a broader view of executive leadership and possessed a more articulate philosophy than his immediate predecessors. The contrast was not so evident in the content of policies as in the manner in which Hoover pursued them. All three postwar Republican Presidents believed in a general way that the national government ought to promote prosperity without infringing on the freedom of the individual or stifling the initative of local governmental units. With Harding and Coolidge this outlook was instinctive. They would have been hard-pressed to formulate it in theoretical terms and would not have worried unduly about violations that suited the interests of their political supporters. Hoover, on the other hand, knew exactly what he believed and why. His program was predicated on basic doctrines about the nature of man and his institutions. Urgent practical problems never tempted Hoover to deviate consciously from his philosophy. When the lines of demarcation which he had drawn between spheres of individual and institutional activity grew blurred, Hoover invoked principles as a guide to action, although occasionally he might have made unconscious rationalizations in line with his wishes.

Undoubtedly Hoover's devotion to principles stood out with such stark clarity because he was forced to apply them under difficult circumstances. Nevertheless, with the possible exception of Theodore Roosevelt, no previous Republican President had enunciated his philosophy as often or embedded it in speeches and state papers as frequently as Hoover. To be sure, nothing before or after had rivaled the intensity of Lincoln's mystical devotion to the Union, but both Roosevelt and Lincoln had displayed a pragmatic streak missing from Hoover's make-up. They had worried little about whether a principle might be destroyed by the method used to implement it, whereas this problem constantly preoccupied Hoover. Like other virtues, consistency can be overdone, and it seemed especially obnoxious to critics of Hoover's philosophy. Yet the court of history has always yielded a grudging admiration to the political leader who makes a determined effort to spurn counsels of expediency.

In print the Hoover philosophy lacks the dramatic, urgent tone that Americans nursed on the bitter ideological disputes of the late-Depression era have come to regard as indispensable. Consequently, it is difficult to realize that much of what Hoover said had been recorded in political science and economic textbooks, and endorsed as emphatically by academicians as the opposite theories of a later generation. In essence, Hoover's position was based on classical nineteenth-century liberalism, qualified by overtones of economic nationalism which had become fashionable both in Europe and America in the 1880's. Like the orthodox liberal, Hoover believed that society should be organized to provide the maximum opportunity for individual initiative and self-development. In theory, he approved of the eighteenth-century constitutional devices which built fences around the citizen to protect him from arbitrary action by government. But Hoover was sufficiently aware of the interdependence between the various elements in society arising out of the industrial revolution to make adjustments in his philosophy. Besides, his faith in engineering and scientific planning predisposed him to favor an enlarged role for government. In this respect he was willing to abandon Thomas Jefferson and Adam Smith, and employ subsidies, tariffs, and various regulatory devices that would promote national welfare.

Hoover's program bore a superficial resemblance to the new nationalism of Theodore Roosevelt and the neo-mercantilism of Europe, but its emphasis was different. By national welfare Hoover still meant the protection of the rugged individualist under twentieth-century conditions, rather than the promotion of group living standards which would thwart initiative at the grass roots. Thus, government should refrain from activities that either private enterprise or local administrative units were capable of handling. Although Hoover experienced some difficulty in drawing the line, he favored government participation in the development of natural resources, power projects, farm marketing agencies, and labor conciliation machinery to the extent that these measures would enable private groups eventually to take over the responsibility. The critical point for Hoover was that government action ought to be indirect rather than direct. He had no particular bias against labor unions or other organizations for the betterment of underprivileged groups. The weakness of Hoover's approach was that business invariably benefited more than other groups from the kind of government action that he endorsed.

The limitations of Hoover's credo might not have become so obvious if the President had been a more magnetic leader. Unfortunately, some of the qualities which made him useful in subordinate posts disappeared in the more exacting environment of the White House. Neither his knack for securing favorable publicity nor his ability to promote teamwork survived his departure from the Commerce Department. It was much easier to gain a reputation for wisdom and candor in a department relatively sheltered from political sniping than in the Presidency. Hoover had looked good by comparison to most of the cabinet members of the Harding and Coolidge Administrations, and had found it simple to place the blame for unpopular policies elsewhere. Once this immunity disappeared, Hoover found press conferences an ordeal and became progressively more aloof and uncommunicative. Reporters retaliated by representing the tribulations of the President in the worst possible light.

Hoover also met with difficulties when he tried to employ the techniques of the administrator in his dealings with Congress. Accustomed to dealing with businessmen, who reverently accepted decisions based on statistical data, the President imagined that politicians would submit as readily to enlightenment. The assumption was a dangerous one at any time, but hopelessly unrealistic in a period of depression when nobody took a rational view of his troubles. A streak of stubbornness prevented Hoover from learning from experience, and he retired from the White House still mystified over the unwillingness of congressmen to share his child-like faith in fact-finding committees.

Other characteristics kept Hoover from becoming an effective politician. Although he had an alert, boyish face that radiated good health, Hoover managed to look abstracted and ill at ease much of the time. He avoided the small talk that promotes confidential relations with politicians. Among intimates Hoover was both brilliant and garrulous, and his excellent mind could range over a variety of subjects. In such an environment, he inspired personal devotion as well as admiration. But Hoover was seldom convivial around anybody who could help him politically.

Most of Hoover's defects became apparent only under stress. At the outset of his Administration people were still under the spell of the campaign propaganda. Inevitably they tended to compare him with Coolidge, which made Hoover look even better. Not only did he work harder than his predecessor, but he showed a wholesome love for the outdoors that had been absent from the White House since the days of Theodore Roosevelt. Hoover's taste ran to big dogs and trout-fishing. He established a weekend camp in the Appalachians a few hours from Washington, and tramped through the woods with the zest of a frontiersman.

Few Presidents encountered less criticism in organizing his government than Hoover did. As usual, the posts were divided between eminent party leaders, campaign workers who deserved recognition, and personal friends of the President. Andrew W. Mellon was asked to stay on as Secretary of the Treasury, as well as "Puddler Jim" Davis, who had presided over the Labor Department since 1921. Hoover wanted Borah for Secretary of State, but the latter recognized that the cabinet did not provide adequate scope for his talents as an obstructionist, and he wisely remained in the Senate. So the post went to Henry L. Stimson of New York, who had served as Secretary of War under Taft. The choice of Walter F. Brown, the chairman of the Republican national committee, as Postmaster General was orthodox enough, while the inclusion of President Ray Lyman Wilbur of Stanford University as Secretary of the Interior assured Hoover of a close friend in his official family. Except for Brown, none of Hoover's selections brought him any political strength. Stimson had been inactive for some time, and Wilbur did not carry much weight with the Republican organization in California. Hoover showed a commendable preference for elder statesmen in other appointments, for he made Charles G. Dawes ambassador to England, and elevated Charles Evans Hughes to the Supreme Court when Taft died in 1930.

Like many of his predecessors who had experienced trouble with Congress, Hoover showed a questionable haste to get acquainted with the lawmakers. He called a special session a month after his inauguration to act on farm relief and tariff revision. Speaker Longworth had the House under effective control, but, as usual, the nominal Republicans from the Great Plains and the Rocky Mountain states held the balance of power in the Senate. The promotion of Curtis to the Vice Presidency necessitated a change in Senate leadership, and the chairmanship of the party conference passed to James Eli Watson of Indiana. From the standpoint of experience, Watson was well suited for the post. He had served as right-hand man to Speaker Joe Cannon in the House from 1902 to 1908, and had reached the Senate in 1916 when the Republicans regained control of Indiana. During the next decade Watson had divided his energy between assisting Lodge and protecting his political position at home. The latter assignment was almost a full-time job, because Watson had to contend with New and Beveridge as well as the Ku Klux Klan, which dominated the state organization. The fact that Watson managed to survive a series of scandals involving Klan officials and Republican office-holders was a tribute to his political shrewdness. Unlike Hoover, he cared little about political principles and a great deal about maintaining the supremacy of the party. He was so adept as a wire-puller that reporters attributed to him a number of older epigrams which glorified political cynicism. He was supposed to have coined the observation that "there is nothing like a majority" and to have revived the witticism: "If you can't beat 'em, join 'em." In any case, Watson was the pragmatist par excellence, and temperamentally at odds with Hoover. Furthermore, Watson had the Midwesterner's suspicion of wealthy men with international connections. He had belonged to the "anyone-but-Hoover" bloc at Kansas City and had contemptuously referred to Hoover as a Britisher. For the sake of the party, Watson tried to co-operate with Hoover, and the President met him halfway, but neither really trusted the other.

Even so, the session started well enough, and within three months Hoover obtained exactly what he had demanded in the way of farm relief. Known as the Agricultural Marketing Act, the new law created a Federal Farm Board of nine members and placed at its disposal a revolving fund of $500 million for loans to bona fide co-operatives. If all went well, the new agency would vindicate Hoover's principle of encouraging farmers to help themselves. Loans would be available to them on a sound business basis, provided that they were willing to organize co-operative marketing organizations. Since the McNary-Haugen supporters denied that the misfortunes of the farmer were solely due to a defective marketing organization, Hoover bought their support with a provision authorizing the Federal Farm Board to establish stabilization corporations. Presumably the purpose of the corporations was to minimize the price fluctuations in key commodities by properly timed buying and selling operations. This kind of operation was dangerously close to the price-fixing devices advocated by the farm bloc, but Hoover indignantly disclaimed any such intention.

The part of the Farm Marketing Act designed to encourage the formation of co-operatives was an immediate success. But neither the centralization of agricultural marketing operations nor the purchases of wheat and cotton by stabilization corporations arrested the drop in farm prices which began in 1929. During the ensuing three years the Farm Board lost $345 million dealing in wheat and cotton, although the fall in prices would probably have occurred more rapidly without its intervention.

That other bugaboo of Republican Presidents, the tariff, produced a far different result in the special congressional session. The President urged the lawmakers to confine rate increases to industrial products suffering from severe competition. The House found over a thousand items in that category, and the Senate a still larger number. The principal trouble came from the farm bloc Republicans, who wanted a government subsidy on agricultural exports. Under the leadership of Borah, they tacked an export debenture provision on the Smoot-Hawley tariff in October 1929, a maneuver which split the party wide open. The surly Moses of New Hampshire characterized the farm bloc senators as "the sons of the wild jackass," while Joseph R. Grundy, who was chairman of the National Association of Manufacturers, snorted that the Western states would never have been "heard from" if the Constitution had not given them two senators.

Eight months later, Hoover managed to knock the debenture provision from the Conference report by threatening a veto. His intervention revived the slumbering distrust of the Chief Executive in the rural areas and jeopardized his other legislative projects. Like several of his predecessors, Hoover did not approve of the final version of the new tariff, which flouted his recommendations and pushed rates to record levels. In the end, he capitulated to the pressure groups clamoring for passage and signed the bill.

VIII

Midway through the debate on the Smoot-Hawley bill, panic gripped the stock market. During the week of October 23 the most frenzied liquidation of stock holdings in American history took place. Republican leaders from the President down expressed confidence that the abrupt break involved only speculators and likened it to the brief Panic of 1907, which had done little damage to the economy. At first, it seemed as if the optimism was justified, but after a few months of hesitation the market began to drift slowly downward. The erosion continued for over three years, and eventually many high-grade stocks were reduced to as little as one-seventh of their peak values. This trend heralded a severe depression, which produced noticeable distress in the fall of 1930 and grew steadily worse during the next two years, until every sector of the economy was engulfed in a common misery. No reliable statistics on unemployment existed, but by 1932 approximately ten million were without jobs.

Hoover was as unsuccessful in his efforts to arrest the deterioration of economic conditions as Grover Cleveland had been after the panic of 1893. The voters reacted to their tribulations between 1929 and 1932, as they had always done in the past, by blaming the party in power. This conditioned reflex dealt a disastrous blow to the Republican party from which it never fully recovered. The generation reaching maturity in the early 1930's came to regard the G.O.P. as the party of depression and refused to return it to power, long after economic problems had been overshadowed by other issues. The intensification of distress during the last three years of Hoover's Administration generated a terrific backfire against the President which was all the more explosive because the public had been convinced by the campaign slogans of 1928 that he was an economic wizard.

In the highly charged emotional atmosphere of the Depression, legends about the incompetence and inactivity of the President were born which bore little relation to the facts. The one accusation which neither Hoover nor his collaborators could dodge was that they had been complacent in the face of the wild speculative activity that preceded the stock market crash of 1929. On the other hand, no previous President, including such a stout friend of the common man as Andrew Jackson, had lectured the people about their indiscretions in the wilder stages of a boom. As in all previous periods of speculative enthusiasm, the primary cause of trouble in 1929 lay with the people themselves, who believed they all could become rich, regardless of whether their investments were sound or not. Before catastrophe struck, few citizens saw anything dangerous in their optimism, and it was wholly characteristic of them to put the blame elsewhere when they gained the sobering perspective of hindsight.

Once the Depression came, Hoover took the intelligent step of trying to restore confidence. He called leaders of industry and labor to the White House and extracted from both groups pledges to carry on economic activity as usual. Then he accelerated public-works programs, and urged state and local officials to do the same. In the fall of 1930 he took two additional steps. He halted immigration and then offered the services of the federal government in co-ordinating scattered relief activities. At the time few people wanted to go further, a fact demonstrated in the 1930 campaign, which was concerned chiefly with the problem of Prohibition enforcement. Republican losses in November were, if anything, relatively low for an off-year election. The results left the Republicans in control of both houses with narrow margins. There were 48 Republicans, 47 Democrats, and one Farmer-Laborite in the Senate, while in the House the Republicans had an over-all majority of three. Before the new Congress met thirteen months later, however, the deaths of several Republicans—including Speaker Longworth—necessitated special elections which went to the Democrats and thus enabled them to organize the House.

Although the outcome in 1930 left it uncertain whether Hoover had been repudiated, Republican losses were sufficiently large to encourage reactivation of the usual coalition between farm bloc Republicans and Democrats in the short session of 1931. Some of them preferred to fight unemployment with large-scale public works and pork-barrel appropriations. Borah, for example, wanted the wealthy to pay for the program in the form of increased income and inheritance taxes. Others anticipated the New Deal with proposals for the establishment of national planning agencies to deal with unemployment, public works, and relief. In the forefront of this movement were two Democratic senators, Edward P. Costigan of Colorado and Robert F. Wagner of New York, plus a Republican maverick, Robert M. La Follette, Jr., of Wisconsin, who now occupied the seat of his father. No common set of principles bound the members of the coalition together. Borah and most of the farm bloc were displaying nothing more than their traditional animus toward Wall Street, which they blamed for all the troubles of America. Most of this group opposed as emphatically as Hoover a genuine enlargement of federal power to fight depression. The Costigan-Wagner-La Follette faction was groping its way toward the type of Progressive program sponsored by Theodore Roosevelt in 1912. As yet, though, they had no clear-cut doctrine of government responsibility for social and economic welfare. In fact, no responsible legislator had reached the point of advocating that relief measures should be undertaken at the expense of a balanced budget.[33]

Hoover was more than a match for the confused army of critics that assailed him during the short session. He vetoed the bills for national planning agencies, and held relief appropriations down to $300 million, a figure twice as large as he had recommended but considerably lower than the one demanded by the coalition. After Congress adjourned, disgruntled members of the bipartisan coalition held a conference in Washington on March 11 and 12, 1931, to frame a program for the next Congress, but broke up without agreement. As usual, Borah had bid for the leadership of the dissidents without presenting any concrete plan of action, which prompted Hiram Johnson to refer to his colleague as "our spearless leader." [34]

During the summer and fall of 1931 economic conditions rapidly grew worse. Five hundred miserable farmers and their wives in drought-ridden Arkansas stormed the business section of England screaming "we are not beggars . . . but we're not going to starve. . . ." [35] Merchants gave food to more than half of them before they quieted down. Elsewhere, the situation in rural areas was just as grave. Some communities established exchanges for the barter of goods, and a few used script or wooden money. Thousands of unemployed roamed the streets of metropolitan areas, lining up at soup kitchens for meals. Large numbers of young unmarried men became vagabonds. They rode around the country in empty railroad boxcars and slept in makeshift dwellings of scrap lumber and tin, settlements bitterly referred to as "Hoovervilles." The year ended with 1600 hunger marchers converging on Congress.

Most of the sufferers were listless and paid little attention to Communist organizers or others urging violent redress of grievances. Nevertheless, the public attitude toward Hoover became increasingly antagonistic. Throughout the country the President was booed when his picture flashed on the screen in movie theaters. Thousands attending a football game at the Los Angeles Coliseum hissed the announcement that Hoover was coming to California the following year to open the Olympic Games.[36] Simultaneously, the whispering campaign about his early career revived, and Hoover was charged with everything from exploiting laborers to reaping enormous profits from business deals.[37] Arthur Train produced a series of articles for *Collier's* dealing with some of these matters. Two full-length books critical of Hoover also had wide circulation: *The Strange Career of Mr. Hoover Under Two Flags* and *Hoover's Millions and How He Made Them*. Despite the ugly demonstrations, Hoover went ahead with plans to deal with the Depression. On the domestic front he launched a variety of projects designed to raise money for private charity, to encourage relief activity by local officials, and to promote odd jobs for the unemployed. The one thing that he stubbornly refused to do was to sponsor direct relief through federal action or provide government jobs in any area that competed with private business. Time and again, he reiterated his basic belief that it was legitimate for the national government to stimulate recovery by indirect measures but not by open intervention in the economy. Just as tirelessly, he insisted that any deviation from his policy would result in regimentation and the destruction of personal liberty.

Hoover professed confidence that his domestic program would produce recovery, but he supplemented it with a series of measures on the international front, since he was convinced that depression was world-wide. On June 21, 1931, he proposed a one-year moratorium on all inter-governmental payments. In effect, he offered a temporary suspension of installments on war and reconstruction debts owed by European powers to the United States, if they would in turn allow Germany to suspend her reparations payments. Hoover's offer was prompted by a desire to stop a series of bank failures in Europe and by a belief that international trade would recover once all states received a brief respite from the obligation to transfer huge balances of gold for debt payments. Simultaneously, he held out the hope of a reduction of debts if the European powers would give up their costly armaments race and balance their budgets.

Neither Hoover's domestic nor his diplomatic program gave any visible lift to the Depression in the fall of 1931, but both provoked much criticism. Opponents ridiculed the private charity drive and charged that the President was indifferent to human misery. Borah, Johnson, and other isolationists took exception just as violently to the moratorium on debt payments, which they branded a devious plot to bail out the international bankers and Wall Street. They loudly accused Hoover of transferring the debt burden from the European governments to the American taxpayer so that the scheming Europeans could pay off their private obligations to Eastern financial houses.[38]

The tempo of political warfare speeded up noticeably when the 72nd Congress convened in December 1931. Only a small bipartisan minority of embryo New Dealers advocated bold government action to cope with the Depression. The vast majority of Republicans and Democrats shared Hoover's philosophy about the proper role of government, but wanted to disassociate themselves from the unpopular President. Lacking any clear ideas about what to do, the Democratic House under the leadership of Speaker John N. Garner of Texas played the double game of defying Hoover on small matters and concurring ungraciously in his major recommendations. Behind this unheroic strategy lurked the fear that an economic revival might take place, and so trap the Democrats in the awkward role of obstructionists. The principal battle arose over the familiar questions of how to provide relief and how to pay for it. Wedded as firmly as ever to the doctrine of helping business to help itself, Hoover sponsored and secured passage of a law establishing a Reconstruction Finance Corporation in January 1932. The new agency was advanced an initial capital of $500,000,000 by the government and empowered to make loans on good security to a wide range of ailing enterprises. The voters overlooked the potential utility of the R.F.C., because it was designed to aid the very groups regarded as responsible for causing the Depression in the first place. Democratic orators in 1932 effectively sneered at the theory of pouring money into big business in the hope that it would "trickle down" to the masses.

After securing passage of the R.F.C. Act, as well as other measures designed to ease the flow of credit, Hoover spent the rest of the session combating proposals that would involve direct relief and thus create an unbalanced budget. In the end he managed to avert an outright government relief program by accepting a compromise in mid-July of 1932 that increased the capital of the R.F.C. and enlarged the purposes for which it could lend money. Altogether, Congress appropriated a record four billion dollars on a variety of projects to combat the Depression, but balked at raising taxes sufficiently to balance the budget. Looking back on the stormy session, the irascible Hiram Johnson confessed to a friend that neither he nor the financial experts had the slightest knowledge of what they were doing: "We have simply taken innumerable shots in the dark in the hope that the enormous sums of money appropriated might accomplish some good." In a final dig at Hoover, Johnson added that, if the President could not re-elect himself with four billion to spend, "he is more unpopular than Judas Iscariot." [39]

IX

Few Republicans believed that Hoover could win in November irrespective of what he did. There was substantial opposition to his renomination, but no organization through which to make it effective. Harold L. Ickes of Chicago tried to rally the old Bull Moosers behind Hiram Johnson or Governor Gifford Pinchot of Pennsylvania. Neither would make the race, although it cost $3500 in public opinion surveys to convince Pinchot that the voters were not interested in him.[40] The regulars made no effort to find a new candidate, so that the Hoover managers were able to secure delegates without much difficulty.

The Republicans opened the convention at Chicago on June 14 in a funereal atmosphere. The only time the delegates showed any enthusiasm was when Permanent Chairman Bertrand Snell of New York delivered a fierce polemic against the Democrats. The convention acquiesced in the renomination of the Hoover-Curtis ticket with a courage born of despair. A number of party leaders thought that some local tickets might be salvaged by abandoning the 18th Amendment. Since the Administration had defended Prohibition too emphatically to abandon it entirely, a floor fight developed. The Hoover managers unveiled a straddle which called for resubmission of the Prohibition question to state conventions, and this plank was sustained by a narrow margin, notwithstanding predictions of disaster in November. The rest of the platform was passed without dispute. It made a blanket defense of the Hoover policies; bravely forecast the end of the Depression; and blamed current pessimism on the unsound proposals of the Democrats in the 72nd Congress. When the convention was over, a distinguished Republican remembered in perplexity that it had nominated a man for whom one did not hear a good word.[41]

The Democrats began gathering at Chicago for their convention on June 27 as soon as the dispirited Republicans had departed. With the smell of victory in the air for the first time since 1916, the old party of Jefferson and Jackson produced an extraordinary number of candidates. Smith thought he deserved another try at Hoover; Speaker Garner wanted the nomination as a reward for his leadership in the 72nd Congress; and a host of favorite-son candidates advertised their availability. Before any of these hopefuls could win, they had to stop Governor Franklin D. Roosevelt of New York, who entered the convention with a majority of the delegates but without the two-thirds necessary for nomination. All orthodox political considerations pointed to the nomination of Roosevelt. He had breasted the Hoover tide in 1928 to win the governorship by 25,000 votes and had increased his margin to 700,000 two years later. Roosevelt was, moreover, the one Democrat likely to attract a significant number of former Bull Moosers and farm bloc Republicans.[42] The "stop Roosevelt" coalition held together for only three ballots, and on the fourth Garner switched the necessary delegates to the New York governor in return for the Vice Presidential nomination.

Roosevelt defied tradition and flew to Chicago to accept the nomination in person. Both he and the Democrats showed more reverence for the political rules in constructing the platform. Indeed, the voters would have found it difficult to distinguish it from the Republican platform. Underlying the various Democratic planks were the same assumptions about the causes and cures of the Depression that the Republicans shared, although, of course, the Democrats promised to implement recovery policies more aggressively than their opponents. Several clauses dealt with security, old-age pensions, and unemployment insurance in lyrical terms, but it was also asserted that jurisdiction over such matters belonged to the states. The sharpest contrast between the two platforms occurred in the treatment of Prohibition, with the Democrats unequivocally committed to repeal of the 18th Amendment. As anticipated, the nomination of Roosevelt brought most of the farm bloc Republicans into the Democratic camp. A Western Independent Republican Committee for Roosevelt was organized by Harold Ickes and received $10,000 from the Democratic national committee.

Inasmuch as both major parties had pledged themselves to solve the Depression in the same way, a host of minor candidates contested their views. The Socialists ran Norman Thomas and campaigned more aggressively than at any time since 1912, when they had polled nearly a million votes. The Communists put William Z. Foster on the ticket in several states, but they were more interested in stirring up trouble than in trying to win an election. "Coin" Harvey and Jacob S. Coxey, two relics from the Populist era, tried to launch a new crusade. Harvey accepted a nomination from a convention of currency cranks who gathered outside their candidate's pyramid at Monte Ne, Arkansas, where he was storing information on the collapse of Western civilization. Coxey revived the Farmer-Labor label and proposed a vast public works program financed by paper money. The Blue Shirts and the Jobless party also entered candidates, but could not get on the ballot in any state. All of these splinter groups were encouraged by the eruption of riots in the Midwest against foreclosures on mortgaged farm property and by the organization of a bonus army which invaded Washington with demands for immediate payment of adjusted service certificates.

The campaign of 1932 featured two major innovations: one was the use of specialists in public relations, a matter hitherto handled by professional politicians; the second was a marked reliance on the radio to carry the message of the candidates. Radio was the largest single item of expenditure for both parties. The Republicans had allocated 10 per cent of their budget to broadcasts in 1928 and doubled the percentage allotment in 1932. The most obvious effect of the new medium was to force the candidates to diversify their speeches. Although both Roosevelt and Hoover spoke about the same basic topics time after time, they had to put their remarks in a variety of contexts so they would avoid tiresome repetition on the air. The single stump speech that could be expanded or contracted survived in dozens of local contests, but the trend toward radio campaigns at every level slowly forced modification of traditional practices. At first, the radio had no perceptible effect on campaign tours, because candidates for major office felt that it was indispensable for them to mingle with local politicians. Roosevelt logged 17,000 miles in 1932, traveling at a clip that compared favorably with the pace of Presidential candidates in a pre-radio age.

The fall campaign featured a long-range debate between Roosevelt and Hoover, with the President winning the arguments and his opponent winning the votes. People did not pay so much attention to what Roosevelt said as to how he said it. His rich, vibrant voice inspired confidence, and in colorful phrases coined by his ghost writers the Democratic candidate promised a "New Deal" for the "forgotten man." Employing the classic strategy of the challenger against an unpopular incumbent, Roosevelt criticized Hoover indiscriminately without committing himself to any novel solutions that might offend migratory voters who had already left the President. Long before the campaign was over, Roosevelt and countless other Democratic orators discovered that the formula worked. The sullen crowds, swelled by thousands who would have preferred to attend a movie but had no money, cheered attacks on Hoover when they responded to nothing else.

The initial intention of the President was to stay on the job in Washington, limiting his campaign to a few major addresses, but the Republican loss of Maine in September drove him into action. The contrast between the platform manner of Hoover and Roosevelt was detrimental to the President. The long months of Depression had eaten away his enthusiasm and made him look perpetually harassed and preoccupied. People differed as to whether adversity had stamped his face with despondency or a scowl, but in any case they gained the impression that Hoover was without hope. This reaction did the President an injustice, because his explanation of Republican policies was learned and clear. He obviously understood economics better than Roosevelt, and he repeatedly bested him in campaign exchanges. Yet Hoover's diagnosis was wasted on voters who wanted an emotional uplift rather than analysis. In the closing days of the campaign, Hoover damaged his cause still further by lashing back at unjustified accusations that he was a do-nothing President. He began to speak of himself as the salvation of the Republic, and predicted that if Roosevelt won "the grass will grow in the streets of a hundred cities; . . . the weeds will overrun the fields of millions of farms . . . their churches and school houses will decay."

The voters went to the polls on November 8 with Hoover's gloomy prophecy ringing in their ears, but approximately 60 per cent of them ignored it. Roosevelt received 22,821,857 popular votes to 15,761,841 for Hoover and slightly over a million in aggregate for all minor party candidates. The outcome was much more lopsided in the electoral college with the Democrats carrying 42 states with 472 electoral votes and the Republicans carrying 6 states with a total of 59 electoral votes. Although Hoover did better than Taft in 1912, the only states that he carried outside of New England were Pennsylvania and Delaware. The results in the South were particularly discouraging to Republicans, who had dreamed of establishing a two-party system there after their spectacular breakthrough in 1928. Despite Hoover's attempt to dislodge the skeletal Republican patronage machines by appointing respectable Southerners to federal office, the region produced its traditional top-heavy Democratic majorities. The turnover in Congress was as drastic as in the country at large. The Democrats wound up with 313 seats in the House to 117 for the Republicans and five for minor-party candidates. In the Senate, where only one-third of the membership had faced the voters, the Democrats controlled 59 seats, the Republicans 36, and the Farmer-Laborites 1. Nevertheless, the G.O.P. oligarchy was cut to bits, the principal casualties being majority leader Watson, Smoot of Utah, and Moses of New Hampshire. Neither the lame ducks nor the holdovers wasted any sympathy on Hoover.[43] Borah sneered that his fellow countrymen had not voted for Roosevelt but against Hoover, while McNary of Oregon thought the repudiation of the President might help business.[44]

The most constructive accomplishment of the lame duck session following the defeat of Hoover was the ratification of the 20th Amendment which abolished such sessions. This anachronism in the American governmental system might have faded out of existence without causing a ripple but for the onslaught of the bank panic and the effort of Hoover to identify Roosevelt with Republican policies. As it was, these related developments turned the deadlock into the most frustrating one since the short session following the election of Lincoln in 1860, and increased the bitterness between the outgoing and the incoming Presidents. Their mutual unwillingness to co-operate during the bank crisis launched a twenty-five year controversy over who was responsible for the penultimate phase of the Depression.

Whatever the ultimate verdict of history on Hoover, one thing is certain: he was not a good loser. Although the voters had rebuked him in unmistakable fashion, Hoover carried on as if he were a man elected to a new term. He bombarded Congress with recommendations and tried to proceed along the lines already charted in the field of international affairs. A political leader with a more sportsmanlike attitude might have asked how he could be of service to his successor, but Hoover was not in a magnanimous mood. With some justification, he felt that his efforts to fight the Depression had been flagrantly misrepresented by his opponent. He believed, moreover, that Roosevelt's campaign professions of devotion to a balanced budget and fiscal responsibility were hollow. Hoover was particularly afraid that Roosevelt intended to abandon the gold standard, turn his back on international measures to solve the Depression, and promote large-scale government intervention in the economy. So Hoover convinced himself that it was his patriotic duty to force the President-elect either to avow his real intentions or acquiesce in the policy of his predecessor.

With debtor states demanding readjustment as early as November 10, 1932, Hoover began pressing for a co-ordinated settlement in which America would lighten the debt burden if European governments committed themselves to reduce armaments, stabilize their currencies in terms of gold, and lower trade barriers. This proposed policy was a logical outgrowth of Hoover's thesis that a real cure for the Depression necessitated remedial measures on an international scale. Any Administration spade work for the World Economic Conference scheduled for the spring of 1933 was futile unless Roosevelt agreed to carry on the Hoover policy. At the President's request, a confrontation between the two men and their advisers took place in mid-November. Roosevelt was amiable but non-committal, and the frustrating sparring on foreign policy continued until inauguration day.

In February 1933, Hoover's attention was distracted by heavy runs on large metropolitan banks that threatened to bring the monetary system to a standstill. As the contagion spread from Detroit eastward, Hoover once more opened negotiations with Roosevelt for joint action. The President was tactless enough to suggest that the bank panic was due to fear of Roosevelt's monetary policy and that confidence would be restored if the President-elect pledged himself to maintain the gold standard. Hoover also wanted Roosevelt to prod congressional Democrats into activating remedial banking legislation which languished in committees. The President-elect declined to intervene, and left the impression that the Administration had caused the trouble and should take sole responsibility for extricating itself. While the deadlock persisted, the banking crisis gained momentum. State after state proclaimed banking holidays, in an effort to stop runs by depositors and to give their financial institutions a chance to recover. As paralysis approached, Hoover redoubled his pleas for help, but Roosevelt declined to assume obligations until he received constitutional responsibility. Thus, Hoover left office on March 4 convinced that his obstructive successor had aggravated the Depression and brought the country to the verge of chaos.

In the light of the subsequent economic revival, it has become fashionable to ridicule Hoover's policies. Yet, it is difficult to demonstrate that Hoover's analysis of the situation was wholly unjustified. The Depression, as he insisted, was a world-wide affair. Hoover was also incontestably right in believing that the failure of the great powers to stabilize currency and remove trade barriers would promote managed societies as well as economic warfare. Perhaps Hoover overdid his devotion to the gold standard, but abandonment of it was certainly one of the many factors that fed the long-term inflation of ensuing decades. It is a moot question whether prolongation of the Hoover policies would have produced an economic revival at home and abroad or averted the drift of the great powers toward war. Considering the money and human life that pursuing recovery on a purely internal basis cost, the historian must question the wisdom of the indiscriminate condemnation lavished on Hoover. His real sin did not lie so much in his economic policies as in his uninspired way of pursuing them. Despite his insistence on "indirect" intervention in the economy, both his budgets and his expenditures had grown steadily larger by 1932 and approached the New Deal level. The trouble was that Hoover could not inspire confidence or give people enough faith in the future to make the hundreds of small, individual decisions necessary for recovery. His successor knew far less about economics than Hoover but was a master in the difficult art of giving pessimistic Americans a dramatic psychological boost.

XII

The Long Years of Frustration

The inauguration of Roosevelt on March 4, 1933, marked the beginning of an era which was to prove as disheartening for the Republican party as the post-Civil War decades had been for the Democrats. The unfamiliar frustrations of minority status embittered G.O.P. leaders, clouded their judgment, and goaded them into political errors. Each blunder led to mutual recriminations and the deterioration of morale, which in turn provoked a fresh disaster at the polls. Like a groggy, bewildered football team, the Republicans never escaped from the shadow of their own goal posts. In their hour of adversity, all their sins of omission in the 1920's were there to plague them. Having limited the party to the role of custodian of prosperity, the Republicans lacked principles which could be employed to slow down defections during the Depression. No pressure group but big business remained loyal, and its continued support became a liability when congressional investigations uncovered a multitude of dishonest financial transactions dating back to the hectic days before the stock market crash.

The consequence of Republican misdeeds was magnified by the fact that during its first twelve years in the political wilderness the party faced the shrewdest antagonist in its history. Estimates regarding the character and motives of Franklin D. Roosevelt differ widely, but nobody has ever disputed his ability to capitalize on the errors of his opponents. He had more faces than the Hindu Brahma, and turned upon the Republicans whatever one the occasion required to keep them off balance. Sometimes they were confronted with the face of the dreamy humanitarian clouded by thoughts of war or malnutrition. More frequently they saw the face of the crusader with jaw set and chin tilted upward. On other occasions they beheld the austere countenance of a chief of state who seemed aloof from party and selflessly devoted to public welfare. Just as often a puckish face invited Republicans to believe that politics was only a game, but during the campaign season good-humored smiles gave way to indignant frowns over what Roosevelt branded as the behavior of a malignant opposition. Coupled with a versatile personality were a superb sense of timing, an uncanny ability to stay just ahead of public opinion, and a knack for obtaining sustained favorable publicity from a hostile press.

Whether these qualities would have enabled Roosevelt to assert leadership over the sullen, quarreling pressure groups in 1932 is uncertain. Fortunately for him, Roosevelt did not have to deal with people in an obstructive frame of mind, because the bank panic in the month preceding his inauguration had created a genuine sense of public emergency. Until that time, the chief complaints, as in earlier depressions, had come from farmers and unemployed workers, whose woes left more prosperous groups unmoved. But the sudden evaporation of lifetime savings engulfed smug middle-class citizens in the common ruin, and shattered their illusion that adversity overtook only the wicked, the foolish, and lazy. Overnight, the well educated and the articulate joined the clamor for drastic action by the new President. With all segments of the economy affected deeply, the major groups which habitually thwarted one another were willing to co-operate. The sense of urgency was so overwhelming that people followed Roosevelt without inquiring about the direction in which he intended to move.

Capitalizing on this unprecedented situation, Roosevelt called a special session of Congress for March 9, 1933; and in the ensuing 104 days he secured legislation to reorganize the banks, inflate the money supply, and provide aid for agriculture, business, labor, homeowners, and the unemployed. Never had the congressional mill ground out laws so rapidly. The House passed the Banking bill of March 9 before it was printed, and some congressmen wandered over to the Senate to find out what was in it. True to its reputation for moving at a more deliberate pace, the Senate spent two hours and fifteen minutes on the bill, whereas the House had disposed of it in thirty-eight minutes. The pace slowed down somewhat in April, but during the so-called "hundred days" it was not unusual for complex bills introduced on one day to become laws the next. The legislators were so docile that they accepted measures drafted at the White House without making the customary protests about the encroachment of the executive on congressional prerogatives. In the process, party lines broke down completely, although fifteen Republican senators voted against all Administration proposals. As usual, the former Bull Moosers and members of the farm bloc compiled erratic records, which proved nothing except that they were still individualists. Of this group, Borah gave Roosevelt the least support and Norris gave the most.

When Congress adjourned, it was clear that no segment of the economy had been overlooked in the distribution of relief. As a matter of fact, the Administration had allowed each pressure group to prescribe its own cure. Yet nobody was any wiser about the ultimate goals of the New Deal. Some measures, such as the National Industrial Recovery Act (N.I.R.A.) and the Agricultural Adjustment Act (A.A.A.), envisaged the national government in a more ambitious role as planner and co-ordinator of productive activity. Legislation conferring power on the President to devalue the dollar and to provide direct relief for the unemployed pointed in the same direction. On the other hand, a number of laws seemed to aim merely at the correction of abuses which many people thought were responsible for the stock market crash and the bank panic. Thus, it was possible at the end of the "hundred days" for some people to believe that Roosevelt favored the purification of capitalism and for others to believe that he wanted to destroy it. Subsequent New Deal legislation only hardened the beliefs on either side and did little to determine the Administration's basic direction. Repeated statements that the New Deal felt responsible for promoting human welfare provided little illumination, because every previous American President had paid homage to this objective. The only unmistakable trend of the Roosevelt years was the increase of both direct and indirect governmental influence over the national economy.

Hoover and his Republican predecessors had tried to stimulate economic activity by protective tariffs, public works, and other governmental policies. As a rule, these subsidies had been indirect, and the principal beneficiaries had been business groups. As a result, the Republicans did not object strenuously to New Deal measures which followed traditional paths. What did arouse their wrath were policies involving direct subsidies to additional groups such as labor, agriculture, migratory workers, homeowners, debtors, the aged, and the unemployed. Many Republicans accepted the principle that people in these categories were entitled to better conditions, but denounced aid which involved government planning as regimentation and the destruction of the American way of life.

II

There was little debate along these lines while the crisis atmosphere of 1933 prevailed. Indeed, during the first year of the New Deal most voters regarded criticism of the President as unpatriotic. With the approach of the 1934 congressional elections, however, Republicans found their voices. They were especially violent in their criticism of the Reciprocal Trade Agreements Act, which authorized the President to negotiate limited tariff reductions. But the Republicans knew that they could not wage the campaign on this issue, and they disagreed about other issues. One faction coalesced behind Hoover, who aspired to the role of minority leader and favored a blanket indictment of the New Deal. An opposing group rallied behind Republican congressional leaders, most of whom feared that Hoover's strategy would backfire on the party. Disharmony was aggravated by the absence in our constitutional system of any provision for centralized leadership of the minority. According to custom, a defeated Presidential candidate was titular leader of his party, but he neither sat in Congress nor possessed any power to shape the legislative policy of the minority. Hitherto the problem of a divided command had never been very serious for the Republicans, largely because they had been in power 56 of the preceding 72 years. The only Republican ex-President who had tried to speak for the party was Theodore Roosevelt in 1916, and the results had been disastrous.

Nevertheless, Hoover ignored precedent and tried to assert his authority in the only way that was possible, by bidding for control of the national committee. The showdown came in the spring of 1934 when the national committee met at the Palmer House in Chicago to select a successor for national chairman Everett Sanders, who had managed the 1932 campaign. The Hoover forces prevailed after a brief struggle and selected Henry P. Fletcher, with the result that the national committee issued a series of violent broadsides against the New Deal during the campaign that fall. At Jackson, Michigan, Fletcher celebrated the eightieth birthday of the Republican party by assailing the 73rd Congress as an assembly of rubber stamps. Since many Republicans had voted for New Deal measures, they bridled at Fletcher's blanket indictment as well as at his reference to the feeble minds of the lawmakers. Yet nothing could stop the denunciations from national headquarters. Hoover joined the chorus with a series of speeches exhorting the voters to save the Constitution by voting the Republican ticket. In September he also published a book entitled *The Challenge to Liberty*, which proclaimed that a New Deal dictatorship was imminent. Just before Hoover's book appeared, a group of wealthy industrialists had organized the Liberty League. Ostensibly nonpartisan, the Liberty League—as one of its sponsors confided to a friend—was created for the purpose of "encouraging people to work; encouraging people to get rich." [1] The sentiments expressed in the leaflets of the new organization coincided so closely with those of Hoover that nobody could doubt which party they favored.

The crusade of the national committee and its "nonpartisan" supporters was carried on amidst mounting evidence of grass-roots support for the New Deal. A redcap in the Washington railroad station, when asked if he favored it, replied: "Well suh, I don't know nothin' about the New Deal, but if it's that what's gettin' us bigger tips then I'm for it." [2] Republican Senator Fess of Ohio reported in dismay that many of his constituents had been urging him to support the President. Caught in this rip tide, many Republicans up for re-election secretly cursed the national committee, professed their sympathy for the objectives of the New Deal, and confined their criticism to pious laments about the concentration of power in Washington. Hiram Johnson, Robert M. La Follette, Jr., and a few other mavericks solicited and received endorsements from Roosevelt.

Their precaution was justified, because the 1934 elections produced an even greater Democratic landslide than in 1932. For the first time since 1866 the party in power increased its margin in both Houses in an off-year election. Democratic strength rose from 313 to 332 in the House, and from 59 to 69 in the Senate. State races went equally strongly against the Republicans, as only a few G.O.P. governors secured re-election. Most observers interpreted the result as a vote of confidence in the President rather than an endorsement of specific New Deal measures. Roosevelt's energetic leadership, buoyant manner, and willingness to experiment had produced a tonic effect on the economy and had revived the people's confidence in the country.

There were limits, however, to recovery based on optimism alone. By the beginning of 1935 cracks appeared in the solidarity of the "all-pressure group" coalition which had dominated the first phase of the New Deal.

Having overcome their alarm, the various pressure groups resumed their traditional warfare and thereby doomed the Roosevelt policy of indiscriminate aid to all sectors of the economy. Businessmen were the most restless and vocal. Some objected to the N.R.A. codes; others concentrated their fire on the inflationary trend of the New Deal, which was underwritten by deficit spending and the abandonment of the gold standard. Nearly all businessmen feared that emergency expenditures for relief would be continued, and they recoiled from the idea of the government employing people directly in competition with private enterprise.

Thus, Roosevelt was confronted with a basic choice between a conservative coalition and a radical one. Either he could bid for white-collar groups, conservative craft workers, and the more well-to-do farmers or for the depressed elements who had profited least from his initial recovery program. The problem was complicated by a serious difference of opinion among Roosevelt's advisers. One set ignored the increased tempo of infighting between pressure groups and proposed to harmonize diverse interests by bigger and better N.R.A.'s. Doctrinal enthusiasm sustained the advocates of national planning, although the N.R.A. seemed likely to collapse under its own weight before June 30, 1935, when it was slated to end. Within this group there was considerable discord between those who regarded the co-operation of business as essential to the success of any plan and those who thought in socialistic terms. A second set of "brain trusters" was more clear about what it wanted. They urged the President to embark on an old-style Populistic reform program, featuring punitive legislation against groups deemed responsible for the Depression.

Neither the planners nor the reformers worried very much about the practical effect of their proposals on political alignments. Roosevelt had every incentive to be more realistic, because a number of radical spellbinders raised the specter of a national third party just as he was threatened by the defection of conservative supporters. Minnesota's militant Farmer-Labor governor, Floyd B. Olson, had just won a third term on a platform advocating state ownership of key industries, while in neighboring Wisconsin the newly organized Progressive party of the La Follette brothers had captured the state with the same kind of appeal. Huey P. Long, a Louisiana senator who had established a virtual dictatorship at Baton Rouge, was attracting national attention with a murky program "to share the wealth." Three other would-be political messiahs bidding for the limelight were Dr. Francis E. Townsend, a retired physician who advocated a pension of $200 a month for every person over sixty; Father Charles Coughlin, a Detroit radio priest with a vast audience and some fanciful ideas about currency inflation; and Gerald L. K. Smith, a sort of fundamentalist version of Father Coughlin.

Nobody could tell in early 1935 whether a national third party could be built upon the conflicting doctrines and ambitions of the radicals, but fear of defections on the left was undoubtedly a factor in Roosevelt's decision to forge a new coalition out of the depressed and disgruntled elements in the population. He was also encouraged to sever his connections with business by the enormous unpopularity of industrialists and bankers revealed in the election of 1934. Since they had taken credit for the prosperity of the 1920's, businessmen inherited the blame for the ensuing Depression. The subsequent exposure by congressional committees of corrupt market transactions on Wall Street converted public distrust into a blind unreasoning hatred of business and all of its works. Under the circumstances, Roosevelt could not resist the temptation to make war on the group that had run the American economy, with brief exceptions, since the Civil War.

It was characteristic of the President to reassure both the planners and the reformers that he supported their viewpoints. The legislative program of the 74th Congress, however, gave the most comfort to the reformers. It included the celebrated Wagner Act, which forced management to bargain collectively with labor unions; an amendment to the Securities Act, which outlawed certain categories of utilities holding companies; and a revision of the tax laws designed to chastise corporations and individuals in the high income brackets. Besides bidding for the votes of workers and other foes of the wealthy, the President tried to outflank his left-wing critics by securing a social security act which featured a complicated system of federal-state co-operation on old-age pensions and unemployment insurance. The only consolation the planners derived from the Administration program was increased relief appropriations and the establishment of the Tennessee Valley Authority, which involved government promotion of dam construction, soil conservation, recreational facilities, homesteads, and generation of cheap electric power in the area. Roosevelt supported the planners by vague professions of devotion to the theories of John Maynard Keynes, who advocated government management of economic life through spending and taxation policies. There was little relation, however, between the disorderly spending habits of the New Deal, which funneled money through a variety of agencies, and the sophisticated system of deficit finance advocated by Keynes. At first the new relief organizations of 1935, the Civil Works Administration (C.W.A.) and the Works Progress Administration (W.P.A.), provided jobs without reference to political considerations; but this policy broke down as the 1936 election approached. Particularly in the W.P.A., relief projects were tailored by its chief administrator, Harry Hopkins, to the needs of the large urban Democratic machines.

The Roosevelt stand between the reformers and planners forced some of the latter, such as Raymond Moley and Hugh S. Johnson, to leave the Administration. On the other hand, the spate of legislation in 1935–36 made grateful New Deal supporters of such diverse groups as farmers, organized labor, the unemployed, and the aged. Simultaneously, Roosevelt was cultivating such ethnic and religious minorities as the Negroes, the Jews, the Italo-Americans, and the Poles by artful use of the appointing power. During the twelve preceding years Republican Presidents had conferred only 16 out of 216 federal judgeships on Catholics and Jews, while in the same length of time Roosevelt drew 51 out of 196 judicial appointments from these two groups.

Political observers were sharply divided as to whether Roosevelt acted from expediency or humanitarian impulse in formulating legislative and patronage policies. Undoubtedly he felt genuine sympathy for the suffering of underprivileged groups and desired to help them. Yet he moved in such a methodical way to cultivate groups the Republicans had ignored and to organize new interest groups that political considerations must have played some part in his calculations. In any case, Roosevelt was so effective that it took the Republicans nearly twenty years to make substantial inroads in the coalition that he created.

The only effective opposition to Roosevelt in 1935–36 was provided by the Supreme Court, which invalidated the N.I.R.A., and the A.A.A., and several other important New Deal measures. The Republican minority in the 74th Congress displayed no cohesiveness whatever. The more excitable partisans exploded in protests which suggested that they were opposed to recovery. Others followed the example of Senate Minority Leader Charles McNary of Oregon and absorbed their punishment in silence. The situation was particularly difficult for them because they approved of many New Deal measures but regarded the huge expenditures as a thinly concealed effort to buy votes.[3]

III

Although the Republicans were unable to display a united front in Congress, they realized that the party would suffer an overwhelming defeat in 1936 unless Hoover retired from control. A coterie of personal supporters preferred another catastrophe at the polls to the abandonment of the ex-President. A much larger group, which was responsive to Eastern business leaders, believed that the party could win on a flat anti-New Deal platform, provided that it offered the voters some new faces. This view found little support among G.O.P. politicians in Congress. Confronted with massive support of the New Deal as reflected in mail from their constituents, most legislators concluded that the party needed new leaders and new principles. As Borah expressed it after the 1934 elections: "You can't eat the Constitution."

Meanwhile, in the summer of 1935 Hoover continued to make what he regarded as authoritative definitions of party doctrine through the national committee. He also stumped the country tirelessly. Despite his disclaimers of interest in the nomination, nobody was fooled.[4] His strategy was to promote a deadlock, and he worked behind the scenes for unpledged delegations full of Hoover sympathizers. He achieved his purpose in California but did not succeed elsewhere.

The Eastern faction ran into an equal amount of difficulty. Ogden Mills, Winthrop Aldrich, ex-Senator David A. Reed of Pennsylvania, and Connecticut boss J. Henry Roraback could not decide whether to back an anti-Roosevelt Democrat like Al Smith or Bainbridge Colby or to rally behind one of their own group. They soon discovered that most Republicans would not vote for any Democrat and that nobody acceptable to the business leaders had any national following. To their dismay, the Eastern conservatives also found that most potential candidates considered their support to be a liability. Faced with the prospect of accepting an unresponsive Western candidate, the conservatives could do nothing but await developments. It was a humiliating situation for the section which had controlled the party during much of its history.

Borah was the most famous member of the group committed to a qualified endorsement of the New Deal, but he had little following among the convention delegates. For over thirty years "the Lion of Idaho" had harassed the party from the inside. He had adroitly fanned sectional grievances and obstructed the party program in Congress. With maddening regularity he had incited others to bolt and then disassociated himself from their action. Worse still, Borah had never supported Republican Presidential candidates when he was up for re-election in Idaho and in a position to benefit from the votes of dissidents. He had no strength whatever in the East, where his antique Progressivism was regarded as a cloak for the appetites of his section. Borah's voting record left everybody bewildered. He had assailed the N.R.A. and the A.A.A. for centralizing power in Washington, but had supported spending programs which tended in the same direction. Nevertheless, the seventy-year-old Senator announced his candidacy in January 1936 and waged a rancorous campaign against the Wall Street monopolists, whom he accused of dominating the Republican party.

A migratory newspaper publisher named Frank Knox came forward to compete with Borah for the allegiance of the prewar Republican Progressives. As a wide-eyed youth of 24, Knox had joined the Rough Riders in 1898 and become a life-long worshipper of Theodore Roosevelt, whom he had followed into the abortive Bull Moose movement. Knox never recovered from his exposure to Roosevelt, and after Roosevelt's death he seemed like a reincarnation of him. Not only did Knox pose as an advocate of the strenuous outdoor life, but he appropriated the personality and vocabulary of Roosevelt. People who encountered Knox were engulfed in waves of enthusiasm and sprayed with a variety of colorful expressions. Leaving Michigan before the war, Knox had launched a paper in Manchester, New Hampshire, only to abandon it in 1927 when he was offered an opportunity to manage the Hearst papers in Boston. Knox possessed too much independence to last long in the Hearst organization, and in 1931 he purchased the *Chicago Daily News*. He arrived in Chicago just as the Cook County organization of Mayor William Hale Thompson was falling apart. Knox moved into the vacuum by establishing his own political organization, while the *Daily News* attacked the New Deal. Even with the memory of the first Roosevelt to inspire him, Knox was no match for Colonel Robert R. McCormick and his *Chicago Tribune* in castigating the Roosevelt Administration. Knox's greater self-restraint proved to be an asset in the long run, for it enabled him to enter the Presidential contest as both an old-fashioned reformer and a critic of Roosevelt.

Many Republican leaders were drawn to Governor Alfred M. Landon of Kansas, a survivor of the New Deal tidal waves in both 1932 and 1934. At first glance Landon appeared to be the perfect candidate for Republi-

cans who wanted to combine praise of basic New Deal objectives with outspoken denunciation of its methods. Although he had been too young to
attract attention in the Bull Moose campaign, the 48-year-old Landon
carried the same credentials of insurgency as Borah and Knox. Landon's
father had battled at Armageddon with Roosevelt, and young Alf had
voted for La Follette in 1924. Thereafter he had fought the regulars in
Kansas until he wrested power from them in 1932. Landon did not
possess an original stock of ideas, but he was open-minded and willing to
discuss everything from the New Deal to Russian Communism in a dispassionate fashion. The universal misery arising out of the Depression
convinced him that government would have to take a larger responsibility
for the welfare of its citizens. In general, he believed that most of the new
functions ought to be assumed by state governments, but he was not doctrinaire on this point and emphatically supported federal aid to agriculture.
What particularly irked Landon about the New Deal was deficit spending.
He thought it inefficient and wasteful, feared that it would degenerate into
vote-buying, and expected it to generate runaway inflation. Existing law
forced Kansas to balance her budget, but Landon would have pursued
such a policy in any case. It was the one feature of his philosophy that
attracted conservative Republicans and hurt him with the more radical
elements in the party as well as the irresolute New Dealers. Landon's
tight rein on the state budget exposed him to charges that state facilities
were shockingly inadequate. Critics paid particular attention to the low
salaries of Kansas grade school teachers, which averaged $615 per year.
This situation was hardly Landon's fault, because the state had never
adopted the policy of providing aid to public schools.

Although Landon's stand for fiscal responsibility cut both ways, his
personality was a decided asset for the kind of campaign that most Republicans wanted to wage. His accumulation of a modest fortune as an
independent oil operator had done nothing to alter his easy-going, modest
bearing. In looks and action he was an honest small-town citizen with
considerable common sense. His face was typical of Midwestern pioneer
stock, weather-beaten, friendly, and strong. People felt at ease with his
flat, unassertive drawl which assured them that their opinions would receive a courteous hearing. Landon was far more shrewd and calculating
than his manner suggested, but he offered a perfect contrast to the sophisticated squire in the White House. Moreover, he displayed a sanity in word

and deed that set him off from Senator Capper, William Allen White, and the other erratic Kansas reformers.

Landon had begun to think seriously about the Presidency in the summer of 1935, at which time he allowed Roy Roberts and Lacy Haynes of the *Kansas City Star* to begin organizational work. The conservative national committeeman for Kansas, John D. M. Hamilton, and William Allen White soon joined the movement. Despite their lack of experience, these Kansans operated a professional campaign. They spent little money, ostentatiously spurned the support of Wall Street, and avoided primary contests that might offend other candidates.[5] Soon *Cosmopolitan, Good Housekeeping,* and *Harper's* were sending staff writers to interview Landon. William Randolph Hearst visited Kansas in December 1935, announced that Landon was another Lincoln, and tendered the support of his vast newspaper chain. With the great and the lowly coming to Landon's support, he seemed certain to win the nomination when he announced his candidacy in January 1936.

The only serious dark-horse candidate was Senator Arthur H. Vandenberg of Michigan, who had first won his seat in 1928 and then had barely been re-elected in 1934. During the later phase of a senatorial career that was to last more than two decades, Vandenberg displayed great capacity for mental growth, but on the eve of the 1936 convention people dismissed him as a narrow-minded, windy doctrinaire. Along with Frank Knox, he had started to work in 1898 on the *Grand Rapids Herald,* which was the leading preparatory school for Michigan politicians. Newspaper work ought to have sharpened both Vandenberg's wits and his style, but unfortunately he had fallen under the influence of William Allen Smith, one of Michigan's prewar nonentities in the Senate, who was known for solemnly delivered redundancies and non sequiturs. Vandenberg never completely recovered from his exposure to Smith, but his florid prose proved to be an asset in 1936 because everyone knew he was hostile to the New Deal without having any idea what he stood for. Vandenberg merely hinted he was available, if there was a deadlock, but did not actively seek the nomination.

Borah and Knox contended with each other in the primaries. Borah offered to rescue the Republican party from sinister monopolistic influences, but only in Wisconsin did this appeal find support. Elsewhere he produced bitterness and reinforced the determination of party leaders to stop him. In the New Jersey primary Borah was thoroughly beaten by Landon, 311,143 to 74,620, although Landon had done no campaigning. A favorite-son delegation headed by Robert A. Taft, the son of the former President, took the bulk of the delegates away from Borah in the Ohio primary. Finally, in Illinois Knox defeated Borah, 491,575 to 420,780. Both men were eliminated in this primary, for Knox had failed to carry his own state conclusively and Borah had lost a constituency which could have been expected to support his isolationism.

When the party delegates assembled in Cleveland early in June, it was expected that Landon would win a first-ballot nomination. Knox still made wild promises to save the country from the Communists he saw masquerading as New Dealers. Hoover waited hopefully for deadlock, and took some comfort from the noncommittal attitude of the large New York and Pennsylvania delegations. The Landon managers were so sure of themselves that they spent the initial days of the convention trying to prevent the platform committee from writing a conservative document. Their backstage maneuvers were aimed at forestalling a bolt by Borah, as well as securing resolutions in harmony with the views of their candidate. Accordingly, William Allen White interrupted his dispatches about the "starry-eyed young Kansas idealists" long enough to sound out Borah. But Borah demanded an extreme isolationist plank as well as an omission of any reference to the gold standard. He was probably relieved at being turned down, because he was running for a sixth term as senator and looking for an excuse to avoid supporting the national ticket.

The final draft of the party platform demonstrated anew the vitality of the two-party system. Since the 1932 election the country had acquiesced in a new concept of governmental responsibility, and the Republicans accepted the verdict by grudgingly endorsing New Deal objectives. The Republican platform concealed the abandonment of traditional positions behind a smoke screen of rhetoric. It announced that a New Deal victory would jeopardize "the welfare of American men and women, and the future of our youth." It also slashed indignantly at reciprocal trade agreements and deficit spending, but the underlying theme was one of capitulation to a new order.

The delegates vented their frustration over what they felt obliged to do by cheering wildly at Hoover's blanket denunciation of the New Deal. Time after time they interrupted his appeal for a new crusade with shouts of "We want Hoover." Each time he attempted to leave the platform, he was greeted with a fresh round of applause. Delegations lifted their standards and marched around the hall. The bewildered Hoover did not understand that the convention was paying final tribute to the old order. Misconstruing the demonstration as the prelude to a stampede, he tried to bring it to a head by persuading Permanent Chairman Bertrand Snell of New York to announce that he was leaving for New York. Instead of going to the railroad station, though, Hoover returned to his hotel room and contacted Vandenberg and Knox. With Chester Rowell of the California delegation acting as an intermediary, messages went back and forth between Hoover and the two candidates.[6] Vandenberg and Knox had no particular love for Landon, but believed that the nomination of Hoover would lead to disaster at the polls. When both men ignored Hoover's hint of availability, Hoover realized there would be no stampede for him, and so boarded the train.

Once the delegates had relieved their pent-up emotions, they nominated Landon on the first ballot. Vandenberg was offered second place on the ticket and declined. Then the convention turned to Knox, who received the news of his nomination in a hotel dining-room where he had stopped on his way back to Chicago. Knox composed a telegram of acceptance in Bull Moose terms, as he informed the delegates that they stood "at Armageddon." It was an ironic exhortation to a convention which had nominated a standard bearer and adopted a platform which precluded a crusade.

Later in June the Democrats renominated the Roosevelt-Garner ticket with a great display of enthusiasm in Philadelphia. They also wrote a platform lauding the achievements of the New Deal and eliminated the ancient party rule requiring a two-thirds majority for a Presidential nomination. A splinter group of Jeffersonian Democrats bolted the ticket, but it was clear that the conservatives had little support from the party as a whole. The prospects for a national third party drawing away the radicals from Roosevelt likewise looked dim in the summer of 1936. Huey Long had been assassinated by one of his numerous enemies in September 1935, and Governor Olson, another leader of the radicals, was slowly dying of cancer. To make matters worse, Olson announced from his hospital room that his own Farmer-Labor party in Minnesota would back Roosevelt to forestall the election of Landon. Deprived of their leaders, the quarrelsome followers of Townsend, Father Coughlin, and Gerald L. K. Smith chose William Lemke, an obscure North Dakota congressman, to a third-party ticket. The selection of Lemke was made in such clandestine fashion that it was said he had been nominated in a phone booth. The new organization took the unimaginative name of Union party and during the campaign only provided comic relief. "The jitney messiahs," as H. L. Mencken called the third-party leaders, could agree about nothing and seldom sat together on the same platform. Their efforts to dramatize the colorless, bald-headed Lemke were equally unfortunate. At first they unveiled him as "Liberty Bell Bill" but hastily dropped the nickname when the Democrats jeered that the Liberty Bell was cracked.

For all practical purposes the fall campaign was a two-party contest between Roosevelt and Landon. It turned out to be even more bitter than the 1928 campaign as both sides stirred up class hatred while piously deploring the practice. If Landon had been able to control his party, he would have prevented the polarization of debate along class lines. Not only was he a moderate by conviction, but he saw that it would be fatal to the Republicans if the Democrats succeeded in identifying him with big business. Consequently, Landon struggled valiantly at the outset to set a temperate tone.[7] He repudiated the support of the Liberty League and managed to keep the resentful Hoover from more than a token participation in the campaign. He repeatedly impressed upon local leaders the necessity of including labor leaders on reception committees and exiling businessmen to the fringes of Republican rallies.[8] These efforts were thwarted by the violent partisanship of his own followers, fanned in turn by the crafty tactics of Roosevelt, who denounced them as "economic royalists." In the closing stages of the campaign Landon partially succumbed to the hysteria surrounding him and went further than he had intended in denouncing the New Deal.

Lesser Republicans showed no restraint whatever. Senator Lester J. Dickinson of Iowa charged that the agricultural policies of the New Deal had raised prices to the point where large numbers of citizens lived off dog food. Others related with relish accounts of A.A.A. officials driving chickens and turkeys into the water in the presence of starving people. National chairman John Hamilton charged in the Hearst papers late in the campaign that the New Deal intended to put dog tags on the 26,000,000 people who would soon be eligible for social security. At the same time handbills predicted that workers would never receive a cent of the money withheld from their pay checks for social security. Conservative Republicans also filled the air with charges that Roosevelt was a Communist. Many businessmen could not refer to him without using expletives, while frail old ladies prayed to God "to remove him from our midst." [9] The Republicans had no monopoly on bitterness or scandal-mongering. Persistent rumors circulated that Landon was a drunkard and that he paid his workers in the oil fields only 50 per cent of the prevailing wages.[10] He also had to contend with charges that he advocated $1.08 per week for families on relief and had reduced the pay of Kansas schoolteachers to $9 per week.[11]

It is doubtful if all these recriminations changed many votes. Roosevelt could rely on a large body of voters who were grateful to him for the improvement in their economic circumstances. Some of them saw the point of Republican arguments against the New Deal, but they invariably countered with the unanswerable rebuttal: "I don't know what would have become of us if it hadn't been for Roosevelt and the Government." [12] Knowing he was ahead, Roosevelt adopted the posture of the statesman aloof from petty politics. He spent much of August and September making "nonpolitical" tours of areas devastated by flood or drought. In October, Roosevelt began to campaign formally, but he ostentatiously ignored his opponent and carried on a casual long-term chat with the voters. Occasionally he dropped the mask of detachment and revived the crusade against entrenched wealth, but most of the time he chided business half-humorously for its lack of gratitude.

There was no way for Landon to break the backbone of Roosevelt's support or to shatter a self-confidence that stopped just short of arrogance. What the Republican candidate gambled on was the chance that the country would prefer a folksy, small-town citizen who groped for words to the fluent cosmopolite. Landon deliberately emphasized the contrast of personalities between him and Roosevelt. He delivered speeches in a dry methodical fashion and systematically concealed his shrewdness. Another year Americans might have turned on an uncommon man, but not in 1936.

Did everyone expect a Roosevelt landslide victory? On the contrary, many people thought it would be a fairly close election. *The Literary Digest,* which had been reliable in its past polls, predicted a Landon victory by a substantial majority. Two newer pollsters, George Gallup and Elmo Roper, reached the opposite conclusion on the basis of more scientific samples than *The Literary Digest* employed, but its reputation made the *Digest* influential. The heavy preponderance of Republican papers, particularly in metropolitan areas, kept up the hopes of the party faithful with slanted stories. Thousands of businessmen who never ran into a Democrat on their commuter trains were unaware of the inarticulate millions behind the President. Most people in Roosevelt's immediate entourage expected him to win, but only national chairman James A. Farley predicted a landslide victory. The most disquieting sign from the Republican standpoint was the unwillingness of veteran senators up for re-election to tie their campaign to Landon's. Trimming by Borah could be expected, but politicians raised their eyebrows when Capper of Kansas reminded the voters that they were free to split their tickets.[13] In Oregon hard-pressed Senate Minority Leader Charles McNary remained "as silent on the Presidential issue as a sea coast mist." [14]

The tension broke within three hours after the polls had closed in the East on election night. Medium-sized Connecticut cities that had not gone Democratic since before the Civil War reported comfortable margins for Roosevelt. As the New Deal tide rolled westward, it swept over almost all of the ancient Republican citadels. Landon had not intended to issue a statement until morning, but at 1 a.m. Topeka time he conceded the election in a gracious telegram to Roosevelt. Considering the bitterness of the campaign, Landon took his defeat serenely. He wasted little time in recriminations and confessed to his friends that he hoped Americans could "gain a shirt without losing their souls." [15] The final returns gave the Democrats every state but Maine and Vermont. The popular vote was 27,476,673 for Roosevelt and 16,679,583 for Landon.

The Democrats made their largest gains in urban areas. With rare exceptions, in previous elections organized labor had remained neutral, and the Republicans had enjoyed substantial support from the workers. Even in 1932 their widespread desertion of the party had been a rebuke to the Republican Administration rather than a pledge of allegiance to the Democrats. But by 1936 the low-income groups, including the older native stock, the newer arrivals, and the Negroes, were voting solidly Democratic. Roosevelt had captured some of them by legislative policy and patronage. Labor leaders had done the rest, particularly John L. Lewis through his new federation of industrial unions, the Congress of Industrial Organizations. Along with George L. Berry and several of the older craft union leaders, Lewis had organized Labor's Nonpartisan League for the 1936 elections. Nobody knows exactly how much the various labor organizations contributed to the Roosevelt campaign fund, but it was in the neighborhood of three-quarters of a million dollars, and it came close to matching the donations of businessmen to the Republican party. The impact of labor was also felt in the congressional elections in which the Democrats captured 333 out of 435 House seats and 76 out of 96 Senate seats. Never before had the Republicans been reduced to such a helpless position.

At the outset of the Presidential campaign, Landon had confided to his running mate that he intended to smoke Roosevelt out in regard to Democratic plans for dealing with a number of issues, including the Supreme Court. On that occasion, Landon had observed that, if Roosevelt refused to speak, he could not subsequently claim a mandate for new policies.[16] Whether or not Roosevelt saw the intended trap is uncertain, but he ignored the challenge for obvious reasons and simply promised to extend the benefits of the New Deal. As one observer wryly put it on the day after the election: "The people have spoken and in the fullness of time Roosevelt will tell us what they have said." [17]

IV

There was much speculation during the final weeks of 1936 as to how Roosevelt would interpret his mandate. Some commentators found a parallel in Monroe's overwhelming victory of 1820 and predicted an era of good feeling, as well as the break-up of the Republican party. Others, like the aging skeptic H. L. Mencken, expected Roosevelt to press forward to an economic New Jerusalem. "Give your mind seriously to the question of the Second Coming," he scornfully wrote a friend, "the signs and portents are upon us." Despite his customary exaggeration, Mencken correctly sensed the mood of many confident New Dealers with their top-heavy majority in Congress. Roosevelt doubtless shared their elation, but he also had many reasons to hesitate. His party still suffered from its traditional instability, since it was composed of a Northern urban wing with a pro-labor orientation and a Southern rural wing hostile to Catholics, labor unions, and radicals. These mutually suspicious factions had co-operated well during the opening months of the New Deal, but by 1936 many Southern leaders were in a rebellious frame of mind. The only part of the Roosevelt program that they really liked was the subsidy for cotton. Deficit spending, social security, and the Wagner Act aroused their apprehension because they seemed likely to unsettle the ancient social structure and improve the status of Negroes as well as poor whites. This program had great support in the North, but in the South the prosperous planters and middle-class citizens who controlled the party were unsympathetic and wanted to stop the New Deal from progressing any further.

Restlessness in the South coincided with the revival of an independent spirit in Congress. The unprecedented co-operation which the lawmakers had accorded Roosevelt during his first term was due to urgent instructions from their constituents. The President did not make obedience any more enjoyable than had his predecessors. On the contrary, his habit of transmitting orders and drafts of bills to Congress through "brain trusters" irritated leaders of his own party, to say nothing of Republicans. With the sense of urgency and crisis receding, Congress began to exhibit its normal reflexes and sought to reclaim powers yielded to the President in the early 1930's.

On February 5, 1937, Roosevelt unwittingly provided the lawmakers with the perfect issue, when he requested authority to enlarge the Supreme Court from nine to fifteen members. The overconfident President had failed to consult congressional leaders before transmitting his special message, but more damaging than this oversight was his attempt to conceal the true purpose of the bill. What Roosevelt really wanted was a New Deal majority on the Supreme Court to stop the invalidation of New Deal laws. Instead of saying so, he buried the proposal in a larger bill to overhaul and speed up judicial procedure. Although the tactic fooled nobody, it did leave the unfavorable impression that Roosevelt was trying to slip through Congress a major change in the constitutional system without public discussion. The result was an immediate outcry that the President wanted to become a dictator by packing the Supreme Court and destroying the separation of powers. A number of Southern Democrats, including hitherto faithful Roosevelt supporters like Senators James F. Byrnes of South Carolina and Tom Connally of Texas, came out flatly against the Court bill. More significant and surprising was the defection of Senator Burton K. Wheeler of Montana, who had run on the third-party ticket with La Follette in 1924 as a foe of the Supreme Court. Several Midwestern Democrats followed his example, and Wheeler also exercised considerable influence on farm bloc Republicans as well as the handful of surviving Bull Moosers.

With the Democratic party split, the Republican minority in Congress decided on a policy of silence so that Roosevelt could not say he was being opposed by reactionaries.[18] McNary easily secured the compliance of the 16 Republican senators, but silencing national leaders was another matter, especially with the Lincoln Day ceremonies in the offing. Landon proved to be the most co-operative. Following the lead of senators, he confined himself to brief statements on the Court plan and stated his oppo-

sition in nonpartisan fashion. At the same time Landon gave anti-Administration Democrats private assurances that he would support them for
re-election in 1938 if they ran as independents.[19] Hoover was more difficult to control, and more difficult yet was national chairman Hamilton. As
the legislative battle over the enlargement of the Supreme Court dragged
on from winter into spring, rank-and-file Republicans became increasingly
critical of party policy.[20] The only thing that kept the party leaders quiet
was the fear that an attack on the President would drive rebellious Democrats back to the fold.[21]

Difficult and unnatural as Republican strategy seemed to the party
faithful at the grass roots, it eventually proved successful in the Senate,
where the principal struggle took place. By mid-March Democratic opponents of the Court plan forced the President to avow his real reason for
pushing the legislation. The Supreme Court helped to wear away Roosevelt's support by reversing the trend of anti-New Deal decisions and sus-
taining both the Social Security and Wagner Acts. Summer found the
President on the run and his majority leader, Joseph Robinson of Arkansas, working for a compromise that would add two justices to the Supreme
Court. The sudden death of Robinson from overwork in mid-July of 1937
left the New Dealers completely demoralized, and after his funeral a coalition of Republicans and defiant Democrats killed the Court plan. It was a
decisive defeat for the President and shattered the myth of his invincibility. Moreover, the bitterness of the accompanying controversy produced
a permanent cleavage in the Democratic majority. A Wages and Hours law
as well as new farm legislation cleared Congress, but the New Deal offensive was at an end. Thereafter, Roosevelt had to fight to preserve his program from counterattacks by a resurgent Republican minority co-operating with the bulk of the Southern Democrats. After the successful Court
fight, some Republicans were optimistic enough to believe that a realignment of parties impended. Landon remained skeptical, and subsequent
events justified his attitude.[22] However logical it seemed for Republicans
and Southern Democrats to coalesce into a single party, two major obstacles stood in the way: the historic aversion of Southerners to the Republican party and the unwillingness of rebellious Dixie Democrats to
jeopardize their committee chairmanships in Congress by leaving their
party. Political reorganization might have been easier if the Republicans
had given up their name, but the revival of the party's prospects killed
their incentive to do so. Nevertheless, the informal coalition of congres-

sional Southern Democrats and Republicans that emerged during the fight over the Supreme Court was to be the dominant force in national politics for the next generation. Irrespective of who occupied the White House, the coalition would exercise life-and-death power over domestic legislation.

It was just as well that the Republicans concentrated on fighting the Court bill, because they could agree on nothing else. Although titular leadership of the party presumably belonged to Landon, the Kansan was soon engaged in a bitter struggle with Herbert Hoover. Both personal and political differences separated the two men. Hoover regarded Landon as a mediocre, prairie politician, while Landon dismissed the "great engineer" as a stuffy egotist and a perpetual Presidential candidate.[23] Moreover, Hoover thought the 1936 campaign should have been waged in defense of his Administration, and he resented Landon's effort to stifle a discussion of constitutional issues.[24] The ex-President considered the election results a vindication of his strategy and an invitation to wrest control of the party from the Landon liberals who had flirted with the New Deal. A mid-term party convention was the instrument chosen by Hoover for a comeback. In late April he enlisted the support of national chairman Hamilton, Frank O. Lowden, and other party leaders. Landon was not informed of their plans for a June convention until the last minute, but succeeded in killing it temporarily by refusing to sign the call. The enraged Hoover then launched a systematic grass-roots campaign to hold a convention in the fall of 1937, as he wrote hundreds of letters and visited local leaders in some twenty states.[25]

Landon had many reasons for doubting the wisdom of a mid-term convention, aside from the obvious fact that he distrusted Hoover's motives. No party had held a mid-term convention since 1866, when a series of such gatherings accelerated the break-up of the Union party. With Landon determined to preserve his redefinition of Republican principles and Hoover equally determined to revive the constitutional issues of 1932, a convention would promote factionalism just at the time that solidarity was needed to attract dissident Democrats. House Minority Leader Snell favored a convention, but most Republicans in Congress did not want to be bound by a declaration of principles.[26] They felt that they had to make the party record on "the legislative battlefield," and they were just as suspicious of guidance by a party convention as by the titular leader of the party.[27] Landon saw the futility of trying to shape legislative strategy from Topeka and was intent on blocking the ambitions of Hoover. For several months the two men were not on speaking terms; [28] and although Frank O. Lowden managed to bring them together that fall, Landon still resisted the convention.[29] In the end, a compromise was arranged by creating a Republican policy committee under the chairmanship of Glenn Frank of Wisconsin. Composed of 215 members, the policy committee sent out an elaborate questionnaire for local leaders to answer and organized some 35 regional conferences to discuss the replies as well as the comments of experts. This activity was climaxed by a five-day series of conferences in August 1938. Landon boycotted the entire operation, but was relieved when the policy committee limited itself to a vaguely worded preliminary report calling for an "adequately regulated system of private enterprise," plus reasonable protection "to the weaker members of society." [30] Two months before the 1940 convention Frank issued a final report to the national committee which was intended to provide the basis for a dynamic platform, but had little influence on the politicians.

Landon undoubtedly performed a service to the party by blocking a divisive mid-term convention. As a result, the Republicans presented a united front in the 1938 elections, while the Democrats increased their party differences that had begun with the Court fight. Roosevelt aggravated these disruptive tendencies by an unsuccessful effort to block the renomination of Democrats who had defied his leadership. The Republicans helped to thwart the President in Iowa, Idaho, and Indiana through clandestine but well-organized support of conservative candidates in Democratic primaries.[31] These efforts proved successful in November when Democratic membership in the House dropped from 333 to 262 and in the Senate from 75 to 69. The magnitude of the New Deal setback was partially concealed by the fact that many Democrats had won re-election as open foes of Roosevelt. The most noteworthy Republican victory occurred in Ohio, where Robert A. Taft beat the incumbent Democrat senator after a frontal attack on the New Deal. Party leaders took almost as much comfort from the showing of Thomas E. Dewey, a young and virtually unknown prosecuting attorney, in the New York gubernatorial contest. Pitted against the popular Herbert Lehman, who was running for a fourth term, Dewey captured over 49 per cent of the total vote.

A close look at the election maps indicated that the Republican revival was more pronounced in the industrial East than in the farm states. Nevertheless, the Landon wing of the party had high hopes of capturing the White House in 1940 by coupling a reaffirmation of Republican concern for the economic welfare of the masses with a counterattack on the deficit financing policy of the New Deal. This strategy was based on the belief that most voters accepted New Deal objectives but opposed the administration of relief on a political basis and the centralization of power in Washington. The dominant coalition of Republicans and conservative Democrats in the 76th Congress fought the President along these lines, but all calculations were upset by the outbreak of World War II in Europe and its repercussions on American opinion.

Historically, the Republican party had been identified with a virile nationalism in foreign affairs, although there was persistent disagreement as to the desirability of entanglements abroad in peacetime. Roosevelt and Lodge had taken a larger view of American responsibilities than the isolationists, but the latter were just as willing to fight in defense of national interests as the expansionists. Nobody had protested more vigorously against naval disarmament in the late 1920's and early 1930's than Hiram Johnson. What separated him from the internationalist wing of the party was his belief that America could protect her interests without participation in collective security arrangements. As long as both wings of the G.O.P. discussed foreign policy from the standpoint of national welfare, the party's isolationist tendencies offered little political risk. During the mid-'30's, however, a dangerous note of pacifism was incorporated into the isolationist position. It drew its stimulus from an investigation of the munitions industry by a special Senate committee under the chairmanship of Gerald Nye of North Dakota. In effect, the Nye committee popularized the old Socialist doctrine that all wars are fomented by international capitalists. It was only one step further to the conclusion that war only benefited international bankers and munitions makers and, conversely, could not serve the nation's best interests. Accordingly, proposals flowed from the Nye committee to the foreign relations committees of both houses for legislation designed to prevent American participation in a new war by banning various forms of economic intercourse with belligerents, at the very time that the Hitler government in Germany was repudiating the Versailles pact and rearming. A large bipartisan majority in Congress followed the recommendations of the Nye committee and passed successive neutrality laws in 1935, 1936, and 1937.

The enthusiastic Republican support for neutrality laws based on socialistic assumptions about the cause of war was all the more remarkable since business groups constituted the backbone of the party. The central role of an old farm bloc senator like Nye in the agitation ought to have made neutrality laws suspect in the mind of the average Republican. If his sponsorship was not enough to brand the scheme, the endorsement of neutrality legislation by the New Dealers should have made him doubly cautious. Yet virtually all Republicans backed proposals to keep Americans off the high seas in time of war and to prevent businessmen from getting an economic stake in a European conflict. Committed to the syllogism that peace depended on the extinction of the profit motive when others were at war, many Republicans also accepted the corollary that the nation had fought in World War I solely for the purpose of protecting sinister economic interests. This attitude was too much for old Hiram Johnson, who grumbled about "the half-baked ideas of the peace societies" and insisted that America ought to rely on international law rather than neutrality legislation.[32] Johnson was as isolationist as ever, but he resented the fatuous argument that adequate armaments and defense of national rights on the high seas played into the hands of munitions makers.

There was not much risk in the posture of the Republicans as long as Roosevelt and the Democrats took the same extreme position. The President, however, had always qualified his dedication to neutrality legislation by seeking authority that would permit him to invoke neutrality bans on a selective basis against aggressors. In 1937 he roused the ire of Republicans by asking for a "quarantine" of aggressors. He did not press energetically on this point until the spring of 1939, when it appeared as if Italy and Germany would attack the European democracies. Inasmuch as the outbreak of war would automatically force the United States to suspend the sale of arms to either side, Roosevelt reasoned that this provision of the neutrality law was detrimental to Great Britain and France, who controlled the seas. He asked Congress for the repeal of the arms embargo and predicted that its retention would encourage Hitler to launch World War II by autumn. Congress adjourned in midsummer without taking action, after it heard Borah assert that his sources of information told him there would be no war. When Hitler invaded Poland in September 1939, Roosevelt called a special session of Congress and secured repeal of the arms embargo. Although the President had done much to encourage pacifistic sentiment of the mid-'30's, he now switched to a policy of aiding the democracies "short of war," and he carried most of his party with him.

Many Republicans suspected Roosevelt of wanting to take the United States into the war. In the light of subsequent developments, their apprehension was justifiable. But instead of drawing a line between the desirability of rearmament in a warlike world and the undesirability of other Administration measures, they clung to the questionable pacifist jargon of the Nye committee. Not only did the bulk of Republicans vote indiscriminately against increased defense appropriations, but they denied that America had any interests worth fighting for. In fact, their mistrust of Roosevelt even drove some of them to speak well of America's potential enemies. Indeed, at times they managed to sound as if they opposed the welfare of their own country. Landon viewed this trend with genuine alarm. He lamented the way that Republicans in Congress were abandoning the traditional nationalist position of the party, but he remained silent rather than risk a split with the legislative leaders.[33] His worst fears were realized after the Germans overran the Low Countries and France in May of 1940, when the bulk of Republican congressmen continued to oppose selective service as well as other defense measures, despite mounting evidence that the country favored them.

V

Roosevelt had been making preparations to run for a third term as a selfless patriot who would arm the country and preserve peace. To promote faith in his intentions, Roosevelt opened negotiations with Landon and Knox in September 1939 for their inclusion in the cabinet.[34] Knox was interested but unwilling to join the Administration by himself. Although Landon displayed more skepticism, he agreed to take a cabinet post, provided Roosevelt made a specific pledge that he would not run for a third term. Discussions broke down because Roosevelt refused to give the necessary assurance, but the President reopened them again after the fall of France. Neither Landon nor Roosevelt had changed his position, and the Kansan stoutly denied that a cabinet could be nonpartisan unless the President agreed to retire from politics at the end of his current term.[35] By this time Roosevelt knew that Knox would accept if another Republican could be persuaded to join the cabinet at the same time. After further discussions, the President secured the services of Henry L. Stimson, a G.O.P. elder statesman who had served in the cabinets of Taft and Hoover. With his customary adroitness, Roosevelt held up the announcement of his cabinet changes until four days before the Republican national convention. Then on June 20, as the delegates were converging on Philadelphia, he announced the appointment of Knox as Secretary of the Navy and Stimson as Secretary of War. Once again, Roosevelt had outmaneuvered the Republicans, for he had deprived them of two leaders who might have blunted their reputation for obstructionism in foreign affairs.

Although the rumors about a coalition cabinet had been circulating for nine months, the pre-convention sparring of Republicans over the nomination indicated that they expected to wage a campaign on purely domestic issues. Except for Hoover, most leaders of the Depression era were either dead or in retirement. Landon saw the urgent need for new faces and used his influence as titular head of the party to thwart a Hoover comeback. As early as 1938 Landon had become interested in Thomas E. Dewey, the 38-year-old district attorney of New York County, because of his spectacular performance against racketeers in New York City. It was Landon who had helped persuade Dewey to run for governor against Lehman,[36] and Dewey's narrow defeat in the race for governor of the nation's most populous state made him the leading candidate for the Republican nomination. As a fearless foe of crime and corruption, Dewey attracted Republicans who hoped to win by condemning the huge urban New Deal machines. With Boss Thomas J. Pendergast of Kansas City already in jail, it seemed as if the G.O.P. might be successful in emphasizing the tie between relief expenditures and the rise of corrupt Democratic machines. Dewey also appealed to people clamoring for a reorganization of the party, for in his gubernatorial campaign he had replaced New York's sluggish, conservative Republican leaders with aggressive young men. The Republican legislature showed the effects of the change in 1939, when it abandoned its negative attitude toward New Deal proposals and introduced constructive counterproposals. Dewey's candidacy gained momentum when he carried several Presidential primaries, and he entered the convention with more than three hundred pledged delegates.

Unfortunately for Dewey, his youth ceased to be an asset early in 1940 when it became apparent that the country wanted a leader with experience in foreign affairs.[37] Landon warned Dewey in late spring that he would have to take a constructive stand on the new issue, and old C. Bascom Slemp grumbled that Dewey ought to "denounce Germany and quit stalling." [38] But Dewey merely continued to attack the New Deal, and brought about retaliatory sneers that he had thrown his diaper into the Presidential ring. Dewey also hurt his chances by quarreling with Kenneth Simpson,[39] the Republican county chairman in Manhattan, who quipped that the New York City delegates "would be solidly and continuously for Dewey until the end of the first ballot." The mutinous attitude in a portion of the New York delegation pointed to a defect in Dewey's personality that would attract more attention in subsequent years. He impressed people as cold and calculating, and there was something mechanical about his gestures, which provoked the famous remark that he looked like the little man on the wedding cake. Undoubtedly, this characterization did Dewey an injustice, but there was an unmistakable air of aloofness in his face.[40] Simpson proved to be the first of several collaborators who thought Dewey ungrateful, insincere, and egotistical. Dewey possessed unrivaled powers as an organizer, but he was utterly lacking in the spirit of fellowship which generates personal loyalty.

Dewey faced a formidable number of rival candidates. Senator Robert A. Taft of Ohio had inherited most of Hoover's conservative followers. What impressed intimates about Taft was the brilliance of his mind, but in 1940 he used it for the sole purpose of denouncing the New Deal. His emotional outbursts were disconcerting, because they emerged from behind a face singularly free from passion or warmth. Taft's candor won him the admiration of the delegates, who welcomed his assaults on pressure groups, but most of them considered him an impossible candidate because of his negative attitude. Nevertheless, Taft accumulated nearly 200 delegates, mostly from the South and Ohio. After Taft came a string of favorite-son candidates, including House Minority Leader Joseph Martin of Massachusetts, Senators Vandenberg of Michigan, McNary of Oregon, H. Styles Bridges of New Hampshire, and Hanford MacNider of Iowa. Even Hoover once more discreetly advertised his availability.[41]

Besides indicating a vacuum at the top of the Republican party, the large number of delegates tied to favorite-son candidates represented a tacit expression of dissatisfaction at the grass roots. Most Republican voters did not know what they wanted, but they sensed the futility of ignoring foreign affairs. They also felt uneasy about the marketability of isolationism, particularly when all the candidates were identified with a position which verged on opposition to self-defense. The feelings of the party followers could not be translated into anything more rational than a predisposition to favor a candidate aloof from conventional partisan politics. The existence of this impulse paved the way for the phenomenal rise of Wendell Willkie, who was not in the running in April but became the Republican nominee two months later.

At first glance Willkie appeared to be a sheep dog in a business suit:

disheveled, clumsy, and good-humored. Closer observation suggested that he was an intellectual of the 1920's who had become a financial success in spite of his principles. Not only did Willkie show interest in a variety of academic topics that most businessmen ignored, but his conversation was sparkling and persuasive, and, although he loved an argument, he wore his learning lightly. Above all, Willkie behaved like an amateur; he left the impression that there was no element of calculation in his make-up. A native of Rushville, Indiana, and a graduate of Indiana Law School, he had started his business career at the Firestone Rubber Company in Akron, Ohio, after brief service in the army. Subsequently he had joined an Akron law firm specializing in utilities and moved on to Wall Street in 1929.

Willkie had first attracted attention during the mid-1930's as a representative of Commonwealth and Southern, a utilities holding company, engaged in a long legal battle with the Tennessee Valley Authority. In the process, Willkie had emerged as an articulate champion of private enterprise, even though Commonwealth and Southern eventually capitulated and sold its properties to the T.V.A. Once in the news, Willkie had remained in it. In January 1938 he debated Assistant Attorney General Robert H. Jackson in "Town Meeting of the Air," a popular radio program, and appeared regularly on the banquet circuit thereafter. During the early months of 1940 Willkie began to get as much attention as avowed Presidential candidates, but hardly through the customary media. He appeared on another famous radio program, "Information Please," and wrote a strong article for the April issue of *Fortune* entitled "We the People," received a foundation award "for distinguished service to humanity," and accepted an honorary degree from Colgate University.

Midway through the spring, Oren Root, a twenty-nine-year-old lawyer from Princeton, New Jersey, was so impressed by the extraordinary public response to a petition he had circulated advocating Willkie's candidacy that he abandoned his legal practice in mid-April and devoted his entire time to launching "Willkie for President" clubs. Simultaneously, Russell Davenport left his editorial duties on *Fortune* to manage Willkie's pre-convention campaign. A number of publishers and public relations men imitated Davenport, but professional politicians steered clear of Willkie, with the exception of a few disillusioned New Dealers and Jeffersonian Democrats.

Republican leaders found it difficult to take Willkie seriously. As late as May 10 Landon dismissed the grass-roots agitation as "simply absurd." [42] Like other Republicans, Landon objected to bestowing the highest party honor on an amateur who had been a registered Democrat until 1936. During the next month no prominent party leader came out for Willkie, but growing public support plus the aggressive campaigning of his backers brought numerous pledges of second choice votes from Eastern delegations. [43] Spokesmen for the major candidates took note of the fact that the Willkie boom was gaining momentum by attacking the Hoosier repeatedly on the eve of the convention.

When the delegates gathered for the opening session at Philadelphia on June 24, they faced an extraordinary situation. The streets around the hall were thronged with members of Willkie clubs, waving petitions, passing out pamphlets, and pinning buttons on bystanders. Postmen delivered additional bales of Willkie petitions to hotels housing delegates. Part of the enthusiasm was genuine, but by this time an element of professional management had crept into the spontaneity. In retrospect, it was clear that some of the petitions had been put together hastily and that names had been drawn from phone books and other readily available sources. [44] The sustained Willkie clamor nevertheless made a profound impression on even the most skeptical delegates.

Besides the unsettling threat of Willkie's candidacy, the convention faced a crisis over the platform as a result of the announcement that Knox and Stimson were joining Roosevelt's cabinet. Until that time a subcommittee headed by Landon had been proceeding harmoniously with a foreign policy plank which took a strongly patriotic line on national defense and aid "short of war" to the democracies. The establishment of the coalition cabinet, however, goaded the isolationist senators on the subcommittee into blind fury. They promptly made the plank more noninterventionist and more critical of the President. Landon even had difficulty persuading them to delete a sentence proclaiming that World War I was a failure. [45] Sentiment outside the subcommittee proved to be just as explosive, and the cooler heads barely averted a formal resolution reading Stimson and Knox out of the party. The controversy postponed adoption of the platform until the evening of June 26. The planks dealing with domestic issues resembled those of the 1936 platform, for they made a qualified endorsement of New Deal objectives and an unrestrained condemnation of New Deal methods. The obstructionist tone of the pronouncements on foreign policy caused misgivings, but the moderates acquiesced rather than risk more inflammatory statements in a floor fight.

It required six ballots for the convention to nominate a President. Each successive vote saw steady gains by Willkie at the expense of Dewey and the numerous favorite-son candidates. After Dewey had dropped from 360 to 315 and Willkie had gained from 105 to 259 during the initial three ballots, the professionals tried to stem the tide by swinging all of their available votes behind Taft, whose total was 212 at that point. On the fourth ballot Taft picked up 43 and Willkie 47, while on the fifth ballot both men gained 123. With Willkie polling 429 votes and Taft 377 of the 501 necessary for the nomination, the professionals made a vain effort to force an adjournment. At this juncture the multimillionaire oilman, Joseph Pew, who controlled the bulk of Pennsylvania's 70-odd delegates, might have decided the contest. However, on the sixth roll call, Pennsylvania unwisely passed, and Willkie won the necessary votes for the nomination by continuing to make steady inroads on the smaller delegations, as he had done throughout the day. His backers had contributed to this erosion process by packing the galleries and chanting: "We want Willkie." Never before had a convention responded so readily to what it thought was the will of the people. The nomination was not so much a tribute to Willkie as it was a rebellion against the quality of the party's professional leadership. In 1934 the Republicans had tried to defeat the New Deal by opposing it directly; in 1936 they had accepted most New Deal principles; and in 1940 they had taken the final step by nominating a renegade Democrat. It was an imaginative decision, but only time would tell whether it was a wise one. After the tense struggle over the nomination, the weary delegates agreed in record time to the selection of Senate Minority Leader Charles L. McNary of Oregon for Vice President.

The Democrats met at Chicago July 15 and, to the surprise of nobody, nominated Roosevelt for a third term. The President had professed outward indifference over his political future, while skillfully killing off the chances of his conservative opponents from behind the scenes. He had even sent the convention a message on July 16 expressing his preference for retirement, so that his nomination would appear to be a spontaneous demand from an apprehensive country. There were a few sour notes at Chicago, especially when Roosevelt chose Secretary of Agriculture Henry A. Wallace to replace Vice President Garner as his running mate. The

President had nevertheless breached a third-term tradition with a skill that minimized the political damage.

The campaign of 1940 was a series of frustrations for Wendell Willkie, aggravated by his inexperience and his unwillingness to accept advice from professional politicians. Aside from his lack of a voting record, Willkie's greatest advantage lay in the numerous manifestations that people were tired of New Dealers. They showed no sign of wanting to give up the legislative benefits of the previous eight years, but their capacity for indignation had been exhausted and they remained unresponsive to agitation for fresh reforms. Some were disturbed by both the prominence and the militance of labor leaders in the New Deal coalition. Others resented the burgeoning of urban Democratic machines and thought a Republican Administration would curtail the relief expenditures on which they fed. Farmers were beginning to feel prosperous enough to grumble about the complex federal controls over agriculture. If Willkie had been able to exploit this dissatisfaction without raising the specter of a new depression, he might have won the election. Unquestionably, Willkie saw his opportunity and tried to capitalize on it. Aside from an occasional lapse into the idiom of big business, he made temperate criticisms of the New Deal and held out the hope that he would administer the Roosevelt program more efficiently. This formula did not carry as much conviction as Willkie anticipated, because he suffered from association with the bankers and businessmen who clustered around him on campaign tours, and there were not enough Republican orators in sympathy with New Deal reforms to discuss them intelligently.[46] Besides, the Democrats ignored Willkie and ran against Hoover, as they had done in the two preceding campaigns.

Despite these handicaps, Willkie made some headway and would have made a great deal more if Roosevelt had allowed the campaign discussion to focus on domestic issues. But Roosevelt ceased to be a New Dealer and allowed his subordinates to remind the various pressure groups of their blessings. He took full advantage of his dual role as President of the country and leader of the Democratic party. For the most part, Roosevelt posed as the commander in chief of a beleaguered country, above partisan strife and preoccupied with the preservation of peace. Even after the campaign was in full swing, he made eight nonpolitical tours of defense installations at government expense. Whenever Roosevelt took up the cudgels as a party leader, he did so with expressions of regret and protestations that he spoke in political terms only to correct the malignant misrepresentations of the Republicans. Secretary of the Interior Harold Ickes set the Democratic campaign theme when he replied to Willkie's demand for a series of debates with Roosevelt by observing, "The President cannot adjourn the Battle of Britain in order to ride circuit with Mr. Willkie." [47]

Willkie was also handicapped by the record of his party on foreign policy. If he flatly repudiated isolationism, he would repudiate the majority of the Republicans in Congress. If, on the other hand, he endorsed their outspoken isolationist position, he ran the risk of seeming to support foreign leaders against the head of his own government. Landon warned Willkie in a long letter on August 31 that foreign policy was the critical issue in the campaign.[48] He earnestly advised Willkie to confine himself to general statements of patriotic support for national defense which could not be construed as criticism of congressional leaders. To his detriment, Willkie ignored this advice. He took specific positions on conscription, the transfer of over-age destroyers to Great Britain, and other issues which placed him in direct opposition to his party's legislators. As a result, he found himself damning the President for past mistakes and echoing him on current policy. In assuming this internationalist posture, Willkie missed the chance to capture the voters who feared that Roosevelt would involve the country in war. The President made extravagant efforts to reassure them that his policy would not lead to war, particularly in a speech at Boston where he promised that no American soldier would have to fight on foreign soil. Why Willkie did not meet head-on an assertion at odds with the underlying trend of Roosevelt's policy is perplexing. Perhaps the Republican candidate felt that he had the isolationist vote, irrespective of what his opponent said. It is more probable that Willkie shared Roosevelt's unspoken conviction that it would be better to aid Britain at the risk of war than to fight alone later. In any case, neither candidate cared to speak candidly about the inherent dangers in the policy of aiding the democracies "short of war," and the fuzziness of exposition redounded to the benefit of the incumbent.

Willkie's many errors in strategy were more damaging than his errors in technique. He ignored emphatic warnings to take a complete vacation before the start of the campaign.[49] Overflowing with vitality and an insatiable thirst for politics in July, Willkie simply could not believe that he would be exhausted in October. He established himself at the Broadmoor Hotel, a resort hotel in Colorado Springs, and courted intrusions on his privacy from the press, office-seekers, and miscellaneous groups of supporters. His entire campaign was marred by lack of co-ordination between the amateur groups formed to aid him and the regular party organization. Chaos reigned on the Willkie campaign train. Amateurs clogged the aisles, giving advice and interposing a physical barrier to local Republican workers who boarded the train for a word with the candidate.[50] Willkie also made mistakes when he was speaking. He had an addiction to the pronoun "I," and, in addition, persisted in calling attention to his previous Democratic affiliation by referring to "you Republicans" rather than "we Republicans." His voice was hoarse, for he had never learned how to avoid straining his throat. At times he appeared tired and as harassed as Hoover in 1932.

With all of his handicaps, Willkie had a boyish charm that attracted many voters. In parades he grinned from ear to ear and waved his arms like a man bent on giving a personal greeting to each spectator. Hecklers left him unruffled, and at Detroit he good-humoredly dodged a barrage of cantaloupes, phone books, and bedspreads. Determined to see and be seen, Willkie crisscrossed the country, traveling 20,000 miles and visiting every section but the deep South. Meanwhile, Roosevelt limited his formal campaign to a dozen major speeches in large cities. As it was, Roosevelt won a third term on November 5, 1940, but Willkie had the satisfaction of making a better showing than any Republican candidate since 1928. The final count gave Roosevelt 27,243,000 popular votes and 449 electoral votes to Willkie's 22,304,400 popular votes and 82 electoral votes.

The bulk of Willkie electors came from states in the upper Midwest, traditionally strong Republican areas. Antagonism between city and country was much more pronounced in 1940 than in 1936. Outside the Solid South, farmers returned to the Republican party in large numbers. The influx was especially pronounced in German-American areas of the Midwest where isolationist sentiment predominated. The Democrats made compensating gains among the Poles and other ethnic minorities whose homelands had been overrun by Germany or Russia. The large cities stayed with Roosevelt, and thus emphasized again the durability of the coalition which he had forged in 1936. Neither the defection of John L. Lewis nor the third-term issue had any visible effect on the labor vote. Outspoken isolationism had hurt the G.O.P. in 1940, despite the evident opposition of a vast majority of the nation to participation in the European war.

VI

A political paradox appeared in Roosevelt's third term. During most of it America was fighting for her life, and yet the upheavals produced by World War II had little perceptible effect on the fortunes of the major parties. The period opened with Willkie trying to impose his leadership on the Republican minority in Congress. Aside from the intrinsic difficulty of operating as a parliamentary leader without being in a parliament, Willkie had placed himself in a difficult position because during the campaign he had tried to purge Republican congressmen of their isolationist sentiments. In 1941 he not only supported Administration measures that drew the United States closer to war with Germany, but he actually moved beyond the President's position. When Roosevelt contended that increased aid to Great Britain would keep America out of war, Willkie, who favored the policy, frankly conceded that it might involve us in the world conflict; and whereas Roosevelt made piecemeal assaults on the neutrality laws, Willkie demanded their repeal.

The Republicans in Congress made no effort to conceal their displeasure over Willkie's activities. At the Lincoln Day dinners in February 1941 they denied that he was speaking for the party, and throughout the year they repudiated his position by their votes in Congress. If anything, they became more isolationist than before. They climaxed their obstruction in November 1941 by voting heavily against extension of the draft, which squeaked through the House by a single vote. Although Borah was dead and Hiram Johnson silenced by poor health, Taft, Vandenberg, and Nye militantly carried on the isolationist tradition, and the House leadership supported them. At the same time the party directed its isolationism only against Europe; in Asia, on the contrary, many Republicans urged a stronger stand against Japanese encroachments. This attitude simplified matters for Roosevelt, because, when the Japanese attacked Pearl Harbor in December 1941, the Republicans found it hard to argue that the President's European policy had precipitated the war.

The entrance of the United States in the world conflict temporarily suspended the rivalry between Willkie and the Republican minority in Congress. The party closed ranks behind the President in support of mobilization measures. Inevitably, price-fixing, rationing, and other war controls stirred up popular unrest which the Republicans exploited in the 1942 congressional elections. Their campaign strategy was unusually successful, partly because many Democratic workers had migrated to take war jobs and did not register or vote, and partly because of popular reaction against wartime regimentation. As a result, the Republicans made their sharpest gains since the 1920's, as they increased their seats in the House from 162 to 209 and in the Senate from 28 to 38. The most heartening development was the election of Thomas E. Dewey as the first Republican governor of New York since 1920.

Immediately after the election, G.O.P. congressional leaders renewed their efforts to destroy Willkie, who had persisted in offending them by undertaking a series of war missions for the President. National chairman Joseph Martin resigned and was replaced on December 6, 1942, by Harrison Spangler of Iowa, a Taft supporter, who advertised himself as a neutral. Willkie struck back indirectly at his tormentors in his book *One World,* published in April 1943, which sold more than a million copies. In it he took an uncompromising stand for a strong postwar international organization. Spangler promptly appointed a Republican advisory council to develop "a realistic peacetime program," from which Willkie was pointedly excluded. The advisory council produced a resolution at Mackinac Island on September 7, 1943, which committed the party in guarded language to a postwar League. A similar resolution cleared both houses of Congress the same year with emphatic Republican and Democratic support. These gestures were primarily designed to outflank Willkie and to placate public opinion, which had begun showing interest in a world organization. Many Republicans still harbored serious reservations about the feasibility of a League, but they wanted to remove the issue from the impending Presidential election.

A Gallup poll in August 1943 showed that 37 per cent of the Republican voters favored Dewey as their nominee and only 28 per cent were for Willkie. But when Dewey announced that he was not a candidate in November and Willkie began to stump the country for delegates, the national committee sent John Hamilton on a seventeen-state tour to encourage the organization of favorite-son delegations. After the beginning of the new year, Willkie announced plans to enter several Presidential primaries. He also made it clear that he would regard Wisconsin, a state famous for its isolationist sentiments, as the acid test of his candidacy. Willkie entered Wisconsin on March 18, traveled 1500 miles, and made 40 speeches. He told Republicans that it was time for them to abandon narrow partisanship and speak out firmly in behalf of a world organization. The voters emphatically rebuked him on April 4, when they elected a full slate of Dewey delegates, despite the fact that the name of the New York governor had been entered in the primary over his protest. Willkie subsequently withdrew from the race.

The Wisconsin primary also derailed General Douglas MacArthur and Commander Harold Stassen. MacArthur was in the midst of plans to recapture the Philippines and could hardly be regarded as a serious candidate. The general commanded great support among Republicans who believed that the nation's real interests lay in the Pacific rather than in Europe. Stassen proved to be the first of a new political type that would become popular in the late 1950's: the earnest young man with a sense of mission. He had been elected governor of Minnesota in 1938 at the age of thirty, and was re-elected twice before resigning to accept a commission in the navy. Stassen was aloof and majestic. He possessed an icy self-assurance and pursued an objective single-mindedly, once committed to it. He regarded a strong international organization as the salvation of the world, which made him as far removed from the bulk of his party as Willkie.

The only other candidate who rose above the level of a favorite son was John W. Bricker, a three-term governor of Ohio. He had stepped aside for Taft in 1940 with the understanding that the senator would reciprocate in 1944. Bricker was a handsome, silver-haired orator of considerable ability who clung to the orthodox G.O.P. doctrines of the 1930's. He was dismissed by William Allen White as "an honest Harding." The phrase may not have been accurate, but it crystallized the fears of many Republicans that Bricker was not dynamic enough to serve as a war leader.

Dissatisfaction with the avowed candidates brought renewed interest in Governor Dewey of New York, who began to seek the nomination actively after his stunning victory in Wisconsin. The odds always favor the selection of a popular governor from a large pivotal state, and Dewey had gained in stature since 1940 by giving New York an aggressive, imaginative administration. Not only had he sponsored some labor laws with a vaguely New Deal flavor, but he had edged cautiously toward internationalism. With an alert, youthful group of managers headed by Edwin Jaeckle and Herbert Brownell, the Dewey forces moved so effectively that by June virtually all opposition to his candidacy had melted, and he was nominated on the first ballot by the staggering margin of 1056 to 1. The Chicago convention balanced the ticket by choosing Bricker for Vice President. Dewey's managers supervised the writing of a platform that hedged on almost everything but New Deal centralization and inefficiency, which it opposed.

The Democrats met in mid-July and nominated Roosevelt for an unprecedented fourth term after receiving a message from the White House with the usual protestations of reluctance. A lively fight ensued over the Vice Presidential nomination, because some Southern Democrats threatened to withhold the electoral votes of their states from Roosevelt unless he dropped Wallace from the ticket. The Vice President had offended them by actively sponsoring various wartime measures to undercut racial segregation. He had also disturbed Roosevelt by dabbling in theosophy and quarreling with other members of the Administration. Since Wallace was exceedingly popular with organized labor, the President felt obliged to manage matters with unusual care, and he endorsed Wallace while at the same time undercutting him. In the end, Harry S. Truman, an obscure Missouri senator acceptable both to the South and organized labor, was chosen for Vice President.

The campaign of 1944 was more frustrating to Republicans than any campaign since the origin of the party, because they lacked any safe subjects to discuss. With military victories piling up throughout the summer and fall, it was pointless, if not dangerous, to criticize the conduct of the war. Denunciation of New Deal legislation in the 1930's carried a heavier risk than usual, for it might give workers who had migrated during the war more incentive to reregister and vote. Foreign policy issues were as unpromising as ever. The public remembered the prewar isolationist record of the Republicans, and Roosevelt had already begun to make headway with the diabolical argument that the Republicans were responsible for World War II because they had blocked American participation in the League of Nations. His argument ignored the militant isolationism of his own party in the mid-'30's, and also ignored the instability of the European power structure that dated back to the Treaty of Versailles.

Deprived of the more conventional issues, Dewey had nothing to fall back on but carping criticism of the New Deal and veiled expressions of concern over the President's health. The latter topic, while legitimate, was a dangerous one to discuss. During the winter of 1943–44 Roosevelt had suffered from a persistent bronchial ailment. If other factors complicated his illness, White House physicians gave no hint of them. The President had been put on a diet until he had lost 15 pounds, which made his cheeks sag badly during the summer of 1944. Roosevelt's stubborn refusal to purchase shirts with smaller necks heightened the impression that he was failing physically and stimulated a whispering campaign that he was mortally ill. Although Dewey wisely avoided a direct statement about Roosevelt's health, he pounded incessantly on the theme that the Democratic Administration was staffed by tired old men. This strategy alarmed Roosevelt so much that he enlarged his speaking program to demonstrate his robustness, and climaxed this approach with a slow drive through New York City with the automobile top down in a pouring rain. Whether this performance influenced any doubters is uncertain, but on November 7 Roosevelt won a fourth term by a somewhat smaller margin than in 1940. His popular vote of 25,602,505 was approximately a million and a half less than four years earlier, but the 22,006,278 polled by Dewey came within 200,000 of duplicating Willkie's showing. The margin in the electoral college was one-sided: Roosevelt received 432 electoral votes and Dewey 99. As usual, the President had swept all of the large industrial states, where organized labor provided him with the indispensable pluralities. The man responsible for the labor vote was Sidney Hillman, whose Political Action Committee of the C.I.O. functioned as the electioneering arm of the unions. Dewey piled up substantial leads in the rural areas and in small towns of the North, which were swallowed up in the metropolitan areas. The sharpness of the cleavage was apparent from the fact that Roosevelt carried every city with a population of more than 500,000 except Cincinnati. Despite the abnormality of a wartime election waged under conditions that favored the incumbent, the Republicans could take little comfort from the results. During the 1930's it had been possible to believe that many potential Republicans voted against the party to rebuke it for the Depression. But by 1944 there was no way to escape the unpleasant conclusion that there were more Democrats than Republicans in the country. What started out as a repudiation of Hoover by the new generation of voters in the 1930's had become a firm loyalty on their part to the Democratic party. Judging by the tenacity of party affiliations in the past, it would require a major political upheaval, coupled with an abrupt enlargement of the electorate, to bring the Republicans back to power.

On April 12, 1945, Roosevelt was felled without warning by a massive cerebral hemorrhage. Before his death he had launched policies which would have a decisive effect on the character of the postwar world. His unconditional surrender policy assured Russia of a commanding position on the European continent and was predicated on the belief that the United States and the U.S.S.R. held similar ideas about the organization of the postwar world. Serene in his conviction about the good intentions of Russia and the other Allied powers, he had moved cautiously toward a world organization like Woodrow Wilson's League, safeguarding his rear by securing bipartisan support in the United States Senate. Six weeks before his death, Roosevelt had also obtained the assent of Churchill and Stalin to a collective security system at Yalta as well as to territorial arrangements that the President believed would be durable. Popular support for Roosevelt's program was overwhelming, and most Republicans joined in assent. Vandenberg, who was soon to be the ranking Republican on the Senate foreign relations committee, repudiated isolationism in January 1945, and, while many colleagues had misgivings about the projected United Nations, they did their grumbling in private.[51]

VII

Roosevelt had generated so much momentum behind his foreign policy program that his successor was assured of bipartisan support. The new President, Harry S. Truman, would probably have enjoyed it in any case, because the circumstances surrounding his elevation released an outburst of public sympathy. Truman had not gotten drunk at his inaugural as Vice President as Andrew Johnson had done, but he had recently attended the funeral of his disgraced political mentor, Boss Tom Pendergast of Kansas City, and thus the public thought of him as a mediocre machine politician. When Truman promptly showed every intention of shouldering the monumental responsibilities of the Presidency, Americans were both grateful and relieved. The spectacle of an unsure, humble man promising to do his best moved even the most partisan Republicans to impulsive pledges of support. Senator Taft responded by calling at the White House with a delegation of Republican legislators. Hoover followed his example, and most of the Republican press adopted a restrained bipartisan tone.

The *union sacré* lasted until the end of the war in August 1945. During this interval the Republicans and Southern Democrats engaged in hopeful speculations about the kind of domestic program Truman would pursue. His Border-state antecedents suggested that he might discontinue the wartime program for improving the social and economic status of the Negro so obnoxious to Southerners. His occasional statements on patriotic occasions indicated he might have doubts as to the advisability of deficit financing, subsidy programs, and other New Deal legislation. The optimism of the Republicans reached its peak immediately after V-J Day when the President dismantled a number of wartime controls.

With the end of the world conflict, however, Truman had to abandon platitudes and take a stand that was bound to end his political honeymoon. Whatever his real convictions might have been, Truman had no intention of disrupting the politically potent New Deal coalition. He broke the spell on September 6, 1945, in a message to Congress with twenty-one specific recommendations. Some bore the New Deal trademarks; others went beyond the New Deal; and all were justified as measures to fight an imminent depression. This message reactivated the coalition of Republicans and Southern Democrats which had blocked the extension of New Deal domestic legislation since 1938. Virtually all of his recommendations were pigeonholed, except his request for the extension of executive war powers over prices and wages. Fearful of reconversion stresses, Congress renewed this authority, but it did so grudgingly for one year.

The period between V-J Day and the elections of 1946 was one long nightmare for Truman. The Russians breached the Yalta agreements by establishing satellite governments in Eastern Europe. They also demonstrated their disagreement with American war aims and stubbornly stalled in negotiations for peace treaties. For the moment, their unmannerly behavior did not bother America as much as the series of nation-wide strikes for higher wages which disrupted production and caused scarce consumer goods to flow into black markets at prices far above the official government ceilings. Delighted by this turn of events, Republicans strongly criticized the Administration. They argued that price control stifled production and predicted plentiful supplies and lower prices if controls were scrapped. When Truman sought another extension of price controls, the congressional coalition riddled it with amendments which raised some ceilings and eliminated others. Businessmen, farmers, and consumers blamed the Administration for reconversion miseries; and for the first time since 1928, the Republicans captured both houses of Congress in the off-year elections, as their Senate seats increased from 39 to 51 and their House seats from 188 to 246.

Immediately after the Republican victory, Landon warned "that people will expect more of us than we can probably deliver"; [52] and his apprehensions were correct. Largely because of the restraining influence of Vandenberg, the Republicans pursued a patriotic, bipartisan foreign policy. By this time the expansionist appetite of Russia was so unmistakable and the inadequacy of the United Nations to thwart it so obvious that the Truman Administration began to act outside the framework of the world organization. The essence of the new policy was to provide independent countries with economic aid that would thwart Communist subversion from within and military aid that would discourage the Russians from making a direct attack. Known as "containment," the Administration program spawned entangling alliances on an ever larger scale. Although most Republicans refrained from raising the old isolationist objections to the alliance system, they grumbled about the cost of armaments and foreign aid, which prevented sharp tax reductions. They also blamed the disappearance of central European countries behind the iron curtain on the secret diplomacy of Roosevelt at Yalta. Republican orators unlimbered their heaviest political guns in 1948 when Truman made preparations to abandon massive American aid for the regime of Chiang Kai-shek in the face of mounting evidence that the Communists would take over China.

There is no particular evidence that the Republicans damaged themselves politically by coupling their co-operation in containment policy with peripheral sniping at the Administration. Ironically, however, the party compiled an acceptable record on foreign affairs just at the time it would do the party the least good. Despite the deterioration of America's world position, concern over domestic affairs was reviving, and the 80th Congress irritated much of the nation. Part of the trouble stemmed from the leadership of Senator Taft, the most conspicuous Republican in Congress. Taft hardly qualified as a defender of the prewar status quo, but his personality made him seem more conservative than he was. Intimates knew him to be a shy, magnanimous man; but the only emotion he displayed in public was a volcanic antipathy to the New Deal. He had no patience with flowery oratory from either side of the chamber and exploded his views in short, harsh sentences. When queried about the solution to high food prices, he had replied: "Eat less." As leader of the Senate he added many other maladroit political epigrams which the Democrats were quick to exploit. Yet his program did not justify the strictures which it provoked. The most important feature of it was a series of amendments to the Wagner Act, known collectively as the Taft-Hartley Act. This legislation sought to reduce the incidence of nation-wide strikes imperiling national health and welfare as well as to outlaw costly jurisdictional strikes. Some of the Taft-Hartley provisions envisaged a curtailment of union power, but it was hardly "a slave-labor law," as union leaders contended. The Taft-Hartley law did alienate organized labor, though, and Truman's unsuccessful veto held workers to the Democratic party.

The Republicans handled farm policy in equally clumsy fashion. The extraordinary demand for food during World War II had temporarily eliminated the troublesome prewar surpluses. In 1948, however, they were becoming evident once more. The Democrats could not resist the opportunity to claim credit for current high prices. In addition, they demanded the reactivation of their prewar system of price floors in order to ensure farmers against a disastrous break in the market. Taft had always been against agricultural subsidies, but many of his colleagues from the farm states co-operated with the Democrats to pass a law calling for a sliding scale of supports between 60 per cent and 90 per cent of parity. Having supported the law, the Democrats then charged that the support levels were inadequate. They also represented reduced appropriations for grain-storage facilities as a crafty plot to deprive farmers of income.

The G.O.P. high command in the 80th Congress by cutting taxes and expenditures alienated more people than it pleased. Consumers welcomed tax reduction, but they reacted badly to concurrent lower appropriations for government services. Resentment ran particularly high in the West because of deep cuts in reclamation projects. The Republicans might have won compensatory support by befriending the Negroes, who had migrated to the North in large numbers during the war and were demanding full civil rights. Instead, the G.O.P. turned a deaf ear to this huge bloc of voters and allowed Truman to gain their support with a variety of proposals for combatting racial discrimination. The Republicans also permitted the Administration to make political capital out of the admission of displaced persons, mainly from Eastern Europe.

The careless attitude of the Republicans to all these pressure groups was not wholly a product of political philosophy, since some groups could have been helped without violating it. Over-confidence and resentment played a large part in the attitude of the party. Relying on voter behavior in the past, Republicans felt that victory was certain to follow an off-year election which gave them control of both houses. Moreover, they could not resist using the rhetoric of the 1930's to retaliate against their Democratic tormentors. House leaders like Jonkman and Hoffman of Michigan, Knutson of Minnesota, and Halleck of Indiana vied with Taft in diatribes against the New Deal. The foolish optimism of the Republicans was nursed by favorable Gallup polls.

VIII

Republican candidates for the 1948 Presidential nomination fell into two categories. One group was committed to an all-out fight against the New Deal, and the other believed that a more moderate posture would be necessary to win the Presidency. Speaker Martin of Massachusetts and House Majority Leader Halleck of Indiana bid for the support of the first group, but its real champion was Senator Taft, who held a sizable bloc of delegates from the Midwest and South. Douglas MacArthur hoped to inherit Taft's support in case of a deadlock, but he had been badly hurt by a defeat in the Wisconsin primary. The second group featured three aspirants: Harold Stassen, Senator Vandenberg, and Governor Dewey. Both Stassen and Vandenberg appealed to people who thought that world problems were more critical than domestic ones. Stassen had recently visited Moscow and other European capitals, which allowed him to pose as an expert on international affairs. He favored a bold approach to end the deadlock on disarmament and was cautiously hopeful about dealing with the Russians. Unfortunately, in an effort to avoid being tagged as an appeaser, Stassen had advocated outlawing the Communist party at home and been beaten on the issue by Dewey in the Oregon primary. Vandenberg was by this time an elder statesman who co-operated with the Democrats in the containment of Russia and said as little as possible about domestic questions. He was as pompous and windy as ever, but the years had mellowed him and improved his judgment. Like a true elder statesman, Vandenberg did not believe in taking an active role in securing delegates. He modestly acknowledged his availability and waited for the people to call him. Inasmuch as the Republicans had never renominated a defeated Presidential candidate, many politicians underestimated the potency of Dewey. He had been re-elected governor of New York by a good margin in 1946 and had rammed through the state legislature a number of laws appealing to minority groups that the party had ignored nationally. As titular leader of the minority, Dewey had avoided interference in congressional politics, although the tactics of the party's legislative leaders distressed him. Nevertheless, Dewey's self-restraint kept him from being a target of congressional leaders and also relieved him of the embarrassment of a record on national issues.

The Dewey strategy showed to advantage when the Republican convention convened at Philadelphia in June. The Governor received 434 votes on the first ballot to 224 for Taft and 157 for Stassen. Neither Dewey's major opponents nor the lesser favorite sons could agree on an alternate candidate. As a result, the New York governor came so close to a majority on the second ballot that the convention gave him a unanimous nomination on the third and final roll call. The delegates decided on an East-West ticket by selecting Governor Earl Warren of California for Vice President. Once again, the Dewey managers managed to secure the adoption of a platform that sounded more moderate than the pronouncement of Republican leaders in the 80th Congress. The party promised to uphold the United Nations as well as the containment program which operated outside its framework. Other planks promised to continue the party's program of cutting expenditures and taxes. The platform also endorsed many schemes that the 80th Congress had blocked, including broadened civil rights, inflation control, public housing, minimum wages, and aid to displaced persons.

The Democrats met two weeks later in the same hall at Philadelphia, amid mounting evidence that the delegates expected a crushing defeat in November. Although Truman ostensibly possessed enough votes to assure his nomination, he was embarrassed by the frantic effort of party leaders to find a more popular substitute. General Dwight D. Eisenhower, the architect of victory in the European war, attracted some, while Supreme Court Justice William O. Douglas attracted others. Neither wanted the nomination, and after forty-eight hours of wild intrigue the convention chose Truman. Few party leaders were anxious to be his running mate, but Truman finally prevailed upon the long-time Senate majority leader, Alben W. Barkley of Kentucky, to accept. A new organization of youthful radicals known as the Americans for Democratic Action (A.D.A.) caused the convention to break up in discord by forcing through a platform plank calling for legislation to enforce Negro rights.

Angry Southerners met at Birmingham, Alabama, on July 17, adopted resolutions endorsing continued segregation of Negroes, and nominated Governor J. Strom Thurmond of South Carolina for President. Calling themselves States' Rights Democrats, the new party organized tickets in all

Southern states and a few Northern ones. A few days later, the followers of Henry Wallace, who were more radical than the A.D.A., also broke away from the Democrats and founded a Progressive party at Philadelphia. Neither Wallace nor his running mate, Senator Glen H. Taylor of Idaho, were Communists, but they attracted the Communist-infiltrated labor unions in the urban East and assorted intellectuals who favored a softer foreign policy toward the Soviet Union. Although Wallace had little chance to win, he wanted to retaliate against Truman, who had ousted him from the cabinet in 1946. Most observers felt he would achieve this limited objective by drawing critical votes away from the President in New York City, Philadelphia, and Chicago.

The fall campaign ended in one of America's greatest political upsets. Believing that his opponents were hopelessly split, Dewey adopted the classic strategy of saying nothing that would drive the two splinter parties back to the Democratic fold. He restricted himself to platitudes and innocuous appeals for national unity. His instinctive caution was reinforced by the belief that the tone—if not the legislative record—of the 80th Congress repelled people otherwise disposed to vote Republican. Not wanting to take issue with the Republicans in Congress as Willkie had done, Dewey tried to take refuge in silence. Truman countered by calling the Republican Congress into special session after the convention season and urging it to enact the more New Deal-like recommendations of the Republican platform. It was a foregone conclusion that the G.O.P. majority would do nothing, but Truman reaped a twofold advantage from the maneuver. He convinced some people that the Republicans were insincere about their platform resolutions, and he generated friction between Dewey and the party's congressional leadership. Recognizing the danger of inaction, Dewey urged Congress to pass measures that he thought would gain votes in critical areas. His interference only generated intra-party bitterness and made Dewey more determined than ever to campaign as an independent.[53] Under the circumstances, Dewey's customary chilliness only made matters worse. He was barely courteous to obstructionist senators like C. Wayland Brooks of Illinois, Chapman Revercomb of West Virginia, and Edward V. Robertson of Wyoming who were seeking re-election.[54] They reciprocated in kind, and thus reduced the incentive of local workers to get out the vote. By mid-October strange predictions were beginning to circulate that Dewey would win, but would face a Democratic Congress.

Meanwhile, Truman—who had been counted out by everybody but

himself—stumped the country more thoroughly than any previous incumbent seeking re-election. The President appeared to be an average small-town citizen, and he took full advantage of the American instinct to sympathize with the comman man who has risen above his early environment. He spoke with authority about bread-and-butter issues, but his delivery was folksy and intimate. The old-fashioned rear-platform speech suited him ideally, and he made numerous "whistle stop" talks as his campaign train crisscrossed America. Everywhere, he indicted the 80th Congress as a "do-nothing Congress," thus giving the impression that the Republicans were actually the party in power.[55] He also followed the well-worn grooves by pretending that the G.O.P. stood on its old 1932 platform and would start a depression if the voters returned it to power.

Each Truman campaign promise was aimed at a key pressure group. He bid for the Northern Negro vote, which had increased 80 per cent since 1940, by an all-out advocacy of civil rights. He championed the cause of organized labor with an impassioned denunciation of the Taft-Hartley Act and with promises for broadened social security, low-cost public housing, and inflation controls. At the same time he artfully exploited the apprehension of farmers by criticizing Republican legislation and forecasting a break in agricultural policies comparable to 1929–33. His approach showed a calculated humanitarianism. The President was a new-style "adding machine" liberal, who methodically singled out the pressure groups essential to his success and appealed to them. Nobody thought Truman was being very effective, because the hitherto reliable Gallup polls predicted a Dewey victory throughout the campaign.

The early returns reaching Republican headquarters on election night seemed to confirm the professional forecasts. Wallace drew enough votes away from Truman in New York to give Dewey the state. Elsewhere in the Northeast Dewey ran well, if not spectacularly. A note of anxiety crept into Republican victory celebration, however, when the Midwest began to report. Early in the morning of November 3, Truman pulled ahead in several large Midwestern states, and Republicans began to insist nervously that returns from the rural areas would save Dewey. At sunrise Truman's small pluralities had remained firm, and he stunned the professionals by carrying such traditional Republican strongholds as Ohio, Iowa, Wisconsin, and Illinois. These states plus the Rocky Mountain area, the West, and the bulk of the Solid South elected Truman. Altogether, the President carried 28 states with 304 electoral votes; Dewey captured 16 states with 115 electoral votes; and Thurmond took 4 of the smaller Southern states with 38 electoral votes. The total popular vote was in the neighborhood of 50,000,000, as it had been since 1940; and the Democrats received only slightly less than their customary share of it. Thurmond drew 1,169,021 votes away from Truman, and the bulk of the 1,157,172 polled by Wallace would otherwise have gone to the President. The defections left Truman with a popular vote of 24,105,812 and a comfortable edge over Dewey, who got 21,970,065.

Surprising as the returns were to professional politicians, they confirmed a traditional pattern. In the absence of any overriding reason for a change, Democrats had voted Democratic, and Republicans had clung just as tenaciously to their party. The same twenty-two million who had voted for Willkie in 1940 stayed with Dewey in the next two elections, but there were not enough of them to elect him President. Truman helped his own cause with pungent reminders to the various pressure groups of why they had been voting Democratic since 1932. Wallace made fractional inroads on the New Deal labor vote, but Truman counterbalanced these losses by picking up some farmers who had drifted back to the Republicans in 1940. The President also held four-fifths of the ever-growing Negro vote, which had become a mainstay of the Democratic party in the North. The Republicans emerged from the 1948 election more discouraged than ever, for they knew that they had been beaten by a far less formidable candidate than Roosevelt.

XIII

New Issues and New Leaders

The election of 1948 demonstrated again how desperately the Republican party needed fresh issues. It could not win by opposing the New Deal, by echoing it, or by making equivocal statements about it. The fault did not lie wholly with the Republicans. Only rarely can winning issues be manufactured by party theoreticians or precinct workers; almost always they are generated by the larger forces of history. Once an issue emerges, however, everything depends upon the ability of a party to exploit it. The Republicans did not create the slavery issue in 1860 or the monetary issue in 1896, but on both occasions they took maximum advantage of the political opportunity presented to them. At some point between 1932 and 1948, the Republicans might have won an election by capitalizing on the country's temporary weariness with familiar faces. Yet it is doubtful that they could have converted any great number of Democrats into Republicans on that basis. Their real opportunity during the New Deal era lay in the field of foreign policy, but they permitted the Democrats to make the most of isolationism while the issue was popular, and then they clung to it with a perverse stubbornness after it ceased to have any real utility.

The political horizon did not look very promising for the Republicans in the weeks following the re-election of Truman. But at the end of the 1948 campaign Richard M. Nixon, a freshman congressman from California, had raised a new issue that promised well for the party. At a routine hearing of the House un-American activities committee on August 3, 1948, Nixon had been impressed by the testimony of Whittaker Chambers, a senior editor of *Time,* who freely described his activities as a Communist before he broke with the party in 1938. What startled Nixon was an assertion by Chambers that Alger Hiss also belonged to the Communist party before World War II. As Nixon recognized immediately, Hiss had not been a plodding, prewar government bureaucrat but a leading New Deal intellectual. The Hiss credentials and record were remarkable. He had been graduated from Johns Hopkins and the Harvard Law School, served for a year as secretary to Justice Oliver Wendell Holmes, and moved to the State Department in 1936, where he climaxed a decade of brilliant service by participating in the Yalta Conference. At the time of the hearings in 1948, Hiss was president of the Carnegie Foundation for Peace.

The Chambers accusation had no effect on the November election because of the unpopularity of the un-American activities committee, the doubtful reputation of Chambers, and the convincing denials of Hiss. Nevertheless, Nixon persuaded other Republicans on the committee to persist with the case. Eventually Chambers substantiated his charges with copies of secret State Department documents allegedly turned over to him by Hiss in 1937. The case featured all the drama of an international spy story, for Chambers produced the documents in the dead of night from a hollowed-out pumpkin. The Truman Administration jeered at the inquiry, and Hiss continued to protest his innocence. But the documents plus the circumstantial evidence convinced a federal grand jury of New York City that it ought to prosecute Hiss. Since the statute of limitations protected him from indictment for espionage, the grand jury charged Hiss with perjury.

The first trial ended in a hung jury on July 8, 1949, but a retrial led to the conviction of Hiss in January 1950. The extended proceedings in court commanded wide publicity and generated much bitterness. Hiss had many articulate defenders, but the evidence left no reasonable doubt about the justice of the verdict. Particularly damning was the similarity between the handwriting of Hiss and the handwriting on some of the stolen documents. The persistent refusal of Hiss to admit his guilt heightened the impression that a traitor had participated in the formulation of American policy during a critical period.

Ever since 1936 Republican campaigners had charged that the New Deal was infiltrated by Communists, but until the Hiss trial the issue had always backfired, partly because the accusations came from intemperate conservatives who offered no proof. Both Roosevelt and Truman had dealt effectively with these denunciations by branding them as transparent efforts to distract public attention from worthwhile reforms. The Hiss trial, however, revolutionized public opinion. Hitherto, most Americans had accepted the explanation of the Truman Administration that the disappearance of countries behind the Iron Curtain after 1945 was either due to poverty which made people Communists or to Russian fear of a common frontier with unfriendly neighbors. Presumably foreign aid programs would make people more prosperous and less Communistic, while military firmness, plus a willingness to negotiate, would eventually overcome the security phobia of the Soviet Union.

Most Americans had been disturbed and later confused by the spread of Soviet Communism since the war, and had experienced growing frustration at the seeming inability of the Administration to counteract this expansion. A Communist coup in early 1948 that had destroyed the democratic government of Czechoslovakia intensified this feeling. It was a simple step from this frustration to the belief that Russian expansion resulted from the activities of Communist policy makers in the State Department. For one thing, Hiss had been at Yalta, and for several years Republicans had denounced the Yalta agreements as having sold out American interests. In addition, the Truman Administration was systematically curtailing aid to the Nationalist regime in China and thereby assuring the ultimate triumph of the Communist regime of Mao Tse-tung. Many conscientious State Department officials doubted that any aid short of war would have saved Chiang Kai-shek, but the timing of the decision to abandon him only reinforced public suspicion about the existence of Communist conspiracy in high places.

Truman might have come closer to salvaging the reputation of his Administration by expressing indignation over the behavior of Hiss and launching a well-publicized investigation of government departments. At this point, however, he displayed the stubbornness and obtuseness that the Republicans had exhibited on other issues. His casual attitude reflected advice from New Deal advisers, who had either sympathized with or were oblivious to the dangers of Communism before the war. Few of them had belonged to the party, and their support of Communist objectives had been pardonable during the mid-'30's when Communist propaganda called loudly for peace, civil liberties, and co-operation with democratic parties engaged in economic reforms. Some New Deal intellectuals had seen the grim visage of international Communism behind the mask when the Soviet

Union partitioned Eastern Europe with Hitler and invaded Finland in 1939. Others had persisted in a stubborn unwillingness to admit that they were wrong and had continued to find a justification for aggressive Soviet behavior in the postwar era. With these people at Truman's elbow, the Administration handled matters badly. To accusations that they had tolerated Communist infiltration of the government, the New Dealers replied that their intentions had been pure, and they demanded that they be judged in terms of their motives. When this argument failed to silence critics, they adopted a contradictory line of defense. On the one hand, they contended that there were no Communists in the government, and, on the other, they admitted the possibility but stoutly denied that American interests had been affected. Several defended Hiss's innocence and in the process destroyed the little confidence that remained in the loyalty board set up by Truman in 1947 to detect Communist spies in the government.

Once citizens concluded that the government was trying to cover up its behavior, they made an explosive demand for corrective action. By the beginning of 1950 the question of whether there had been one Communist or fifty in the government no longer seemed important. People simply doubted that the Truman Administration was a safe custodian of the national interest, and they clamored for action against alleged Communists in government. The base of support for a Red scare was considerably broader than in the 1920's. The Catholics and the new immigrants from Central Europe had been persecuted along with the Communists after World War I. In 1950 both groups were violently anti-Communist. To make matters worse for the Administration, they normally voted Democratic.

The Republican who converted public fear about Communism into a winning issue against the Democrats was Senator Joseph R. McCarthy of Wisconsin. Nobody will ever know whether McCarthy's alarm was genuine at the outset, but he repeated his charges about a massive Communist infiltration of the American government so often that he wound up believing his own indictment. His special assets were a resonant voice, a vitriolic tongue, and a crusading zeal that turned others into fanatics. McCarthy started his campaign on February 9, 1950, in a speech to the Women's Republican Club of Wheeling, West Virginia, in which he charged that there were 205 Communists in the State Department. His accusations launched a four-year cycle of investigations that made him the most controversial figure in America.

People who watched McCarthy in his role of grand inquisitor learned to expect certain gambits: irresponsible accusations, incessant juggling of statistics, the introduction of inflammatory irrelevancies, the browbeating of adversaries, and the editing of documents introduced as evidence. His initial feat in 1950 was to force a subcommittee of the Senate foreign relations committee to investigate a Far Eastern expert. McCarthy dominated the subsequent hearings even though he did not belong to the committee. The performance seemed even more awesome in retrospect because McCarthy's victim, Owen Lattimore, had been only an occasional adviser of the State Department and was not currently a government employee. Even with these handicaps, McCarthy managed to discredit Lattimore and to secure the defeat of Senator Millard Tydings, a conservative Maryland Democrat, who had presided over the subcommittee hearings and absolved Lattimore. Heartened by the unmistakable evidence of popular approval for McCarthy, other Republicans concentrated their attention on Communism in the off-year elections.

Truman would have liked to focus the 1950 campaign on the Fair Deal, which was his version of the New Deal. He had secured bipartisan support for enlarging the federal housing program and the coverage of the social security law. Democratic orators emphasized these measures as well as Republican opposition to bills for national health insurance and federal aid to education, which had been shelved by Congress. They also lauded the President for sending American troops to Korea on June 30, 1950, when the Communist-dominated North Korean regime had invaded South Korea. Making the most of a successful October counteroffensive by American and South Korean troops, the Democrats advertised the President as a staunch foe of Communist aggression abroad. Nothing the campaigners said, however, distracted the voters from their concern with Communist infiltration at home. As a result, the Republicans made substantial gains in the November elections, increasing their Senate membership from 42 to 47 and their House membership from 171 to 199. Several Senate races showed the direct impact of the Communist issue. Richard M. Nixon, the hero of the Hiss investigation, won a Senate seat against Democratic Congresswoman Helen Gahagan Douglas after a bitter campaign in which Nixon charged his opponent with receiving widespread Communist support. The Democrats never forgave Nixon for casting doubt on the loyalty of Mrs. Douglas. In Idaho an outspoken admirer of McCarthy, Herman Welker, replaced Glen H. Taylor as senator. Although the Communist issue did not play as much of a part in Ohio as the Taft-Hartley Act, the smashing victory of Senator Taft, over the strenuous protests of organized labor, made him a leading candidate for the Republican nomination in 1952.

Matters went from bad to worse for Truman after the off-year elections, despite the fact that the Democrats were in nominal control of both houses. Hitherto, the Southern Democrats had co-operated with Republicans in limited warfare against the Fair Deal; but in the 82nd Congress the coalition made an all-out attack on the Administration, and conducted more than 130 investigations into its activities. Veteran Southern Democrats, who held most of the committee chairmanships, either took the lead or stood politely aside while the minority brought forth information detrimental to the Administration. The Southerners' vengeful mood was the cumulative result of Truman's repeated efforts to ram civil rights legislation down their throats. Irrespective of national issues, the state Democratic machines in the South had stoutly defended white supremacy since the Civil War. Now that the President of their own party was trying to wreck the key principle of the regional party organization, Southern Democrats regarded him as a more dangerous antagonist than the Republicans. It was clear that the Solid South had begun to crumble and that many congressmen from the Gulf states thought a Democratic defeat in the Presidential election would relieve the pressure on their state organizations. As a result, the bipartisan coalition in Congress functioned more effectively than ever before.

Two or three committees probed Communist subversion, with Southerners loudly contending that native Reds were behind the agitation for Negro rights. The new atmosphere favored McCarthy, and the Democratic chairman of the committee on government operations permitted him to launch a new series of investigations. By this time most of the public was as hysterical about Communist infiltration as McCarthy, and had become complacent about his methods. It no longer mattered whether people under investigation had ever worked for the federal government or influenced foreign policy. Any radical was fair game for McCarthy, and most of his victims emerged from committee hearings with their reputations in tatters. The Senator attracted many imitators at the state and local level. Legislatures established committees to hunt for Communists in state agencies and in school systems. Private organizations of right wingers did what they could to keep the agitation alive.

There was no doubt the Communist investigation helped the Republican party more than any single issue since the pre-Depression era. Leading G.O.P. senators like Taft and Eugene Millikin of Colorado who might have restrained McCarthy, allowed him free rein. A number of colleagues abetted his activities, and some who wanted to speak out were afraid of him. Few of the silent Republican leaders thought the investigations endangered civil liberties. Since congressional committees had seldom shown any regard for judicial standards of fair play, they were happy to see the inquisitorial machinery turned against the left wing. Republicans with long memories recalled the persecution of bankers and businessmen by congressional committees in the New Deal era, and thought that turnabout was fair play. In tolerating McCarthy, the Republican high command was creating a Frankenstein monster that it might not be able to control. Moreover, the spectacle of McCarthy spraying wild accusations in all directions undoubtedly damaged American prestige abroad. Clearly the Republicans had lost their perspective, but they were not the first to push partisanship beyond the limits of sanity and good taste.

Other investigations disclosed corruption at several levels in the Truman Administration. Some officials had accepted valuable gifts from lobbyists in return for favors; others had made money at public expense; and a few had developed close connections with underworld figures. The agencies hit by scandal included the Bureau of Internal Revenue, the Reconstruction Finance Corporation, and the White House staff. Several friends of the President violated the spirit if not the letter of the law, and in certain ways Truman did not seem to be a much better judge of character than Harding had been. Like his Republican predecessor, Truman had appointed competent men to the critical posts in his Administration, but he had also shown a fondness for genial mediocrities who abused his trust.

In addition to all his other troubles, Truman faced a frustrating stalemate in Korea. At the time of the 1950 elections, it had seemed as if the United Nations forces, composed mostly of Americans and South Koreans, would reunify Korea; but, shortly thereafter, forces from Red China intervened when the U.N. army crossed the 38th parallel, the dividing line between North and South Korea. Caught by surprise, the U.N. forces under General MacArthur were driven back. Some Republicans demanded that the United States withdraw from what they called "Mr. Truman's War." A more vocal group demanded that America bomb Chinese bases in Manchuria and support an invasion of the mainland by Chiang Kai-shek, who had fled to Formosa after the collapse of his regime. Truman disarmed neither set of critics, but followed a middle course of continuing limited warfare against the North Koreans and Chinese.

Opposition to the President became more heated in April 1951 when he removed General MacArthur from command for insubordination. Not only was MacArthur the hero of World War II in the Pacific but a militant Republican as well. After his return to the United States, MacArthur aired his differences with Truman. He insisted that limited warfare was futile, and he advocated a full-scale offensive in Korea. The General had no patience with the timid officials in the State Department who feared that his policy would lead to war with China and Russia. Most Republicans echoed MacArthur's views, and a number went beyond him. The fire-brands expressed unwarranted confidence in the striking power of Chiang Kai-shek's army on Formosa and demanded that the United States support a civil war against the Communist regime in China, irrespective of the consequences. There was no evidence that the public really wanted to risk a third world war over Korea or China, and Truman might have eliminated a troublesome issue if he had been able to secure an armistice in Korea. When a Russian delegate in the U.N. suggested a cease-fire on June 23, 1951, Truman promptly held exploratory talks with the North Koreans and Chinese. Despite the apparent simplicity of arranging a cease-fire, negotiations dragged on unsuccessfully throughout the remainder of Truman's term.

Long before the 1952 election Americans had lost patience with the President. Besides producing a high casualty rate and draft calls averaging 47,000 men per month, the Korean war kept taxes high. Worst of all, it had seemingly reached a dead end where neither victory nor defeat was possible. To the alliterative Republican chant of "corruption and Communism," party orators added "Korea."

II

The bright prospects of the Republicans would have assured a spirited contest for the nomination in any case, but the pre-convention skirmishing was carried on with unwholesome enthusiasm because of factional differences dating back to the 1948 election. A substantial element of the party felt that it was time to stop nominating liberal Republicans, since the strategy had backfired three times in a row. This view drew its greatest support from the Middle West, although to call it a sectional position would be an oversimplification. Many congressmen favored the selection of an orthodox Republican, because both Willkie and Dewey had apologized for the legislative record of the party. A number of leaders outside Congress also believed a candidate committed to tax reduction and a balanced budget would attract more voters than at any time since the 1920's. There was some merit to this reasoning in view of the obvious public dissatisfaction with the costly containment policy of Truman. The proponents of retrenchment did not expect the electorate to support old-style isolationism, but they thought it would approve of a program which combined cuts in foreign aid with vigorous national security measures. Such a formula dovetailed nicely with the argument that America would be more secure once Communists were weeded out of the government. The whole approach sounded appropriately patriotic, particularly if combined with the postwar Republican demand for a more vigorous American policy in Asia.

The candidate best qualified to carry the banner of Republican orthodoxy was Senator Taft. He still flew into towering rages whenever he got involved in a debate about New Deal philosophy, and his denunciations of government spending were similar to those of the aging Herbert Hoover. Moreover, Taft had been the undisputed architect of Republican domestic policy in successive postwar Congresses. His attitude toward legislation was not nearly so rigid or doctrinaire as some of his admirers supposed. He actively supported federal subsidies for low-cost housing and tolerated the social security program. In fact, he was far more interested in curtailing the power of pressure groups which had been nurtured by the New Deal than in indiscriminately repealing New Deal legislation. His Taft-Hartley Act did not envisage a destruction of unions but was an effort to restore a balance between labor and management. Although Taft was the darling of the conservatives, he appealed to a broader segment of the party. Many Republicans admired his blunt honesty in an era when most politicians lived in mortal fear of offending a pressure group. Taft awed others who disagreed with him by his extraordinary ability to master every detail in a piece of legislation.

Despite his many virtues, Taft still possessed the defects that had interfered with his Presidential aspirations since 1940. His timidity was often mistaken for stuffiness, and his indignation for unyielding conservatism. Even when he discussed bread-and-butter issues, he sounded like a logician pyramiding syllogisms rather than a politician concerned with human problems. In short, Taft displayed all of the characteristics which made a large segment of the electorate think that Republicans were cold-blooded and Democrats were warm-blooded. Various public opinion polls confirmed the fact that Taft would not be an outstanding vote-getter. Yet he announced his candidacy in October 1951 and began to gain substantial delegate support in the months before the convention. The distribution of Taft's strength demonstrated his handicaps afresh. For the most part his delegates came from states that always went Republican or never went Republican. The populous doubtful states of the East, which were essential for a Republican victory, showed no interest in him.[1]

The delegations immune to the Taft influence either opposed his brand of Republicanism or felt that he could not win the election. The ideological critics of the Ohio senator took a more dispassionate view of the New Deal and the Fair Deal as well as of Truman's foreign policy. The leading spokesman for this faction was Governor Dewey of New York, who had been re-elected by an impressive majority in 1950. He was anathema to the Taft people both as an Easterner with internationalist leanings and as a political strategist. They blamed him for the loss of the 1948 election and had no intention of taking any candidate who wore the Dewey colors. But it was easier to denounce Dewey than to outmaneuver him. He knew that the convention would not nominate him a third time, and he began to look for a replacement after the 1950 election. The most eager candidate was Harold Stassen, but he had begun to seem a little shopworn, even at the youthful age of 44. Another possibility was Governor Earl Warren of California, who had been Dewey's running mate in 1948. Warren had established a remarkable reputation as a vote-getter. Due to the peculiarity of California election laws, it was possible for a candidate to cross-file, and Warren had twice swept both the Republican and Democratic primaries. Warren had the further asset of coming from a rapidly growing state with an electoral vote equal to that of Ohio. His greatest handicap was the widespread belief that he had purchased Democratic support by demoralizing the Republican party in California. Like most governors with Presidential aspirations, he had avoided pronouncements on national issues which could be used against him, but his state legislative program was too New Deal in tone for even the liberal wing of the party.

The liabilities of Stassen and Warren convinced Dewey that he would have to go outside the ranks of the professional politicians. His choice fell on General Dwight D. Eisenhower, the most popular military leader since Grant. The Eisenhower biography featured all the traditional ingredients of the American success story. He was born into a poor, upright, and deeply religious home on October 14, 1890. As the third of five sons, he had been obliged to divide his time as a youth in Abilene, Kansas, between attending school and contributing to family income. Without any pronounced career objectives, he entered West Point in 1911 and graduated 61st in a class approximately three times as large. Eisenhower failed to go overseas in World War I, and during the inter-war period he received the usual routine assignments of the career officer. He was well liked, but nobody had any reason to think Eisenhower was brilliant until the spring of 1942, when General George C. Marshall, the Army Chief of Staff, made him Commander of American forces in the European theater. The transition from obscurity to fame came abruptly for Eisenhower. He presided over the successful North African invasion in the fall of 1942, and subsequently became the Supreme Commander of the Allied forces which conquered Germany. By the time Eisenhower reached the apex of his fame as a military leader in 1945, he had been promoted over 366 officers who outranked him in seniority. In the ensuing two years Eisenhower served as Chief of Staff in Washington, and then had been for two years president of Columbia University. In October 1950 Truman appointed him Supreme Commander of the North Atlantic Treaty Organization, which had its headquarters in Paris. Eisenhower had no sooner arrived at his new job than Republican politicians began approaching him about 1952.

It was not the first time that the politicians had shown interest in Eisenhower. Prominent Democrats had tried to draft him in 1948, and he had escaped only by dictating a public refusal in terms almost as emphatic as those used by General William T. Sherman in 1884. None of his Democratic sponsors had bothered to inquire about Eisenhower's political affiliations, and the General saw no reason to enlighten them or the public. Many politicians supposed that Eisenhower was a Democrat, since he owed his rapid promotion to them and also appeared to be identified with their policies in Europe. The fact that Eisenhower had enjoyed good relations with Roosevelt, Churchill, and other Allied statesmen also encouraged the inference that he had been consulted about the peace terms. On the other hand, prominent Republicans promoted his appointment to the presidency of Columbia University. Some Republicans thought that Truman had called Eisenhower back to active duty to ruin his chances for the G.O.P. nomination in 1952, while others thought the President was grooming him for the Democratic nomination. In December 1951 the county clerk of Abilene, Kansas, was asked if Eisenhower had ever been registered with either party and delivered a negative answer, "I don't think he has any politics." [2]

This observation probably came close to the truth. Like most career army officers, Eisenhower had avoided politics and developed an allergy to politicians. On several occasions he had been outside the country at election time. Even when he was in the United States, the army moved Eisenhower around so often that the maintenance of voting residence would not have been easy. There is no evidence that Eisenhower made the effort to cast a ballot in a Presidential election before World War II. Although Eisenhower lacked the normal partisan instincts, he did possess the normal distaste of a military man for quarreling pressure groups. Their incessant pursuit of self-interest seemed unpatriotic to Eisenhower, while their noisy complaints about government policy affronted his sense of discipline. He emphasized this view repeatedly in postwar speeches, as well as the corollary proposition that Americans were too concerned about self-indulgence and not concerned enough about self-sacrifice. It was difficult to fit these pronouncements in a precise political context, but no one could mistake the conservative tenor of Eisenhower's remarks. Politicians found Eisenhower appealing precisely because he had no record on such volatile questions as civil rights and labor legislation.

Although Eisenhower seemed to be all things to all men, he had a persistent grass-roots popularity quite apart from the synthetic enthusiasm drummed up by professionals. He was one of the few generals in World War II genuinely admired by his troops, and they coined the nickname "Ike" out of pure affection. Soldiers and civilians alike were struck by an informality rare in a career army officer. This trait would not have been so striking if it had not been accompanied by a warm, outgoing personality. Eisenhower approached people with the idea of liking them, and his face radiated good will. The most distinctive feature of it was a broad grin which disarmed the hostile, reassured the nervous, and charmed the noncommittal. Looking pleased came easily to Eisenhower, and his cheerfulness contained no hint of calculation or the strained conviviality of the politician. He would have been less than human not to recognize that his infectious smile was an asset. Eventually the grin became an Eisenhower trademark, but it never ceased to be a reliable indicator of his state of mind. Basically, he was an optimistic man, and his buoyant personality generated confidence and a spirit of teamwork in others.

It is difficult to fix the time when Eisenhower's interest in the Presidency finally overcame his distaste for politics, but after the 1950 elections emissaries of Dewey and other anti-Taft Republicans pursued him in Paris. By this time most of his intimates knew Eisenhower would not accept a Democratic nomination. He had always disapproved of Truman and was unwilling to be indebted to the President. Family tradition, temperament, and postwar associations may have drawn Eisenhower toward the Republicans. It was one thing, however, to secure his consent to be a candidate, and quite another to make him fight for the nomination. Not only did Eisenhower feel that he should refrain from politics while he was in uniform, but he believed that he should finish out his army career unless the party drafted him. The urgent plea of Senator Henry Cabot Lodge, Jr., of Massachusetts, who was soon to become Eisenhower's pre-convention manager, coaxed the General into making a statement in January 1952 that he belonged to the Republican party. The Dewey forces promptly brought their organizational strength to Eisenhower's campaign.

Until Eisenhower announced his political affiliation, some Republican leaders feared that if the G.O.P. did not nominate him the Democratic convention would. Once this threat was removed they felt free to express their secret preference for Taft. In March the Eisenhower forces showed their strength by defeating Taft in the New Hampshire primary and accumulating an unprecedented 100,000 write-in votes in the Minnesota primary. Taft rallied in April by winning a three-cornered contest from Stassen and Warren in the Wisconsin primary, and the same day the Ohio senator carried Nebraska by a large margin. Although neither primary had involved a direct test between Taft and Eisenhower, the convincing Taft victories dispelled the notion of his ineptness as a campaigner. It was obvious that Taft had a head start and could not be overtaken by a passive candidate in Paris. So Eisenhower wrote a letter to the Defense Secretary, Robert A. Lovett, the day after Taft's primary victories requesting release from his duties as Supreme Commander. Truman responded to Eisenhower's letter by granting the General his release as of June 1. As a result, Eisenhower would have only five weeks for pre-convention campaigning. It appeared that the Taft and Eisenhower forces would enter the convention with almost equal delegate strength.

Conflict between the Eisenhower and Taft factions came to a head at the Texas Republican convention the end of May. Taft had cultivated the dominant faction, headed by national committeeman Henry Zweifel, but so many county conventions instructed their delegates for Eisenhower that Zweifel found it difficult to control the state convention. After a series of acrimonious disputes, the Eisenhower supporters bolted and held a rump convention. Similar contests developed in Georgia and Louisiana, with the result that the national convention faced the unpleasant task of deciding which set of delegations from these three states should be seated.

Eisenhower reached the United States in the midst of the uproar; resigned from the army on June 2; and flew to Abilene, Kansas, two days later for a homecoming celebration and political speech in which he made a platitudinous defense of American ideals. This was the prelude to a month of intensive conferences between him and party leaders. At first neither Eisenhower nor his managers said too much about the contests in the three Southern states. But when it became apparent that Taft would be close to a first ballot nomination if the convention seated his delegates, the Eisenhower camp began to raise the issue of fraud. By June 21 Eisenhower had embarked on a crusade to prevent "the betrayal of the whole Republican party and its principles." His sincerity was unquestioned, but people familiar with the long history of Republican politics in the South knew that it would take more than the seating of the Eisenhower delegations to purify the party. It was easy to demonstrate that a majority of the delegates to the Texas state convention favored Eisenhower, but not at all clear that the people who elected them at the county conventions were Republicans. Zweifel claimed, with some justification, that disgruntled Democrats stampeded the conventions for Ike. In fact, Southern Republicans conducted party business in such irregular fashion that it was impossible to make an objective judgment about their conflicting claims.

When the G.O.P. national committee convened a week before the opening of the convention to conduct hearings on the delegate contests, Eisenhower occupied roughly the same position as Theodore Roosevelt in 1912. Like Roosevelt forty years earlier, Eisenhower was the choice of rank-and-file Republicans, but he needed more than a hundred additional delegates to win the nomination. The parallel between the two conventions was all the more remarkable because the younger Taft enjoyed the identical advantage possessed by his father before him. Taft not only controlled more delegates than Eisenhower but the convention machinery as well. This advantage, reinforced by precedent, seemed to assure the seating of the 68 contested Taft delegates from the three Southern states. The similarity between the two conventions failed at one critical point, inasmuch as the bloc of delegates pledged to favorite sons or uncommitted was much larger in 1952 than in 1912. At the 1952 convention it exceeded 300 and included the bulk of the delegates from such large states as California, Michigan, Pennsylvania, and Minnesota. These delegates held the balance of power.

The sustained charges of dishonesty from the Eisenhower camp seemed to be influencing public opinion, because the Taft-controlled national committee behaved with unexpected restraint. It turned down a plea that the contests over the delegates be televised, listened respectfully to a telegram from Hoover offering his services as a mediator, and proposed a compromise whereby Eisenhower would receive 16 of the 38 Texas delegates. Senator Lodge rejected both the Hoover and Taft offers with a touch of indignation, whereupon the national committee adopted the Taft formula on all three of the contested states.

As everybody expected, Lodge vowed to contest the decisions of the national committee on the floor of the convention. Eisenhower kept up the pressure at "whistle stops" en route to the convention with denunciations of "star-chamber methods" and "smoke-filled rooms." His managers also had in their possession a letter signed by 23 of the 25 Republican governors which urged that no contested delegates be allowed to vote in the convention until all contests had been decided. Accompanying this recommendation was the demand that the convention go to the country with clean hands. The formula proposed by the governors was the one that Theodore Roosevelt had unsuccessfully attempted to force on the 1912 convention.

The contests over delegations had been so heated that the 1206 delegates assembled in a grim mood for the opening session of the Chicago convention on July 7. The initial showdown came when Senator Bricker of Ohio offered the customary motion to adopt the previous rules. Governor Arthur B. Langlie of Washington promptly leaped to his feet and offered the substitute proposed by the governors. Congressman Clarence J. Brown of Ohio in turn offered an amendment which would have made the Langlie rule more palatable to Taft. So the test vote actually came on the Brown amendment after a furious two-hour debate. It lost by a count of 658 to 548, whereupon the convention adopted the Langlie rule without a roll call. The initial test vote was the beginning of the end for Taft. Many of the delegates nominally committed to favorite sons had voted with the majority, and they would hardly have overturned the traditional rule governing contests unless they intended to support Eisenhower. The one hope of keeping these delegates out of the Eisenhower column was a deadlock between the two candidates, but this development would help a dark horse rather than Taft.

After the crucial victory of Monday, the Eisenhower managers wisely refrained from any effort to interfere with the election of the convention officers nominated by the Taft-dominated national committeeman. Keynoter and temporary chairman Douglas MacArthur delivered a speech which must have pleased Taft, although the General was himself a dark horse candidate. Permanent chairman Joe Martin followed MacArthur and spoke in more restrained fashion. Tuesday and Wednesday the credentials committee reviewed the conflicting claims of the Southern delegates before a television audience but, to the surprise of nobody, ratified the verdict of the national committee. When the contest was carried to the convention floor, it produced a bitter exchange. At one point Everett Dirksen, a staunch Taft man and senator from Illinois, pointed a finger at Governor Dewey and solemnly said: "We followed you before and you took us down the path to defeat." A chorus of boos followed the reference to Dewey, but Dirksen changed few votes. In fact, he managed to sound unctuous, when his purpose was to deliver a battle cry. The second test vote came on the motion to accept the minority report of the credentials committee seating the Eisenhower delegation from Georgia. The motion passed by a vote of 607 to 531, with the Eisenhower forces mustering 3 more votes than the number necessary to nominate their candidate. With the margin so close, Taft did not contest the Texas and Louisiana delegations, which were promptly awarded to Eisenhower.

The delegates were restless during the nominating speeches on Thursday night, and Martin tried to cut them short by limiting them to ten minutes. Despite the fact that only five names went before the convention, the evening was a long one. The climax came on Friday morning, July 11, when Martin started the first roll call. There were few surprises, although Eisenhower did better than some observers had expected when he picked up some votes at the expense of favorite sons. Throughout the roll call Eisenhower gradually built up his lead, but it was never overwhelming. When the votes were tallied at the end of the ballot, Eisenhower had 595, Taft 500, Warren 81, Stassen 20, and MacArthur 10. With Eisenhower only 9 votes from victory, Senator Edward Thye secured recognition for the Minnesota delegation and announced it was changing its vote to Eisenhower. A number of other states followed suit, but some 280 die-hard Taft men, along with most Warren and MacArthur delegates, resisted. Later in the day, after Taft had met with Eisenhower and pledged his support, the convention adopted a motion making the nomination unanimous.

The outcome was a bitter blow to Taft. Not only did he regard Eisenhower as an interloper with little loyalty to Republican principles, but he was violently resentful of the reflections on his integrity raised in the contest over the Southern delegations. Taft had the consolation of knowing that many delegates who wound up in the Eisenhower column preferred him. Among other things, the Gallup poll of June 19 had caused some admirers to desert Taft, because it indicated that, whereas he would lose to the two leading Democratic aspirants, Eisenhower would beat them easily. The truth was that after twenty years in the political wilderness a majority of Republicans were not in a mood to gamble. They preferred a candidate who looked like a sure winner to their uncrowned champion who faced uncertain treatment at the hands of the voters. The fate of Taft demonstrated afresh the reluctance of American parties to nominate senators or congressmen with long records on controversial issues. In a country where parties build a national majority out of sections with conflicting viewpoints, a forthright position continues to handicap an aspirant for the Presidency.

Most Republican delegates were so preoccupied with the tense contest over the nomination that they were only dimly aware of the Vice Presidential candidate they selected and the platform they adopted. At the request of Eisenhower, who wanted adequate emphasis on the Communist issue, they gave Senator Nixon of California second place on the ticket. The platform turned out to be an unexceptional document, criticizing the conduct of the Democratic Administration at home and abroad without being specific about remedial measures. One plank bore down hard on corruption in government, and another promised to balance the budget by eliminating unnecessary expenses and subsidies. The voter was allowed to guess where the cuts would be made. With an eye to the votes of Texas and Louisiana oilmen, the Republicans also proposed that the title to offshore oil be transferred from the federal government to the states.

Democratic delegates moved into the International Amphitheater at Chicago a week after the departure of the Republicans. Truman had withdrawn his name from consideration in early spring, and, despite official proclamations of neutrality, he favored the nomination of Governor Adlai Stevenson of Illinois. It proved difficult, however, to persuade Stevenson that he ought to run, although he weakened just before the third and decisive ballot. Senator John J. Sparkman of Alabama was nominated for Vice President in the hope of averting a Southern revolt on the civil rights issue. The platform also handled the issue more diplomatically than in 1948. These efforts averted a walkout but did not prevent several Southern governors from declaring for Eisenhower.

Stevenson was an unfortunate candidate for the Democrats to nominate in a year when the Republicans emphasized the menace of Communist infiltration. Nobody charged Stevenson with being a Communist, but he looked and acted like one of the Fair Deal intellectuals whom McCarthy had taught many Americans to distrust. The Democratic candidate wore bow ties, spoke as fluently as a newscaster, and displayed the subtle wit of a *New Yorker* cartoonist. Labor leaders and Democratic precinct workers were unhappy when he used terms like "admonish" and "vilify." Voters did not think it was funny when he ridiculed the talk about Eisenhower's middle-of-the-road supporters by characterizing them as "middle-of-the-gutter" supporters. Sophistication and levity are doubtful assets to the American politician under the best of circumstances, and they backfired badly on Stevenson, because he left the impression that he did not take the charges against the Democratic party seriously. Stevenson was also hurt by the fact that few voters had heard of him before the campaign. A systematic publicity build-up might have helped Stevenson overcome this handicap, but Truman drew attention away from him by embarking on an extended "whistle-stop" tour, which only projected his own Administration's record further into the campaign.

By contrast the Eisenhower campaign was a triumphal tour. Tremendous crowds turned out to cheer him everywhere, even in the deep South. He engaged in little mudslinging and talked mostly about his crusade for clean government, appealing in patriotic fashion to men of good will. Far from being a defect, his jerky delivery and apparent groping for words impressed hearers with his sincerity. They knew he was competent and hence felt enormously pleased when he stumbled through a speech as clumsily as they might have. It was an unintended form of flattery, but Americans found it politically irresistible. Some voters immune to Eisenhower's personal appeal were won over by his promise to visit Korea immediately after the election. A number of self-styled independents claimed that Eisenhower had destroyed his own crusade by appearing on the same platform with two such hysterical Communist hunters as Senators McCarthy and William R. Jenner of Indiana. Since it was no secret that Eisenhower disapproved of both men, critics jeered at him for lacking political courage. The decision probably cost Eisenhower few votes. In any case, he salved his conscience by endorsing the Republican ticket without a word of personal commendation for the two senators who were seeking re-election.

The only real sensation of the campaign was the revelation that a group of California businessmen had made funds available to Nixon to help cover his administrative expenses as senator. Demands for his resignation from the ticket snowballed, and Eisenhower remained noncommittal several days while his organization tested voter reaction. Nixon made a highly emotional speech on television, after which Eisenhower acclaimed his running mate. Subsequent exposure of the fact that Stevenson, when governor, had used a similar fund to supplement the salaries of his aides at Springfield helped to take the pressure off Nixon.

The 1952 campaign marked the end of the era when Presidential candidates did most of their traveling on railroads. Henceforth, they were to make long airplane hops and hold some of their rallies at airports. Television was largely responsible for the change, because candidates could be seen by much of the electorate, without having to make rear-platform appearances in innumerable small communities. Party managers tried to reproduce the atmosphere of the "whistle stop" at airport rallies, but were not very successful. Safety regulations prevented the audience from drawing close to the candidate when he debarked, while the roar of departing planes frequently drowned out the greetings of local dignitaries and the candidate's response. The loss of intimacy was not so serious as the fact that key campaign workers were deprived of the exciting experience of a personal chat with the candidate. Fast travel by air released time for mammoth receptions in hotel ballrooms, but such occasions were not conducive to unhurried discussions of local political conditions in the privacy of a railroad compartment. The old arrangement had given the candidate first-hand information and the campaign worker the zeal generated by direct contact. Under the new arrangement the lesser party leaders were obliged to get their inspiration either in a fast-moving reception line or on the television screen. The effect of these changes was difficult to measure, but they undoubtedly put a premium on effective television appearances.

A candidate who looked tired and disagreeable at Peoria, Illinois, lost little if he recovered his radiance the next day at St. Louis. But by 1952 a substantial number of Americans owned television sets; and when the candidate appeared to be dispirited on the screen, he ran serious risks of losing a substantial number of votes.

The Republicans relied more heavily than ever before on the public relations experts of Madison Avenue, New York City, to grind out campaign material. As part of a general trend in American life to put everything in the hands of a specialist, the Eisenhower managers gave the advertisers a key role in selling the G.O.P. The Democrats protested against the practice of taking the control over political propaganda away from the politicians, but their own National Committee had started the practice in 1931 by hiring Charles Michelson, a shrewd journalist, to belittle the policies of Herbert Hoover. Nevertheless, both parties broadened their expenditures for professional advice on publicity in the 1950's and became increasingly preoccupied with "the image" projected by their candidates. For the moment, the voters accepted with complacency the assaults on their intelligence by the advertising men. Nobody seemed to know whether tolerance was limitless or whether the politicians would use their superior knowledge to regain control of their own profession.

The innovations of the campaign did nothing to check the Eisenhower ground swell. Long before midnight on November 4 it was clear that Eisenhower had won a smashing victory. Returns from key counties in Connecticut and New York established the trend, which continued throughout the night. Eisenhower received 33,936,252 popular votes to 27,314,992 for Stevenson. The Democrats received their customary popular vote, but over 11,000,000 more people had gone to the polls than in 1948 and apparently most of them supported Eisenhower. If the Republicans could make dedicated party members out of their new voters, the long dry spell was over. In the electoral college, the Republicans carried 39 states with 442 votes and the Democrats 9 states with 82 votes. The results confirmed earlier indications that the Solid South was crumbling, for Eisenhower carried Texas, Florida, and Virginia as well as several Border states. The shift appeared to be far more significant than Hoover's inroads on the South in 1928. For one thing, the Republicans put up many more candidates for state and local office than they had done twenty-four years earlier. The party won only a trifling percentage of these contests, but the accelerated activity of the G.O.P. organization indicated that the

Republican label was losing its odious identification with oppression of the South. Part of the change was due to the large influx of Northern Republicans who retained their old voting habits. Some had migrated to retire in Florida and others to participate in the rapid postwar development of Southern industry. At the same time, a number of Southerners were shifting their allegiance in protest against the Truman policy on civil rights. The bulk of the people in this category had backed Eisenhower through independent organizations with the word "Democratic" somewhere in their names. Only time would tell whether they were willing to take the next step and become Republicans.

The one feature of the election that took the edge off Republican rejoicing was the narrow party margin in Congress. Although the G.O.P. carried both houses, it wound up with an edge of only 49 to 47 in the Senate and 221 to 214 in the House. Eisenhower had captured 55.1 per cent of the popular vote, but Republican legislative candidates received only slightly more than 50 per cent.

III

Eisenhower's Presidency invites a comparison with Grant's. Both men's popularity was based on brilliant military records. Both were reluctant to enter politics, and unwilling to take up the full burdens of party leadership when they finally did so. Grant was more successful in insisting on a genuine draft as the condition for his acceptance of a Presidential nomination, but both believed that they had made a distinct sacrifice in answering the call of the people. Like his nineteenth-century predecessor, Eisenhower took office in a turbulent postwar period of party strife when voters were irked by an accumulation of unsolved problems and believed that only a military hero aloof from partisan strife could restore tranquillity. Just as Grant conceived his mission to be the restoration of amity between North and South, so Eisenhower dedicated himself to ending the cold war abroad and discord at home. Because of their military background, both men tried to establish a chain of command in the White House and delegate broad areas of responsibility to subordinates. They were also affected by the tempo of army life, in which short bursts of intense activity interrupted longer periods of virtual inactivity. Eisenhower drove himself without respite during a crisis, but he was bored by the routine tasks of the Presidency and took refuge in golf, bridge, painting, and hunting, preferably under conditions that involved extended travel. Prolonged rest became a necessity for him, however, after his heart attack in 1955. His previous career had generated an abiding interest in foreign affairs, national defense, and disarmament. As President, he developed just as much concern about agriculture, the budget, and the broader aspects of economic policy. On all of these topics he was knowledgeable. Concluding sensibly that he could not inform himself about everything, Eisenhower left most of the remaining problems to subordinates. The choice of areas to be delegated reflected a practical streak in Eisenhower's make-up. He lacked the preoccupation of the intellectual with the problems of labor, social security, and public housing. In such matters he allowed himself to be guided almost entirely by professional advisers.

Despite his sociability, Eisenhower found most of the ceremonial tasks of the Presidency irksome. He was even more allergic to the responsibilities of party leadership. Although he tried very hard to become acquainted with Republican congressmen and to win their good will, his gestures were doomed because of his apathy toward all aspects of political management. He simply had no interest in patronage problems or the organizational rivalries dear to the heart of the average congressman. Politics was another area that Eisenhower turned over to others whenever possible.

Eisenhower was much more fortunate in the choice of his subordinates than Grant, and as a result his Administration introduced a commendable tone of honesty and efficiency to government service. Yet, Eisenhower shared Grant's unlimited reverence for businessmen, and his cabinet, and other sensitive posts as well, was filled with them. These men did little to advance the President's political education. Aside from the Secretary of the Treasury, George M. Humphrey, and one or two others who offered intelligent—if somewhat cautious—advice, the businessmen were an unpredictable quantity. Defense Secretary Charles E. Wilson, a General Motors executive, began by informing Congress the first week that what was good for his firm was good for the country. Secretary of State John Foster Dulles, upon whom Eisenhower relied heavily, possessed considerable political experience and knowledge of diplomacy. Although a Dewey protégé, Dulles had received several diplomatic assignments from Truman. He took office with a huge reservoir of good will, but soon lost his popularity with both the American public and with foreign governments. He did not have the kind of personality that invites intimacy, and his manner was unnecessarily brusque. The unfavorable impression created by these qualities was aggravated by Dulles's attempt to be both a moralist and a practitioner of *Realpolitik*. Hence, his policy statements often were provocative when they were merely intended to sound firm. Eisenhower delegated much of his administrative responsibility to Sherman Adams, a former congressman and governor of New Hampshire. Adams had a stern visage and could say "no" more emphatically than any other politician in Washington. He kept a great many troublesome details away from the President and in so doing earned the cordial hatred of many people who thought they ought to have direct access to Eisenhower.

In his first term, Eisenhower probably came closer to fulfilling the letter of his personal campaign promises than any President in the twentieth century. He succeeded in negotiating a truce that ended the Korean war; he cut expenditures enough to balance the budget after three years of unremitting effort; he improved the tone of public service; and he managed to convince the voters that there were no Communists working in the government. His cautious sparring with McCarthy in 1953 disappointed a great many people, but the Eisenhower tactic of allowing McCarthy to overreach himself ultimately worked. By the end of 1954, the Wisconsin senator had lost most of his followers and had been censured by the Senate for unbecoming conduct.

Unfortunately for the Republican party, Eisenhower's specific achievements were not the stuff from which durable issues can be made. In dealing with the larger problems of the 1950's, he experienced considerable frustration. Both the President and Dulles imagined that the United States could take the initiative away from the Soviet Union, promote freedom movements behind the Iron Curtain, and eradicate the Communist threat in uncommitted countries. Eisenhower also believed that real progress could and ought to be made in the field of nuclear disarmament. These hopes died slowly of exposure to the grim reality of the cold war. In 1954 the Administration faced the disagreeable problem of whether to intervene with force in Indochina or allow part of it to become Communist. It chose not to intervene. Two years later, a complicated series of developments enabled Russia to establish herself in the Middle East by making an alliance with Egypt. Still later, a revolution in Iraq strengthened Russian influence in the area, and caused Eisenhower to retaliate by sending marines temporarily to Lebanon. Throughout the 1950's Communist China repeatedly threatened a war over Formosa. In May 1960 Eisenhower's hopes of a final contribution to world stability were smashed when Soviet Premier Nikita Khrushchev refused at the last minute to attend a summit meeting in Paris. Projects for disarmament went as badly awry as American plans to assume the initiative in the cold war. The inability of Eisenhower to do more than fall back on containment represented a response to conditions that had been created by American strategic and diplomatic decisions during World War II. Within this context the possible alternatives were limited, and, while Eisenhower did as well as his Democratic predecessor, there was nothing distinctive enough about his foreign policy to help the Republican party.

On the domestic front the President had just as much difficulty identifying his party with any dramatic departures in policy. Although Eisenhower approached the task of curtailing governmental activity with amateurish enthusiasm, he soon discovered that nothing substantive could be accomplished except at heavy political cost. Until the New Deal era only big business and the war veterans had been strong enough to apply sustained pressure on Washington. In helping the underprivileged, however, Roosevelt had not only centralized power but had organized a host of new pressure groups. As might have been expected, they helped to perpetuate the swollen administrative machine by clinging to emergency relief payments after the emergency was over. Subsidies originally granted as curative measures during the Depression became vested interests which the beneficiaries protected through ever tighter organization and discipline. Inasmuch as most of the expanded governmental functions helped some pressure group, a tenacious resistance to decentralization was built into the system. By 1953 the pressure groups had multiplied to the point where Eisenhower could reduce neither expenditures nor services without risking organized retaliation. His misery was compounded by a growing awareness that the Republicans would have to detach some pressure groups from their customary Democratic allegiance if they were to become the majority party. So Eisenhower spent much of his time struggling to hold the line. In attempting to deal with agricultural surpluses, the President had a broad choice between reducing price supports and government controls on production, or raising floors and restricting output. Secretary of Agriculture Ezra Benson persuaded him to embrace the first alternative, but convincing Congress was another matter. Since farm politicians in both parties wanted high support prices and token controls, they would not support any clear-cut policy. In 1954 Eisenhower managed to secure passage of a law which took a short step in the direction proposed by Benson. Later legislation established a soil bank to take some acreage out of production, but Benson was so unpopular with Republican congressmen that Eisenhower spent his last years in office combating attempts to raise price supports. In spite of his efforts, the problem of surpluses persisted. Indeed, it was aggravated by the spread of scientific farming methods that increased productivity.

Neither Eisenhower nor the G.O.P. energetically championed the Negro in his fight against racial discrimination, although a Republican crusade for civil rights in the 1950's might have attracted many votes. In May 1954 the Supreme Court in a unanimous decision declared segregation in the public school systems unconstitutional. No time limit was set on the implementation of its decision; the Court only insisted that responsible judicial authorities act with reasonable speed in their respective districts. Cautious as it was, the opinion of the Court had been read by Chief Justice Earl Warren, an Eisenhower appointee, and revitalized the 14th Amendment as an instrument for protecting civil rights. With Northern Negroes holding the balance in large pivotal states, the Republicans possessed every incentive to spearhead the drive for enforcement of the desegregation decision. Historically, the party had identified itself with the cause of the Negro. Moreover, it was easy to demonstrate that a Democratic President could not do much about civil rights, since Southerners controlled key committees by virtue of seniority and bottled up such legislation. Even if the Republicans made only fractional inroads on the Negro vote, which normally went Democratic in a ratio of 4 to 1, they would revolutionize the character of Northern elections. Such tactics were bound to slow up the exodus of whites from the Democratic party in the South, but the potential loss was negligible compared to the potential gain.

Instead, the Eisenhower Administration took the legally defensible but politically dubious position of acquiescing in delaying tactics on desegregation. Eisenhower never put the moral prestige of his office behind the Court's decision but only took notice of it as "the law of the land." The President did send army units to Little Rock, Arkansas, in 1957 when state authorities refused to enforce a federal court order for token integration; but the unhappy repercussions of this incident discouraged Eisenhower from further action. Although he was undoubtedly right in rejecting integration by bayonet, he was unwise in not showing more interest in other methods. Most Republicans in the Senate followed the short-sighted policy of co-operating with Southern Democrats to block rule revision which would have ended filibusters on civil rights legislation. The party that had initiated Negro rights now, a century later, refused to take the lead in implementing them.

Throughout his Administration, Eisenhower had trouble with Republicans in Congress. At the outset, he annoyed G.O.P. senators by neglecting to consult them about cabinet appointments and by following a variable policy on patronage. To make matters worse for the President, most government employees had been granted civil-service status during the preceding twenty years and could not be ousted despite their Democratic leanings. The only places open to large numbers of political job seekers were in the state governments, but many Republicans illogically blamed the President for the paucity of federal jobs. The former supporters of Taft made loud complaints that the Administration was discriminating against them, although they got a reasonable share of the positions available.

The party's ideological cleavage posed a still more serious problem for Eisenhower. Despite the orthodoxy of his views on domestic policy, the President was an internationalist identified with the Roosevelt-Truman program of promoting democracy abroad by foreign aid and tariff reduction. Moreover, much as Eisenhower wanted to cut government expenditures, he would not do so by jeopardizing what he regarded as an adequate foreign-aid and defense program. Most Eastern Republicans and the bulk of the Democrats shared his outlook, but the President found himself in violent conflict with the Taft wing of his party. This faction questioned the usefulness of foreign aid, resented any kind of economic intercourse with countries behind the Iron Curtain, and believed that enormous savings could be made in defense expenditures without damaging national security. The tendency to minimize the importance of American commitments in Europe was coupled with a decided preference for a more aggressive policy in Asia. Most Republicans who took this position also wanted Eisenhower to denounce Yalta and other secret agreements. To prevent a recurrence of such alleged executive indiscretions, they made an abortive effort to pass a constitutional amendment sponsored by Senator Bricker, restricting Presidential power in foreign affairs.

As senior congressmen and the chairmen of the most important congressional committees, Eisenhower's Republican critics possessed a power out of proportion to their numbers. Most of the obstructionists came from the Midwest, but the older and more conservative Eastern Republicans shared their view. At first, it seemed as if Taft, who became majority leader of the Senate, would coax his followers into grudging support of the President's foreign policy. McCarthy made the task doubly hard because he was at the height of his power in the summer of 1953 and used it to harass Eisenhower on many fronts. Unfortunately for the President, the conscientious Taft died of cancer in August. Leadership of the Senate then devolved on a triumvirate composed of William F. Knowland of California, Eugene Millikin of Colorado, and H. Styles Bridges of New Hampshire. As the new majority leader, Knowland was a perpetual thorn in the side of the President. Gruff, opinionated, and so dedicated to the cause of Chiang Kai-shek that he was dubbed the senator from Formosa, Knowland dragged his feet and voted against Eisenhower recommendations at least half the time. The House was more tractable than the Senate, although occasionally Speaker Martin of Massachusetts had difficulty extricating Administration bills from hostile committees.

The mid-term congressional elections were conducted in the most unorthodox manner imaginable. The Democrats were not only afraid to attack Eisenhower, but many of them took the line that a Democratic Congress would give the President more support than one controlled by his own party. Even with these tactics, the Democrats picked up only 21 House seats and a single Senate seat. These negligible gains gave them control of both houses, but hardly constituted a mandate for obstruction. Most observers thought the voters had endorsed Eisenhower, and the Democrats seemed to agree, for they provided him with more reliable support for his foreign policy than did the Republicans.

IV

It was taken for granted that Eisenhower would run for a second term until he suffered a heart attack in late September 1955, while vacationing in Colorado. The President was confined to the hospital for seven weeks and worked on a restricted schedule for several months thereafter. During this period party leaders alternated between hope and despair as they tried to interpret conflicting reports about Eisenhower's state of mind. When the specialists informed the President in February that he would be able to bear the physical burdens of another term, he announced his candidacy. An operation for ileitis on June 9, 1956, again raised doubts about Eisenhower's health, but he recovered well in advance of the national convention.

Uncertainty about the ability of the President to survive a second term increased the importance of the Vice Presidential nomination. Nixon wanted to be on the ticket again and had the support of most Republican leaders. But he was anathema to the Democrats, who regarded him as a "McCarthy in a white collar." They especially objected to Nixon's style of campaigning in the 1954 election, when he had served as hatchet man for the Administration and had predicted that a Democratic victory would promote socialism. Normally what the Democrats thought would not have had very much influence on the choice of a Republican candidate. In this case, however, some Republican strategists believed the renomination of Nixon would frighten away thousands of discerning, independent Democrats who were presumed to be fretting about the President's health. How much impression this argument made on Eisenhower is a matter of conjecture. He had talked to Nixon in January and had explored the possibility of another post for him. Nixon gained the impression that Eisenhower was trying to ease him off the ticket, and the equivocal tone of Presidential statements at a succession of press conferences reinforced his misgivings.[3] Although Eisenhower had told Nixon "to chart his own course" and report back, matters were up in the air until the end of April, when the President emphatically endorsed his running mate. The subterranean anti-Nixon sentiment had not completely spent itself, however, because Harold Stassen tried to substitute Governor Christian Herter of Massachusetts for Nixon on the eve of the convention. By this time the sniping at Nixon had begun to annoy the President, who gave no encouragement whatever to Stassen and was obviously relieved when Stassen decided not to press his project from the convention floor.

The aversion of Eisenhower to long campaigns caused the Republicans to postpone their convention until August 20, with the result that the Democrats met first. The last time they had done so was in 1888, but this innovation proved to be the only unorthodox point about their convention. The delegates assured a rematch by nominating Adlai Stevenson and selected Senator Estes Kefauver of Tennessee as his running mate.

The Republicans proceeded smoothly at the Cow Palace in San Francisco. Mindful of the need to produce a good television show, the convention transacted its business at record speed and renominated the Eisenhower-Nixon ticket within 48 hours of the opening session. There was no quarreling over the platform, but the Republicans spurned an opportunity to take a firmer stand on the enforcement of school desegregation than the Democrats. In fact, the platform of the two parties were so similar that the campaign amounted to nothing more than a popularity contest between two Presidential candidates.

The pace of the transactions more than met the demands of restless television viewers, who had complained about the tedious exchanges on the floor and the long delays for polling delegations in the 1952 conventions. The drastic restrictions placed on the length of convention speeches at the Cow Palace could probably be repeated in later years, but there were limits to the concessions that political parties were willing to make to television. Whenever a convention faced a spirited contest over nominations or its platform, there was bound to be a certain amount of stalling on the floor while party leaders negotiated behind the scenes. Yet the pressures for change generated by television were constructive in some respects. The prolonged demonstrations and convention horseplay had originated in a period when politics and recreation were intertwined. But the element of spontaneity had disappeared from most of these activities by World War I, and these lifeless traditions were mercilessly exposed by the television cameras.

In the four years since his first nomination, Stevenson had tried to shed his reputation as a wisecracking intellectual and replace it with the conventional image of the homespun, healthy, outdoor man. Neither Stevenson nor the Democratic national committee criticized Eisenhower directly, which was a tacit confession that the President was too popular to be beaten. Relying on a more subtle approach, the Democrats pictured Eisenhower as an amiable, well-meaning stuffed shirt who provided a respectable front for the sinister activities of Nixon and other Red-baiters. The voter was supposed to draw the conclusion that Eisenhower would die in office and that his power would pass to angry, unscrupulous partisans. The Democrats made so little headway with this theme that Stevenson in desperation proposed to end the draft and suspend H-bomb tests, views that provoked retaliatory cries of irresponsibility.

As usual, Eisenhower left the more obvious forms of party warfare to his subordinates. He made a dignified defense of the Republican Administration and a patriotic appeal for votes. To safeguard his health, the President limited his campaigning to air hops between large cities with national television hook-ups. Stevenson did some touring by rail, but his campaign also reflected the continuing impact of the airplane and television on political techniques.

Long before November 6 it seemed certain that Eisenhower would win, but the magnitude of his victory surprised the country. He carried 41 states and 451 electoral votes, while Stevenson won only 7 states and 74 electoral votes. The President increased his portion of the popular vote from 55 per cent in 1952 to 58 per cent. He also made deeper inroads on Democratic strength in the Solid South and Border, where the voters again rebuked their party for the continuing agitation over civil rights. The one thing that Eisenhower could not do was carry his party to victory in Congress. Four out of ten voters split their tickets, and the Democrats were able to retain their 49 to 47 majority in the Senate and acquire a 234 to 201 majority in the House. For the first time since 1848 the country had simultaneously chosen a President of one party and houses of Congress of another. Inasmuch as the 22nd Amendment, sponsored by the Republican Congress as a retrospective rebuke to Roosevelt and adopted in 1951, barred Presidents from serving more than two elective terms, the result raised a grave question about Republican prospects in 1960. It seemed as if the Republicans were in the same condition as the Whigs in the 1840's, who had been unable to win except with popular generals aloof from partisanship. More than ever before, the Republicans needed issues which would overcome the predisposition of the majority to vote Democratic.

Despite the persistence of Democratic strength, there was evidence of considerable fluidity in party alignments. The South appeared to be on the verge of developing a two-party system, and the same trend was observable in areas hitherto monopolized by the Republicans. Even at the height of the New Deal there had been no Democratic state organizations worthy of the name in Michigan, Wisconsin, Minnesota, and the Dakotas. Voters had rebuked the Republicans by organizing third parties, like the Farmer-Labor party in Minnesota and the Progressive party in Wisconsin, which were in effect second parties. This pronounced aversion to the Democrats stemmed from tradition as well as the reluctance of older Protestant elements to support a party which drew the bulk of its support from Irish and German Catholics. Representatives of the "new immigration" from the Catholic areas of Europe had started trickling into these states about 1900 and had raised larger families than the native population. As in the urban East, most of them had become Democrats, but they did not affect the political complexion of these states until after World War II.

Minnesota led the way in 1948 by electing a Democratic senator, Hubert H. Humphrey, for the first time in the twentieth century. The same year G. Mennen Williams won the first of six consecutive terms as a Democratic governor of Michigan. Urbanization and the growth of labor unions accelerated the trend, but there was no dramatic turn against the Republicans until 1957 and 1958. A special election in Wisconsin to fill the seat of Senator McCarthy, who had died in 1957, chose a Democrat, William Proxmire. Minnesota and Michigan imitated Wisconsin in 1958, and Iowa elected several Democrats to its congressional delegation. Most of the state Houses in the upper Midwest also passed into the control of the Democrats the same year. A similar upheaval took place in Maine and Vermont, which had been private preserves of the Republicans since the Civil War. Maine elected Edmund Muskie, a Catholic and a Democrat, governor in 1954, and sent him on to the Senate in 1958 after he had completed his second term. Vermont broke a record of more than a century by electing a Democratic congressman the year Muskie went to the Senate.

Long before the 1958 off-year elections, Eisenhower had discovered the unassailable political fact that Presidents suffer more harassment in their second terms than in their first. There were long and unproductive fights over the budget, farm legislation, and foreign-aid appropriations. The Democrats stepped up their investigations of executive departments, and forced the retirement of several Presidential aides, including the valuable Sherman Adams. It was not clear that Adams had been guilty of anything more than friendship with a slippery New England textile manufacturer named Bernard Goldfine. But over the years the two men had exchanged gifts, and Adams left the Administration in the wake of charges that he had tried to save Goldfine from prosecution for a variety of misdemeanors.

The voters reacted in their customary fashion to bickering and confusion in Washington by chastising the Administration. The Democrats increased their Senate seats from 49 to 66 and their House seats from 234 to 280, and thus the Republicans were left with a minority as helpless as in the early days of the New Deal. Two solitary figures breasted the Democratic tide: one was Senator Barry Goldwater of Arizona, an outspoken conservative who won re-election over a strong opponent; the second was Nelson A Rockefeller, a multimillionaire philanthropist who upset Governor W. Averell Harriman of New York by the incredible margin of 573,034 votes.

Emboldened by what they regarded as a mandate for obstruction and by the knowledge that Eisenhower could not succeed himself, the Democrats stepped up their attacks on the Administration. They complained that the United States was falling behind Russia in the development of missiles and other weapons of the space age. The Democrats also blamed Eisenhower for the increasing tension between Fidel Castro's left-wing dictatorship in Cuba and the United States. Some said the President was too provocative, and others that he was not firm enough; but both sets of critics agreed that the short-sighted policies of the State Department were driving Castro into the arms of the Communists. Democratic orators likewise tried to establish an unflattering connection between American foreign policy and the political instability of dependent allies like Korea and Japan. A similar spirit characterized the sniping at the Administration on the domestic front. It was accused of being niggardly in its support of welfare programs and hostile to the farmer.

V

Under the astute management of Lyndon Johnson in the Senate and a co-operative fellow Texan, Speaker Sam Rayburn, in the House, the Democrats steered their course on dead center. Since Johnson hoped to reunite the two wings of the party behind his candidacy, he worked through Congress some innocuous bread-and-butter legislation, as well as a Negro voting law to which even the Southerners agreed. Johnson also advertised his party as patriotic by appropriating more money for national defense than Eisenhower had requested. Having tailored the program to fit his own candidacy, Johnson suffered the misfortune of losing the Democratic nomination to a fellow Senator, John F. Kennedy of Massachusetts. After some hesitation, Johnson swallowed his disappointment and accepted second place on the ticket at the Los Angeles convention, which was held early in July 1960. The fact that Kennedy was a Catholic and only 43 years old assured some voter realignment, but the Democratic candidate courted more by forcing the convention to adopt a controversial platform plank on civil rights. This plank noted with approval the sit-in strike, a new technique being used by Negroes to force desegregation of lunch counters in the South. In addition, the party declared against discrimination in hiring procedures and promised federal intervention if necessary to secure equal opportunity for Negroes.

Months before the meetings of the Republican convention national chairman Leonard W. Hall had begun arousing support for Vice President Richard M. Nixon. Delegates were quietly approached, and press releases picturing Nixon as a far-sighted man of experience were sent to Republican newspapers. Eisenhower co-operated by dispatching Nixon on several ceremonial assignments outside the country. An extended tour of South America in the spring of 1958 had almost ended in the death of the Vice President at the hands of a Communist mob. During this terrifying incident at Caracas, Venezuela, and on other occasions when heckled by Communists, Nixon had behaved with courage and dignity. Throughout the South American tour newspaper dispatches had lauded him for being cool under fire. In July 1959 Nixon had turned an extemporaneous exchange with Khrushchev into a demonstration of his adeptness at diplomatic repartee. Not only had the unpredictable Khrushchev forced a confrontation in public during Nixon's visit to the International Exposition in Moscow, but he had done so in front of the television cameras. Films of the exchange demonstrated that Nixon had responded firmly as well as courteously to provocative remarks from the Soviet premier.

In January 1960 he was given an opportunity in domestic affairs as he participated in the settlement of a crippling 115-day steel strike. The unremitting effort to portray Nixon as a mature national leader was pursued with the election rather than the nomination in mind. Most Republicans did not need to be persuaded of his virtues, but the thousands who had voted for Eisenhower and a Democratic Congress in 1956 did. If anything could bring these wobblers to Nixon, it would be the belief that he had outgrown his particular brand of partisanship.

By spring 1960 it seemed as if the Republican strategy might work. Aside from the volatile question of Negro rights, there was no domestic issue pressing enough to stimulate remobilization of the old Fair Deal coalition. Eight years of reasonable prosperity under Eisenhower had demonstrated that a Republican victory did not automatically trigger a disastrous depression. Voters had also discovered that Republicans did not attempt to tamper with the major New Deal programs. Thus, what Nixon needed to do was to keep the focus of the campaign on international affairs and to stress the contributions of the Eisenhower Administration to peace.

This promising strategy received a sharp setback when Khrushchev suddenly decided to boycott a May summit conference with Eisenhower at Paris. The shooting down of an American U-2 plane over Russia provided the excuse for Khrushchev's action, but it is probable that he did not want to attend a meeting unlikely to result in American concessions. The break-up of the summit conference shattered the prospects for stability on which the Republicans had counted. It provoked Democratic criticism of Eisenhower for jeopardizing peace with the U-2 flights. An even more disconcerting by-product was an eleventh-hour effort by Governor Nelson Rockefeller of New York to wrest the leadership of the party from Nixon. On June 8 Rockefeller released a long statement which complained about the complacent leadership of the party, proposed a nine-point program to rectify matters, and indicated that he would be available for a draft. In view of the fact that virtually all Republican delegates had been chosen and pledged to Nixon, it appears more likely that Rockefeller was seeking modification of the party principles rather than the nomination. Yet supporters of the Governor opened a Rockefeller headquarters in Chicago and waged a feverish pre-convention campaign in the style of the Willkie volunteers of 1940.

If Rockefeller's basic purpose was to extract concessions from Nixon, he succeeded unquestionably. After long-distance negotiations with the platform committee, which had assembled in Chicago the week before the convention, Rockefeller announced on Friday, July 22, that the tentative draft lacked "in strength and specifics." That evening Nixon met Rockefeller at the Governor's New York apartment. By midnight they had worked out a compromise dubbed "The Fourteen Point Compact of Fifth Avenue," and had telephoned the substance of the agreement to Chicago. The major changes secured by Rockefeller were in the area of civil rights and national defense. He forced on Nixon a civil rights plank almost as strong as the one adopted by the Democrats. The reworded national defense plank called for urgent measures to improve both offensive and defensive armaments.

Rockefeller's attempt to dictate the platform produced a violent reaction in Chicago. Many Republicans who did not object to the changes in principle stoutly resisted the compromise because it by-passed the platform committee. The conservative Goldwater disliked the proposed intervention of the federal government in the area of civil rights, which he thought should remain under the jurisdiction of the states. Eisenhower resented the implied criticism of his stewardship as commander in chief in the defense plank. Nixon arrived in Chicago on Monday morning, July 25, and, after endless conferences, managed to subdue what he called the "almost cannibalistic urge" of Republicans "to destroy and consume one another." [4] Once again the platform was reworded, but it retained in essence the firm Rockefeller stand on civil rights and national defense. With the platform controversy disposed of on Tuesday, the convention nominated Nixon the following evening. He received all but the ten votes of the Louisiana delegates, who were disturbed about the civil rights plank and supported Goldwater. With the approval of Eisenhower, Nixon, and the bulk of the party's leaders, the convention selected Henry Cabot Lodge, Jr. for Vice President. The choice of Lodge, who had served as ambassador to the United Nations for eight years, indicated that the Republicans would emphasize foreign affairs in the fall campaign.

Although a Gallup poll immediately after the Republican convention gave Nixon a 53 per cent to 47 per cent lead over Kennedy, the Vice President faced an uphill fight and knew it. Despite his efforts to erase the impression that he had been the hatchet man of the Eisenhower Administration, Nixon possessed more than his share of enemies. New Deal intellectuals believed that he had ridden to power by pinning the Communist label on innocent liberals. Many newspapermen disliked Nixon and lost no opportunity to portray him in an unfavorable light. The reasons for their hostility varied. A few shared the grudge of the intellectuals, while a much larger number thought the Vice President was a man without convictions. The contrast between his incisive manner in private conversation and his windy, cliché-ridden platform style struck reporters as unmistakable proof of his insincerity. This impression was heightened by Nixon's lack of spontaneity and warmth. Reporters who covered him day after day thought that his joviality was forced. Watching his mind at work, they concluded that each statement and gesture was contrived with a view to its probable political effect.

The public did not see Nixon in as unfavorable a light as the reporters. Some people thought he was a little out of character when he indulged in sentimental boyhood reminiscences. Others noted his extraordinary facility for taking divergent positions simultaneously. Nobody who watched him dedicate a federal housing project could miss the fact that he deplored government action in this area, recognized that slum clearance was needed, and felt proud that the job had been done so well. Voters unable to observe the Vice President on such occasions could count on the Democrats to remind them that Nixon was shifty and had frequently changed his position on key issues.

Like all hostile estimates of political leaders, the emphasis on Nixon's indifference to principles was overdone. He was not the first politician to modify his views after close contact with the thorny problems of his generation. Indeed, some of the adjustments in his thinking did credit to the Vice President and indicated that he had broadened his perspective. The trouble was that too many people refused to take anything Nixon said at face value, especially the independents, whose votes he needed to win the election. His enemies may have been unfair, but over the years they had smeared him effectively.

In Kennedy the Vice President faced a more dangerous antagonist than he imagined. Although Nixon at 47 was young as Presidential candidates go, he looked his age; while Kennedy, who at 43 looked thirty, managed to turn a potential handicap into an asset. Kennedy had the fresh appearance of the "All-American" boy, trim, athletic, alert, and wholesome. But the lines in his face were just hard enough to suggest maturity, and he strengthened the impression that he was ready for the highest responsibility by his sober bearing. Kennedy's face could light up with a gracious smile when he was waving to a crowd or making his way to a rostrum. Once he began to speak, however, Kennedy stiffened into the conscientious young statesman. His delivery was almost telegraphic, enabling him to compress the maximum number of points into the fewest possible words. He used humor sparingly and seldom relied on autobiographical material for illustrations. His arms moved ceaselessly as he emphasized points. Although Kennedy evaded concrete issues as artfully as Nixon, the Massachusetts senator was not handicapped with a reputation for equivocation as the Vice President was.

Kennedy's youth might have been an unqualified asset except for the fact that he had so few accomplishments to his credit after eight years of service in the Senate. No major piece of legislation bore his name, nor had he taken an outspoken stand on the more volatile issues of the 1950's. His record could not have been a very controversial one, since it received the blessing of a party hitherto unwilling to nominate a senator for President. In any case, Kennedy's previous career left him vulnerable to the charge that he had displayed little leadership, an accusation which supplemented Republican efforts to represent Nixon as a mature statesman. At the outset, Republican claims about the superior qualifications of their candidate were worth something in a campaign dominated by public concern over world tensions. Unfortunately, the Vice President surrendered this advantage by agreeing to a series of television debates with Kennedy. For Nixon to gain anything from such an encounter he would have to score an unmistakable victory. Anything resembling a stand-off would convince the voters that Kennedy was just as effective under pressure as his more experienced opponent. Moreover, it was a political axiom that a famous candidate should not help one less known by appearing on the podium with him. Nixon was under some pressure to hold debates, since the three major television networks had offered the major parties 19 hours of free time. The two national committees had concurred in these arrangements but not in language that was binding on the candidates. Although it is a certainty that a President would have rejected a debate, Nixon found it easier to accept because both he and Kennedy were "outcumbents." Besides, the Vice President excelled at extemporaneous encounters and felt confident of winning. As a result, the candidates agreed to four debates and the first was held at Chicago on September 26.

The timing turned out to be most unfortunate for Nixon. He had injured his kneecap, and a subsequent infection put him in Walter Reed Hospital from August 29 until September 9. This misfortune had disrupted his campaign schedule and forced him to overwork during the next two weeks. On the day of the debate Nixon was exhausted and nervous. Television cameras never flattered him because they made the lower part of his face look dark and unshaven. On this occasion he also seemed unnaturally pale, and the loss of five pounds during his illness had caused a perceptible sag in his cheeks. Although Kennedy was doubtless just as nervous, he managed to look fresh and rested.

Nearly 70,000,000 Americans watched the debate. They saw an alert, fluent Kennedy describe in general terms how he hoped to promote national progress and watched Nixon counter with a series of courteous rejoinders. Quite apart from his ghostly appearance, Nixon was at a disadvantage, because he could not take the position that he opposed progress. Furthermore, he had to agree with Kennedy's incontestable proposition that things could be better, but he was obliged to do so grudgingly, lest his concession seem to be a criticism of the Eisenhower Administration. Unfortunately, the agreed-upon questions encouraged vague responses, whereas Nixon's case would have been stronger had specific issues been discussed. Nixon could do nothing but concur with Kennedy's objectives and oppose his methods. Although nobody won the debate, Kennedy was clearly the more zealous friend of progress. Being outpointed in platitudes did not hurt Nixon as much as the demonstration that Kennedy had as much stage presence and equanimity under trying circumstances as the

Vice President. Thenceforward, the argument that Nixon was the more experienced leader fell on deaf ears.

Nixon never recovered from the damage inflicted on him by the first television debate, although he performed creditably in the ensuing three. He was not much more successful in overcoming the impression that he lacked the physical stamina and vitality to cope with the problems of world leadership. Hoover had looked sour and discouraged in the closing days of the 1932 campaign, and Willkie had groped his way through the last stages of the 1940 campaign more dead than alive. Nixon ought to have heeded these lessons, but he stubbornly carried out a convention pledge to campaign in all fifty states, despite the loss of ten days in the hospital. He ended the long ordeal wearily stumbling through his speeches.

There was probably little that Nixon could have done to change votes in most pressure groups traditionally loyal to the Fair Deal. The Negroes constituted an exception, however, even though pollsters indicated that gratitude for past economic favors would influence most of them to vote Democratic. Increasingly, Northern Negroes were responding to agitation against discrimination and applauding the more militant tactics of the various civil rights organizations. In 1956 Eisenhower had made slight inroads into the Democratic Negro vote, and his intervention with federal troops at Little Rock improved Republican prospects for 1960. When Nixon capitulated to Rockefeller on the civil rights plank, he would have been well advised to make an all-out effort for the Northern Negro vote. But the unexpected success of his Southern tour in August apparently caused him to try instead for a sweep in the Solid South. The likelihood of gaining some Southern votes through the religious issue must also have entered into his calculations. In any case, he failed to emphasize his party's civil rights plank and left the implication that discrimination was a local problem. Senator Goldwater crisscrossed the South saying the same thing in quite specific terms. Nevertheless, Nixon had a final chance to bid for the Negro vote when integrationist leader Reverend Martin Luther King was arrested on October 19 for demanding service in the restaurant of an Atlanta department store. Kennedy not only telephoned King's wife to express his concern personally, but his New York headquarters followed up with a plea for King's release on bail, which was granted. By contrast, Nixon remained silent. He must have wondered about the wisdom of this decision on election night when Philadelphia, Chicago, and Detroit with their heavy Negro populations cancelled Republican majorities built up elsewhere in Pennsylvania, Illinois, and Michigan.

One other act of omission hurt Nixon: the decision to keep Eisenhower out of the campaign until the very end. Recalling the way Truman had overshadowed Stevenson in the 1952 campaign, the Nixon managers were determined that their candidate should have the center of the stage. In making the comparison they forgot that Eisenhower was more popular than Truman and that Nixon was better known than Stevenson. When Eisenhower began to make eleventh-hour campaign speeches by pre-arrangement, he stirred up much enthusiasm. Whether he could have con-verted applause into votes for Nixon through a more intensive canvass is a debatable question. Eisenhower's previous efforts to transfer his popu-larity to other Republicans had not been very successful, but in an elec-tion as close as the one in 1960 greater reliance on the President might have changed the outcome.

The sole issue over which Nixon virtually had no control was the reli-gious issue. Both candidates took an official stand against its injection in the campaign, and aside from one outburst by Norman Vincent Peale, a well-known Protestant minister, high religious officials behaved with far more restraint than in 1928. It was clear midway through the campaign, however, that religious feelings would have an important effect on the elec-tion. Judging from the resolutions of the Southern Baptist Convention, pamphlets circulated by smaller denominations, and sermons delivered by individual ministers, many Protestant Democrats intended to desert Ken-nedy. Catholic laymen said little, and church officials limited themselves to guarded pleas for tolerance. Yet there was a good deal of indirect evi-dence that Catholics would behave like Protestants at the polls. It also seemed probable that a substantial number of Jews would support Ken-nedy in order to break the Protestant monopoly on the Presidency. Ken-nedy made a flat pledge to uphold the separation of state and church in a speech to the Greater Houston Ministerial Association on September 12. Thereafter he made no pointed reference to the issue, but lesser Demo-cratic campaigners beat such a steady tattoo for tolerance that Nixon's managers became alarmed. Although some advisers wanted the Republi-can candidate to echo this sentiment, Nixon remained silent.

On election night Massachusetts, Connecticut, and New York went to Kennedy early in the evening. Reports from Kentucky introduced a jarring note, however, as the state went strongly for Nixon. When Tennessee followed suit an hour later and Ohio showed signs of doing the same, it became clear that religious considerations were modifying the customary voting pattern along the same lines as in 1928. Areas with a predominantly Anglo-Saxon, Protestant population in the Solid South, the Border, the Middle West, and the Rocky Mountains began to pile up pluralities for Nixon comparable to the Kennedy margins in the Catholic sections of the Northeast. After 1 a.m. the spotlight focused on Illinois, Michigan, and Minnesota, where there were heavy concentrations of first- and second-generation Catholics in the big cities, and a Protestant majority in the hinterlands. Kennedy's lead in all three states continued to be so slim that Nixon refused to concede the election when he made a statement in Los Angeles at 3:15 a.m., Eastern time. The early morning hours of November 9 drifted in with no change in the status quo; midway through the morning the Vice President finally telegraphed his congratulations to Kennedy. The election had been the closest in the twentieth century. Kennedy had a plurality of 113,000 out of nearly 69,000,000 votes cast, or only one-tenth of one per cent more than Nixon. In the electoral college, however, the Democrats won 23 states with 303 votes, to 25 states with 219 votes for the Republicans. All of the Mississippi electors, plus six from Alabama and one from Oklahoma, cast their ballots for Senator Harry F. Byrd of Virginia, for a total of 15. The outcome was so close that the switch of a few thousand votes in Illinois and Texas would have given the election to the Republicans. Kennedy carried nine states with a total of 120 electoral votes by a majority of less than 51 per cent.

The Democrats won by sweeping the Northeast except for Maine and Vermont, carrying seven Southern states by comfortable margins, and winning narrow victories in Michigan, Minnesota, and Illinois. Nixon took most of the Midwest and all the states beyond the Missouri River but New Mexico, Nevada, and Hawaii. Post-election studies of strongly Catholic and Protestant precincts demonstrated that religious prejudice played a critical role in the outcome. Kennedy received 78 per cent of the Catholic vote and carried 7 of the 10 states with 30 per cent or more Catholic voters.[5] Undoubtedly the religious issue worked in his favor, because Catholics were concentrated in the populous Northeast, whereas the most militant foes of Catholicism were in Southern and Midwestern states with smaller electoral votes. Moreover, the Protestant Democrats who swung to Nixon had little effect on the outcome. They either swelled majorities in

Midwestern states that he would have carried anyway, or fell short of over-coming Kennedy's lead in the South. The Negroes shared responsibility with the Catholics for defeating Nixon. In fact, some Negro wards in pivotal Northern states gave Kennedy majorities of more than 8 to 1.

Apparently more Independents and disgruntled Protestants were willing to vote for Nixon than were willing to support Republican candidates for Congress, for the Democrats won both houses by comfortable margins. They did not do as well as the 1958 landslide but still held an edge of 259 to 178 in the House, and of 64 to 36 in the Senate. At all events, 1960 was a good year for incumbents, as veteran legislators in both parties secured re-election.

VI

The first two years of the Kennedy Administration did not look very different from any two-year period after the war when the Democrats con-trolled both the Presidency and Congress. There were the same bold pro-posals for extending social and economic benefits and the same pleas for generous foreign-aid appropriations and for authority to cut tariff barriers. The Kennedy program was called the New Frontier to distinguish it from Truman's Fair Deal, but the philosophy behind the legislative recom-mendations of both Presidents and the sources of their support were identical. Kennedy made more of an effort than Truman to swing Southern Democrats behind his program by proceeding cautiously on Negro inte-gration. He requested and secured congressional authorization for a Fed-eral Commission on Civil Rights, but otherwise did nothing except estab-lish a Committee on Equal Employment Opportunities under Vice Presi-dent Lyndon Johnson.

The conciliatory behavior of the President did not prevent the re-emergence of the old coalition between Southern Democrats and Repub-licans. As in every Congress since 1939, this group exercised a life-and-death power over legislation; it killed much of the President's domestic program. The principal casualties were a government sponsored medical insurance measure popularly known as Medicare, a project to establish a Department of Urban Welfare with cabinet status, and an agricultural bill based on the traditional Democratic formula of high price supports and rigid production controls. On the administrative front the President launched a series of anti-trust suits with the energetic assistance of his brother Robert, the Attorney General. The harassment of business reached a climax in the spring of 1962 when Kennedy forced the major steel companies to rescind a general price increase by threatening them with prosecution under the anti-trust laws.

Kennedy would have preferred to wage the off-year elections on the familiar bread-and-butter issues, and it appeared as if he would do so successfully when two Southern Democratic opponents of Medicare lost primary elections to avowed supporters of the President. In mid-September, however, the Republicans' concerted attack on the Administration's Cuban policy registered considerable popular support. The problem of Cuba reached serious proportions in the last months of the Eisenhower Administration, when Premier Fidel Castro ostentatiously strengthened his ties with the Soviet Union and Khrushchev warned the United States that he would not tolerate an attack on Cuba. In the spring of 1961, Kennedy had helped an army of Cuban exiles to launch an invasion at the Bay of Pigs but withheld the support of the American Air Force, with the result that Castro crushed the rebels and strengthened his grip on the island. Criticism of Kennedy's ill-advised action, which came both from people who believed American power should have been placed behind the invasion and from others who considered it a provocative act endangering world peace, died out quickly.

Save for an occasional reminder of the episode in the opposition press, little was heard about Cuba until Republican Senator Kenneth Keating of New York reopened the subject on August 31, 1962. In a Senate speech Keating warned that Russian troops and equipment were being landed on the island. For a time the Administration professed ignorance of what was being sent to Cuba, but at a press conference on September 13 Kennedy confirmed Keating's assertion and minimized its importance. "The shipment of Communist weapons," said the President, "does not constitute a serious threat to any other part of this Hemisphere." A week later, Congress passed a joint resolution reaffirming the determination of the United States to prevent the Marxist-Leninist regime in Cuba from extending its activities by force or the threat of force. At the behest of the Administration, this bold resolve was qualified by a weak statement to the effect that the government would co-operate with the Organization of American States and with "freedom-loving Cubans" to promote self-determination on the island. Having ruled out unilateral American intervention or the use of force against Castro, the Administration waited hopefully for the agitation over Cuba to subside.

The Republicans were aware that they had a winning issue, however, and they injected it into the congressional elections. Keating and other Republicans began to charge that the Russians were establishing missile sites on Cuba. Republican congressional candidates also rediscovered the Monroe Doctrine and reminded the voters that the Kennedy Administration was ignoring its injunction against the establishment of "unfriendly systems" in the Western Hemisphere. A variety of solutions ranging from blockade to outright military intervention was urged, depending on the bellicosity of Republican nominees and their constituents. The Democrats replied feebly to this withering assault by asserting that it would be unworthy of the United States to use force against a small neighbor, by evoking the specter of another bloody, indecisive Korean-type war in Cuba, and by talking of the danger of nuclear war.

By mid-October the Administration had discovered that Americans felt differently about Cuba than Korea, but it was reluctant to undercut its congressional candidates by reversing itself and adopting a bellicose posture. Matters drifted until October 22 when Kennedy made a television speech to the country. He confessed that Cuba was capable of making a nuclear attack on the United States, announced the imposition of a partial blockade on Cuba, and asserted that all missiles would have to be dismantled and removed. The substance of the Kennedy stand on missiles was delivered to the Soviet Union in the form of an ultimatum which stated that noncompliance would provide justification for American military intervention in Cuba.

The tension was acute for the next 48 hours, but Russian merchant ships carrying armaments to Cuba turned back and Khrushchev agreed to remove the missiles. In the process, Kennedy slowly converted his ultimatum into a document for negotiation. He also accepted the dubious Soviet distinction between "offensive" and "defensive" arms and conceded that the latter could remain in Cuba. The President even pledged himself to discontinue attempts to overthrow the Castro regime, once the removal of missiles had been verified. The mulishness of Castro, who refused to permit American inspectors on Cuba, ultimately enabled the President to back away from positions that involved a tacit repudiation of the Monroe Doctrine. In the end, missiles and some Russian troops were removed from Cuba, but Castro remained defiant, amidst indications that the Soviet military force would remain on the island.

The sparse fruits of the Kennedy ultimatum did not ripen in time to affect the 1962 elections. The fact that Khrushchev backed away from war and agreed to remove the missiles was represented as a great victory for the Administration. Democrats, who had been praising the peaceful Kennedy policy in Cuba, reversed themselves without any trace of embarrassment and clamored for the country to back the President. Since Kennedy had been shown pictures of Soviet military installations on Cuba at least a week before his ultimatum, some people thought his sense of diplomatic timing was defective. Nobody questioned his political sense of timing, because it saved the Democrats in the November elections. The relative strength of the two parties in the House remained virtually unchanged, and the Democrats actually picked up two Senate seats. In so doing, they made the best mid-term showing of any party in power since 1934.

The one bright spot for the Republicans was the South. Throughout the 1950's their share of the Presidential vote in the region had grown steadily, demonstrating that the South was no longer exclusively Democratic territory. The emergence of a genuine two-party system, however, depended upon Republican effectiveness in organizing at the precinct level. Signs of such activity had been most evident in Texas where Republican John G. Tower won the Senate seat vacated by Lyndon B. Johnson shortly after the 1960 election. The G.O.P. showed greater vitality in 1962, electing several congressmen and coming within a few thousand votes of unseating Senator Lister Hill of Alabama. Still more significant was a sharp rise in the number of G.O.P. candidates for state legislatures.

VII

The success of the Democratic party elsewhere was all the more remarkable because the Kennedy Administration had suffered its share of reversals. The Administration had irritated segregationists without satisfying civil rights leaders, and had experienced a series of reversals in Congress. The record in foreign affairs was hardly more reassuring. It had weathered a succession of crises, but no respite was in sight. The disposition of the public to condone or overlook these shortcomings was partly due to the phenomenal personal popularity of the President. The fact that voters found him appealing was not as remarkable as their reasons for doing so. Some worshiped him as an American Adonis. They lavished on the President the mindless adulation ordinarily reserved for movie stars. Others were captivated by his manifestations of concern for the underprivileged masses at home and abroad. This quality attracted the intellectuals, who were also intrigued by Kennedy's preoccupation with up-grading the cultural tastes of fellow Americans. From the perspective of the intellectuals he came into focus as a modern Lorenzo il Magnifico bent on enhancing all aspects of human life. Something resembling a Renaissance court emerged at the White House, with the intellectuals assuming the advisory function of the fifteenth-century humanists, and Jacqueline Kennedy presiding over cultural functions, banquets, and fox hunts.

The identification of the intellectuals with Kennedy was a mixed blessing. It had great appeal for people who were responsive to the humanitarian aspects of the Administration, but it disturbed voters with conservative inclinations. The conspicuous role of the intellectuals made no difference to segregationists and neo-isolationists who would have opposed Kennedy in any case. The real trouble came from a more flexible element in the political spectrum that distrusted the sentimental enthusiasm of the intellectuals for socialistic experiments abroad. This group no longer believed, as it had in the McCarthy era, that the intellectuals took orders from Moscow. But it was disturbed by what it regarded as sympathy for leftist regimes, particularly those at odds with American foreign policy. It was willing to swallow a foreign aid program but not the related notion that left-wing dictatorships deserved preferential treatment and could be converted into democracies more readily than right-wing dictatorships. Whether Kennedy operated on the premise of the intellectuals is a matter of conjecture, but many conservatives thought that he did. Since most of these conservatives were Republicans, their apprehensions raised the possibility that they would acquiesce in the selection of a doctrinaire anti-Communist presidential candidate in 1964.

Other factors promoted the polarization of opinion at the extremes of the political spectrum. Negro demonstrations in Birmingham, Alabama, in April 1963, followed by Kennedy's prompt demand for comprehensive civil rights legislation, brought the controversy over integration to one of its periodic peaks. At first the general indignation over the brutal tactics of the Birmingham police strengthened the President's hand. But by fall the sense of urgency had subsided and the civil rights bill languished in Congress. Extremists took over the debate, but outside of the South they did not seem to have much of an audience.

The reversion of the majority to a state bordering on indifference highlighted a trend that had been gaining momentum for over a decade. Public opinion polls reported a record number of Independents and ticket-split-ters flanked by nominal Democrats and Republicans. The growth of an ambivalent center in American politics was less a sign of moderate opinions than of boredom.[6] The bulk of the Independents did not bother to vote unless their economic interests were affected in unmistakable fashion. The nominal Republicans and Democrats retained their traditional affiliations without enthusiasm. The former saw little prospect of arresting the piecemeal encroachments of the welfare state, while the latter despaired of achieving genuine reform. From the standpoint of both, the major parties had become coalitions of pressure groups pursuing their respective interests without regard to national needs. Repelled by what they sensed rather than understood to be a struggle for control of an overdeveloped state machine, the centerists had lapsed into a consensus of apathy. They took the accumulated legislative benefits of the New Deal and subsequent Democratic Administrations for granted. They also tolerated selective extensions of government service to new groups. The only thing capable of galvanizing the centerists into an energetic display of Democratic proclivities was a threat to the economic status quo. Such a challenge would materialize in the 1964 election, evoking a negative enthusiasm which subsided into torpor as soon as the challenger was defeated.

There was nothing novel about American parties being temporarily becalmed on a vast Sargasso Sea. Cyclical changes in the political weather had been the rule rather than the exception. The trouble was that each successive onslaught of the doldrums lasted longer than the alternate periods of brisk political winds. The long-term forces at work were easy to identify: the relegation of politics to the periphery of American life, and the corresponding decline of interest in the obligations of citizenship. It was not that the apathetic had no interest in issues, although surely some fell into that category. The bulk of them, however, had reached the conclusion that the vital issues were either insoluble or too complex for the voter. The typical citizen of the 1960's was a century removed physically —and eons spiritually—from the milieu in which "almost the only pleasure" of the American was "to take part in government and discuss its issues." [7] At the heart of his progressive disengagement from politics was a diminution of faith in democracy and in the party system that sustained it. The most obvious danger to the political party from the consensus of apathy was that it would be captured by the vigilant minority. The Republicans were to experience the bitter fruits of such indifference during the 1964 pre-convention campaign.

As in previous phases of the consensus of apathy, the inevitable con-
comitant was the politics of personality: a style that dominated the post-
Reconstruction era, the 1920's, and the period after the Korean war.
Diverse as they were in other respects, Blaine, Coolidge, and Eisenhower
would be remembered because of their personalities rather than because of
their identification with issues. It is futile to speculate about the effect of
modern communications on the style of a Blaine or a Coolidge. The
former lived before the emergence of the tabloid mind that fed on a diet
of intimacies, and the latter before the advent of the public relations firm
or television that aggravated the obsession with personalities. In any case,
the pressing issues raised by depression, World War II, and its aftermath
would have prevented exclusive use of these instruments in the projection
of public images. But the termination of the Korean war and the McCarthy
controversy removed the last barriers against the application of modern
communications to political personalities. The subsequent revolution mod-
ified the concepts of political availability, campaign finance, and other
election procedures.

Political commentators heralded the new era with extended speculation
about Eisenhower and the sources of his appeal. They did so with a touch
of condescension, implying that he was a political freak rather than a
pioneer. It was difficult to overlook the importance of the personal image
itself when Kennedy duplicated Eisenhower's feat by projecting a different
kind of image. Whether by chance or design, Eisenhower had identified
himself with the agrarian myth, and Kennedy had done just as well by
repudiating it. The voters had never cherished bumpkins or boors, but
they had always distrusted cosmopolites who deviated from the norms of
republican simplicity. Sooner or later, a Presidential candidate was bound
to develop a style more congenial to the growing urban population. Kennedy's dramatic contribution to the politics of personality was underlined
by the abruptness with which he popularized a type hitherto abhorrent in
American public life: the good-looking, sophisticated, youthful, Ivy
Leaguer.

If Kennedy demonstrated that an image was more important than an
issue, he also pointed the way to a new standard of political availability.
His type had already triumphed in the business world and suburbia.
Moreover, there were 21 million Americans between the ages of 21 and
30 in 1960, and the number below age 40 would increase for at least a
decade. Not all of them would be drawn to Kennedy personally, but they

were numerous enough to force the political parties to lower the age qualification for high office. Television accelerated the trend toward youthful candidates and put a premium on the selection of the actor-politician as well. The elderly baby-kisser could not be displaced if he was already an established politician, but the current began to run strongly against him in the middle 1960's. The accent on youth elevated Mark Hatfield of Oregon, Birch Bayh of Indiana, Frank Church of Idaho, and Charles Percy of Illinois to the top of the party hierarchy in their respective states. As might have been expected, California led the way with actor-politicians, sending George Murphy to the Senate in 1964 and Ronald Reagan to Sacramento as governor in 1966.

The cult of personality affected the political structure in other ways. Candidates relied increasingly on independent committees to enhance their appeal, de-emphasizing their affiliation with regular party organizations and issues. Under the new dispensation, polls became a mandatory guide to political style. Candidates fretted about their images; took repeated soundings; and tried to make the indicated adjustments in behavior and bearing. Expenditures on polls by the two national committees skyrocketed from $1.5 million in 1960 to $5 million in 1964.[8] But that was not the end of it. State and local committees allotted a larger percentage of their more modest budgets for samples of public opinion, and wealthy candidates paid for supplemental expenditures out of their own pockets. The findings were scrutinized with the same awe as horoscopes in the Middle Ages, partly because of a childlike faith in things scientific and partly because candidates did not want to ignore advice for which they had paid. Inevitably the system encouraged candidates to sacrifice or conceal unpopular convictions. There was nothing new about such tactics. Candidates of earlier generations had made the same adjustments on the basis of the informal poll. The scientific poll simply encouraged them to practice dissimulation on a larger scale.

By 1966 a few candidates were beginning to carry matters to their logical conclusion and turn complete control of their campaigns over to pollsters and advertising men. The public-relations firms had first been drawn into politics in the 1930's when corporations paid them to fight unfavorable legislation. After World War II politicians began to consult them on controversial issues, but it was not until the 1960's that the former relied on advertising experts for advice about every aspect of campaign strategy. The political novice willing to pay for the convenience could forget about such tiresome details as the printing of stationery, distribution of literature, and the raising of funds. He could even count on the public-relations firm to produce an appropriate number of "warm bodies" for a political rally. More important was the function of sampling public opinion and rewriting the candidate's speeches along the proper lines. Some public-relations firms helped the candidate to retain his self-respect by refusing to take on a client unless the firm agreed with his political views; while others changed clients and political postures as casually as a sorority girl switches boyfriends. The California firm of Baus and Ross, by managing the state pre-convention of Barry Goldwater, a conservative Republican, in 1964, and the re-election campaign of Edmund G. (Pat) Brown, a liberal Democratic governor, in 1966, illustrated the lengths to which political amoralism could go.[9]

Most candidates dared not entrust their entire campaign to public-relations firms. Quite apart from the tremendous cost of such an operation, they were hardly in a position to bypass the regular party organization or ignore its advice. But the joint participation of professional politicians and public-relations men usually created more problems than it solved. Besides being pulled in opposite directions by the image-makers and the issues-makers, the candidate faced long hours in the role of mediator. More often than not, the new system substituted exhaustion by conference for the exhaustion by travel which the jet age had eliminated. Several Presidential aspirants in 1964 were to be conspicuous victims of the wear and tear of this system.

Similarly, the increasing reliance on television was to make elections more expensive and generate pressure for revolutionary changes in campaign finance. From the era of Mark Hanna until the 1950's, both major parties had relied primarily on wealthy individuals and corporations to fill war chests and pay off deficits. This system had withstood the inroads of inflation and such costly innovations as radio broadcasting. But the first breaches had occurred in the 1930's when national committees hired full-time publicity men to supplement their unpaid professional staffs. This step foreshadowed a change in the function of the national committees, which had hitherto been inactive except at election time. After World War II, overhead costs and the responsibilities of the national committees had grown rapidly. It was the advent of television, however, that provided the *coup de grâce* to the old system of campaign finance. Besides being expensive, television was deemed indispensable to the politics of personality. In 1952 the beginning of the end loomed, with the total cost of the election, including state and local campaigns, reaching the unprecedented figure of $140 million. Twelve years later it would reach $200 million and produce monstrous deficits.[10] The pressure for funds at all levels intensified both the competition and the friction between the national committees, congressional campaign committees, and local party units.

As usual, the politicians were slow to adjust to an urgent problem. First improvisations included increasing reliance on the so-called educational funds dispensed by labor unions, associations of manufacturers, and other pressure groups. Even though such funds were often earmarked by their donors for special use, they enabled the party to release its own funds for other purposes. The pretense that such funds were educational also helped the parties and their candidates to evade the various statutory limitations on campaign spending. Nevertheless, the major parties needed additional revenue directly under their own control: a conclusion underlined by the sizable deficits that both contracted during the Nixon-Kennedy campaign. They took tentative steps to tap new sources after the 1960 election and by 1964 produced what appeared to be durable changes in Mark Hanna's system.

Some techniques were wholly new; others were older devices which had not been methodically exploited. In the latter category was the fund-raising dinner. For over half a century the major parties had held banquets of some sort to commemorate the birthdays of their heroes. Initially, party leaders had wasted little thought on the financial aspect of such affairs, viewing them as an opportunity to compare political notes and to look over promising Presidential aspirants. Franklin D. Roosevelt had stumbled into the future in 1937 by turning the old-style *agape* into a fund-raising enterprise. Guests were charged $100 per plate to dine with the President and hear rhapsodic tributes to the Democratic party. At the time, the financial potentialities of the banquet were limited by the size of the hall and by the fact that the star attraction could not perform simultaneously at several locations. Television removed both restrictions, and by the middle 1950's Eisenhower was speaking at one banquet and being heard at several. Those who watched Eisenhower on closed circuit could not be expected to pay as much as guests favored with a live performance. But an effort was made to increase both the interest and the take at regional banquets by arranging for the participation of a prominent party leader at each. The revenue from the large banquet increased so rapidly in the late 1950's that both parties relied on the device to clear up deficits from the 1960 campaign.

Still more ambitious plans were made for 1964. Each national committee scheduled fifteen major banquets to honor its respective Presidential candidate, hoping to raise half of its total revenue in this fashion.[11] Prices were scaled from $1000 to $5, depending on the prominence and affluence of the participants. In general, the quality of a dinner varied inversely with its cost, because the rank and file expected something for their money, whereas the well-to-do did not. Because of this circumstance, the profit margin was higher on the $1000 per plate banquet than on more modest affairs. Inevitably party managers were tempted to push the profits on the former still higher by limiting the menu to hors d'œuvres and highballs. As one commentator waspishly observed: "the politicians would really like phantom banquets which nobody would attend and where no food would be served." [12] Barring such an eventuality, the banquet seemed destined for a long life. There was less chance that the fund-raisers would overdo the displays of greed at the luaus, hootenannies, rodeos, and other variations to raise money at the local level. Such affairs had been employed sparingly before 1966, but every aspirant from sheriff to congressman took a look at the "entertainment—fund-raising" formula in the off-year election.

The Republican party achieved unusual success in 1964 by reviving an old idea: the mass solicitation of the party faithful. Professional fund-raisers had always been skeptical of the technique, believing that the administrative costs of mass solicitation would sponge up most of the money. So gestures were half-hearted and results negligible until a major drive for $10 contributions enabled the Republicans to finish their 1964 campaign in the black. Besides direct appeals over television, the G.O.P. national committee mailed out an unprecedented 10 million requests for aid. The compilation of a proper mailing list was a key factor in its success. The files of active party workers provided the most obvious source of potential contributors, but the G.O.P. national committee showed exceptional ingenuity by purchasing additional lists from brokers who ordinarily compiled them for mail-order houses and magazines. Some junk mail lists are obviously better than others. The Republicans drifted into a bonanza by purchasing the names of people who order Kozak Drywash Cloths to clean their own automobiles. Apparently parsimony in car maintenance was accompanied by liberality in political contributions as well as a propensity to vote Republican.[13] In any case, G.O.P. solicitations from the Kozak list and others produced 40 per cent of the money spent by the national committee.[14]

The Democrats approached the matter of mass solicitations obliquely. Mindful of the fact that there were more Democrats than Republicans, they urged government employees to make small contributions to the party of their choice. President Kennedy's committee on campaign costs encouraged corporations to promote a similar program among their employees. Some 300 firms responded in 1964.[15] The results were modest but encouraging enough to stimulate Democratic proposals for a law making contributions up to $50, tax deductible. Congress failed to act at once, but Senator Russell Long of Louisiana attached a rider to a foreign investors' tax bill in 1966, authorizing citizens to earmark $1 of their income-tax payments for financing Presidential elections. The new law restricted the use of such funds to the fall campaign and divided them equally between the major parties. It has been estimated that they could realize as much as $30 million in 1968, but this legislation may be repealed before it is tested.

Prior to this experiment, the Democrats had concentrated their efforts on capitalizing the advantages derived from their possession of the White House. With the enthusiastic approval of President Kennedy, they had organized a President's Club. Membership was open to anybody who would contribute $1000 per year to the party. The visible benefits of membership were nominal: autographed photographs of the President and occasional invitations to White House functions.[16] Predictably, Republicans charged that there were invisible benefits as well, including special consideration for members doing business with governmental agencies. These objections did not prevent Kennedy's successor from continuing the club or Republicans from creating their own pale imitation of it: The G.O.P. Congressional Boosters Club.

The Democrats also reached potential contributors through utilization of the Presidential power to make appointments. In the process, they staffed some 2000 advisory units to the federal government, ranging from the Beet Leafhopper Advisory Committee to the Committee for the Preservation of the White House.[17] Known as "honoraries," such posts carried no salary and few responsibilities. Office-holders were paid in prestige, which served both as a reward for past donations and an invitation for new ones. Since there were no overhead costs connected with the dispensing of prestige, the returns from such operations could be considerable. The Eisenhower Administration had been the first to see the vast possibilities of the "honorary" as a substitute for the vanishing patronage job. The Democrats broadened the system by adding the category of "personal representative of the President." Recipients of this honor were numerous because they often functioned but a single day.

Nothing as artful as these innovations had taken place since Avignon Popes reorganized the fiscal machinery of the Catholic church in the fourteenth century. It is possible to admire the ingenuity of party fund-raisers without subscribing to the theory that the ever-growing expenditures stimulated interest in politics. There had always been a distracting element of pageantry associated with American campaigns, but until the beginning of the twentieth century it was a symptom of mass participation in politics. Thereafter the citizen slowly changed his role from participant to spectator. In the process, pageantry and the related expenditures lost their tenuous connection with political education. The advent of television completed the evolution by converting conventions and rallies into extravaganzas staged as carefully as a Hollywood movie. Such gatherings provided much entertainment but little information. The development, however, was wholly consistent with the consensus of apathy and the politics of personality.

XIV

The Amateur Hour and After

During the three years that Kennedy spent harassing Congress and charming the voters, the Republicans were seldom able to command the limelight. Under the leadership of Everett M. Dirksen in the Senate and Charles A. Halleck in the House, the minority co-operated quietly with Southern Democrats but advanced few proposals of its own. This outward show of solidarity concealed an intense struggle for the control of the party that commenced immediately after the 1960 election. As titular head of the G.O.P., Nixon ought to have been a key factor in the backstage maneuvers, but his narrow defeat had discredited him as completely as a similar misfortune had destroyed Charles Evans Hughes in 1916. Each faction assumed that Nixon would have won if he had embraced its strategy more forthrightly. So it was apparent to the ex-Vice President that he needed a fresh vote of confidence from the people to restore his authority and prestige. Accordingly he returned to his native California, ran for governor in 1962, and suffered an unexpected defeat at the hands of Edmund G. (Pat) Brown. Then Nixon compounded the consequences of his reversal in a post-election television interview. Criticizing his tormentors in the news media, he announced his unconditional withdrawal from politics. Shortly thereafter, he moved from California to New York and joined a Manhattan law firm. Opinion differed as to whether his retirement was permanent, but at the time nearly everybody agreed that Nixon would not be a factor in the Republican pre-convention contest.

Before the 1962 election it was easier to identify the factions bidding for control of the G.O.P. than the leaders destined to direct them. The retirement of Eisenhower had freed the Taft faction from an irksome tutelage. Some of the old leaders and the old issues were dead. Moreover, the McCarthyites who had been both a help and an embarrassment were temporarily inactive. The most durable attitude of erstwhile Taft men was an opposition to further extensions of government welfare programs. A few nursed the hope of curtailing existing services, but the rest were content to defend the remaining enclaves of free enterprise. There was less consensus on foreign policy, although the entire faction resented what it regarded as the supine posture of the United States abroad. To some, a harder line meant withdrawing aid from ungrateful allies and insolent neutralist powers. To the rest, it meant intensifying the cold war, whatever the consequences. The first position pointed to a kind of neo-isolationism; the second to a new version of gunboat diplomacy.

It would be an oversimplification to represent the conservatives as a purely sectional faction. Outside of the urban Northeast, they either held the upper hand or fought on equal terms for control of G.O.P. state organizations. As always, sectionalism and personalities impeded polarization along ideological lines, but several factors helped to generate a conservative revival. For one thing, the loss of the 1960 election had partially discredited the strategy of bidding for the moderates and liberals. Because they had acquiesced in the tactic since 1936, the conservatives felt entitled to name the candidate in 1964. Secondly, their bargaining power was augmented by the upsurge of conservative and racist sentiment in the South, which opened up the possibility of victory without the electoral votes of the populous Northeast.

The Republican liberals were a more amorphous group than the conservatives. Some liberals wholeheartedly embraced the concept of the welfare state and saw no alternative but to outbid the Democrats. Others were ambivalent toward big government but prepared to tolerate it in areas that were popular with the voters. This posture appeared most frequently in the Middle Atlantic states and New England, which contained a diversity of well-organized ethnic and economic groups. Depending on the individual Republican leader and his constituency, bids might be made for the support of Negroes, Jews, immigrants from Central Europe, organized labor, or some combination of these elements. The same impulse might lead to the advocacy of slum clearance, anti-poverty measures, and medical insurance programs. The confusion was compounded in foreign affairs by selective emphasis on parts of the world that interested a particular constituency. Concern about foreign trade blurred matters still further.

Thus, practical considerations provided liberals and conservatives alike with an excuse for abandoning doctrinal rigidity. Hard-headed organization men like Ray Bliss of Ohio and Senator Thruston Morton of Kentucky, who were sometimes called moderates, provided the party with an objective and a route map. Scattered and feuding Republicans were to be encouraged to converge on a nonideological task: the recruitment of party workers in cities that had gone to Kennedy in 1960. Rebuilding rickety urban organizations was not a very inspiring goal, but it seemed like a safe one. Counsels of caution, however, did not enjoy very much popularity. Between them, the fire brands and the schemers overwhelmed the moderates, jeopardizing the prospects of party solidarity.

The conservatives were especially preoccupied with doctrine and believed that they had found their standard-bearer right after the 1960 election. Their choice fell on Senator Barry Goldwater of Arizona, who had been a department store executive and community leader in Phoenix before entering the Senate in 1952. Elected as an Eisenhower supporter, he had gradually become critical of the President for "running a dime-store New Deal." Spurning Eisenhower's coattails, Goldwater had won re-election six years later by a bigger majority in the face of a strong Democratic tide. During this period Goldwater had made more of an impression on local party workers than on the Senate, primarily because of his service as chairman of the Senatorial campaign committee in 1956 and 1960. In the latter year, he had bid for a wider audience with a book entitled *The Conscience of a Conservative* and with a thrice-weekly newspaper column. Ghost-writers assisted Goldwater with both enterprises, but he generated his own momentum on the banquet circuit, where he was a tireless performer. The country, as distinct from G.O.P. professionals, first became aware of him at the Republican convention of 1960, where he electrified the conservatives with a fighting speech. Affirming his loyalty to the Nixon-Lodge ticket, Goldwater went on to tell conservatives that they were in the majority and to urge them to take over the G.O.P. in 1964. A manifesto in January 1961 called for a crusade in behalf of the common man, whom Goldwater identified as the bewildered, apathetic citizen burdened by the exactions of pressure groups.

Increasing popularity usually makes a politician more timid, but it had the opposite effect on Goldwater, who spent the next two years behaving like the absurdist hero of Camus. In a country where it was good form to be some sort of progressive, Goldwater advertised himself as a conservative. He was just as defiant about other matters. He took a perverse pleasure in forgetting the names of obvious admirers, and in spurning a compensatory device like the political card file. He directed his oratory at small groups, some of which contained neither politicians nor voters. His most disconcerting habit was to court controversial questions and then respond with forthright, pungent answers. In so doing he said publicly what many businessmen believed but would not admit except in the privacy of a country club over a couple of drinks. Goldwater behaved like a man trying to convert a candidacy into a noncandidacy, driving the point home by discouraging offers of organized support.

It is impossible to do more than speculate about his state of mind between 1961 and 1963. But if actions meant anything, he was trying to mobilize support for a cause rather than a candidate. Perhaps he believed that the problem of leadership would solve itself if conservatives demonstrated that they were worthy of leadership. In any case, there were numerous objections to a Goldwater candidacy, and he must have been aware of them. Precedent frowned on the selection of senators as well as of party leaders from small states, and on both counts Goldwater was disqualified. Moreover, Presidential nominees did not normally emerge out of controversy, and the Senator was one of the most controversial figures in the party. Finally, party leaders were supposed to have an appetite for administrative and legislative detail. Goldwater had a positive aversion to both.

Irrespective of what Goldwater thought about himself, the liberals and moderates decided that he was not available. Indeed, they discounted him so completely that they were unable to launch a "stop Goldwater movement" until it was too late. Their most obvious candidate in 1961-62 was Governor Nelson A. Rockefeller of New York, who gave unmistakable signs that he coveted the honor. His entire career had been identified with philanthropic causes of one kind or another. But he had paid a heavy price for his liberalism at the 1960 convention, arousing the enmity of both the conservatives and the Eisenhower men. Perhaps Rockefeller could have prevailed by a consistent adherence to his original position, because he was persuasive as a crusader. Unfortunately, his ambition and his childlike faith in the image-makers tempted him to equivocate. Like many of his contemporaries, Rockefeller imagined that he could sell anything by turning his battalions of public-relations men loose on the voters. A Rockefeller operation was as thorough as the Allied saturation bombing of Dresden in 1944 and just as difficult to forget. So he was really tempting the Fates when he made a fresh debut as a responsible conservative in the spring of 1961. He warmed up with a series of philippics against Kennedy. George Hinman, the agreeable New Yorker and G.O.P. national committeeman, crisscrossed the country, carrying a more subdued version of the conversion to local party leaders. The next step was a rapprochement with Goldwater, and Rockefeller, with an excellent sense of timing, pulled the Arizonian into his orbit on the eve of the 1962 elections. The erstwhile antagonists discovered a mutual admiration for free enterprise and a mutual antipathy to the New Frontier. They also regaled each other with denunciations of Eisenhower liberals for spawning citizens' committees outside the regular party organization. Party unity was their watchword during the campaign season.

The net effect of the new Rockefeller image on the voters was not very reassuring. He won re-election as governoi against a weak candidate by a smaller margin than in 1958. Yet he consoled himself with the belief that there were compensations outside New York: the good will of conservatives and their quixotic noncandidate. In December 1962 the *Wall Street Journal* took the same view, insisting that Rockefeller had neutralized his opposition on the right and was far ahead for the nomination.[1] So the Rockefeller-Goldwater alliance against schismatics continued throughout the winter of 1962-63, with the principals holding intimate breakfast sessions on Sunday mornings.[2] In retrospect, it is easy to see that Rockefeller had offended the liberals without disarming important conservatives, except Goldwater. The incident that exposed the precarious base of the Rockefeller boom was the decision of the Governor to remarry. Few politicians had been openly critical when he divorced the first Mrs. Rockefeller in 1961, but there was an explosive reaction following his marriage on May 4, 1963, to Mrs. Margaretta Fitler Murphy, herself a divorcée and mother of four children. Some of the indignation could be traced to middle-aged wives who resented Rockefeller's decision to marry a younger woman. But the persistence of criticism indicated that other Republicans had been looking for an excuse to desert Rockefeller. Some of the more vocal complaints came from conservatives, and Rockefeller without very much supporting evidence concluded that Goldwater was

behind the agitation. Up to this point, the alliance with the Arizona senator had been to Rockefeller's advantage, but the repercussions of the marriage reduced the utility of the relationship. So Rockefeller concluded that
the only way he could gain the nomination was to reverse his strategy and
wage a violent war on the conservatives. A midsummer convention of the
Young Republicans, which contained an articulate minority of segregationists, provided him with the excuse for a break. So on Bastille Day,
1963, he issued a withering blast at the conservative wing of the party. No
doubt he had found the cultivation of conservatives distasteful and felt
more comfortable after resuming his old role. But the results were disastrous. He had weathered one change of image but could not survive a
second. The residual impression that persisted was of a Rockefeller who
discarded unprofitable political positions as cold-bloodedly as his grand-
father had discarded unprofitable oil leases.

Despite unmistakable signs that even the liberals had deserted him,
Rockefeller announced his candidacy in October 1963 and made preparations for a crusade against the right wing of the G.O.P. Except for
Goldwater, few of the conservatives were surprised. The Arizonian, however, had received only a misleading telegram before Rockefeller's July
salvo on the conservatives and believed that he was a victim of treachery.[3]
It is one thing to oppose a colleague on grounds of principle, and quite
another to break with him abruptly after courting close personal relations.
The first type of disagreement does not preclude some measure of co-
operation and trust; the second one assures a peculiarly intense form of
antagonism. It is well to bear the distinction in mind, because it helps to
account for the subsequent lethal warfare in the G.O.P. If Rockefeller had
been the only liberal to cultivate Goldwater and then discard him, then
the latter would have been unjustified in questioning the good faith and
integrity of his factional opponents. But other liberals were to duplicate
Rockefeller's behavior pattern sooner or later, with the result that Goldwater became suspicious of the entire faction. In driving Goldwater to the
verge of paranoia, the liberals were paving the way for the fatal confrontation at San Francisco.

The most immediate effect of Rockefeller's maneuvers was to convert
his erstwhile breakfast companion from a gospeller into a Presidential
candidate. No immediate announcement was forthcoming, but the Goldwater camp began to show unmistakable signs of activity in the fall of
1963. Denison Kitchel, a fifty-five-year-old Washington lawyer and in-

timate friend of Goldwater, arrived in Washington and opened an office. The taciturn Kitchel would not say what he was doing, but nobody supposed that he was there to run another senatorial campaign for Goldwater. Simultaneously, a volunteer Goldwater organization headed by F. Clifton White of New York, which had been operating since 1961 without the slightest encouragement from the Senator, began to function more energetically. White's most urgent responsibility was to eliminate members of the John Birch Society and other elements of the extreme right from the volunteer movement. He approached this delicate task with his customary efficiency, but neither White nor Goldwater could silence embarrassing supporters outside the organization.

II

Meanwhile, the political kaleidoscope had begun to spin wildly. Analysts were predicting a Goldwater-Kennedy contest, and with it a significant political realignment, when an assassin's bullet felled President Kennedy at Dallas, November 22, 1963. The universal sense of shock and grief terminated political discussion for a month. Subsequent reappraisals suggested that Goldwater's prospects had been badly damaged by the assassination.

The character and antecedents of the new President, Lyndon B. Johnson, were thought to be responsible for the change in the political weather. As a Texan he was expected to be a beneficiary of regional pride—the more so, since the deep South had not placed one of its sons in the White House since Zachary Taylor.* His legislative record was acceptable to labor and other pressure groups that normally voted Democratic. Moreover, many people remembered that Johnson had intervened in the Senate to weaken civil rights legislation of the Eisenhower Administration. So it was assumed that Johnson would hurt Goldwater in the South, without jeopardizing Democratic prospects elsewhere. Some analysts counted Goldwater out of the race, and others took the more extreme view that the Republican nomination was worthless.

The first moves of the new President seemed to confirm this diagnosis. He placed himself solidly behind the Kennedy welfare programs so appealing to Northern pressure groups. He also managed to endorse the civil rights bill pending in Congress without arousing visible opposition in the

* Woodrow Wilson was born in Virginia but had become a Northerner by the time he launched his political career.

South. At the same time, Johnson bid for the support of business groups by cutting $500 million from the projected Kennedy budget and by ostentatiously conserving the use of electricity in the White House. During the ensuing months, he enhanced his reputation for political astuteness by breaking the legislative log jam that had stalled the Kennedy program. Before Congress adjourned in 1964 he was able to secure federal aid for higher education and urban transportation, a new farm subsidy act, and the first comprehensive civil rights law since 1875. His effectiveness seemed to constitute a pledge that he would, if re-elected, secure medicare and other benefits for the underprivileged. Johnson gave these expectations his distinctive stamp by announcing a war on poverty which would presumably end in a Great Society. Both the program and the slogan identified him with the New Deal, the Fair Deal, and the New Frontier.

Johnson's exhibition of political wizardry owed something to the fact that he was the first from the inner circle in the Senate to reach the White House. Harding, Truman, and Kennedy had been peripheral figures as lawmakers but Johnson belonged to the select group of Senate wire-pullers like John Sherman and William B. Allison. For one thing, he knew exactly where power was located in the baffling tangle of congressional committees. In addition, he had done numerous favors over the years for conservative Southern legislators and drew repeatedly on his accumulated political credit in 1964. His most convincing demonstration of political virtuosity occurred just before the conventions were to open, when he secured the co-operation of the Republican minority to break the Southern filibuster against the civil rights bill in the Senate. By that time he had become as odious to segregationists as Kennedy. In so doing, he helped to revive Goldwater's candidacy, which had faltered temporarily in the wake of Kennedy's assassination.

While Johnson was establishing an election platform in Washington, the Republicans pursued their bitter pre-convention fight. If the Gallup polls can be regarded as a reliable index of sentiment, then no more than 27 per cent of the Republicans favored Goldwater at any time after the death of Kennedy. The periodic samples by the Gallup organization also indicated that in April and May, when most delegates were being chosen, support for Goldwater dropped as low as 14 per cent. On the eve of the Republican convention it rebounded to slightly more than 20 per cent. Although small variations appeared in other polls, the findings were so uniform as to raise the question of how Goldwater secured a first-ballot nomination.

There is a simple explanation: Goldwater's supporters knew what they wanted, whereas his opponents did not. The consensus of apathy provided an opportunity for effective action by a determined minority. As Richard Rovere put it: "The Goldwater people were the sort to arrive early at meetings, endure the tedium and stay on, bright-eyed after adjournment, to fold the chairs and put away the coffee cups."[4] They did more than that: taking over precinct and county G.O.P. organizations long before the delegates were chosen. Once they had gained control of the machinery, they could not be routed, because only 541 of the 1308 delegates to the Republican convention were chosen in Presidential primaries.

The success of the Goldwaterites in dominating the selection machinery does not explain their pre-convention immunity to divisive tactics, adverse public opinion polls, and other manifestations of the unpopularity of their candidate. Three factors nerved the conservatives for their inflexible stand: (1) devotion to Goldwater; (2) conviction that a conservative posture offered the best prospect for victory; and (3) bitterness at the disruptive tactics of the liberal faction of the party, which prevented them from pursuing their strategy under optimum conditions.

The conservatives were attracted to Goldwater because he cut through complex questions and offered simple answers in traditional terms. The crux of his position was a faith in individual responsibility illuminated by self-criticism: "Ask yourself," Goldwater urged his followers on one occasion, "did I live with hate? Did I steal, cheat, hate, take shortcuts? If you answer, yes, you haven't been a good American."[5] Woven into this typical exhortation were strands of nationalism, conservatism, and traditional Puritan activism. Such a credo assumed that mutual respect for personal rights would solve more problems than legislation. If government action became necessary, it should be at the local level where the emphasis on individual initiative was preserved. Presumably, even the ancient evil of race prejudice would disappear if local people launched a grass-roots crusade along the lines of a Community Chest drive. Goldwaterites far from the sites of racial friction beguiled themselves with visions of door-to-door canvasses and parades composed of monster floats featuring willowy blondes waving integration posters. Pageantry and persuasion were likewise expected to produce funds for the war against ignorance, poverty, and disease. Neither Goldwater nor his followers thought that the conduct of foreign affairs could be similarly decentralized. They hoped to revitalize diplomacy, however, by a straightforward emphasis on American interests. This twofold formula for domestic and foreign problems could never have been applied in the stark way that it was advocated. Some people embraced it through naïveté, and others did so for discreditable reasons. But what seems most probable is that the bulk of Goldwaterites did not take the formula seriously. Rightly or wrongly, they were disaffected by the trend toward bigger government and hoped that a man who denounced all functions of the welfare state would manage to eliminate a few.

It was to be expected that the Goldwater personality would have some appeal, particularly to an electorate preoccupied by the politics of personality. He projected the image of the man who disliked images. Indeed, he was the first major politician since Benjamin Harrison to express open contempt for the pomposity and evasiveness so characteristic of his own profession. This impulse prompted his statement that "political platforms are packets of lies."[6] It also accounted for his whimsical confession to the press on one occasion that his bulging brief-case "was full of Mickey Spillane."[7] His scorn for political expediency was to express itself in campaign speeches against medicare in Florida, against T.V.A. in Tennessee, and against poverty programs in West Virginia. Voters who missed the point were later told on a national television hook-up that they would not be treated as pocketbooks "surrounded on all sides by self-seeking concerns."[8] Goldwater showed the same open disdain for hand-shaking and baby-kissing.[9] More than once he strode through an airport with scarcely a glance at his shouting retainers. Yet his personal—as opposed to his political—image was that of a well-adjusted businessman with a host of hobbies. As a golfer, ham-radio operator, pilot, amateur anthropologist, and student of Southwestern history, he displayed the new cultural style of suburbia.

If the Goldwater principles and personality commanded the intense loyalty of a minority, they generated an equally intense antipathy on the part of a far larger group. It is possible to write about most elections as if the outcome were in doubt until the polls closed, but the Goldwater candidacy was doomed long before it became official. Although the terms of the political consensus prevailing in the early 1960's elude a compact summary, Goldwater stood beyond the frontiers in some respects. His narrow view of governmental responsibilities was repugnant to a majority, composed of voters with humanitarian impulses and specific economic interests. It was less clear that Goldwater defied the broad but fluid sentiment for the improvement of the status of Negroes. His abstract statements on race relations radiated good will, but people discounted them on the theory that his real preference was to perpetuate the status quo. His pugnacious way of embracing national interests in foreign policy likewise struck the average voter as a breach of consensus. Most Americans were as national-istic as Goldwater in the sense that they placed the welfare of the United States above the welfare of other countries, but they wanted to believe that the welfare of the United States and that of the world were closely identified. Goldwater would not cater to this need, and his statements on specific issues of foreign policy were a disconcerting compound of bluster and common sense. Finally, Goldwater aroused the same apprehensions in the area of civil liberties. His abhorrence of Communism was regarded as unmistakable evidence that he possessed a fascistic mentality, and he en-joyed as secure a place in the demonology of the liberals as the late Senator Joseph R. McCarthy.

It is improbable that Goldwater was as badly out of step with the ma-jority of his fellow countrymen as his own rhetoric and that of his enemies suggested. When the events of 1963-64 recede into a better perspective, it will be possible to judge the degree to which Goldwater was a victim of his own indiscretions and the misrepresentations of his enemies. Whatever the facts in the situation, it is clear that a decisive number of voters regarded Goldwater as an anachronistic figure from the 1920's. Under the circum-stances, it could do his party no good to nominate him. But there was a vacuum in the upper levels of the G.O.P. The few capable of filling it were not interested, and the few interested in filling it were not capable! So Goldwater became the Republican standard-bearer, after the party leaders had conducted a pre-convention campaign that resembled an amateur hour.

III

Goldwater had spoken so often and incautiously over the years that he would have been wise to avoid controversy while rounding up delegates. He dared not go as far as Prahbu Dutt Bramachari, a Hindu holy man, who had not uttered a single word during his campaign for an Indian parlia-mentary seat in 1952. Yet he would have been well advised to imitate McKinley, who had won the nomination in 1896 by being inconspicuous. At the outset, Goldwater contemplated something of the sort: a minimum of oratory and a concerted backstage effort to secure delegates. The only deviation from this strategy was to be participation in the California primary, where Goldwater expected to demonstrate his vote-getting prowess under favorable circumstances.[10] By the time he made a formal declaration of his candidacy, however, he had been persuaded to enter several primaries, including the March primary in New Hampshire. This decision committed him to six months of continuous exposure, and was in part forced on him by the ambitious primary schedule of Rockefeller. The burgeoning Goldwater headquarters also bore some responsibility for the revised strategy. As his central strategy board expanded, it became noisy with politicians, braintrusters, and public-relations experts working at cross-purposes. The one thing about which everybody agreed was that Goldwater should do some more talking: a remarkable conclusion considering the fact that he had already expressed himself on every conceivable subject from disarmament, which he opposed, to college fraternities, which he favored.[11] Of all his advisers, Clifton White was the best suited to tell Goldwater what to say and where to say it. But White's volunteer committee had been absorbed and relegated to a secondary role by an Arizona triumvirate composed of Denison Kitchel, Dean Burch, and Richard Kleindienst. This trio was shrewd but parochial in outlook, being accustomed to operating in "Marlboro country," with its wide-open spaces, where ethnic and class problems were negligible. The Arizonians also placed excessive faith in the charismatic powers of Goldwater, and believed that the format of informal speeches to small groups would work everywhere. Consequently, the triumvirate did not initially perceive the difference between off-the-cuff remarks by a senatorial candidate that were likely to go unreported, and those by a Presidential candidate that were certain to be reported.

Because of its early primary and unpredictable electorate, New Hampshire had replaced Ohio as the snake pit of Republican politics. The state party was faction-ridden and full of adventurers, but the triumvirate was led on by promises of support and the alleged similarities between Arizona and New Hampshire. The Goldwaterites relied heavily on the individualistic psychology of the New Hampshire voter and the custom of a coffee hour following a speech, during which the Senator could exercise his well-advertised charm. Unfortunately for Goldwater, the average Republican Yankee was as glacial as his winter landscape and allergic to relaxed politicians. He also showed an inquisitiveness about the practical consequences of conservative philosophy that was uncongenial to Goldwater. These factors and others became apparent as Goldwater spent late January grimly plowing through the eighteen-hour days scheduled by his managers. His formal speeches made less trouble than his habit of dealing with a bewildering variety of subjects in coffee sessions and press conferences. Unfavorable publicity came to a focus on: (1) his criticism of social security; (2) his proposal that the United States withdraw from the United Nations if Red China became a member; and (3) his contention that the N.A.T.O. commander should be vested with discretionary authority to use tactical nuclear weapons in case of an enemy attack.

There was much subsequent controversy about what Goldwater said on these topics. Many reporters wanted to believe and print the worst. They might have done so out of their own resources, but Goldwater gave them an unintentional assist by unduly compressing his treatment of issues or by restating them in ambiguous language. His tactics in New Hampshire simply saved the Democratic national committee the inconvenience of digging similar material out of old newspaper files. Over the years the context for Goldwater's remarks had changed but not the principles that motivated them: the curtailment of the welfare state at home, and the practice of *Realpolitik* abroad. So the counterassault was bound to come sooner or later. The only possible advantage for Goldwater in precipitating matters himself was to select the areas where he wanted to receive the attack. If he thought in these terms, he chose badly. Of all the federal subsidies, those to the aged caused the least controversy and were the most justifiable on humanitarian grounds. Whether Goldwater wanted to reform social security or abolish it, his unmistakable dislike of the existing system was apparent. He also showed questionable judgment in proposing any decentralization of control over nuclear weapons. His stand was contrary to tradition and collided with a deep-seated suspicion of military power. The latter had been further stimulated by novels and moving pictures depicting the hypothetical dangers from nuclear weapons under the control of unbalanced commanders.

Thus, Goldwater provided his enemies with an early opportunity to characterize him as impulsive, bellicose, and indifferent to human welfare. The Democrats did not have to make these points in New Hampshire because Rockefeller did the job for them and gave encore performances in later primaries. Goldwater never recovered from the initial impression that he created, nor did the New Hampshire primary reveal the full extent of the damage. There were three avowed candidates besides Goldwater and Rockefeller. Richard M. Nixon and Henry Cabot Lodge, Jr., for whom write-in campaigns had been organized, provided the most competition for

Goldwater and Rockefeller. Computors accurately predicted the result minutes after the polls closed on March 10. Lodge won with 35 per cent of the vote, followed by Goldwater with 22 per cent, Rockefeller with 21 per cent, and Nixon with 17 per cent.

The popular verdict lent itself to several interpretations, the most obvious being that the party wanted neither Goldwater nor Rockefeller as its standard-bearer. The large vote for the write-in candidates also reflected disapproval of the bloodletting in New Hampshire, but the principals went ahead with plans for re-runs in Oregon and California. Of the two, Rockefeller's position was the more untenable. He lacked visible support in the Midwest and had been repudiated in his own region.

During the three months between the New Hampshire primary and the California primary, the situation was perfect for dark horses. Presumably neither Goldwater nor Rockefeller could win; nor could they be expected to join forces. But Goldwater was certain to enter the convention with enough votes to veto any candidate who displeased him. Accordingly, it was mandatory for dark horses to avoid an anti-Goldwater posture and desirable for them to say nothing. Four prominent Republicans adopted this strategy: Henry Cabot Lodge, Jr., who was serving as American ambassador to South Vietnam; Governor George W. Romney of Michigan; Governor William W. Scranton of Pennsylvania; and former Vice President Nixon. Within the group there were differing degrees of aloofness, but all were available for a draft.

Any one of them might have been persuaded to become an active candidate by ex-President Eisenhower. It was an open secret that he detested Goldwater, but he had an even greater distaste for all aspects of political jobbery. His formula called for the encouragement of fresh entries without a pledge of open support. No takers materialized, but conservative Republicans kept an apprehensive eye cocked on Eisenhower's farm at Gettysburg throughout the spring.

Meanwhile, Goldwater had begun to rebound from the New Hampshire disaster. For one thing, the Arizona triumvirate learned by doing and hence, put a firm muzzle on its candidate. There was only one subsequent slip, on May 24. It came in a televised interview, when Goldwater speculated about the possibility of using low-yield atomic weapons to defoliate jungle supply routes in Vietnam. Otherwise he plodded successfully through several primaries against token opposition. Ironically enough, his most important boost came from Democratic primaries in Wisconsin

(April 7) and Indiana (May 5). On both occasions, Governor George C. Wallace of Alabama won approximately a third of the vote as a states' rights candidate. Avoiding explicit reference to racial problems, Wallace ran strongly in the Polish wards of Milwaukee[12] and polled 71 per cent in the Aetna district of Gary, which had a heavy concentration of steel workers.[13] The result seemed to indicate that the Democrats would lose a sizable number of second-generation Americans and industrial workers on the civil rights issue. Nobody missed the fact that Goldwater was the Republican best suited to exploit a white backlash. If the trend continued, he could conceivably build a victorious coalition on the states of the Old South, the Midwest, and the Rocky Mountains. This combination would also free him from dependence on the hostile Republican organizations in New England and the Middle Atlantic. Accordingly, a succession of state conventions chose Goldwater delegates in May, despite the fact that he lost the Oregon primary to Rockefeller during the same month.

The Oregon primary eliminated Lodge, who had intrigued the political handicappers since New Hampshire. The rest of the dark horses were still officially unavailable and unofficially available. But it became apparent that their hopes rested on a Goldwater defeat in the California primary. Otherwise the Arizona senator would be within reach of the 655 delegates needed for the nomination. Only Goldwater and Rockefeller had entered the California primary, and both sides tried to enlist the elusive dark horses. Rockefeller was the boldest, issuing a pamphlet which—among other things—claimed that Lodge, Nixon, Romney, and Scranton were in the mainstream of Republicanism along with him. On May 26—a week before the primary—Goldwater countered with a query to the dark horses. Lodge was not easy to reach, but the other three received identical notes asking whether they had authorized the use of their names by Rockefeller.

At this point, an honest avowal of anti-Goldwater sentiments from the dark horses would have left the conservatives without an excuse for subsequent cries of treachery. None of the dark horses, however, cared to be so forthright. On the contrary, Scranton and Nixon were so determined to placate the Arizonian that they repudiated the Rockefeller pamphlet before Goldwater's letter arrived.[14] Romney took more time to reply, but made the same response. Whatever they told themselves, the actions of the dark horses indicated that they foresaw a fatal setback for Goldwater in California and wanted to inherit his strength.

The California primary campaign was so bitter that the party could not help losing, irrespective of the outcome. Goldwater avoided, as he had from the beginning, personal attacks on his opponent; his overzealous rightist supporters were not restrained. His managers watched in dismay as the superpatriots ran "through the woods like a collection of firebugs. . . ." [15] Rockefeller courted the attacks of the rightists, using them as an excuse for vituperative thrusts at his opponent. Unlike Goldwater, who still nursed the hope of leading a united party in the fall campaign, Rockefeller had lowered his sights. Intent on stopping Goldwater, he stormed through the state like a blind Samson.

As usual, nobody knew how the volatile Californians would vote, but everybody expected a close election. This expectation was more than justified: on June 2 the unpredictable electors chose the slate of 86 Goldwater delegates by 1,083,133 votes to 1,030,180. For a moment, it seemed as if the California primary had cleared the air. Of the major G.O.P. leaders, only Rockefeller had behaved like a schismatic. He had saved the Democrats a dress rehearsal, but something could be salvaged if the Republicans closed ranks.

As matters turned out, however, neither Eisenhower nor the dark horses were willing to accept the consequences of their noninterventionist policy. Having failed to take a stand on principle when it might have counted, they embarked on a series of improvisations. The aging Warwick at Gettysburg was the first to stir. He invited Governor Scranton for a conference the Saturday after the California primary. It is not clear what took place, but Scranton thought he had a pledge of support. So he flew to Cleveland for the Governors' Conference with the idea of announcing his candidacy on the Sunday television program "Face the Nation."

There were nearly twice as many Democratic as Republican governors at Cleveland, but the Republicans made all the news. The fireworks began at a Sunday morning breakfast on June 8, when Romney of Michigan announced a crusade against Goldwater. For a start, Romney proposed that Goldwater submit to questions the coming Tuesday. Mark Hatfield, the liberal governor of Oregon, reminded Romney that the fighting season was over and urged him to desist for the good of the party. Scranton supported the inquest, however, but promptly regretted it because of a phone call from Eisenhower after breakfast. The latter, having been harassed by conservatives, had reverted to his old distinction between encouragement and public endorsement. Scranton was given his blessing but denied open support. The Pennsylvanian was so shaken that he tore up the announcement of his candidacy and spent a miserable half hour on "Face the Nation" conceding that Goldwater would be an acceptable candidate.

It would have been merciful for all parties concerned if the amateur hour had ended on Sunday. But Nixon appeared in Cleveland the next day, criticized Goldwater's stand on a host of issues, and conferred privately with Romney. The latter had pioneered the compact car as head of American Motors, but he could not reform the nomination system on such short notice. Whatever the Republican governors thought of Goldwater, they regarded Romney as a loner who had won in Michigan by advertising his freedom from party ties. It took only an additional twenty-four hours to demonstrate that Romney lacked tangible support. So he left Cleveland Tuesday morning and put his crusade into cold storage.

Presumably the rebellion of the dark horses was over. Scranton was in an especially unfavorable position to make trouble. He had come close to taking himself out of the race in April and was virtually unknown outside Pennsylvania. After the California primary he had indicated that he was available for second place on a Goldwater ticket. Then, in his unhappy interview on "Face the Nation," he had explicitly promised to support Goldwater, even if the latter voted against the then pending cloture motion on the civil rights bill. "One vote," Scranton had contended, "does not prove how a man stands on a whole issue." [16] Yet twenty-four hours after Goldwater voted against the motion to end the filibuster, Scranton announced his candidacy for President. His belated campaign began June 12 at Baltimore, starting with restrained attacks on Goldwater that became more abusive as uncommitted delegations climbed on the Goldwater bandwagon. This futile operation consumed a month, and its net effect was a majority of approximately 200 delegates for Goldwater.

When the G.O.P. convention opened at the Cow Palace in San Francisco, Monday, July 13, Goldwater had been under fire from his fellow Republicans for seven months. The climax had come the preceding evening when Scranton headquarters released a letter, bristling with insults, that challenged Goldwater to debate. Rewarming old issues, it accused him of paving the way for nuclear war and a racial holocaust. Scranton denied that he had seen the document bearing his signature, but declined to make amends by calling off the hopeless agitation. Along with Rockefeller, Romney, and a handful of delegates, he waged a futile fight to liberalize the Goldwater platform. The majority would have been well advised to acquiesce in a stronger civil rights plank and in an explicit condemnation of the Ku Klux Klan and the John Birch Society. But by this time, all basis for accommodation had disappeared. The liberals believed that they were making a desperate effort to rescue the party from oblivion, whereas the Goldwaterites regarded the wrangle over the platform as a final effort to discredit their standard-bearer before a national television audience. The episode triggered a deplorable display of bad manners by Goldwater's supporters in the galleries, who interrupted the speeches of the liberals with protracted boos. The Goldwater delegates on the floor behaved with more restraint, but the result of the outburst was to provide fresh support for the belief that conservatives possessed authoritarian personalities. The sequel to the "insultfest" was the adoption of the Goldwater platform without amendment.

Considering the divisive influence of the platform, it turned out to be a surprisingly tame document. The civil rights plank was a terse pledge to enforce the legislation of 1964. Other sections dealing with domestic matters envisaged a decentralization of power but stopped short of enunciating a doctrinaire position on states' rights. Although the foreign policy pronouncements were nationalistic in tone, they were also antiseptic by comparison to Goldwater's pre-convention statements. Yet nothing had been settled. Liberals found sinister intentions lurking in colorless words, and extremists considered the platform too noncommittal. It was conservative, but hardly a manifesto for a crusade.

Despite the fact that the nomination of Goldwater was a foregone conclusion, 7 hours were consumed in placing 8 names before the convention. Goldwater received 883 votes on the first ballot, and Scranton made a belated bid for solidarity by moving that the nomination be made unanimous. Again, concessions were in order, but Goldwater ignored the opportunity. It would have been difficult for him to accept one of his leading tormenters in the liberal camp as a running mate, but he was still on speaking terms with Hatfield of Oregon and Dr. Milton Eisenhower, the brother of the ex-President. Although neither had a large public following, there was more point to taking an obscure liberal than an obscure conservative. But rational considerations no longer prevailed at the Goldwater headquarters. As a result, the convention was ordered to swallow one of Goldwater's fellow conservatives, Congressman William E. Miller of upstate New York. As chairman of the Republican national committee, Miller was a familiar figure in the upper circles of the party, but he was virtually unknown to voters outside his congressional district. The country would soon learn that he had an abrasive oratorical style. Beyond that dubious asset, he brought nothing to the ticket that could strengthen Goldwater with elements that distrusted him.

It would have been better for the party if the convention had adjourned without further oratory. But since the days of Franklin Roosevelt, it had been customary for Presidential candidates to address the convention in person. Although Goldwater acquiesced in this tradition, he was in no mood to conciliate the opposition. On the contrary, he climaxed his speech with a challenge as unfortunate in its repercussions as the one issued by Andrew Johnson to Radical Republicans on February 22, 1866. Defiance was concentrated in two sentences:

> I would remind you that extremism in the defense of liberty is no vice. And let me remind you also that moderation in the pursuit of justice is no virtue.

These words were not prompted by a mere canon of rhetoric, but by the frustration of a man who had been called an extremist once too often. As might have been expected, they produced an effect opposite to the one intended. Gleefully appropriated by the opposition, they were hailed as proof that Goldwater was an extremist.

The momentum of his counterattack carried Goldwater into a final act of retaliation against the liberals. He conducted a systematic purge of hostile and lukewarm Republicans in the national organization. Then he elevated the inexperienced, youthful Dean Burch to the chairmanship of the national committee, which was tantamount to putting the campaign in the hands of the Arizona triumvirate.

IV

Aside from the obvious conclusion that the convention and its aftermath was a disaster for the G.O.P., these tangled developments do not lend themselves to dispassionate evaluation. As usual, both factions felt justified from their own viewpoint. The conservatives believed that they had loyally supported a repugnant strategy since 1936; hence, they thought themselves entitled to a reciprocal display of teamwork on the one occasion when they controlled the national convention. Viewed from this perspective, the liberals had continued the fight long after their position was demonstrably hopeless, and in so doing had simply provided the Democrats with extra ammunition. Outraged conservatives could point to the contrast between this tactic and their own deportment in 1952 when they had rallied to the support of General Eisenhower, whom they detested. Conservatives were just as unimpressed by the argument that the defence of principles justified disruptive behavior, for they had often swallowed their own principles in the interest of party solidarity. These factors operated with special force in the case of Goldwater, who had repeatedly placed the party welfare above his own feelings. So when the liberals waged the futile eleventh-hour fight against his candidacy, Goldwater believed that he was a victim of flagrant treachery. His retaliatory gestures were unjustified but understandable. Convinced that schismatics had destroyed his chance for victory, he preferred to lose badly rather than placate men who had misused him. The most conspicuous parallel was 1912, when the Taft forces preferred a party disaster to accommodation with factional opponents.

Two considerations nerved the liberals for their bitter fight against Goldwater: (1) the belief that he could not win the election, and (2) the conviction that he stood for principles harmful to the Republican party and the country. Their assumption about the hopelessness of his candidacy was undoubtedly correct, although he would have made a better showing if they had given up their fight after the California primary. It is also clear that the liberals continued the hopeless fight because they did not believe it was hopeless. In some intuitive way, they concluded that Goldwater's unpopularity in the public-opinion polls was bound to express itself through the convention machinery. This feeling had little factual basis, for the candidate was chosen by convention delegates, not by the public at large, and the liberals lacked an outstanding candidate who could rally their forces at the convention. Nevertheless, they felt obliged to struggle for control of the party, whatever the odds, because they regarded Goldwater as an alien force in the heart of Republicanism. It was this proprietary concern for the party that caused them to claim its shelter during the fall campaign rather than to defect to the Democrats. The future of the G.O.P. was safer in their hands, and they ultimately ousted the Goldwaterites from key positions in the organization. Even so, it is pardonable for the conservatives to believe that Goldwater was not as far outside the mainstream of American politics as the liberals imagined. He was not the first Presidential candidate to espouse abstractions that had no chance of implementation. Nor was he the first to accept support from elements that he ought to have repudiated. His personal entourage was not composed of wide-eyed fanatics but of sober, methodical men who would have felt just as comfortable in the service of Robert A. Taft. Nevertheless, if one conclusion stands out in the no-man's land of controversy, it is that Goldwater was a freak candidate—perhaps the most unconventional one in the history of the Republican party.

V

Like the fall campaign of 1912, the Johnson-Goldwater campaign in 1964 was an anticlimax and moved to a foregone conclusion. Every issue that the Democrats could raise against Goldwater had already been aired by his Republican opponents. With the rest of the country, the candidate knew what was coming, and an atmosphere of defeat hung over his head-quarters. Goldwater went through the motions of placating the liberals in a conference at Hershey, Pennsylvania, but he insulated himself from their advice. Like a man on his deathbed, Goldwater preferred to be surrounded by his friends. Defeatism was infectious, and many Republican candidates for state and national office disassociated themselves from Goldwater in an effort to survive.

The Democratic convention, which nominated Johnson at Atlantic City in late August, was a routine affair. The managers relied on pageantry as a substitute for business. The television audience witnessed a spectacle on the scale of the triumphal scene from *Aïda,* but the view of most partici-pants was obstructed by video cameras. In an effort to introduce some sus-pense into the transactions, Johnson concealed his preference for the Vice Presidential nomination until the last possible moment. But nobody was surprised when he selected Senator Hubert H. Humphrey of Minnesota, an orthodox supporter of welfare programs and civil rights. The Democratic platform endorsed the civil rights law enthusiastically, promised to create the Great Society, and pointed with pride to the pacific tone of administra-tion foreign policy.

The popular impression of the platforms was vague, but most voters had a positive and unflattering view of the candidates. They pictured Goldwater as a humorless, conservative Cromwell, and Johnson as a master manipu-lator whose clandestine operations had been exposed. As one woman put it succinctly: "Johnson counts the votes first and then acts. Goldwater acts and then counts the votes—if there are any." [17] Of the two caricatures, the one of Goldwater was more exaggerated; close contact with Johnson did leave the impression that he lived by Dale Carnegie's *How To Win Friends and Influence People.* He was always dispensing favors, perhaps spontaneously and without ulterior motives. Yet he did so in the style of the salesman-politician who is trying to promote his product or himself. For Johnson, the credo of personal relations was a substitute for principles, partly because fidelity to the latter would limit his political maneuverability. On occasion he could get testy about efforts to probe his doctrinal affiliations, as in 1958 when he wrote: "At the heart of my beliefs is a rebellion against this very process of classifying, labeling, and filing Americans under headings." [18] In view of his attitude, Johnson was ideally suited to lead the conglomerate of pressure groups that composed the Democratic party.

Although the majority had negative feelings about both candidates, they were apathetic about Johnson and violently opposed to Goldwater. This distinction may not have been flattering to Johnson, but it helped him to an election victory. His own references to Goldwater were indirect and didactic: broad warnings about the hazards of putting an unstable, bellicose personality in power. The Democratic national committee felt no obligation to adopt such a statesmanlike tone. It exploited popular anxiety about social security and nuclear war with a variety of visual aids. Posters depicted Goldwater tearing up social security cards. Short television film clips carried a more frightening message. The viewer saw small children eating ice cream cones or picking daisies against a background of clicking Geiger counters or mushrooming atomic clouds. Then an unseen commentator with a ghostly voice insinuated that such ghastly scenes would materialize if Goldwater was elected. The Republicans could produce nothing to match this material. Even so the national committees of both parties showed indecent enthusiasm for facilitating the circulation of publications produced by various hate groups. This literature varied from routine misrepresentation of the candidates to vile attacks on their characters. From the standpoint of quantity and effectiveness, honors were evenly divided between extremists of the right and left.[19] A larger segment of the news media backed the Democrats than in any campaign since 1932. The defection of traditionally Republican journals like the Kansas City *Star* and the *Saturday Evening Post* strengthened the impression that the G.O.P. had been infiltrated by extremist elements.

Virtually every factor at work in the campaign helped to keep the Republicans on the defensive. Goldwater and Miller started bravely enough, dwelling on coruption in high places, crime in the streets, and iniquities of centralized government. But as the campaign progressed they were forced to spend more time dealing with the charges of the Democrats. By mid-

October the crusade of January had turned into a prosaic struggle against demoralization.

Politicians are obliged to assume that the outcome of a campaign is doubtful, if only to sustain the zeal of party workers. The Democrats would have found it hard to feel any sense of insecurity, had it not been for the civil rights issue. Johnson suggested and Goldwater accepted the proposal that both parties avoid the topic. The ostensible reason for doing so was to minimize the chances for racial violence, but the real reason was that neither side knew who would benefit from playing with such an explosive question. The civil rights law had accelerated the drift of Southern whites to the G.O.P. and of Northern Negroes to the Democrats. What frightened the politicians was uncertainty as to the attitude of blue-collar workers and ethnic groups that normally voted Democratic. Pollsters kept reassuring the Democratic high command that it had nothing to fear, because open expression of racial prejudice had gone out of style. Yet professionals feared that the sentiment was still alive. The ambivalent seemed to be numerous: irresolutely balancing their dislike of Negro aspirations against their fear of losing social security benefits. As late as October, the mood of potential backlashers was changing with every headline.[20] Clearly, the basic predisposition of lower-class urban whites was to swallow their resentment of the Negro and vote the Democratic ticket. But race riots in Harlem and Rochester, New York, as well as the threat of similar eruptions elsewhere, made Democrats extremely nervous all the way through to election day. Their instinctive response was to step up the twofold barrage against Goldwater as the foe of social security and human brotherhood. They insisted that reference to "crime in the streets" and "states' rights" were code phrases employed by bigots to conceal racial bias.

The Democrats enjoyed their customary good luck in advancing the claim that they were the party of peace. Just as Woodrow Wilson had been obliged by the German inactivity in 1916, Lyndon Johnson was obliged by the Viet Cong's concentrating on guerilla operations against the American-supported South Vietnamese regime in 1964. This deceptive calm seemed to vindicate the contention of the Administration that its policy carried little risk of involving American soldiers. The only direct intervention by Washington was a retaliatory naval bombardment of North Vietnamese gunboats that followed an attack on the destroyer *Maddox* on August 2. So isolated an incident actually helped the Democrats by providing them with an opportunity to make alarming speculations about what

Goldwater would have done. In view of subsequent developments in Vietnam, it must be assumed that the Administration was either poorly informed about actual conditions or misrepresented them.

VI

There was no longer a September election in Maine to measure trends, but the available indicators pointed to a Democratic landslide. Besides the reassuring evidence provided by the pollsters, the registration of new voters everywhere revealed a marked preference for the Democrats.[21] Even at convention time TV rentals in Michigan hospitals were higher during the Democratic convention than the Republican convention.[22]

In November more than 70 million people went to the polls and confirmed the dire predictions about the Republican party. Johnson carried 44 states with 486 electoral votes, and Goldwater carried 6 states with 52 electoral votes. The Democrats captured nearly two-thirds of the popular vote, restricting the Republicans to a hard core of 26.8 million supporters. Outside of the five states in the deep South, which constituted the shrinking citadel of all-out segregationists, Goldwater was able to carry only his native Arizona. Subsequent analysis indicated that he had lost many farmers and businessmen who normally voted Republican as well as the smaller group of Negroes hitherto affiliated with the party. Moreover, a larger percentage of industrial workers, ethnic minorities, and the aged had supported the Democrats than in any Presidential election since 1936. Johnson carried a lot of congressional candidates to victory on his coattails. As a result, the Democrats made a net gain of 38 seats in the House and 2 seats in the Senate, giving them a margin of 295 to 140 in the former, and 68 to 32 in the latter. The magnitude of the landslide was underlined by the fact that the Democrats captured control of both houses in 32 state legislatures, including such normally Republican states as Iowa, Colorado, and Indiana. This achievement was especially significant, because the Supreme Court had ordered these and other states to reapportion their legislatures. The Democrats in general, and suburban areas in particular, seemed certain to benefit, opening the way for fresh changes in the party structure.

The G.O.P. debacle was more the product of an anti-Goldwater than an anti-Republican vote, although the total vote of the Arizonian ran only 500,000 behind the total vote for Republican congressmen. Governor Romney had survived the Democratic tide in Michigan by disassociating himself from Goldwater. The same strategy had saved John V. Lindsay in

New York and several other Republican congressmen representing preponderately urban districts. Goldwater asserted that he had been defeated the preceding July by the behavior of his fellow Republicans.[23] His analysis was true, but it was not the whole truth. The Republicans undoubtedly would have had fewer losses had they avoided the lethal pre-convention vendetta. The decisive factor, however, was Goldwater's erroneous belief that he could win the common man by attacking all pressure groups. The common man devoid of group interests existed only in Goldwater's imagination. There was something of the Ibsen hero in his posture, but he overdid his defiance of political convention. He might, for example, have successfully exploited racial discontent in the North by stifling his reservations about social security and medicare and appealing directly to the backlash vote. Voters in California, Ohio, and Maryland—to mention three states—turned down proposals for fuller implementation of civil rights.[24] Undisturbed by threats to their economic interests, they might have vented their racial bias in the Presidential election as well. But Goldwater, to his credit, refused to give them that kind of choice. A final factor in the Republican defeat was the rigidity displayed by local leaders who had outlived their usefulness. Bud Wilkinson, an ex-football coach and unsuccessful G.O.P. senatorial candidate in Oklahoma, had this situation in mind when he noted that listening to the politicians "was like listening to the alumni before a football game—suicide." [25]

The Republican party seemed certain to regain some of its lost supporters in the North once the controversial Goldwater had vacated the center of the stage. Matters were much more perplexing in the South. A genuine two-party system existed in the Border states, but the same could not be said of the lower South, where the G.O.P. was like a head without a body. Starting with Eisenhower, each Republican Presidential candidate had polled a larger percentage of the regional vote than his predecessor. The trouble was that G.O.P. state and congressional tickets did not make proportionate gains. The situation was still more discouraging at the local level. A few enclaves like St. Petersburg, Florida, and Dallas, Texas, had flourishing Republican organizations and fielded a full slate of candidates. Elsewhere systematic activity was the exception rather than the rule. In both Louisiana and Mississippi, which Goldwater carried by large majorities, practically all the registered voters were Democrats. Indeed, the Mississippi Democratic organization tried to formulate legislation that woud keep the Republican party off the ballot.[26] Prodded by Lyndon

Johnson and Governor John Connally, the Texas Democrats worked successfully behind the scenes in 1964 to arrest the rise of an effective G.O.P. organization in Texas.

The key to this bewildering pattern was racial politics, with foes of integration dominating most Democratic state parties. Few Southerners felt the impulse to defect as long as these organizations were reliable custodians of white supremacy. So they supported the Democrats locally and rebuked the national party ticket. The influx of Northerners, which accompanied the industrialization of the South, did not upset existing alignments as much as courthouse politicians had feared. Newcomers soon discovered that they would waste their votes unless they participated in Democratic primaries, and many of them made the necessary adjustment. They also found it easy to tolerate Southern views on the race question, particularly after the battleground shifted from integration of lunch counters to more sensitive areas such as housing and public schools. Like the migrants from the North, most of newly enfranchised Southern Negroes acquiesced in the political status quo. Of the 2 million Negroes registered in 1964, 40 per cent had no definite affiliation; nearly 50 per cent considered themselves Democrats; and only 10 per cent, Republicans. Some identified the G.O.P. with hard times; others believed that the national Democratic party, as distinct from its state organizations, was more committed to civil rights than the Republicans; and still others voted Democratic in response to pressure from Southern whites. The persistence of the one-party system in the lower South militated against the competitive bidding for Negro votes so prevalent in the North. The fact that there were 17 million whites and only 5 million Negroes of voting age in 1964 discouraged the formation of a racial party. Moreover, the effort of various civil rights organizations to register Southern Negroes, which had doubled their bloc of eligible votes between 1952 and 1964, merely stimulated the white population to execute more successful registration drives.[28]

Under the circumstances, the Republicans did not have much cause for elation over the 1964 election in the lower South. They did elect a few more congressmen and state legislators by running candidates who professed to be more conservative on the race question than their Democratic opponents. The gains from this policy, however, were more than counterbalanced by its adverse effect on the larger Negro population in the North. Besides, the bulk of Southern Democratic candidates for Congress won re-election and protected their seniority by taking no part in the Presidential election. The transitory character of Republican gains was to be demonstrated in the 1966 elections, when the Democrats, unembarrassed by a Presidential contest, recaptured a number of offices with militant racists. The continuing flow of migrants to the South and the increasing pugnacity of Southern Negroes may ultimately revolutionize regional politics. Yet the emergence of a genuine two-party system there in the near future is by no means assured.

VII

There is nothing like failure to generate momentum for a change in party leadership. No sooner had the votes been counted in 1964 than the liberal Republicans who survived the Goldwater debacle began to clamor for the scalp of Dean Burch, the chairman of the national committee. The agitation was seconded by conservatives excluded from Goldwater's inner circle during the campaign and irritated by what they regarded as a ruinous posture. At first Goldwater tried to save his subordinate, but he finally capitulated on January 12, 1965. It was agreed that Burch would step down in April and be replaced by Ray Bliss, who had studiously avoided ideological quarrels with his antiseptic emphasis on salvation through the rebuilding of urban G.O.P. machines. Bliss had his work cut out for him. Factional quarrels had disrupted the continuity of local leadership. In fact, when Bliss took office there were only two G.O.P. state chairmen whose tenure dated back to 1960. Fortunately, the Republicans were solvent at the end of the 1964 campaign, with the result that Bliss devoted his full energies to organizational problems. Progress turned out to be slow and uninspiring, but Bliss managed to ease the most rabid factionalists out of key positions in the national organization long before the mid-term elections.

Dean Burch was not the only casualty of the 1964 campaign. House Republicans replaced minority leader Charles A. Halleck of Indiana with Gerald Ford of Michigan. The principal objection to Halleck had nothing to do with ideology, because he was a typical middle-of-the-roader. But he was getting old himself, and showed no particular haste about honoring the claims of younger Republican congressmen for promotion in the House hierarchy. His ouster had no perceptible effect on the policy of the minority. The new leader defended decisions with more dash and less fluency than Halleck. On the other side of Capitol Hill, Dirksen of Illinois continued to preside over the minority, entertaining the country if not his colleagues with the spread-eagle oratory of the 1890's.

It really did not matter who led the Republicans, because the Democratic majority was large enough to do anything it wanted. In the House, conservative Southerners were inundated in a sea of freshman Democrats from such improbable places as Iowa, Michigan, and Colorado. Since the Southerners had been outflanked in the Senate during the 1964 battle over civil rights, they were in no better position than their House collaborators to revive the old coalition of Republicans and conservative Democrats. Accordingly, the Great Society program cleared Congress with a minimum of difficulty in 1965. The legislative mill ground almost as rapidly as it had during the first phase of the New Deal. Johnson secured generous appropriations to wage war on poverty and to stimulate economic diversification in the poor but scenic area known as Appalachia. He also won legislative approval of medicare, financial aid for education and housing, plus a law to facilitate the registration of Southern Negroes.

Few people bothered to note what the Republicans were doing. The spotlight remained on the White House, where the President displayed his customary legislative wizardry and professed to be governing by consensus. Throughout 1965 there were sporadic expressions of dissent, but on the whole the voters accepted the achievements and the claims of the Administration at face value. The political climate began to change soon after the beginning of the new year. The war in Vietnam was dragging on as inconclusively as ever and voters became increasingly disturbed by rising draft calls and American casualties. For once, prominent Democrats took the lead in criticizing the foreign policy of their own Administration and denouncing the President for misleading voters about his Vietnamese policy in 1964.

A simultaneous rise in Negro demonstrations and riots offended many citizens who had looked favorably on token gestures of integration. Increasing militance split the Negro movement and focused attention on the Student Nonviolent Coordinating Committee. Under the leadership of Stokely Carmichael, it took the line that American Negroes were a colonial people under a white imperialism like their brethren in Africa. Contemptuous of legislative solutions, Carmichael urged Negroes to resist the draft, oppose the war in Vietnam, and fight for their rights at home. Just what "fighting" involved was not made clear, but the deportment of Carmichael and his followers indicated that they had gone beyond the tactic of peaceful demonstrations. Some Negro leaders disagreed publicly with Carmichael, but voters came to think of him as the principal spokesman of the civil rights movement, especially in the wake of widespread Negro riots during the summer of 1966.

The celebrated war on poverty also generated disagreeable repercussions. Local politicians wanted greater control over the dispensing of funds than Washington cared to give them. Well-to-do taxpayers resented the costliness of various projects and the meager progress made by unpromising recipients, many of whom were Negroes. Even the poor complained bitterly that they were getting less out of the program than the army of officials who administered it. These grievances seemed certain to backfire against the Democrats in the mid-term elections, especially since people were free to vote their racial biases without jeopardizing social security or welfare legislation.

The heaviest skirmishing took place in a few crucial gubernatorial contests and in the congressional districts of the forty freshman Democrats. Redistricting had improved the prospects of some in the latter category, and the Administration tried to save them all by flooding their districts with money for federal projects.[29] Bliss countered with an unprecedented effort to prevent elderly Republican ex-congressmen from contesting their old seats. With promises of generous financial support from the G.O.P. national committee, he coaxed a number of dynamic, and photogenic young Republicans to make the race.[30] For the most part, President Johnson stayed out of the campaign, whereas ex-Vice President Nixon plunged into it wholeheartedly. There was no single Republican party line, but cautious criticism of the Vietnam war, race riots, and the high cost of food.

As usual in off-year elections, the discontented voted in larger numbers than the satisfied or the apathetic. Approximately 15 million less went to the polls in November 1966 than had done so two years earlier. Dissatisfaction with the Administration showed up most clearly in the House, where the Republicans recaptured 47 seats, cutting the Democratic margin to 248-187. The Senate was almost a standoff, although the Republicans picked up three widely scattered seats. Their most notable victory was in Illinois, where the handsome, articulate Charles Percy won over the three-term veteran, Paul H. Douglas. Several statehouses returned to Republican control, the most important being California. There the debonair, movie actor-politician Ronald Reagan won by nearly a million votes. The party also picked up governorships in Arkansas and Florida. Nonetheless, the 1966 election perpetuated the tendency of the voters to retain incumbents and split tickets. A Republican governor and a Democratic senator won re-election in Rhode Island, both by approximately a two-thirds majority.

Prophecy in the wake of the off-year elections was as hazardous as ever. Plainly, the Republicans had a large crop of Presidential hopefuls. It included newcomers like Reagan of California, Percy of Illinois, and more established leaders such as Richard M. Nixon and George W. Romney, who had been re-elected in Michigan by an impressive majority. But the real difficulty for the Republican party was not the choice of an appropriate candidate but the rehabilitation of its image. George Gallup pointed to the magnitude of this problem when he noted that a quarter of a century earlier nearly half the voters had considered themselves Republicans, whereas by 1966 only 26 per cent indicated the same preference. If his survey was accurate, the number of people with no party allegiance equaled the number of Republicans.[31] This state of affairs, as Gallup pointed out, has been due to the fact that the G.O.P. gradually developed a fatal reputation of being opposed to progress of any kind. How much this unpromising situation is due to the mistakes of the party is a debatable question. Clearly, the G.O.P. did not make an energetic effort to find new sources of support when its coalition based on Midwestern farmers, big business, native-born workers, and the old middle class lost its numerical importance. The danger first became apparent in 1928 when the Democrats captured the bulk of first- and second-generation Americans in the large Eastern cities. It would have been difficult to arrest the process of erosion during the subsequent depression, which the Democrats attempted to blame on the Republicans, but the Republicans did not really try. The continued increase in the size of the disaffected groups, coupled with the loss of the Negroes and the decrease of the farm vote, doomed the Republicans to minority status.

Once important voting blocs had been lost, the Republicans found it as hard to win them back as the Democrats had found it to retrieve their old Northern supporters after the Civil War. There was nothing new about the frustrations of the G.O.P. after 1940. Americans have always been tenacious in their party allegience. Long periods of one-party supremacy have been the rule rather than the exception. Within such periods the voter may occasionally rebuke his party, but he rarely deserts it until it fails to deal with some new and vital issue. The Republicans can draw comfort from the inherent tendency of major parties to rest on their oars and from the existence of so many apathetic voters. A crisis precipitating new issues is needed by the Republicans, but it is unlikely that the minority can do much to create its own opportunities. What it must do is deal energetically and imaginatively with opportunities whenever they materialize.

The prolongation of the Vietnamese war might cause the voters to rebuke the Democrats, but unless it spreads elsewhere it is no more likely to produce a lasting realignment than the Korean war. The burgeoning problems of the city offer the G.O.P. more opportunity for constructive action, inasmuch as they generate antagonism between important elements of the Democratic coalition. Thus preconditions for a change in political attitudes already exist. For such a shift to materialize, the Democrats would have to take the loyalty of their dissidents for granted, and the Republicans would have to offer dynamic leadership. Otherwise the G.O.P. seems certain to occupy its current role as a minority party for the foreseeable future.

Notes

Wherever the location of personal papers is not specified in the following notes, these papers reside in the Library of Congress, Washington, D.C. (See page viii for complete listing.) The reliance on the Landon Papers in Chapter XII and the seeming lack of thorough documentation in Chapters XII and XIII is a result of the fact that many of the principals in the political events of the past few decades have not yet released their private papers for investigation by scholars. Much of the material in these chapters was by necessity taken from the newspapers and periodicals of the time and from secondary sources.

CHAPTER I

1. Alexis de Tocqueville, *Democracy in America*, 2 vols. (New York, 1890), I:271–2.
2. *Peoria Transcript*, July 13, 1860.
3. Alton B. Parker Papers, *The Occasional Reminiscences of Bertha Parker Hall*, p. 3.
4. J. W. Forney, *The Philadelphia Press*, Aug. 26, 1858.
5. Clayton S. Ellsworth, "Oberlin and the Anti-Slavery Movement up to the Civil War" (unpublished Ph.D. thesis, Cornell University, 1930), p. 105.
6. Lyman Trumbull Papers, E. J. Tichenor to Trumbull, Feb. 22, 1858.
7. Tyler Dennet, *John Hay: From Poetry to Politics* (New York, 1934), p. 141.
8. James Bryce, *Modern Democracies*, 2 vols. (New York, 1912), I:102.
9. George H. Knoles, *The Presidential Campaign of 1892* (Stanford University Publications: History, Economics and Political Science, Vol. 5, No. 1, 1942), p. 122.
10. Theodore Roosevelt Papers, Roosevelt to Morris Jastrow, Nov. 14, 1914, c.c.

11. Carl Schurz, *The Reminiscences of Carl Schurz*, 3 vols. (New York, 1907), II:73.
12. Mary S. Logan, *Reminiscences of a Soldier's Wife: An Autobiography* (New York, 1913), p. 102.
13. Jeter A. Isely, *Horace Greeley and the Republican Party 1853–1861* (Princeton University Press, 1947), p. 4.
14. Abraham Lincoln Papers, J. S. Winter to Lincoln, Sept. 9, 1858.
15. David Lindsey, "Samuel Sullivan Cox 1824–1899" (unpublished Ph.D. thesis, University of Chicago, 1950), p. 38.
16. Gustave Koerner, *Memoirs (1809–1896)*, 2 vols. (T. J. McCormack, editor, Cedar Rapids, 1909), I:26–8.
17. Thurlow Weed, *Autobiography of Thurlow Weed* (Harriet A. Weed, editor, Boston, 1884), p. 491.
18. Harold P. James, "Lincoln's own State in the Election of 1860" (unpublished Ph.D. thesis, University of Illinois, 1943), p. 324.
19. Ibid. p. 327.
20. Whitelaw Reid Papers, Thomas Collier Platt to Reid, Dec. 15, 1877.
21. Roger H. Van Bolt, "The Rise of the Republican Party in Indiana, 1840–56" (unpublished Ph.D. thesis, University of Chicago, 1950), p. 32.
22. O. J. Hollister, *The Life of Schuyler Colfax* (New York, 1886), p. 102.
23. William Ritchie, "The Public Career of Cassius M. Clay" (unpublished Ph.D. thesis, George Peabody College for Teachers, 1934), p. 110.
24. Charles Roll, *Colonel Dick Thompson: The Perpetual Whig* (Indianapolis, 1948), p. 86.
25. Don E. Fehrenbacher, "The Origins and Purpose of Lincoln's House Divided Speech," *Mississippi Valley Historical Review*, Vol. 46, No. 4, March 1960, p. 621.
26. George Fort Milton, *The Eve of Conflict: Stephen A. Douglas and the Needless War* (Boston and New York, 1934), p. 316.
27. James A. Garfield Diary, Sept. 21, 1866.
28. John C. Spooner Papers, Spooner to H. M. Kutchin, July 11, 1896, c.c.
29. Charles B. Johnson, *Illinois in the Fifties* (Champaign, 1918), p. 143.
30. John Sherman Papers, Henry D. Cooke to Sherman, Nov. 8, 1864.
31. John Sherman to William T. Sherman, Nov. 9, 1889 (R. S. Thorndike, editor, *The Sherman Letters: Correspondence between General and Senator Sherman from 1837 to 1891*, New York, 1894).
32. W. M. Dickson to Rutherford B. Hayes, May 23, 1876 (Charles R. Williams, *The Life of Rutherford Birchard Hayes*, Boston and New York, 1914, p. 437).
33. Carl Russell Fish, *The Civil Service and the Patronage* (New York, 1905), p. 166; Dorothy G. Fowler, *The Cabinet Politician: The Postmaster General 1829–1909* (New York, 1943), p. 106.
34. Weed, p. 584.
35. Leland Sage, *William Boyd Allison: A Study in Practical Politics* (Iowa City, 1956), p. 107.
36. Thomas H. Carter Papers, O. M. Landstrum to Carter, Nov. 23, 1908.
37. Russell K. Nelson, "The Early Life and Congressional Career of Elihu B. Washburne" (unpublished Ph.D. thesis, University of North Dakota, 1953), p. 112.
38. Ralph A. Straetz, "The Progressive Movement in Illinois, 1910–1916" (unpublished Ph.D. thesis, University of Illinois, 1951), p. 114.

39. Adlai E. Stevenson, *Something of Men I Have Known* (Chicago, 1909), p. 4.
40. Albert J. Beveridge, *Abraham Lincoln (1809–1858),* 4 vols. (Boston and New York, 1928), II:221.

CHAPTER II

1. Gideon Welles Papers, Salmon P. Chase to Welles, Oct. 26, 1855.
2. John B. Stabler, "A History of the Constitutional Union Party: A Tragic Failure" (unpublished Ph.D. thesis, Columbia University, 1954), p. 310.
3. Burton J. Hendrick, *Lincoln's War Cabinet* (Boston, 1946), p. 50.
4. Jesse Macy, *The Anti-Slavery Crusade* (New Haven, 1919), p. 58.
5. Henry L. Dawes Papers, Moses Kimball to Dawes, Aug. 28, 1854.
6. Gordon S. P. Kleeberg, *Formation of the Republican Party as a National Political Organization* (New York, 1911), p. 18.
7. C. Maxwell Myers, "The Rise of the Republican Party in Pennsylvania, 1854–1860" (unpublished Ph.D. thesis, University of Pittsburgh, 1940), p. 59.
8. Godfrey T. Anderson, "The Slavery Issue as a Factor in Massachusetts Politics from the Compromise of 1850 to the Outbreak of the Civil War" (unpublished Ph.D. thesis, University of Chicago, 1944), pp. 100–101, 122–8.
9. John Sherman, *Recollections of Forty Years in the House, Senate and Cabinet,* 2 vols. (New York and Chicago, 1895), I:104.
10. Mildred C. Stoler, "Influence of the Democratic Element in the Republican Party of Illinois and Indiana" (unpublished Ph.D. thesis, University of Indiana, 1938), p. 58.
11. John McLean Papers, Hector Orr to McLean, Dec. 25, 1854.
12. Anderson, p. 111.
13. Hamilton Fish Papers, D. D. Barnard to Fish, Jan. 30, 1855.
14. Russell K. Nelson, "The Early Life and Congressional Career of Elihu B. Washburne" (unpublished Ph.D. thesis, University of North Dakota, 1953), p. 112.
15. Welles Papers, Welles to Preston King, Nov. 25, 1854, c. c.
16. Ibid. Preston King to Welles, Oct. 21, 1854; Welles to James F. Babcock, March 14, 1855, c.c.
17. Albert J. Beveridge, *Abraham Lincoln, 1809–1858,* 4 vols. (Boston and New York, 1928), III:354, Abraham Lincoln to J. F. Speed, Aug. 24, 1855.
18. Fish Papers, R. A. West to Fish, Jan. 13, 1856.
19. Hendrick, p. 270.
20. Josiah B. Grinnell, *Men and Events of Forty Years* (Boston, 1891), p. 179.
21. Henry Adams, *The Education of Henry Adams* (Boston, 1918), p. 104.
22. Kleeberg, p. 30.
23. George W. Julian, "The First Republican National Convention," *American Historical Review,* Vol. 4, No. 2, Jan. 1899, p. 318.
24. R. H. Luthin, *The First Lincoln Campaign* (Harvard University Press, 1944), p. 3.
25. Salmon P. Chase Papers, A. P. Stone to Chase, March 31, 1855.
26. William E. Smith, *The Francis Preston Blair Family,* 2 vols. (New York, 1933), I:327.
27. Hamilton Fish Papers, Fish to D. D. Barnard, March 6, 1856 c.c.; Robert C. Winthrop to Fish, March 26, 1856.

28. John G. Nicolay Papers, Nicolay to Paul Selby, Aug. 24, 1886 c.c.
29. Ruhl J. Bartlett, *John C. Frémont and the Republican Party* (Ohio State University Bulletins, Columbus, 1930), p. 34.
30. Francis P. Weisenburger, *The Life of John McLean: A Politician on the United States Supreme Court* (Ohio State University Studies #15, Columbus, 1937), p. 147; Bartlett, p. 12.
31. Trumbull Papers, Orville H. Browning to Trumbull, May 19, 1856; McLean Papers, Caleb B. Smith to McLean, Oct. 30, 1855.
32. R. R. Wilson, *New York Post,* June 16, 1900.
33. Grace Julian Clarke, *George W. Julian* (Indianapolis, 1923), p. 180.
34. Bartlett, p. 36.
35. Jeter A. Isely, *Horace Greeley and the Republican Party 1853–1861* (Princeton University Press, 1947), p. 177.
36. Thaddeus Stevens Papers, Stevens to E. D. Gazzam, Dec. 4, 1856, c.c.
37. O. J. Hollister, *The Life of Schuyler Colfax* (New York, 1886), p. 106.
38. Ernest Paul Muller, "Preston King: A Political Biography" (unpublished Ph.D. thesis, Columbia University, 1957), p. 581.
39. Trumbull Papers, William Fessenden to Trumbull, Nov. 16, 1856.

CHAPTER III

1. *New York Tribune,* March 7, 1857.
2. *Congressional Globe,* 3rd session, pp. 103–14; Don E. Fehrenbacher, "Lincoln, Douglas, and the Freeport Question," *American Historical Review,* Vol. 63, No. 3, April 1961, pp. 609–10.
3. John B. Stabler, "A History of the Constitutional Union Party: A Tragic Failure" (unpublished Ph.D. thesis, Columbia University, 1954), p. 56; Stanton L. Davis, "Pennsylvania Politics, 1860–1863" (unpublished Ph.D. thesis, Western Reserve University, 1935), p. 35.
4. John Nicolay Papers, Lyman Trumbull to Nicolay, Dec. 26, 1857; Gideon Welles Papers, Preston King to Welles, Jan. 2, 1858.
5. Henry L. Dawes Papers, Dawes to Anna Dawes, March 28, 1858.
6. Joshua Giddings–George W. Julian Papers, Giddings to Laura Giddings, April 30, 1858.
7. Dawes Papers, Dawes to Mrs. Dawes, April 2, 1858.
8. Carl Schurz, *The Reminiscences of Carl Schurz,* 3 vols. (New York, 1907), II:93.
9. Walter C. Woodward, *The Rise and Early History of Political Parties in Oregon, 1843–1868* (Portland, 1913), p. 148.
10. Ernest Paul Muller, "Preston King: A Political Biography" (unpublished Ph.D. thesis, Columbia University, 1957), p. 632; Welles Papers, Dixon to Welles, April 26, 1860.
11. Glyndon G. VanDeusen, *Thurlow Weed: Wizard of the Lobby* (Boston, 1947), pp. 245–7.
12. McLean Papers, R. M. Corwine to McLean, March 19, 1860; Lincoln Papers, Sam Galloway to Lincoln, March 15, 1860; Wade Papers, R. F. Paine to Wade, March 22, 1860, H. E. Parsons to Wade, Feb. 19, 1860.
13. Lincoln Papers, J. M. Lucas to Lincoln, May 6, 1860.

14. Chase Papers, John A. Bingham to Chase, May 10, 1860.
15. Ibid. A. C. Gray to Chase, March 19, 1860.
16. Trumbull Papers, G. A. Norse to Trumbull, May 13, 1860.
17. R. H. Luthin, *The First Lincoln Campaign* (Harvard University Press, 1944), p. 106.
18. Davis, p. 103.
19. Lincoln Papers, Mark W. Delahay to Lincoln, March 21, 1860.
20. Nicolay Papers, Norman Judd to Nicolay, notes on a personal interview, Feb. 23, 1876.
21. Hamilton Fish Papers, D. D. Barnard to Fish, Jan. 22, 1859.
22. *Springfield Republican*, May 11, 1860.
23. *New York Tribune*, May 11, 1860.
24. Stabler, p. 397.
25. John J. Crittenden Papers, A. A. Lawrence to Crittenden, May 25, 1860.
26. Murat Halstead, *Caucuses of 1860* (Columbus, 1860), p. 121.
27. Harold P. James, "Lincoln's Own State in the Election of 1860" (unpublished Ph.D. thesis, University of Illinois, 1943), p. 337.
28. C. Maxwell Myers, "The Rise of the Republican Party in Pennsylvania, 1854–1860" (unpublished Ph.D. thesis, University of Pittsburgh, 1940), p. 276.
29. John Sherman Papers, John Longs to Sherman, May 20, 1860.
30. Muller, p. 646.
31. George Fort Milton, *The Eve of Conflict: Stephen A. Douglas and the Needless War* (Boston and New York, 1934), p. 482.
32. James, p. 146.
33. Lincoln Papers, James S. Harvey to Lincoln, July 4, 1860.
34. Chase Papers, Mrs. R. L. Hunt to Chase, Nov. 23, 1860.
35. William H. Gist–Frank P. Blair Papers, Blair to Montgomery Blair, Jan. 21, 1861.
36. Richard Taylor, *Destruction and Reconstruction: Personal Experiences of the Late War* (Richard B. Harwell, editor, New York, 1955), p. 8.
37. Nicolay Papers, Abraham Lincoln to John F. Fry, Aug. 15, 1860.
38. *New York Tribune*, Nov. 10, 1860.
39. Russell K. Nelson, "The Early Life and Congressional Career of Elihu B. Washburne" (unpublished Ph.D. thesis, University of North Dakota, 1953), p. 206.
40. Wade Papers, Lyman Trumbull to Wade, Nov. 9, 1860.
41. Joseph Hawley Papers, O. S. Ferry to Hawley, Dec. 11, 1860.
42. Welles Papers, King to Welles, Dec. 11, 1860.
43. Dawes Papers, Dawes to Mrs. Electa A. Dawes, Dec. 9, 1860.
44. Fish Papers, Fish to W. P. Fessenden, Dec. 11, 1860, c.c.
45. Lincoln Papers, Elihu Washburne to Lincoln, Dec. 9, 1860.
46. Fish Papers, Fessenden to Fish, Dec. 15, 1860.
47. Sherman Papers, Simon Rush to Sherman, Dec. 17, 1860; Trumbull Papers, Gustave Koerner to Trumbull, Dec. 10, 1860; Washburne Papers, John Montelins to Washburne, Dec. 5, 1860; Wade Papers, J. D. Cox to Wade, Dec. 21, 1860.
48. Henry Adams, *The Education of Henry Adams* (Boston, 1918), p. 83.
49. Trumbull Papers, W. Kitchell to Trumbull, Dec. 18, 1860.
50. Allan Nevins, *The Emergence of Lincoln*, 2 vols. (New York, 1950), II:394.

51. David N. Potter, *Lincoln and His Party in the Secession Crisis* (New Haven, 1962), pp. 287–8.
52. Ibid. p. 314.
53. James A. Garfield Papers, Garfield to B. A. Hinsdale, Feb. 17, 1861, c.c.
54. John Russell Young, *Philadelphia Evening Star,* Aug. 22, 1891.
55. Ibid.
56. Nicolay Papers, Nicolay to Therena Bates, April 7, 1861, c.c.

CHAPTER IV

1. Maurice G. Baxter, "Orville H. Browning: Conservative in American Politics" (unpublished Ph.D. thesis, University of Illinois, 1948), p. 131.
2. Abraham Lincoln Papers, O. H. Browning to Lincoln, April 30, 1861.
3. Martin Lichterman, "John Adams Dix, 1789–1879" (unpublished Ph.D. thesis, Columbia University, 1952), p. 476.
4. William Salter, *The Life of James W. Grimes* (New York, 1876), p. 140.
5. Dorothy G. Fowler, *The Cabinet Politician: The Postmaster General 1829–1909* (New York, 1943), p. 106.
6. William B. Allison to G. M. Dodge, April 19, 1861 (Leland Sage, *William Boyd Allison: A Study in Practical Politics,* Iowa City, 1956, p. 47).
7. Fred Messamore, "John A. Logan: Democrat and Republican" (unpublished Ph.D. thesis, University of Kentucky, 1939), p. 133.
8. W. L. Garrison to J. S. Gibbons, April 28, 1861 (*Essex Institute Collections,* 1906, Vol. 42, p. 310).
9. Henry L. Dawes Papers, Dawes to Mrs. Electa A. Dawes, July 7 and 10, 1861.
10. Horace White, *The Life of Lyman Trumbull* (Boston, 1913), p. 428; Zachariah Chandler Papers, Chandler to Ben Wade, Oct. 8, 1861 (Ralph J. Roske, "The Post Civil War Career of Lyman Trumbull," unpublished Ph.D. thesis, University of Illinois, 1949, p. 42).
11. Roger B. Taney Papers, W. P. Fessenden to J. S. Pike, Sept. 8, 1861.
12. Charles E. Hamlin, *The Life and Times of Hannibal Hamlin* (Cambridge, 1899), p. 423.
13. Zachariah Chandler Papers, Chandler to Mrs. Letitia Grace Chandler, Sept. 17, 1861.
14. John G. Nicolay Papers, copy of the John Hay Diary, Oct. 27, 1861.
15. Zachariah Chandler Papers, Chandler to Mrs. Chandler, Oct. 27, 1861.
16. Edward L. Pierce, *Memoirs and Letters of Charles Sumner,* 4 vols. (London, 1893), IV:49; Harriette M. Dilla, *The Politics of Michigan, 1865–1878* (New York, 1912), p. 31.
17. Harris L. Dante, "Reconstruction Politics in Illinois, 1860–72" (unpublished Ph.D. thesis, University of Chicago, 1950), p. 20; Frank James Munger, "Two-Party Politics in the State of Indiana" (unpublished Ph.D. thesis, Harvard University, 1955), p. 35.
18. Dante, p. 46.
19. George H. Porter, *Ohio Politics During the Civil War* (New York, 1911), pp. 77–8.
20. Joshua Giddings–George W. Julian Papers, Giddings to Julian, Jan. 18, 1863.

21. Giddings–Julian Papers, Wade to Julian, Sept. 29, 1862.
22. William E. Smith, *The Francis Preston Blair Family*, 2 vols. (New York, 1933), II:134.
23. Giddings–Julian Papers, Giddings to Julian, June 16, 1862.
24. George W. Julian, *Political Recollections, 1840–1872* (Chicago, 1884), p. 213.
25. Adam Gurowski, *Diary*, 3 vols. (Boston, 1862), March 1862, I:166.
26. Dawes Papers, Dawes to Mrs. Dawes, May 29, 1862; *Chicago Tribune*, June 2, 1862.
27. Robert B. Warden, *An Account of the Private Life and Public Services of Salmon Portland Chase* (Cincinnati, 1874), p. 486; Ben Butler Papers, Salmon P. Chase to Butler, Sept. 23, 1862.
28. John Sherman to William T. Sherman, Aug. 24, 1862 (R. S. Thorndike, editor, *The Sherman Letters: Correspondence between General and Senator Sherman from 1837 to 1891*, New York, 1894).
29. Orville H. Browning, *Diary*, 2 vols. (Springfield, Ill., 1925), July 8, 1862, I:555.
30. John Sherman, *Recollections of Forty Years in the House, Senate, and Cabinet*, 2 vols. (New York and Chicago, 1895), I:330.
31. Baxter, p. 171.
32. J. Robert Lane, *Connecticut During the Civil War* (Catholic University Press, 1941), p. 229.
33. Zachariah Chandler Papers, Lyman Trumbull to Chandler, Nov. 9, 1862.
34. Ibid. Chandler to Mrs. Chandler, Dec. 10, 1862.
35. Hamilton Fish Papers, Lafayette Foster to Fish, Dec. 16, 1862.
36. Zachariah Chandler Papers, Chandler to Mrs. Chandler, Feb. 4, 7, and 10, 1863.
37. Manton Marble Papers, Clement L. Vallandigham to Marble, Aug. 13, 1863.
38. Guy James Gibson, "Lincoln's League: The Union League Movement in the Civil War" (unpublished Ph.D. thesis, University of Illinois, 1957), p. 121.
39. Thaddeus Stevens Papers, Stevens to Col. S. Stevens, Sept. 5, 1862.
40. Carl Sandburg, *Abraham Lincoln: The War Years* (New York, 1939), III:120.
41. James Welch Patton, *Unionism and Reconstruction in Tennessee, 1860–1869* (University of North Carolina Press, 1934), p. 43.
42. John Hay Diary, Vol. I, July 4, 1864.
43. Thomas G. Belden, "The Salmon P. Chase Family in the Civil War and Reconstruction: A Study in Ambition and Corruption" (unpublished Ph.D. thesis, University of Chicago, 1952), p. 7.
44. Salmon P. Chase Papers, T. Brown to Chase, Jan. 4, 1864.
45. John Sherman Papers, W. D. Bickham to Sherman, March 1, 1864.
46. Andrew D. White, *Autobiography of Andrew Dixon White*, 2 vols. (New York, 1905), I:117.
47. John Russell Young, *Philadelphia Evening Star*, Aug. 22, 1891; Josiah H. Drummond, *Portland Express*, July 16, 1891; Gov. William Stone of Iowa, *Washington Post*, July 20, 1891.
48. Hay Diary, Vol. I, June 5, 1864.
49. Lane, p. 275.
50. Nicolay Papers, Nicolay to Therena Bates, Aug. 21, 1864; Nicolay to John Hay, Aug. 25, 1864.
51. Lincoln Papers, Henry J. Raymond to Lincoln, Aug. 22, 1861.
52. Zachariah Chandler Papers, Chandler to Mrs. Chandler, Aug. 27, 1864.

53. Ibid. Henry Winter Davis to Chandler, Aug. 24, 1864.
54. Charles R. Wilson, "McClellan and the Peace Plank," *American Historical Review*, Vol. 38, No. 1, Oct. 1952, p. 503; George B. McClellan Papers, George T. Curtis to McClellan, Sept. 1, 1864.
55. Edward McPherson Papers, P. E. Sawerwein to McPherson, Oct. 8, 1864.
56. Zachariah Chandler Papers, Chandler to Mrs. Chandler, Sept. 24, 1864; John C. Frémont to Chandler, May 23, 1878.
57. Lincoln Papers, Henry Wilson to Lincoln, Sept. 5, 1864.
58. Paul G. Hubbard, "The Lincoln-McClellan Presidential Election in Illinois" (unpublished Ph.D. thesis, University of Illinois, 1949), p. 135.
59. Kenneth M. Stampp, "The Milligan Case and the Election of 1864 in Indiana," *Mississippi Valley Historical Review*, Vol. 31, No. 1, June 1944, p. 42.
60. Hubbard, p. 200.
61. Munger, p. 434.
62. Washburne Papers, Joe Medill to Washburne, Oct. 18, 1864.

CHAPTER V

1. George W. Julian Journal, *Indiana Magazine of History*, Vol. 11, No. 4, Dec. 1915, p. 334.
2. Ibid. p. 335.
3. Ernest Paul Muller, "Preston King: A Political Biography" (unpublished Ph.D. thesis, Columbia University, 1957), p. 719.
4. Robert F. Durden, "James Shepherd Pike and His Career as a Republican Journalist and Diplomat" (unpublished Ph.D. thesis, Princeton University, 1952), Chap. VI, p. 6.
5. John Bigelow, *Retrospections of an Active Life,* 5 vols. (New York, 1909), III:229.
6. Charles Sumner to F. W. Bird, April 25, 1865 (Edward L. Pierce, *Memoir and Letters of Charles Sumner,* 4 vols., London, 1893, IV:241).
7. George Fort Milton, *The Age of Hate* (New York, 1930), p. 163.
8. Julian Journal, loc. cit. p. 337.
9. *36th Congressional Globe,* Part II, p. 1367.
10. Richard Taylor, *Destruction and Reconstruction: Personal Experiences of the Late War* (Richard B. Harwell, ed., New York, 1955), p. 297.
11. Muller, p. 719.
12. Carl Schurz, *The Reminiscences of Carl Schurz,* 3 vols. (New York, 1907), III:157.
13. Henry L. Dawes Papers, Charles Sumner to Dawes, July 20, 1865.
14. Milton, p. 217.
15. Richard Current, *Old Thad Stevens: A Story of Ambition* (Madison, 1942), p. 213.
16. Willard H. Smith, "The Political Career of Schuyler Colfax to His Election as Vice President in 1868" (unpublished Ph.D. thesis, University of Indiana, 1939), p. 229.
17. Elihu Washburne Papers, James Harlan to Washburne, June 12, 1865.
18. Gideon Welles, *Diary of Gideon Welles,* 3 vols. (Boston and New York, 1911), June 24, 1865, II:322.

19. Murray M. Horowitz, "Ben Butler: The Making of a Radical" (unpublished Ph.D. thesis, Columbia University, 1955), p. 294; Fred Messamore, "John A. Logan: Democrat and Republican" (unpublished Ph.D. thesis, University of Kentucky, 1939), p. 227.

20. Ben L. Wade Papers, Ben Butler to Wade, July 26, 1865.

21. Edwin M. Stanton Papers, Francis Lieber to Stanton, Oct. 31, 1865.

22. Orville H. Browning, *Diary*, 2 vols. (Springfield, Ill., 1925), July 23, 1865, II:39.

23. John Sherman to William T. Sherman, May 16, 1865 (R. S. Thorndike, editor, *The Sherman Letters: Correspondence between General and Senator Sherman from 1837 to 1891*, New York, 1894).

24. Edward McPherson Papers, T. Parsons to McPherson, Nov. 7, 1865.

25. Thurlow W. Barnes, editor, *Memoir of Thurlow Weed* (Boston, 1884), p. 451.

26. Edna M. Colman, *White House Gossip: From Andrew Johnson to Calvin Coolidge* (New York, 1927), p. 33.

27. Shelby M. Cullom, *Fifty Years of Public Service* (Chicago, 1911), p. 144; James A. Garfield Papers, Garfield to B. A. Hinsdale, Dec. 11, 1865, c.c.

28. James W. Neilson, "The Senatorial Career of Shelby Moore Cullom" (unpublished Ph.D. thesis, University of Illinois, 1958), p. 18.

29. William A. Russ, Jr., "Congressional Disfranchisement, 1866–1898" (unpublished Ph.D. thesis, University of Chicago, 1933), p. 11.

30. Johnson Papers, Ransom Balcom to Johnson, Jan. 2, 1866.

31. Charles R. Williams, *Diary and Letters of Rutherford B. Hayes,* 5 vols. (Columbus, 1924), III, Jan. 10, 1866.

32. *39th Congressional Globe,* 1st Session, Part I, p. 746.

33. Howard K. Beale, *The Critical Year: A Study of Andrew Johnson and Reconstruction* (New York, 1930), p. 173.

34. Francis Fessenden, *Life and Public Services of William Pitt Fessenden,* 2 vols. (Boston, 1907), II:21.

35. Charles A. Jellison, "William Pitt Fessenden, Statesman of the Middle Ground" (unpublished Ph.D. thesis, University of Virginia, 1956), p. 355.

36. Manton Marble Papers, P. Ripley to Marble, Feb. 8, 1866.

37. John H. and LaWanda Cox, "Andrew Johnson and His Ghost Writers," *Mississippi Valley Historical Review,* Vol. 48, No. 3, Dec. 1961.

38. Eric McKitrick, *Andrew Johnson and Reconstruction* (Chicago, 1960), pp. 286–7.

39. Welles, *Diary,* Feb. 16, 1866, II:454.

40. Browning, footnote of letter from James R. Dolittle to Orville H. Browning, Oct. 7, 1866, II:93.

41. Dawes Papers, R. A. Chapman to Dawes, Feb. 23, 1866.

42. Gideon Welles Papers, J. R. Hawley to Welles, Feb. 26, 1866.

43. Dawes Papers, Dawes to Mrs. Electa A. Dawes, Feb. 22, 1866.

44. Ibid. Dawes to Mrs. Dawes, Feb. 20, 1866; Joseph Hawley Papers, H. B. Harrison to Hawley, Feb. 23, 1866.

45. Dawes Papers, Dawes to Mrs. Dawes, March 31, 1866.

46. John Sherman to William T. Sherman, late March 1866 (Thorndike, op. cit.).

47. Justin Morrill Papers, B. G. Benedict to Morrill, April 5, 1866.

48. Walter C. Woodward, *The Rise and Early History of Political Parties in Oregon, 1843–1868* (Portland, 1913), p. 246.

49. Johnson Papers, Joseph H. Geiger to James R. Dolittle, Feb. 11, 1866.

50. Ibid. Jacob D. Cox to Johnson, March 2, 1866.

51. William D. Foulke, *Life of Oliver P. Morton,* 2 vols. (Indianapolis and Kansas City, 1899), I:466.
52. Welles, *Diary,* March 9, 1866, II:449.
53. Dawes Papers, Dawes to Mrs. Dawes, April 8, 1866.
54. Fessenden, II:66.
55. Horace White, *The Life of Lyman Trumbull* (Boston, 1913), p. 272; Welles, *Diary,* April 19, 1866, II:489.
56. Dawes Papers, Dawes to Mrs. Dawes, April 8, 1866; Rutherford B. Hayes to Mrs. Hayes, April 8, 1866 (Williams, III).
57. Claude G. Bowers, *The Tragic Era* (Boston, 1929), p. 112.
58. Joseph B. James, "The Framing of the Fourteenth Amendment," *Illinois Studies in the Social Sciences* (Illinois University Press, 1956), 37:137.
59. James Gordon Bennett, *New York Herald,* June 12, 1866.
60. Benjamin B. Kendrick, *The Journal of the Joint Committee of Fifteen on Reconstruction* (New York, Columbia University, 1914), p. 327.
61. Dawes Papers, Dawes to Mrs. Dawes, July 12, 1866.
62. Ibid. Dawes to Mrs. Dawes, July 19, 1866.
63. Browning, June 11, 1866, II:79.
64. Dorothy G. Fowler, *The Cabinet Politician: The Postmaster General 1829–1909* (New York, 1943), p. 133.
65. John Sherman to William T. Sherman, Oct. 26, 1866 (Thorndike, op. cit.).
66. Hugh McCulloch, *Men and Measures of Half a Century* (New York, 1888), p. 392.
67. Martha B. Caldwell, "The Attitude of Kansas Toward Reconstruction of the South" (unpublished Ph.D. thesis, University of Kansas, 1933), p. 44.
68. Dawes Papers, Dawes to Mrs. Dawes, Dec. 7, 1866.
69. Bigelow, IV:45.
70. James, pp. 174–6.
71. Ralph Korngold, *Thaddeus Stevens* (New York, 1955), p. 392.
72. *40th Congressional Globe,* Session 1, pp. 749–50.
73. Hambleton Tapp, "Three Decades of Kentucky Politics, 1870–1900" (unpublished Ph.D. thesis, University of Kentucky, 1950), pp. 7, 32; John R. Lambert, Jr., *Arthur Pue Gorman* (Baton Rouge, 1953), p. 18.
74. William F. Zornow, *Kansas: A History of the Jayhawk State* (Norman, 1957), p. 124.
75. Harold Hyman, "Johnson, Stanton, and Grant: A Reconsideration of the Army's Role in the Events Leading to Impeachment," *American Historical Review,* Vol. 66, No. 1, Oct. 1960, pp. 89–93.
76. Welles, *Diary,* Sept. 17, 1866, II:570.
77. Washburne Papers, J. B. Grinnell to Washburne, Oct. 26, 1867; T. B. Shannon to Washburne, Oct. 27, 1867.
78. *New York Tribune,* Nov. 9, 1867.
79. Jeremiah Black Papers, W. D. Umstead to Black, Sept. 10, 1867.
80. Thaddeus Stevens Papers, Thaddeus Stevens to Colonel S. Stevens, Aug. 3, 1867, c.c.
81. J. R. Hawley Papers, Horace Greeley to Hawley, Nov. 17, 1867.
82. John Russell Young Papers, Schuyler Colfax to Young, Feb. 16, 1868.
83. John Sherman Papers, F. Hassaurek to Sherman, Jan. 27, 1868.
84. Messamore, p. 245.

85. Ibid. p. 244.
86. George W. Julian, *Political Recollections, 1840–1872* (Chicago, 1884), p. 313.
87. Marble Papers, Louisa G. Arnold to Marble, Feb. 2, 1863.
88. Garfield Papers, Garfield to General Irwin McDowell, Feb. 26, 1869, c.c.
89. Ben Butler Papers, Butler to J. H. Chadwick, March 21, 1876, c.c.
90. James G. Blaine, *Twenty Years of Congress: From Lincoln to Garfield,* 2 vols. (Norwich, Conn., 1884), I:376.
91. Smith, p. 286.
92. Young Papers, Colfax to Young, April 28, 1868.
93. Garfield Papers, Garfield to Dr. S. E. Shepherd, May 6, 1868, c.c.
94. Ibid. Garfield to L. W. Hall, May 20, 1868, c.c.; Selig Adler, "The Senatorial Career of George Franklin Edmunds" (unpublished Ph.D. thesis, University of Illinois, 1934), p. 51.
95. W. W. Clapp Papers, Ben Perley Poore to Clapp, April 24, 1868.
96. Welles, *Diary,* III:338,
97. Fessenden, II:205.
98. Edwin M. Stanton Papers, Young to Stanton, May 6, 1868.
99. Milton, p. 553.
100. Horace White, p. 317.
101. Salmon P. Chase Papers, Chase to Mrs. Kate Chase Sprague, May 10, 1868.
102. Caldwell, p. 76.
103. Louis Taylor Merrill, "General Benjamin F. Butler as a Radical Leader During the Administration of President Andrew Johnson" (unpublished Ph.D. thesis, University of Chicago, 1936), p. 173.
104. Caldwell, p. 90.
105. S. Coben, "Northeastern Business and Radical Reconstruction: A Reexamination," *Mississippi Valley Historical Review,* Vol. 46, No. 1, June 1959, p. 68.
106. William Salter, *The Life of James W. Grimes* (New York, 1876), p. 313.
107. William C. Hudson, *Random Recollections of an Old Political Reporter* (New York, 1911), p. 20.
108. Bigelow, Bigelow to W. H. Huntington, July 30, 1868, IV.
109. Chauncey M. Depew, *My Memories of Eighty Years* (New York, 1922), p. 28.
110. James R. Dolittle to Charles A. Dana, April 16, 1880 (*Wisconsin Magazine of History,* VI, 1922).
111. Marble Papers, M. C. Kerr to Marble, Nov. 8, 1868.
112. W. E. Chandler Papers, Norman B. Judd to Chandler, Aug. 18, 1868.
113. Russell K. Nelson, "The Early Life and Congressional Career of Elihu B. Washburne" (unpublished Ph.D. thesis, University of North Dakota, 1953), p. 544.
114. W. E. Chandler Papers, Senator James Harlan to Chandler, June 24, 1868.
115. Ibid. Chandler to Whitelaw Reid, Nov. 1, 1904, c.c.; Leon B. Richardson, *William E. Chandler: Republican* (New York, 1940), p. 98.
116. W. E. Chandler Papers, J. S. Runnells to Chandler, July 25, 1868.
117. James G. Wilson, editor, *General Grant's Letters to a Friend, 1861–1880* (New York, 1897), Grant to Washburne, p. 57.
118. Richardson, p. 95.
119. Harris L. Dante, "Reconstruction Politics in Illinois, 1860–1872" (unpublished Ph.D. thesis, University of Chicago, 1950), p. 227; Chase Papers, Chase to J. Jewett, Aug. 24, 1868, c.c.
120. W. E. Chandler Papers, J. M. Tomeny to Chandler, Dec. 27, 1868.

121. Whitelaw Reid Papers, Jacob Brinkerhoff to Reid, Dec. 24, 1872.
122. J. Borden Harriman, *From Pinafores to Politics* (New York, 1923), p. 217.

CHAPTER VI

1. Harris L. Dante, "Reconstruction Politics in Illinois, 1860–1872" (unpublished Ph.D. thesis, University of Chicago, 1950), p. 323.
2. Charles R. Williams, *Diary and Letters of Rutherford B. Hayes,* 5 vols. (Columbus, Ohio, 1924), *Diary,* July 1, 1870; Charles R. Williams, *The Life of Rutherford Birchard Hayes,* 2 vols. (Boston and New York, 1914), I:419.
3. Whitelaw Reid Papers, Reid to Horace Greeley, Dec. 27, 1868, c.c.
4. W. W. Clapp Papers, E. B. Wright to Clapp, Jan. 24, 1876.
5. John R. Young, *Men and Memories; Personal Reminiscences,* 2 vols. (New York, 1901), I:220.
6. Williams, Hayes *Diary,* April 19, 1888; Williams, Hayes *Life,* II:234.
7. Young, I:216.
8. Henry Adams, *The Education of Henry Adams* (Boston, 1918), p. 264; Dawes Papers, Diary entry of Jan. 4, 1876.
9. Gustave Koerner, *Memoirs, 1809–1896,* 2 vols. (T. J. McCormick, editor, Cedar Rapids, 1909), II: 528; John Sherman, *Recollections of Forty Years in the House, Senate and Cabinet,* 2 vols. (New York and Chicago, 1895), I: 474; Dawes Papers, Dawes to Anna Dawes, June 16, 1870.
10. James A. Garfield Papers, Garfield to J. D. Cox, Feb. 29, 1872, c.c.
11. Koerner, II: 527.
12. Wilson (ed.) *General Grant's Letters to a Friend 1860–1880* (New York, 1897); Grant to Elihu Washburne, May 26, 1872.
13. Garfield Diary, May 31, 1872.
14. W. B. Hesseltine, *Ulysses S. Grant: Politician* (New York, 1935), p. 289; Williams, Hayes *Letters,* III, Rutherford B. Hayes to Sardis Birchard, Sept. 22, 1872; Garfield Diary, Sept. 27, 1872.
15. Earle D. Ross, *The Liberal Republican Movement* (New York, 1919), p. 151.
16. Ben Butler Papers, Blaine to Butler, Nov. 19, 1872.
17. Garfield Diary entries of Oct. 8 and 9, 1872, after victories in October elections.
18. Dawes Papers, Dawes to Anna Dawes, Feb. 26, 28, 1873.
19. Chester L. Barrows, *William M. Evarts: Lawyer, Diplomat, Statesman* (Chapel Hill, 1941), p. 297.
20. John Bigelow, *Retrospections of an Active Life,* 5 vols. (New York, 1909), V: 227.
21. Clapp Papers, B. P. Poore to Clapp, January 15, 1876 to Feb. 29, 1876.
22. J. R. Hawley Papers, Hawley to Mrs. Harriet Hawley, March 15, 1875.
23. Clapp Papers, E. B. Wright to Clapp, Feb. 28, 1876.
24. Garfield Diary, June 5, 1876.
25. W. E. Chandler Papers, James N. Tyner to Jay Gould, Nov. 1, 1876, c.c.
26. Ibid. W. S. Dodge to Chandler, Dec. 19, 1876.
27. James S. Clarkson Papers, J. N. Tyner to Clarkson, Nov. 23, 1884.
28. Sherman, I:558–9.
29. Thomas Jessup Papers, A. C. Janin to Mrs. F. B. Blair, Nov. 21, 1876, c.c.
30. Garfield Papers, Garfield to Hayes, Dec. 13, 1876, c.c.

31. Ibid. Garfield to Hayes, Dec. 18, 1876, c.c.
32. Alfred R. Conkling, *The Life and Letters of Roscoe Conkling, Orator, Statesman, Advocate* (New York, 1889), p. 528.
33. Harry E. Pratt, *David Davis: 1815–1886* (unpublished Ph.D. thesis, University of Illinois, 1930), p. 145–7.
34. Williams, Hayes *Diary*, III, Aug. 5, 1877; Dorothy G. Fowler, *The Cabinet Politician: The Postmaster General, 1829–1909* (New York, 1943), p. 163.
35. Carl Russell Fish, *The Civil Service and Patronage* (New York, 1905), p. 204.
36. Williams, Hayes *Diary*, III, Feb. 14, 1879.
37. Vincent P. DeSantis, *Republicans Face the Southern Question: The New Departure Years, 1877–1897* (Baltimore, 1959), pp. 100–102; Williams, Hayes *Letters*, IV, Hayes to Mrs. B. T. Tanner, Feb. 20, 1883.
38. Garfield Papers, C. E. Henry to Garfield, Feb. 20, 1880.
39. William C. Hudson, *Random Collections of an Old Political Reporter* (New York, 1911), p. 95; John Sherman Papers, W. A. Conoday to Sherman, Feb. 3, 1880.
40. Garfield Diary, March 16, 1875.
41. Ibid. Feb. 11, 1880; April 24, 1880; Thomas M. Nichol, *Chicago Daily News*, Sept. 13, 1887; Robert G. Caldwell, *James A. Garfield: Party Chieftain* (New York, 1931), p. 278.
42. Mary S. Logan, *Reminiscences of a Soldier's Wife: An Autobiography* (New York, 1913), p. 404.
43. Garfield Papers, Garfield to Mrs. Lucretia Garfield, June 4, 1880.
44. Sherman Papers, Sherman to William Dennison, May 31, 1880 c.c.
45. Williams, Hayes *Diary*, II, June 15, 1880.
46. Dawes Papers, Dawes to Mrs. Dawes, June 15, 1880.
47. Smith, II:1009–10.
48. Garfield Diary, Aug. 6 and Aug. 9, 1880.
49. Matthew Josephson, *The Politicos* (New York, 1938), p. 297.
50. L. T. Michener Papers, James N. Tyner to Michener, Sept. 21, 1888.
51. Caldwell, p. 295.
52. Garfield Papers, Garfield to Reid, Aug. 30, 1880, c.c.; Reid Papers, Garfield to Arthur, Aug. 30, 1880, c.c.
53. Wharton Barker Papers, Marshall Jewell to Barker, Sept. 30, 1880.
54. Paul T. Smith, "Indiana's Last October Campaign," *Indiana Magazine of History*, Vol. 19, No. 4, Dec. 1923, p. 341.
55. Garfield Papers, Hinsdale to Garfield, Oct. 9, 1880.
56. Herbert J. Clancy, "The Presidential Election of 1880" (unpublished Ph.D. thesis, Georgetown University, 1949), p. 310.
57. Clancy, p. 345.
58. David S. Muzzey, *James G. Blaine, a Political Idol of Other Days* (New York, 1934), p. 180.
59. Reid Papers, Garfield to Reid, March 30, 1881.
60. Wharton Barker Papers, Morrill to Barker, March 10, 1883.
61. Sherman Papers, C. L. Kurz to Sherman, June 8, 1884.
62. Theodore Roosevelt Letters, Roosevelt to Anna Roosevelt, June 8, 1884.
63. Earl Ray Beck, "The Political Career of Joseph Benson Foraker" (unpublished Ph.D. thesis, Ohio State, 1942), pp. 26–7; Sherman Papers, C. L. Kurz to Sherman, June 8, 1884, and Marcus Hanna to Sherman, June 10, 1884.

64. Sherman Papers, Sherman to Murat Halstead, May 5, 1884, c.c.; Justin Morrill Papers, Morrill to Redfield Procter, April 26, 1884, c.c.
65. Allan Nevins, *The Evening Post: A Century of Journalism* (New York, 1922), p. 459.
66. Butler Papers, Ralph W. Pope to Butler, Aug. 6, 1884.
67. Reid Papers, Blaine to Reid, postscript July 27, 1880.
68. Ibid. Reid to W. W. Phelps, July 24, 1884, c.c.
69. Claude M. Fuess, *Carl Schurz: Reformer, 1829–1906* (New York, 1932), p. 289.
70. Reid Papers, Reid to Blaine, Oct. 18, 1884, c.c.
71. Adler, pp. 250–62.
72. William F. Zornow, *Kansas: A History of the Jayhawk State* (Norman, 1957), p. 195.
73. Hudson, p. 199.
74. Donald B. Chidsey, *The Gentleman from New York: A Life of Roscoe Conkling* (New Haven, 1935), p. 377.
75. Reid Papers, Blaine to Reid, June 14, 1884.
76. Harry W. Baehr, Jr., *The New York Tribune since the Civil War* (New York, 1936), p. 190.
77. Butler Papers, T. E. Major to Butler, July 16, 1884; Butler to W. E. Chandler, Sept. 24, 1884, c.c.
78. Depew, p. 144.
79. John R. Lambert, Jr., *Arthur Pue Gorman* (Baton Rouge, 1953), p. 106.
80. J. S. Clarkson Papers, F. B. Loomis to Clarkson, Nov. 17, 1884 (quotes letter from Blaine to Francis Fessenden, Nov. 17, 1884: "I should have carried New York by 10,000 if the weather had been clear on election day and Dr. Burchard had been doing missionary work in Asia Minor or Cochin China.").
81. Beck, p. 71.
82. Sherman Papers, Sherman to Benjamin Harrison, Sept. 12, 1888, c.c.
83. Benjamin Harrison Papers, Wharton Barker to Harrison, Feb. 5, 1888.
84. Sherman Papers, Sherman to Murat Halstead, April 10, 1888, c.c.; Beck, pp. 106–28; Barker Papers, Barker to Sherman, Jan. 13, 1888, c.c., and Sherman to Barker, Jan. 20, 1888.
85. Sherman Papers, W. H. Bateman to Sherman, June 6, 1888; Harrison Papers, S. B. Elkins to Harrison, Feb. 14, 1888.
86. Harrison Papers, L. T. Michener to D. Halford, May 25, 1888, c.c.
87. Edward A. White, "The Republican Party in National Politics, 1888–1891," (unpublished Ph.D. thesis, University of Wisconsin, 1941), p. 65.
88. Roosevelt Papers, James Clarkson to Roosevelt, Sept. 23, 1904.
89. Reid Papers, Blaine to Reid, Oct. 11, 1887; Jan. 12, 1888; Jan. 26, 1888.
90. Reid Papers, Reid to Hay, March 20, 1888, c.c.
91. Clarkson Papers, S. B. Elkins to Clarkson, May 6, 1888.
92. Edward White, p. 7.
93. Sherman Papers, Hanna to Sherman, June 23, 1888.
94. Edward White, p. 157.
95. *New York World,* June 25, 1888; C. Joseph Bernardo, "The Presidential Election of 1888" (unpublished Ph.D. thesis, Georgetown University, 1949), p. 224.
96. Edward White, pp. 65–6.
97. Ibid. p. 138.
98. Barker Papers, Barker to Benjamin Harrison, October 9, 1888, c.c.

99. Edward White, p. 175.
100. Ibid. p. 247.
101. Barker Papers, Barker to Harrison, July 14, 1888, c.c.; Barker to Levi P. Morton, July 12, 1888, c.c.
102. Ibid. Dr. William Carroll to Barker, Oct. 1, 1888; John Devoy to Barker, Oct. 18, 1888; Edward White, p. 196.
103. Joseph Bernardo, "The Presidential Election of 1888" (unpublished Ph.D. thesis, Georgetown University, 1949), p. 303.
104. Edward White, p. 235.
105. Ibid.
106. Michener Papers, notes on the campaign of 1888.
107. R. C. Buley, "The Campaign of 1888 in Indiana," *Indiana Magazine of History,* Vol. 10, No. 2, June 1914, p. 48.
108. Williams, Hayes *Diary,* IV, Dec. 10, 1890.

CHAPTER VII

1. L. T. Michener Papers, undated memo on Benjamin Harrison; Chauncey M. Depew, *My Memories of Eighty Years* (New York, 1922), p. 133.
2. Wharton Barker Papers, Barker to Benjamin Harrison, Feb. 8, 1889, c.c.
3. Edward A. White, "The Republican Party in National Politics, 1888–1891" (unpublished Ph.D. thesis, University of Wisconsin, 1941), pp. 269–70.
4. Ibid. p. 275.
5. William M. Stewart, *Reminiscences of Senator William M. Stewart of Nevada* (New York, 1908), p. 310.
6. Shelby M. Cullom, *Fifty Years of Public Service* (Chicago, 1911), p. 126.
7. Whitelaw Reid Papers, L. E. Quigg to Reid, May 24, 1892.
8. Michener Papers, J. S. Clarkson to Michener, May 29, 1890.
9. Dorothy G. Fowler, *The Cabinet Politician: The Postmaster General 1829–1909* (New York, 1943), p. 214.
10. Selig Adler, "The Senatorial Career of George Franklin Edmunds" (unpublished Ph.D. thesis, University of Illinois, 1934), pp. 352–3.
11. James W. Neilson, "The Senatorial Career of Shelby Moore Cullom" (unpublished Ph.D. thesis, University of Illinois, 1958), p. 207.
12. George S. Boutwell, *Reminiscences of Sixty Years in Public Affairs,* 2 vols. (New York, 1902), II:155.
13. John Sherman, *Recollections of Forty Years in the House, Senate, and Cabinet,* 2 vols. (New York and Chicago, 1895), II:1071.
14. Adler, p. 338.
15. Reid Papers, Benjamin Harrison to Reid, Sept. 27, 1888.
16. Edward White, p. 386.
17. Elmer Ellis, *Henry Moore Teller: Defender of the West* (Caldwell, 1941), p. 191.
18. Stewart, p. 310.
19. Ibid. p. 299.
20. Michener Papers, memo for Colonel Halford, Feb. 9, 1912, c.c.
21. Reid Papers, Chauncey Depew to Reid, Aug. 30, 1891.
22. Ibid. R. G. Horn to Reid, Nov. 24, 1891.
23. Ibid. Blaine to Whitelaw Reid, Jan. 13, 1892, c.c.

24. Michener Papers, memo to Colonel Halford, Feb. 9, 1912, c.c.
25. Neilson, pp. 215, 220.
26. John Sherman Papers, Sherman to F. F. D. Albery, May 19, 1892, c.c.; Sherman to Frank B. Wiberg, June 7, 1892, c.c.
27. Michener Papers, "Minneapolis Convention: June 7 to 10, 1892."
28. George H. Knoles, *The Presidential Campaign of 1892,* Stanford University Publications: History, Economics, and Political Science, Vol. 5, No. 1, 1942, p. 58.
29. Michener Papers, typewritten notes on the Minneapolis Convention.
30. Malcolm C. Moos, *The Republicans; A History of Their Party* (New York, 1956), p. 192.
31. John Sherman Papers, Marcus Hanna to Sherman, June 14, 1892.
32. Michener Papers, clipping from the *National Republican,* April 21, 1923, "The Republican Party: A Brief History," by Frank P. Litschert.
33. John D. Hicks, *The Populist Revolt* (Minneapolis, 1931), p. 218.
34. Ibid. p. 244.
35. Henry L. Stoddard, *Presidential Sweepstakes* (Francis W. Leary, editor, New York, 1948), p. 117.
36. Carl Henry Chrislock, "The Politics of Protest in Minnesota, 1890–1901, From Populism to Progressivism" (unpublished Ph.D. thesis, University of Minnesota, 1955), p. 180.
37. Barker Papers, Barker to Harrison, Nov. 9, 1892, c.c.
38. William E. Connelley, *The Life of Preston Plumb* (Chicago, 1913), p. 422.
39. James S. Clarkson Papers, Clarkson to Welker Given, Aug. 18, 1894, c.c.
40. John R. Lambert, Jr., *Arthur Pue Gorman* (Baton Rouge, 1953), p. 184.
41. Jeanette P. Nichols, "The Politics and Personalities of Silver Repeal in the United States Senate," *American Historical Review,* Vol. 41, No. 1, Oct. 1935, pp. 30–33.
42. Michener Papers, Harrison to Michener, Aug. 24, 1893.
43. Barker Papers, W. P. Frye to Barker, Dec. 4, 1894.
44. Louis A. Coolidge, *An Old Fashioned Senator: Orville H. Platt of Connecticut* (New York and London, 1910), p. 244.
45. Thomas Richard Ross, *Jonathan Prentiss Dolliver* (Iowa City, 1958), p. 112.
46. Henry Cabot Lodge Papers, Lodge to Henry Blanchard, Nov. 24, 1886, c.c. (Massachusetts Historical Society Library, Boston).
47. Ross, p. 107.
48. Nelson W. Aldrich Papers, W. E. Chandler to Aldrich, Oct. 9, 1893; Michener Papers, Harrison to Michener, Aug. 24, 1893.
49. Francis C. Warren Papers, Warren to E. A. Slick, Jan. 17, 1896, c.c.; Warren to W. E. Gleason, Feb. 25, 1896, c.c. (University of Wyoming Library, Laramie).
50. Lambert, p. 201.
51. Elihu Root Papers, T. Roosevelt to Root, May 21, 1904.
52. Thomas Beer, *Hanna* (New York, 1929), p. 132.
53. Ibid. pp. 215–17.
54. John E. Pixton, "The Early Career of Charles G. Dawes" (unpublished Ph.D. thesis, University of Chicago, 1952), pp. 300–301.
55. Charles G. Dawes, *A Journal of the McKinley Years* (Chicago, 1950), Aug. 27, 1902, p. 319.

56. Tyler Dennett, *John Hay: From Poetry to Politics* (New York, 1934), Hay to Henry Adams, Oct. 20, 1896, p. 178.
57. William McKinley Papers, J. M. Swank to Hanna, Feb. 28, 1896, c.c.
58. Moreton Frewen Papers, E. Wolcott to Frewen, April 10, 1896.
59. Clarkson Papers, Clarkson to Samuel Fessenden, July 19, 1907, c.c.
60. Herbert Croly, *Marcus Alonzo Hanna* (New York, 1919), p. 198.
61. Joseph B. Foraker, *Notes on a Busy Life,* 2 vols. (Cincinnati, 1916), I:464; Joseph Schafer, Jr., "The Presidential Election of 1896" (unpublished Ph.D. thesis, University of Wisconsin, 1941), p. 138.
62. W. E. Chandler Papers, Chandler to Charles H. Grosvenor, June 24, 1896, c.c.
63. William Allen White, *The Autobiography of William Allen White* (New York, 1946), p. 276.
64. Schafer, p. 119.
65. Ibid. p. 287.
66. Paolo E. Coletta, "Bryan, Cleveland, and the Disrupted Democracy, 1890–1896," *Nebraska History,* Vol. 41, No. 1, March 1960, p. 24.
67. Schafer, p. 291.
68. W. E. Chandler Papers, O. H. Platt to Chandler, June 26, 1896.
69. Clarkson Papers, Jonathan P. Dolliver to Clarkson, June 3, 1896.
70. Coolidge, p. 424.
71. John Chamberlain, *Farewell to Reform* (New York, 1932), p. 267.
72. John A. Garraty, *Henry Cabot Lodge: A Biography* (New York, 1953), p. 175.
73. Reid Papers, John Hay to Reid, Aug. 31, 1896.
74. Ibid. Marcus Hanna to Reid, July 6, 1896.
75. William C. Beer Papers, Julius Whiting to Beer, July 18, 1896 (Yale University Library).
76. William McKinley Papers, McKinley to C. A. Boutelle, Aug. 1, 1896, c.c.
77. McKinley Papers, W. M. Osborne to McKinley, Aug. 11, 1896; Clarkson Papers, H. C. McMillan to Clarkson, Sept. 5, 1896.
78. Michener Papers, Rep. John Gear to Michener, July 20, 1896; Clarkson Papers, McMillan to Clarkson, Sept. 5, 1896.
79. Pixton, pp. 120–24.
80. Dawes, p. 97.
81. Henry Watterson Papers, W. B. Haldeman to Watterson, Oct. 9, 1896.
82. Clarkson Papers, McMillan to Clarkson, Sept. 5, 1896.
83. Schafer, p. 303.
84. Beer Papers, Henry W. Seney to Beer, Oct. 29, 1896.
85. Reid Papers, F. B. Loomis to Reid, Oct. 5, 1896.
86. Ibid. Oct. 29, 1896.
87. Margaret Leech, *In the Days of McKinley* (New York, 1899), p. 94.
88. Schafer, p. 397.
89. Justin Morrill Papers, B. W. Morrill to Morrill, June 10, 1896.
90. Raymond L. Flory, "The Political Career of Chester I. Long" (unpublished Ph.D. thesis, University of Kansas, 1955), p. 9.
91. For a different view see: James A. Barnes, "Myths of the Bryan Campaign," *Mississippi Valley Historical Review,* Vol. 34, No. 3, Dec. 1947, p. 391.
92. *New York Times,* Oct. 3, 1896.
93. Gilbert C. Fite, "Republican Strategy and the Farm Vote in the Presidential

Campaign of 1896," *Mississippi Valley Historical Review*, Vol. 54, No. 4, July 1959, pp. 787–806.

94. Republican Campaign Text, 1896, p. 73.
95. Lewis W. Rathgeber, "The Democratic Party in Pennsylvania, 1880–1896" (unpublished Ph.D. thesis, University of Pittsburgh, 1955), p. 348; Chrislock, p. 303.
96. W. E. Chandler Papers, E. A. Wolcott to Chandler, Sept. 25, 1896.
97. Schafer, p. 328.
98. Rathgeber, p. 2.
99. Hambleton Tapp, "Three Decades of Kentucky Politics (1870–1900)" (unpublished Ph.D. thesis, University of Kentucky, 1950), pp. 444–7; Lambert, pp. 242–55; Homer Clevenger, "Missouri Becomes a Doubtful State," *Mississippi Valley Historical Review*, Vol. 29, No. 4, March 1943, pp. 542–52.
100. Leech, p. 136.
101. Reid Papers, Hay to Reid, Jan. 22, 1897.
102. W. E. Chandler Papers, Wolcott to Chandler, Nov. 13, 1896.
103. George F. Kennan, *American Diplomacy, 1900–1950* (University of Chicago Press, 1951), p. 17.
104. Beer, p. 209.
105. Garraty, p. 104, 185.
106. Ellis, pp. 308–12; Coolidge, p. 286.
107. Harry S. New Papers, Charles W. Fairbanks to New, March 6, 1898.
108. Dawes, p. 149.
109. Theodore Roosevelt Papers, Roosevelt to Robert Bacon, April 15, 1898, c.c.; Lodge Papers, S. M. Weld to Lodge, Dec. 21, 1896, John T. Morse to Lodge, April 14, 1898.
110. Coolidge, letter of Platt to William B. Carey, March 23, 1898, p. 270.
111. Leech, p. 172.
112. McKinley Papers, H. C. Lodge to McKinley, March 31, 1898.
113. Coolidge, letter of Platt to John H. Flagg, April 2, 1898, p. 276.
114. Dawes, p. 149.
115. Ibid. p. 149.
116. Dawes, p. 152.
117. Roosevelt Papers, Roosevelt to Bacon, April 8, 1898, c.c.
118. W. E. Chandler Papers, Chandler to James H. Ross, December 23, 1898, c.c.
119. Coolidge, p. 289.
120. Leech, p. 544.
121. Roosevelt Papers, Lemuel Quigg to Roosevelt, May 16, 1913.
122. Leech, p. 374.
123. Roosevelt Papers, Roosevelt to H. C. Lodge, Dec. 11, 1899, c.c.
124. Ibid. Feb. 3, 1900, c.c.
125. Dennett, p. 340.
126. Beer, p. 225.
127. Roosevelt Papers, Roosevelt to Seth Low, June 23, 1900, c.c.
128. Croly, p. 330.
129. Ibid. pp. 304–5.
130. W. E. Chandler Papers, Chandler to P. E. Dow, Aug. 17, 1899, c.c.
131. Reid Papers, W. A. White, *Boston Globe*, Nov. 4, 1900 (clipping).

CHAPTER VIII

1. Herman H. Kohlsaat, *From McKinley to Harding; Personal Recollections of Our Presidents* (New York and London, 1923), p. 99.
2. Mark Sullivan, *Our Times,* 6 vols. (New York, 1935), I:98.
3. Theodore Roosevelt Papers, Roosevelt to Bellamy Storer, April 17, 1901, c.c.
4. Ibid. Roosevelt to Charles D. Willard, April 28, 1911, c.c.
5. Ibid. Roosevelt to C. S. Rice, July 3, 1901, c.c.
6. Roosevelt Papers, Roosevelt to P. C. Knox, Nov. 10, 1904, c.c.
7. E. R. Lewis, *A History of American Political Thought from the Civil War to the World War* (New York, 1937), p. 323.
8. Roosevelt Letters, Roosevelt to Ray Stannard Baker, Nov. 20, 1905, c.c.
9. Elting E. Morison, editor, *Letters of Theodore Roosevelt,* 8 vols. (Cambridge, 1951), VI:1560, Appendix II.
10. Roosevelt Papers, Roosevelt to John M. Palmer, Aug. 9, 1900, c.c.
11. A. Kazin, *On Native Grounds* (New York, 1942), p. 103.
12. Roosevelt Papers, Roosevelt to Lyman Abbott, June 17, 1908, c.c.
13. Elihu Root Papers, Root to Henry C. Lodge, Sept. 29, 1911, c.c.
14. Roosevelt Papers, Roosevelt to Anna Roosevelt, Jan. 30, 1887.
15. William R. Gwinn, "Uncle Joe Cannon: A History of the Rise and Fall of Insurgency" (unpublished Ph.D. thesis, University of Notre Dame, 1953), pp. 237–8.
16. Whitelaw Reid Papers, S. B. Elkins to Reid, Feb. 18, 1904.
17. Francis C. Warren Papers, Warren to Willis Van Deventer, April 29, 1896, c.c.
18. Ibid. Warren to W. E. Chaplin, April 22, 1910, c.c.
19. *Minneapolis Journal,* April 14, 1903.
20. Roosevelt Papers, Roosevelt to H. C. Lodge, Aug. 20, 1901, c.c.
21. William Allen White, *The Autobiography of William Allen White* (New York, 1946), p. 339.
22. James S. Clarkson Papers, Clarkson to L. S. J. Hunt, Nov. 17, 1903, c.c.
23. Ibid. Clarkson to L. T. Michener, Dec. 19, 1903, c.c.; Clarkson to George B. Cox, May 27, 1903, c.c.
24. Root Papers, Hanna to Root, Aug. 8, 1903.
25. Clarkson Papers, Clarkson to Hunt, October 19, 1903, c.c.
26. Ibid. Clarkson to Hunt, Oct. 19, 1903, c.c.; John R. Lambert, Jr., *Arthur Pue Gorman* (Baton Rouge, 1953), p. 310.
27. Charles G. Dawes, *A Journal of the McKinley Years* (Chicago, 1950), p. 361.
28. Root Papers, Root to J. S. L. Strachey, March 23, 1904, c.c.
29. Ibid. Root to Roosevelt, June 13, 1904, c.c.
30. Thomas H. Carter Papers, Carter to John Carter, July 8, 1904, c.c.
31. Clarkson Papers, Clarkson to Hunt, Oct. 1, 1904, c.c.
32. Leland Sage, *William Boyd Allison: A Study in Practical Politics* (Iowa City, 1956), p. 303.
33. Ibid. pp. 302–4.
34. Gwinn, p. 148.
35. Roosevelt Papers, Roosevelt to Lyman Abbott, June 18, 1906, c.c.
36. George E. Mowrey, *The California Progressives* (Berkeley, 1951), pp. 87–9;

Calvin P. Armin, "Coe I. Crawford and the Progressive Movement in South Dakota" (unpublished Ph.D. thesis, University of Colorado, 1957), p. 98.

37. Thomas Richard Ross, *Jonathan Prentiss Dolliver* (Iowa City, 1958), p. 141; Armin, pp. 68–70; Albert H. Pike, Jr., "Jonathan Bourne, Jr., Progressive" (unpublished Ph.D. thesis, University of Oregon, 1957), pp. 43–4, 51–2; Raymond L. Flory, "The Political Career of Chester I. Long" (unpublished Ph.D. thesis, University of Kansas, 1955), pp. 126–32, 149–54; M. C. McKenna, "The Early Career of William E. Borah, 1865–1917" (unpublished Ph.D. thesis, Columbia University, 1953), p. 63; Robert S. Maxwell, *La Follette and the Rise of the Progressives in Wisconsin* (Madison, 1956), pp. 1–17.

38. Ross, p. 155.

39. Ibid. p. 141.

40. Flory, p. 126.

41. Ibid. p. 149.

42. McKenna, p. 73.

43. Maxwell, pp. 11–17.

44. Ibid. 175–94; Nils P. Haugen, "Pioneer and Political Reminiscences," *Wisconsin Magazine of History*, Vol. 12, No. 3, pp. 279–80, 388.

45. Maxwell, p. 71.

46. J. Borden Harriman, *From Pinafores to Politics* (New York, 1923), p. 187.

47. Roosevelt Papers, Roosevelt to Lodge, May 31, 1911, c.c.

48. Spooner Papers, Spooner to E. H. Abbott, Nov. 29, 1905, c.c.; Spooner to Charles Nagel, June 14, 1906, c.c.

49. Spooner Papers, Spooner to J. W. McCormick, June 5, 1906, c.c.

50. Flory, p. 126.

51. Walter Johnson, "William Allen White: Country Editor, 1897–1914," *Kansas Historical Quarterly*, Vol. 15, No. 1, Feb. 1947, p. 2.

52. Flory, p. 164.

53. Ibid. p. 164.

54. Ibid. p. 173.

55. Ibid. p. 174.

56. Ross, pp. 221–8.

57. Roosevelt Papers, Roosevelt to Lincoln Steffens, June 5, 1908, c.c.; Roosevelt to William Allen White, July 31, 1906, c.c.; Roosevelt to Kermit Roosevelt, May 30, 1908, c.c.

CHAPTER IX

1. Theodore Roosevelt Papers, Roosevelt to William Howard Taft, June 15, 1907, c.c.

2. C. J. Bonaparte Papers, H. C. Gauss to Bonaparte, Jan. 15, 1913.

3. Robert J. Lee, "The Conventions that Nominated the Presidents, 1896–1944" (unpublished Ph.D. thesis, University of Southern California, 1949), p. 43.

4. Edward A. Hornig, "The Presidential Election of 1908" (unpublished Ph.D. thesis, Stanford University, 1954), p. 156.

5. Roosevelt Papers, Roosevelt to Taft, Sept. 5, 1908, c.c.

6. William Howard Taft Papers, Taft to Charles F. Brocker, Sept. 12, 1908, c.c.; Roosevelt Papers, Roosevelt to Taft, Oct. 12, 1908, c.c.

7. Francis C. Warren Papers, Warren to Messrs. Dewey, Gould & Co., Sept. 2, 1908, c.c.
8. Whitelaw Reid Papers, S. B. Elkins to Reid, Jan. 17, 1909.
9. Kenneth W. Hechler, *Insurgency: Personalities and Politics of the Taft Era* (New York, 1940), p. 53.
10. Joseph L. Bristow Papers, Bristow to Harold T. Chase, March 15, 1909, c.c. (Kansas Historical Society Library, Topeka).
11. Ibid. Bristow to Frank Bristow, March 18, 1909, c.c.; Bristow to C. B. Kirtland, March 20, 1909, c.c.
12. Helen J. Poulton, "The Progressive Movement in Oregon" (unpublished Ph.D. thesis, University of Oregon, 1949), p. 93.
13. Bristow Papers, Bristow to W. Jettmer, April 20, 1909, c.c.
14. Calvin P. Armin, "Coe I. Crawford and the Progressive Movement in South Dakota" (unpublished Ph.D. thesis, University of Colorado, 1957), p. 206.
15. *Congressional Record,* XLIV, p. 1712, May 4, 1909; XLIV, p. 2943, June 8, 1909.
16. Bristow Papers, Bristow to H. T. Chase, May 22, 1909, c.c.
17. Ibid. Bristow to Fred C. Trigg, March 20, 1909, c.c.
18. Ibid. Bristow to Harold T. Chase, June 19, 1909, c.c.
19. Thomas H. Carter Papers, Carter to Mrs. E. L. Carter, July 27, 1909; Carter to Nelson W. Aldrich, July 26, 1909, c.c.
20. Bristow Papers, Bristow to Albert B. Cummins, Aug. 28, 1909, c.c.; Miles Poindexter Papers, Poindexter to John E. Lathrop, Aug. 26, 1909, c.c. (University of Virginia Library).
21. Bristow Papers, Bristow to Col. W. R. Nelson, Aug. 20, 1909, c.c.
22. Ibid. Albert Beveridge to Bristow, Sept. 25, 1909; Cummins to Bristow, Sept. 25, 1909.
23. William R. Gwinn, "Uncle Joe Cannon: A History of the Rise and Fall of Insurgency" (unpublished Ph.D. thesis, University of Notre Dame, 1953), p. 266.
24. Bristow Papers, Bristow to Chase, March 26, 1909, c.c.; Bristow to Fred S. Jackson, Dec. 6, 1909, c.c.
25. Taft Papers, Taft to Otto Bannard, Dec. 20 1909, c.c.
26. Gwinn, p. 266.
27. Bristow Papers, Cummins to Bristow, Sept. 25, 1909.
28. Ibid. Bristow to Chase, Feb. 12, 1910, c.c.; Bristow to Henry J. Allen, June 25, 1910, c.c.
29. Henry C. Lodge Papers, Lodge to W. Sturgis Bigelow, March 25, 1910, c.c.
30. Carter Papers, S. Jordan to Carter, Jan. 29, 1910; Carter to Jordan, Feb. 7, 1910, c.c.; J. B. Collins to Carter, June 30, 1910; J. H. Harris to Carter, March 10, 1910; Mark Sullivan to Carter, Sept. 16, 1910.
31. Reid Papers, W. H. Taft to Reid, April 17, 1910; Poindexter Papers, Poindexter to W. M. Scott, Jan. 3, 1910, c.c.
32. Reid Papers, C. D. Norton to Reid, Sept. 13, 1910.
33. George E. Mowrey, *The California Progressives* (Berkeley, 1951), pp. 119–20.
34. Henry F. Pringle, *The Life and Times of W. H. Taft,* 2 vols. (New York, 1939), I:318–20; Mowrey, p. 121; Mark Sullivan, *Our Times* (New York, 1935), IV:296; Bonaparte Papers, H. C. Gauss to Bonaparte, Jan. 19, 1910.
35. Henry C. Lodge Papers, Lodge to C. G. Washburne, July 11, 1923, c.c.
36. *Washington Post,* March 18, 1912 (reprinted from the *New York Sun*).

37. Lawrence F. Abbott (ed.), *The Letters of Archie Butt,* 2 vols. (New York, 1924), I:271–2, Archie Butt to Clara Butt, Jan. 5, 1909.

38. Belle C. La Follette and Fola La Follette, *Robert M. La Follette, June 14, 1855-June 18, 1925,* 2 vols. (New York, 1953), I:302; Bristow Papers, Bristow to Cummins, July 11, 1910, c.c.

39. Ibid. Bristow to Jonathan Bourne, July 6, 1910, c.c.

40. Amos Pinchot Papers, Gifford Pinchot to Amos Pinchot, July 14, 1910.

41. Chester I. Long Papers, Long to Morton Albaugh, Oct. 31, 1910, c.c.; Claude M. Fuess, "Political Episode: Henry L. Stimson and the New York Campaign of 1910," *Proceedings of the Massachusetts Historical Society,* Vol. 68, Nov. 1945, pp. 398–401.

42. Bonaparte Papers, H. C. Gauss to Bonaparte, Nov. 19, 1910.

43. Amos Pinchot Papers, James R. Garfield to Pinchot, Sept. 28, 1911; Pinchot to T. R. Shipp, Oct. 10, 1911, c.c.

44. Roosevelt Papers, Roosevelt to H. C. Lodge, July 19, 1908, c.c.

45. Ibid. Roosevelt to Trevelyan, Nov. 6, 1908, c.c.; Elting E. Morison, ed., *Letters of Theodore Roosevelt,* 8 vols. (Cambridge, 1951), Vol. VII, Robert Grant to James Ford Rhodes, March 22, 1912.

46. Roosevelt Papers, Roosevelt to Lodge, Dec. 13, 1911, c.c.; Pinchot Papers, Amos Pinchot to Hiram Johnson, March 30, 1912, c.c.

47. Pinchot Papers, Pinchot to Overton W. Price, Feb. 17, 1912 c.c.; Pinchot to Ickes, Jan. 27, 1912, c.c.

48. George H. Lobdell, "A Biography of Frank Knox" (unpublished Ph.D. thesis, University of Illinois, 1954), p. 105.

49. Roosevelt Papers, Roosevelt to William L. Ward, Jan. 9, 1912, c.c.

50. Phillip C. Jessup, *Elihu Root,* 2 vols. (New York, 1938), II:173.

51. Worthington C. Ford, editor, *Letters of Henry Adams,* 2 vols. (Boston, 1930 and 1938), Vol. II, Henry Adams to Elizabeth Cameron, Feb. 25, 1912.

52. John A. Garraty, *Henry Cabot Lodge: A Biography* (New York, 1953), p. 285; Elihu Root Papers, Root to W. H .Taft, Oct. 14, 1910, c.c.

53. Roosevelt Papers, Roosevelt to John C. O'Loughlin, Feb. 8, 1912.

54. Roosevelt Papers, Robert Grant to James Ford Rhodes, March 22, 1912 (Morison, ed., Vol. VII).

55. Lodge Papers, Lodge to G. B. Washburn, July 11, 1923, c.c.; Garraty, p. 287; Warren Papers, Warren to Messrs. Dewey, Gould, & Co., Feb. 29, 1912, c.c.; Bonaparte Papers, Bonaparte to H. C. Gauss, March 16, 1912, c.c.; McKenna, p. 245.

56. *New York Times,* May 5, 1912; see also Pringle, II:783.

57. Bonaparte Papers, Bonaparte to Gauss, July 3, 1912, c.c.

58. Clifford B. Liljekvist, "Senator Hiram Johnson" (unpublished Ph.D. thesis, University of Southern California, 1935), p. 86.

59. Chester Rowell Papers, Rowell to A. B. Hart, Feb. 18, 1932, c.c. (Bancroft Library, University of California).

60. Warren Papers, Warren to Fred Warren, June 10, 1912, c.c.; Warren to C. W. Burdick, June 29, 1912, c.c.

61. Walter Davenport, *Power and Glory, The Life of Boies Penrose* (New York, 1931), p. 191.

62. Amos Pinchot Papers, Pinchot to Hiram Johnson, July 18, 1912, c.c.

63. Donald R. Richberg, *Tents of the Mighty* (New York and Chicago, 1930), p. 38.

64. Arthur Ruhl, "The Bull Moose Call," *Collier's*, Aug. 24, 1912, p. 20.
65. Armin, p. 277; Mowrey, p. 188.
66. James R. Scales, "The Political History of Oklahoma, 1907–1949" (unpublished Ph.D. thesis, University of Oklahoma, 1949), p. 146.
67. Straetz, pp. 299–309.
68. Republican Campaign Text Book of 1912.
69. Root Papers, Root to Robert Bacon, Sept. 11, 1912, c.c.
70. Ibid. Root to Bacon, March 9, 1912, c.c.

CHAPTER X

1. Chester I. Long Papers, Long to Carl C. Marshall, Nov. 29, 1912, c.c.
2. Meyer Lissner Papers, Hiram Johnson to Lissner, Nov. 29, 1912; Amos Pinchot Papers, Harold Ickes to Pinchot, Dec. 2, 1912.
3. Theodore Roosevelt Papers, Roosevelt to Gifford Pinchot, Nov. 13, 1912, c.c.
4. Ibid. Roosevelt to Hiram Johnson, Jan. 28, 1913, c.c.
5. Miles Poindexter Papers, Poindexter to O. H. Martin, Sept. 15, 1913, c.c.
6. M. C. McKenna, "The Early Career of William E. Borah, 1865–1917" (unpublished Ph.D. thesis, Columbia University, 1953), pp. 336–7.
7. Bristow Papers, Bristow to George W. Marble, June 19, 1917, c.c.
8. Philander C. Knox Papers, W. H. Taft to Knox, May 16, 1914.
9. Helen J. Poulton, "The Progressive Movement in Oregon" (unpublished Ph.D. thesis, University of Oregon, 1949), p. 166.
10. William Allen White Papers, White to Roosevelt, April 6, 1916 c.c.
11. Borah Papers, J. H. Gipson to Borah, June 24, 1916; Gifford Pinchot Papers, John J. Parker to Pinchot, July 7, 1916.
12. Amos Pinchot Papers, William Kent to Pinchot, July 26, 1916.
13. Bristow Papers, Bristow to Jonathan Bourne, Sept. 12, 1916, c.c.
14. Henry C. Lodge Papers, Lodge to Charles Evans Hughes, Aug. 3, 1916, c.c.
15. Francis C. Warren Papers, Warren to Patrick Sullivan, Oct. 7, 1916, c.c.
16. Miles W. Dunnington, "Senator Thomas J. Walsh, Independent Democrat in the Wilson Years" (unpublished Ph.D. thesis, University of Chicago, 1940), p. 156.
17. Warren Papers, Warren to Sullivan, Oct. 16, 1916, c.c.
18. Keith A. Murray, "Republican Party Politics in Washington During the Progressive Era" (unpublished Ph.D. thesis, University of Washington, 1946), pp. 273–5.
19. Thomas J. Walsh Papers, William J. Bryan to Walsh, Oct. 6, 1916.
20. Lodge Papers, Reynolds to Lodge, Oct. 17, 1916.
21. Gerald E. Ridinger, "The Political Career of Frank B. Willis" (unpublished Ph.D. thesis, Ohio State, 1957), pp. 74–80.
22. Poindexter Papers, Theodore Roosevelt to Poindexter, Nov. 16, 1918.
23. Lodge Papers, Lodge to Sturgis Bigelow, April 5, 1916. c.c.
24. Edward M. House Diary, July 9, 1918.
25. Lodge Papers, Lodge to Bigelow, April 30, 1917, c.c.
26. Hiram W. Johnson Papers, Johnson to C. K. McClatchy, Sept. 17, 1917, c.c.; May 8, 1918, c.c. (Bancroft Library, University of California).
27. Johnson Papers, Johnson to Meyer Lissner, March 15, 1918, c.c.; Poindexter Papers, Horace Kimball to Poindexter, April 10, 1918.

28. Seward W. Livemore, "The Congressional Elections of 1918," *Mississippi Valley Historical Review,* Vol. 35, No. 1, June 1948, p. 32.
29. Thomas J. Walsh Papers, Walsh to William C. Niblack, Nov. 11, 1918, c.c.
30. Lodge Papers, Will H. Hays, to Lodge, Sept. 25, 1918.
31. Ibid. Lodge to Hays, Sept. 14 ,1918, c.c.; Lodge to Hays, Sept. 27, 1918, c.c.
32. Walsh Papers, T. J. Nolan to Walsh, Oct. 19, 1918.
33. Johnson Papers, Johnson to McClatchy, Jan. 19, 1918, c.c.; Feb. 13, 1918.
34. Roosevelt Papers, Roosevelt to Selden Spencer, Oct. 15, 1918, c.c.; Roosevelt to Ogden Reid, Jan. 1, 1919, c.c.
35. Ibid. Hiram Johnson to Roosevelt, Dec. 27, 1918.
36. *New York Sun,* Jan. 4, 1919.
37. Poindexter Papers, Poindexter to W. H. Cowles, Jan. 29, 1919, c.c.
38. Lodge Papers, Lodge to W. Sturgis Bigelow, Jan. 29, 1919, c.c.
39. William Howard Taft Papers, Taft to Horace Taft, Dec. 31, 1918, c.c.
40. Lodge Papers, Lodge to Bigelow, Feb. 13, 1919, c.c.
41. Ibid. Lodge to Calvin Coolidge, Feb. 24, 1919, c.c.; Lodge to James M. Beck, Feb. 22, 1919, c.c.
42. Ibid. Lodge to Bigelow, Feb. 27, 1919, c.c.
43. Borah Papers, Charles F. Borah to Borah, Feb. 27, 1919.
44. Taft Papers, Judge J. B. Woodward to Taft, March 4, 1919; W. H. P. Faunce to Taft, March 6, 1919.
45. Borah Papers, Albert J. Beveridge to Borah, Jan. 26, 1919.
46. Warren Papers, Warren to John J. Pershing, March 22, 1919, c.c.
47. Edward M. House Diary, Sept. 8, 1918 (Yale University Library).
48. Borah Papers, E. H. Dewey to Borah, April 23, 1919.
49. Johnson Papers, Johnson to McClatchy, Feb. 24, 1919, c.c.
50. Ibid. Johnson to Meyer Lissner, March 14, 1919, c.c.
51. *Literary Digest,* April 5, 1919.
52. Johnson Papers, Johnson to McClatchy, April 25, 1919, c.c.
53. Taft Papers, Gus J. Karger to Taft, April 16, 1919; Horace Taft to Taft, April 23, 1919.
54. Lodge Papers, Lodge to James M. Beck, February 26, 1920, c.c.
55. Roosevelt Papers, Henry C. Lodge to Roosevelt, Dec. 9, 1918.
56. House Diary, Nov. 2, 1916.
57. John A. Garraty, *Henry Cabot Lodge: A Biography* (New York, 1953), p. 362.
58. Lodge Papers, Lodge to J. T. Williams, Jr., May 19, 1919, c.c.
59. Taft Papers, Gus Karger to Taft, May 27, 1919.
60. Johnson Papers, Johnson to McClatchy, July 16, 1919, c.c.; Taft Papers, Karger to Taft, June 14, 1919; July 2, 1919; July 31, 1919; Sept. 24, 1919.
61. Garraty, p. 350; Lodge to Beveridge, Feb. 27, 1919.
62. Taft Papers, Karger to Taft, June 5, 1919.
63. Chester Rowell Papers, Rowell to Meyer Lissner, April 17, 1919, c.c. (Bancroft Library, University of California).
64. Taft Papers, Karger to Taft, May 27, 1919.
65. *Literary Digest,* June 28, 1919.
66. Lodge Papers, Lodge to Albert Beveridge, July 12, 1919, c.c.; Moreton Frewen Papers, Henry C. Lodge to Frewen, Sept. 10, 1919.
67. Taft Papers, Taft to A. Lawrence Lowell, Oct. 5, 1919, c.c.; Karger to Taft, Sept. 8, 1919.

68. Root Papers, Le Baron Colt to Root, Sept. 2, 1919.
69. Taft Papers, Taft to Karger, Sept. 8, 1919, c.c.
70. Root Papers, Henry Cabot Lodge to Root, Sept. 29, 1919.
71. Taft Papers, Taft to Caspar S. Yost, Sept. 16, 1919, c.c.; Karger to Taft, Sept. 24, 1919.
72. Taft Papers, Taft to Mrs. William A. Edwards, Sept. 16, 1919.
73. Meyer Lissner Papers, Lissner to Will H. Hays, Sept. 23, 1919, c.c.
74. Lodge Papers, Lodge to John W. Weeks, Sept. 22, 1919, c.c.; Warren Papers, Warren to John W. Weeks, Sept. 25, 1919, c.c.
75. Root Papers, Lodge to Root, Sept. 29, 1919.
76. Lodge Papers, Lodge to Brooks Adams, Dec. 17, 1919, c.c.
77. Ibid. Lodge to J. T. Williams, Jr., Dec. 20, 1919, c.c.
78. Taft Papers, Taft to Charles McNary, Dec. 22, 1919, c.c.
79. Poindexter Papers, Charles N. Thompson to Poindexter, Oct. 17, 1919; Borah Papers, George W. Hunt to Borah, Nov. 10, 1919.
80. Walsh Papers, A. E. Spriggs to Walsh, Jan. 28, 1920.
81. Will H. Hays Papers, Frederick S. Peck to Hays, Jan. 1, 1920; W. H. Highland to Hays, Feb. 4, 1920 (Indiana State Library, Indianapolis).
82. Wesley M. Bagby, *The Road to Normalcy: The Presidential Campaign and the Election of 1920* (Baltimore, 1962), pp. 94–5.
83. Ibid. p. 264.
84. Walsh Papers, Walsh to Governor S. V. Stewart, Feb. 26, 1920, c.c.
85. Lodge Papers, Lodge to James M. Beck, March 22, 1920, c.c.; Garraty, p. 390.
86. Hays Papers, Hays to Mrs. Maude Wetmore, Jan. 3, 1920, c.c.
87. Ibid. Hays to R. K. Hynicka, March 19, 1920, c.c.
88. Taft Papers, William Howard Taft to Horace Taft, Jan. 12, 1920, c.c.; Bagby, pp. 13–15.
89. Hays Papers, Harry S. New to Hays, April 8, 1920.
90. *New York Times,* Feb. 21, 1920.
91. Root Papers, Lodge to Root, May 17, 1920; Lodge Papers, Lodge to Mrs. Douglas Robinson, June 19, 1920, c.c.
92. Bagby, pp. 200–202.
93. Knox Papers, Warren G. Harding to Knox, Sept. 25, 1920.
94. Walsh Papers, John Clelinpet to Walsh, Sept. 27, 1920; James E. Murray to Walsh, June 7, 1920; Poindexter Papers, Joseph C. Manning to Poindexter, June 22, 1920; Lodge Papers, Harry S. New to Lodge, Sept. 24, 1920; Bagby, p. 574.
95. James R. Scales, "The Political History of Oklahoma, 1907–1949" (unpublished Ph.D. thesis, University of Oklahoma, 1949), p. 215.
96. Lodge Papers, Lodge to John T. Williams, April 21, 1921, c.c.

CHAPTER XI

1. Lodge Papers, L. A. Coolidge to Lodge, Feb. 24, 1921.
2. Diary of Charles Hamlin, March 22, 1921.
3. Lodge Papers, Lodge to Charles G. Washburn, April 24, 1922.
4. Guy B. Hathorn, "The Political Career of C. Bascom Slemp" (unpublished Ph.D. thesis, Duke University, 1950), pp. 176–7.
5. Johnson Papers, Johnson to McClatchy, June 12, 1926.

6. Johnson Papers, Johnson to Fremont Older, Jan. 17, 1921, c.c.; Johnson to Carlos McClatchy, April 27, 1922, c.c.
7. Johnson Papers, Johnson to C. K. McClatchy, Dec. 8, 1922, c.c.
8. K. Schriftgeisser, *This Was Normalcy* (Boston, 1948), p. 205.
9. J. L. Bates, "Senator Walsh of Montana 1918–1924: A Liberal Under Pressure" (unpublished Ph.D. thesis, University of North Carolina, 1952), pp. 330–35.
10. David H. Stratton, "Albert B. Fall and the Teapot Dome" (unpublished Ph.D. thesis, University of Colorado, 1955), p. 227.
11. Ibid. p. 281.
12. Borah Papers, Borah to Frank Wyman, Feb. 29, 1924.
13. Lodge Papers, Lodge to W. Sturgis Bigelow, Feb. 5, 1924.
14. McNary Papers, McNary to Louis Lachmund, Feb. 15, 1924.
15. Hathorn, pp. 211–12.
16. Hathorn, pp. 64–7, 171–8.
17. Ibid. p. 197.
18. Johnson Papers, Johnson to Wm. Wrigley, Jr., Dec. 13, 1923, c.c.
19. Herbert Hoover, *The Memoirs of Herbert Hoover,* 2 vols. (New York, 1952), I:190.
20. James Sheffield Papers, Dewey Hilles to Sheffield, April 12, 1929 (Yale University Library).
21. Johnson Papers to McClatchy, June 22, 1926, c.c. Hoover, I:190.
22. Hays Papers, typed transcript of Hoover statement before Sub Committee of Manufactures in U.S. Senate, January 3, 1918.
23. G. Wayne Smith, *Nathan Goff Jr: A Biography with Some Account of Guy Despard Goff and Brazilla Carroll Reese* (Charleston, 1959), p. 326.
24. S. C. Deskins, "The Presidential Election of 1928 in North Carolina" (unpublished Ph.D. thesis, University of North Carolina, 1944), p. 55.
25. Hathorn, p. 253.
26. Republican Campaign Textbook, 1928, p. 230.
27. Deskins, p. 95.
28. Ibid. p. 103.
29. House Papers, Thomas W. Gregory to House, Nov. 5, 1928.
30. Borah Papers, R. W. Rainey to Borah, Nov. 12, 1928.
31. Harold F. Gosnell, *Negro Politicians: The Rise of Negro Politics in Chicago* (Chicago, 1935), p. 30.
32. Gilbert C. Fite, "The Agricultural Issue in the Presidential Campaign of 1928," *Mississippi Valley Historical Review,* Vol. 37, No. 4, p. 669.
33. Howard Zinn, "Fiorello La Guardia in Congress" (unpublished Ph.D. thesis, Columbia University, 1957), p. 323.
34. Johnson Papers, Johnson to Charles McNary, July 15, 1931, c.c.
35. *Literary Digest,* Jan. 24, 1931.
36. Walsh Papers, J. T. Carroll to Walsh, Oct. 13, 1931.
37. George W. Norris Papers, Jan. 1932; Johnson Papers, Johnson to C. K. McClatchy, Feb. 21, 1932.
38. Ibid. Johnson to George O. MacGregor July 1, 1931.
39. Ibid. Johnson to C. K. McClatchy, July 17, 1932, c.c.
40. Borah Papers, Harold Ickes to Borah, March 14, 1932; Johnson Papers, Johnson to C. K. McClatchy, Feb. 2, 1932, c.c.; Harold L. Ickes, *The Autobiography of a Curmudgeon* (New York 1943), p. 253.
41. Sheffield Papers, J. G. Harbord to Sheffield, June 28, 1932.

42. Johnson Papers, Johnson to C. K. McClatchy, Feb. 14, 1932, c.c.; April 15, 1932, c.c.
43. Ibid. Johnson to C. K. McClatchy, Dec. 4, 1932, c.c.
44. Borah Papers, Borah to R. P. Parry, Nov. 14, 1932, c.c.; Charles McNary Papers, McNary to Mrs. W. T. Stolz, Nov. 10, 1932, c.c.

CHAPTER XII

1. Frederick Rudolph, "The American Liberty League, 1934–1940," *American Historical Review*, Vol. 56, No. 1, Nov. 1950, p. 19.
2. *Literary Digest,* Feb. 24, 1934.
3. Charles L. McNary Papers, McNary to John H. McNary, May 8, 1935, c.c.; May 16, 1935, c.c.
4. Francis V. Keesling Papers, Keesling to Orr M. Chenowith, Nov. 21, 1935, c.c. (Stanford University Library).
5. Landon Papers, Landon to R. O. Deming, Aug. 14, 1935, c.c.; Landon to Stanley High, Sept. 17, 1935, c.c.; Herbert L. Bodman to Landon, March 3, 1936.
6. Chester Rowell Papers, Rowell to Myrtle (niece), June 11, 1936.
7. Landon Papers, Landon to William E. Borah, Aug. 3, 1936, c.c. (Kansas State Historical Society, Topeka).
8. Ibid. Landon to John Hamilton, Aug. 7, 1936, c.c.; Landon to Raymond Moley, Nov. 14, 1940, c.c.
9. Ibid. Blanche M. Tice to Landon, Nov. 8, 1936.
10. Ibid. Carl M. Starr to W. Mayberry, Oct. 14, 1936, c.c.; J. D. Rogers to Landon, Aug. 18, 1936.
11. Ibid. Landon to C. E. Randall, Aug. 20, 1936, c.c.; Landon to Amelia Schweitzer, Oct. 21, 1936, c.c.
12. Ibid. Francis Brown to Landon, April 30, 1936.
13. Arthur Capper Papers, copy of radio broadcast, Nov. 3, 1936 (Kansas State Historical Society, Topeka).
14. Walter K. Roberts, "The Political Career of Charles L. McNary" (unpublished Ph.D. thesis, University of North Carolina, 1954), p. 219.
15. Landon Papers, Landon to Ray Clapper, Nov. 16, 1936, c.c.
16. Ibid. Landon to Arthur A. Ballantine, Feb. 8, 1937, c.c.
17. Ibid. Henry Breckenridge to Landon, Nov. 18, 1936.
18. Burton K. Wheeler with Paul F. Healy, *Yankee from the West* (New York, 1962), pp. 322–4; Pinckney, p. 151.
19. Landon Papers, Landon to Lew Douglas, April 1, 1937, c.c.
20. Ibid.
21. Wheeler, p. 323.
22. Landon Papers, Landon to Jay G. Hayden, June 21, 1937, c.c.; Landon to Bob Johnson, July 29, 1937, c.c.
23. Ibid. Landon to Don Berry, Oct. 14, 1937, c.c.
24. Ibid. Landon to Berry, Oct. 25, 1937, c.c.
25. Ibid. Landon to Jay W. Scovel, Aug. 27, 1937, c.c.; Landon to Berry, Oct. 14, 1937, c.c.
26. Ibid. Bertrand Snell to Landon, Nov. 4, 1947.
27. William E. Borah Papers, Borah to Harrison E. Spangler, Nov. 11, 1937, c.c.
28. Landon Papers, Landon to Hard, June 23, 1937, c.c.

29. William T. Hutchinson, *Lowden of Illinois*, 2 vols. (University of Chicago Press, 1937), II:724.
30. Landon Papers, Landon to Latham Reed, March 29, 1938, c.c.; Landon to Roger W. Strauss, Aug. 10, 1938, c.c.
31. Ibid. W. A. Sheaffer to Frank Gannett, June 10, 1938, c.c.; Landon to Douglas, April 6, 1938, c.c.
32. Hiram Johnson Papers, Johnson to John Bassett Moore, April 14, 1935, c.c.
33. Landon Papers, Landon to Sheaffer, Dec. 27, 1939, c.c.; Landon to H. B. Johnson, Aug. 15, 1941, c.c.
34. Harold Ickes, *The Secret Diary of Harold Ickes*, 3 vols. (New York, 1954). Diary entry for Sept. 9, 1939, II:818.
35. Landon Papers, Landon to Sterling Morton, Jan. 13, 1949, c.c.
36. Ibid. Landon to Edwin D. Canham, Feb. 20, 1940, c.c.
37. McNary Papers, J. M. Devers to McNary, Feb. 21, 1940.
38. Landon Papers, Landon to W. W. Waymack, May 15, 1940, c.c.; Guy B. Hathorn, "The Political Career of C. Bascom Slemp" (unpublished Ph.D. thesis, Duke University, 1950), p. 319.
39. Hugh Ross, "Was the Nomination of Wendell Willkie a Political Miracle?," *Indiana Magazine of History*, June 1962, p. 82.
40. Richard Rovere, "The Man in the Blue Serge Suit," *Harper's Magazine*, May 1944, p. 484.
41. Ibid. Landon to Harold B. Johnson, July 12, 1940, c.c.
42. Ibid. Landon to Harold Robbins, May 10, 1940, c.c.
43. Hugh Ross, loc. cit. p. 87.
44. Ibid. p. 99; Donald B. Johnson, *The Republican Party and Wendell Willkie* (Urbana, 1960), pp. 91–3.
45. Landon Papers, Landon to A. H. Kirchofer, April 26, 1944, c.c.
46. Landon Papers, Landon to Ray Moley, Nov. 14, 1940, c.c.
47. Johnson, p. 125.
48. Landon Papers, Landon to Wendell Willkie, Aug. 31, 1940, c.c.
49. Johnson, p. 114.
50. Landon Papers, Landon to Harold Johnson, Dec. 10, 1940, c.c.
51. Wheeler, pp. 375–6; Landon Papers, Clarence B. Hewes to Landon, July 14, 1945.
52. Ibid. Landon to Harold B. Johnson, Nov. 12, 1946, c.c.
53. Ibid. Landon to William Hard, Sept. 14, 1948, c.c.
54. Ibid. Col. Robert R. McCormick to Landon, Nov. 5, 1948.
55. *1948 Election Report*, Dec. 17, 1948, prepared by George H. E. Smith, Secretary and Staff Director of the Republican Policy Committee.

CHAPTER XIII

1. *New York Times*, April 20, 1952: Arthur Krock, "Eisenhower Now Seems to be Gaining Ground."
2. Sherman Adams, *First Hand Report* (New York, 1961), p. 13.
3. Adams, p. 231; Earl Mazo, *Richard Nixon: A Political and Personal Portrait* (New York, 1959), pp. 152–4.
4. Richard M. Nixon, *Six Crises* (New York, 1962), p. 316.
5. *United States News & World Report*, Dec. 12, 1960, pp. 78–81.

6. Survey Research Center, University of Michigan, April 10, 1963 (mimeographed bulletin). "Who Will Elect the Next President?," *Nation's Business,* April 1964, p. 77.
7. Tocqueville, I, pp. 271-2.
8. *United States News & World Report,* Nov. 9, 1964, p. 41.
9. *Wall Street Journal,* Sept. 15, 1966.
10. *United States News & World Report,* Nov. 9, 1964, p. 41.
11. Ibid. June 8, 1964, p. 164.
12. Ibid.
13. Calvin Trillin, "Onward and Upward with the Arts: You Can't Wear Out a List," *New Yorker,* Sept. 24, 1966, p. 145.
14. *Indianapolis Star,* Nov. 8, 1964.
15. *Wall Street Journal,* Oct. 13, 1964.
16. Ibid. May 15, 1964.
17. Don Oberdorfer, "The New Political Non-job," *Harper's Magazine,* Oct. 1965, p. 108.

CHAPTER XIV

1. December 10, 1962.
2. Robert D. Novak, *The Agony of the G.O.P.: 1964* (New York, 1965), p. 103.
3. Ibid. pp. 211-12.
4. Richard H. Rovere, *The Goldwater Caper* (New York, 1965), p. 114.
5. Theodore H. White, *The Making of the President, 1964* (New York, 1965), p. 99.
6. Rovere, p. 5.
7. Ibid. p. 14.
8. H. Faber, editor, *The Road to the White House* (New York, 1965), p. 232.
9. Novak, p. 307.
10. S. Shadegg, *What Happened to Goldwater?* (New York, 1965), p. 92.
11. Ibid. p. 41; Novak, p. 24.
12. *United States News & World Report,* April 20, 1964, p. 34.
13. *Chicago Tribune,* May 21, 1964.
14. White, p. 149.
15. Ibid. p. 125.
16. Novak, p. 436.
17. *Indianapolis Star,* Oct. 4, 1964.
18. J. Kraft, "Johnson's Next Four Years," *Harper's Magazine,* Nov. 1964, p. 44.
19. *Wall Street Journal,* Oct. 28, 1964.
20. Ben H. Bagdikian, "How Strong Is the Hate Vote?," *Saturday Evening Post,* Oct. 17, 1964, pp. 19-20.
21. *United States News & World Report,* Oct. 12, 1964, p. 40.
22. *Wall Street Journal,* Aug. 27, 1964.
23. *United States News & World Report,* Nov. 23, 1964.
24. Ibid. Nov. 16, 1964, p. 6.
25. *Sports Illustrated,* June 27, 1966, p. 57.
26. *United States News & World Report,* March 30, 1964, p. 8.
27. *Wall Street Journal,* May 8, 1964.

28. Ibid. Sept. 12, 1963.
29. *United States News & World Report,* Oct. 31, 1966, p. 13.
30. *Wall Street Journal,* Oct. 10, 1966.
31. *United States News & World Report,* Sept. 19, 1966, p. 53.

Index

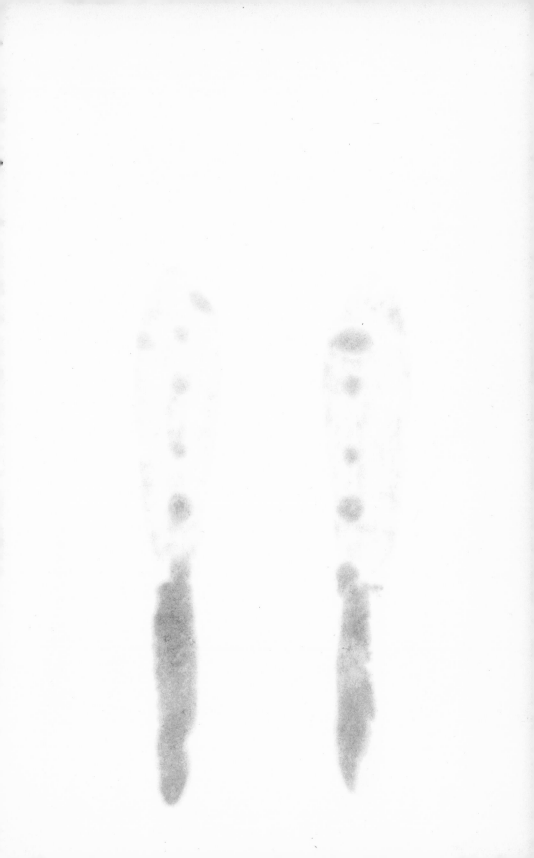

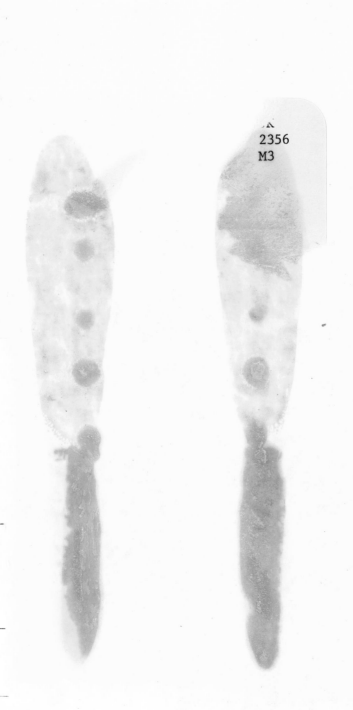

2356
M3